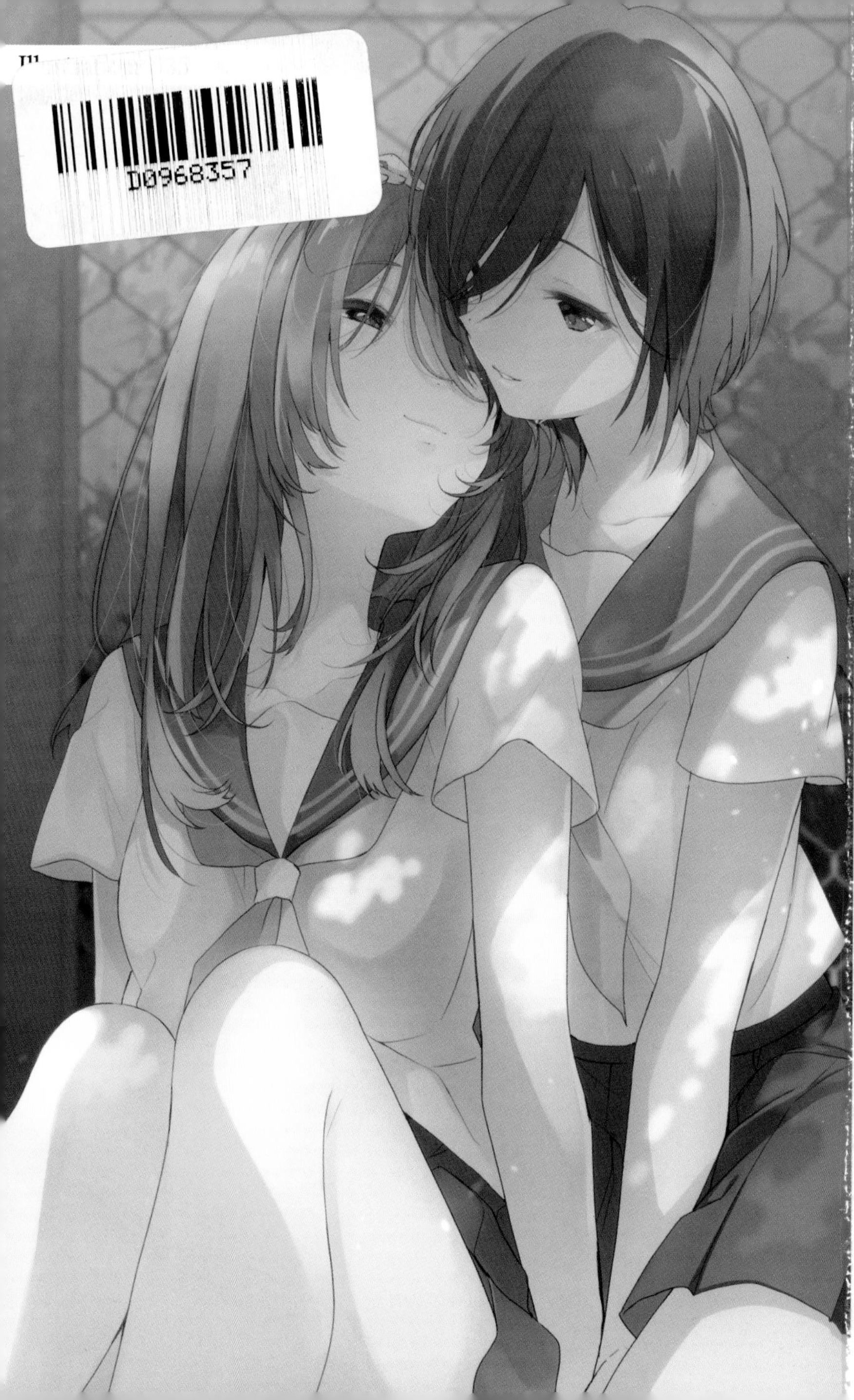

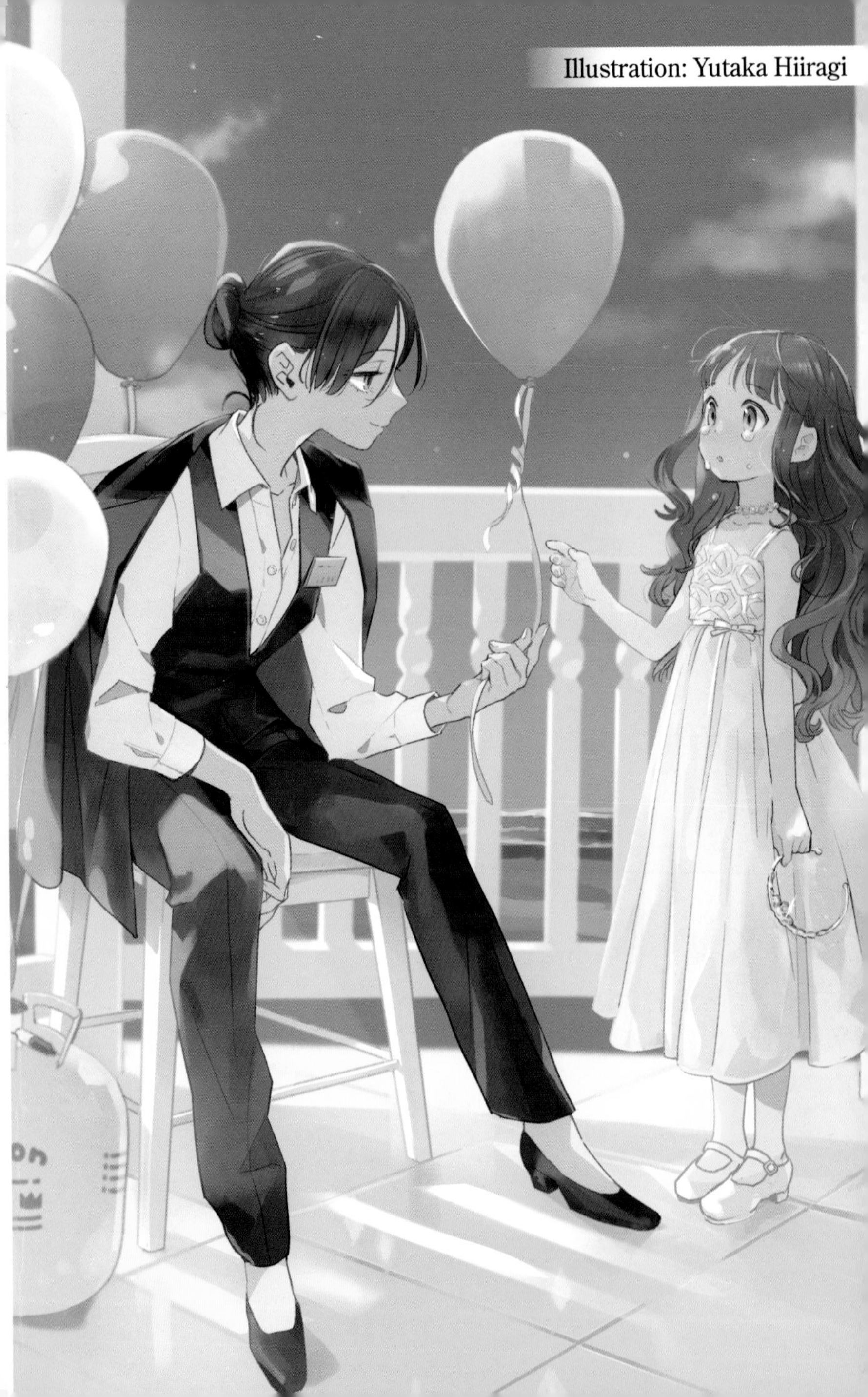

Illustration: Yutaka Hiiragi

Illustration: Non

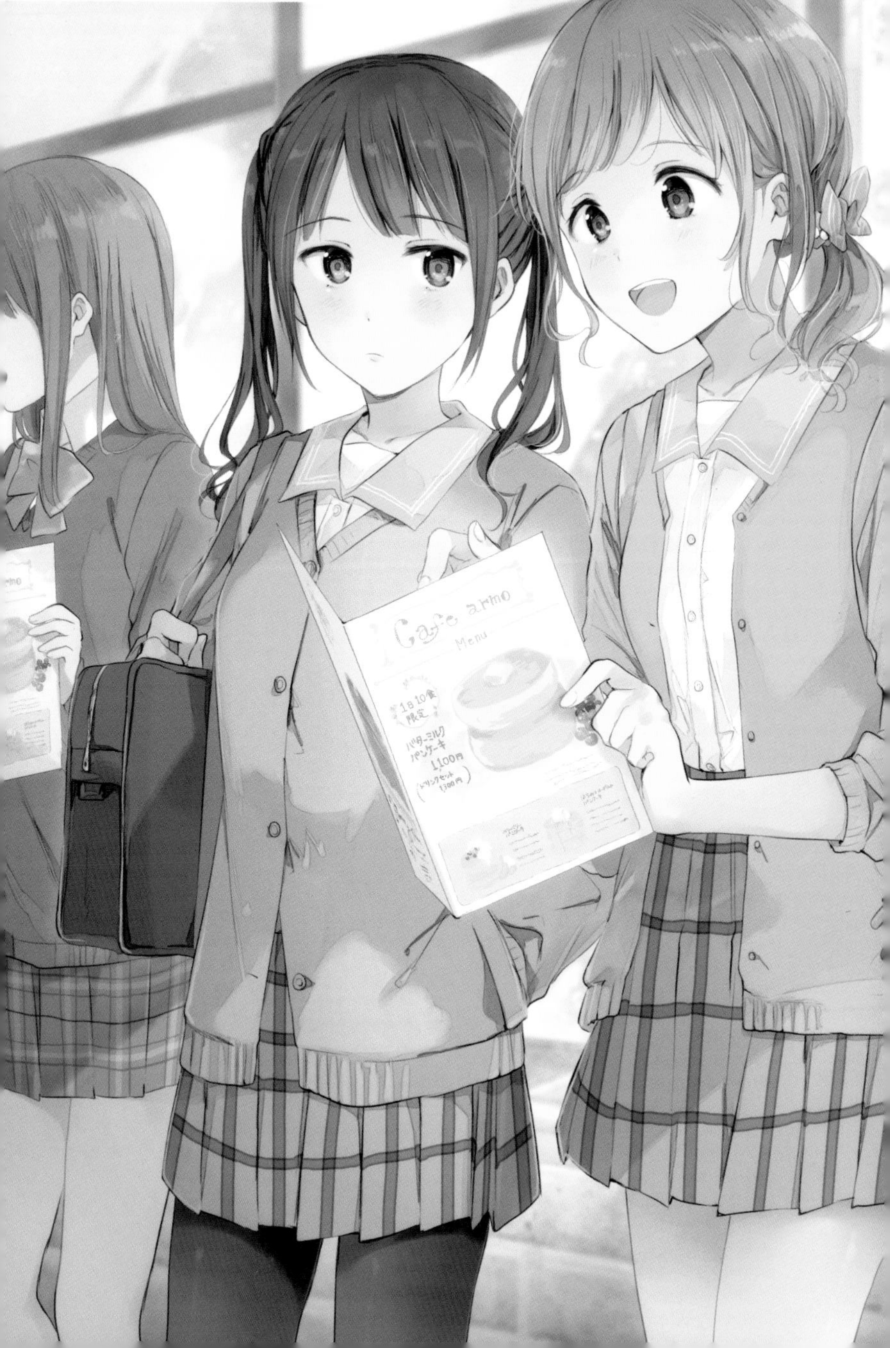
Cafe armo
Menu
1日10食限定
バターミルク
パンケーキ
1,100円

Cover Illustration

Fly

Illustrations

U35.........001

Yutaka Hiiragi.........002

Non.........003

Comics

Fly Flowers in a Storm.........005

Musshu Happy Yellow Chick.........015

Nio Nakatani Always in Profile.........031

Kazuno Yuikawa Azalea Corner.........041

Tamamushi Oku The Evolution of Bed-Sharing.........061

Kagekichi Tadano Something Only I Know.........075

Canno The Unemployed Woman and the High School
       Girl.........093

Kabocha Though Summer Won't Come Again.........105

Fumiko Takada My Mom.........143

Shuninta Amano The Cutest Girl in the Universe.........151

Izumi Kawanami Graduation Piercing.........175

Taki Kitao The Princess and the Knight for Two Days a
          Week.........191

Uta Isaki Sewing Machine.........217

Eri Ejima Let Me Keep This Secret.........233

Auri Hirao Secret Sharing.........255

Contents

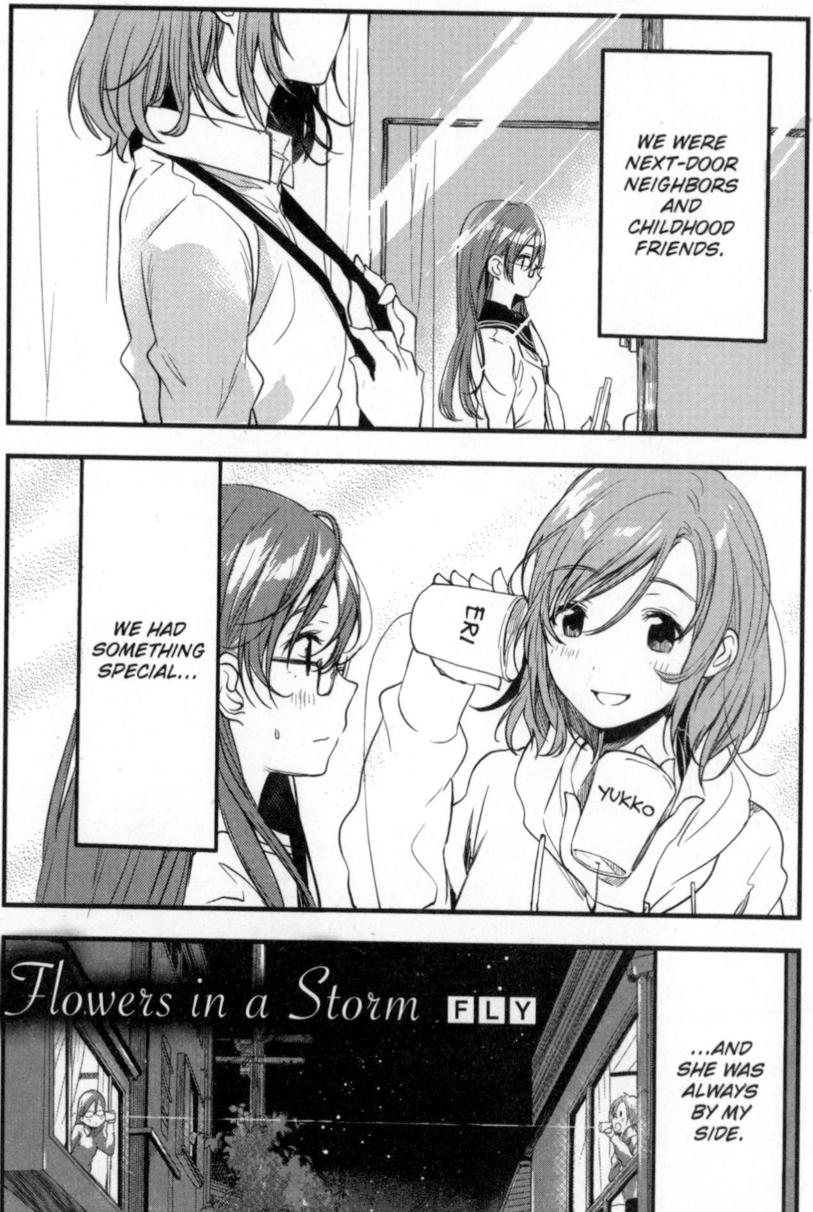
WE WERE NEXT-DOOR NEIGHBORS AND CHILDHOOD FRIENDS.
ERI
YUKKO
WE HAD SOMETHING SPECIAL...
...AND SHE WAS ALWAYS BY MY SIDE.
Flowers in a Storm FLY

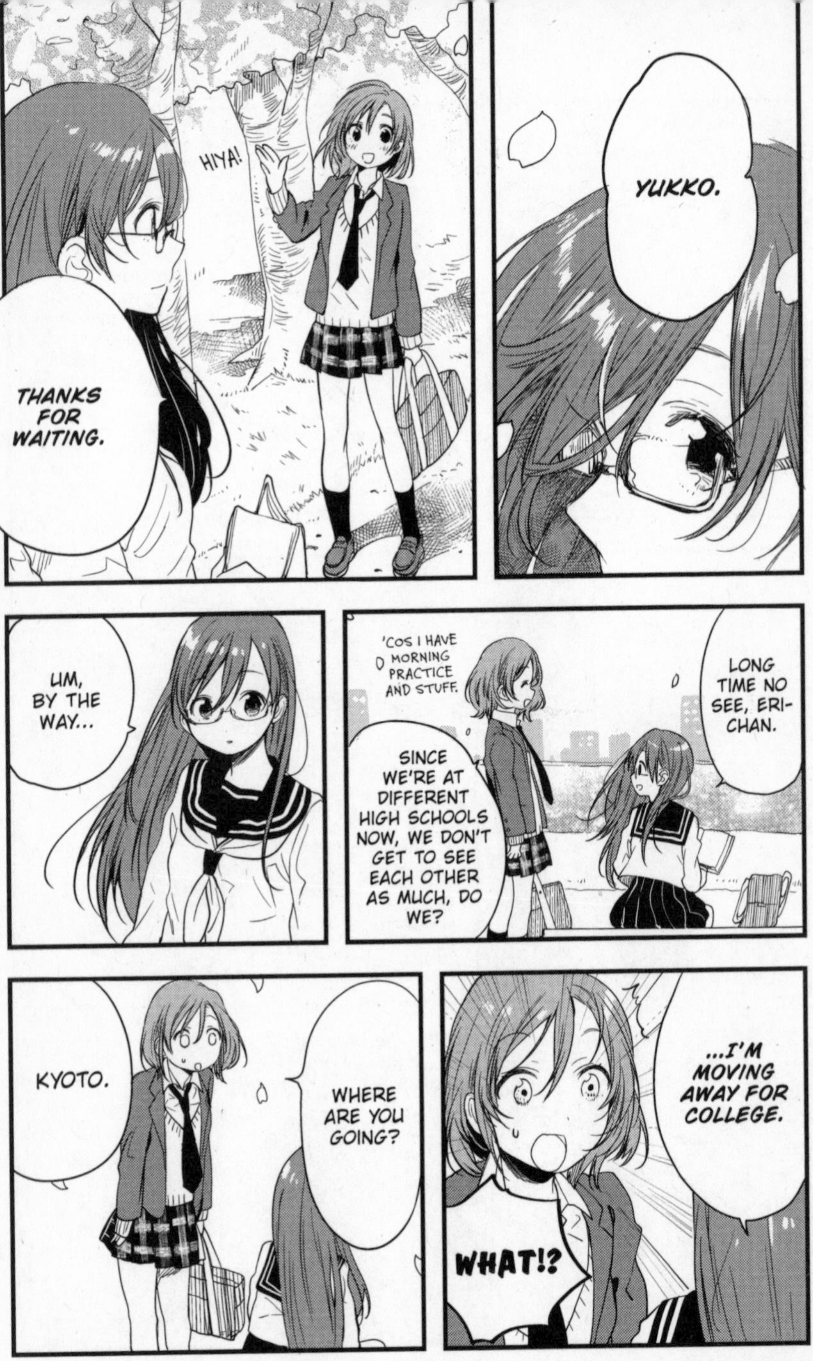
YUKKO.
HIYA!
THANKS FOR WAITING.
LONG TIME NO SEE, ERI-CHAN.
'COS I HAVE MORNING PRACTICE AND STUFF.
SINCE WE'RE AT DIFFERENT HIGH SCHOOLS NOW, WE DON'T GET TO SEE EACH OTHER AS MUCH, DO WE?
UM, BY THE WAY...
...I'M MOVING AWAY FOR COLLEGE.
WHAT!?
WHERE ARE YOU GOING?
KYOTO.

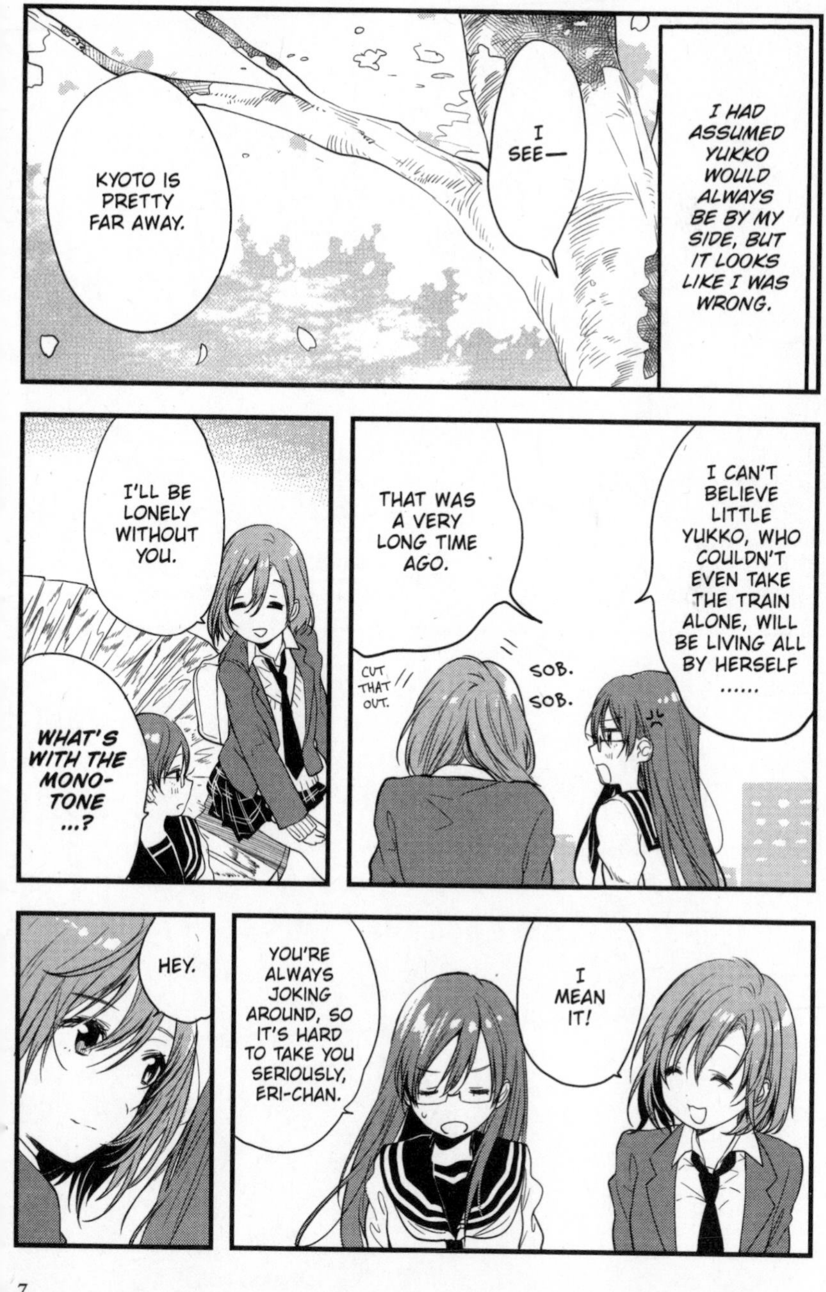
I HAD ASSUMED YUKKO WOULD ALWAYS BE BY MY SIDE, BUT IT LOOKS LIKE I WAS WRONG.
I SEE—
KYOTO IS PRETTY FAR AWAY.
I CAN'T BELIEVE LITTLE YUKKO, WHO COULDN'T EVEN TAKE THE TRAIN ALONE, WILL BE LIVING ALL BY HERSELF ......
THAT WAS A VERY LONG TIME AGO.
SOB. SOB.
CUT THAT OUT.
I'LL BE LONELY WITHOUT YOU.
WHAT'S WITH THE MONO-TONE ...?
I MEAN IT!
YOU'RE ALWAYS JOKING AROUND, SO IT'S HARD TO TAKE YOU SERIOUSLY, ERI-CHAN.
HEY.

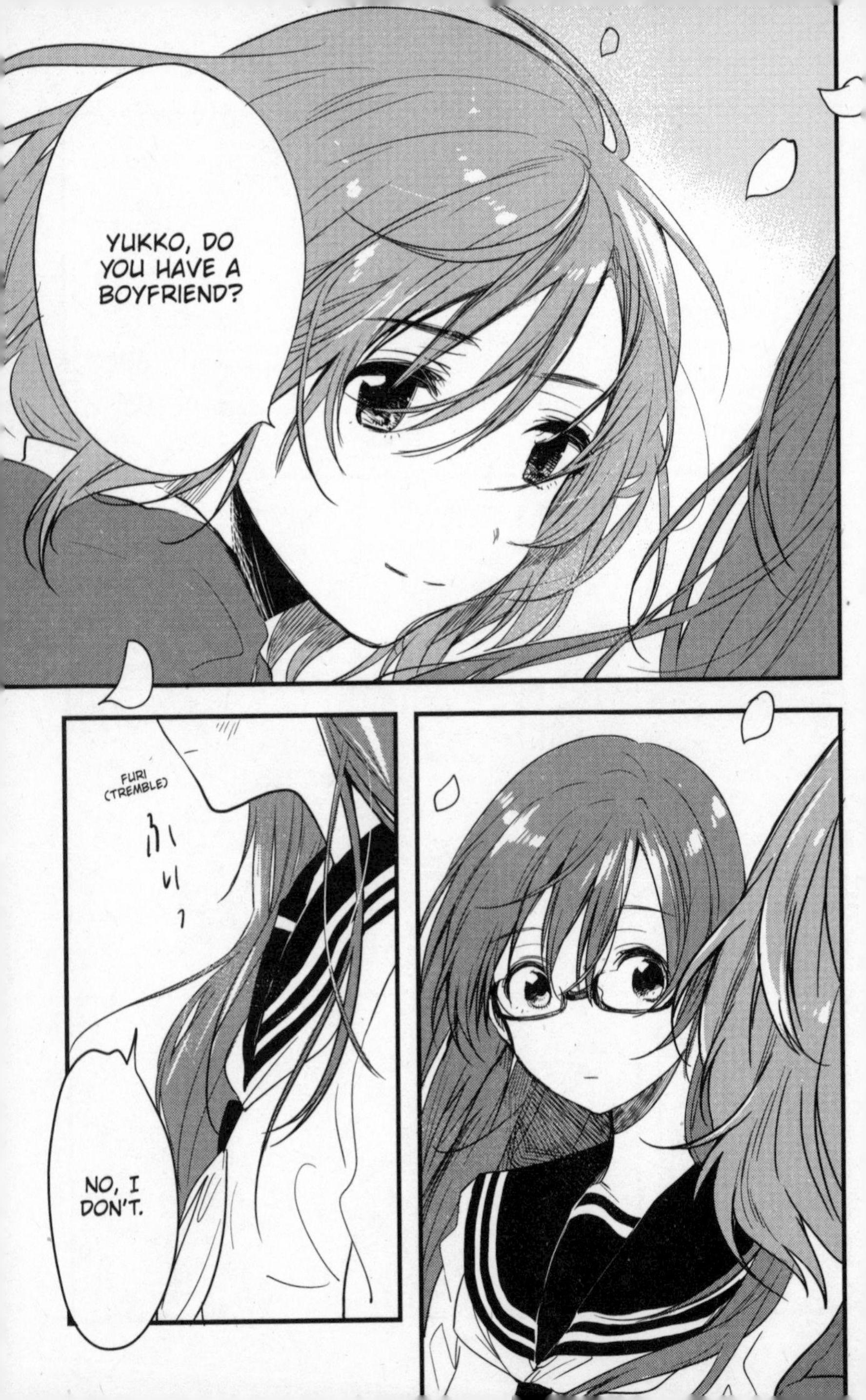
YUKKO, DO YOU HAVE A BOYFRIEND?
FURI (TREMBLE)
ふい
NO, I DON'T.

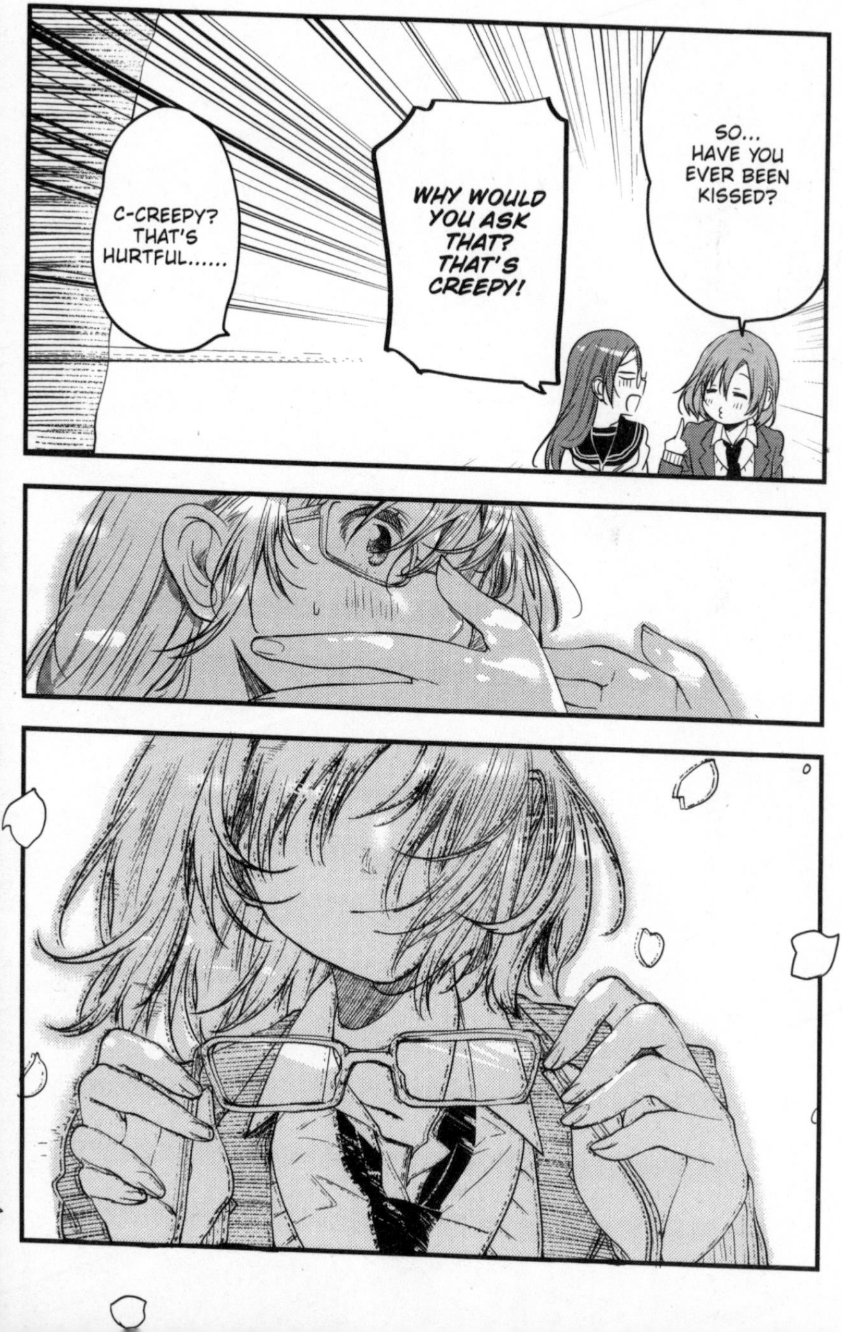
SO... HAVE YOU EVER BEEN KISSED?
WHY WOULD YOU ASK THAT? THAT'S CREEPY!
C-CREEPY? THAT'S HURTFUL......

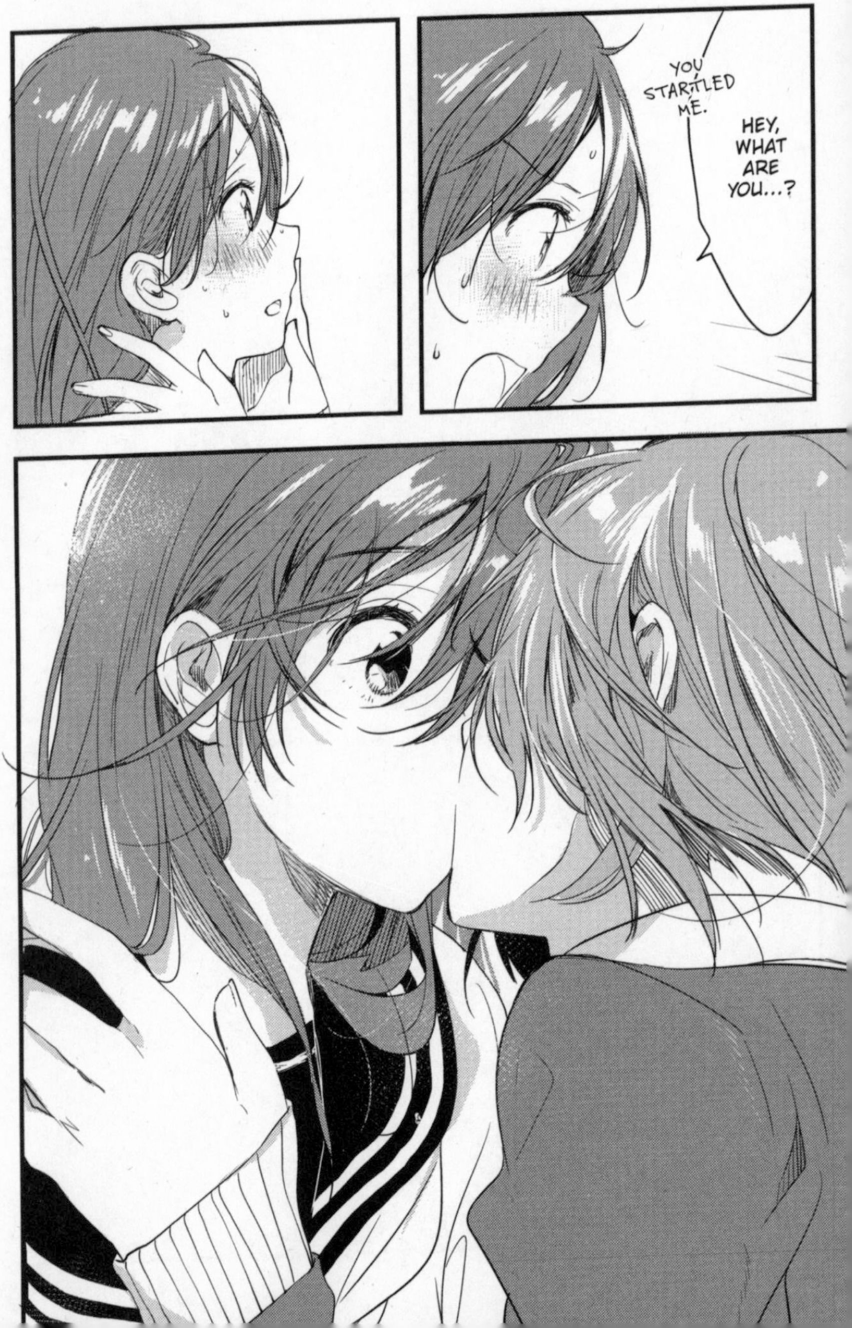
HEY, WHAT ARE YOU...?
YOU STARTLED ME.

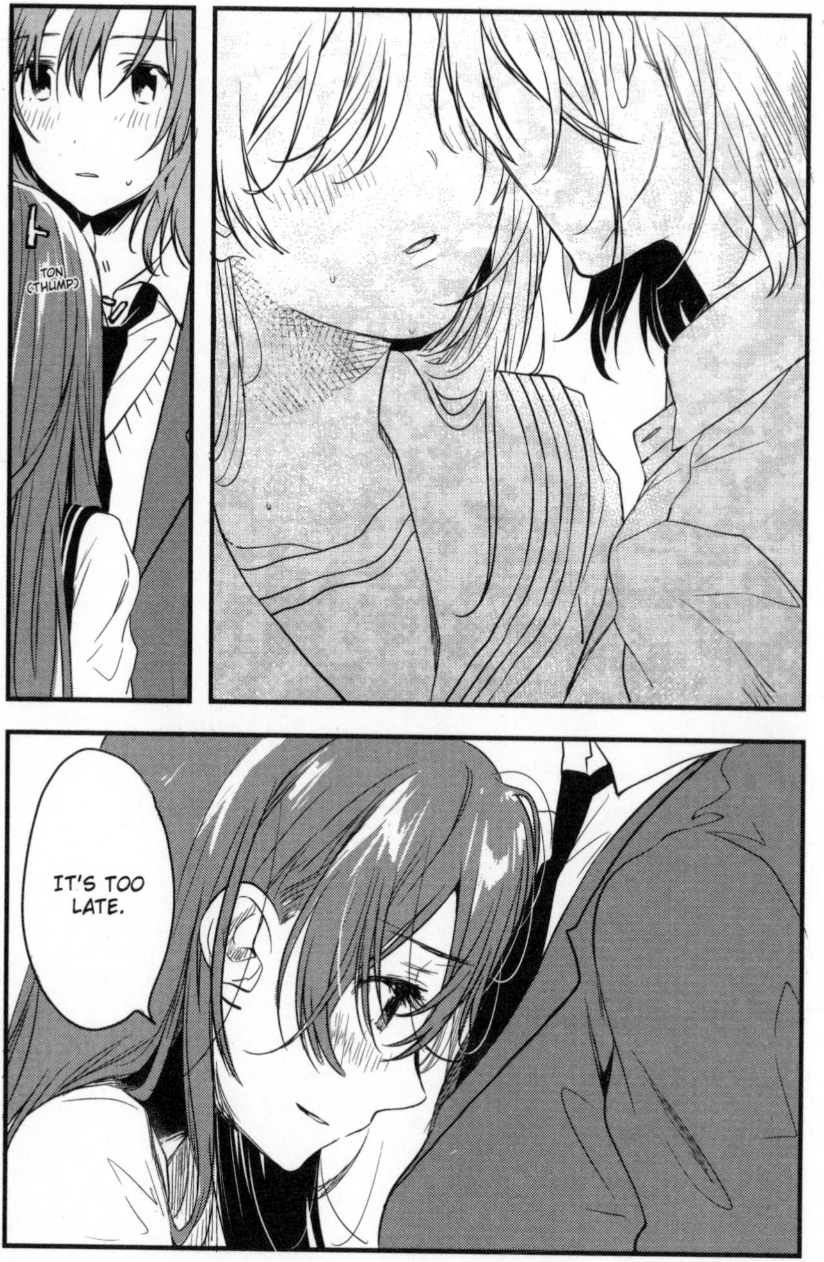
TON (THUMP)
IT'S TOO LATE.

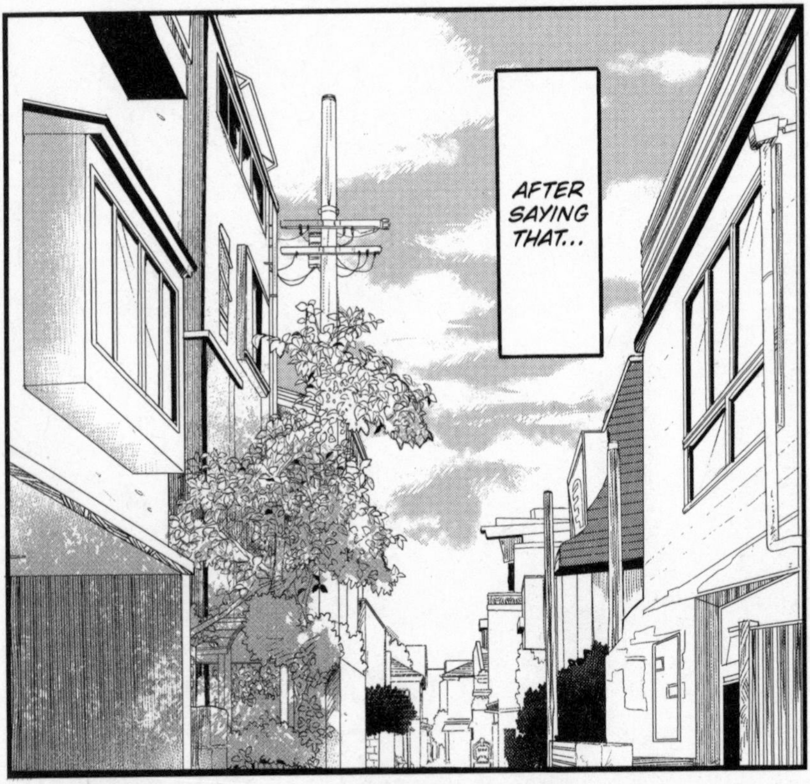
AFTER SAYING THAT...
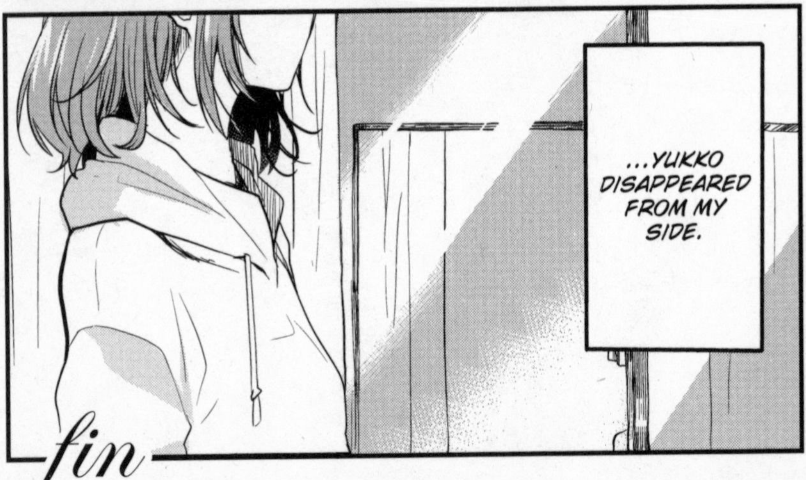
...YUKKO DISAPPEARED FROM MY SIDE.
fin

éclair
blanche

A Girls' Love Anthology
That Resonates in Your Heart

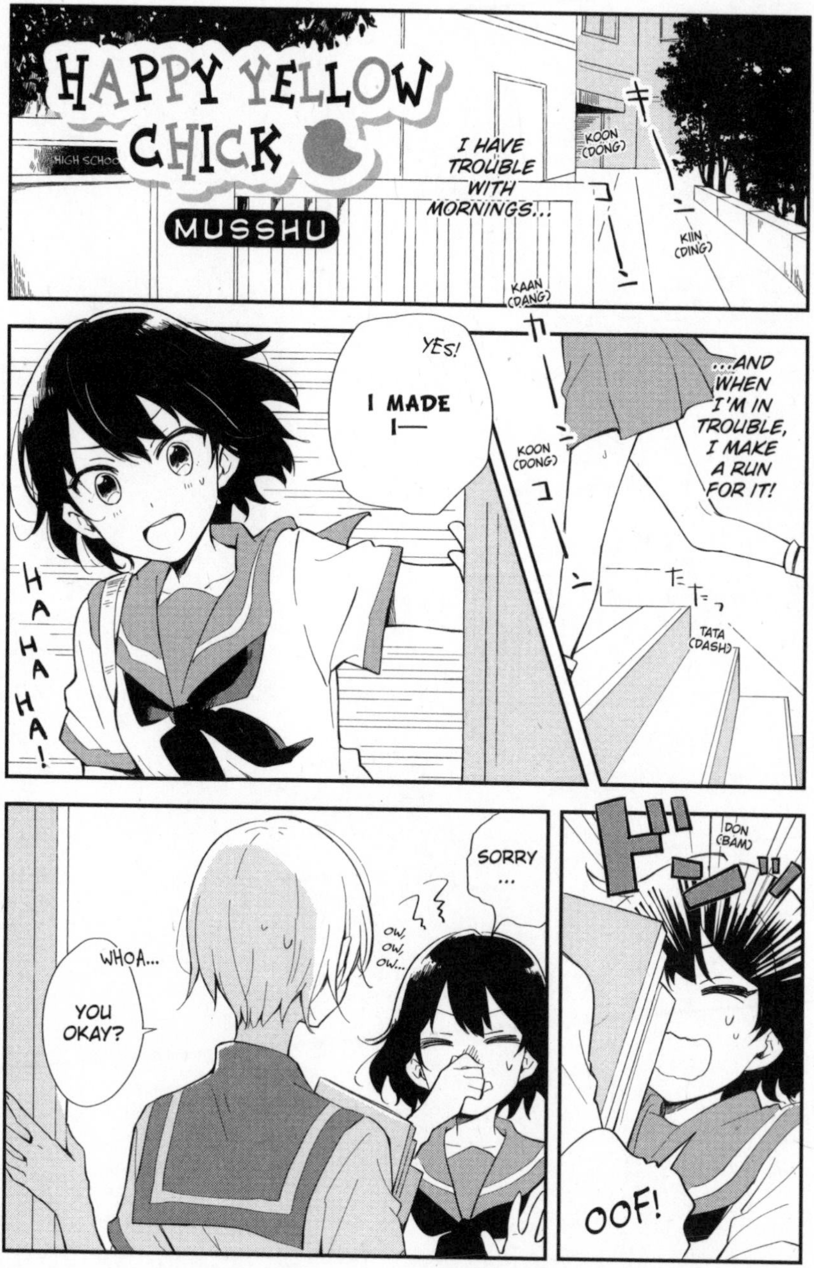
HAPPY YELLOW CHICK
MUSSHU
KOON (DONG)
KIIN (DING)
I HAVE TROUBLE WITH MORNINGS...
HIGH SCHOO
KAAN (DANG)
...AND WHEN I'M IN TROUBLE, I MAKE A RUN FOR IT!
KOON (DONG)
TATA (DASH)
YES!
I MADE I—
HA HA HA HA!
DON (BAM)
OOF!
SORRY...
OW, OW, OW...
WHOA...
YOU OKAY?

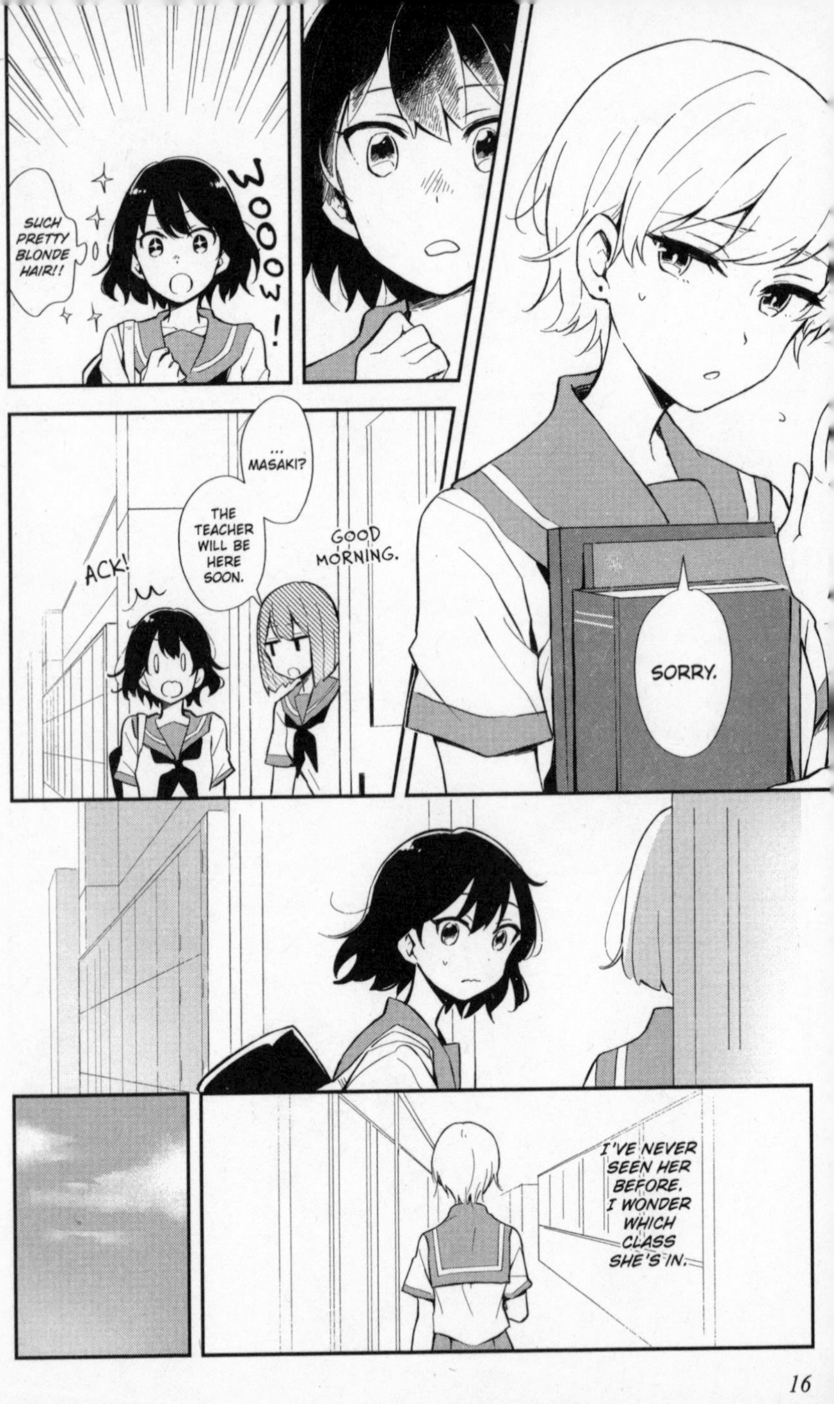
SORRY.
WOOOW!
SUCH PRETTY BLONDE HAIR!!
...MASAKI?
GOOD MORNING.
THE TEACHER WILL BE HERE SOON.
ACK!
I'VE NEVER SEEN HER BEFORE. I WONDER WHICH CLASS SHE'S IN.

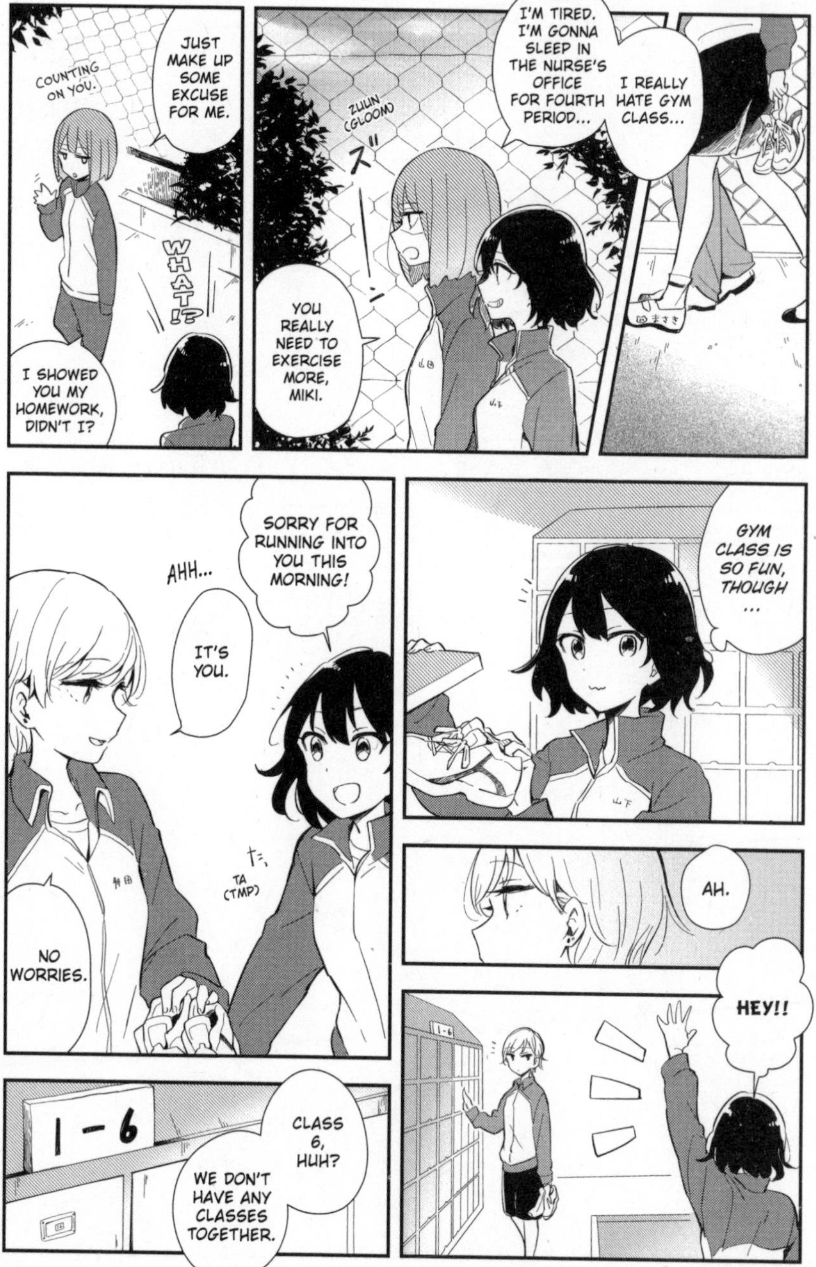
I REALLY HATE GYM CLASS...
I'M TIRED. I'M GONNA SLEEP IN THE NURSE'S OFFICE FOR FOURTH PERIOD...
ZUUN (GLOOM)
YOU REALLY NEED TO EXERCISE MORE, MIKI.
JUST MAKE UP SOME EXCUSE FOR ME.
COUNTING ON YOU.
WHAT!?
I SHOWED YOU MY HOMEWORK, DIDN'T I?
GYM CLASS IS SO FUN, THOUGH...
AH.
HEY!!
SORRY FOR RUNNING INTO YOU THIS MORNING!
AHH...
IT'S YOU.
TA (TMP)
NO WORRIES.
1-6
CLASS 6, HUH?
WE DON'T HAVE ANY CLASSES TOGETHER.

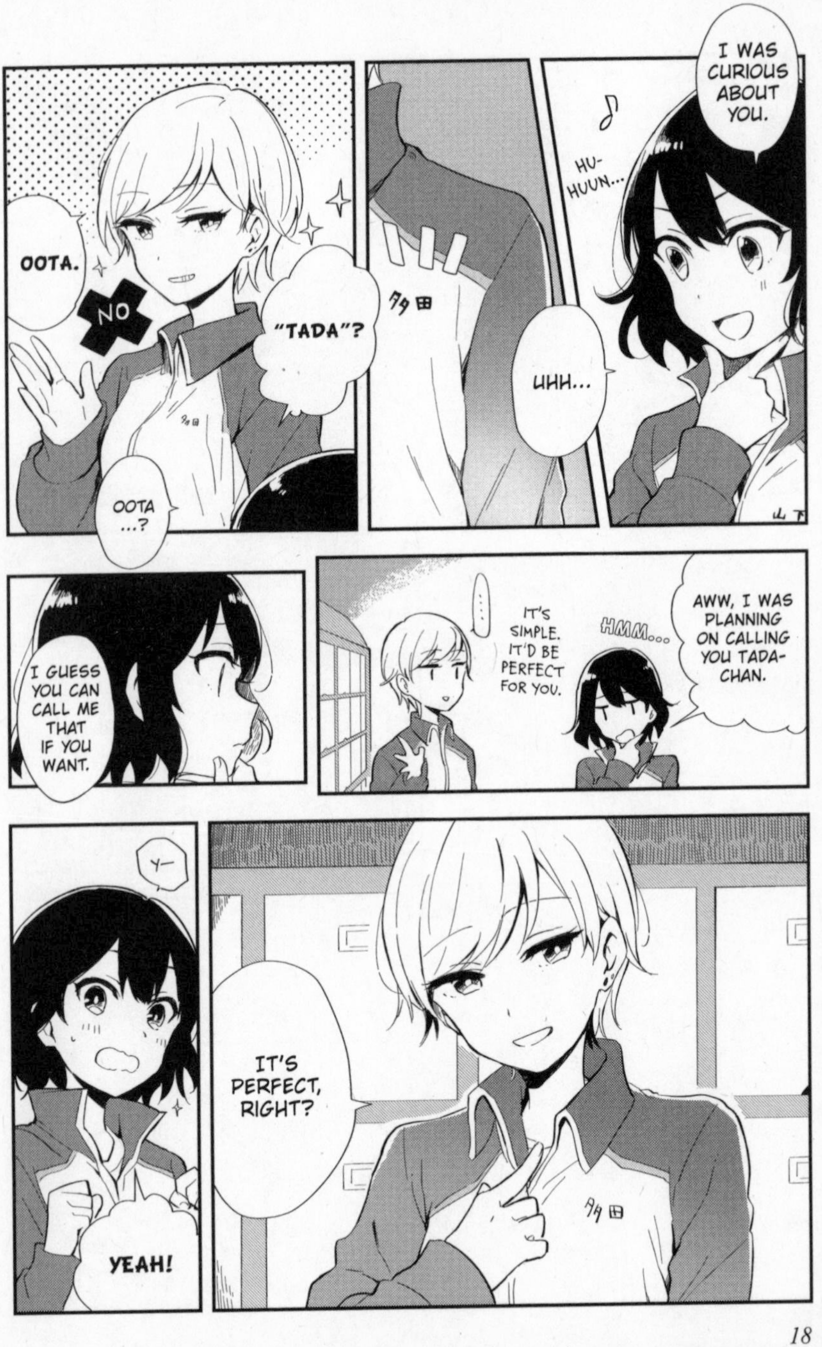
I WAS CURIOUS ABOUT YOU.
HU-HUUN...
UHH...
"TADA"?
OOTA.
NO
OOTA ...?
AWW, I WAS PLANNING ON CALLING YOU TADA-CHAN.
HMM...
IT'S SIMPLE. IT'D BE PERFECT FOR YOU.
...
I GUESS YOU CAN CALL ME THAT IF YOU WANT.
IT'S PERFECT, RIGHT?
Y—
YEAH!

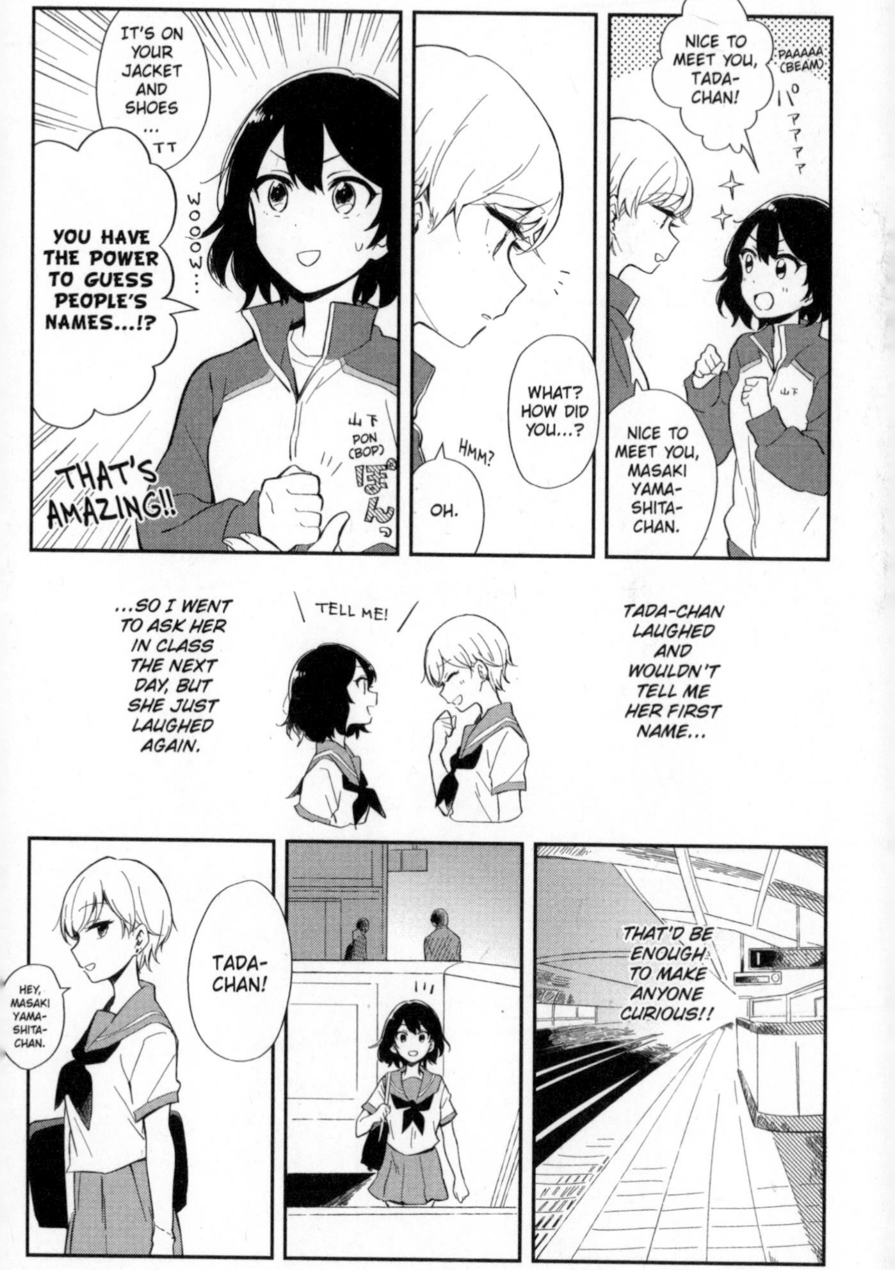
NICE TO MEET YOU, TADA-CHAN!
PAAAAA (BEAM)
NICE TO MEET YOU, MASAKI YAMA-SHITA-CHAN.
山下
WHAT? HOW DID YOU...?
HMM?
OH.
IT'S ON YOUR JACKET AND SHOES ... TT
WOOOOW...
YOU HAVE THE POWER TO GUESS PEOPLE'S NAMES...!?
山下
PON (BOP)
THAT'S AMAZING!!
TADA-CHAN LAUGHED AND WOULDN'T TELL ME HER FIRST NAME...
TELL ME!
...SO I WENT TO ASK HER IN CLASS THE NEXT DAY, BUT SHE JUST LAUGHED AGAIN.
THAT'D BE ENOUGH TO MAKE ANYONE CURIOUS!!
TADA-CHAN!
HEY, MASAKI YAMA-SHITA-CHAN.

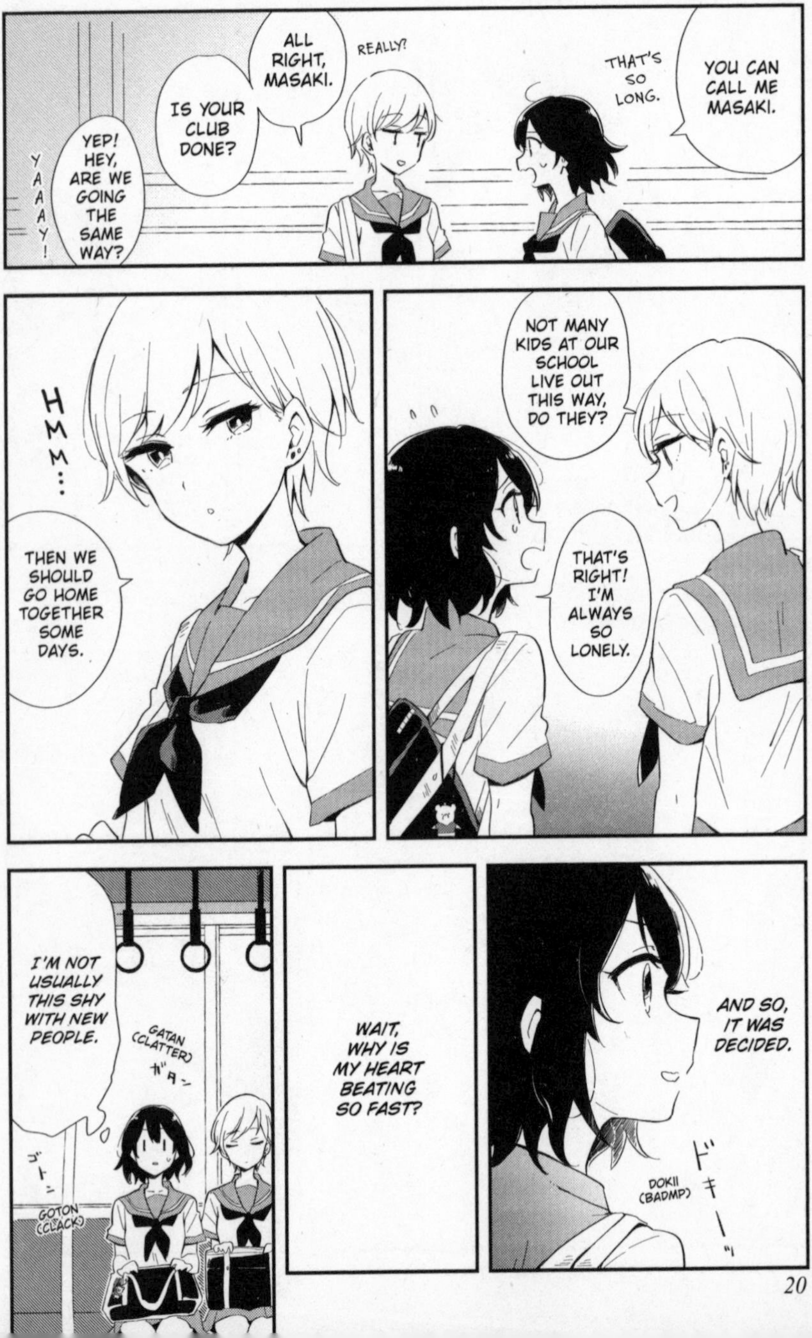
YOU CAN CALL ME MASAKI.
THAT'S SO LONG.
REALLY?
ALL RIGHT, MASAKI.
IS YOUR CLUB DONE?
YEP! HEY, ARE WE GOING THE SAME WAY?
YAAAY!
NOT MANY KIDS AT OUR SCHOOL LIVE OUT THIS WAY, DO THEY?
THAT'S RIGHT! I'M ALWAYS SO LONELY.
HMM...
THEN WE SHOULD GO HOME TOGETHER SOME DAYS.
AND SO, IT WAS DECIDED.
ドキー
DOKII (BADMP)
WAIT, WHY IS MY HEART BEATING SO FAST?
I'M NOT USUALLY THIS SHY WITH NEW PEOPLE.
GATAN (CLATTER)
ガタン
ゴトン
GOTON (CLACK)

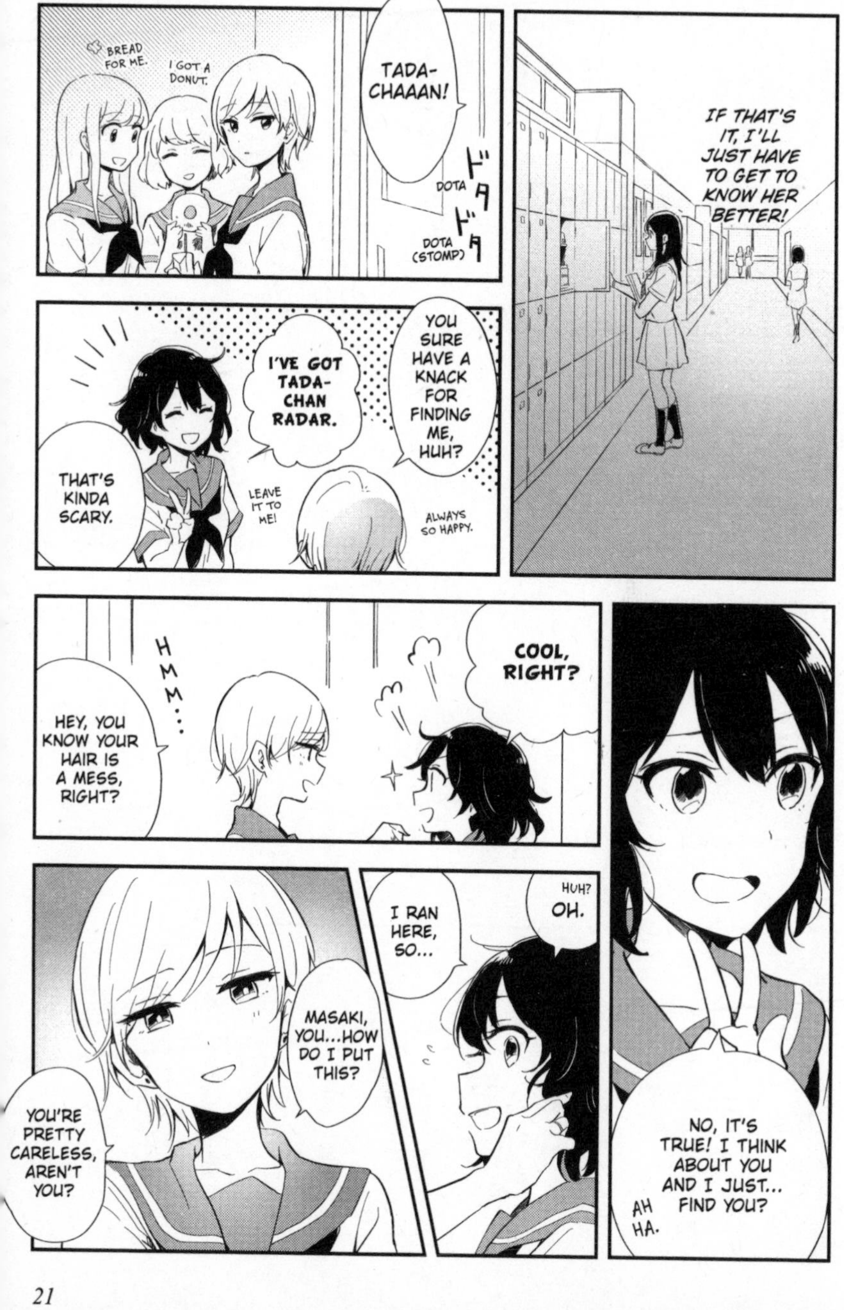
IF THAT'S IT, I'LL JUST HAVE TO GET TO KNOW HER BETTER!
TADA-CHAAAN!
ドタ DOTA
ドタ DOTA (STOMP)
I GOT A DONUT.
BREAD FOR ME.
YOU SURE HAVE A KNACK FOR FINDING ME, HUH?
ALWAYS SO HAPPY.
I'VE GOT TADA-CHAN RADAR.
LEAVE IT TO ME!
THAT'S KINDA SCARY.
NO, IT'S TRUE! I THINK ABOUT YOU AND I JUST... FIND YOU?
AH HA.
COOL, RIGHT?
HMM...
HEY, YOU KNOW YOUR HAIR IS A MESS, RIGHT?
HUH?
OH.
I RAN HERE, SO...
MASAKI, YOU...HOW DO I PUT THIS?
YOU'RE PRETTY CARELESS, AREN'T YOU?

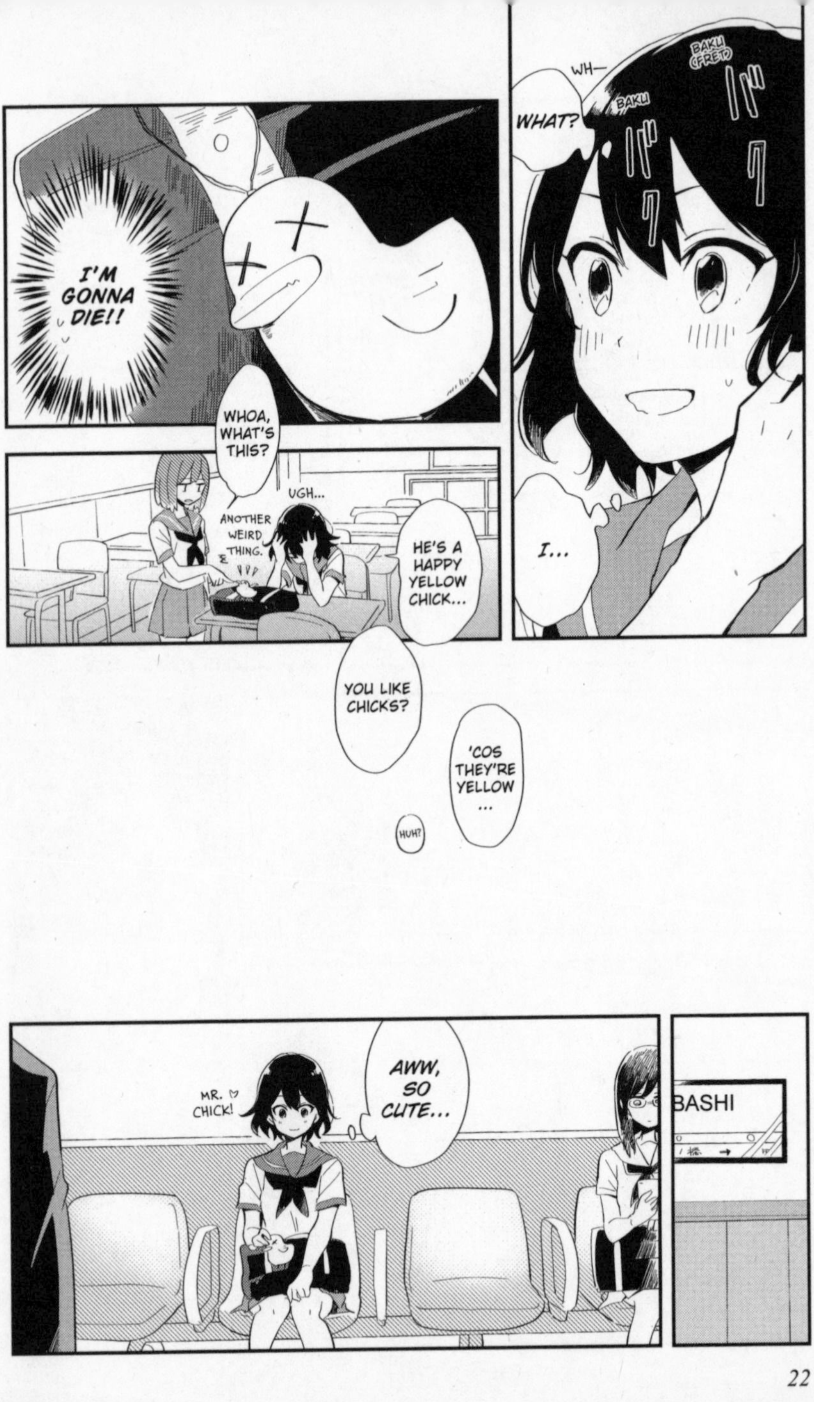
WH—
WHAT?
BAKU BAKU (FRET)
I...
I'M GONNA DIE!!
WHOA, WHAT'S THIS?
UGH...
ANOTHER WEIRD THING.
HE'S A HAPPY YELLOW CHICK...
YOU LIKE CHICKS?
'COS THEY'RE YELLOW ...
HUH?
BASHI
AWW, SO CUTE...
MR. ♡ CHICK!

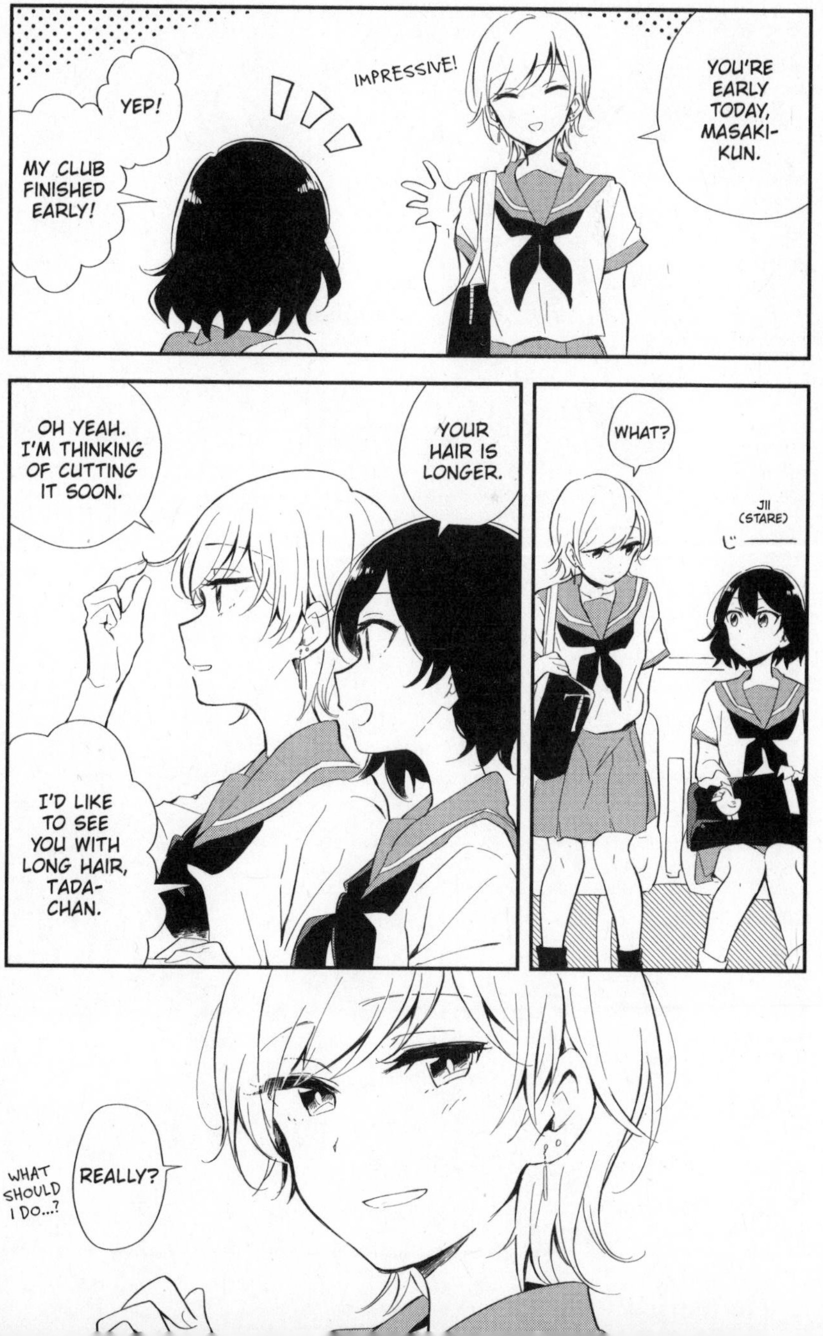
YOU'RE EARLY TODAY, MASAKI-KUN.
IMPRESSIVE!
YEP!
MY CLUB FINISHED EARLY!
WHAT?
JII (STARE)
じ——
YOUR HAIR IS LONGER.
OH YEAH. I'M THINKING OF CUTTING IT SOON.
I'D LIKE TO SEE YOU WITH LONG HAIR, TADA-CHAN.
REALLY?
WHAT SHOULD I DO...?

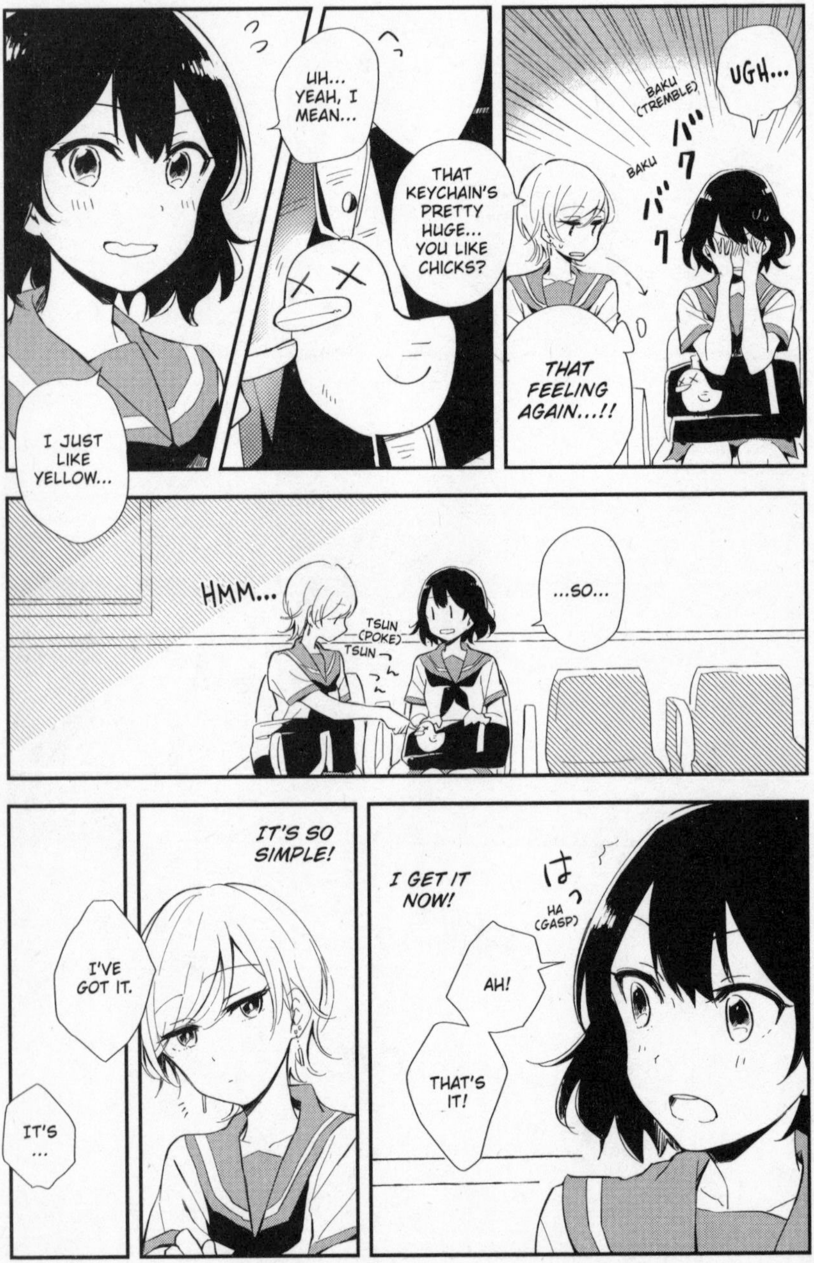
UGH...
BAKU (TREMBLE)
バク
BAKU
バク
THAT FEELING AGAIN...!!
THAT KEYCHAIN'S PRETTY HUGE... YOU LIKE CHICKS?
UH... YEAH, I MEAN...
I JUST LIKE YELLOW...
...SO...
TSUN (POKE)
TSUN
HMM...
はっ
HA (GASP)
I GET IT NOW!
AH!
THAT'S IT!
IT'S SO SIMPLE!
I'VE GOT IT.
IT'S ...

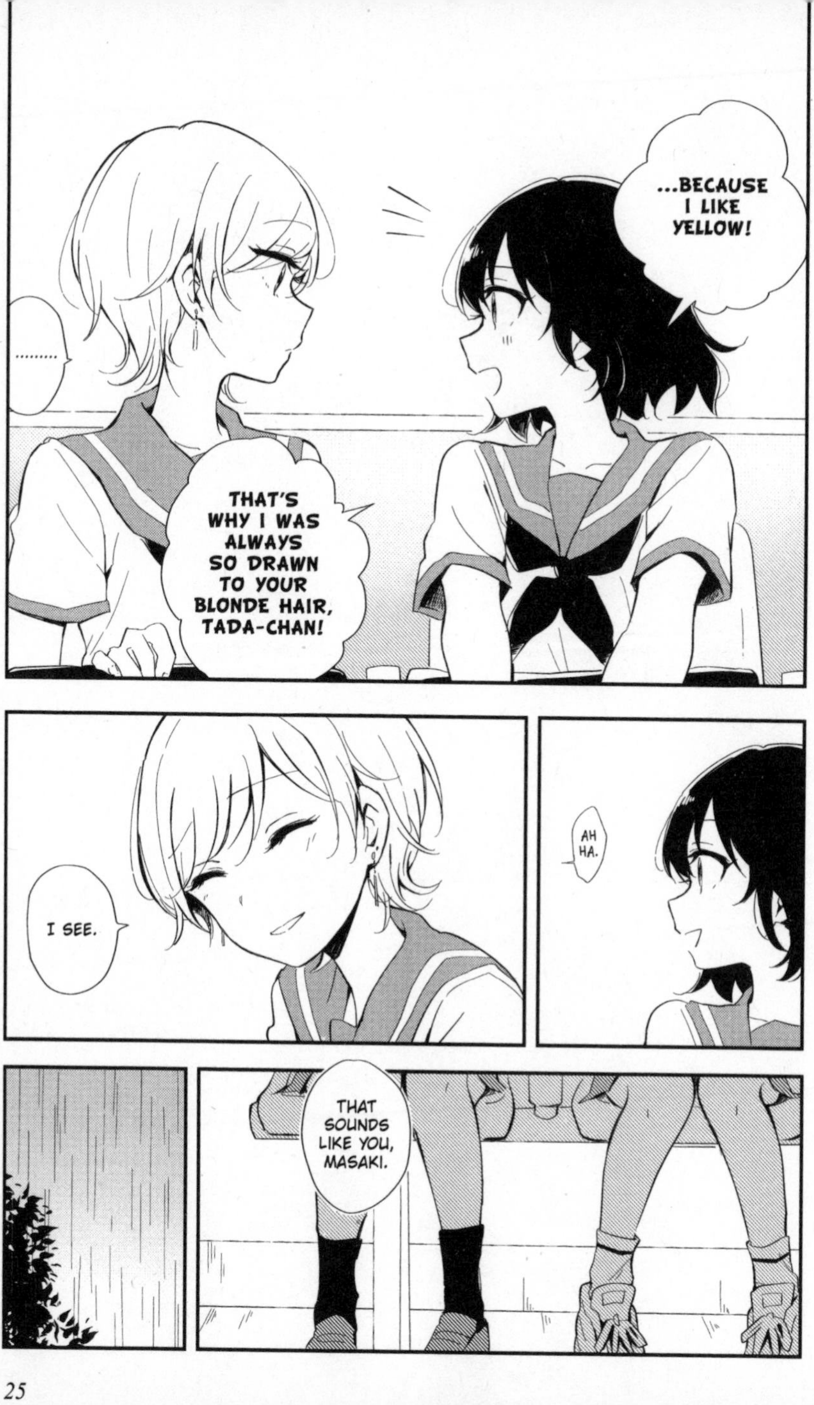
...BECAUSE I LIKE YELLOW!
THAT'S WHY I WAS ALWAYS SO DRAWN TO YOUR BLONDE HAIR, TADA-CHAN!
....
AH HA.
I SEE.
THAT SOUNDS LIKE YOU, MASAKI.

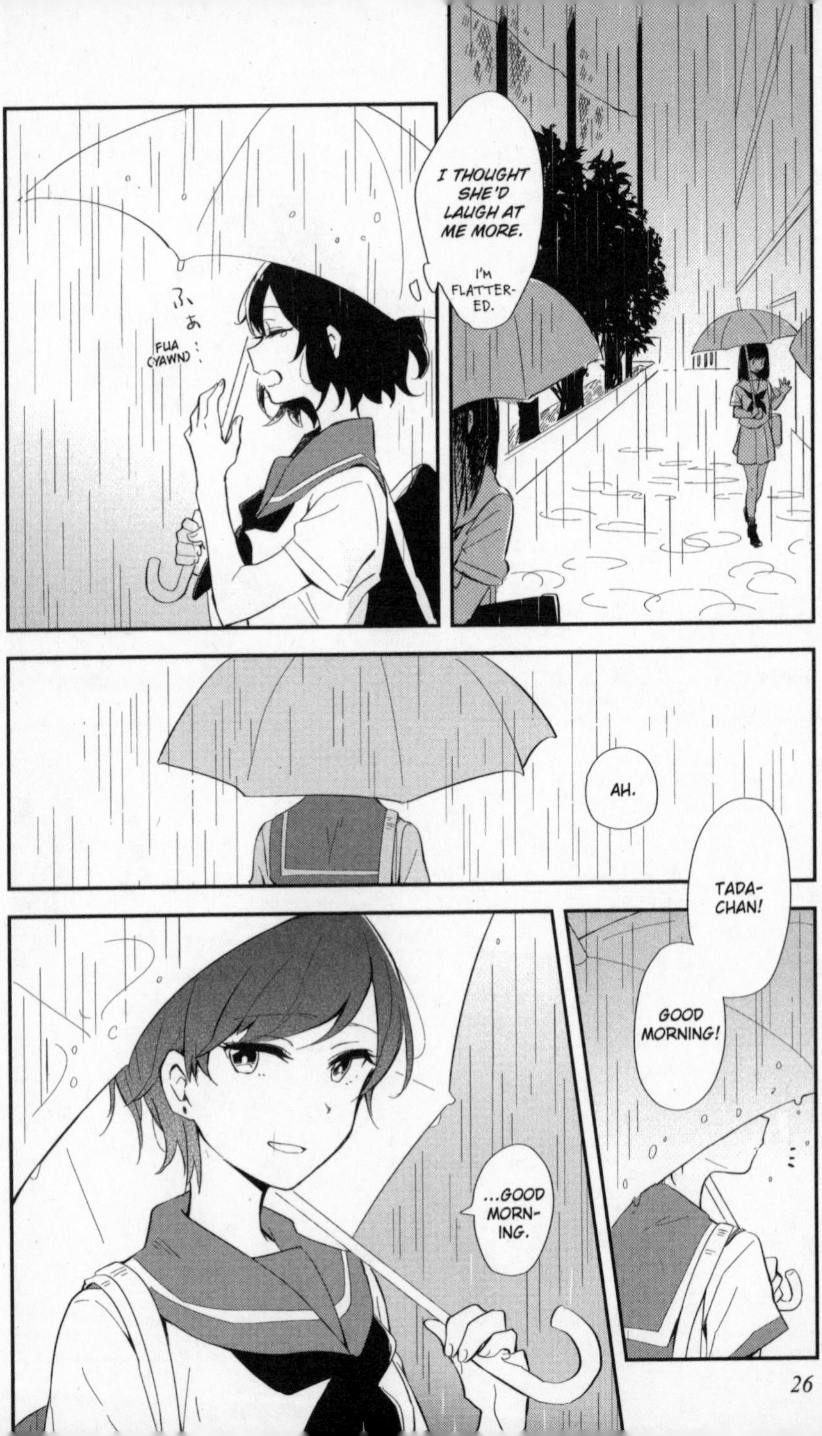
I THOUGHT SHE'D LAUGH AT ME MORE.
I'M FLATTER-ED.
ふあ
FUA (YAWN)
AH.
TADA-CHAN!
GOOD MORNING!
...GOOD MORN-ING.

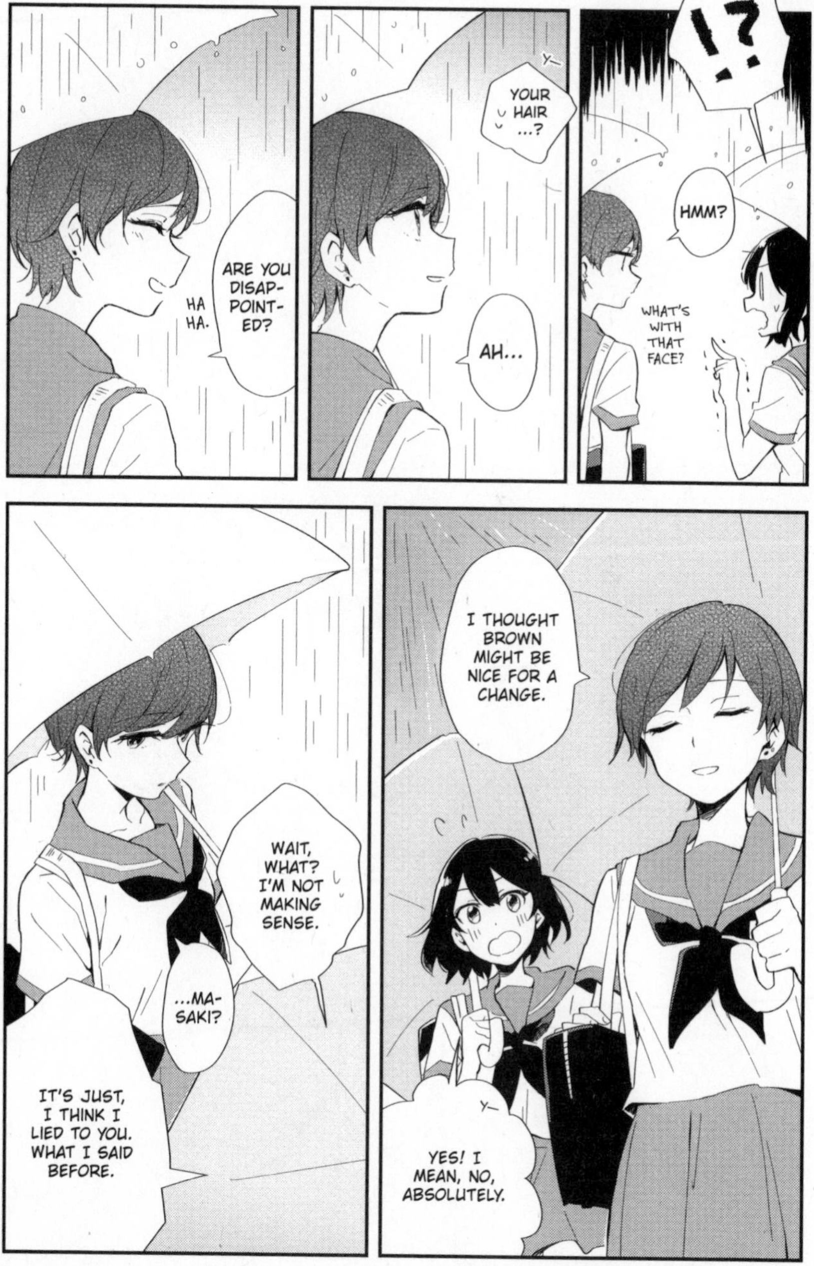
!?
HMM?
WHAT'S WITH THAT FACE?
Y—
YOUR HAIR ...?
AH...
ARE YOU DISAPPOINTED?
HA HA.
I THOUGHT BROWN MIGHT BE NICE FOR A CHANGE.
Y—
YES! I MEAN, NO, ABSOLUTELY.
WAIT, WHAT? I'M NOT MAKING SENSE.
...MASAKI?
IT'S JUST, I THINK I LIED TO YOU. WHAT I SAID BEFORE.

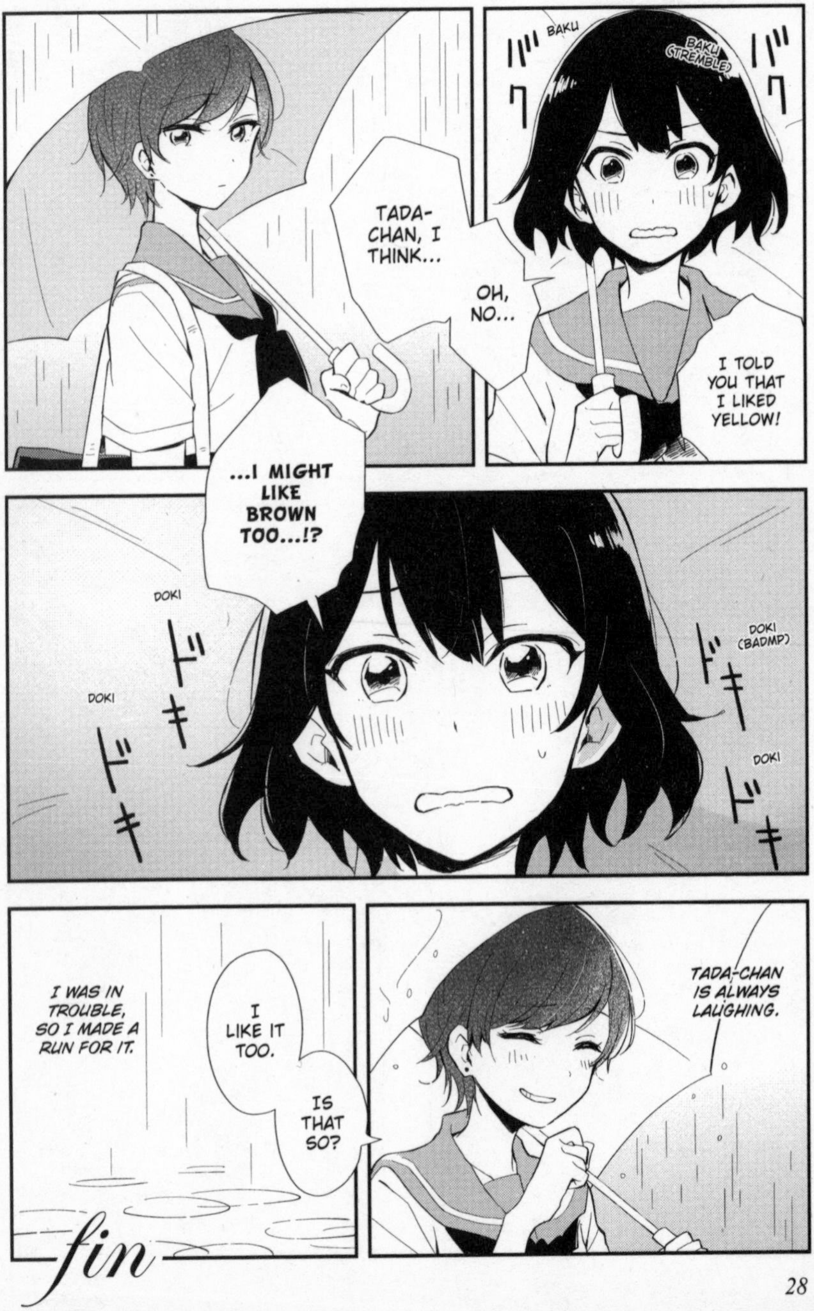
BAKU
BAKU (TREMBLE)
OH, NO...
I TOLD YOU THAT I LIKED YELLOW!
TADA-CHAN, I THINK...
...I MIGHT LIKE BROWN TOO...!?
DOKI (BADMP)
DOKI
DOKI
DOKI
TADA-CHAN IS ALWAYS LAUGHING.
I LIKE IT TOO.
IS THAT SO?
I WAS IN TROUBLE, SO I MADE A RUN FOR IT.
fin

éclair
blanche

A Girls' Love Anthology
That Resonates in Your Heart

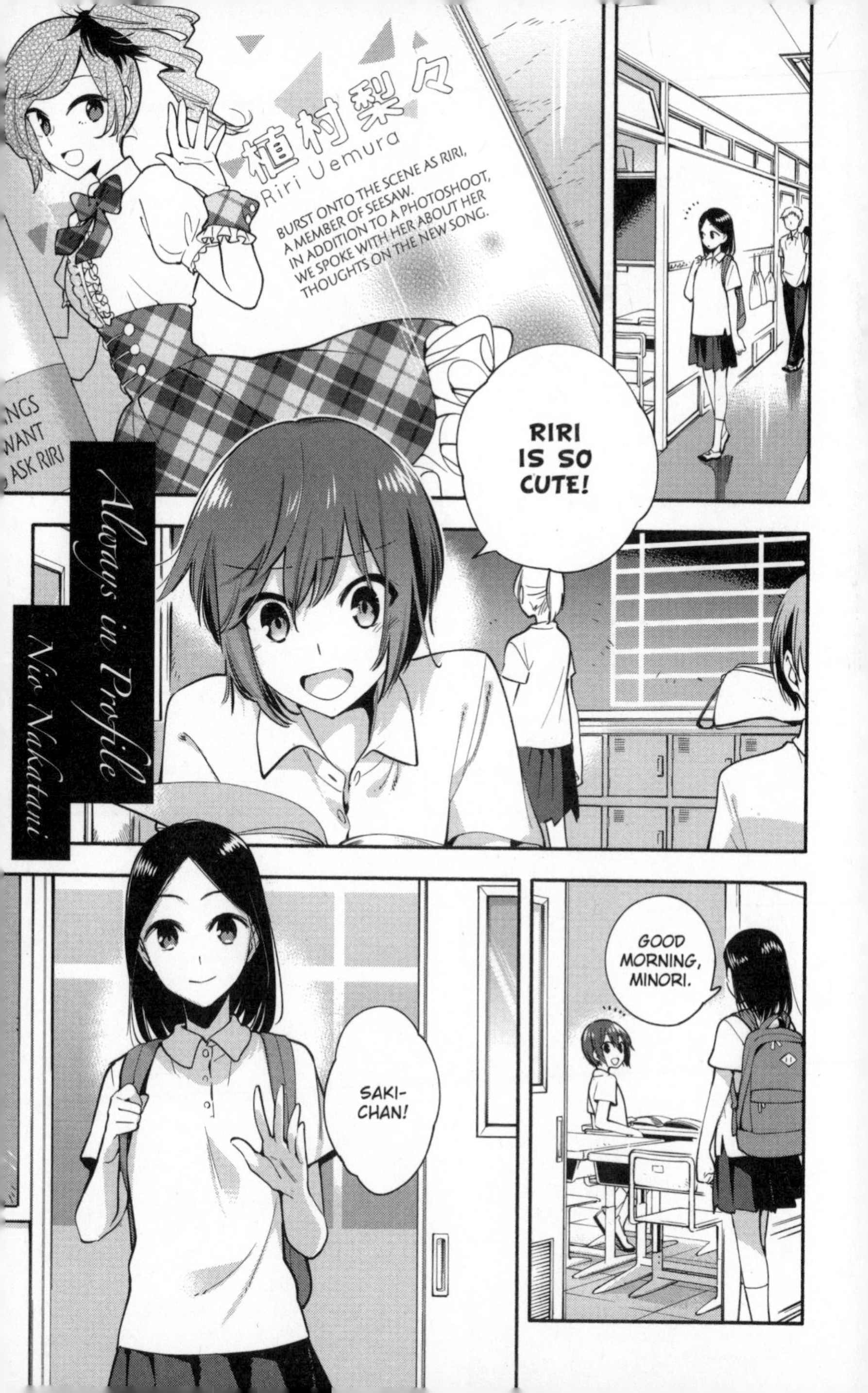

植村梨々
Riri Uemura
BURST ONTO THE SCENE AS RIRI, A MEMBER OF SEESAW. IN ADDITION TO A PHOTOSHOOT, WE SPOKE WITH HER ABOUT HER THOUGHTS ON THE NEW SONG.
RIRI IS SO CUTE!
Always in Profile
Nio Nakatani
GOOD MORNING, MINORI.
SAKI-CHAN!

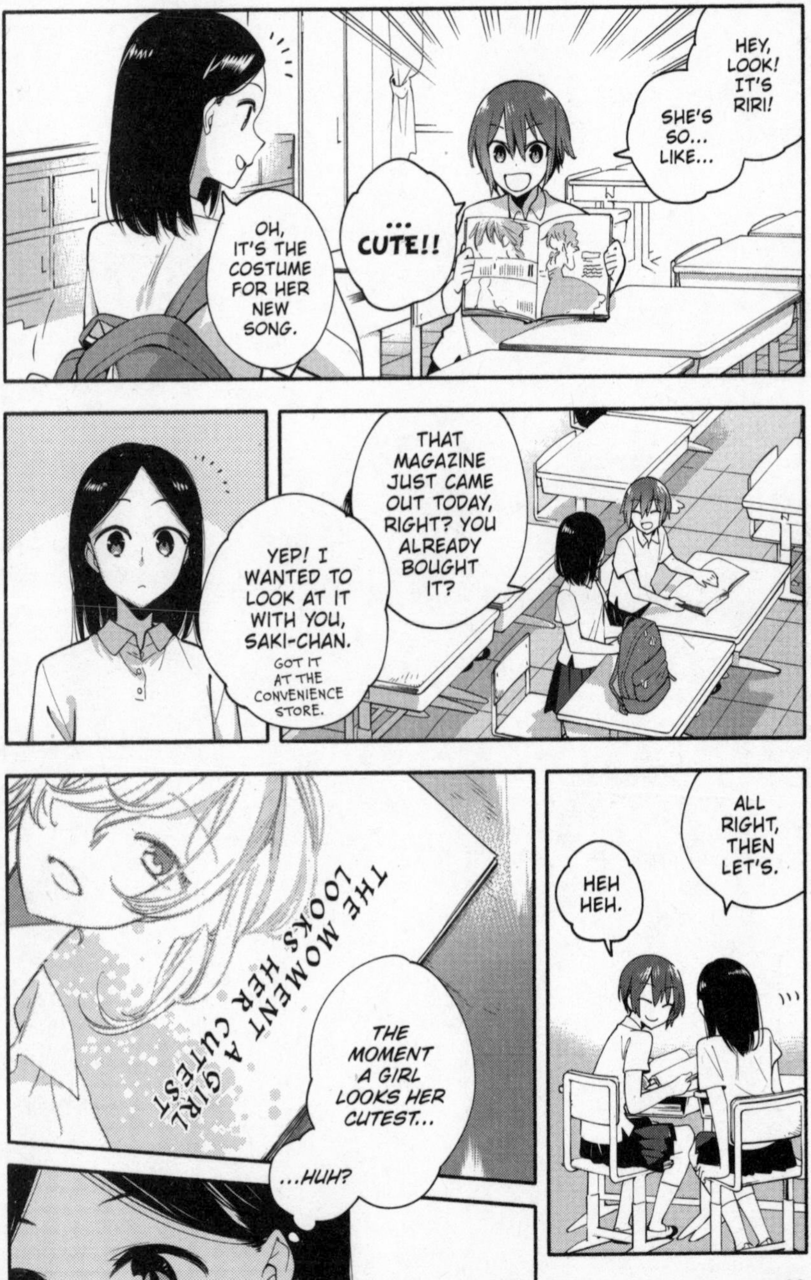
HEY, LOOK! IT'S RIRI!
SHE'S SO... LIKE...
...CUTE!!
OH, IT'S THE COSTUME FOR HER NEW SONG.
THAT MAGAZINE JUST CAME OUT TODAY, RIGHT? YOU ALREADY BOUGHT IT?
YEP! I WANTED TO LOOK AT IT WITH YOU, SAKI-CHAN.
GOT IT AT THE CONVENIENCE STORE.
ALL RIGHT, THEN LET'S.
HEH HEH.
THE MOMENT A GIRL LOOKS HER CUTEST
THE MOMENT A GIRL LOOKS HER CUTEST...
...HUH?

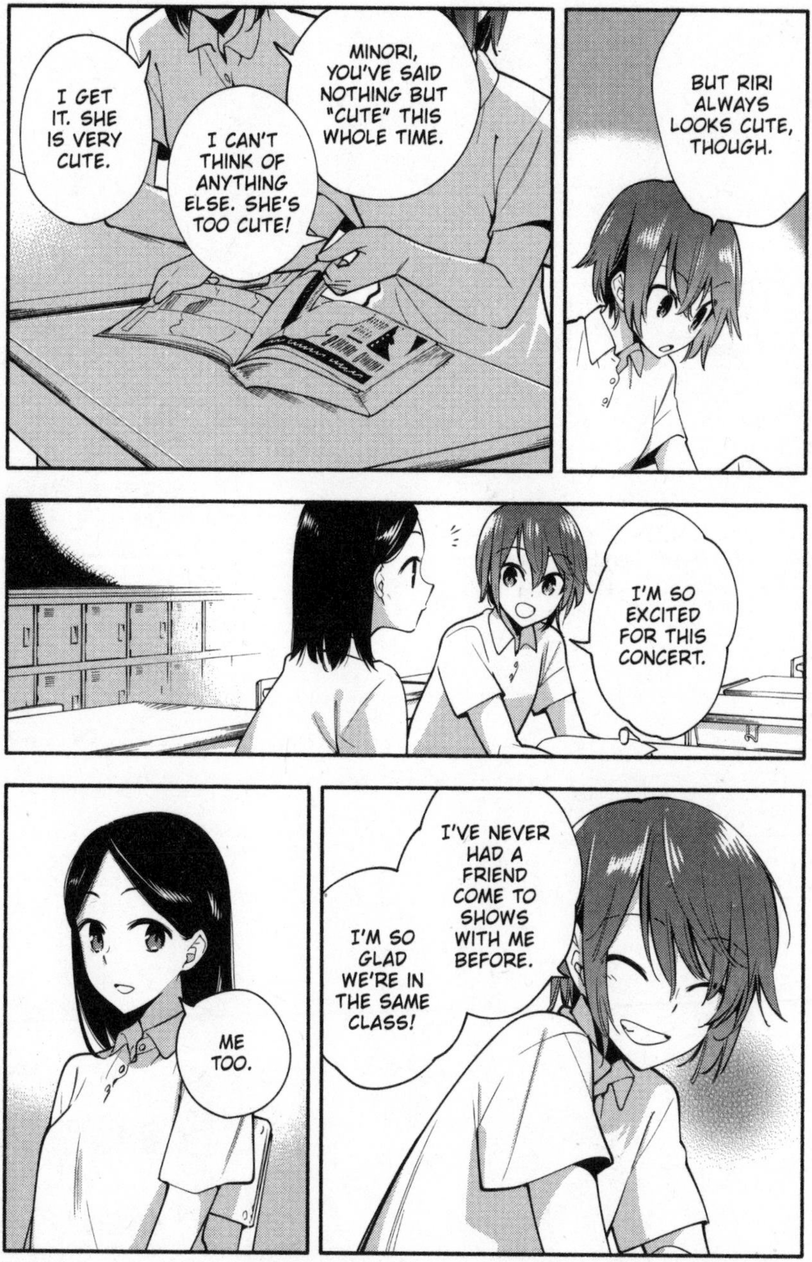
BUT RIRI ALWAYS LOOKS CUTE, THOUGH.
MINORI, YOU'VE SAID NOTHING BUT "CUTE" THIS WHOLE TIME.
I CAN'T THINK OF ANYTHING ELSE. SHE'S TOO CUTE!
I GET IT. SHE IS VERY CUTE.
I'M SO EXCITED FOR THIS CONCERT.
I'VE NEVER HAD A FRIEND COME TO SHOWS WITH ME BEFORE.
I'M SO GLAD WE'RE IN THE SAME CLASS!
ME TOO.

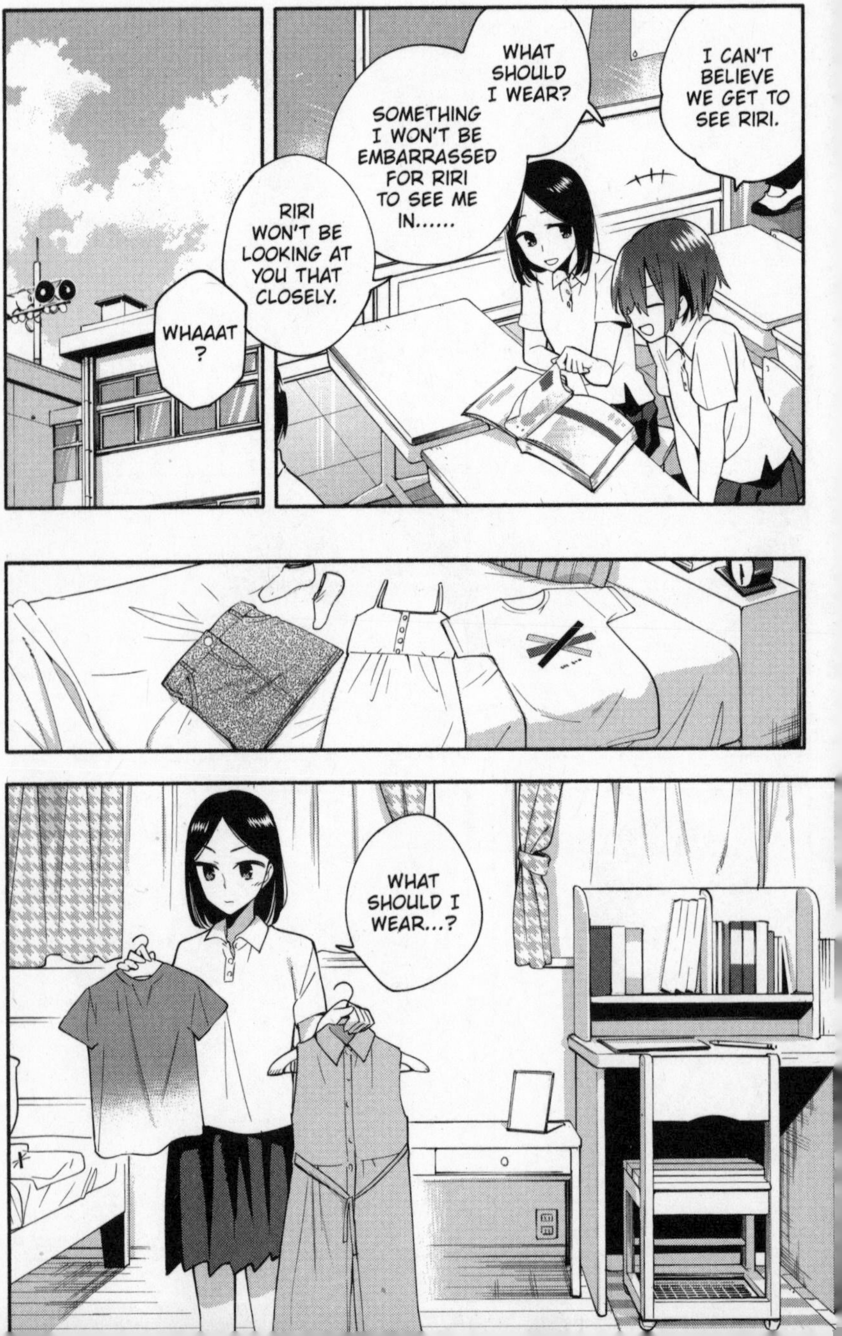
I CAN'T BELIEVE WE GET TO SEE RIRI.
WHAT SHOULD I WEAR?
SOMETHING I WON'T BE EMBARRASSED FOR RIRI TO SEE ME IN......
RIRI WON'T BE LOOKING AT YOU THAT CLOSELY.
WHAAAT?
WHAT SHOULD I WEAR...?

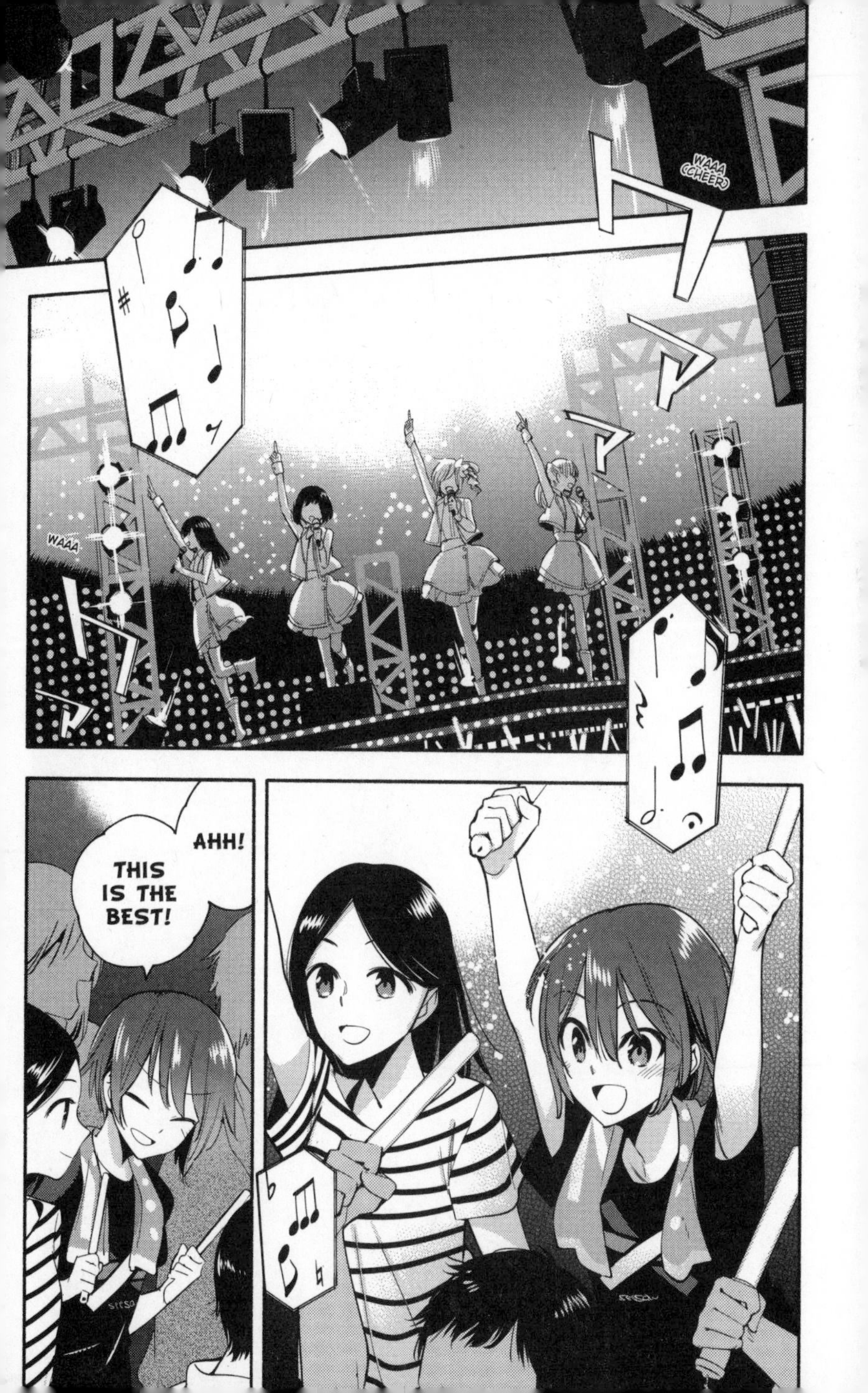
WAAA (CHEER)
WAAA
AHH! THIS IS THE BEST!

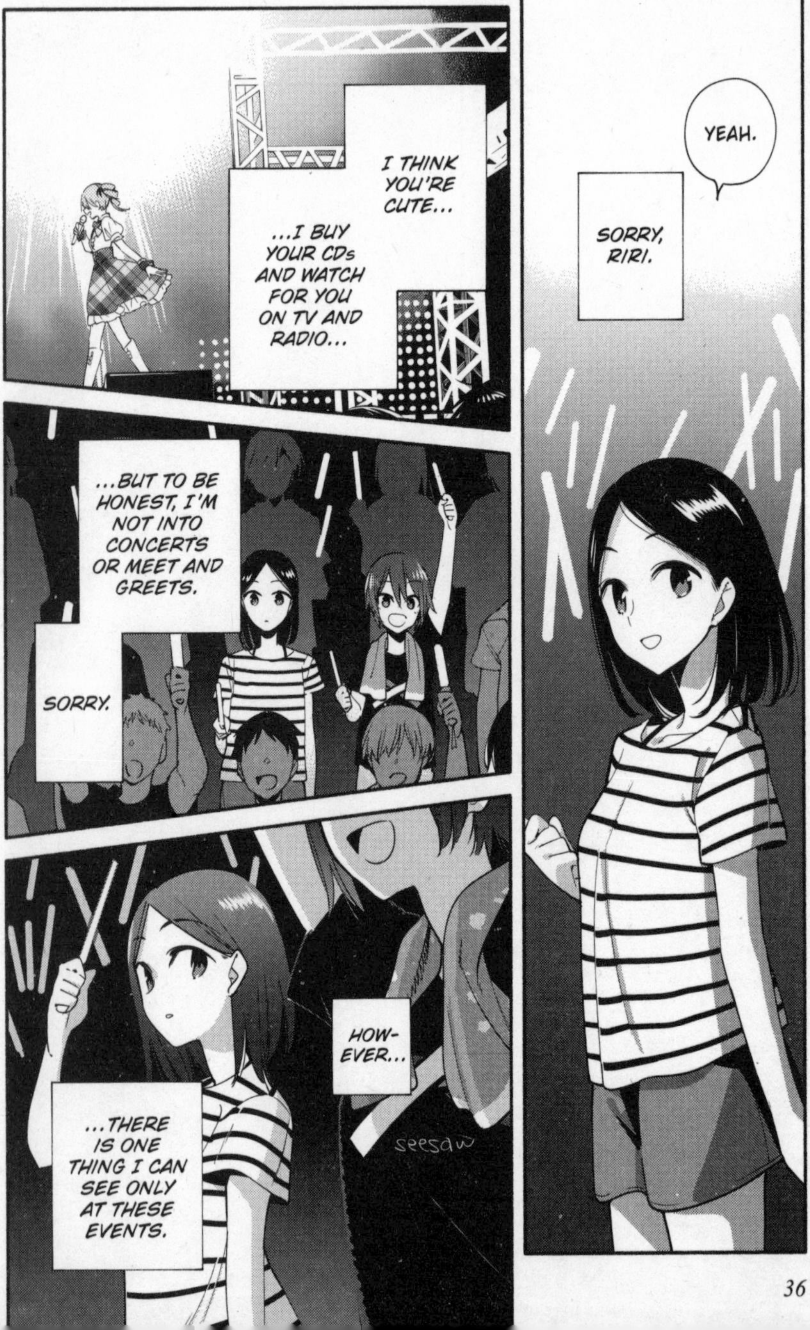
YEAH.
SORRY, RIRI.
I THINK YOU'RE CUTE...
...I BUY YOUR CDs AND WATCH FOR YOU ON TV AND RADIO...
...BUT TO BE HONEST, I'M NOT INTO CONCERTS OR MEET AND GREETS.
SORRY.
HOW-EVER...
...THERE IS ONE THING I CAN SEE ONLY AT THESE EVENTS.
seesaw

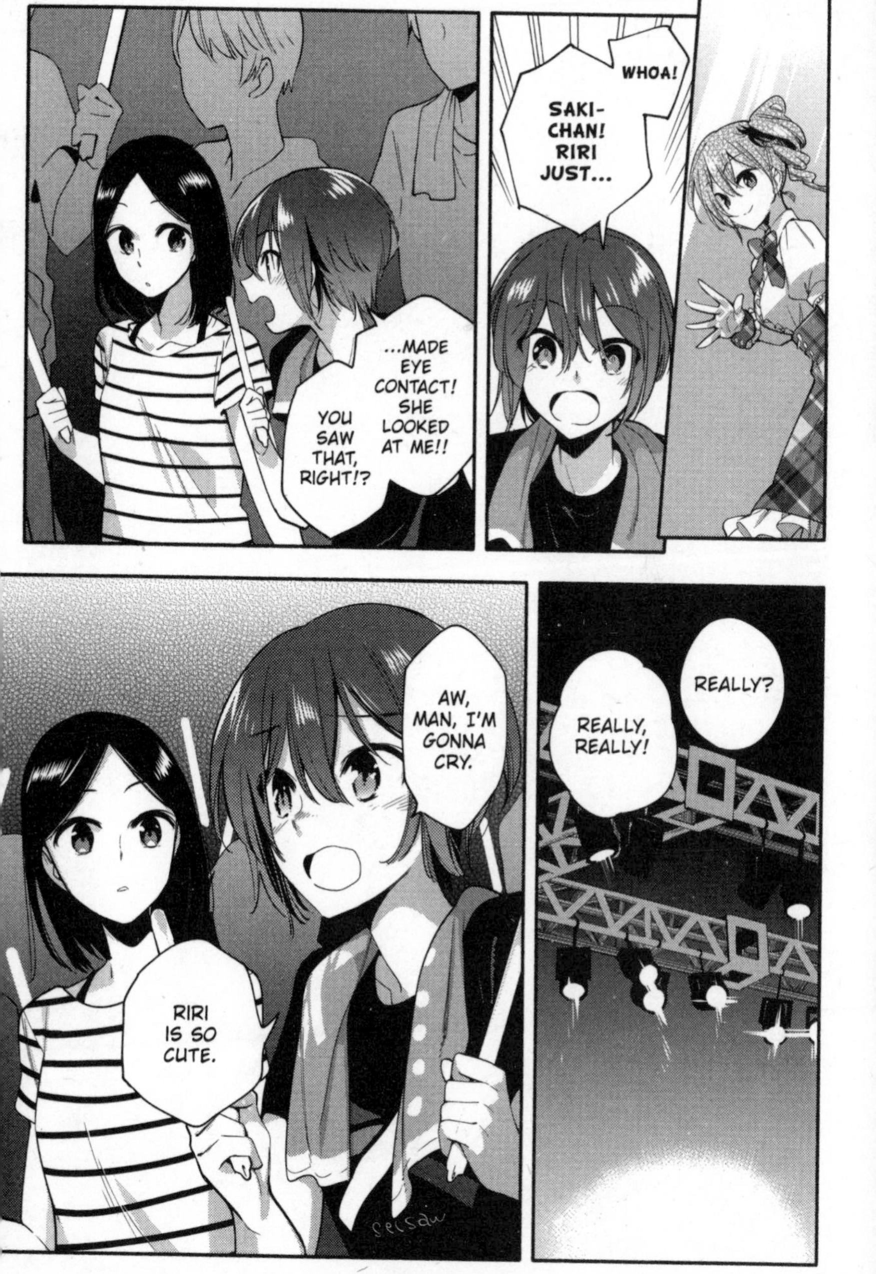
WHOA! SAKI-CHAN! RIRI JUST...
...MADE EYE CONTACT! SHE LOOKED AT ME!!
YOU SAW THAT, RIGHT!?
REALLY?
REALLY, REALLY!
AW, MAN, I'M GONNA CRY.
RIRI IS SO CUTE.

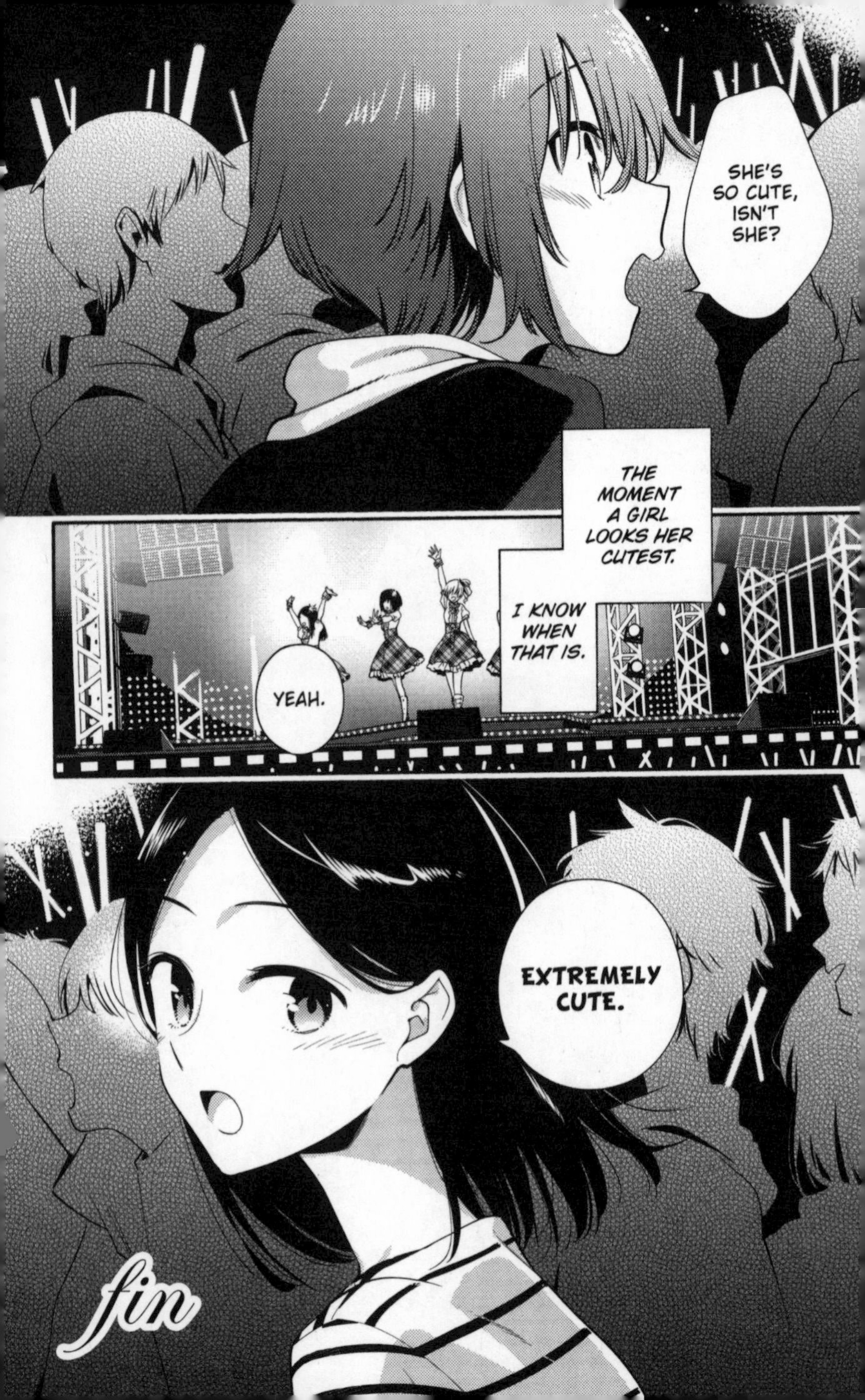
SHE'S SO CUTE, ISN'T SHE?
THE MOMENT A GIRL LOOKS HER CUTEST.
I KNOW WHEN THAT IS.
YEAH.
EXTREMELY CUTE.
fin

éclair
blanche

A Girls' Love Anthology
That Resonates in Your Heart

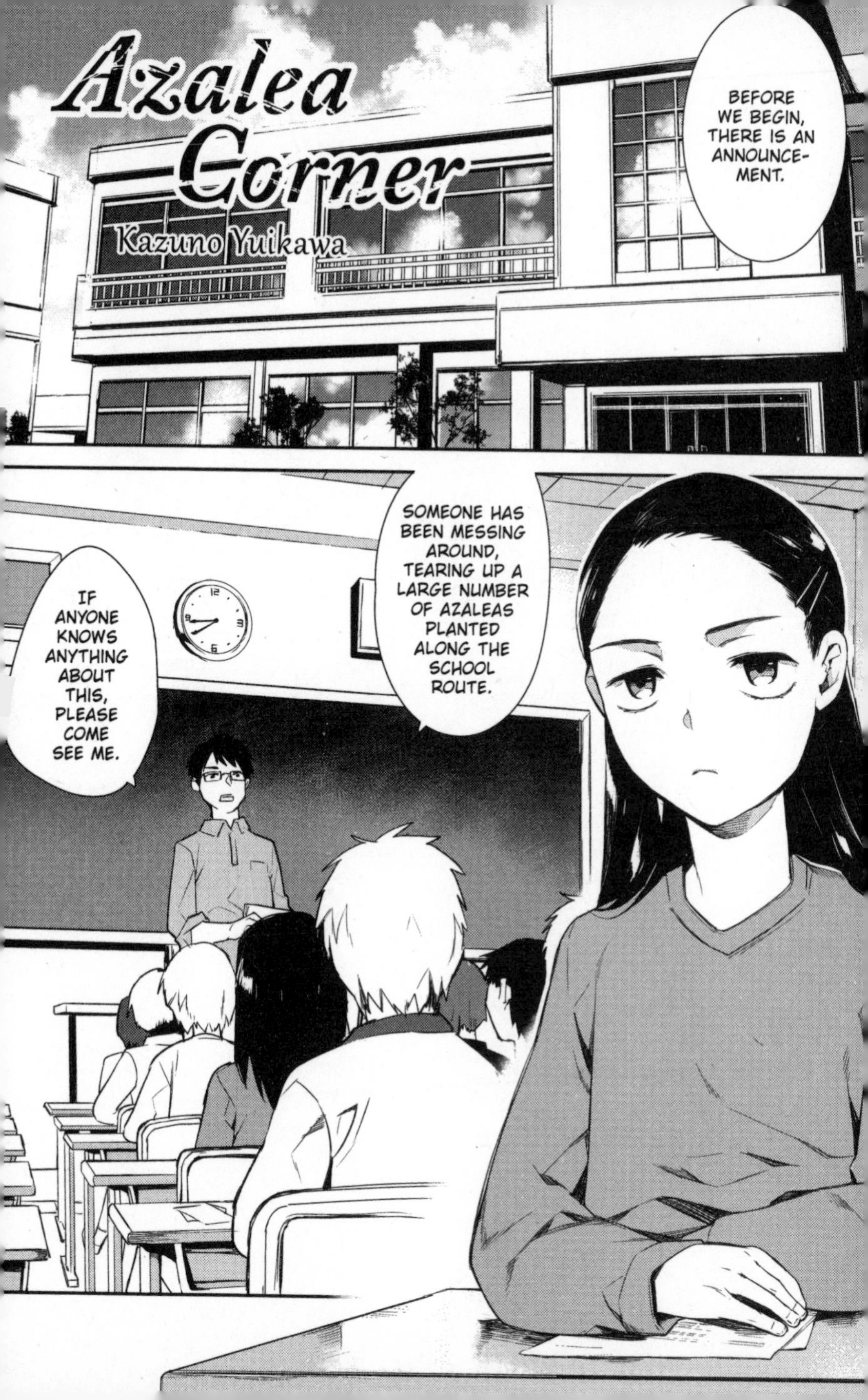
BEFORE WE BEGIN, THERE IS AN ANNOUNCEMENT.
Azalea Corner
Kazuno Yuikawa
SOMEONE HAS BEEN MESSING AROUND, TEARING UP A LARGE NUMBER OF AZALEAS PLANTED ALONG THE SCHOOL ROUTE.
IF ANYONE KNOWS ANYTHING ABOUT THIS, PLEASE COME SEE ME.

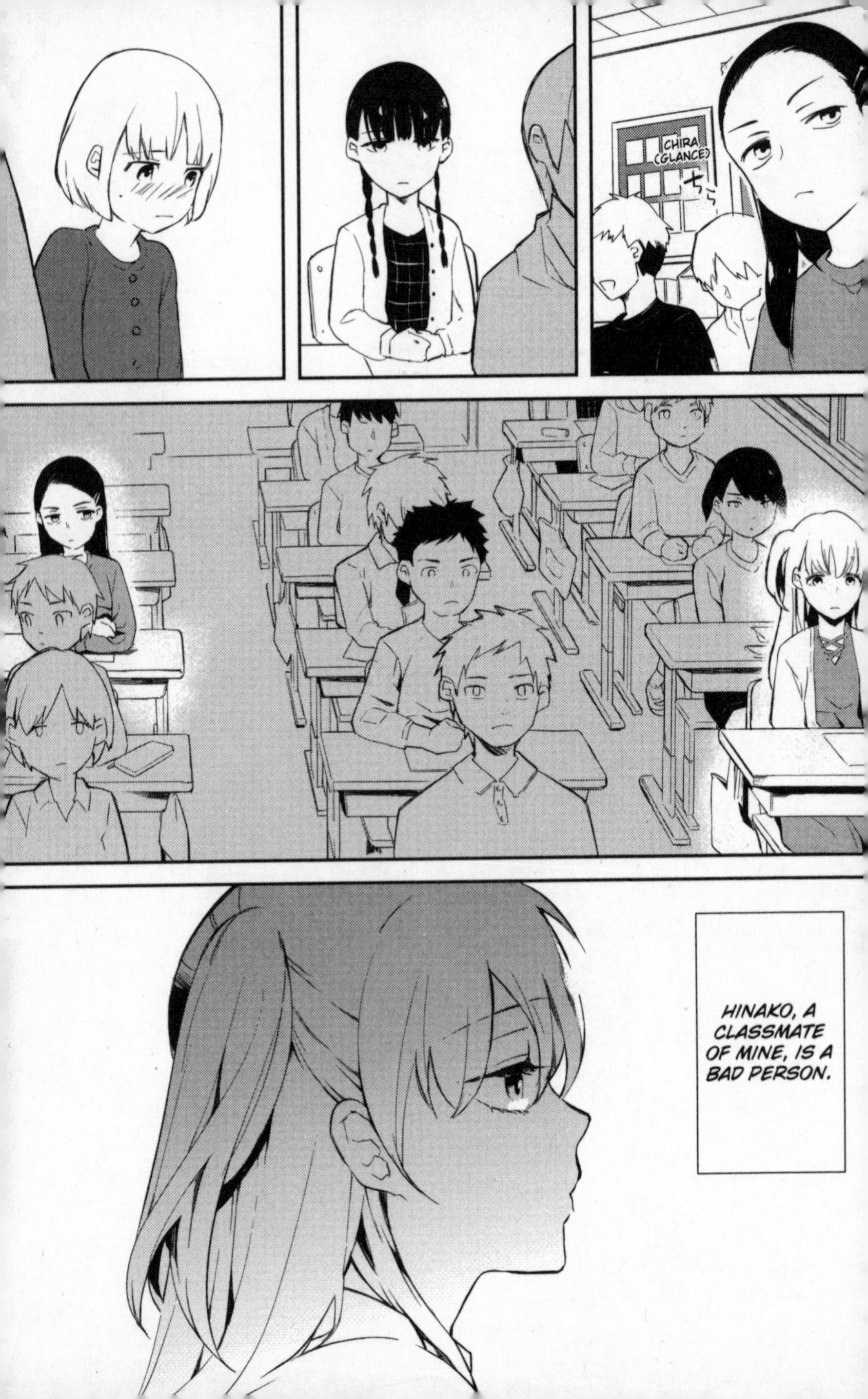
CHIRA (GLANCE)
HINAKO, A CLASSMATE OF MINE, IS A BAD PERSON.

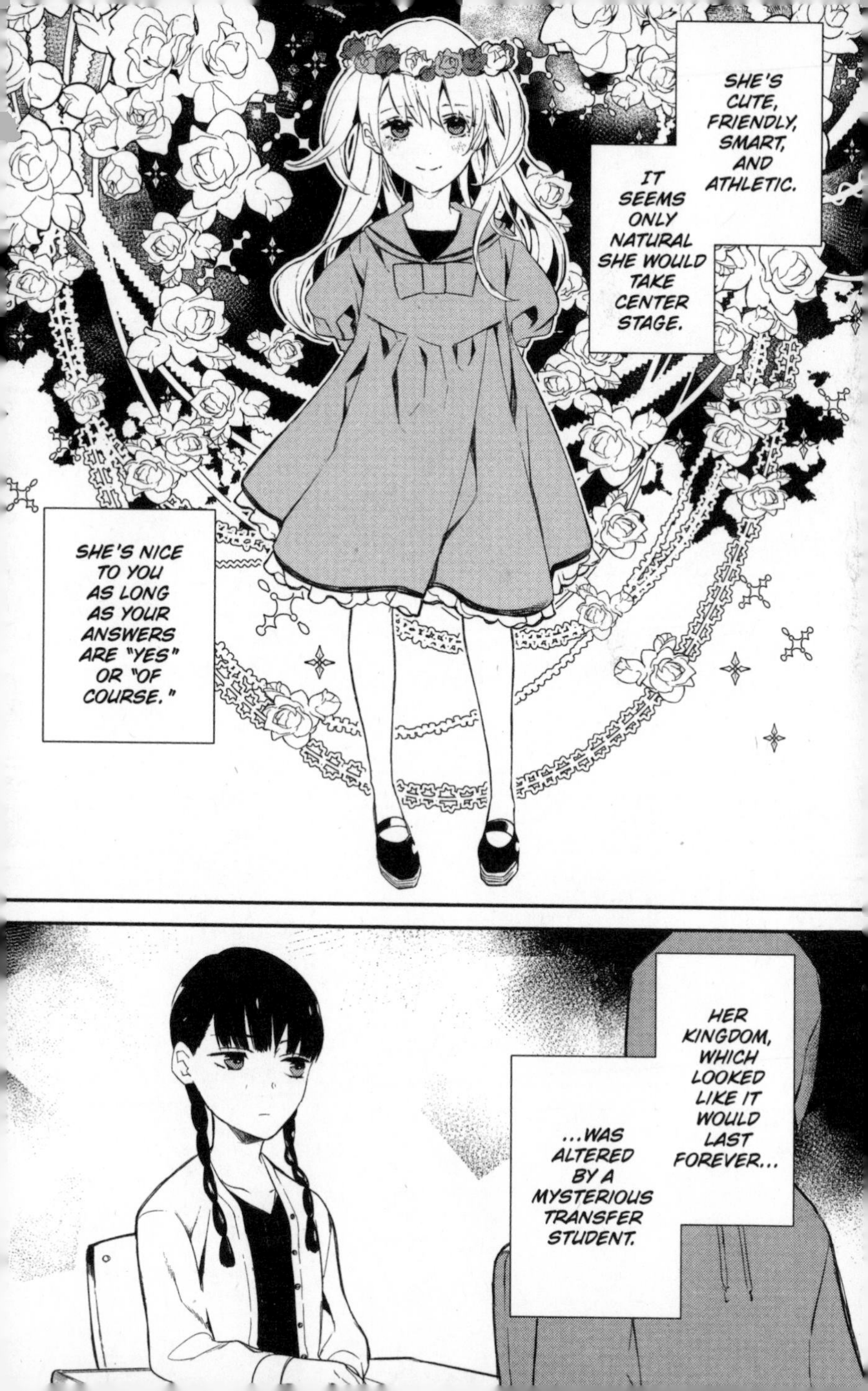
SHE'S CUTE, FRIENDLY, SMART, AND ATHLETIC.
IT SEEMS ONLY NATURAL SHE WOULD TAKE CENTER STAGE.
SHE'S NICE TO YOU AS LONG AS YOUR ANSWERS ARE "YES" OR "OF COURSE."
HER KINGDOM, WHICH LOOKED LIKE IT WOULD LAST FOREVER...
...WAS ALTERED BY A MYSTERIOUS TRANSFER STUDENT.

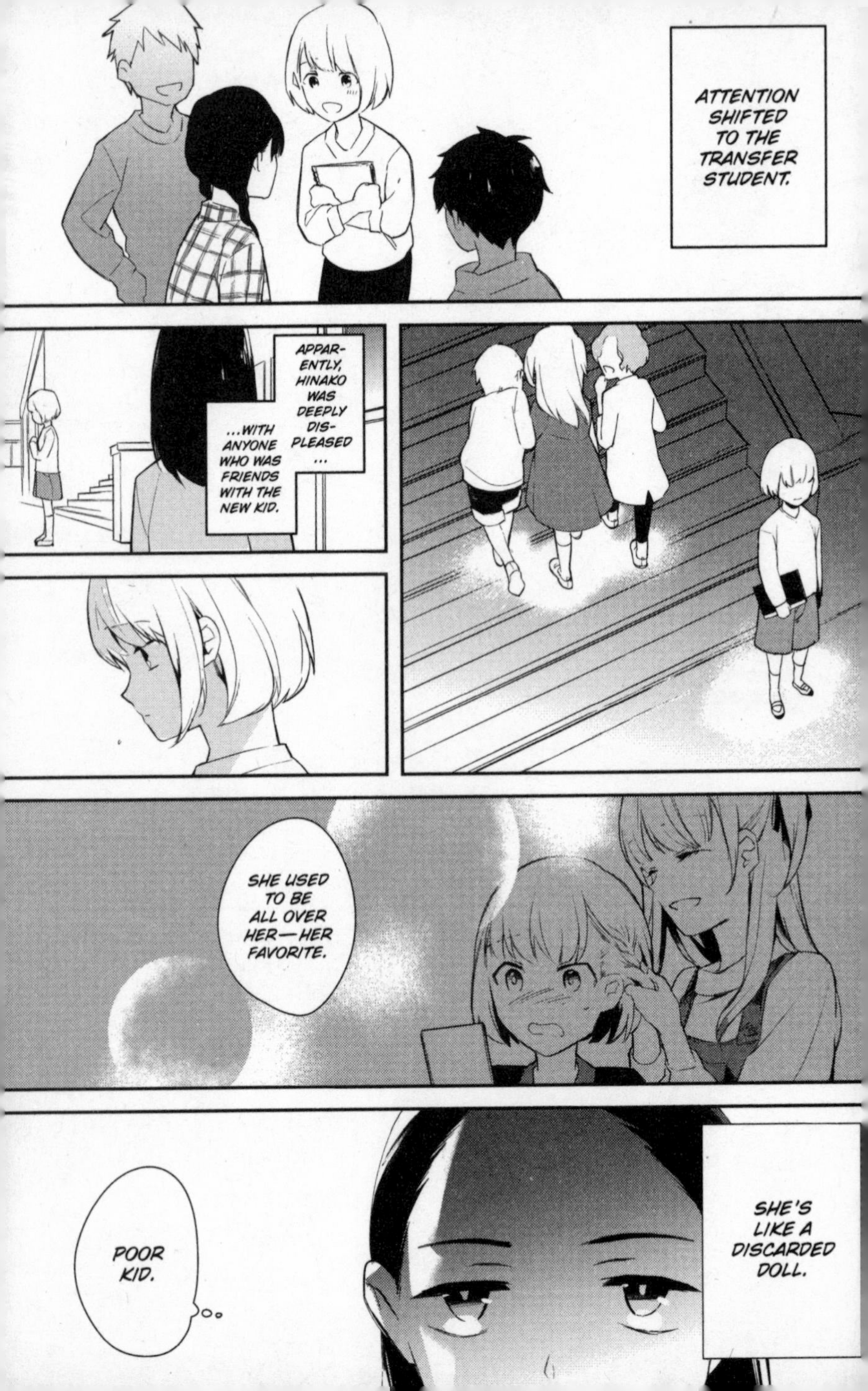
ATTENTION SHIFTED TO THE TRANSFER STUDENT.
APPARENTLY, HINAKO WAS DEEPLY DISPLEASED...
...WITH ANYONE WHO WAS FRIENDS WITH THE NEW KID.
SHE USED TO BE ALL OVER HER—HER FAVORITE.
SHE'S LIKE A DISCARDED DOLL.
POOR KID.

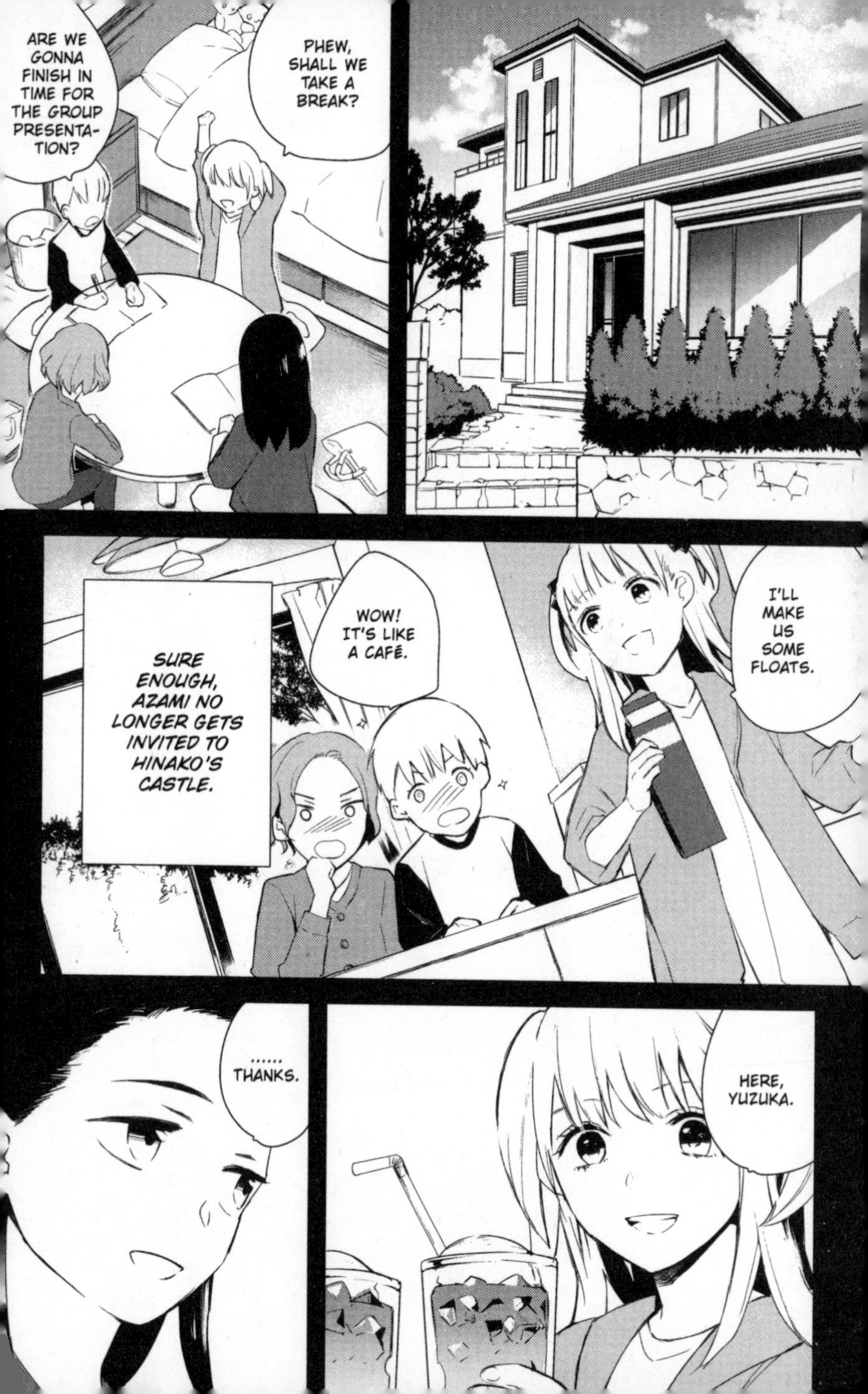
PHEW, SHALL WE TAKE A BREAK?
ARE WE GONNA FINISH IN TIME FOR THE GROUP PRESENTATION?
I'LL MAKE US SOME FLOATS.
WOW! IT'S LIKE A CAFÉ.
SURE ENOUGH, AZAMI NO LONGER GETS INVITED TO HINAKO'S CASTLE.
HERE, YUZUKA.
...... THANKS.

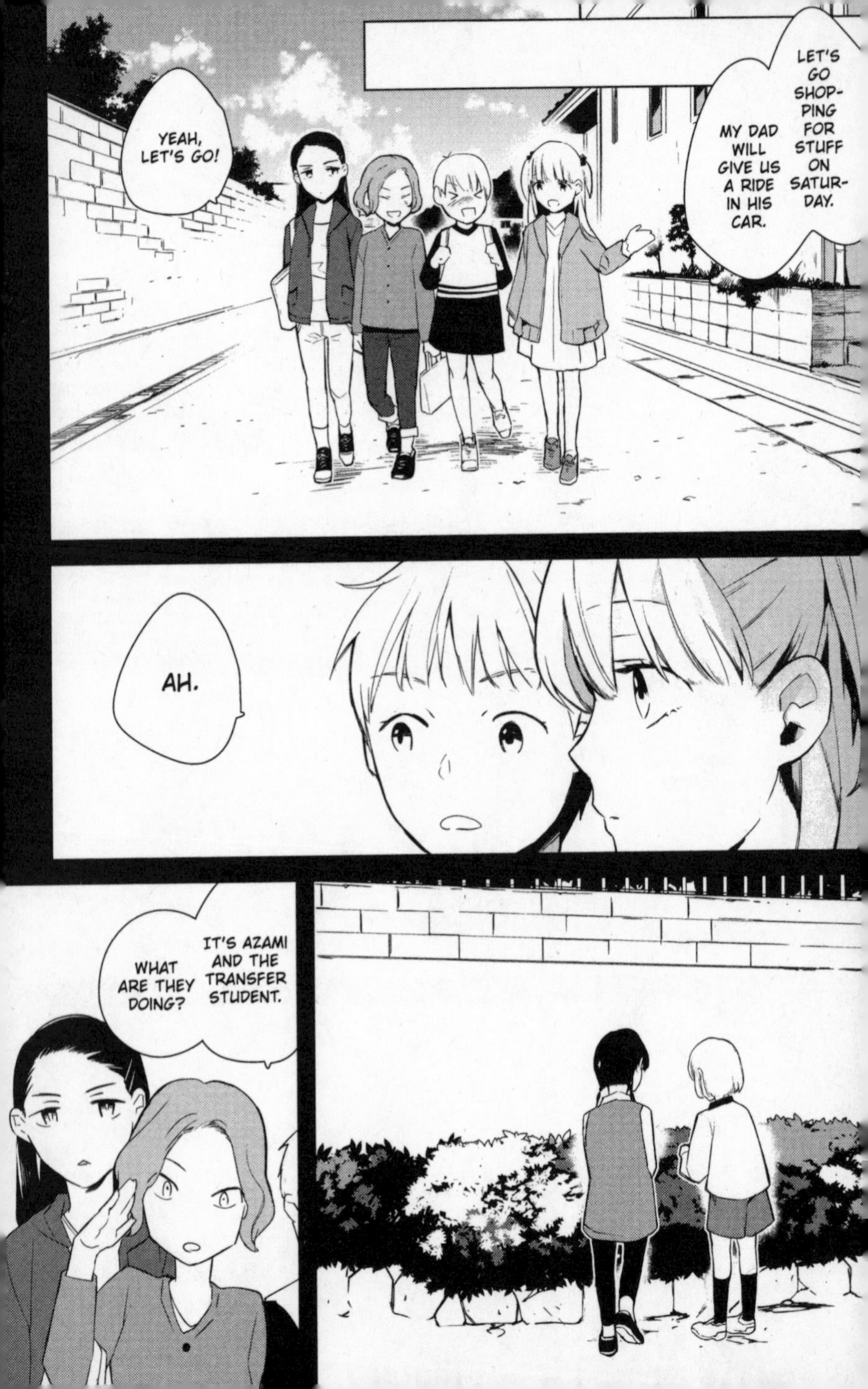
LET'S GO SHOPPING FOR STUFF ON SATURDAY.
MY DAD WILL GIVE US A RIDE IN HIS CAR.
YEAH, LET'S GO!
AH.
IT'S AZAMI AND THE TRANSFER STUDENT.
WHAT ARE THEY DOING?

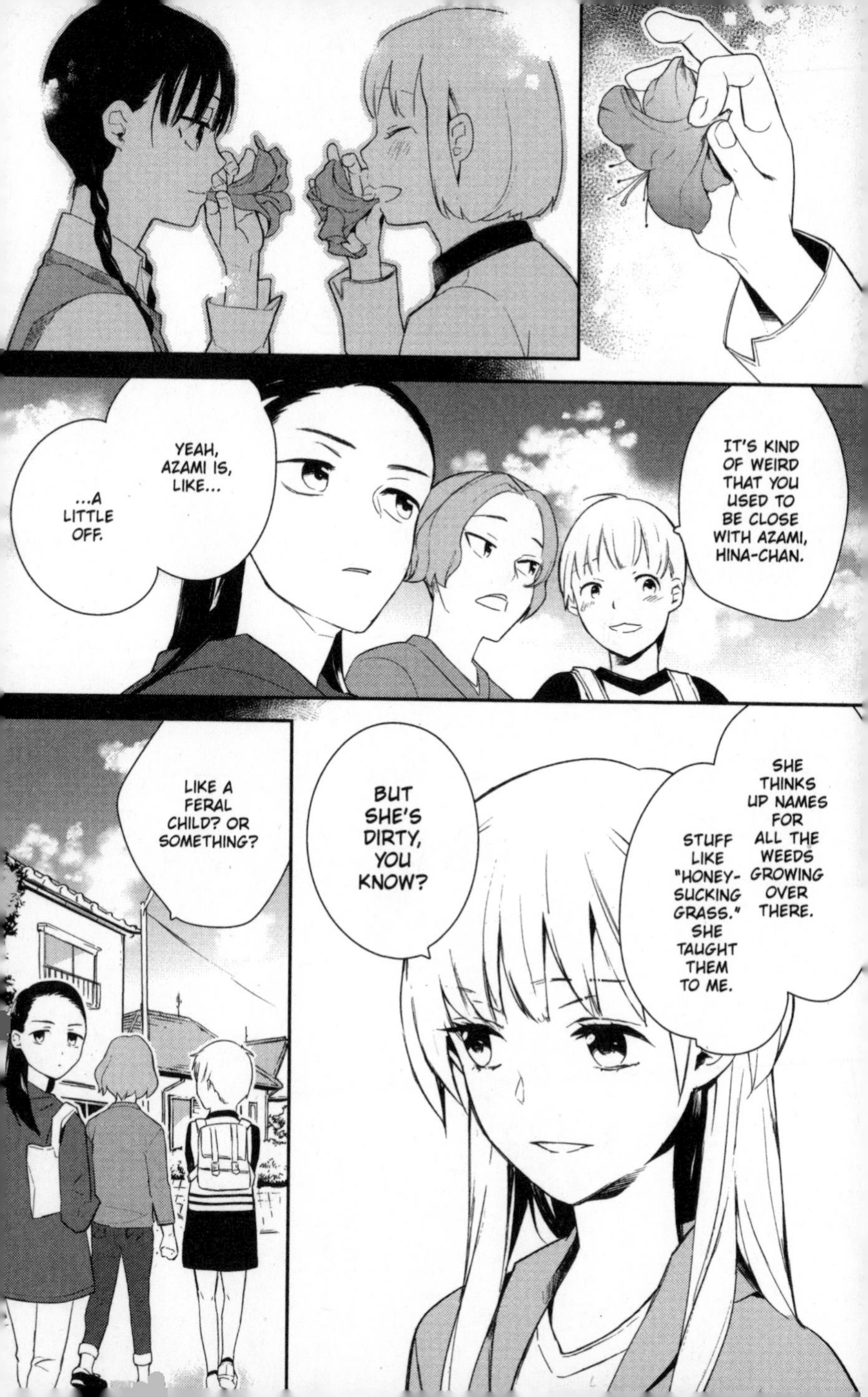
IT'S KIND OF WEIRD THAT YOU USED TO BE CLOSE WITH AZAMI, HINA-CHAN.
YEAH, AZAMI IS, LIKE...
...A LITTLE OFF.
SHE THINKS UP NAMES FOR ALL THE WEEDS GROWING OVER THERE.
STUFF LIKE "HONEY-SUCKING GRASS." SHE TAUGHT THEM TO ME.
BUT SHE'S DIRTY, YOU KNOW?
LIKE A FERAL CHILD? OR SOMETHING?

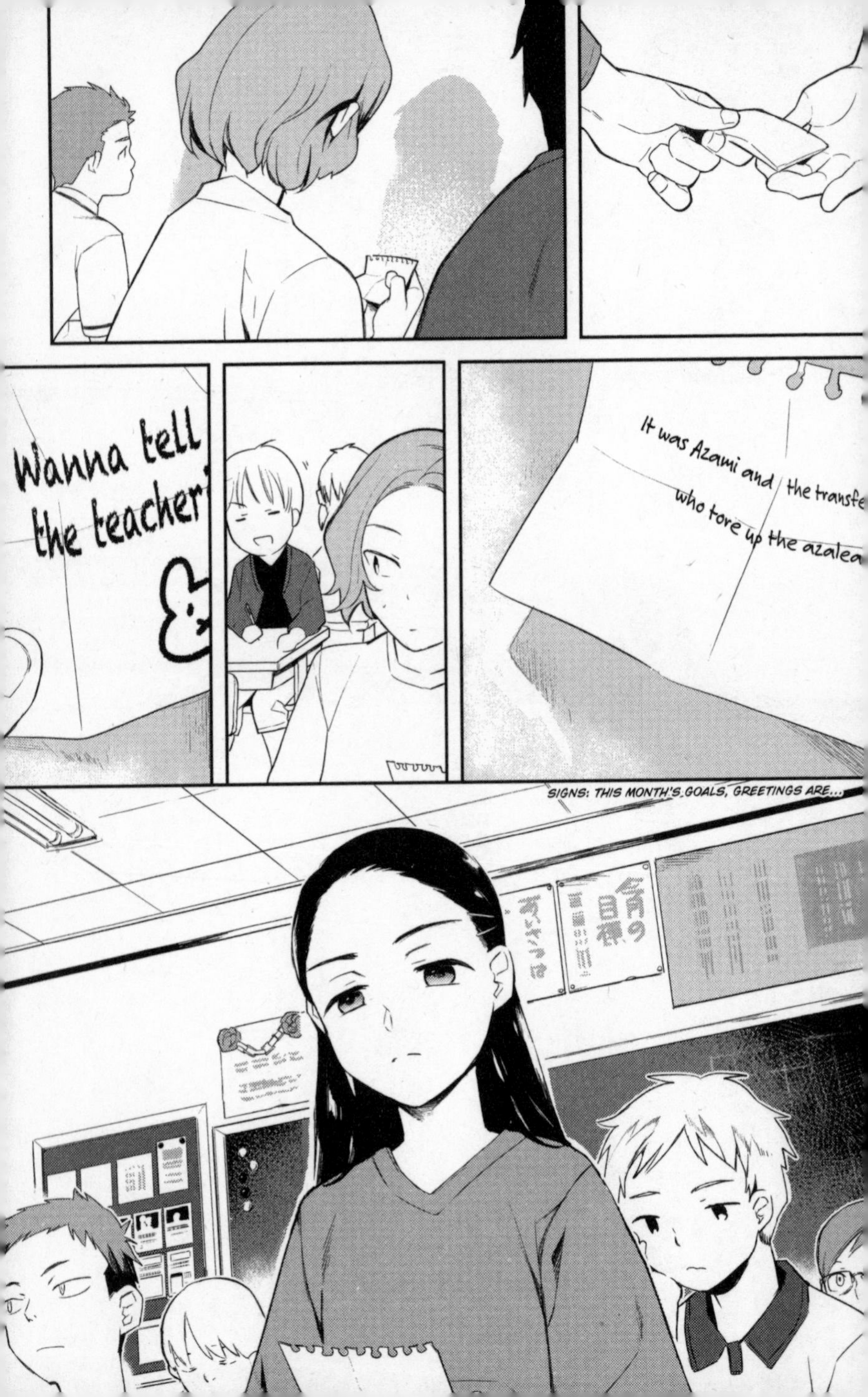
It was Azami and the transfe
who tore up the azalea
Wanna tell
the teacher
SIGNS: THIS MONTH'S GOALS, GREETINGS ARE...
今月の目標
あいさつは

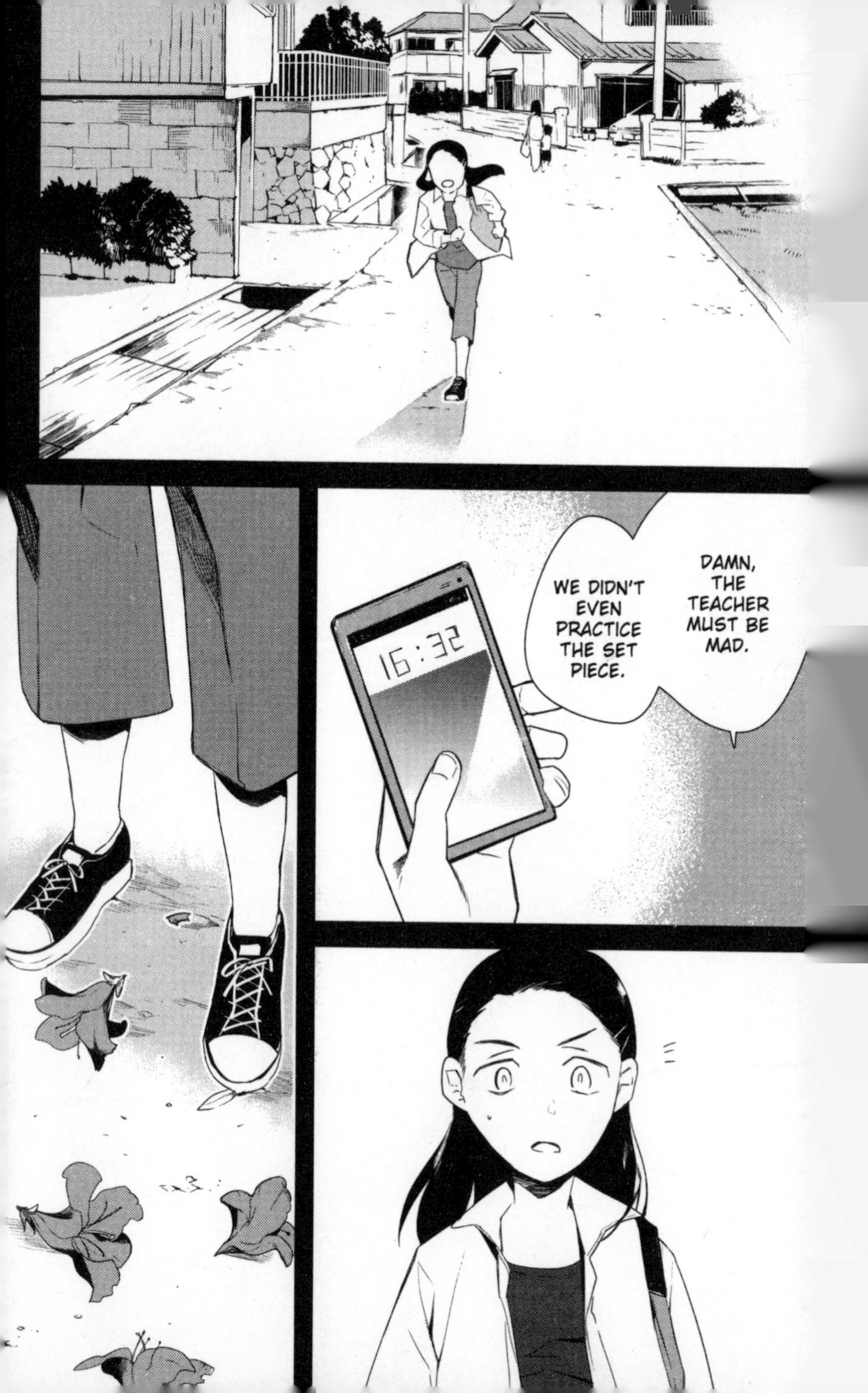
DAMN, THE TEACHER MUST BE MAD.
WE DIDN'T EVEN PRACTICE THE SET PIECE.
16:32

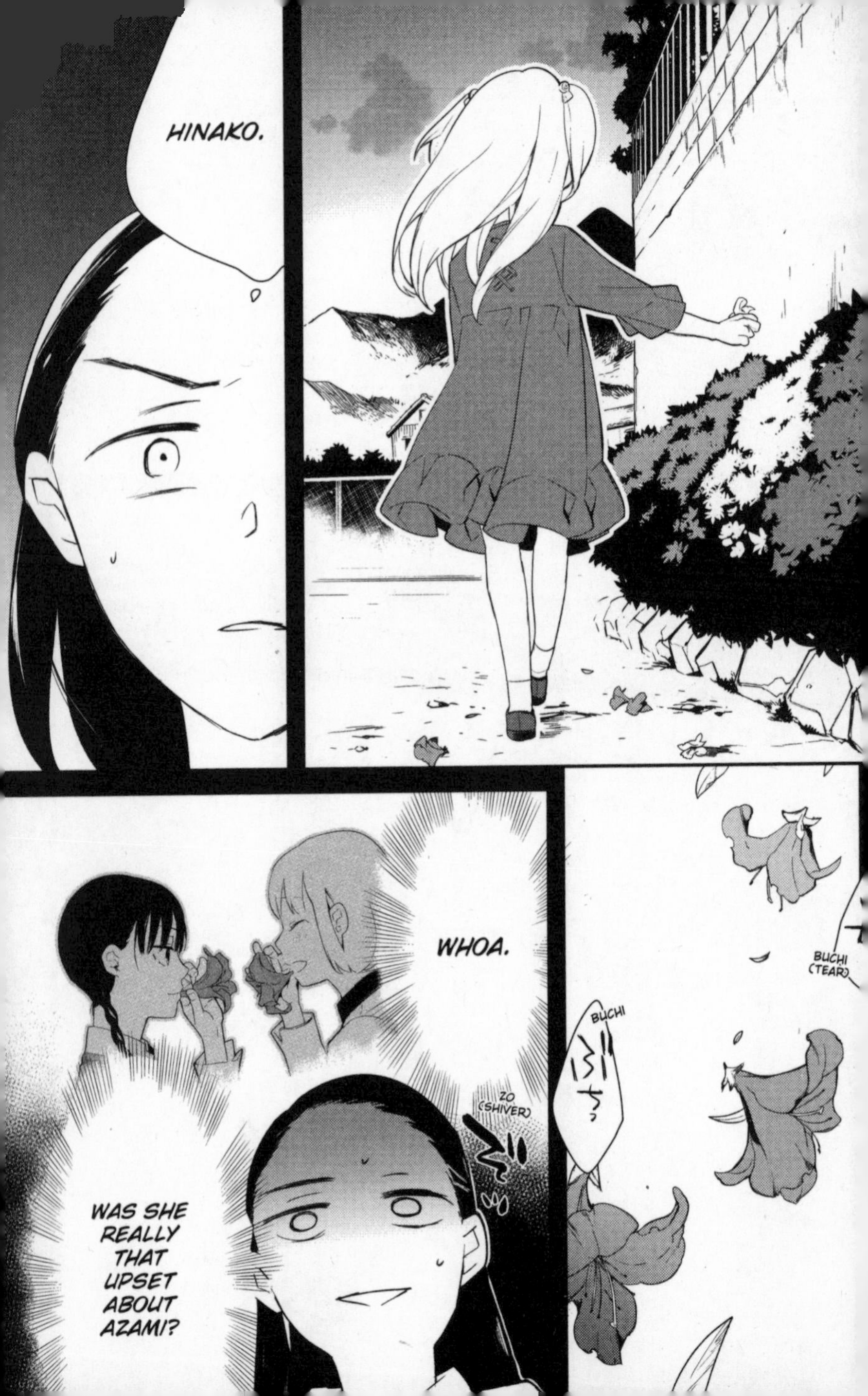
HINAKO.
BUCHI (TEAR)
BUCHI
WHOA.
ZO (SHIVER)
WAS SHE REALLY THAT UPSET ABOUT AZAMI?

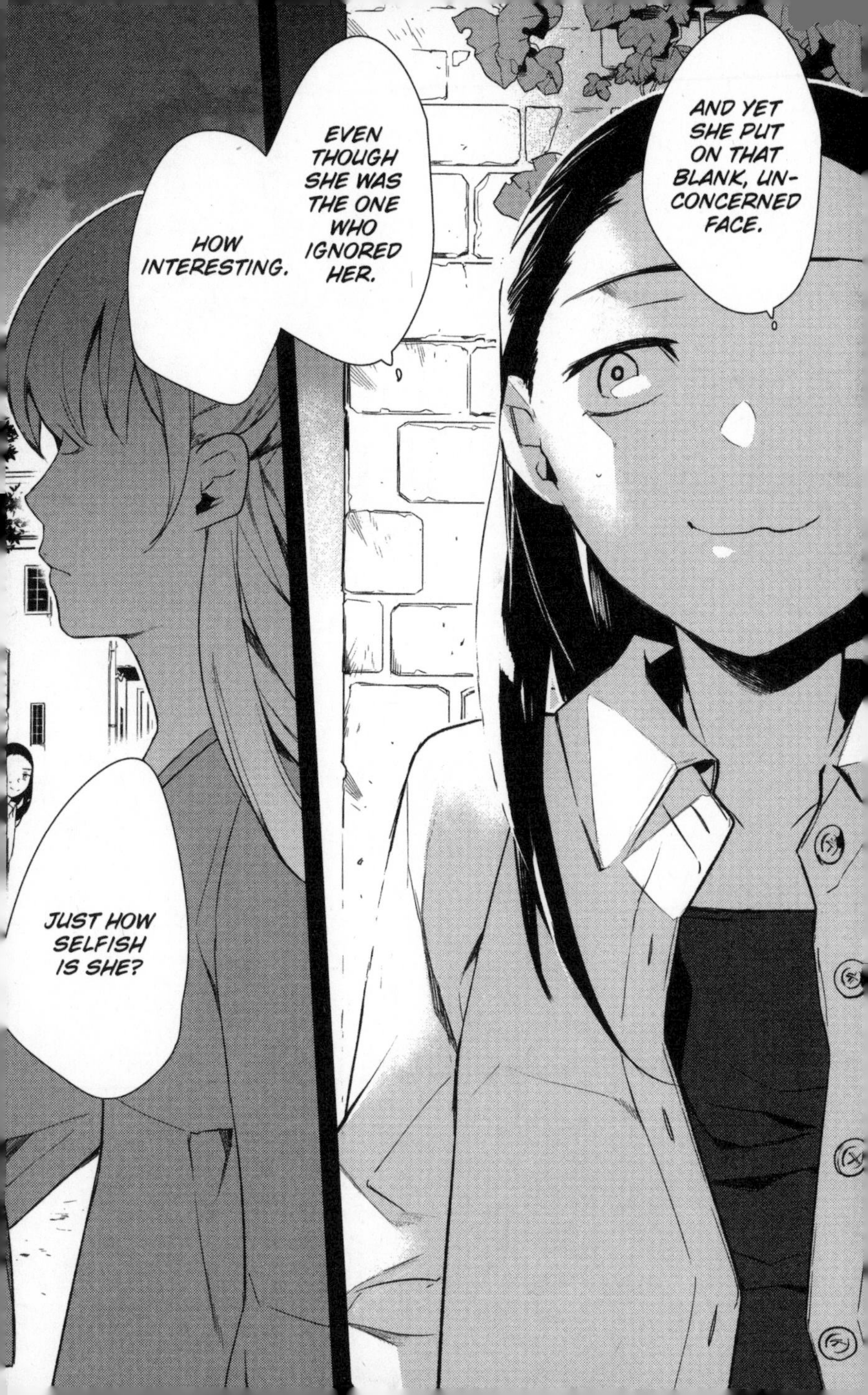
AND YET SHE PUT ON THAT BLANK, UN-CONCERNED FACE.
EVEN THOUGH SHE WAS THE ONE WHO IGNORED HER.
HOW INTERESTING.
JUST HOW SELFISH IS SHE?

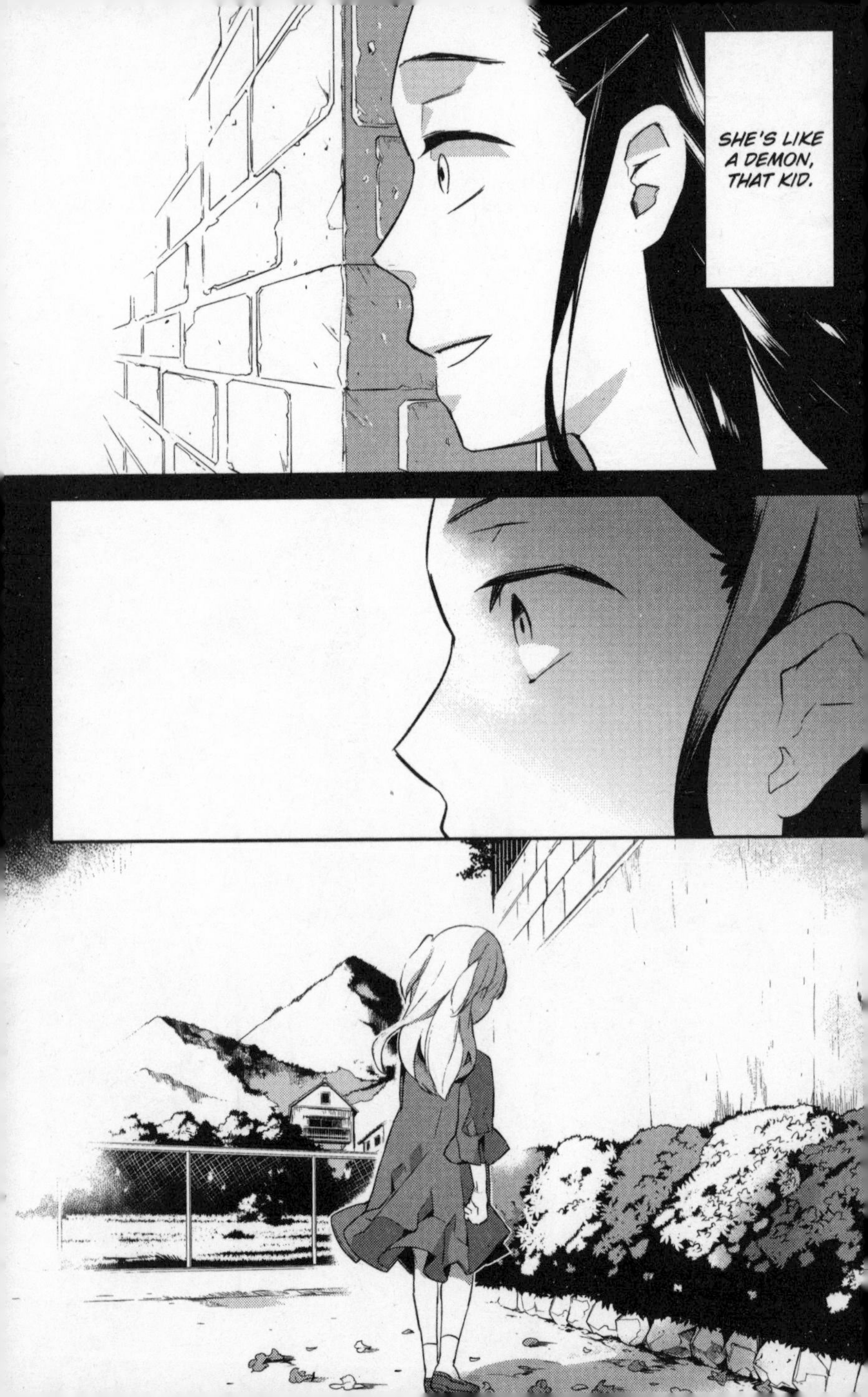
SHE'S LIKE A DEMON, THAT KID.

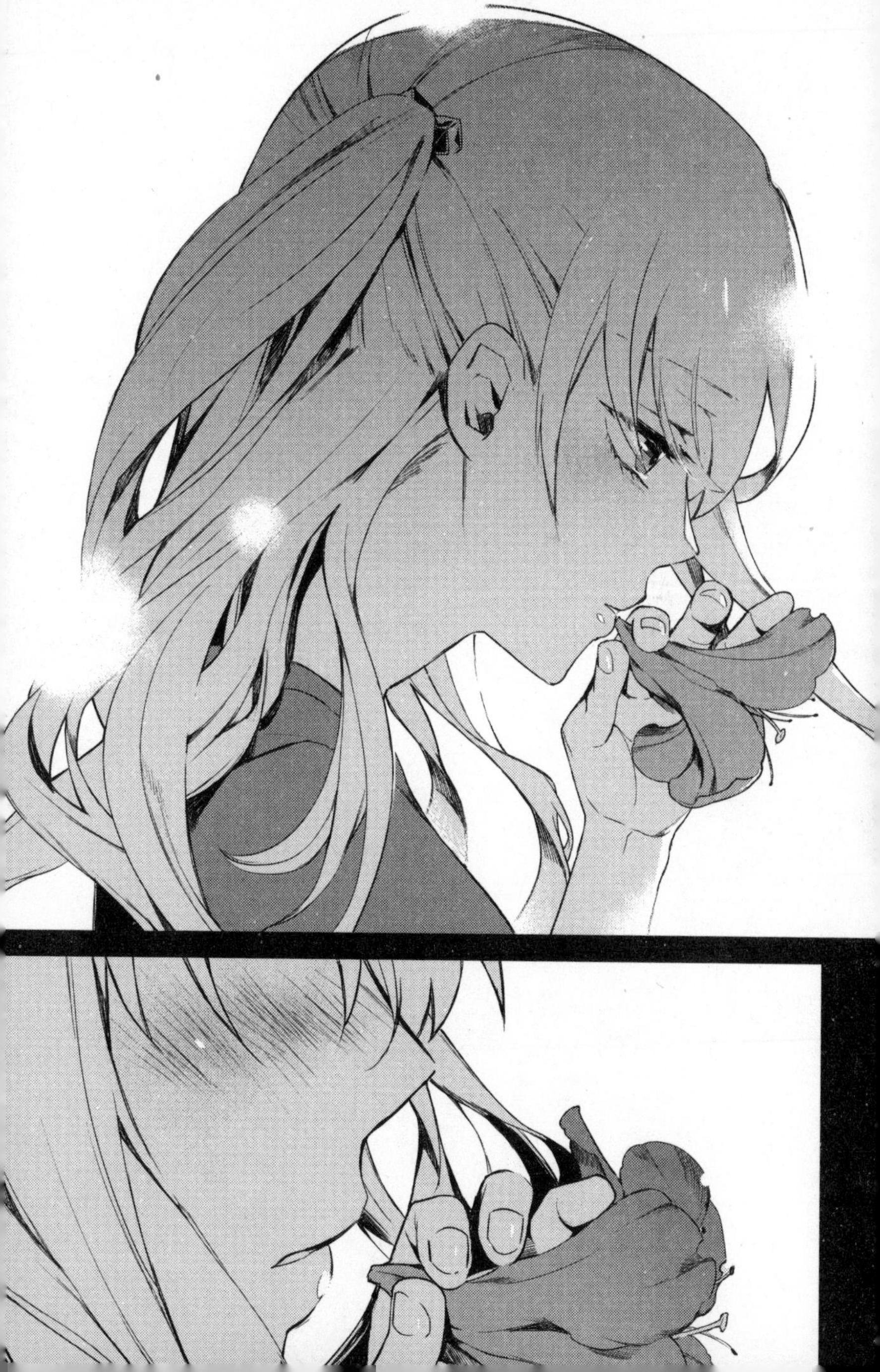

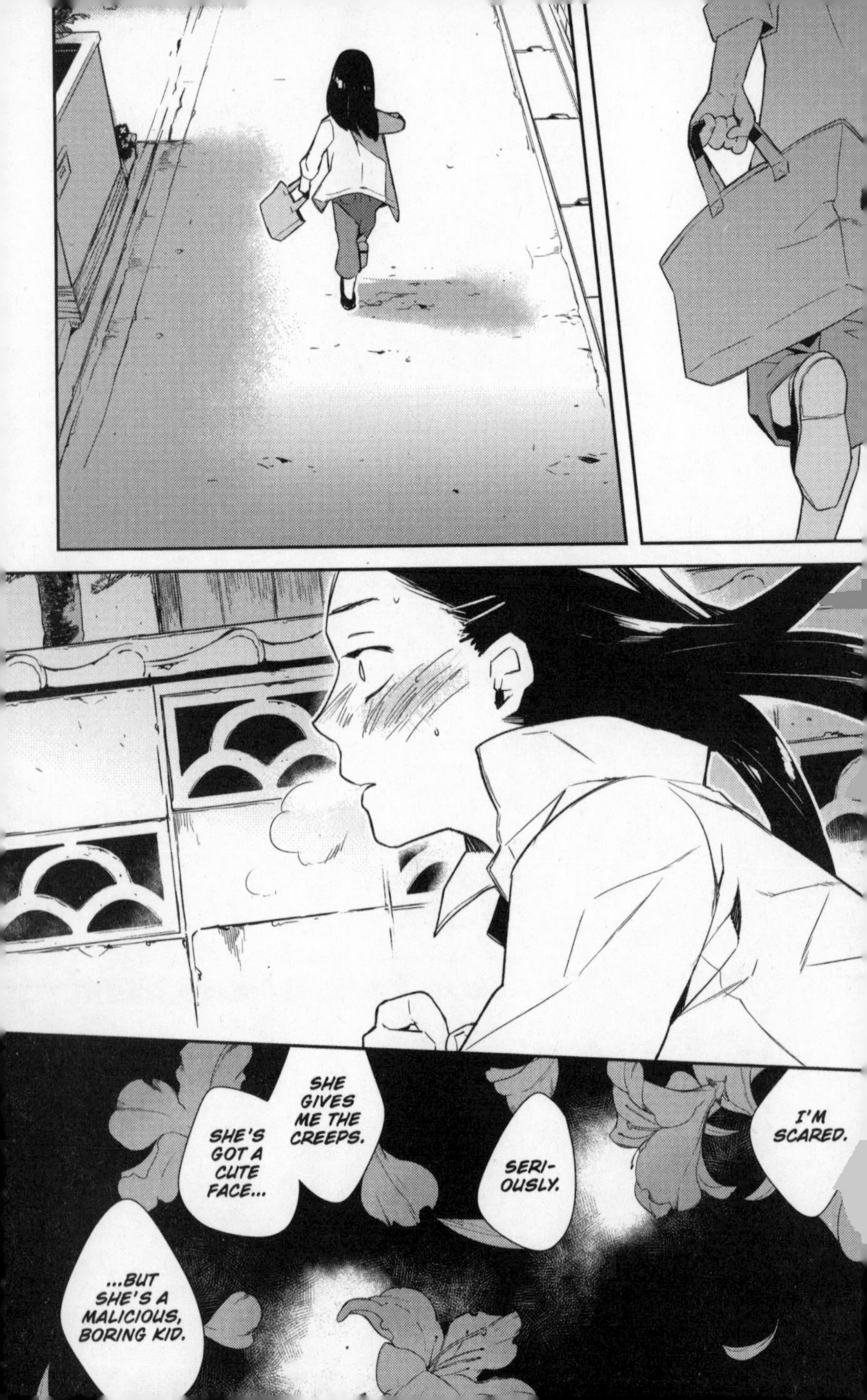
I'M SCARED.
SERI-OUSLY.
SHE GIVES ME THE CREEPS.
SHE'S GOT A CUTE FACE...
...BUT SHE'S A MALICIOUS, BORING KID.

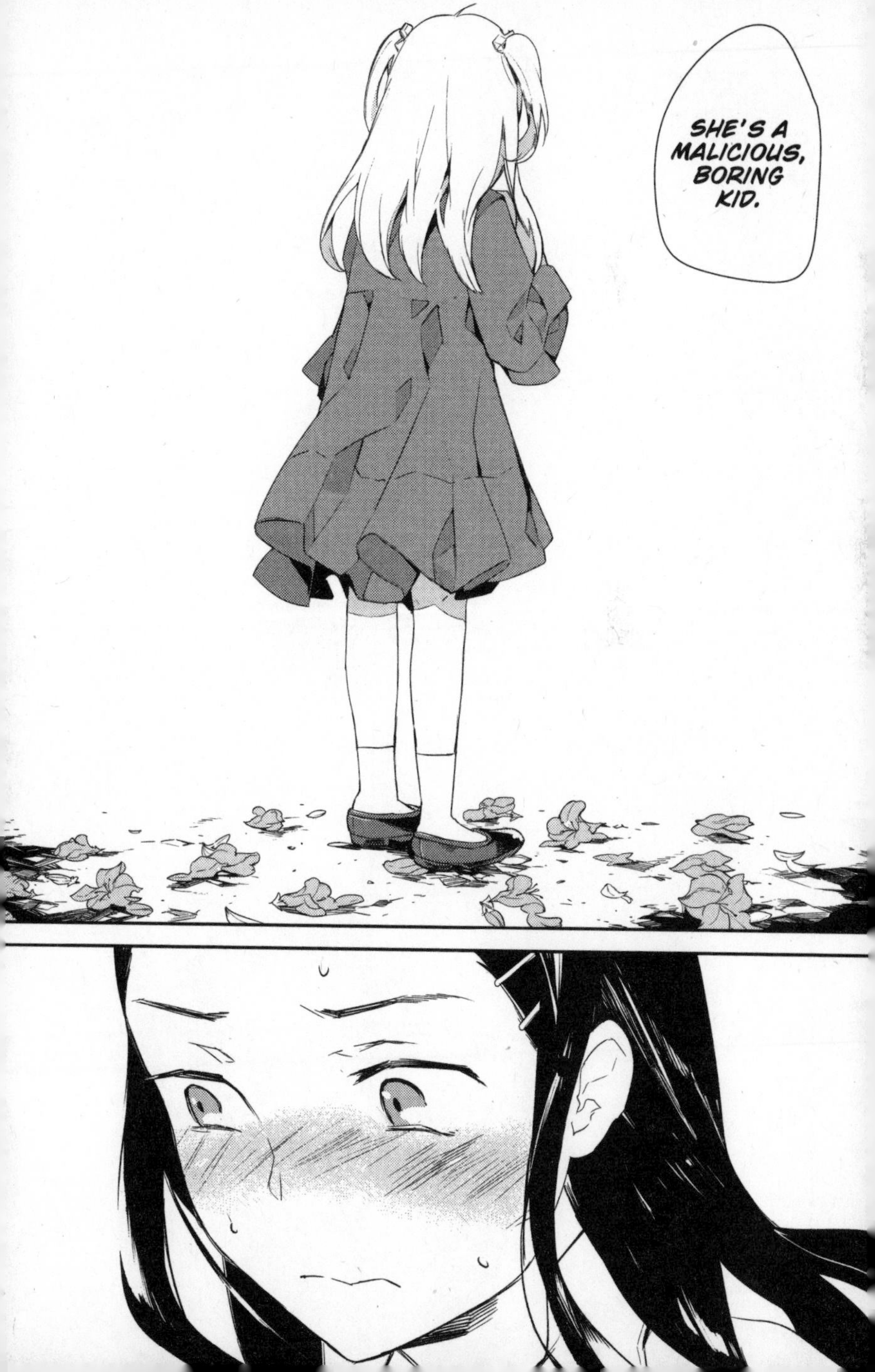
SHE'S A MALICIOUS, BORING KID.

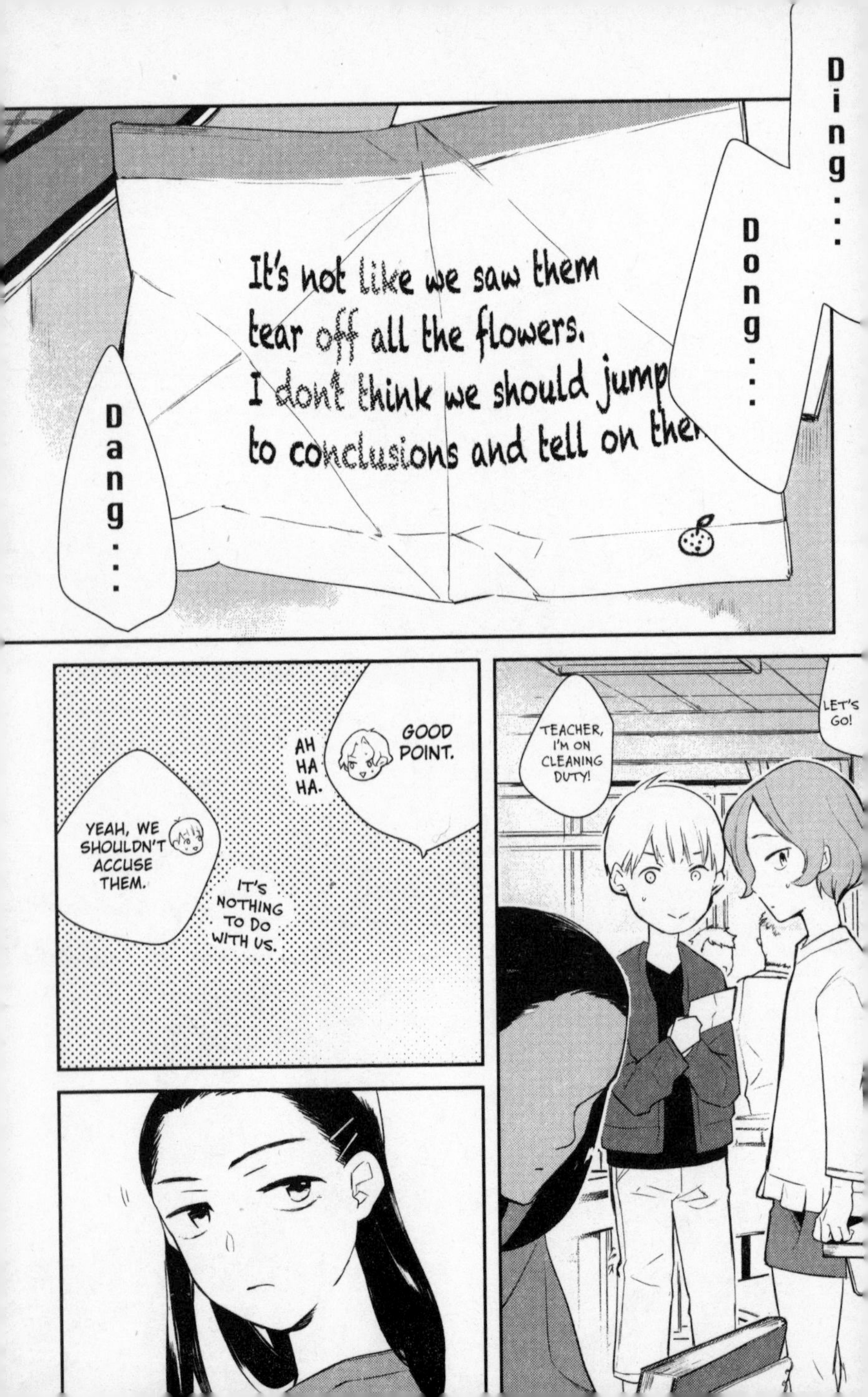
Ding...
Dong...
It's not like we saw them tear off all the flowers. I dont think we should jump to conclusions and tell on the
Dang...
LET'S GO!
TEACHER, I'M ON CLEANING DUTY!
GOOD POINT.
AH HA HA.
YEAH, WE SHOULDN'T ACCUSE THEM.
IT'S NOTHING TO DO WITH US.

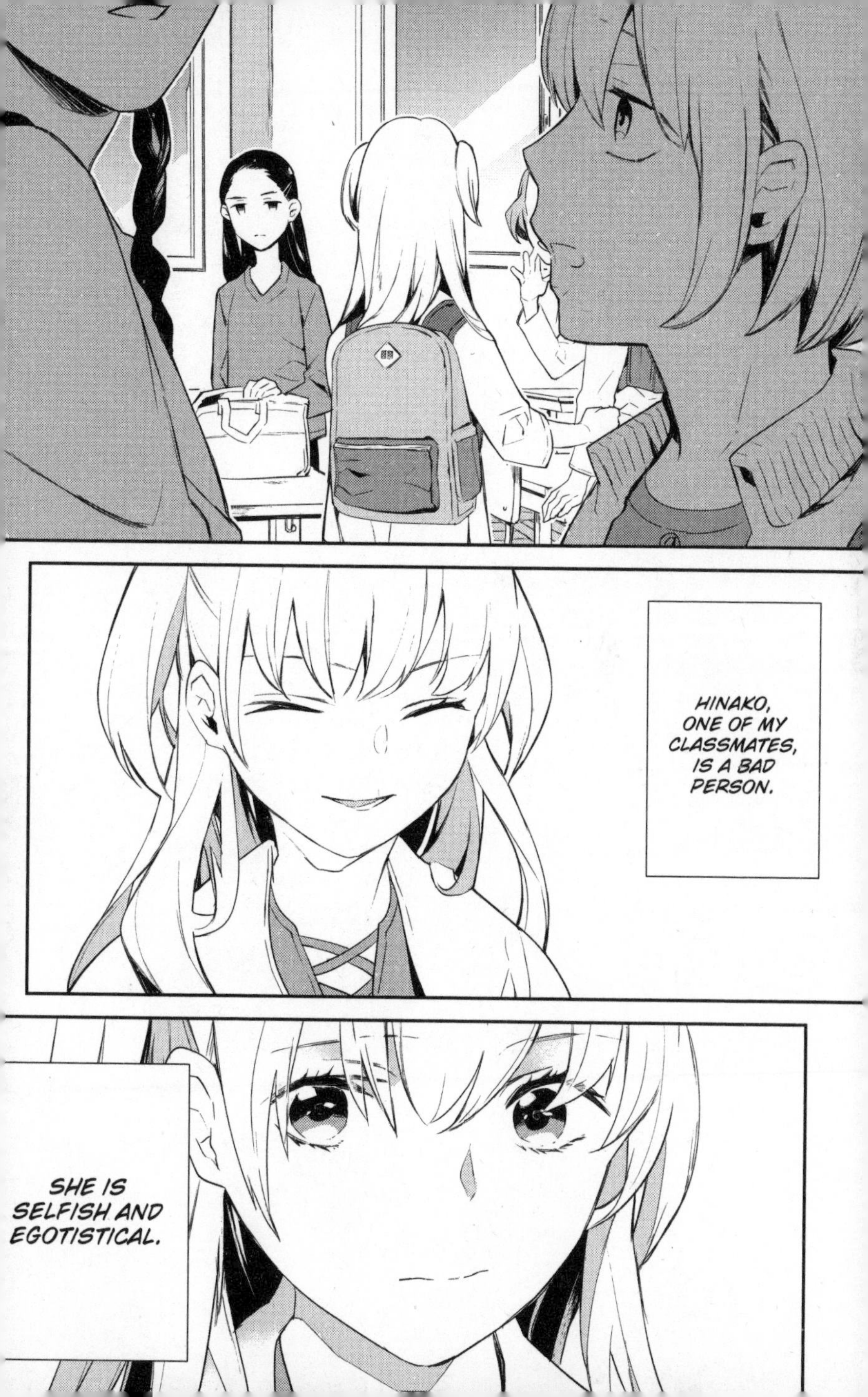
HINAKO, ONE OF MY CLASSMATES, IS A BAD PERSON.
SHE IS SELFISH AND EGOTISTICAL.

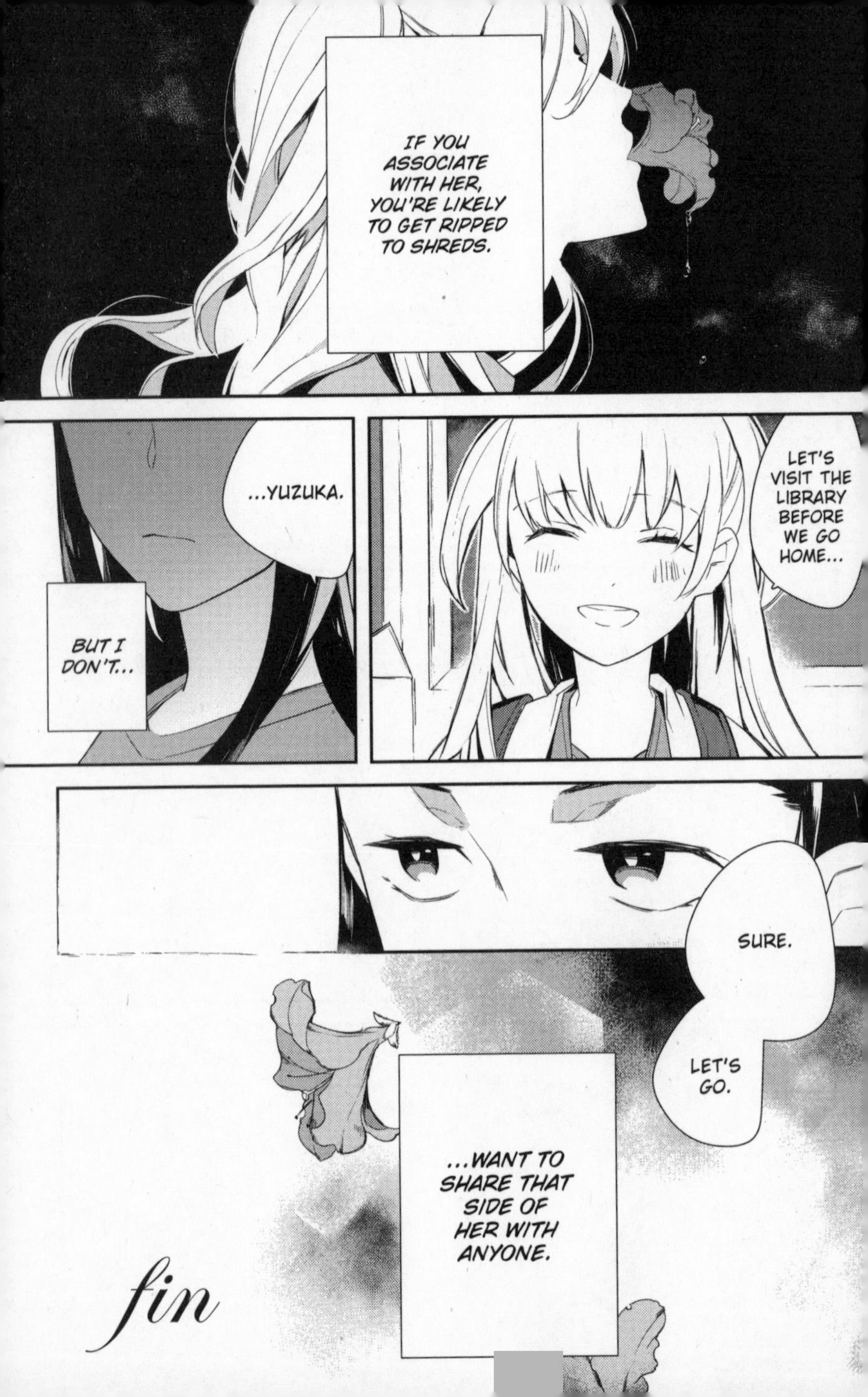
IF YOU ASSOCIATE WITH HER, YOU'RE LIKELY TO GET RIPPED TO SHREDS.
LET'S VISIT THE LIBRARY BEFORE WE GO HOME...
...YUZUKA.
BUT I DON'T...
SURE.
LET'S GO.
...WANT TO SHARE THAT SIDE OF HER WITH ANYONE.
fin

éclair blanche

A Girls' Love Anthology
That Resonates in Your Heart

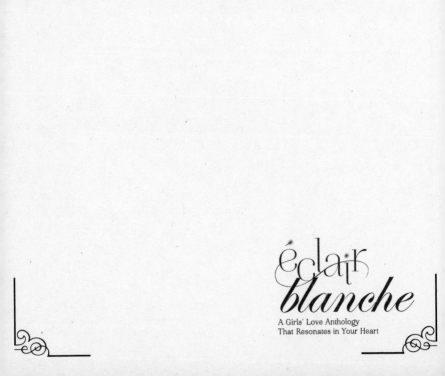

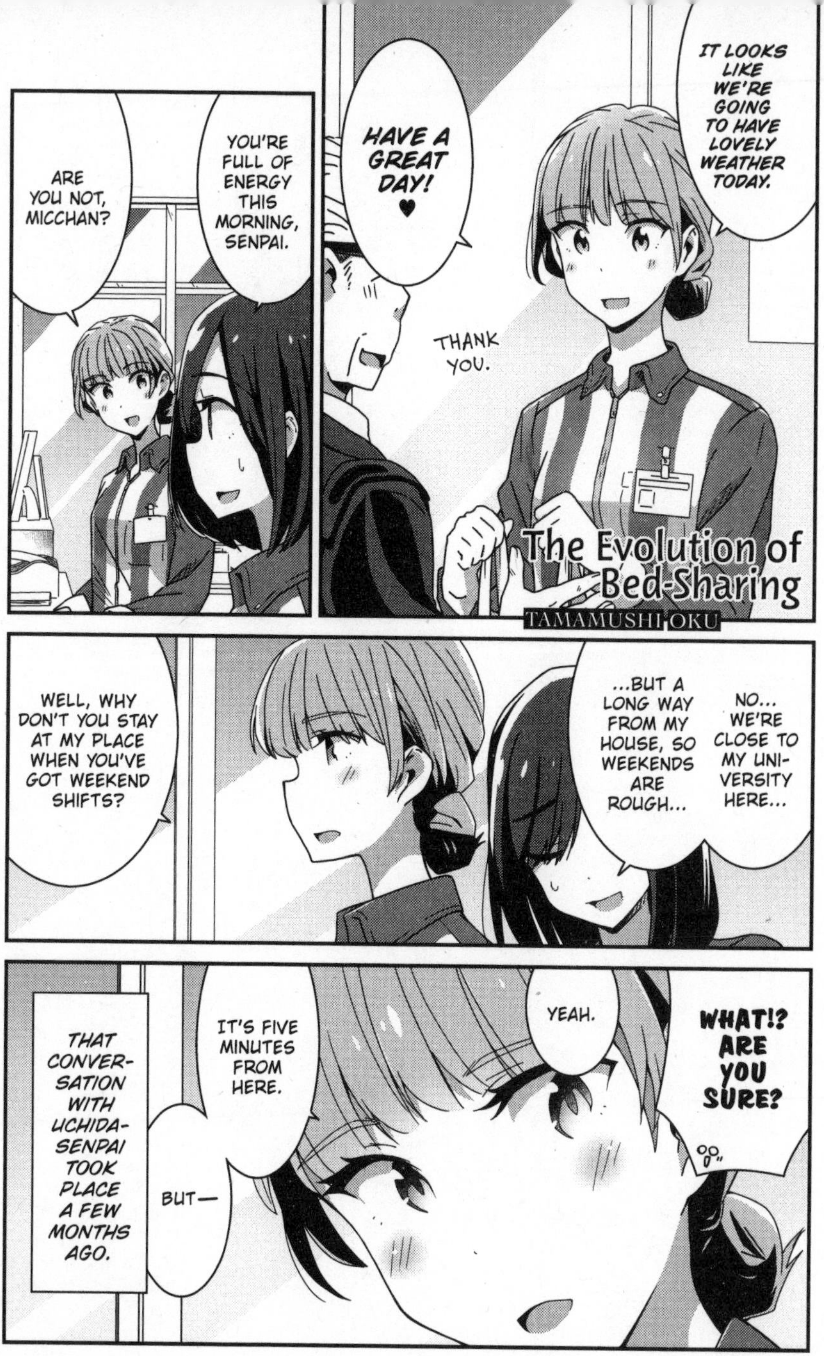

The Evolution of Bed-Sharing
TAMAMUSHI OKU
IT LOOKS LIKE WE'RE GOING TO HAVE LOVELY WEATHER TODAY.
HAVE A GREAT DAY! ♥
THANK YOU.
YOU'RE FULL OF ENERGY THIS MORNING, SENPAI.
ARE YOU NOT, MICCHAN?
NO... WE'RE CLOSE TO MY UNIVERSITY HERE...
...BUT A LONG WAY FROM MY HOUSE, SO WEEKENDS ARE ROUGH...
WELL, WHY DON'T YOU STAY AT MY PLACE WHEN YOU'VE GOT WEEKEND SHIFTS?
WHAT!? ARE YOU SURE?
YEAH.
IT'S FIVE MINUTES FROM HERE.
BUT—
THAT CONVERSATION WITH UCHIDA-SENPAI TOOK PLACE A FEW MONTHS AGO.

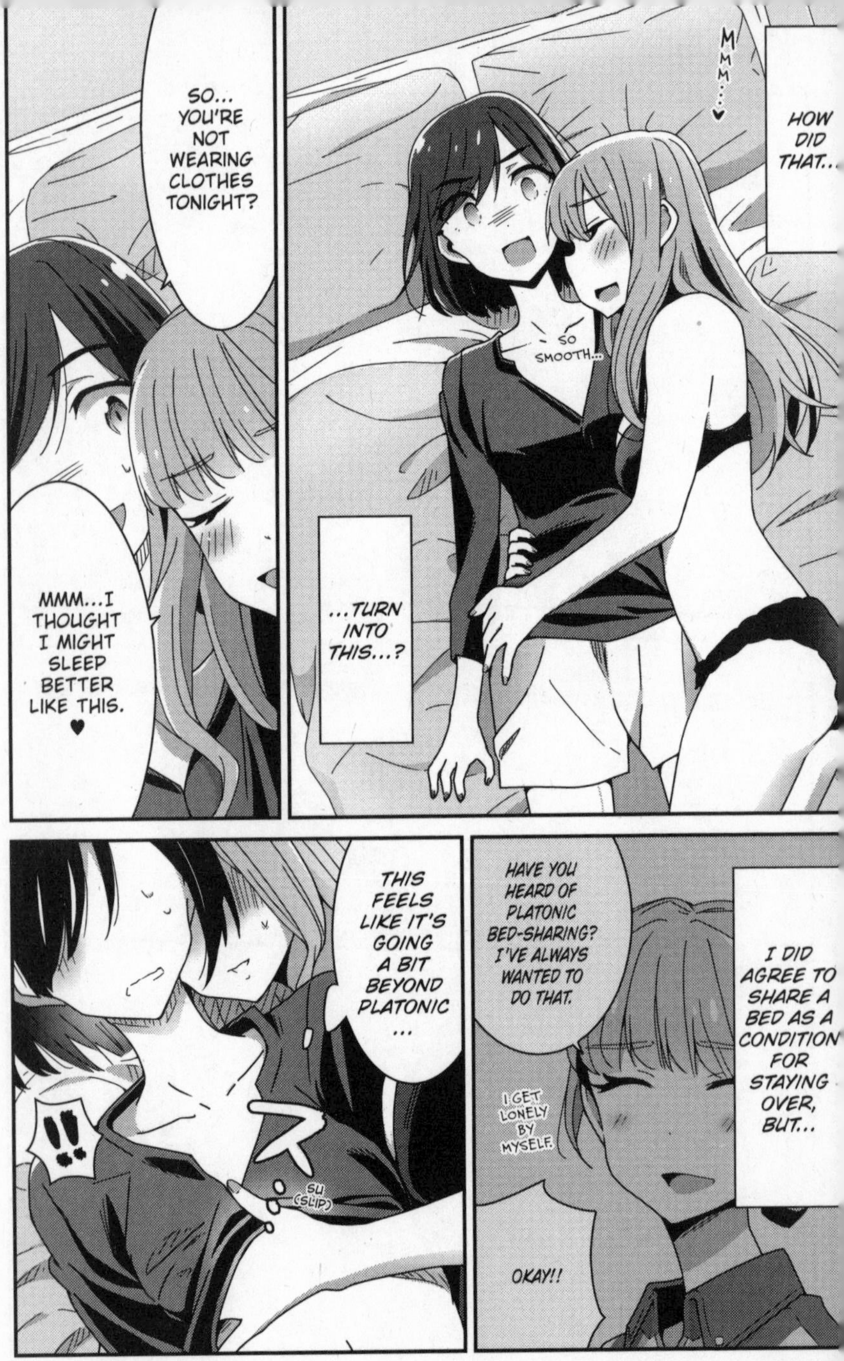
MMM...♥
HOW DID THAT...
SO SMOOTH...
...TURN INTO THIS...?
SO... YOU'RE NOT WEARING CLOTHES TONIGHT?
MMM...I THOUGHT I MIGHT SLEEP BETTER LIKE THIS. ♥
I DID AGREE TO SHARE A BED AS A CONDITION FOR STAYING OVER, BUT...
HAVE YOU HEARD OF PLATONIC BED-SHARING? I'VE ALWAYS WANTED TO DO THAT.
I GET LONELY BY MYSELF.
OKAY!!
THIS FEELS LIKE IT'S GOING A BIT BEYOND PLATONIC...
!!
SU (SLIP)

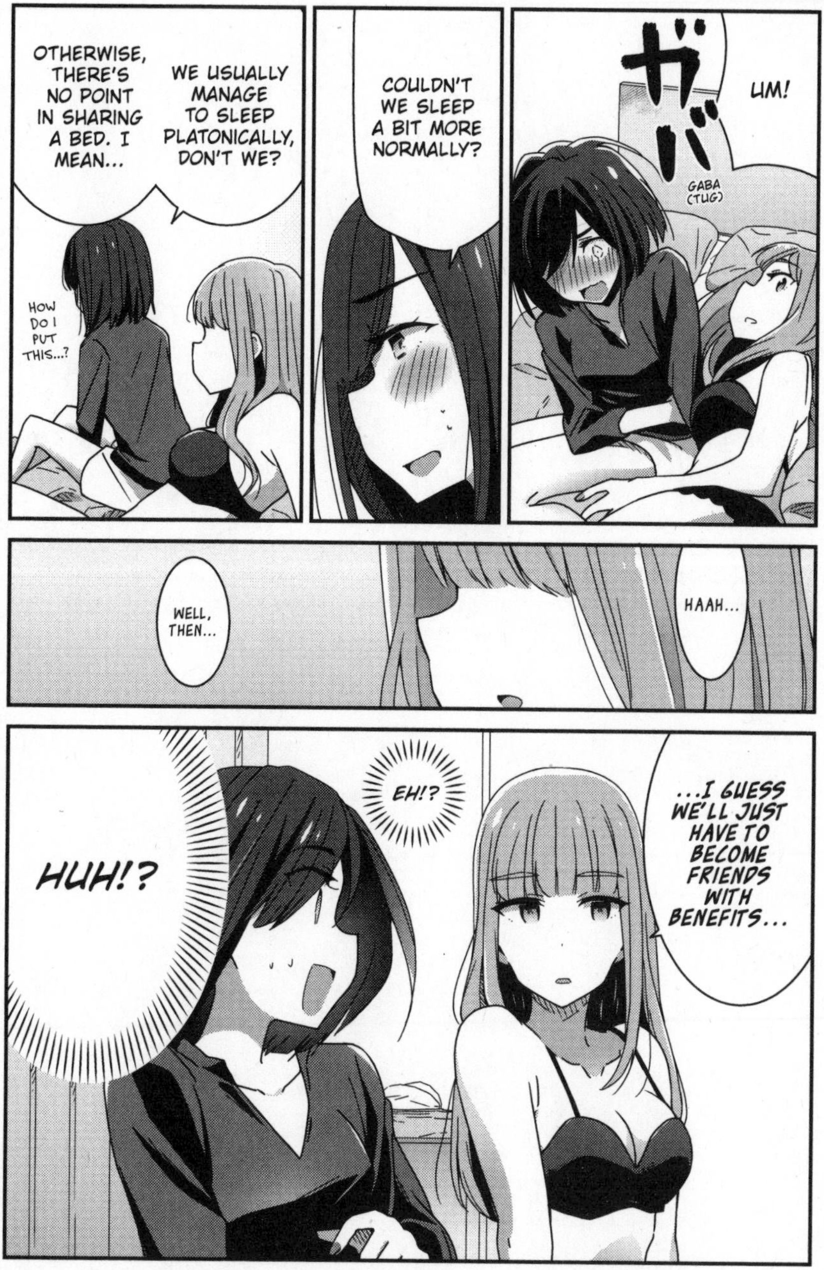
ガバ
GABA (TUG)
UM!
COULDN'T WE SLEEP A BIT MORE NORMALLY?
WE USUALLY MANAGE TO SLEEP PLATONICALLY, DON'T WE?
OTHERWISE, THERE'S NO POINT IN SHARING A BED. I MEAN...
HOW DO I PUT THIS...?
HAAH...
WELL, THEN...
...I GUESS WE'LL JUST HAVE TO BECOME FRIENDS WITH BENEFITS...
EH!?
HUH!?

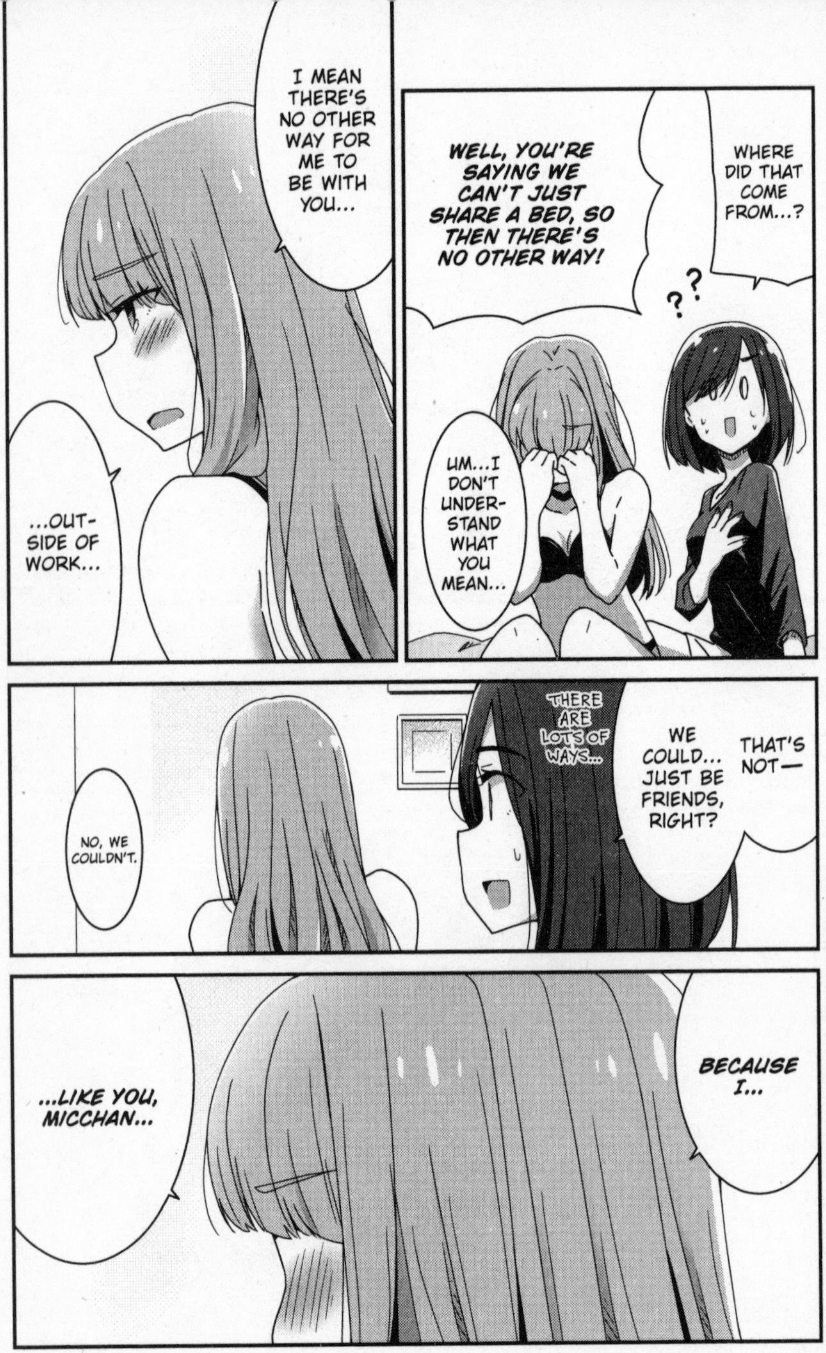
WHERE DID THAT COME FROM...?
WELL, YOU'RE SAYING WE CAN'T JUST SHARE A BED, SO THEN THERE'S NO OTHER WAY!
UM...I DON'T UNDER-STAND WHAT YOU MEAN...
I MEAN THERE'S NO OTHER WAY FOR ME TO BE WITH YOU...
...OUT-SIDE OF WORK...
THAT'S NOT—
WE COULD... JUST BE FRIENDS, RIGHT?
THERE ARE LOTS OF WAYS...
NO, WE COULDN'T.
BECAUSE I...
...LIKE YOU, MICCHAN...

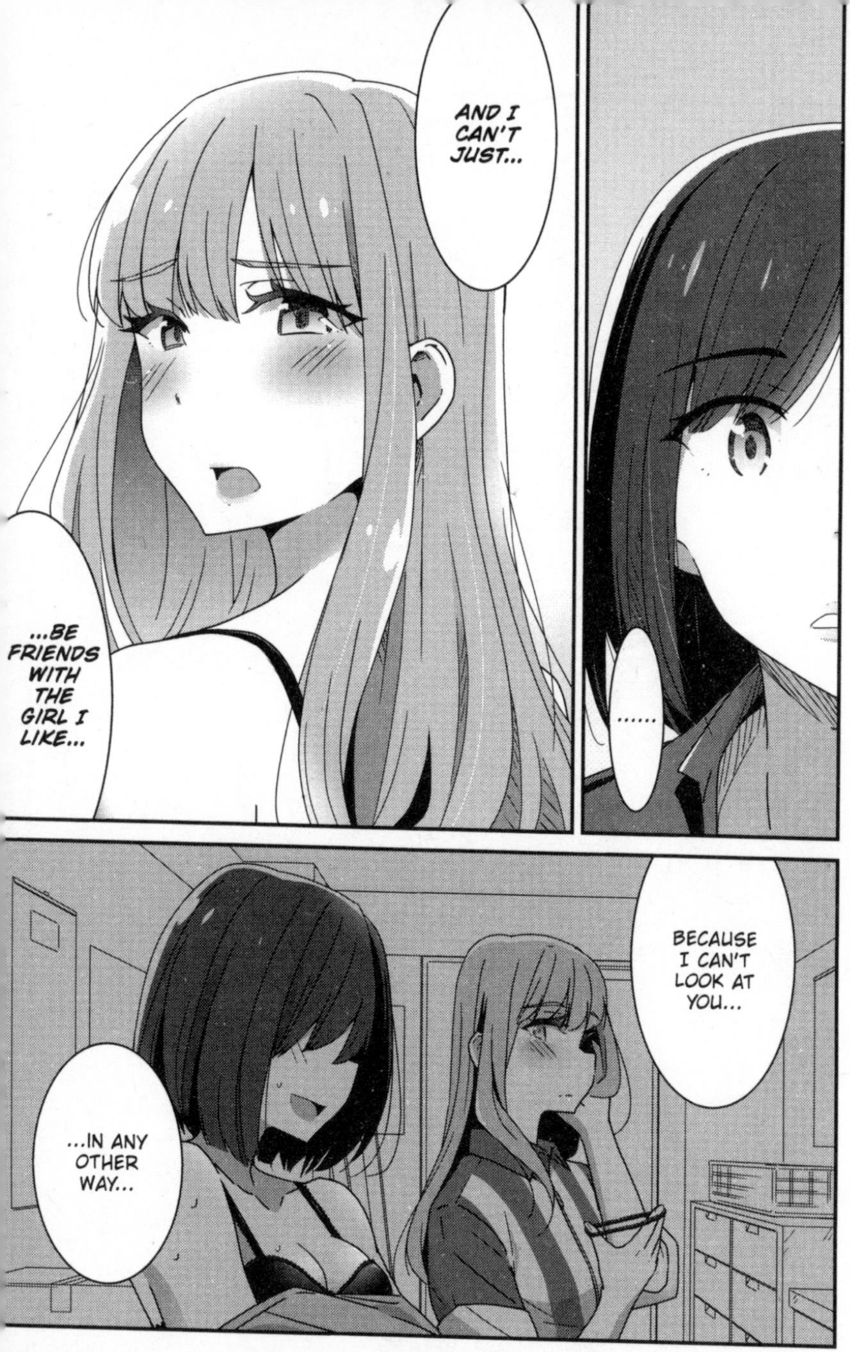
......
AND I CAN'T JUST...
...BE FRIENDS WITH THE GIRL I LIKE...
BECAUSE I CAN'T LOOK AT YOU...
...IN ANY OTHER WAY...

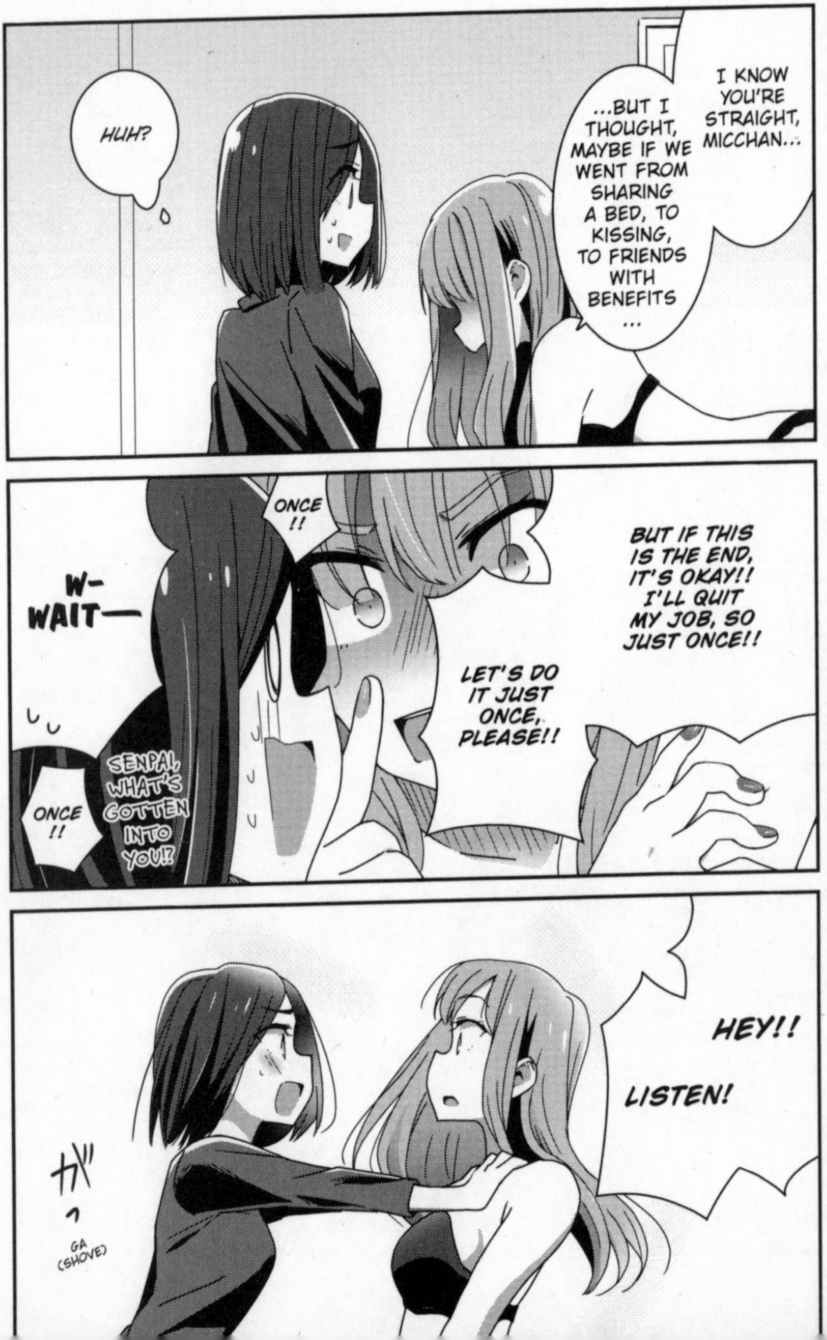
I KNOW YOU'RE STRAIGHT, MICCHAN...
...BUT I THOUGHT, MAYBE IF WE WENT FROM SHARING A BED, TO KISSING, TO FRIENDS WITH BENEFITS ...
HUH?
BUT IF THIS IS THE END, IT'S OKAY!! I'LL QUIT MY JOB, SO JUST ONCE!!
ONCE !!
LET'S DO IT JUST ONCE, PLEASE!!
W-WAIT—
SENPAI, WHAT'S GOTTEN INTO YOU!?
ONCE !!
HEY!!
LISTEN!
GA (SHOVE)

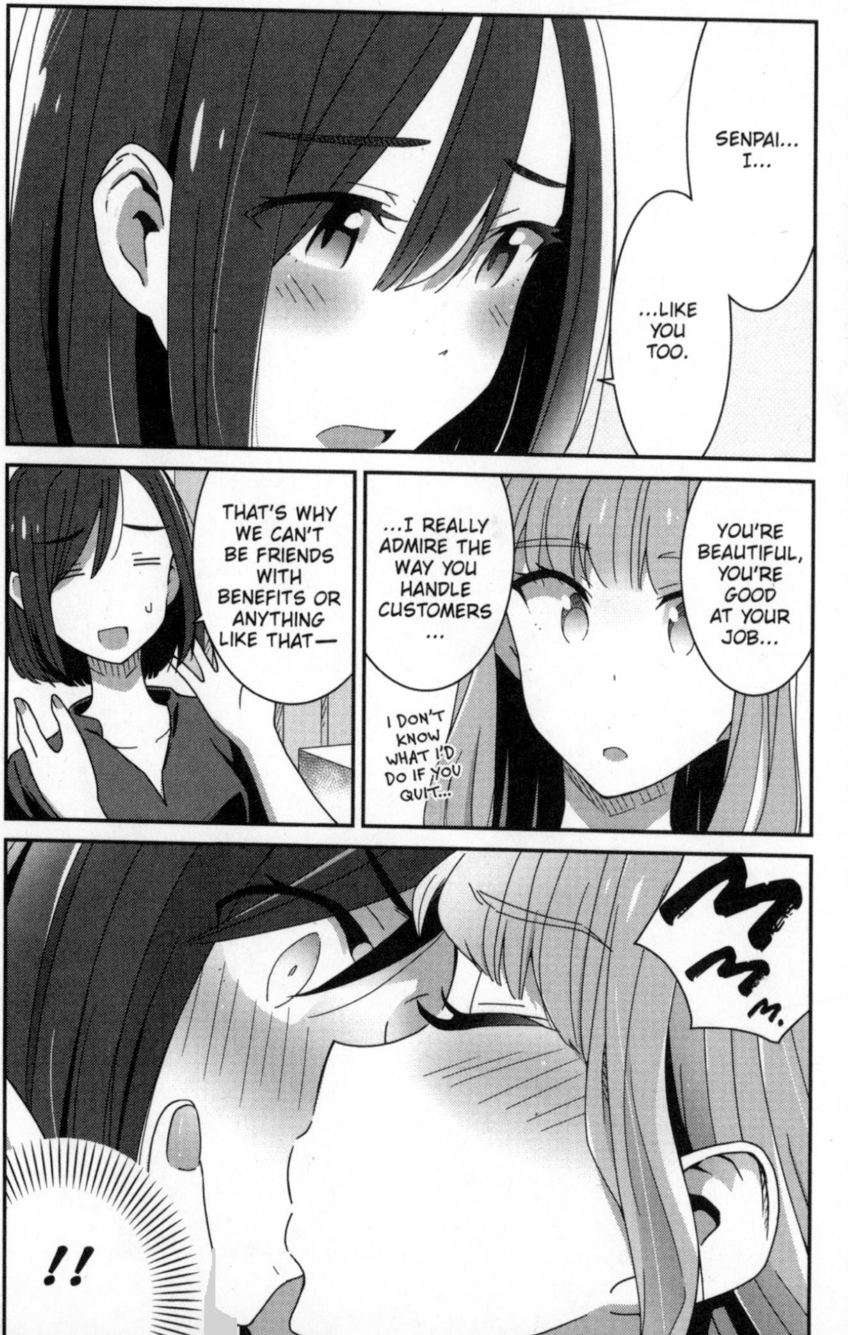
SENPAI... I...
...LIKE YOU TOO.
YOU'RE BEAUTIFUL, YOU'RE GOOD AT YOUR JOB...
...I REALLY ADMIRE THE WAY YOU HANDLE CUSTOMERS...
I DON'T KNOW WHAT I'D DO IF YOU QUIT...
THAT'S WHY WE CAN'T BE FRIENDS WITH BENEFITS OR ANYTHING LIKE THAT—
MMM.
!!

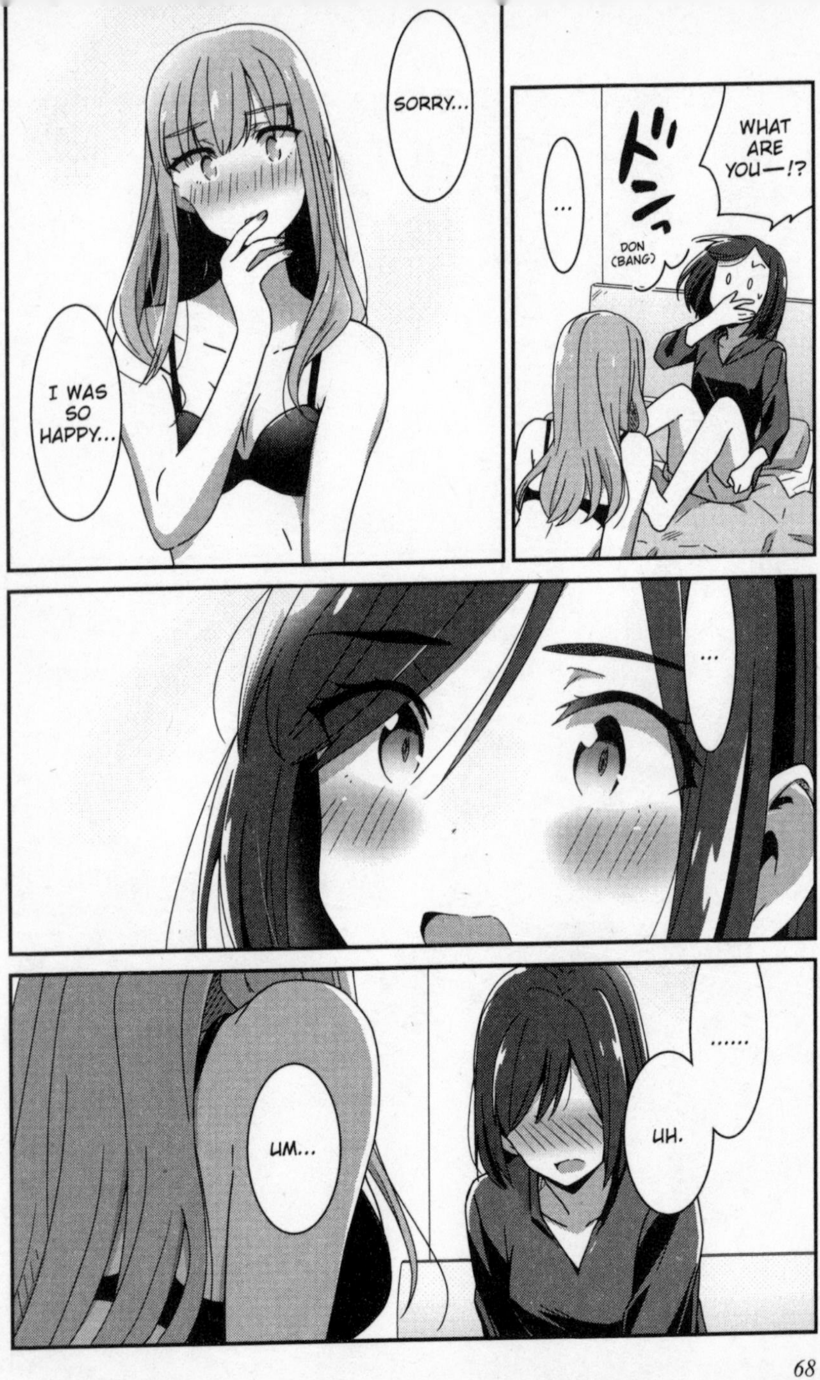
WHAT ARE YOU—!?
ドン
DON (BANG)
...
SORRY...
I WAS SO HAPPY...
...
......
UH.
UM...

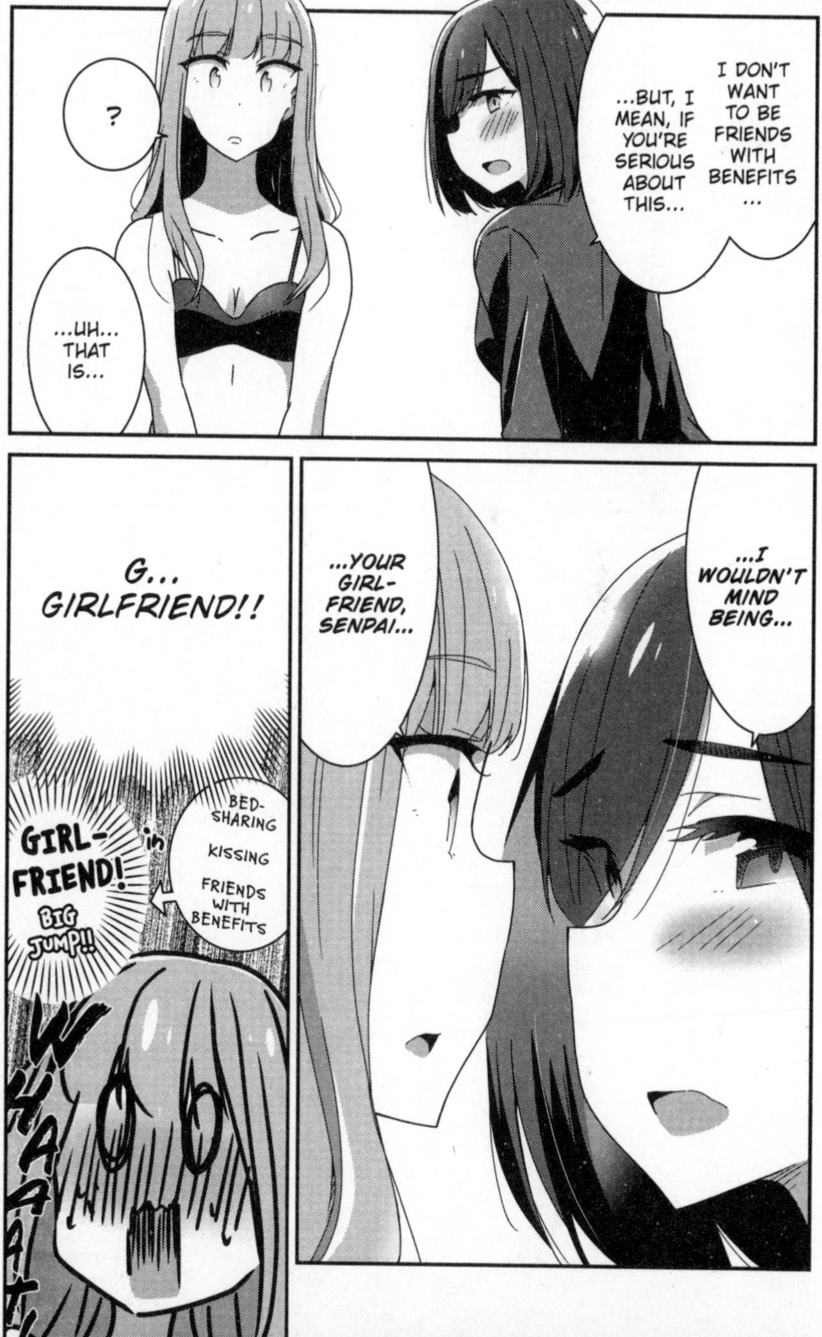
I DON'T WANT TO BE FRIENDS WITH BENEFITS...
...BUT, I MEAN, IF YOU'RE SERIOUS ABOUT THIS...
?
...UH... THAT IS...
...I WOULDN'T MIND BEING...
...YOUR GIRL-FRIEND, SENPAI...
G... GIRLFRIEND!!
BED-SHARING
KISSING
FRIENDS WITH BENEFITS
in
GIRL-FRIEND!
BIG JUMP!!

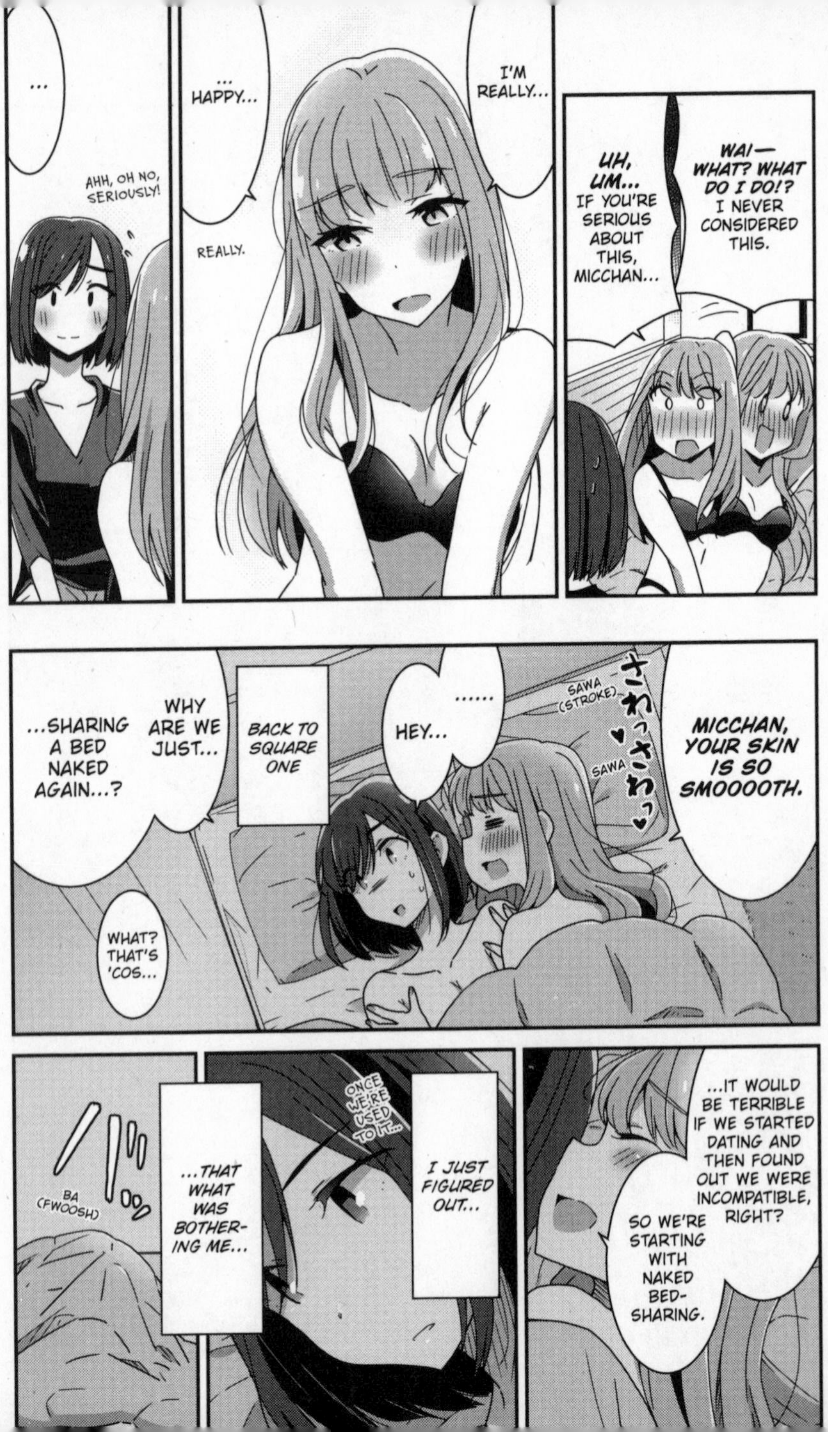
WAI— WHAT? WHAT DO I DO!? I NEVER CONSIDERED THIS.
UH, UM... IF YOU'RE SERIOUS ABOUT THIS, MICCHAN...
I'M REALLY...
...HAPPY...
REALLY.
...
AHH, OH NO, SERIOUSLY!
MICCHAN, YOUR SKIN IS SO SMOOOOTH.
さわっさわっ
SAWA (STROKE)
SAWA
......
HEY...
BACK TO SQUARE ONE
WHY ARE WE JUST...
...SHARING A BED NAKED AGAIN...?
WHAT? THAT'S 'COS...
...IT WOULD BE TERRIBLE IF WE STARTED DATING AND THEN FOUND OUT WE WERE INCOMPATIBLE, RIGHT?
SO WE'RE STARTING WITH NAKED BED-SHARING.
ONCE WE'RE USED TO IT...
I JUST FIGURED OUT...
...THAT WHAT WAS BOTHERING ME...
BA (FWOOSH)

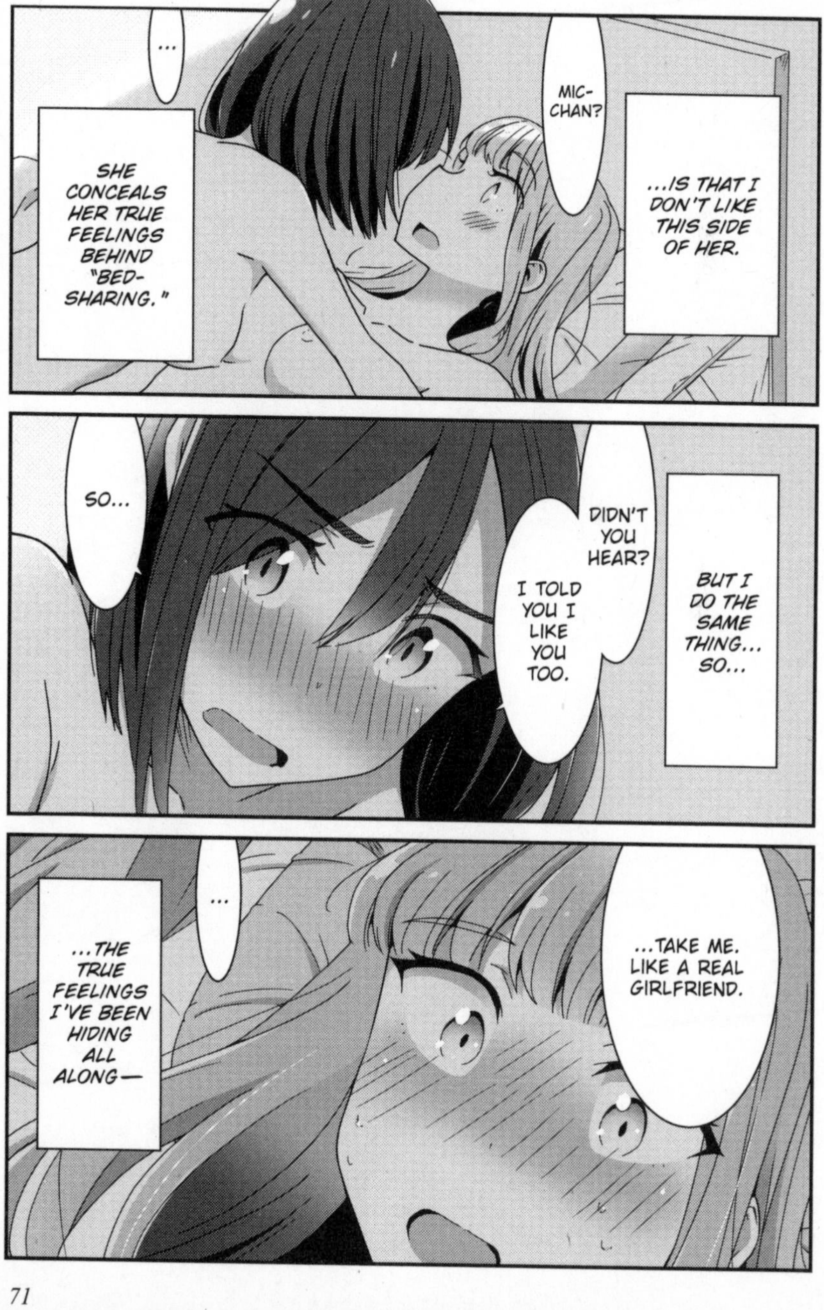
...IS THAT I DON'T LIKE THIS SIDE OF HER.
MIC-CHAN?
...
SHE CONCEALS HER TRUE FEELINGS BEHIND "BED-SHARING."
BUT I DO THE SAME THING... SO...
DIDN'T YOU HEAR? I TOLD YOU I LIKE YOU TOO.
SO...
...TAKE ME. LIKE A REAL GIRLFRIEND.
...
...THE TRUE FEELINGS I'VE BEEN HIDING ALL ALONG—

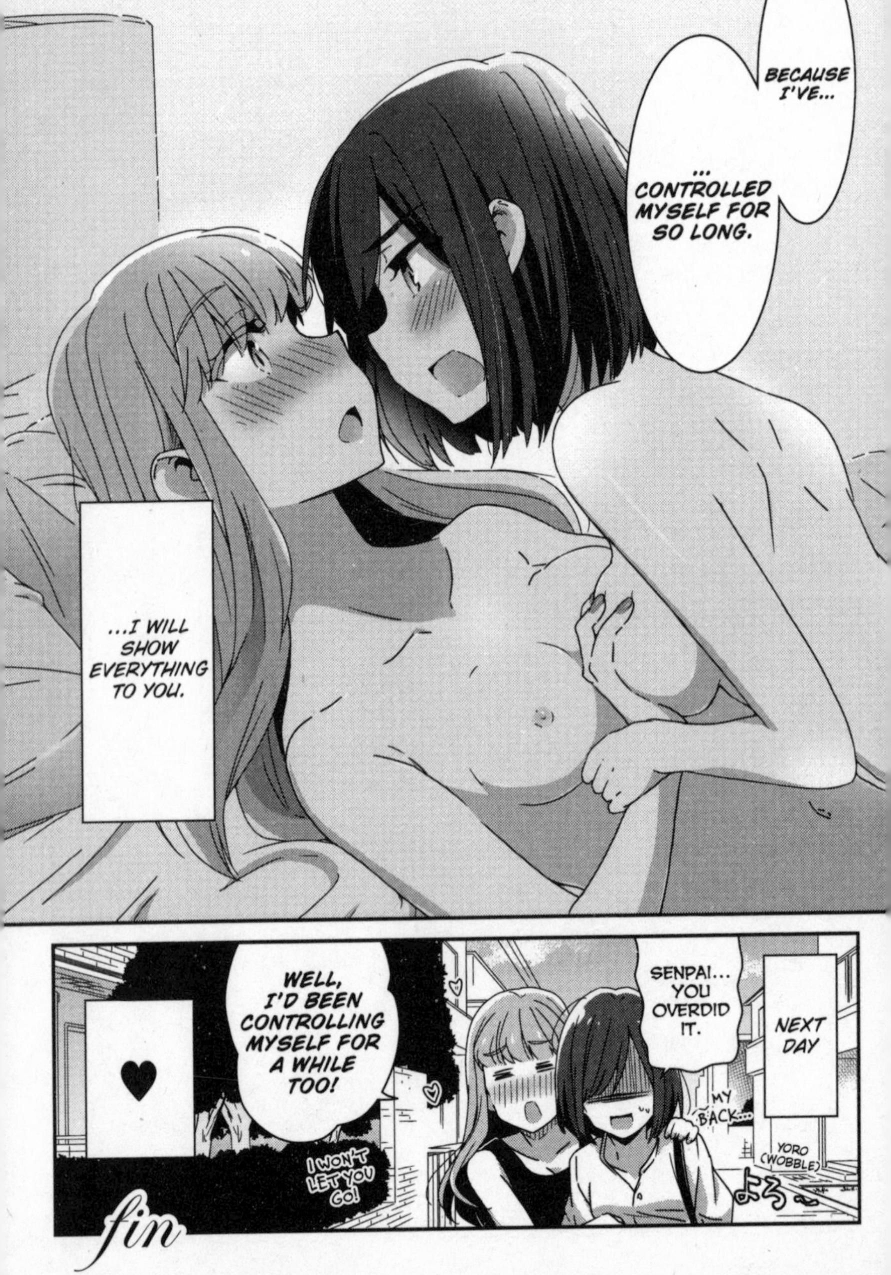
BECAUSE I'VE...
...CONTROLLED MYSELF FOR SO LONG.
...I WILL SHOW EVERYTHING TO YOU.
NEXT DAY
YORO (WOBBLE)
よろ～
SENPAI... YOU OVERDID IT.
MY BACK...
WELL, I'D BEEN CONTROLLING MYSELF FOR A WHILE TOO!
I WON'T LET YOU GO!
♥
fin

éclair
blanche

A Girls' Love Anthology
That Resonates in Your Heart

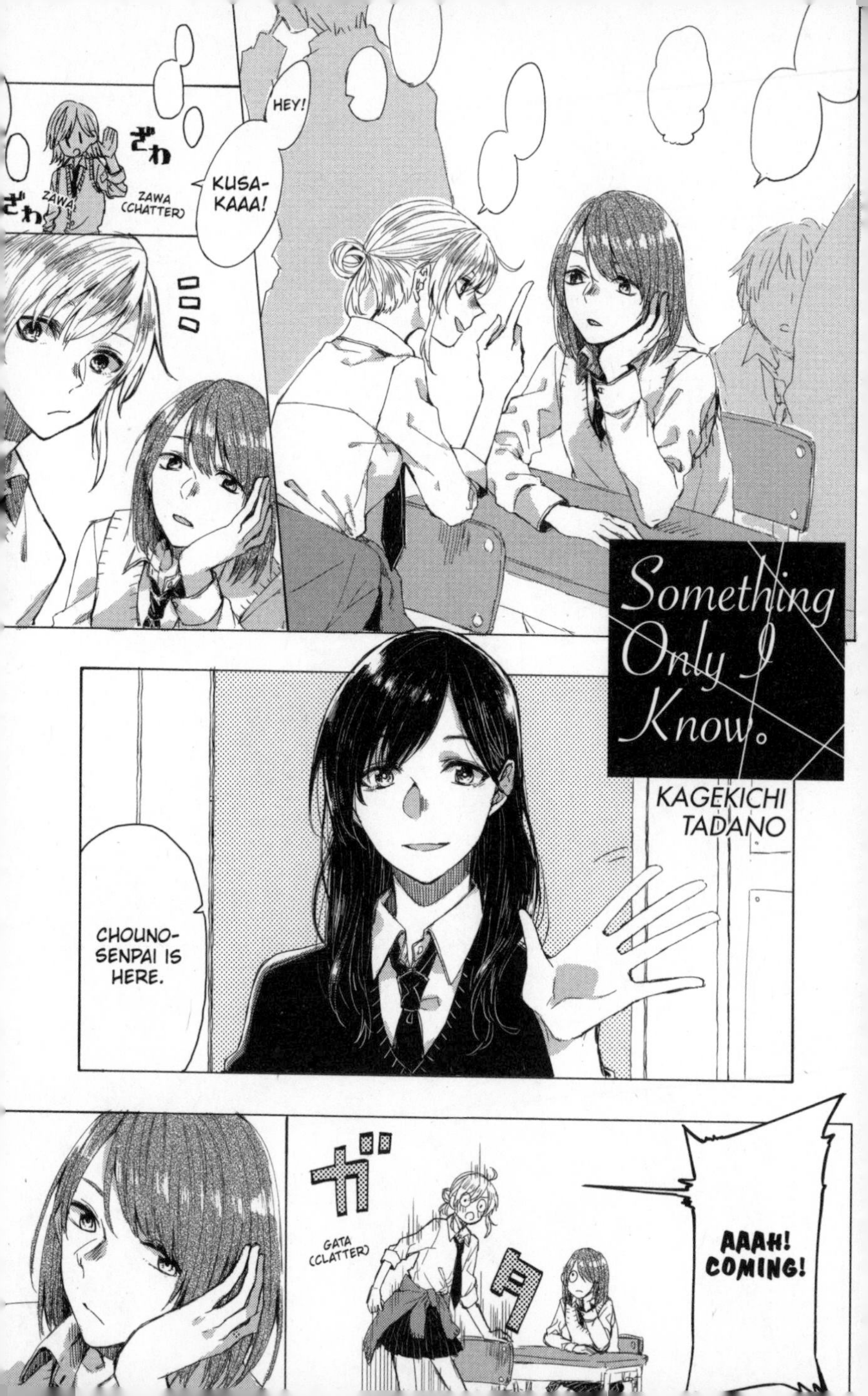
HEY!
KUSA-KAAA!
ざわ
ZAWA
ざわ
ZAWA (CHATTER)
Something Only I Know.
KAGEKICHI TADANO
CHOUNO-SENPAI IS HERE.
AAAH! COMING!
ガ
タ
GATA (CLATTER)

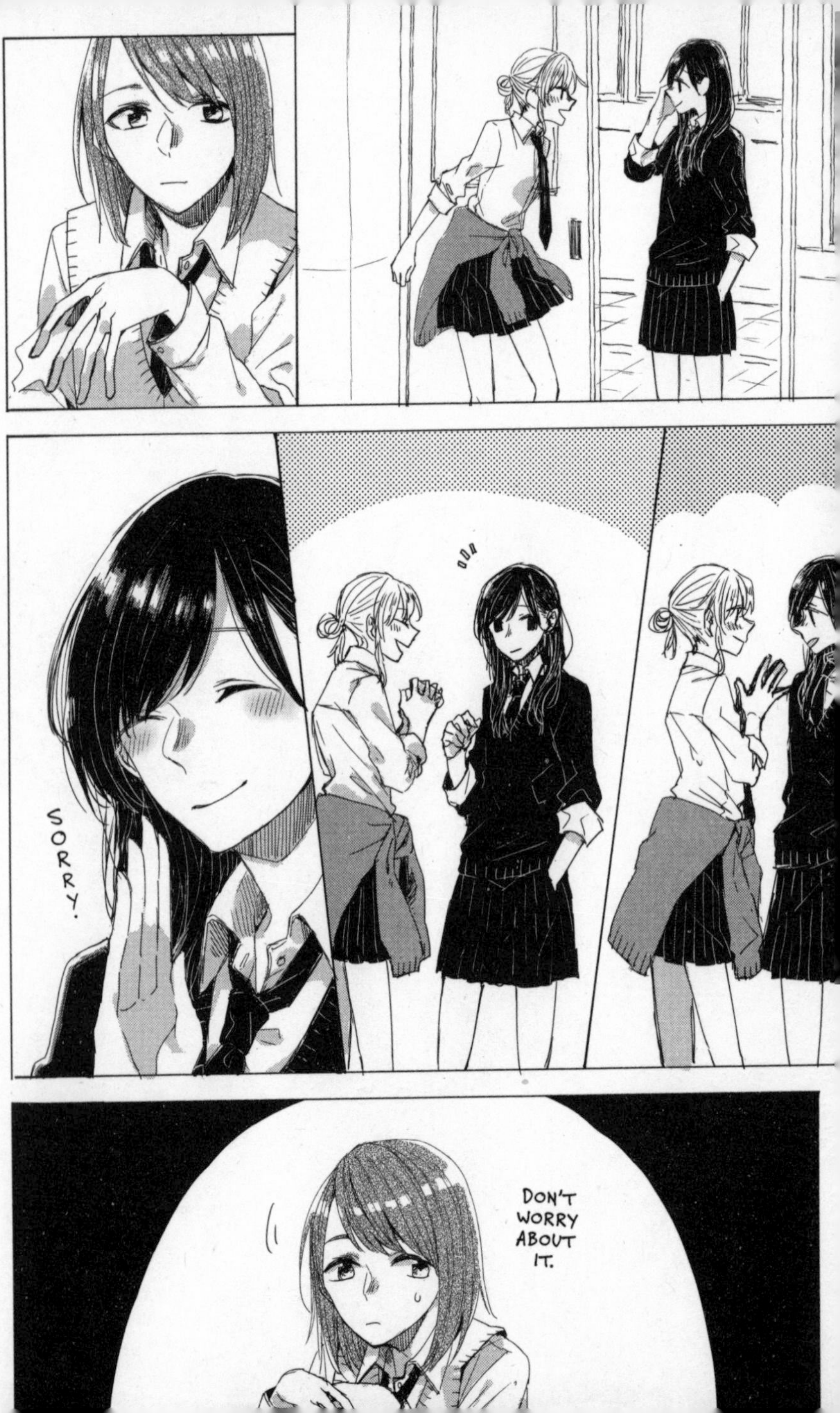
SORRY.
DON'T WORRY ABOUT IT.

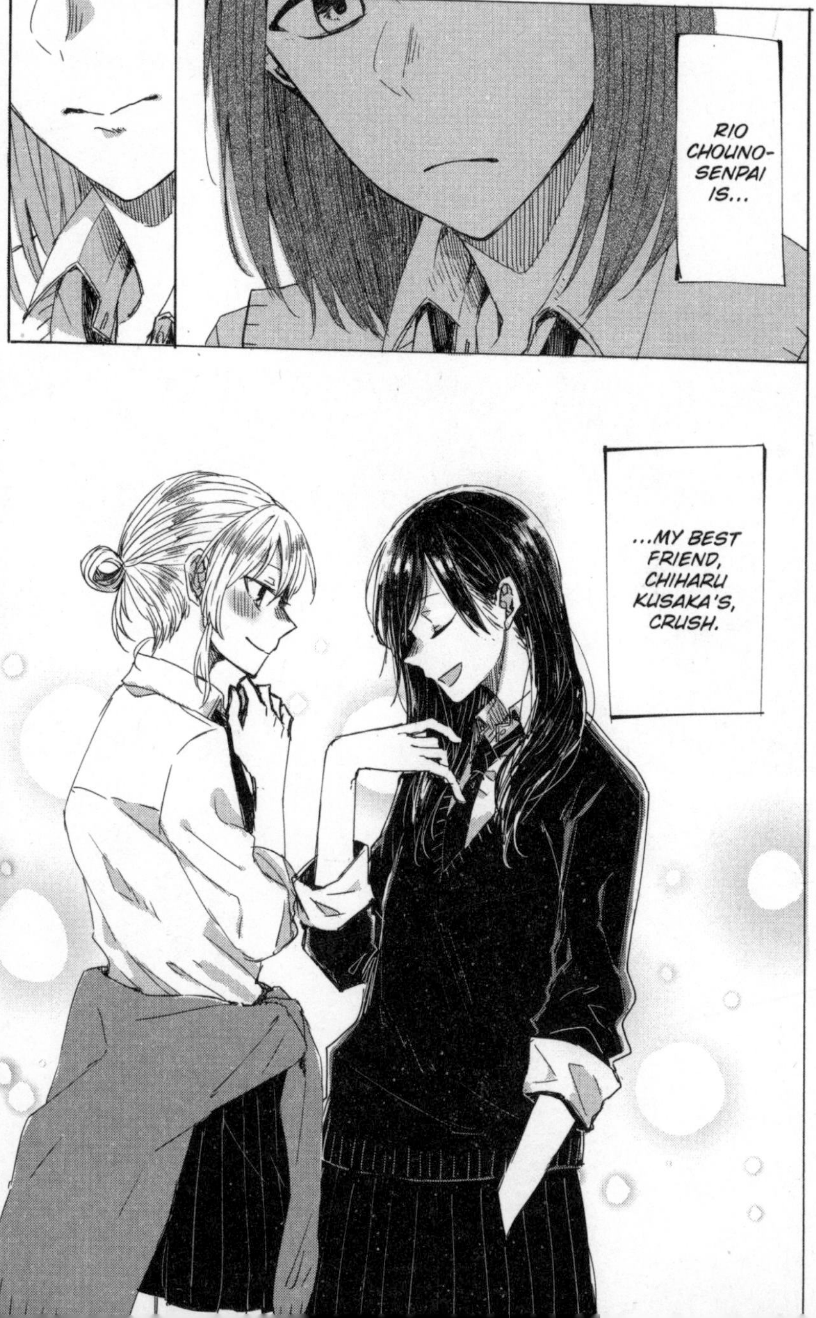
RIO CHOUNO-SENPAI IS...
...MY BEST FRIEND, CHIHARU KUSAKA'S, CRUSH.

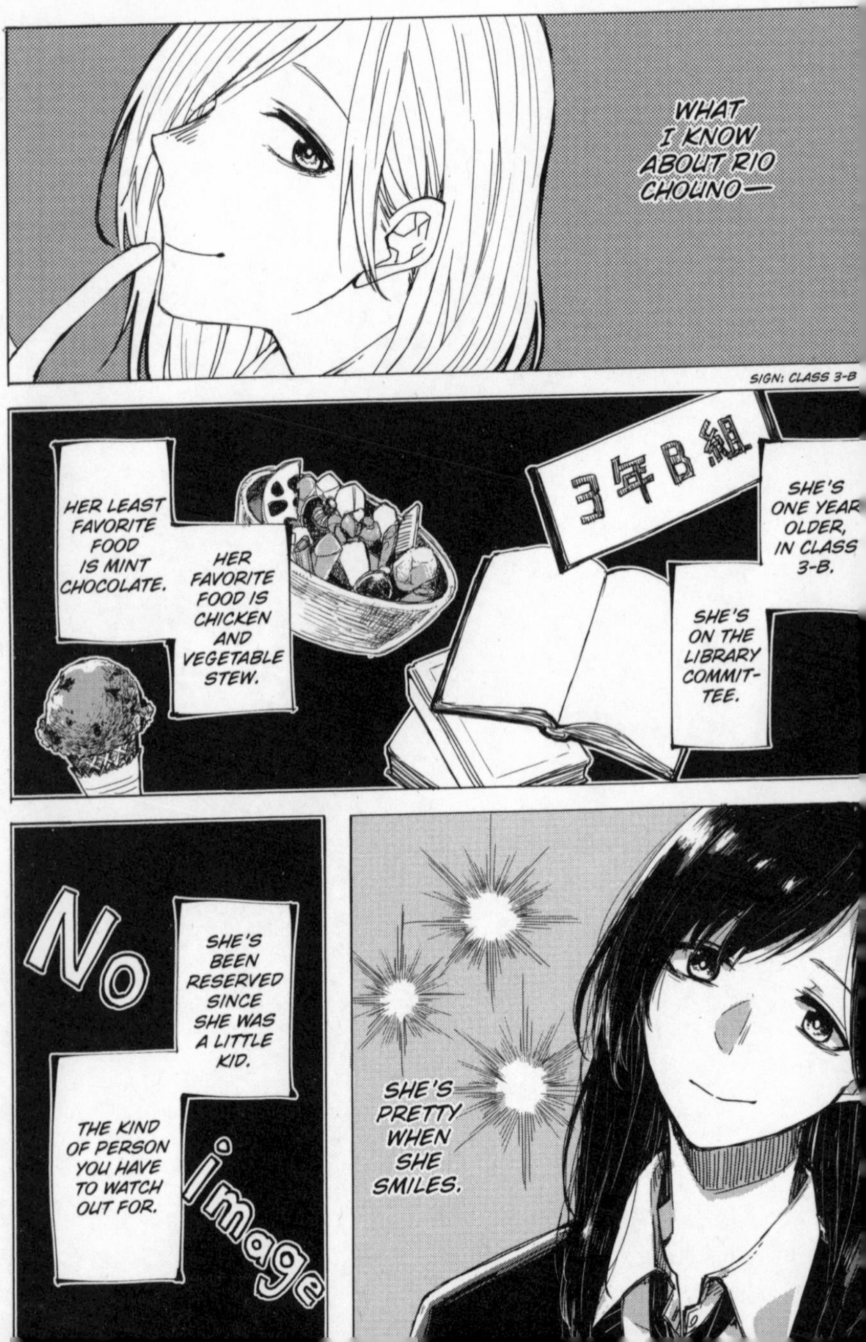
WHAT I KNOW ABOUT RIO CHOUNO—
SIGN: CLASS 3-B
3年B組
SHE'S ONE YEAR OLDER, IN CLASS 3-B.
SHE'S ON THE LIBRARY COMMIT-TEE.
HER FAVORITE FOOD IS CHICKEN AND VEGETABLE STEW.
HER LEAST FAVORITE FOOD IS MINT CHOCOLATE.
SHE'S PRETTY WHEN SHE SMILES.
SHE'S BEEN RESERVED SINCE SHE WAS A LITTLE KID.
THE KIND OF PERSON YOU HAVE TO WATCH OUT FOR.
No image

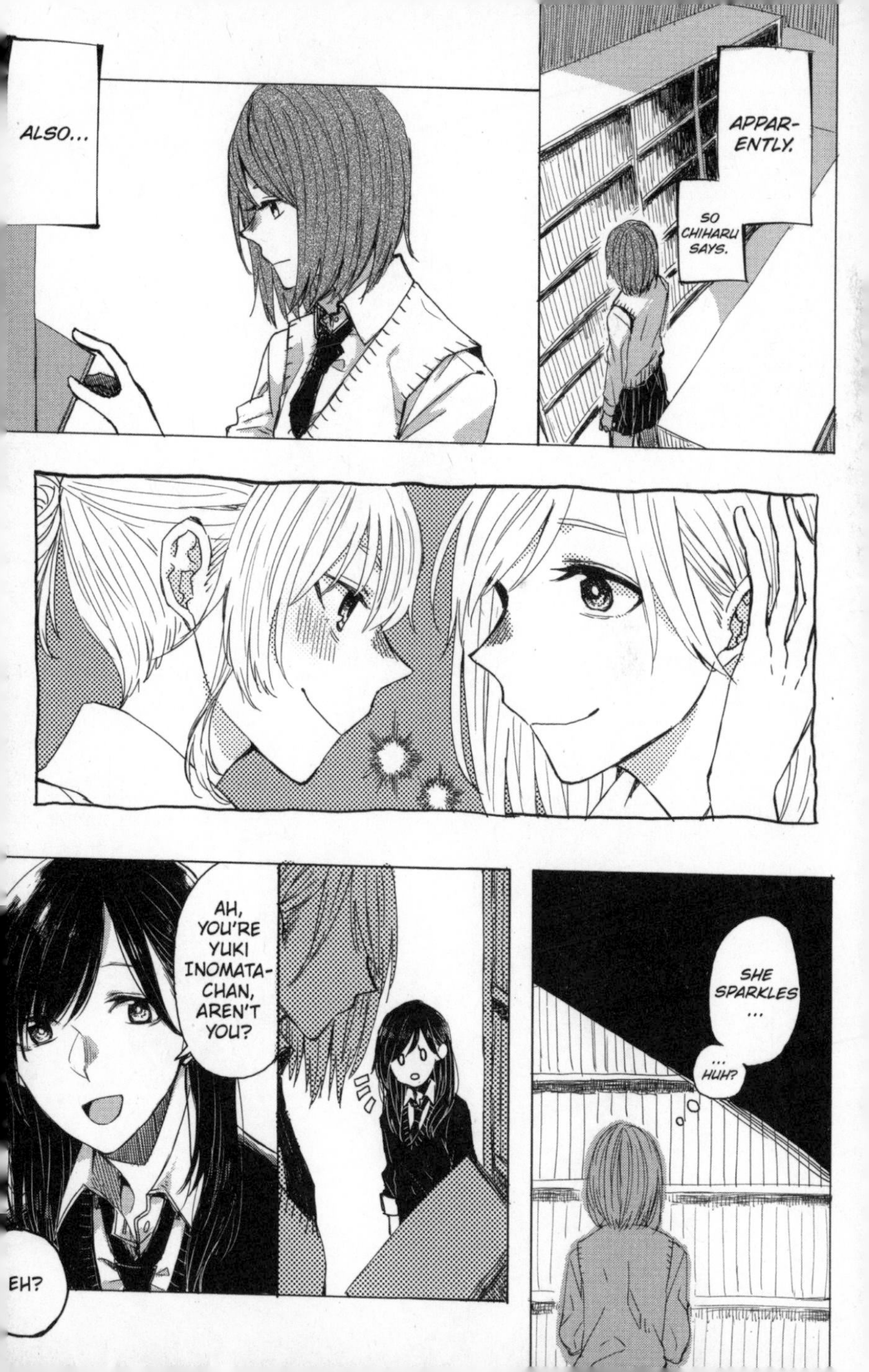
APPARENTLY.
SO CHIHARU SAYS.
ALSO...
SHE SPARKLES...
...HUH?
AH, YOU'RE YUKI INOMATA-CHAN, AREN'T YOU?
EH?

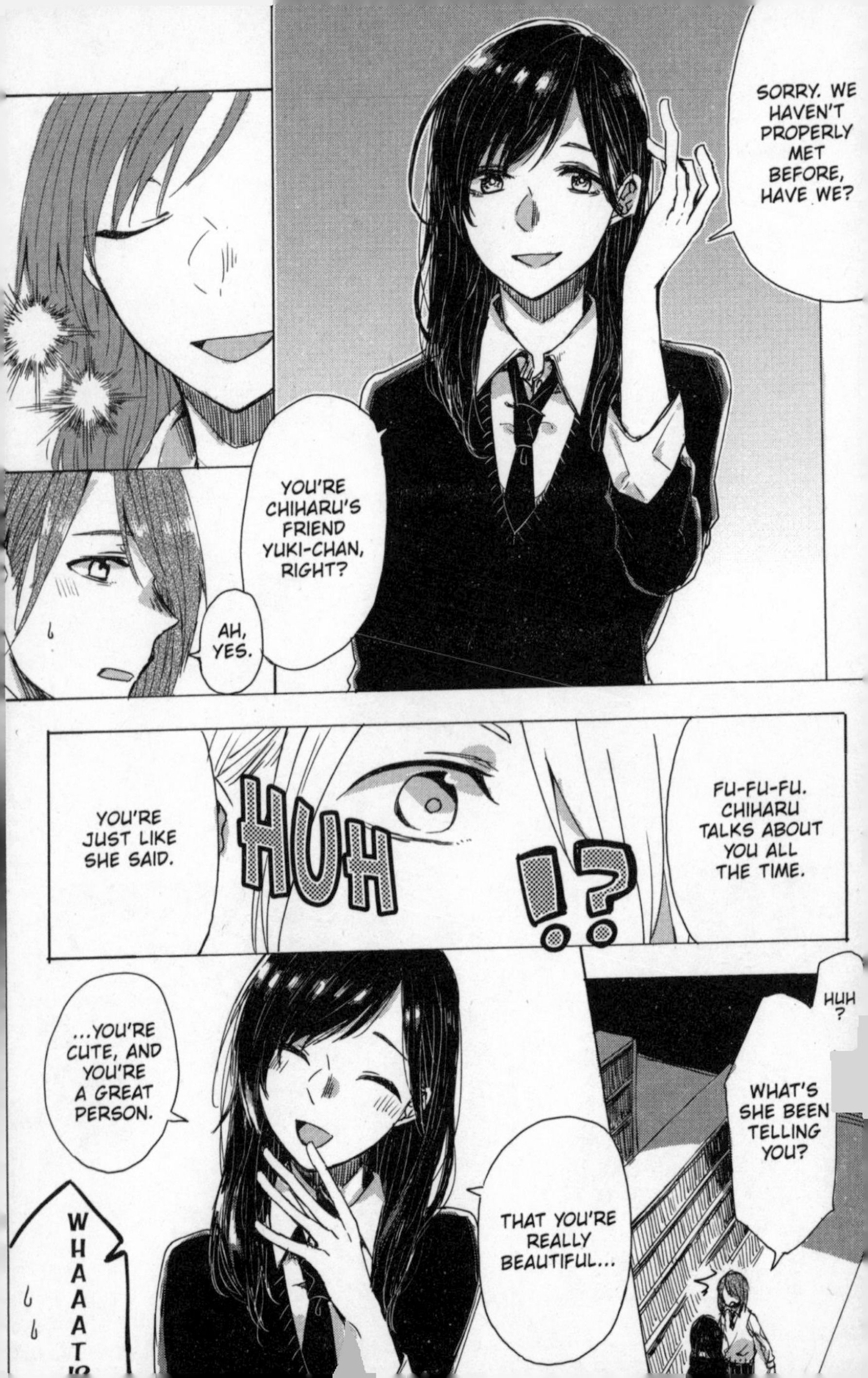
SORRY. WE HAVEN'T PROPERLY MET BEFORE, HAVE WE?
YOU'RE CHIHARU'S FRIEND YUKI-CHAN, RIGHT?
AH, YES.
FU-FU-FU. CHIHARU TALKS ABOUT YOU ALL THE TIME.
HUH !?
YOU'RE JUST LIKE SHE SAID.
HUH?
WHAT'S SHE BEEN TELLING YOU?
THAT YOU'RE REALLY BEAUTIFUL...
...YOU'RE CUTE, AND YOU'RE A GREAT PERSON.
WHAAAAT!?

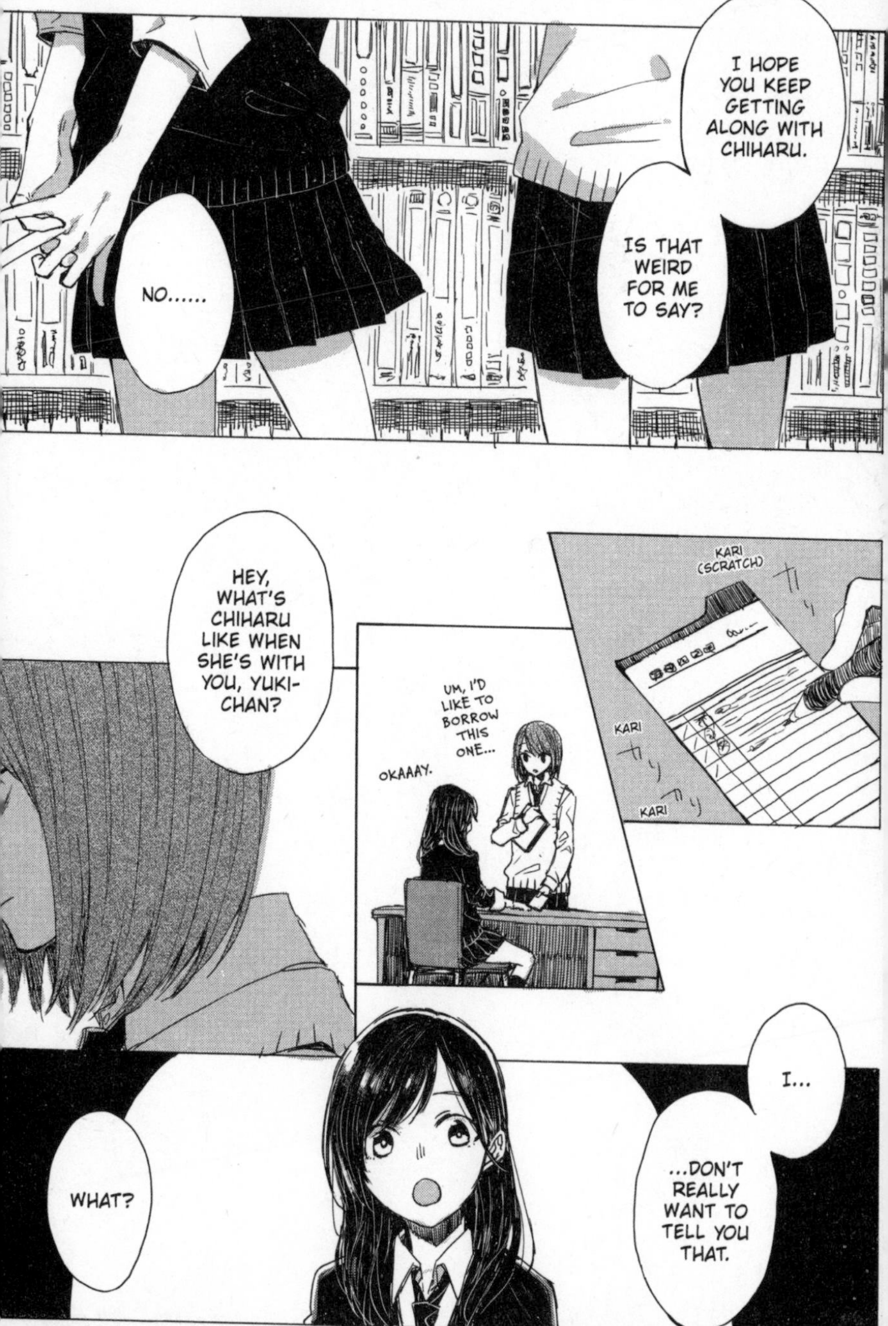
I HOPE YOU KEEP GETTING ALONG WITH CHIHARU.
IS THAT WEIRD FOR ME TO SAY?
NO......
KARI (SCRATCH)
KARI
KARI
UM, I'D LIKE TO BORROW THIS ONE...
OKAAAY.
HEY, WHAT'S CHIHARU LIKE WHEN SHE'S WITH YOU, YUKI-CHAN?
I...
...DON'T REALLY WANT TO TELL YOU THAT.
WHAT?

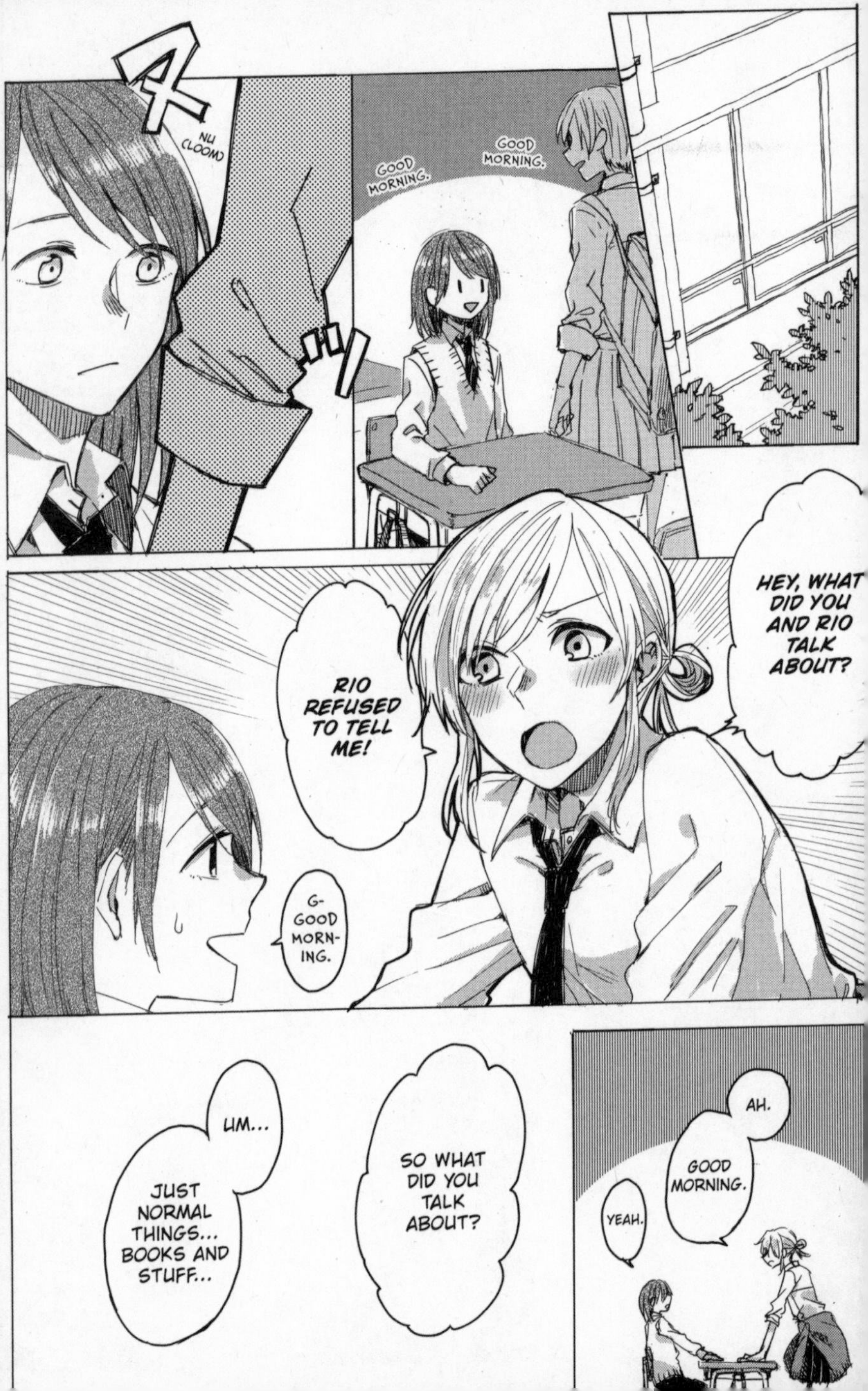
GOOD MORNING.
GOOD MORNING.
NU (LOOM)
HEY, WHAT DID YOU AND RIO TALK ABOUT?
RIO REFUSED TO TELL ME!
G-GOOD MORN-ING.
AH.
GOOD MORNING.
YEAH.
SO WHAT DID YOU TALK ABOUT?
UM...
JUST NORMAL THINGS... BOOKS AND STUFF...

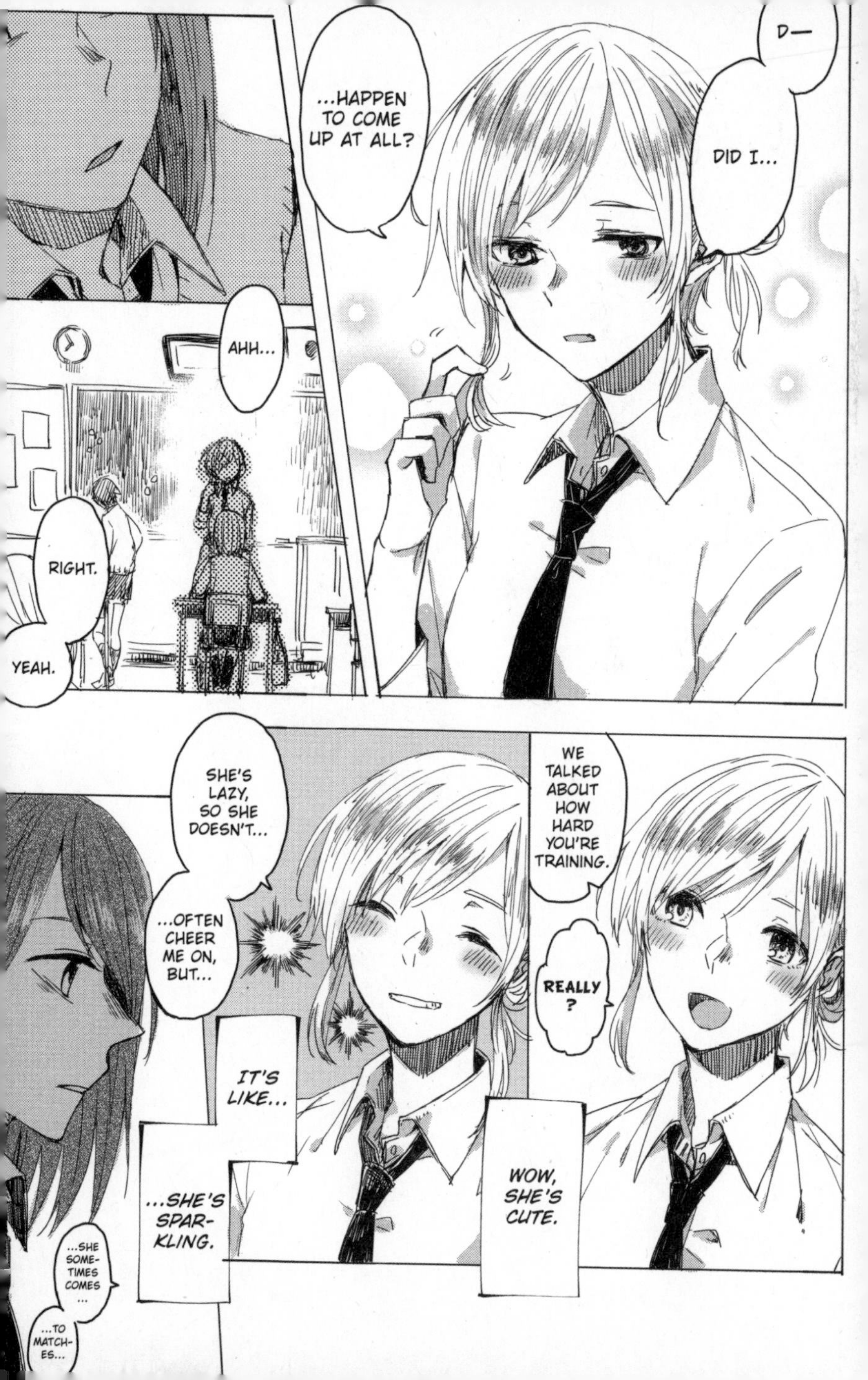
D—
DID I...
...HAPPEN TO COME UP AT ALL?
AHH...
RIGHT.
YEAH.
WE TALKED ABOUT HOW HARD YOU'RE TRAINING.
REALLY?
WOW, SHE'S CUTE.
SHE'S LAZY, SO SHE DOESN'T...
...OFTEN CHEER ME ON, BUT...
IT'S LIKE...
...SHE'S SPARKLING.
...SHE SOMETIMES COMES...
...TO MATCHES...

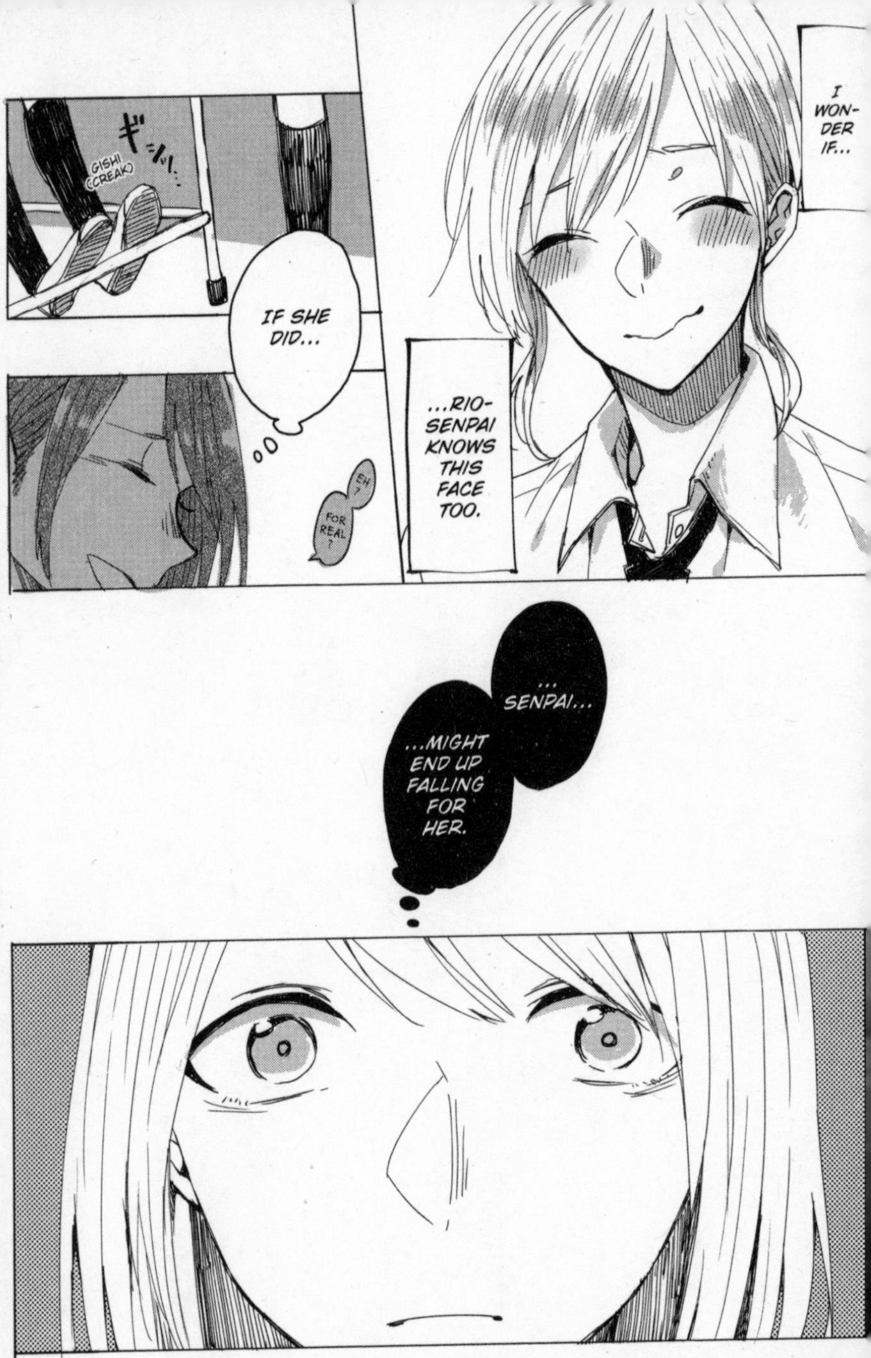
I WON-DER IF...
...RIO-SENPAI KNOWS THIS FACE TOO.
ギシッ
GISHI (CREAK)
IF SHE DID...
EH? FOR REAL?
...SENPAI...
...MIGHT END UP FALLING FOR HER.

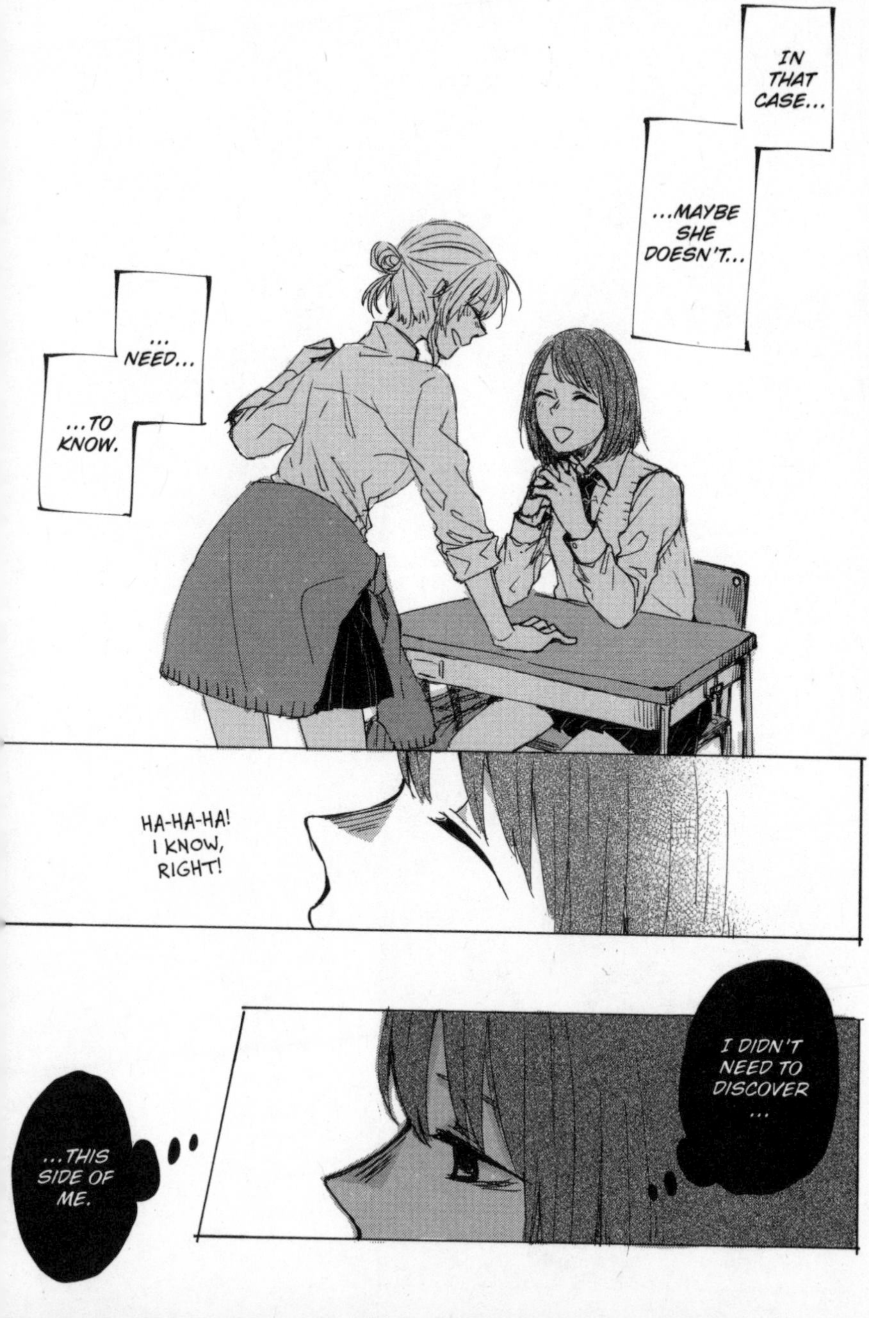
IN THAT CASE...
...MAYBE SHE DOESN'T...
... NEED...
...TO KNOW.
HA-HA-HA! I KNOW, RIGHT!
I DIDN'T NEED TO DISCOVER ...
...THIS SIDE OF ME.

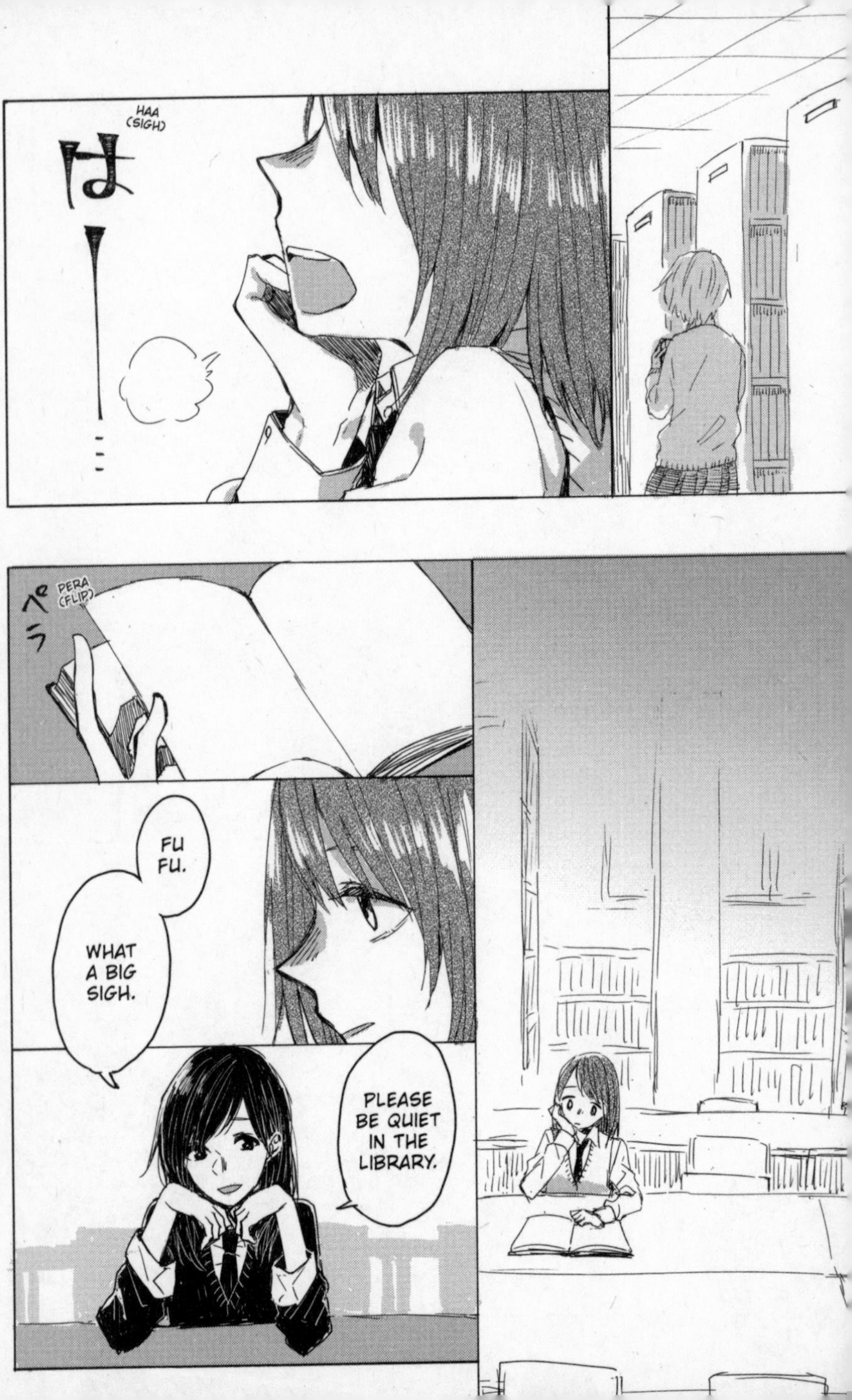
HAA (SIGH)
はー…
PERA (FLIP)
ペラ
FU FU.
WHAT A BIG SIGH.
PLEASE BE QUIET IN THE LIBRARY.

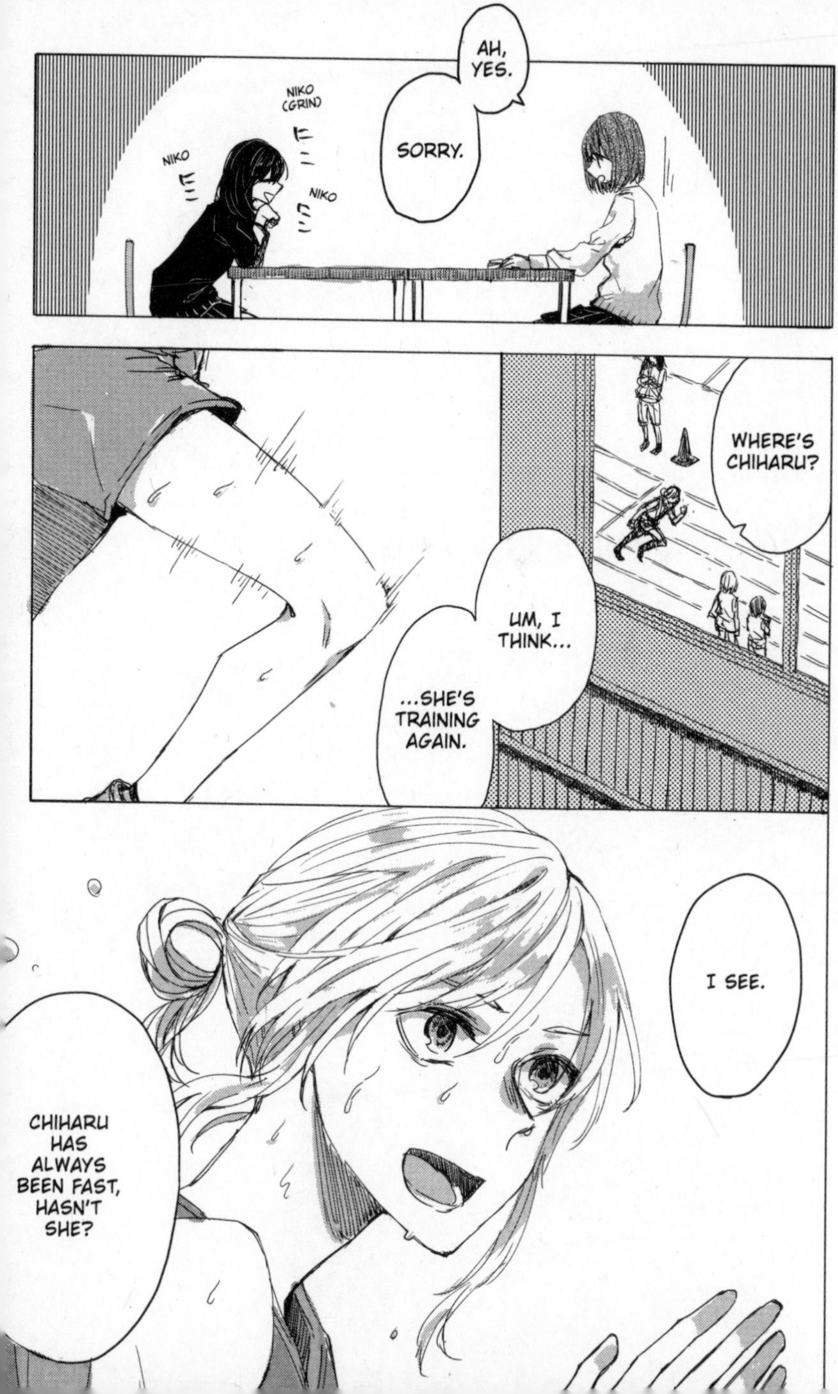
AH, YES.
SORRY.
NIKO (GRIN)
NIKO
NIKO
WHERE'S CHIHARU?
UM, I THINK...
...SHE'S TRAINING AGAIN.
I SEE.
CHIHARU HAS ALWAYS BEEN FAST, HASN'T SHE?

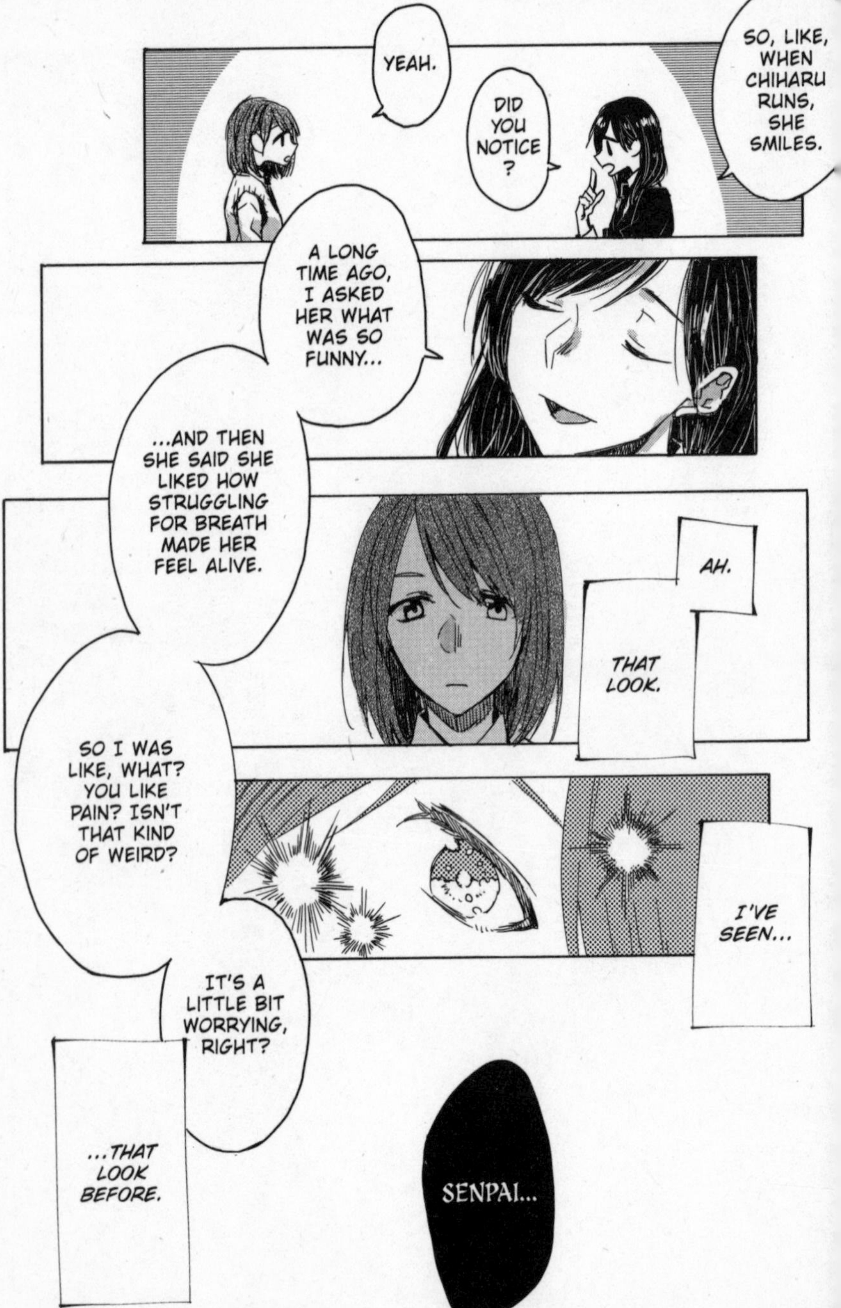
SO, LIKE, WHEN CHIHARU RUNS, SHE SMILES.
DID YOU NOTICE?
YEAH.
A LONG TIME AGO, I ASKED HER WHAT WAS SO FUNNY...
...AND THEN SHE SAID SHE LIKED HOW STRUGGLING FOR BREATH MADE HER FEEL ALIVE.
AH.
THAT LOOK.
SO I WAS LIKE, WHAT? YOU LIKE PAIN? ISN'T THAT KIND OF WEIRD?
I'VE SEEN...
IT'S A LITTLE BIT WORRYING, RIGHT?
SENPAI...
...THAT LOOK BEFORE.

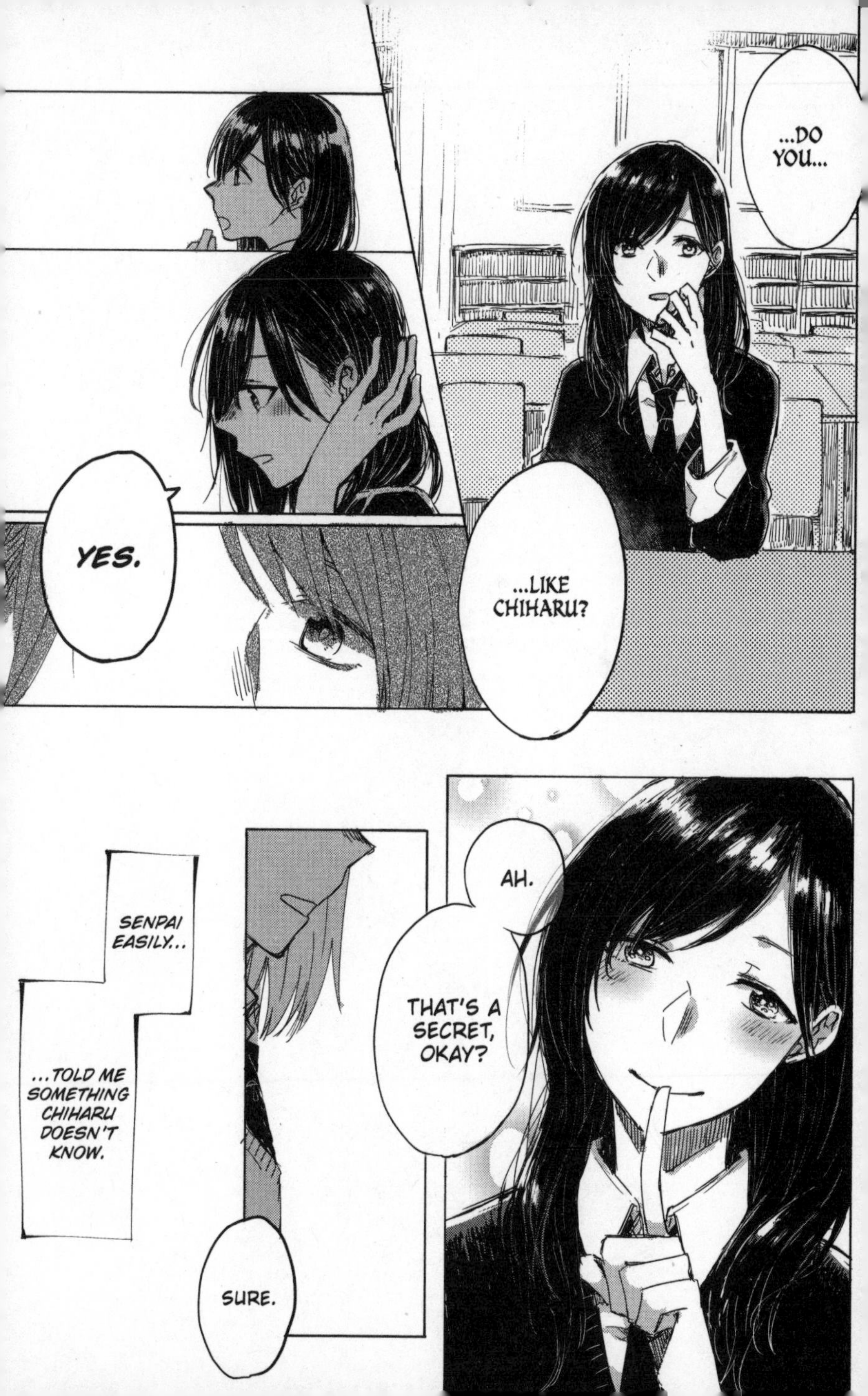
...DO YOU...
...LIKE CHIHARU?
YES.
AH.
THAT'S A SECRET, OKAY?
SENPAI EASILY...
...TOLD ME SOMETHING CHIHARU DOESN'T KNOW.
SURE.

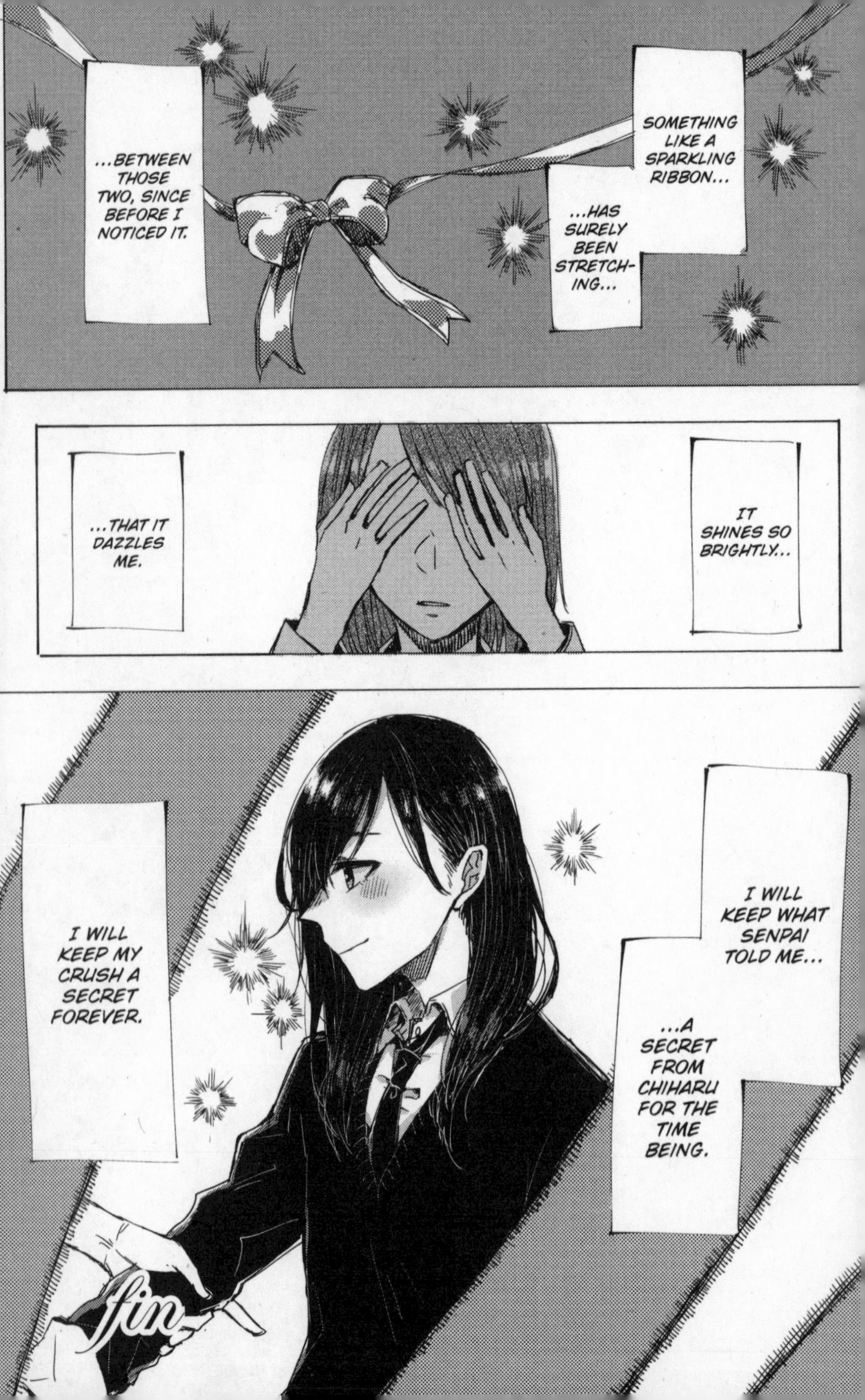
SOMETHING LIKE A SPARKLING RIBBON...
...HAS SURELY BEEN STRETCHING...
...BETWEEN THOSE TWO, SINCE BEFORE I NOTICED IT.
IT SHINES SO BRIGHTLY...
...THAT IT DAZZLES ME.
I WILL KEEP WHAT SENPAI TOLD ME...
...A SECRET FROM CHIHARU FOR THE TIME BEING.
I WILL KEEP MY CRUSH A SECRET FOREVER.
fin

éclair
blanche

A Girls' Love Anthology
That Resonates in Your Heart

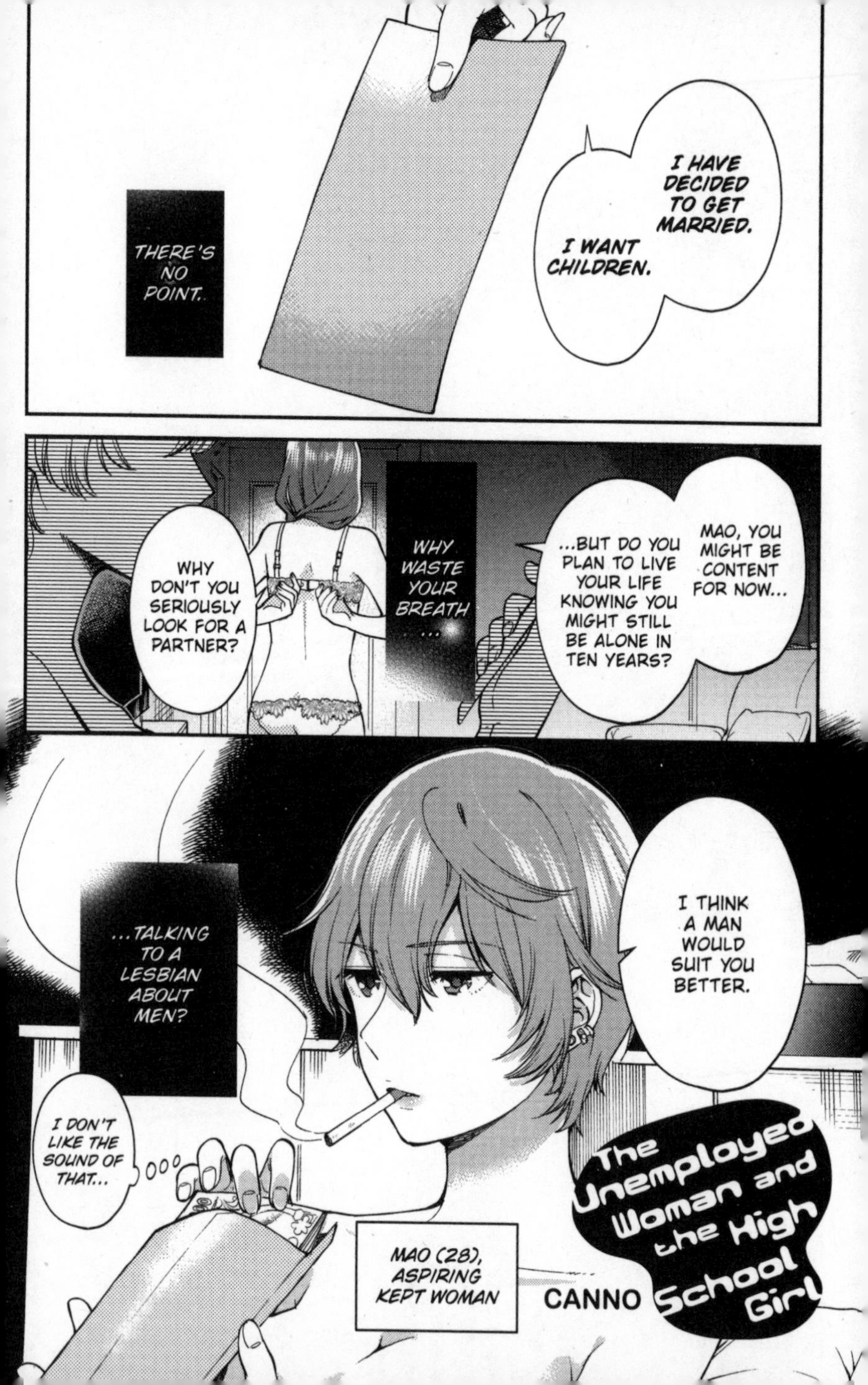
I HAVE DECIDED TO GET MARRIED.
I WANT CHILDREN.
THERE'S NO POINT.
MAO, YOU MIGHT BE CONTENT FOR NOW...
...BUT DO YOU PLAN TO LIVE YOUR LIFE KNOWING YOU MIGHT STILL BE ALONE IN TEN YEARS?
WHY WASTE YOUR BREATH...
WHY DON'T YOU SERIOUSLY LOOK FOR A PARTNER?
I THINK A MAN WOULD SUIT YOU BETTER.
...TALKING TO A LESBIAN ABOUT MEN?
The Unemployed Woman and the High School Girl
CANNO
MAO (28), ASPIRING KEPT WOMAN
I DON'T LIKE THE SOUND OF THAT...

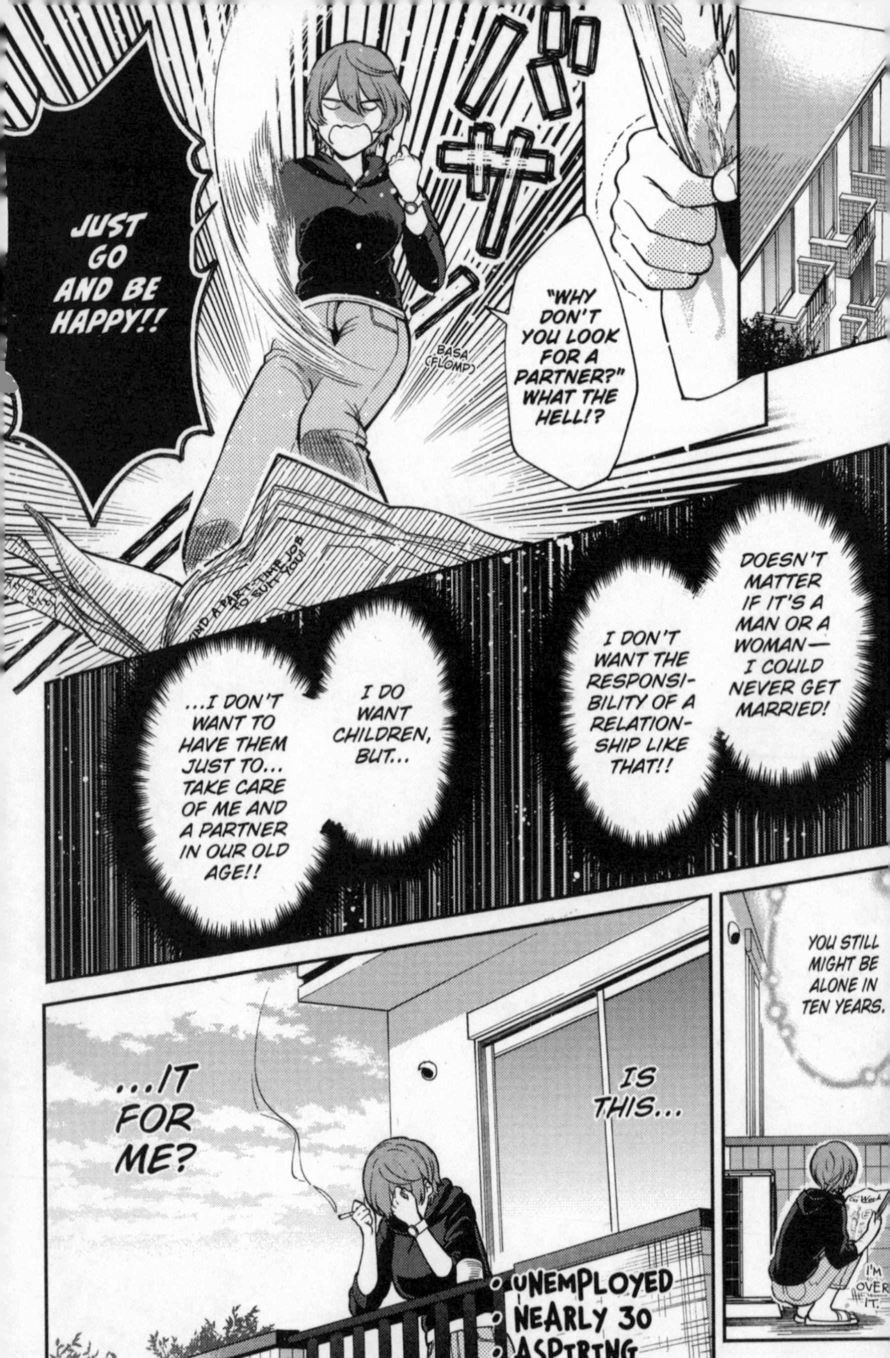
"WHY DON'T YOU LOOK FOR A PARTNER?" WHAT THE HELL!?
BASA (FLOMP)
JUST GO AND BE HAPPY!!
IND A PART-TIME JOB TO SUIT YOU!
DOESN'T MATTER IF IT'S A MAN OR A WOMAN— I COULD NEVER GET MARRIED!
I DON'T WANT THE RESPONSIBILITY OF A RELATIONSHIP LIKE THAT!!
I DO WANT CHILDREN, BUT...
...I DON'T WANT TO HAVE THEM JUST TO... TAKE CARE OF ME AND A PARTNER IN OUR OLD AGE!!
YOU STILL MIGHT BE ALONE IN TEN YEARS.
I'M OVER IT.
IS THIS...
...IT FOR ME?
• UNEMPLOYED
• NEARLY 30
• ASPIRING KEPT WOMAN

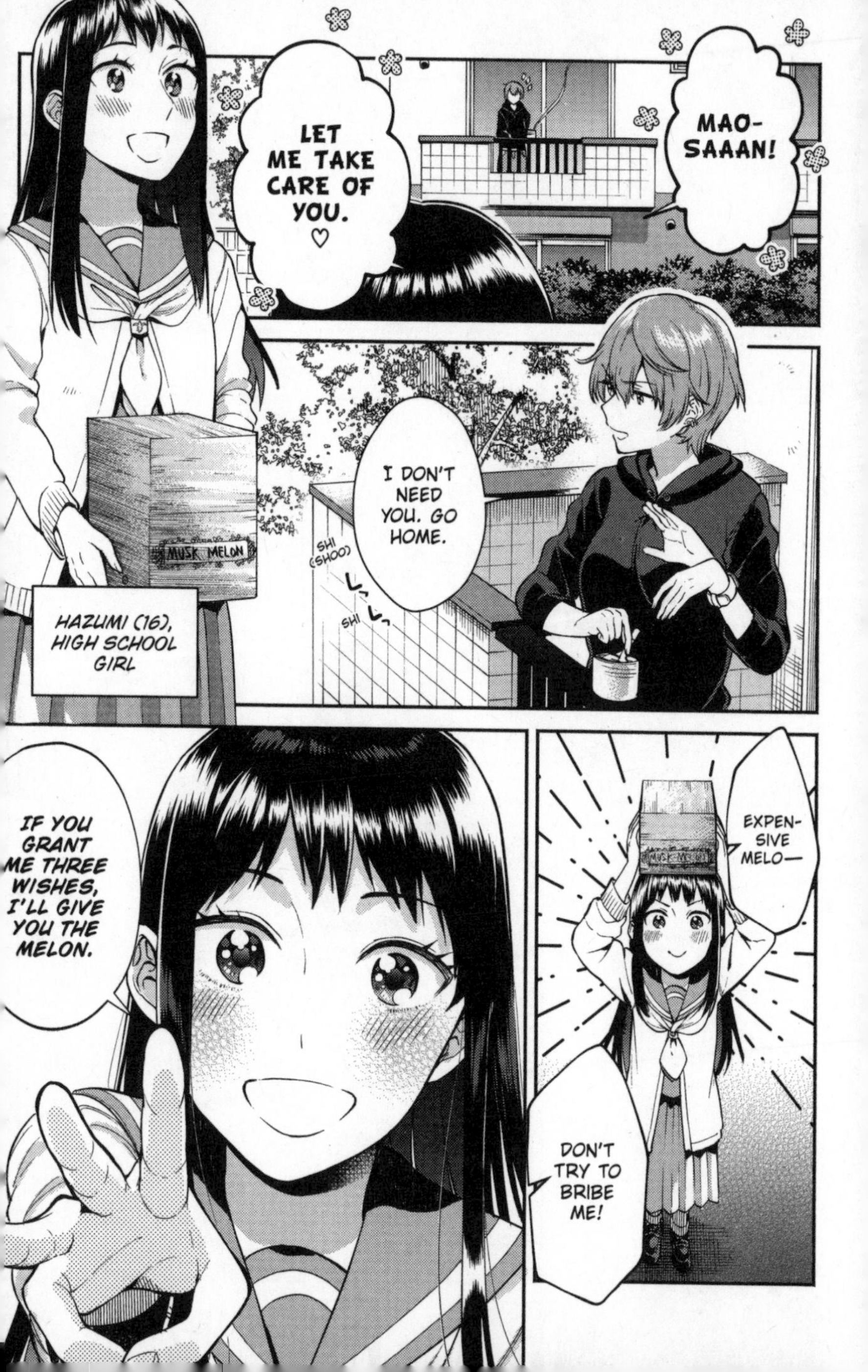
MAO-SAAAN!
LET ME TAKE CARE OF YOU. ♡
I DON'T NEED YOU. GO HOME.
SHI (SHOO)
SHI
MUSK MELON
HAZUMI (16), HIGH SCHOOL GIRL
EXPENSIVE MELO—
MUSK MELON
DON'T TRY TO BRIBE ME!
IF YOU GRANT ME THREE WISHES, I'LL GIVE YOU THE MELON.

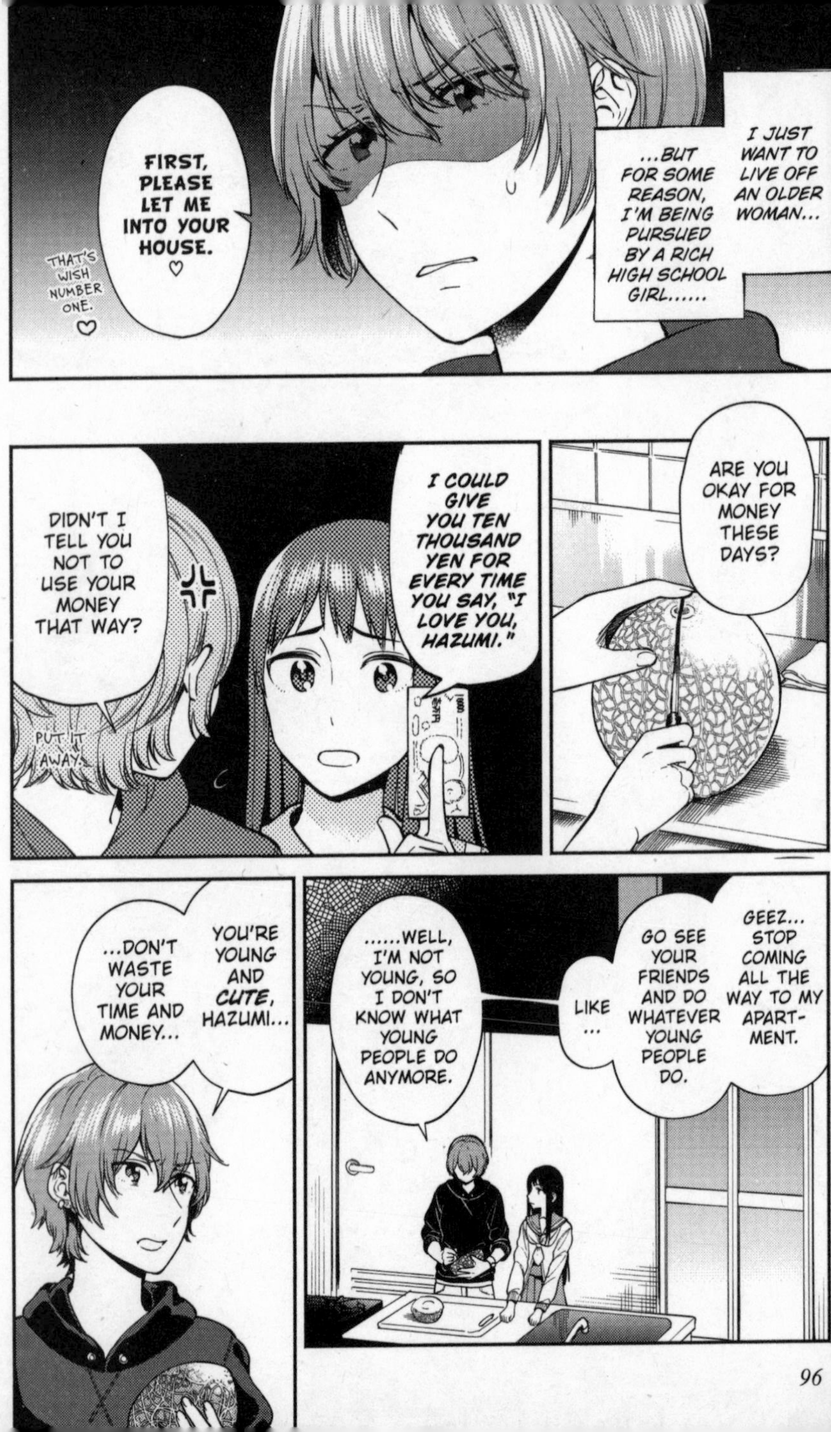
I JUST WANT TO LIVE OFF AN OLDER WOMAN...
...BUT FOR SOME REASON, I'M BEING PURSUED BY A RICH HIGH SCHOOL GIRL......
FIRST, PLEASE LET ME INTO YOUR HOUSE. ♡
THAT'S WISH NUMBER ONE. ♡
ARE YOU OKAY FOR MONEY THESE DAYS?
I COULD GIVE YOU TEN THOUSAND YEN FOR EVERY TIME YOU SAY, "I LOVE YOU, HAZUMI."
DIDN'T I TELL YOU NOT TO USE YOUR MONEY THAT WAY?
PUT IT AWAY.
GEEZ... STOP COMING ALL THE WAY TO MY APARTMENT.
GO SEE YOUR FRIENDS AND DO WHATEVER YOUNG PEOPLE DO.
LIKE...
......WELL, I'M NOT YOUNG, SO I DON'T KNOW WHAT YOUNG PEOPLE DO ANYMORE.
YOU'RE YOUNG AND CUTE, HAZUMI...
...DON'T WASTE YOUR TIME AND MONEY...

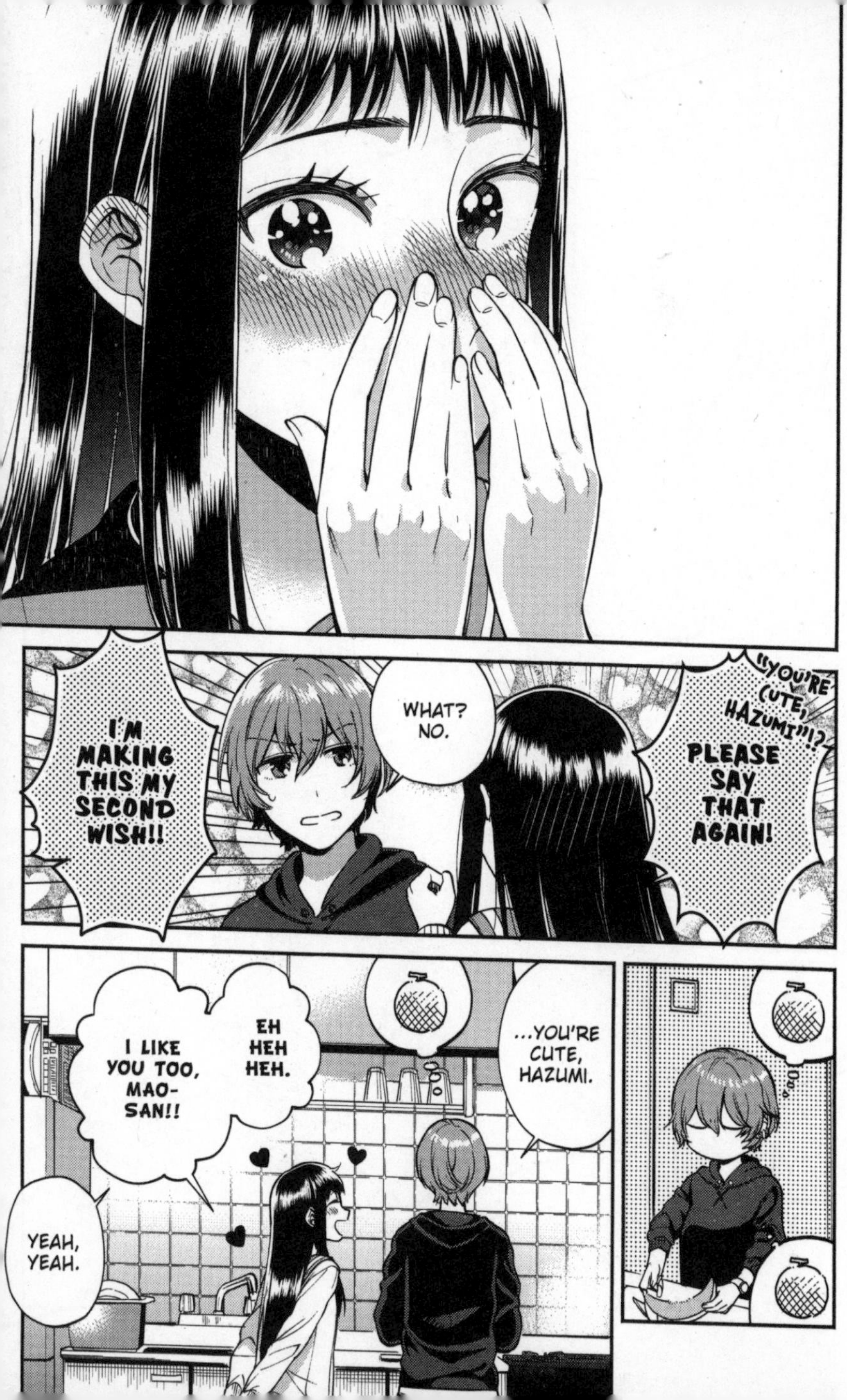
"YOU'RE CUTE, HAZUMI"!?
PLEASE SAY THAT AGAIN!
WHAT? NO.
I'M MAKING THIS MY SECOND WISH!!
...YOU'RE CUTE, HAZUMI.
EH HEH HEH.
I LIKE YOU TOO, MAO-SAN!!
YEAH, YEAH.

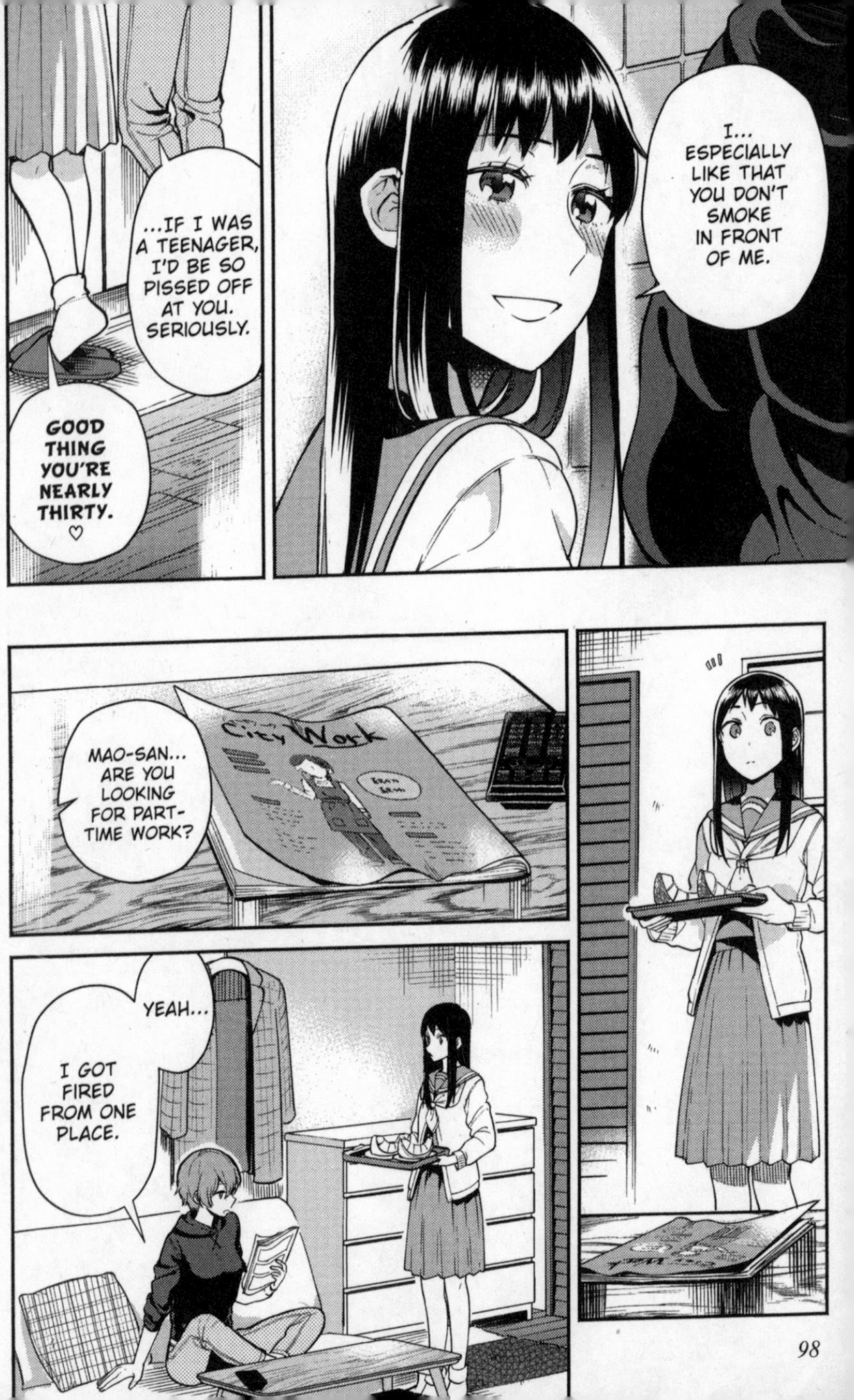

I... ESPECIALLY LIKE THAT YOU DON'T SMOKE IN FRONT OF ME.
...IF I WAS A TEENAGER, I'D BE SO PISSED OFF AT YOU. SERIOUSLY.
GOOD THING YOU'RE NEARLY THIRTY. ♡
MAO-SAN... ARE YOU LOOKING FOR PART-TIME WORK?
City Work
YEAH...
I GOT FIRED FROM ONE PLACE.

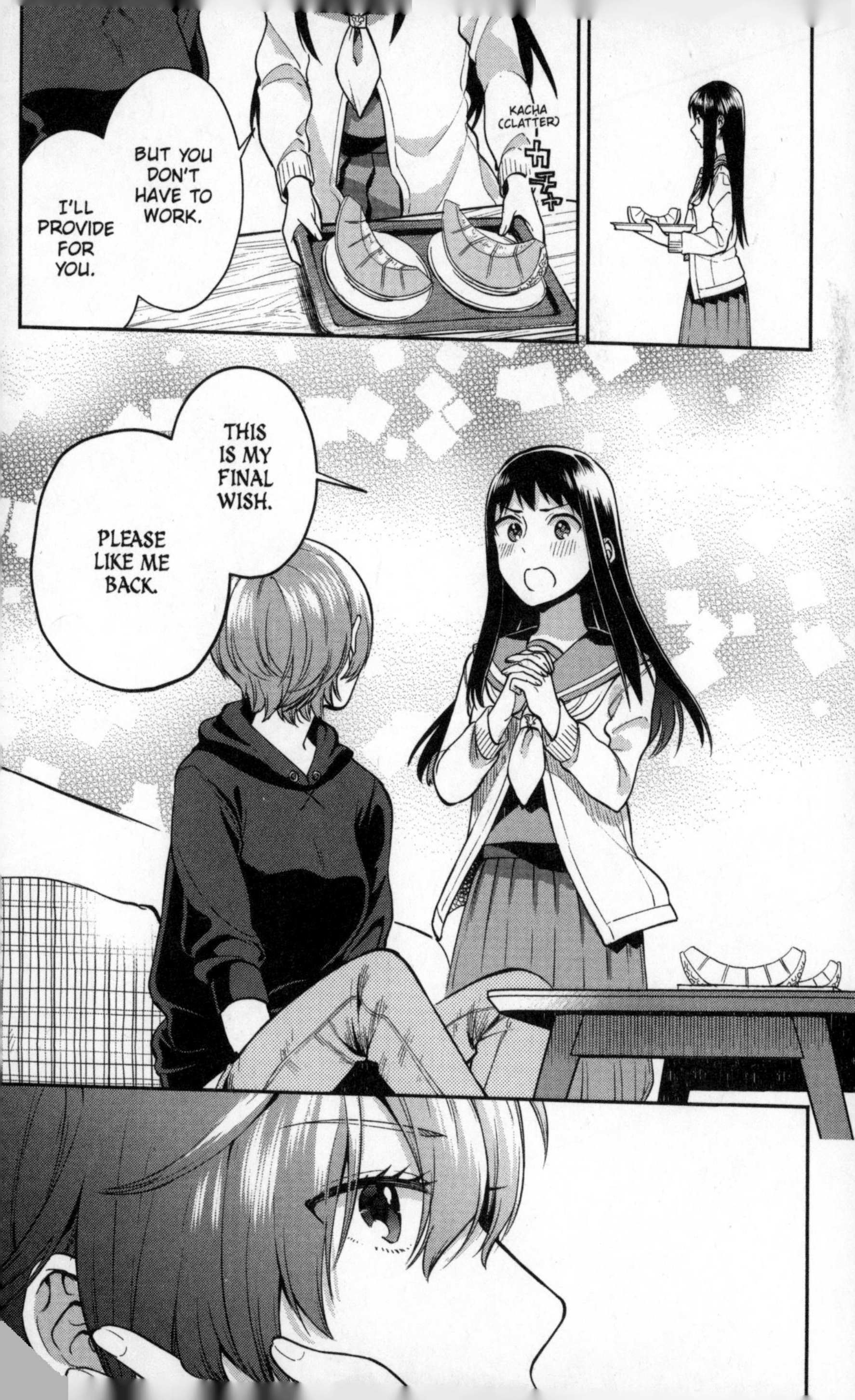
KACHA (CLATTER)
カチャ
BUT YOU DON'T HAVE TO WORK.
I'LL PROVIDE FOR YOU.
THIS IS MY FINAL WISH.
PLEASE LIKE ME BACK.

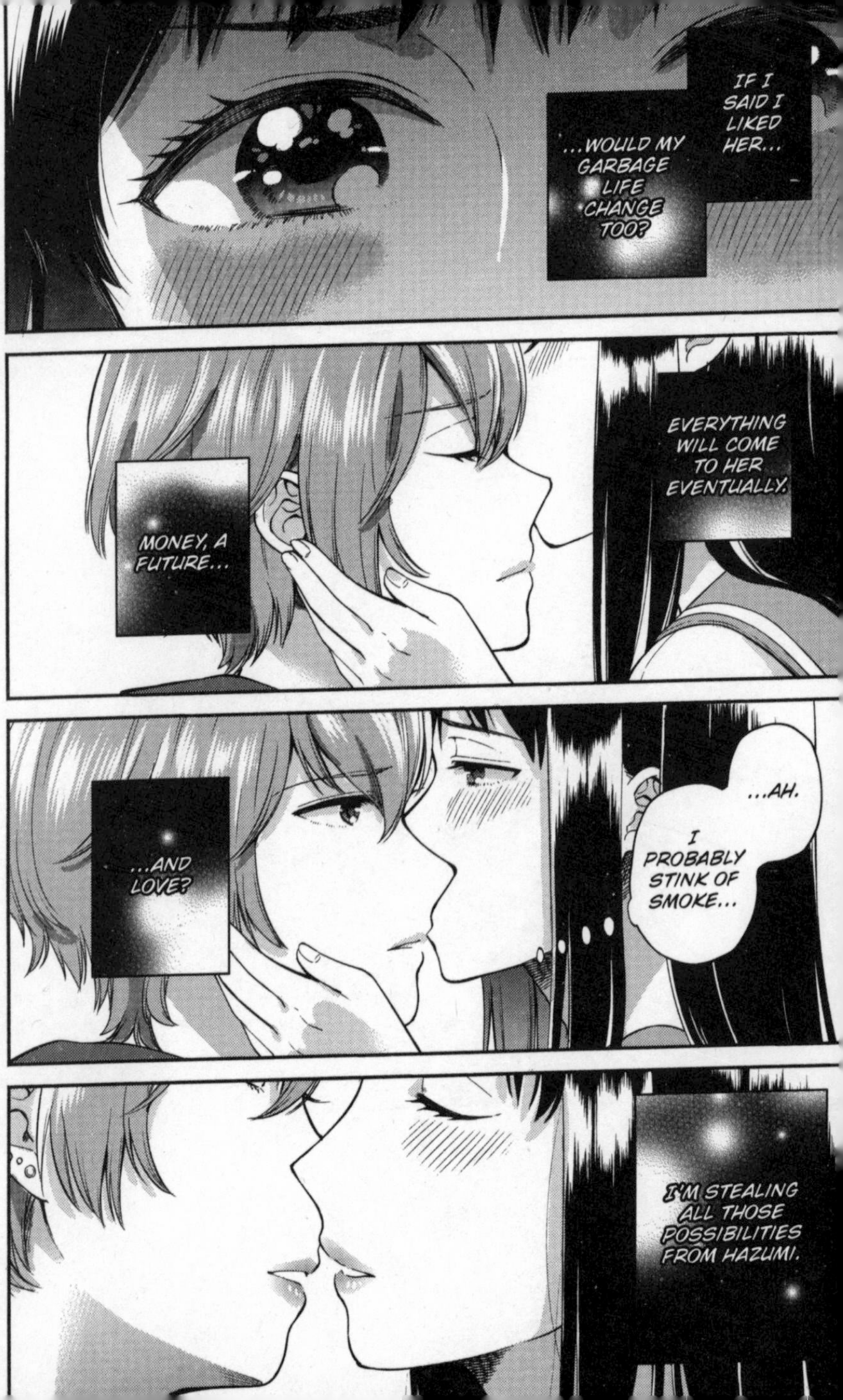
IF I SAID I LIKED HER...
...WOULD MY GARBAGE LIFE CHANGE TOO?
EVERYTHING WILL COME TO HER EVENTUALLY.
MONEY, A FUTURE...
...AH.
I PROBABLY STINK OF SMOKE...
...AND LOVE?
I'M STEALING ALL THOSE POSSIBILITIES FROM HAZUMI.

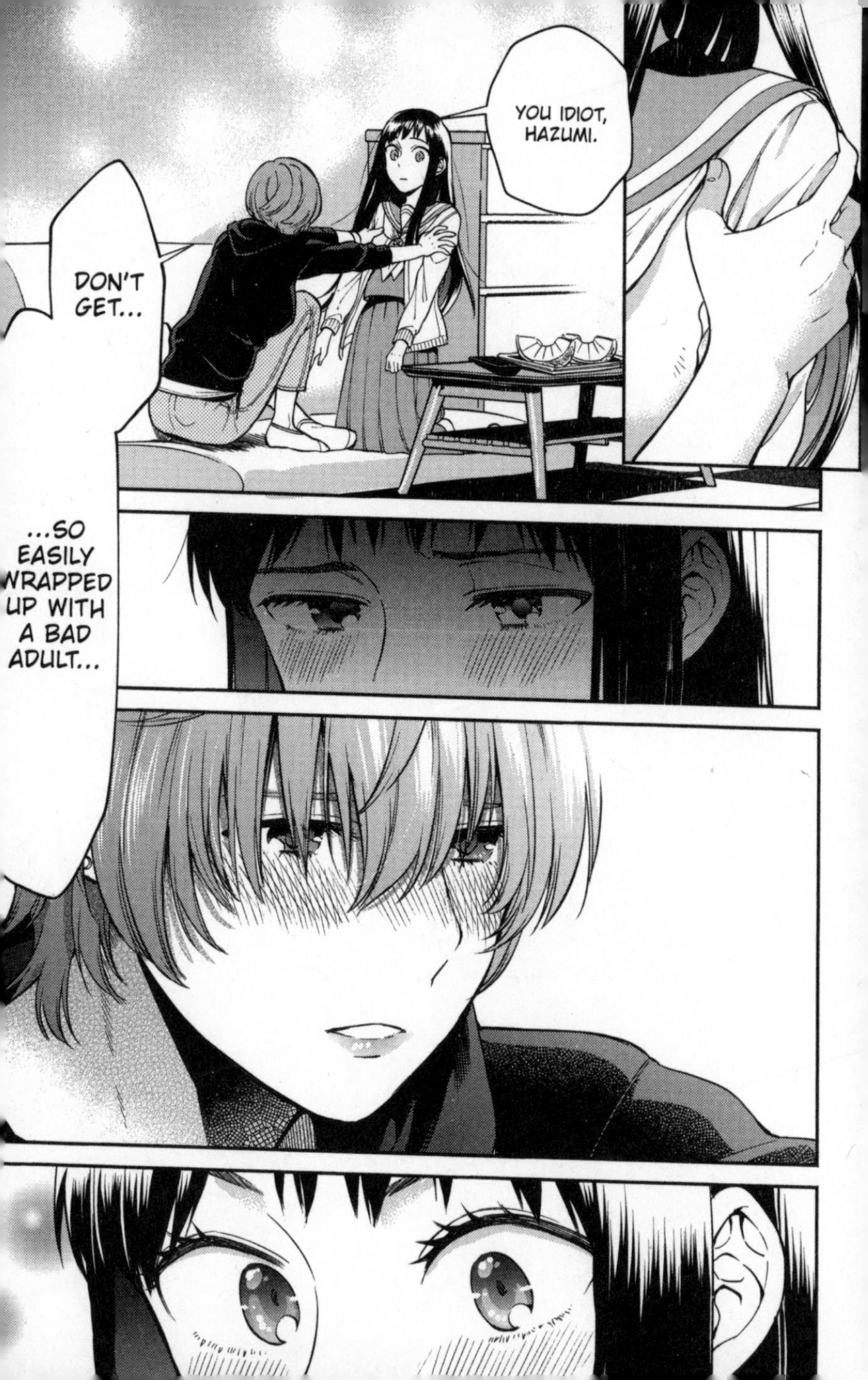
YOU IDIOT, HAZUMI.
DON'T GET...
...SO EASILY WRAPPED UP WITH A BAD ADULT...

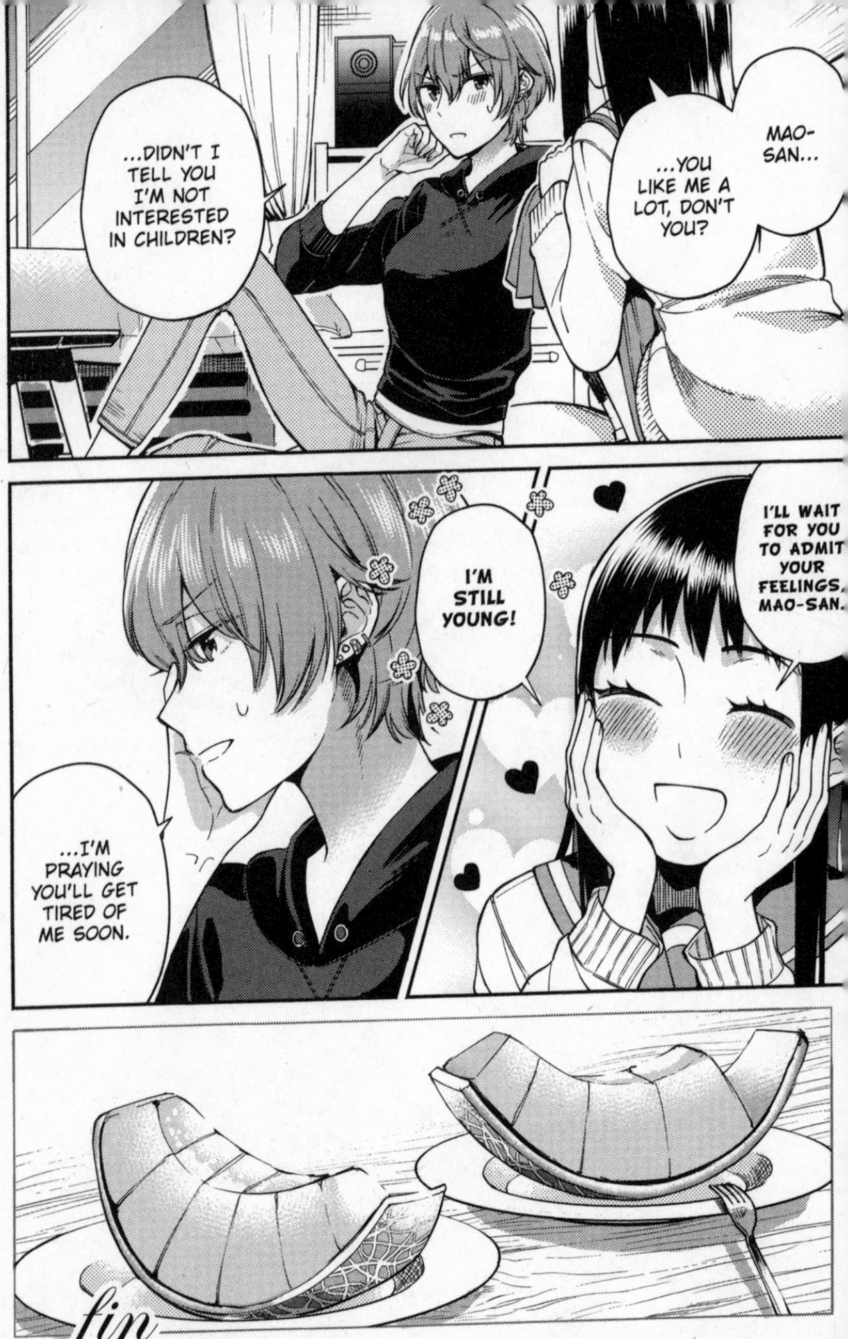
MAO-SAN...
...YOU LIKE ME A LOT, DON'T YOU?
...DIDN'T I TELL YOU I'M NOT INTERESTED IN CHILDREN?
I'LL WAIT FOR YOU TO ADMIT YOUR FEELINGS, MAO-SAN.
I'M STILL YOUNG!
...I'M PRAYING YOU'LL GET TIRED OF ME SOON.
fin

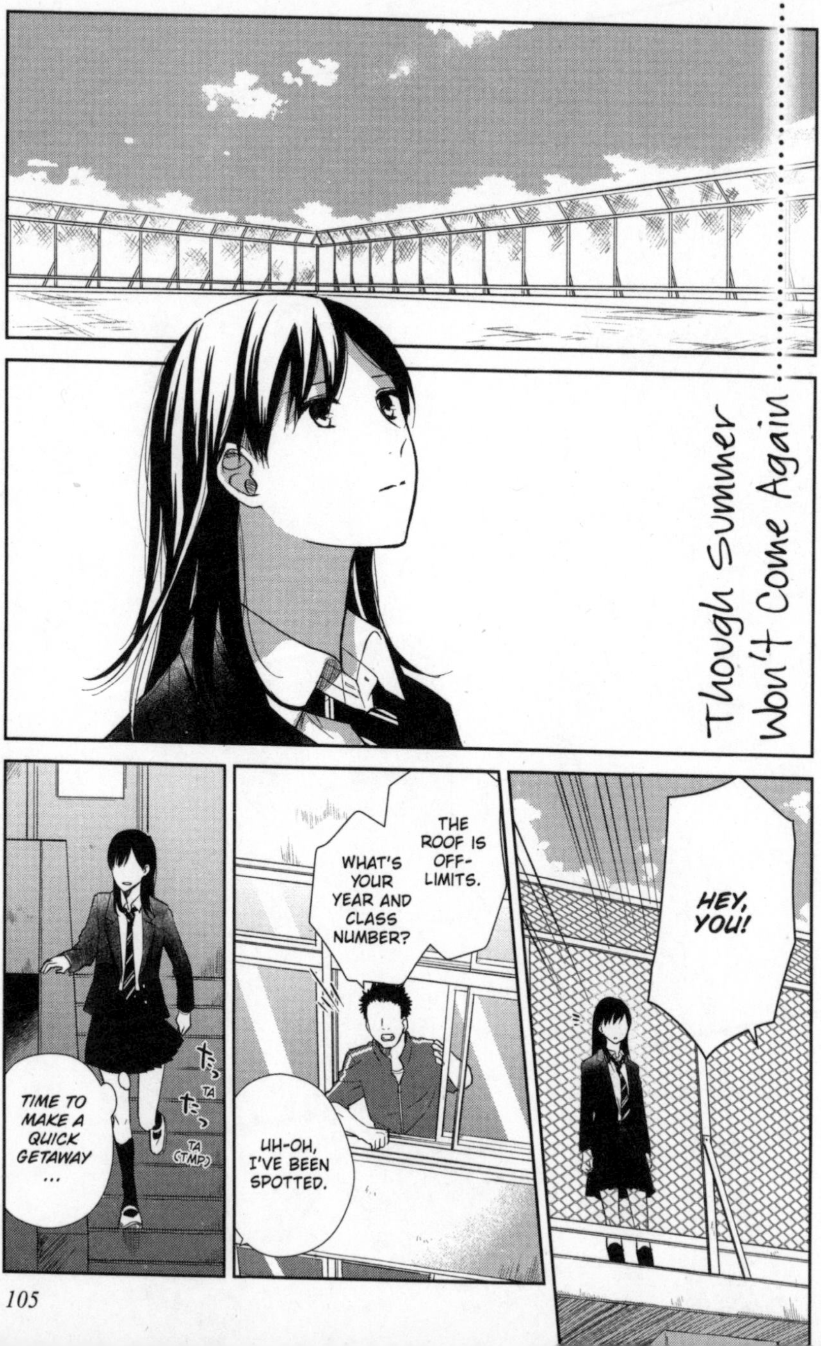
Though Summer Won't Come Again
HEY, YOU!
THE ROOF IS OFF-LIMITS.
WHAT'S YOUR YEAR AND CLASS NUMBER?
UH-OH, I'VE BEEN SPOTTED.
TA
TA (TMP)
TIME TO MAKE A QUICK GETAWAY ...

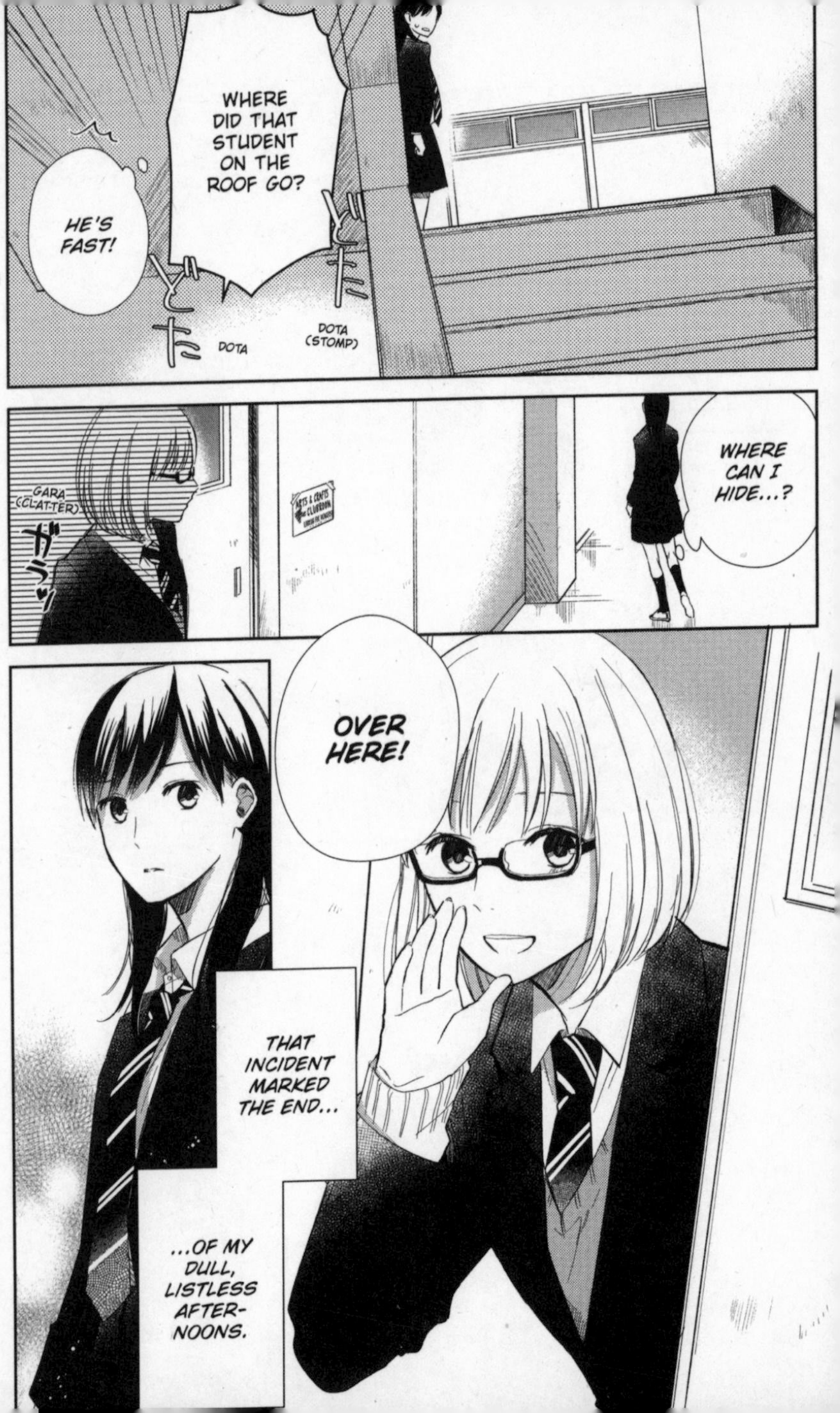

WHERE DID THAT STUDENT ON THE ROOF GO?
DOTA (STOMP)
DOTA
HE'S FAST!
WHERE CAN I HIDE...?
ARTS & CRAFTS CLUBROOM
GARA (CLATTER)
OVER HERE!
THAT INCIDENT MARKED THE END...
...OF MY DULL, LISTLESS AFTERNOONS.

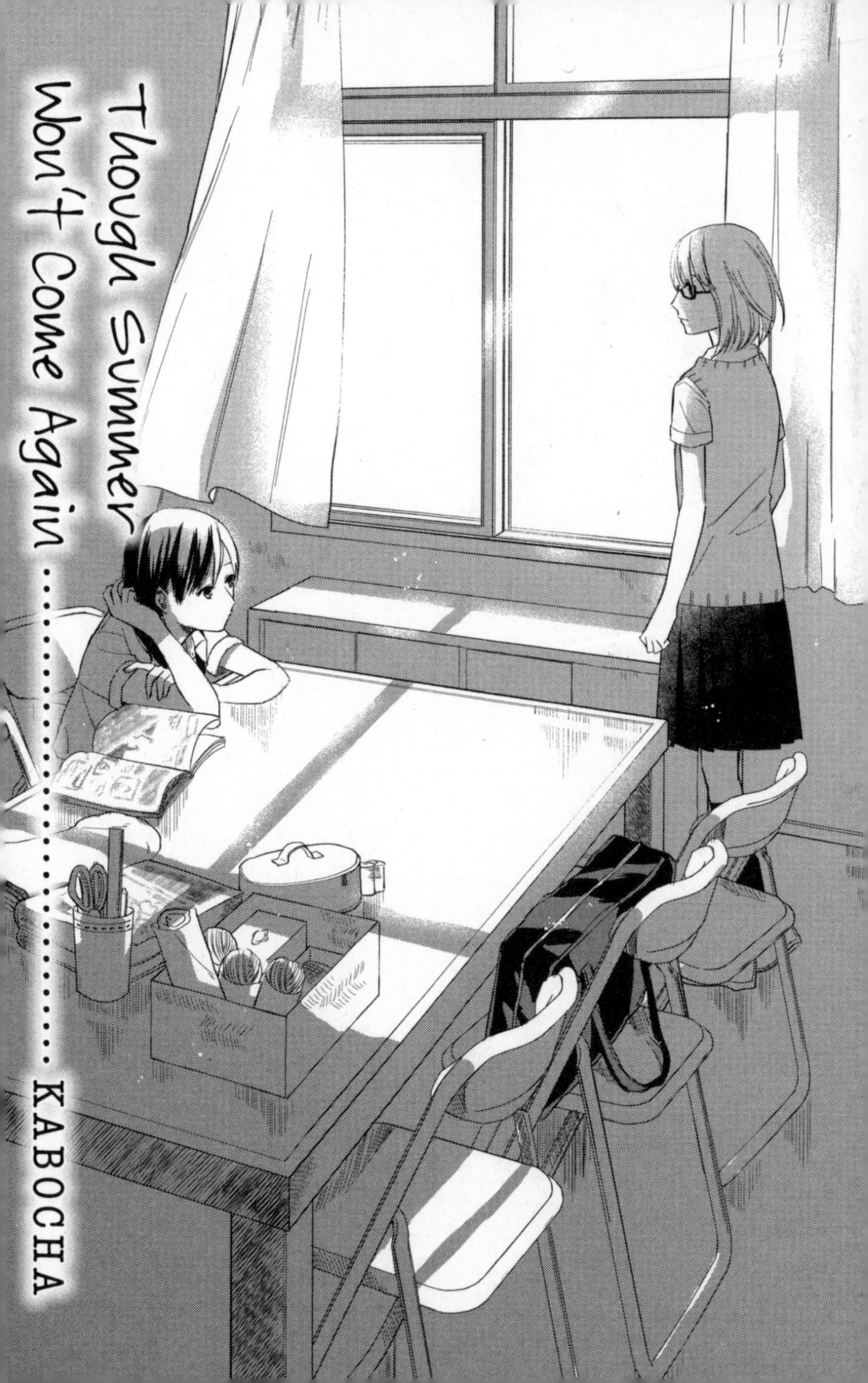
Though Summer
Won't Come Again .... KABOCHA

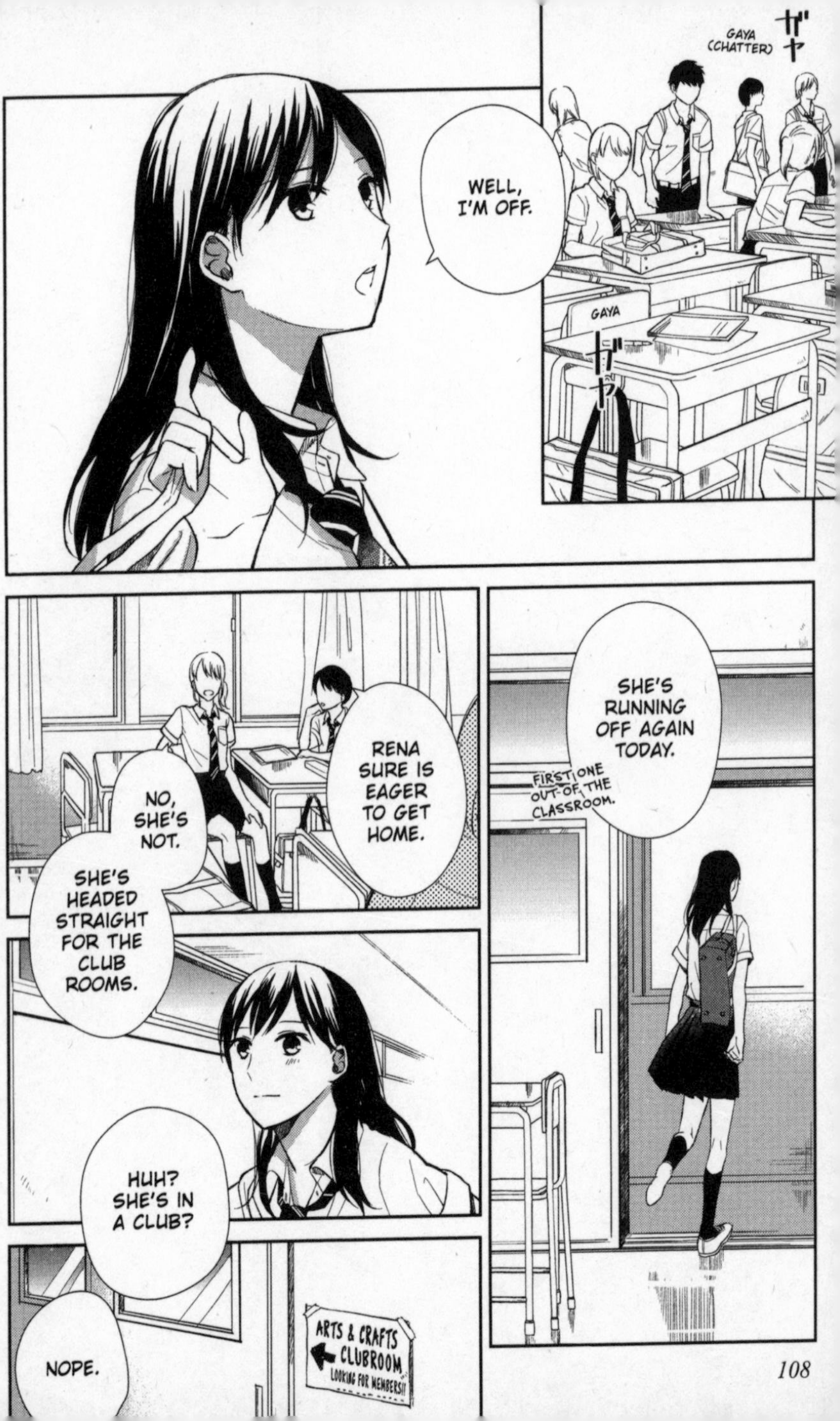
ガヤ
GAYA (CHATTER)
GAYA
ガヤ
WELL, I'M OFF.
SHE'S RUNNING OFF AGAIN TODAY.
FIRST ONE OUT OF THE CLASSROOM.
RENA SURE IS EAGER TO GET HOME.
NO, SHE'S NOT.
SHE'S HEADED STRAIGHT FOR THE CLUB ROOMS.
HUH? SHE'S IN A CLUB?
ARTS & CRAFTS CLUBROOM
LOOKING FOR MEMBERS!!
NOPE.

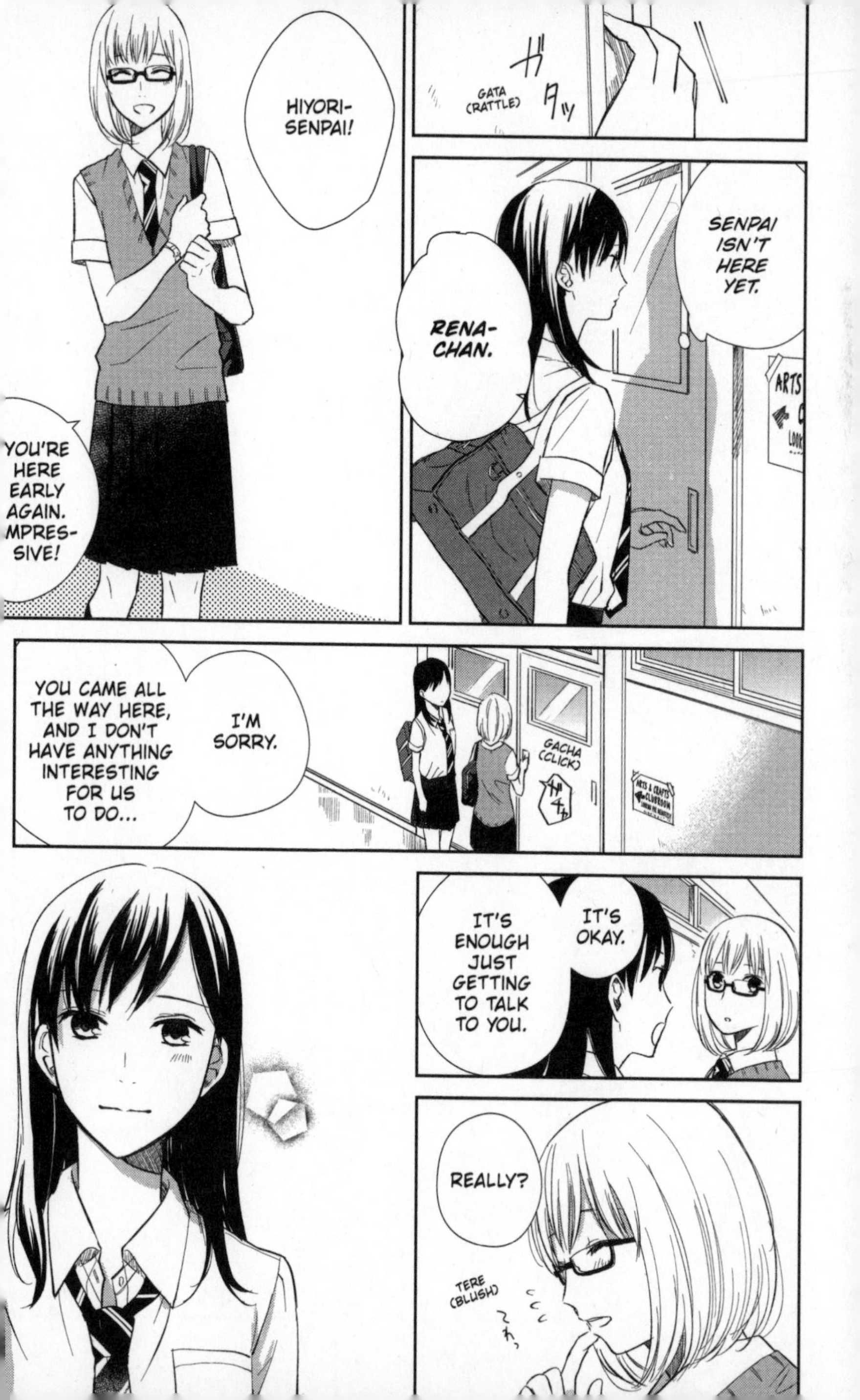
GATA (RATTLE)
SENPAI ISN'T HERE YET.
RENA-CHAN.
ARTS
HIYORI-SENPAI!
YOU'RE HERE EARLY AGAIN. MPRES-SIVE!
GACHA (CLICK)
I'M SORRY.
YOU CAME ALL THE WAY HERE, AND I DON'T HAVE ANYTHING INTERESTING FOR US TO DO...
IT'S OKAY.
IT'S ENOUGH JUST GETTING TO TALK TO YOU.
REALLY?
TERE (BLUSH)

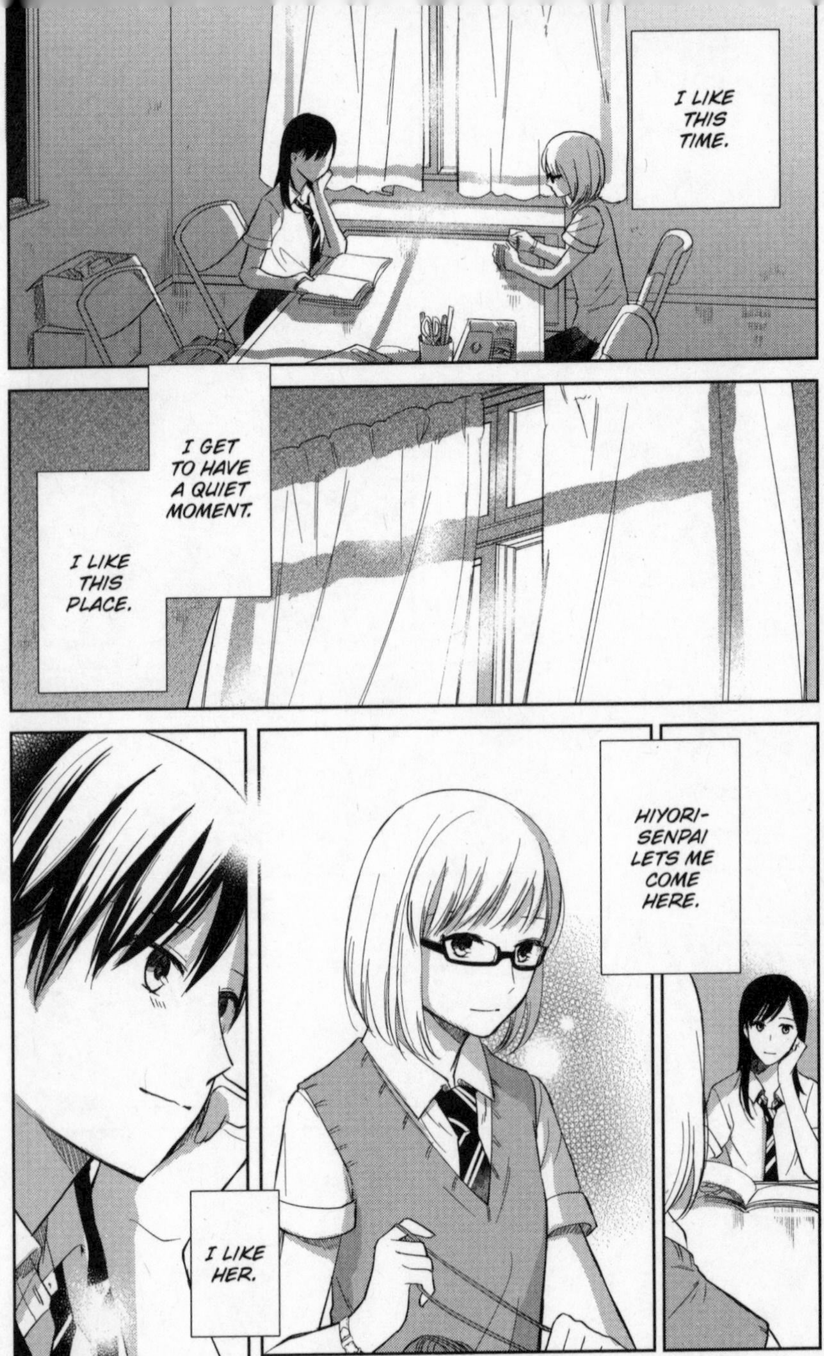
I LIKE THIS TIME.
I GET TO HAVE A QUIET MOMENT.
I LIKE THIS PLACE.
HIYORI-SENPAI LETS ME COME HERE.
I LIKE HER.

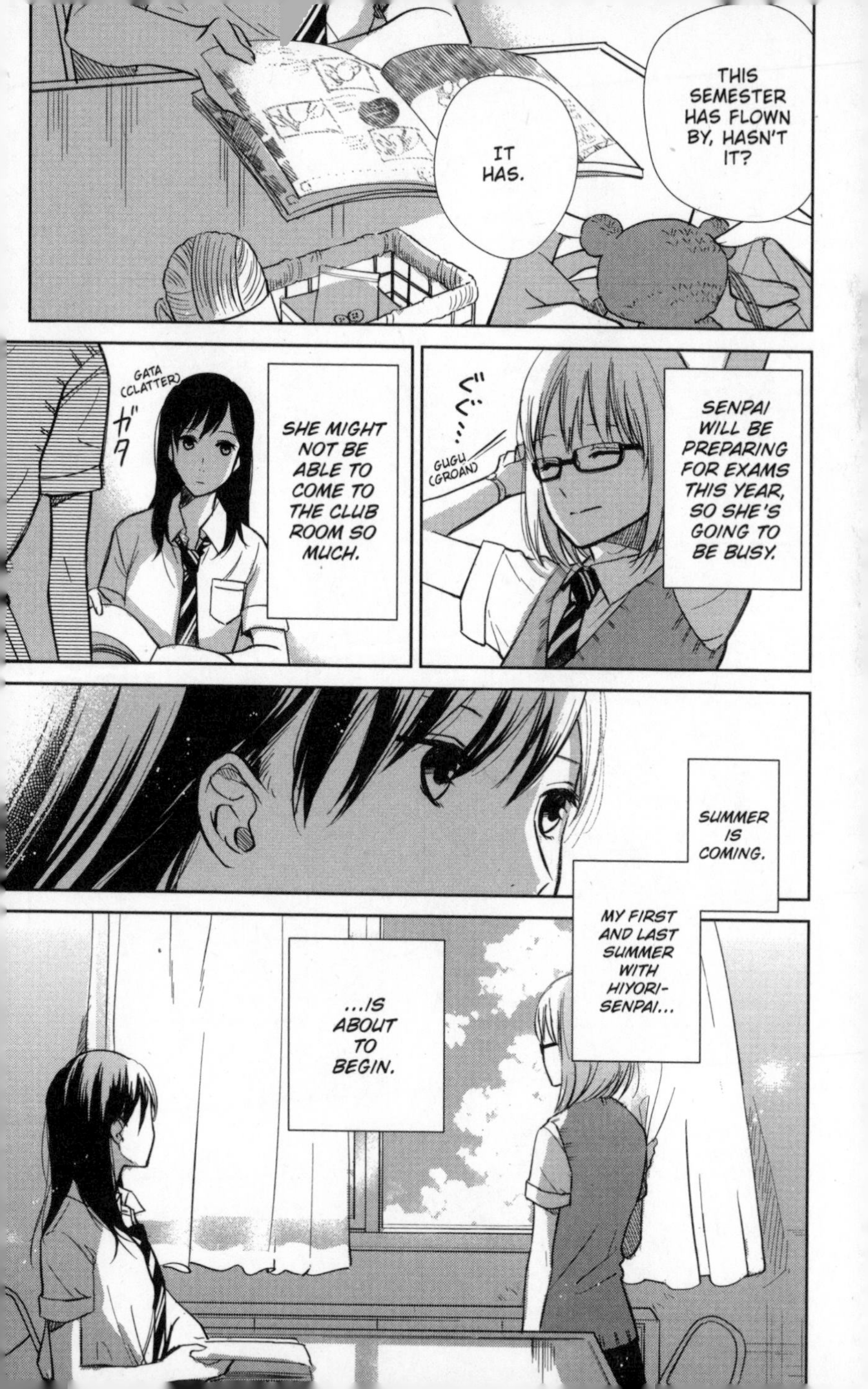
THIS SEMESTER HAS FLOWN BY, HASN'T IT?
IT HAS.
SENPAI WILL BE PREPARING FOR EXAMS THIS YEAR, SO SHE'S GOING TO BE BUSY.
ぐぐ…
GUGU (GROAN)
SHE MIGHT NOT BE ABLE TO COME TO THE CLUB ROOM SO MUCH.
ガタ
GATA (CLATTER)
SUMMER IS COMING.
MY FIRST AND LAST SUMMER WITH HIYORI-SENPAI...
...IS ABOUT TO BEGIN.

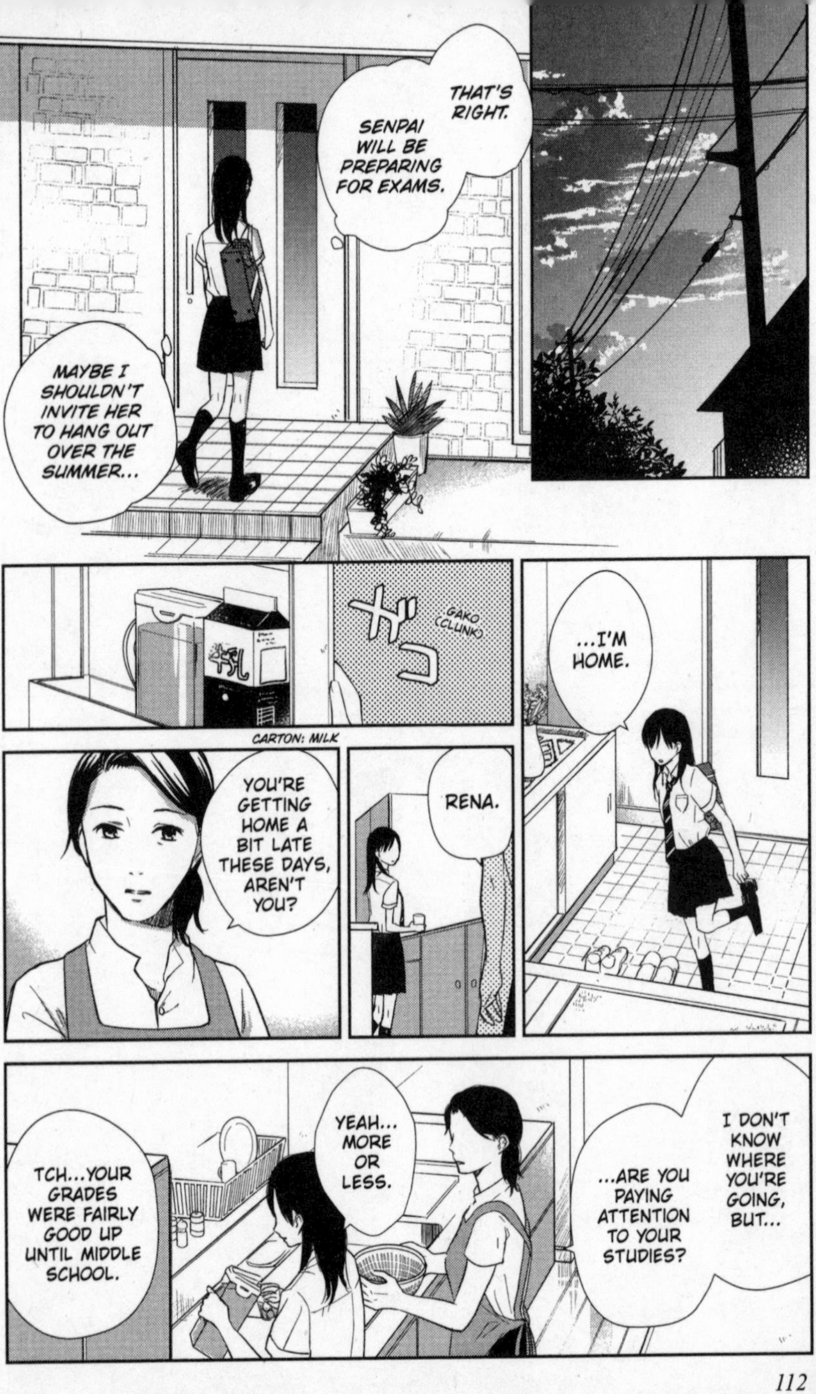
THAT'S RIGHT.
SENPAI WILL BE PREPARING FOR EXAMS.
MAYBE I SHOULDN'T INVITE HER TO HANG OUT OVER THE SUMMER...
...I'M HOME.
GAKO (CLUNK)
CARTON: MILK
RENA.
YOU'RE GETTING HOME A BIT LATE THESE DAYS, AREN'T YOU?
I DON'T KNOW WHERE YOU'RE GOING, BUT...
...ARE YOU PAYING ATTENTION TO YOUR STUDIES?
YEAH... MORE OR LESS.
TCH...YOUR GRADES WERE FAIRLY GOOD UP UNTIL MIDDLE SCHOOL.

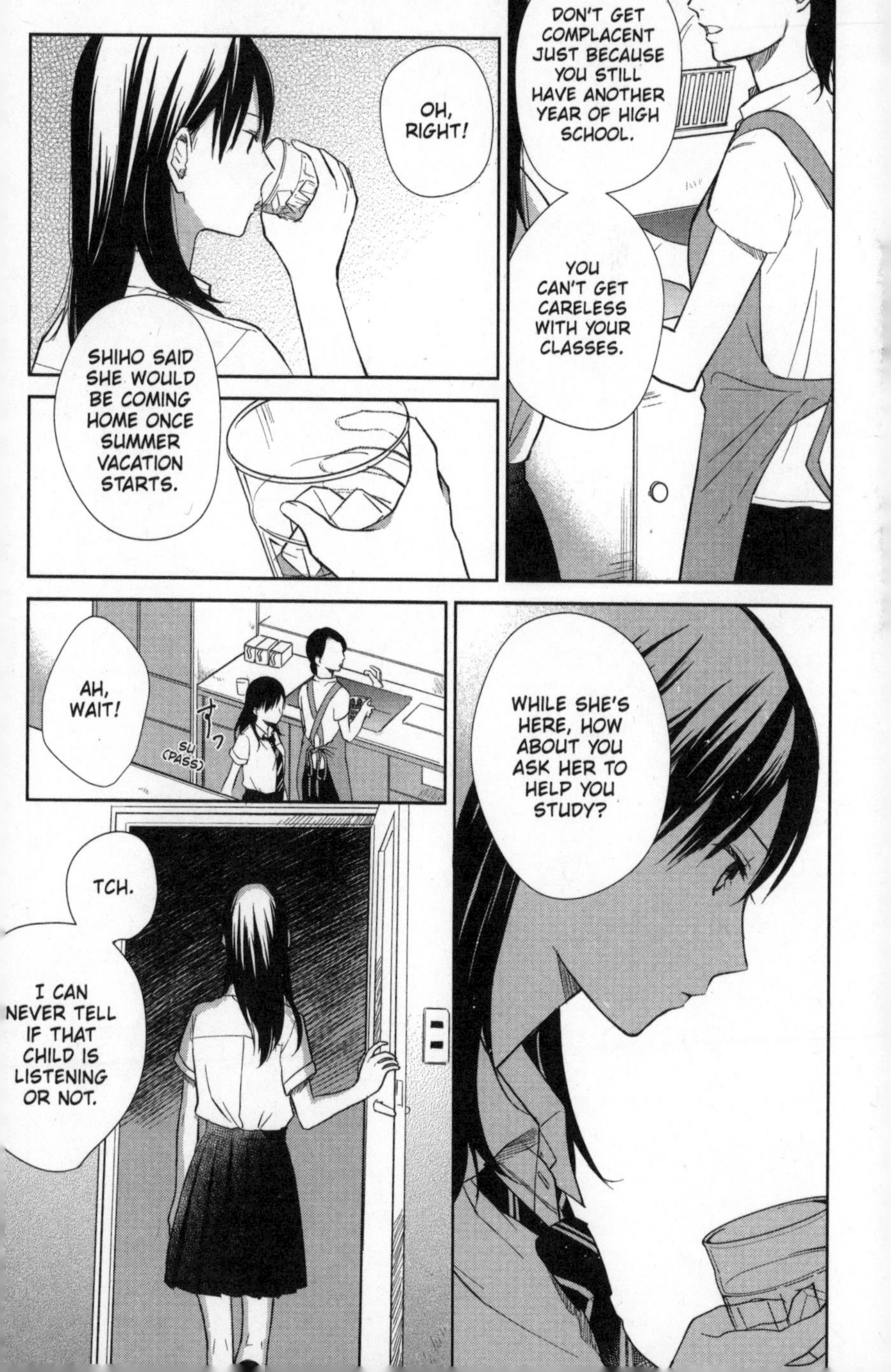
DON'T GET COMPLACENT JUST BECAUSE YOU STILL HAVE ANOTHER YEAR OF HIGH SCHOOL.
YOU CAN'T GET CARELESS WITH YOUR CLASSES.
OH, RIGHT!
SHIHO SAID SHE WOULD BE COMING HOME ONCE SUMMER VACATION STARTS.
WHILE SHE'S HERE, HOW ABOUT YOU ASK HER TO HELP YOU STUDY?
AH, WAIT!
SU (PASS)
TCH.
I CAN NEVER TELL IF THAT CHILD IS LISTENING OR NOT.

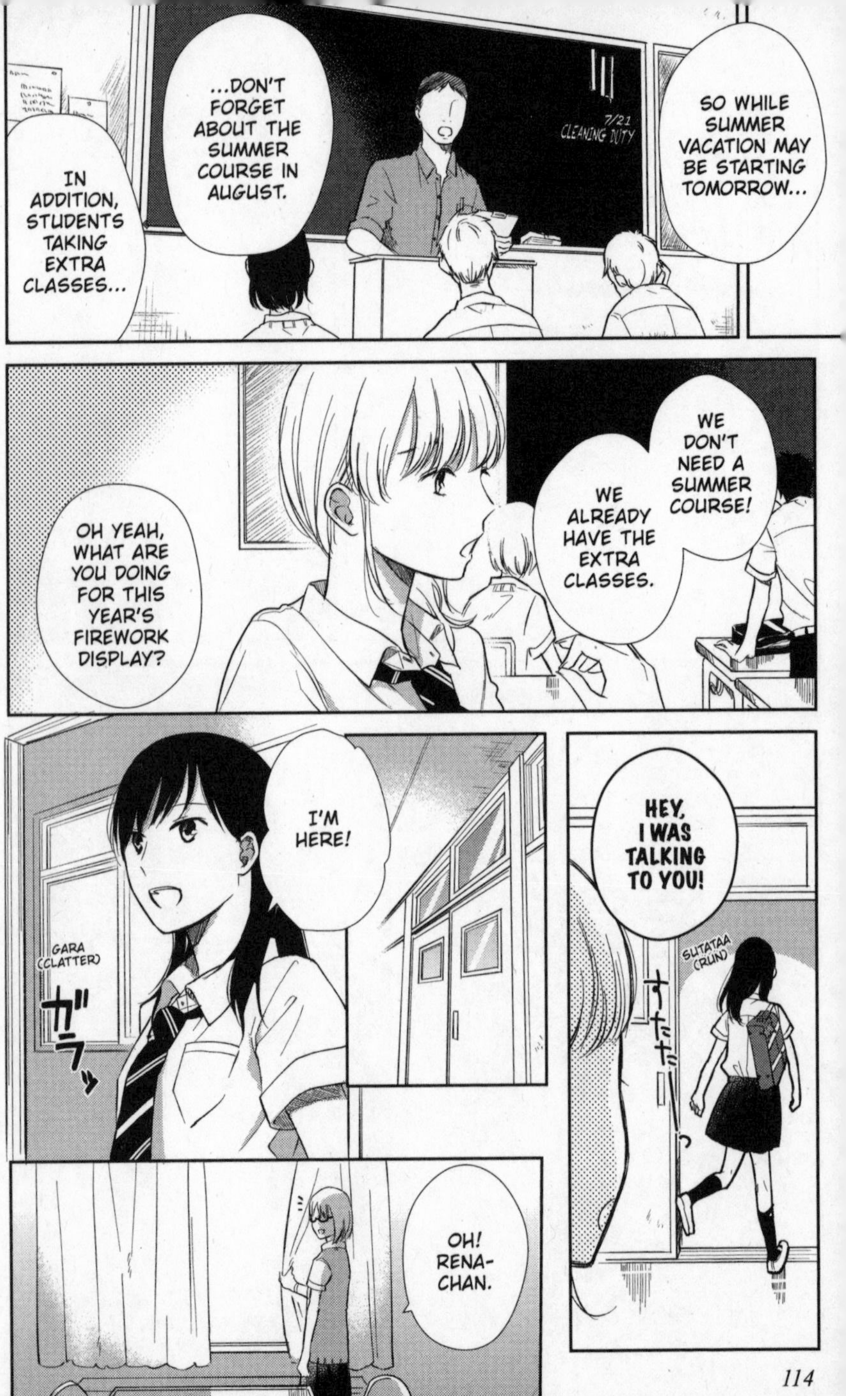
SO WHILE SUMMER VACATION MAY BE STARTING TOMORROW...
7/21 CLEANING DUTY
...DON'T FORGET ABOUT THE SUMMER COURSE IN AUGUST.
IN ADDITION, STUDENTS TAKING EXTRA CLASSES...
WE DON'T NEED A SUMMER COURSE!
WE ALREADY HAVE THE EXTRA CLASSES.
OH YEAH, WHAT ARE YOU DOING FOR THIS YEAR'S FIREWORK DISPLAY?
HEY, I WAS TALKING TO YOU!
SUTATAA (RUN)
I'M HERE!
GARA (CLATTER)
OH! RENA-CHAN.

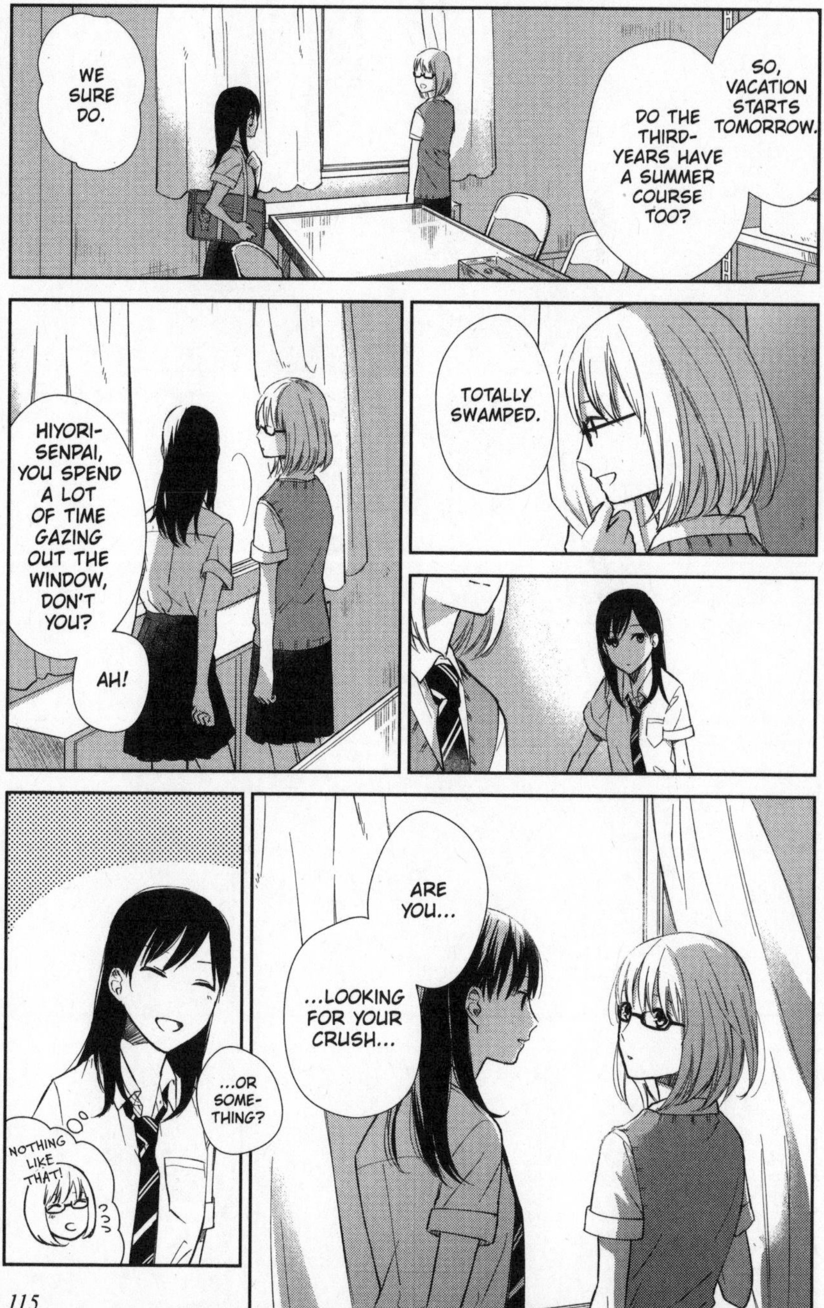
SO, VACATION STARTS TOMORROW.
DO THE THIRD-YEARS HAVE A SUMMER COURSE TOO?
WE SURE DO.
TOTALLY SWAMPED.
HIYORI-SENPAI, YOU SPEND A LOT OF TIME GAZING OUT THE WINDOW, DON'T YOU?
AH!
ARE YOU...
...LOOKING FOR YOUR CRUSH...
...OR SOMETHING?
NOTHING LIKE THAT!

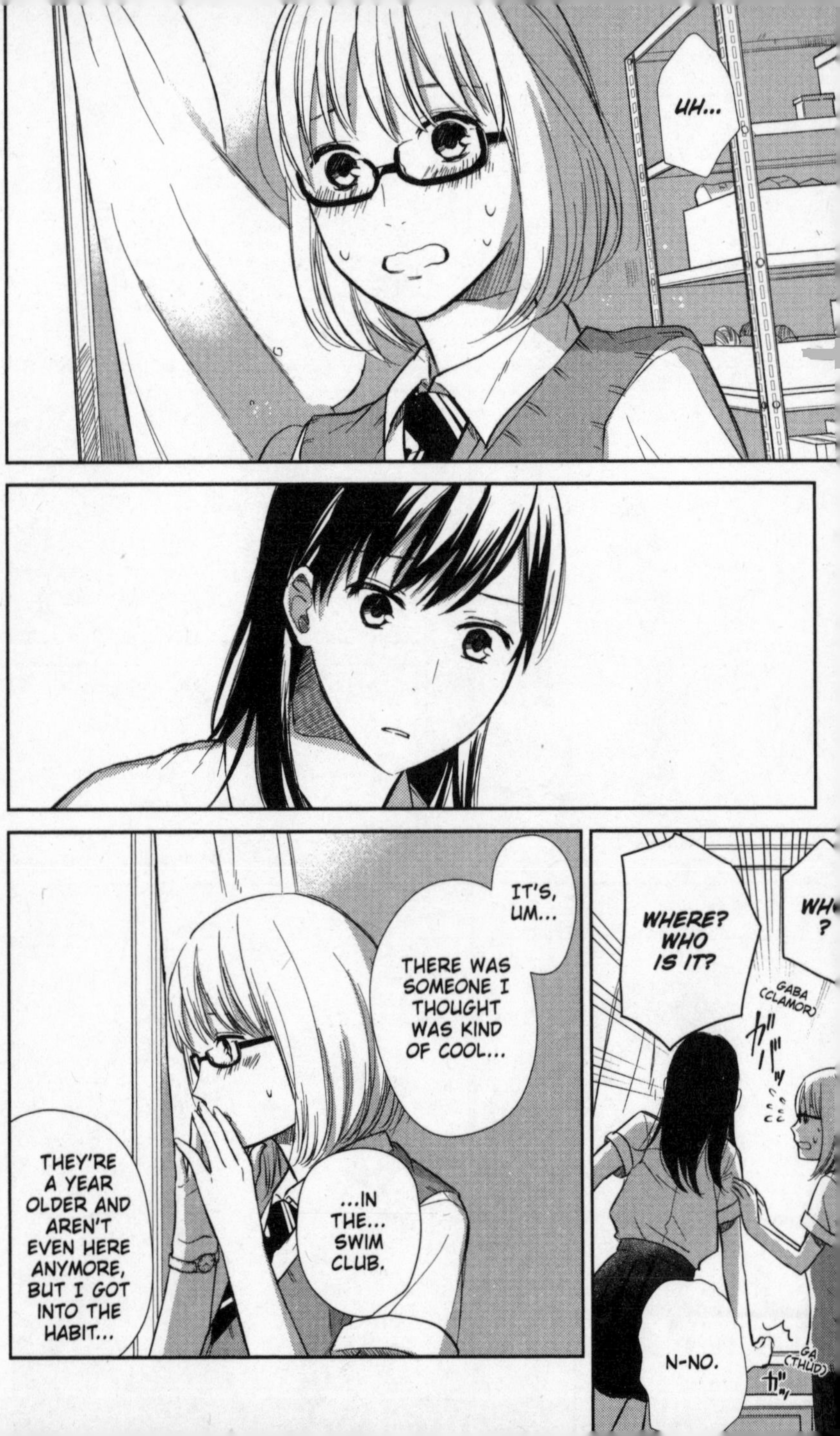
UH...
WH ?
WHERE? WHO IS IT?
GABA (CLAMOR)
N-NO.
GA (THUD)
IT'S, UM...
THERE WAS SOMEONE I THOUGHT WAS KIND OF COOL...
...IN THE... SWIM CLUB.
THEY'RE A YEAR OLDER AND AREN'T EVEN HERE ANYMORE, BUT I GOT INTO THE HABIT...

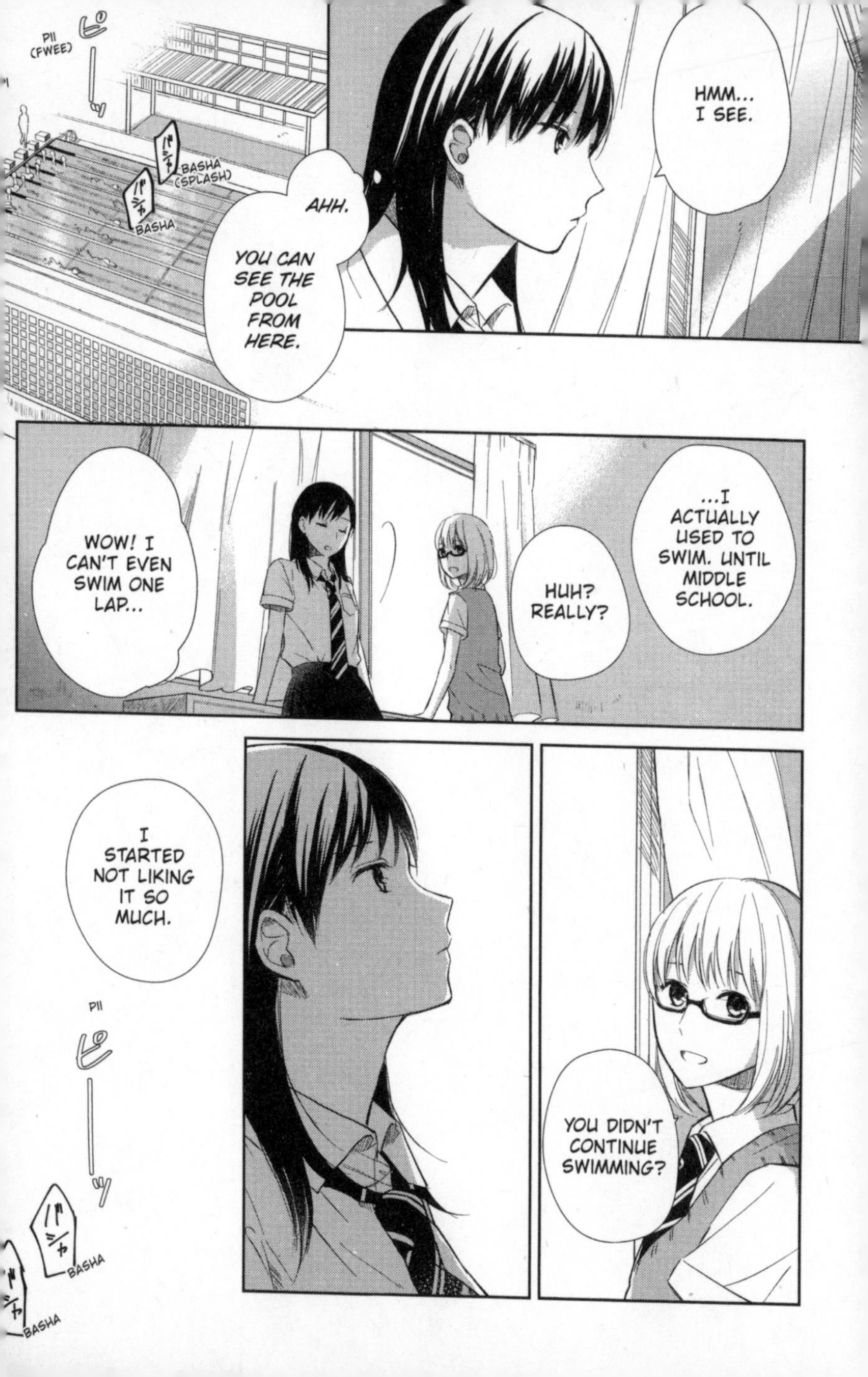
HMM... I SEE.
AHH.
YOU CAN SEE THE POOL FROM HERE.
PII (FWEE)
BASHA (SPLASH)
BASHA
...I ACTUALLY USED TO SWIM. UNTIL MIDDLE SCHOOL.
HUH? REALLY?
WOW! I CAN'T EVEN SWIM ONE LAP...
YOU DIDN'T CONTINUE SWIMMING?
I STARTED NOT LIKING IT SO MUCH.
PII
BASHA
BASHA

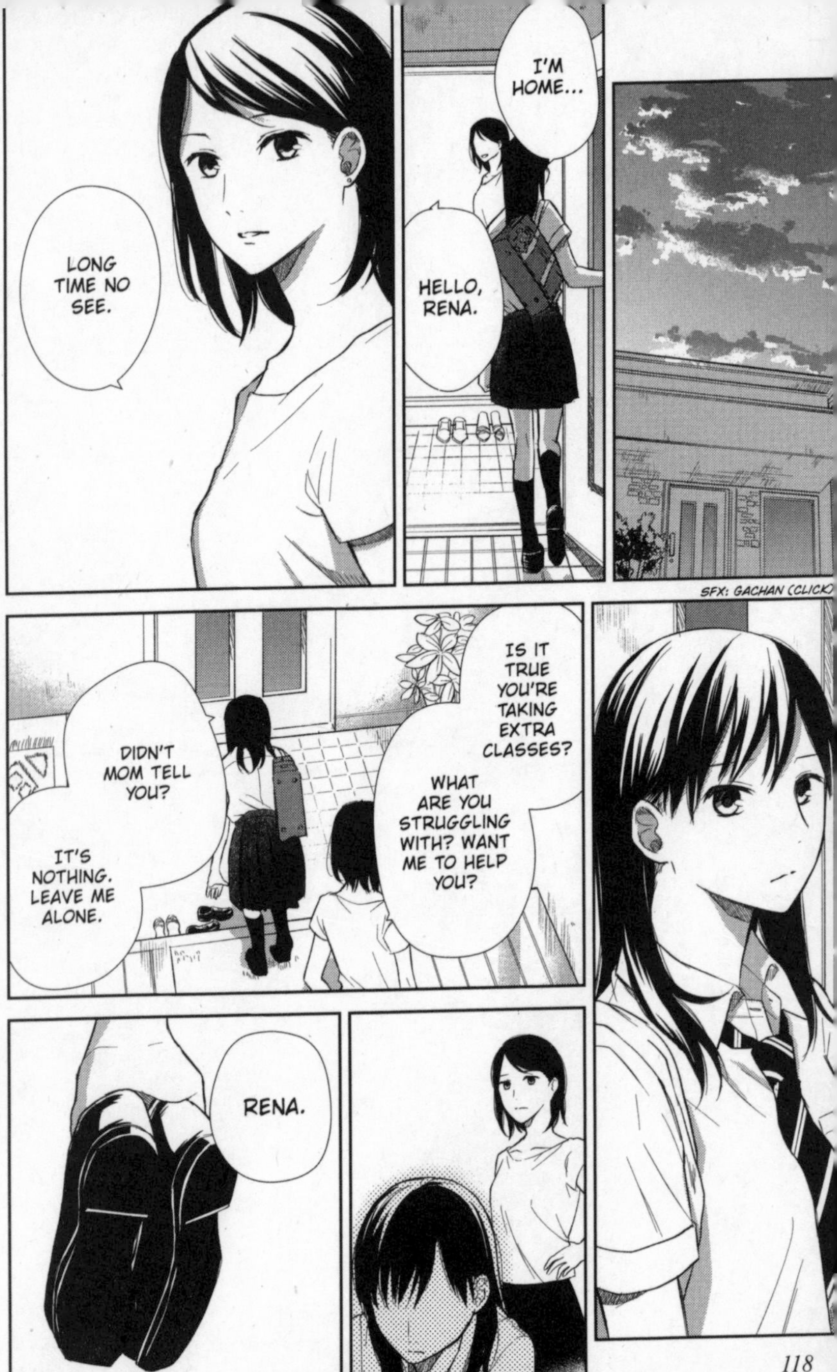
SFX: GACHAN (CLICK)
I'M HOME...
HELLO, RENA.
LONG TIME NO SEE.
IS IT TRUE YOU'RE TAKING EXTRA CLASSES?
WHAT ARE YOU STRUGGLING WITH? WANT ME TO HELP YOU?
DIDN'T MOM TELL YOU?
IT'S NOTHING. LEAVE ME ALONE.
RENA.

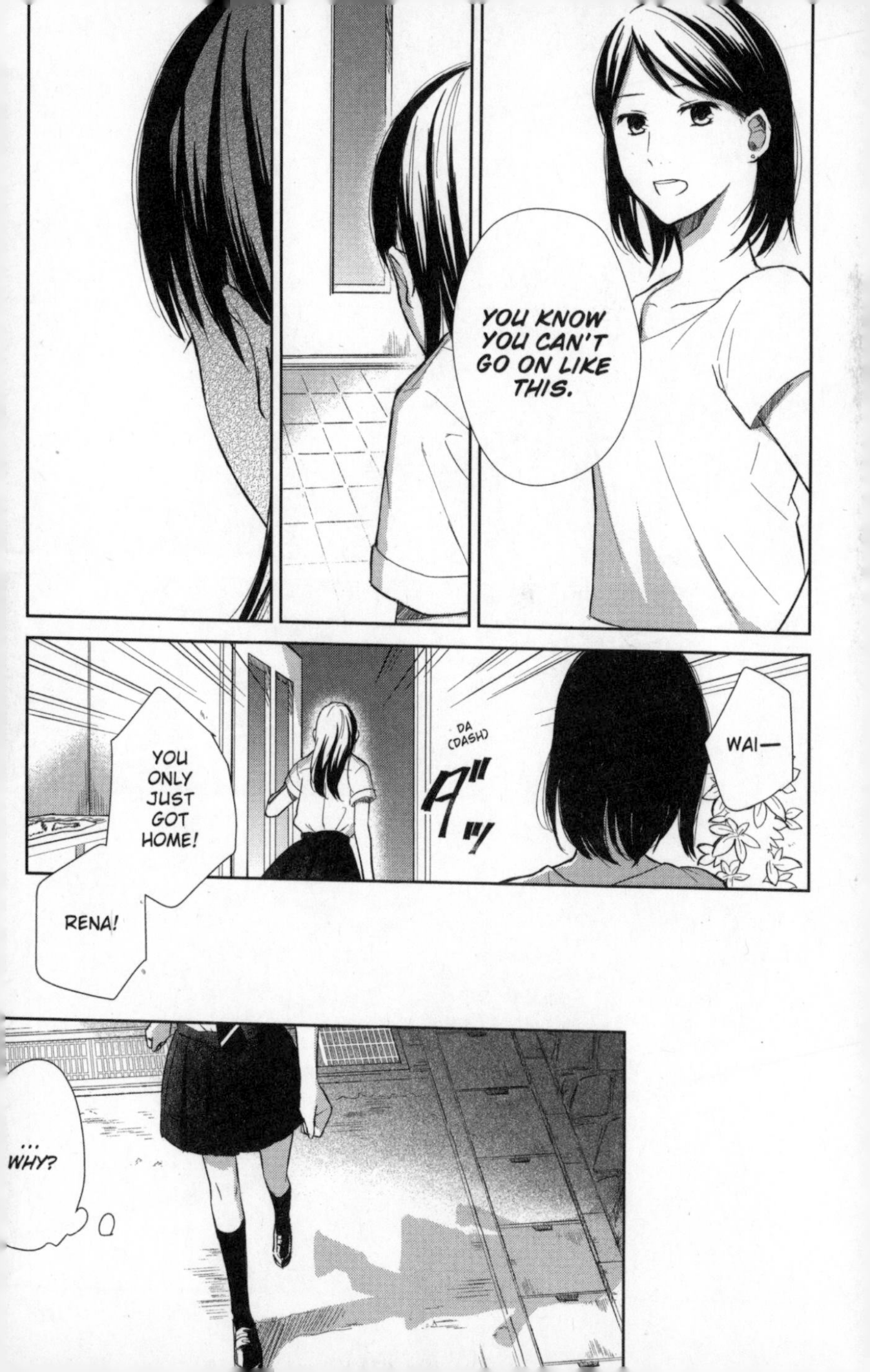
YOU KNOW YOU CAN'T GO ON LIKE THIS.
WAI—
DA (DASH)
YOU ONLY JUST GOT HOME!
RENA!
...WHY?

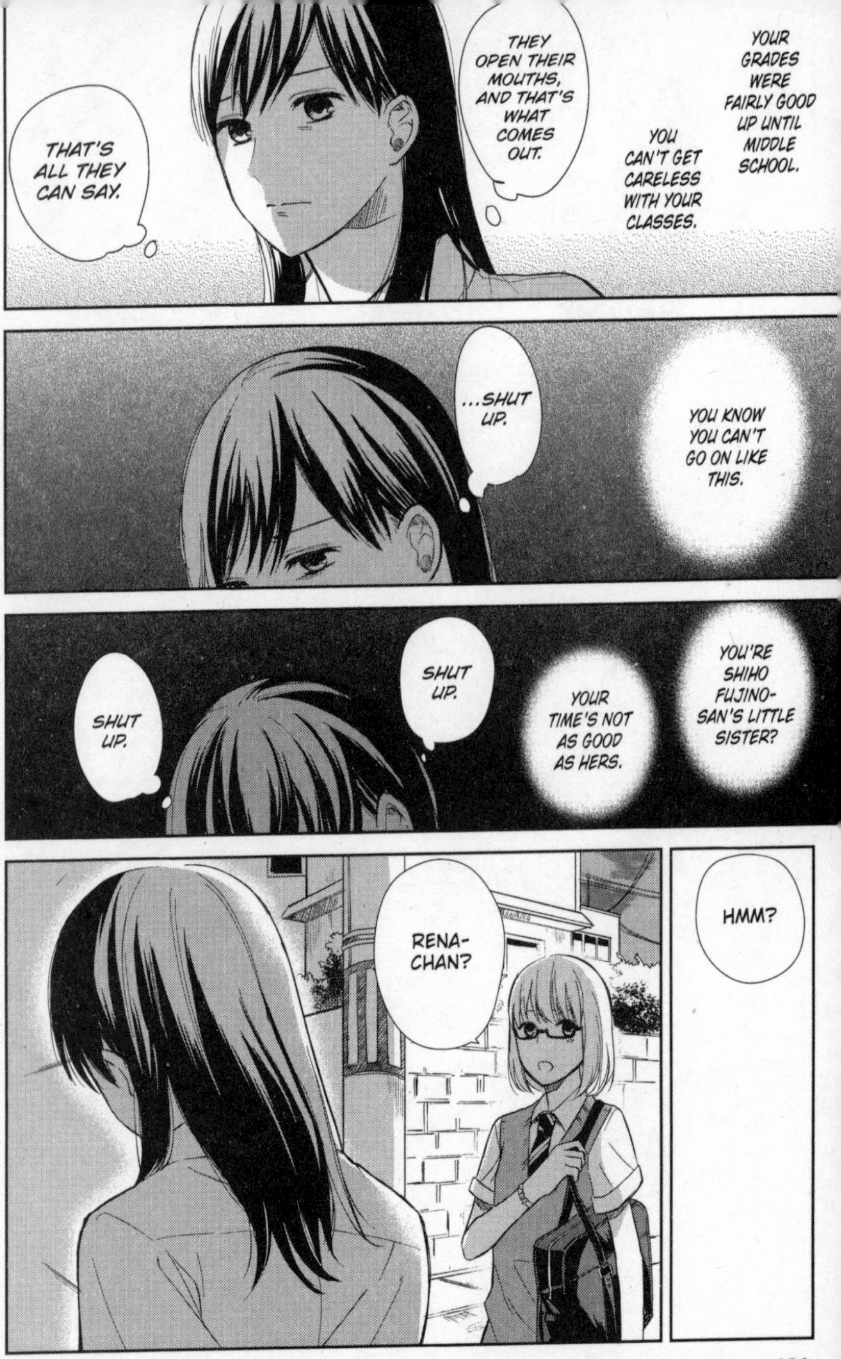
YOUR GRADES WERE FAIRLY GOOD UP UNTIL MIDDLE SCHOOL.
YOU CAN'T GET CARELESS WITH YOUR CLASSES.
THEY OPEN THEIR MOUTHS, AND THAT'S WHAT COMES OUT.
THAT'S ALL THEY CAN SAY.
YOU KNOW YOU CAN'T GO ON LIKE THIS.
...SHUT UP.
YOU'RE SHIHO FUJINO-SAN'S LITTLE SISTER?
YOUR TIME'S NOT AS GOOD AS HERS.
SHUT UP.
SHUT UP.
HMM?
RENA-CHAN?

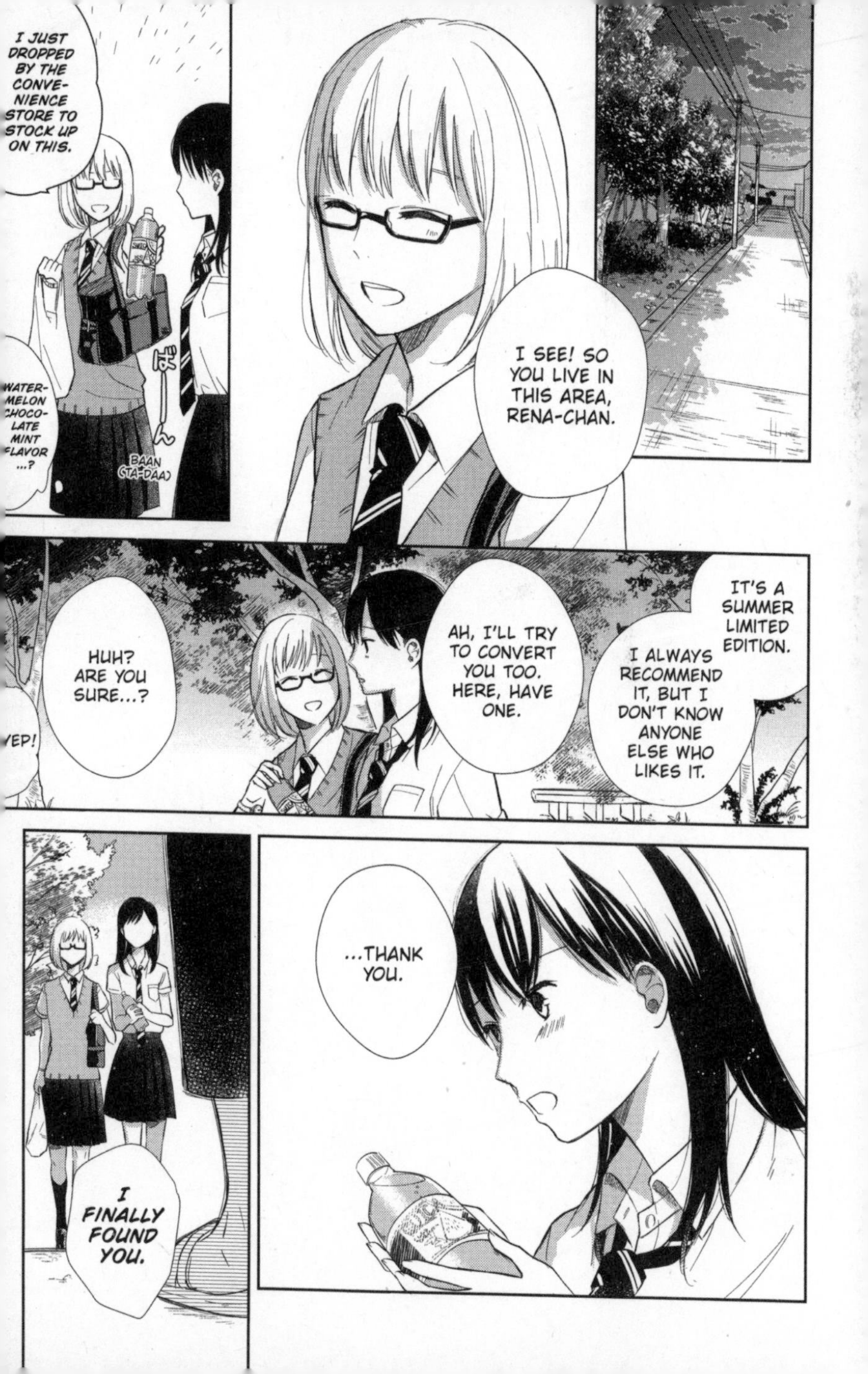
I SEE! SO YOU LIVE IN THIS AREA, RENA-CHAN.
I JUST DROPPED BY THE CONVENIENCE STORE TO STOCK UP ON THIS.
ばーん
BAAN (TA-DAA)
WATERMELON CHOCOLATE MINT FLAVOR ...?
IT'S A SUMMER LIMITED EDITION.
I ALWAYS RECOMMEND IT, BUT I DON'T KNOW ANYONE ELSE WHO LIKES IT.
AH, I'LL TRY TO CONVERT YOU TOO. HERE, HAVE ONE.
HUH? ARE YOU SURE...?
YEP!
...THANK YOU.
I FINALLY FOUND YOU.

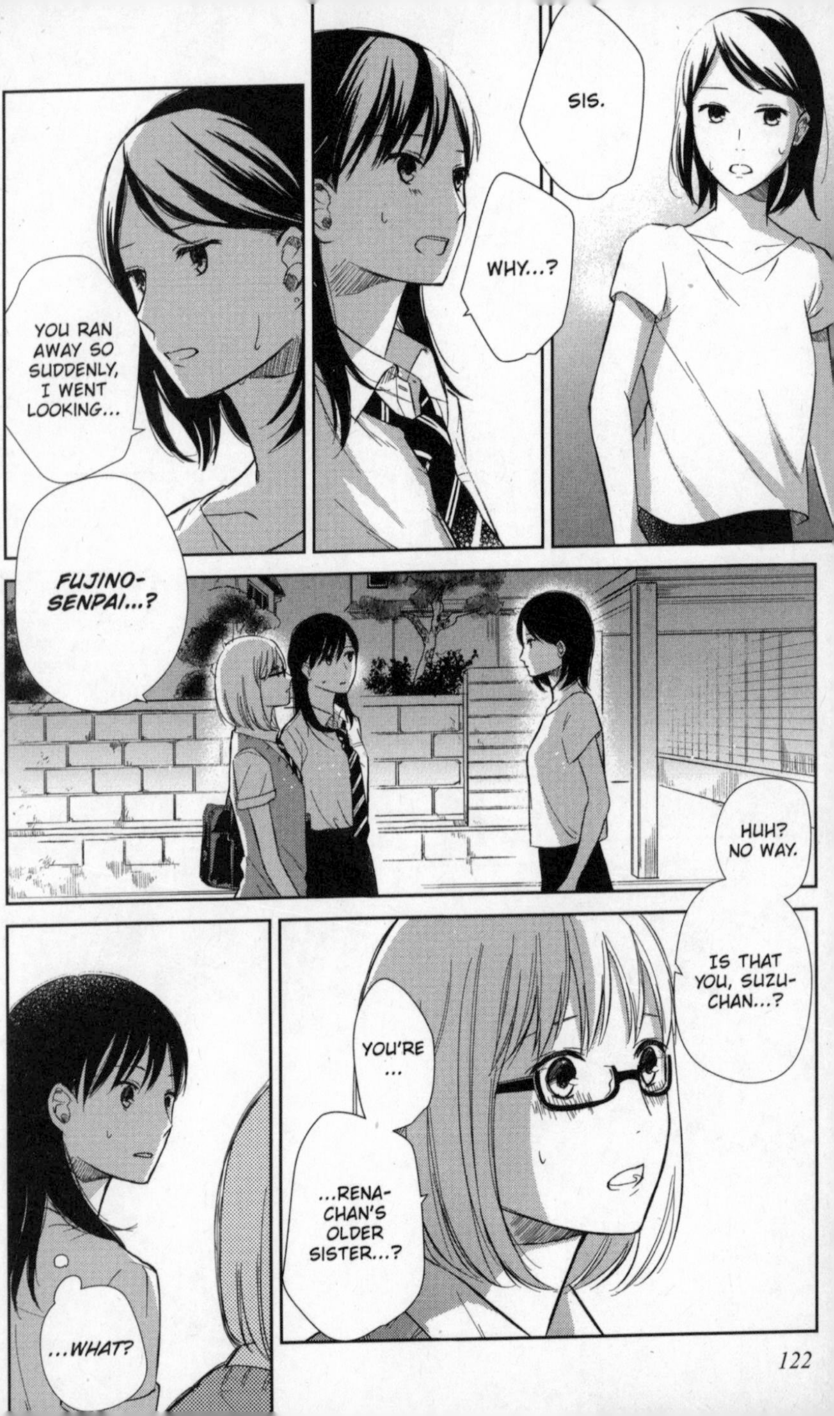
SIS.
WHY...?
YOU RAN AWAY SO SUDDENLY, I WENT LOOKING...
FUJINO-SENPAI...?
HUH? NO WAY.
IS THAT YOU, SUZU-CHAN...?
YOU'RE ...
...RENA-CHAN'S OLDER SISTER...?
...WHAT?

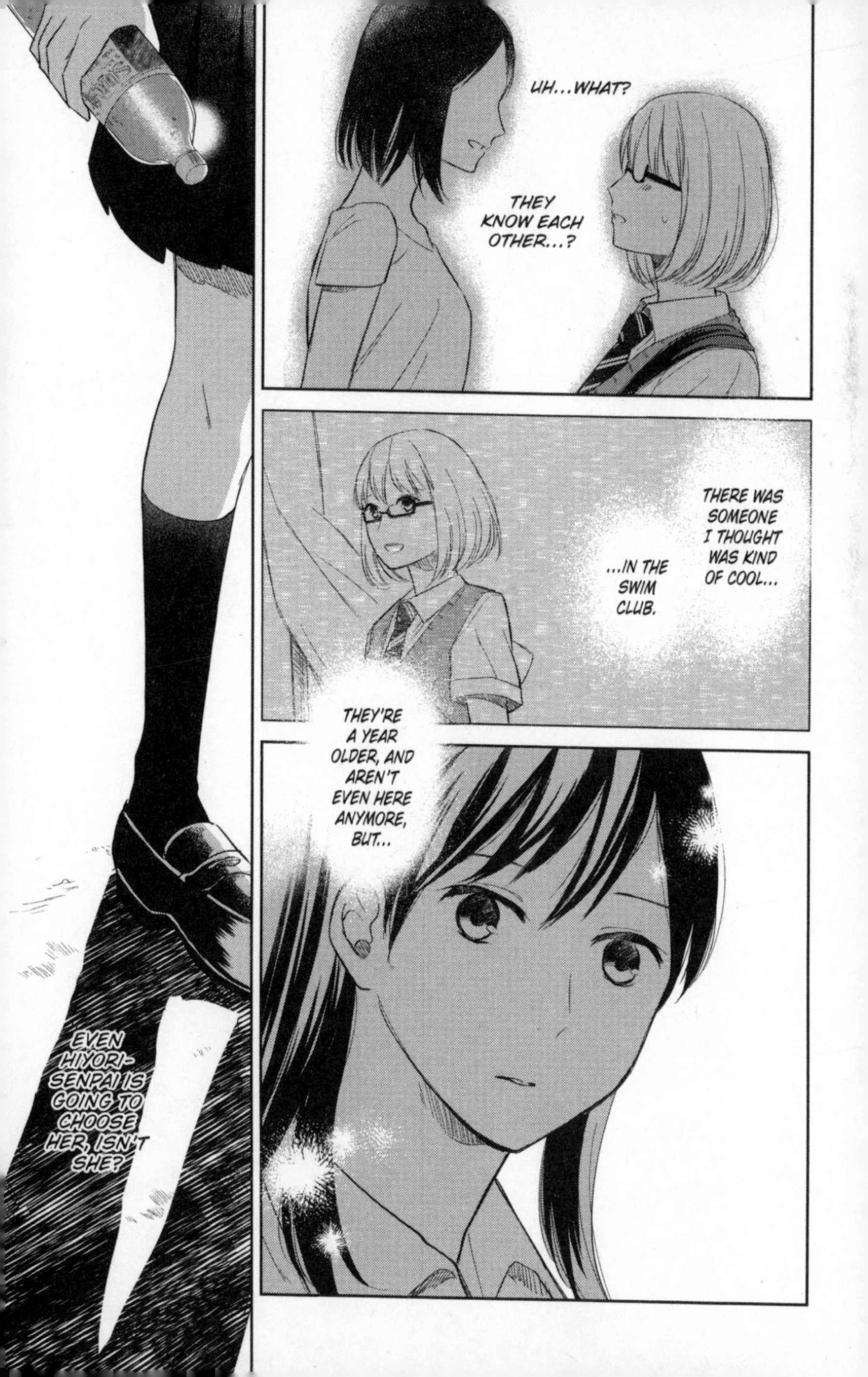
UH...WHAT?
THEY KNOW EACH OTHER...?
THERE WAS SOMEONE I THOUGHT WAS KIND OF COOL...
...IN THE SWIM CLUB.
THEY'RE A YEAR OLDER, AND AREN'T EVEN HERE ANYMORE, BUT...
EVEN HIYORI-SENPAI IS GOING TO CHOOSE HER, ISN'T SHE?

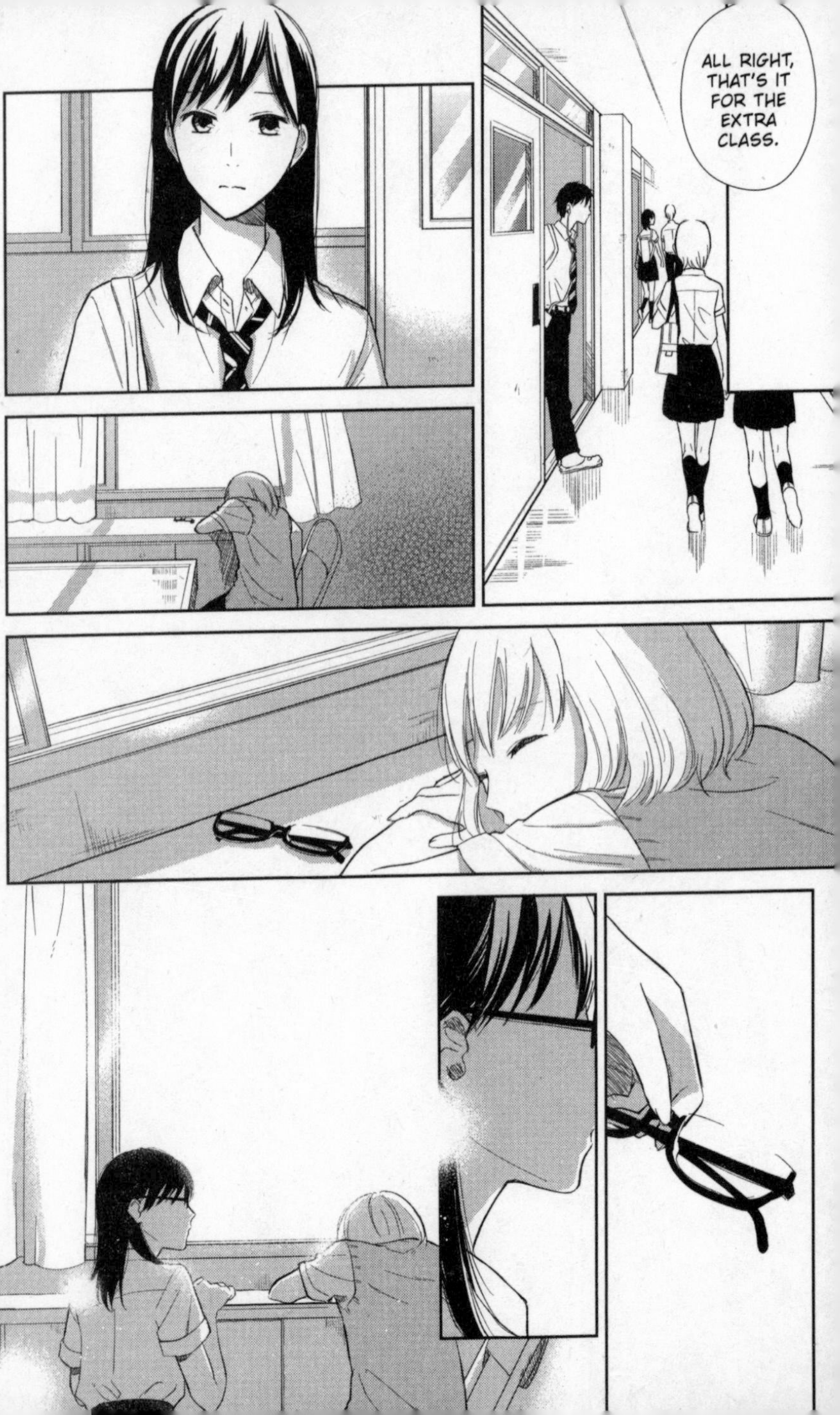
ALL RIGHT, THAT'S IT FOR THE EXTRA CLASS.

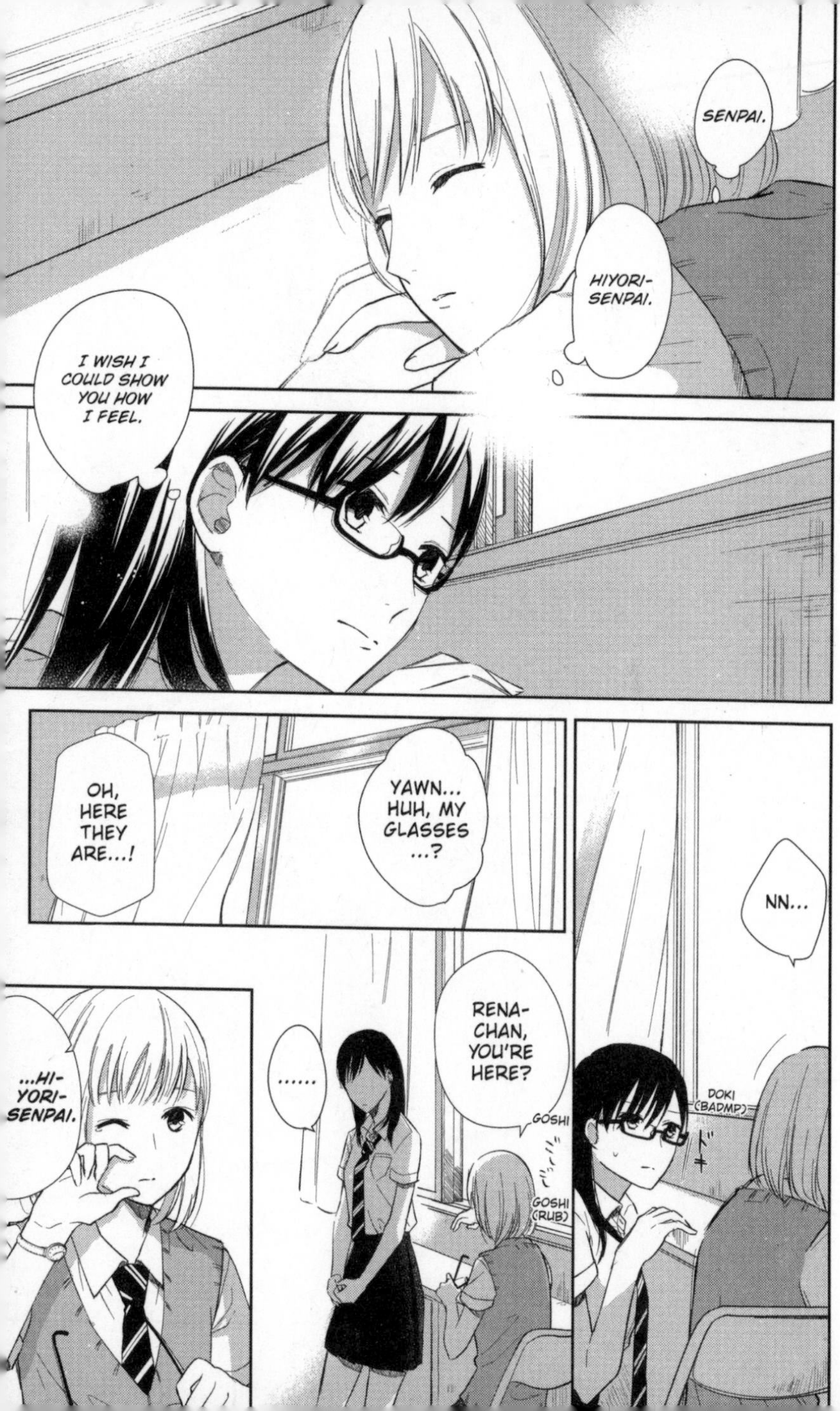
SENPAI.
HIYORI-SENPAI.
I WISH I COULD SHOW YOU HOW I FEEL.
NN...
DOKI (BADMP)
YAWN... HUH, MY GLASSES ...?
OH, HERE THEY ARE...!
RENA-CHAN, YOU'RE HERE?
GOSHI
GOSHI (RUB)
......
...HI-YORI-SENPAI.

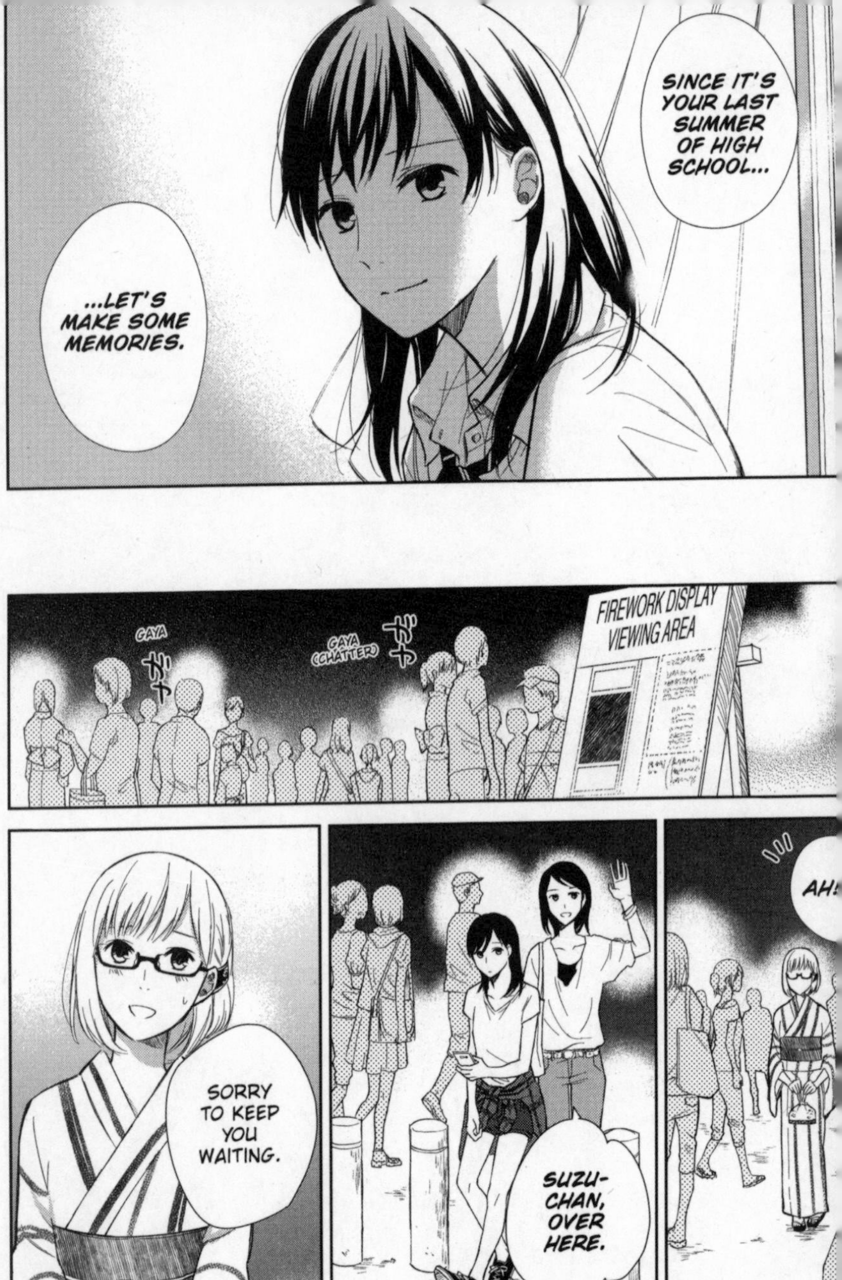
SINCE IT'S YOUR LAST SUMMER OF HIGH SCHOOL...
...LET'S MAKE SOME MEMORIES.
FIREWORK DISPLAY VIEWING AREA
GAYA (CHATTER)
GAYA
AH!
SUZU-CHAN, OVER HERE.
SORRY TO KEEP YOU WAITING.

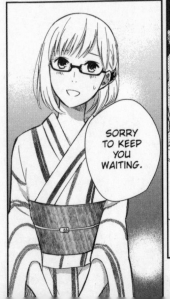

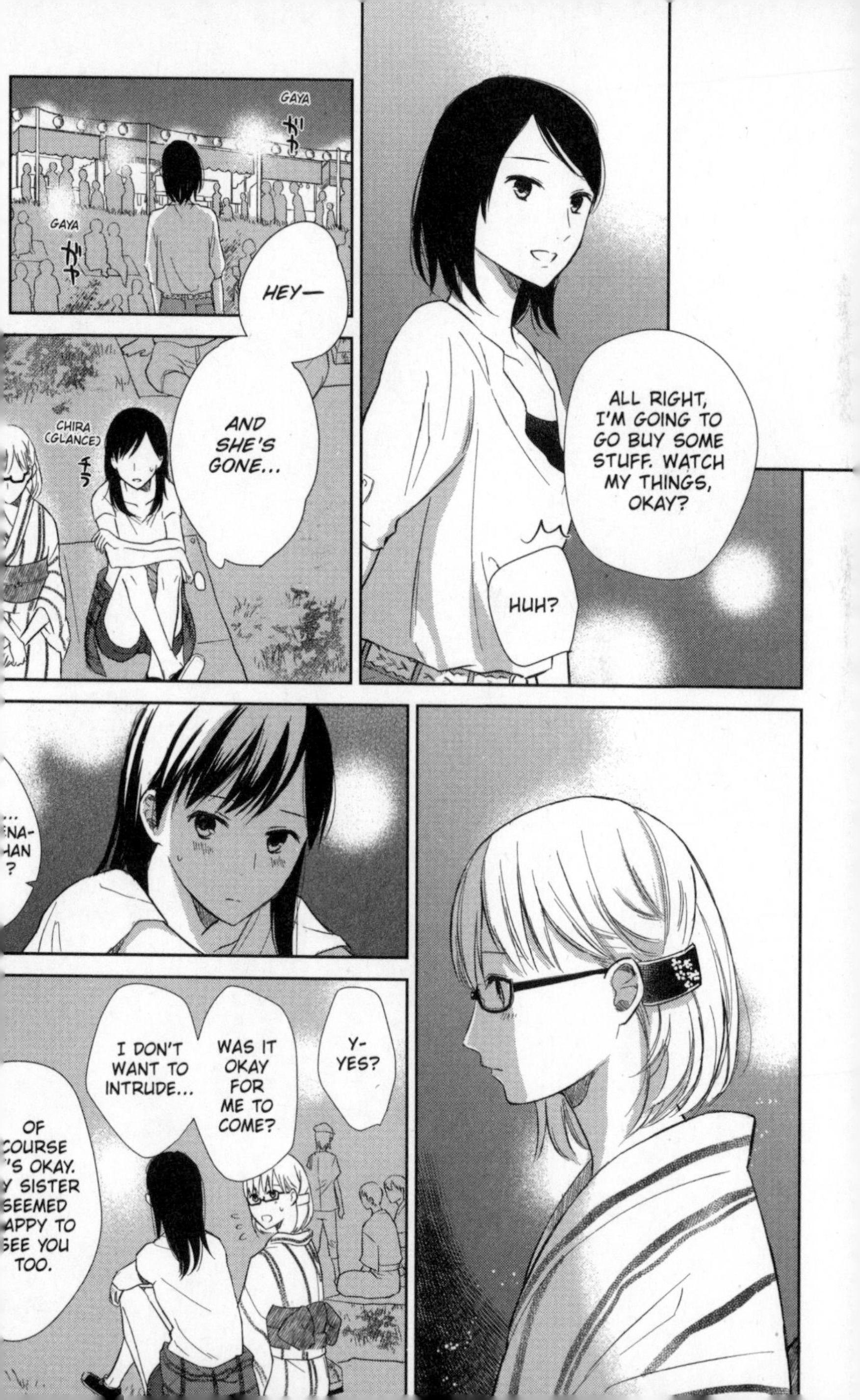
ALL RIGHT, I'M GOING TO GO BUY SOME STUFF. WATCH MY THINGS, OKAY?
HUH?
GAYA
がや
GAYA
がや
HEY—
AND SHE'S GONE...
CHIRA (GLANCE)
チラ
...
ENA-
HAN
?
Y-
YES?
WAS IT OKAY FOR ME TO COME?
I DON'T WANT TO INTRUDE...
OF
COURSE
'S OKAY.
Y SISTER
SEEMED
APPY TO
SEE YOU
TOO.

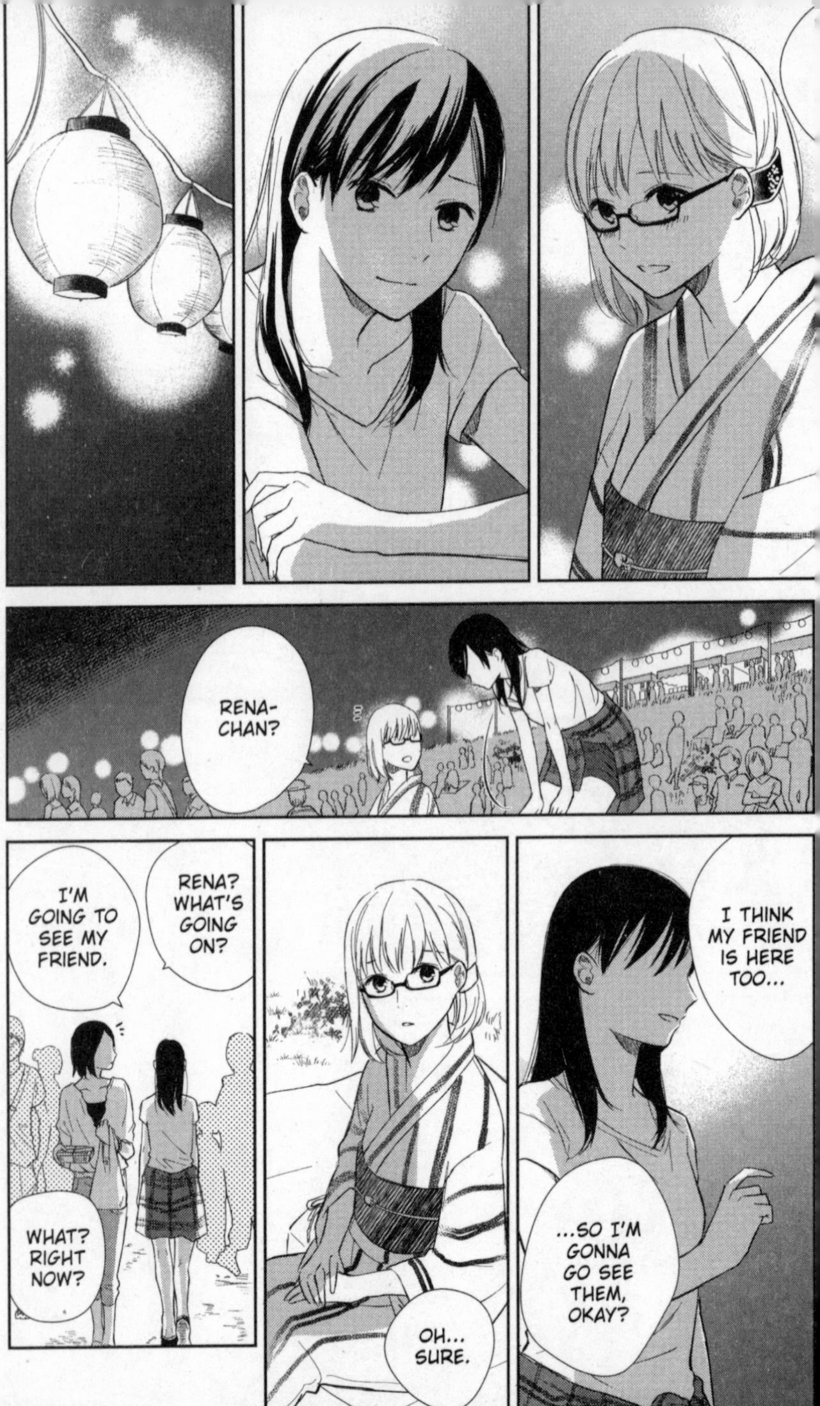
RENA-CHAN?
I THINK MY FRIEND IS HERE TOO...
...SO I'M GONNA GO SEE THEM, OKAY?
OH... SURE.
RENA? WHAT'S GOING ON?
I'M GOING TO SEE MY FRIEND.
WHAT? RIGHT NOW?

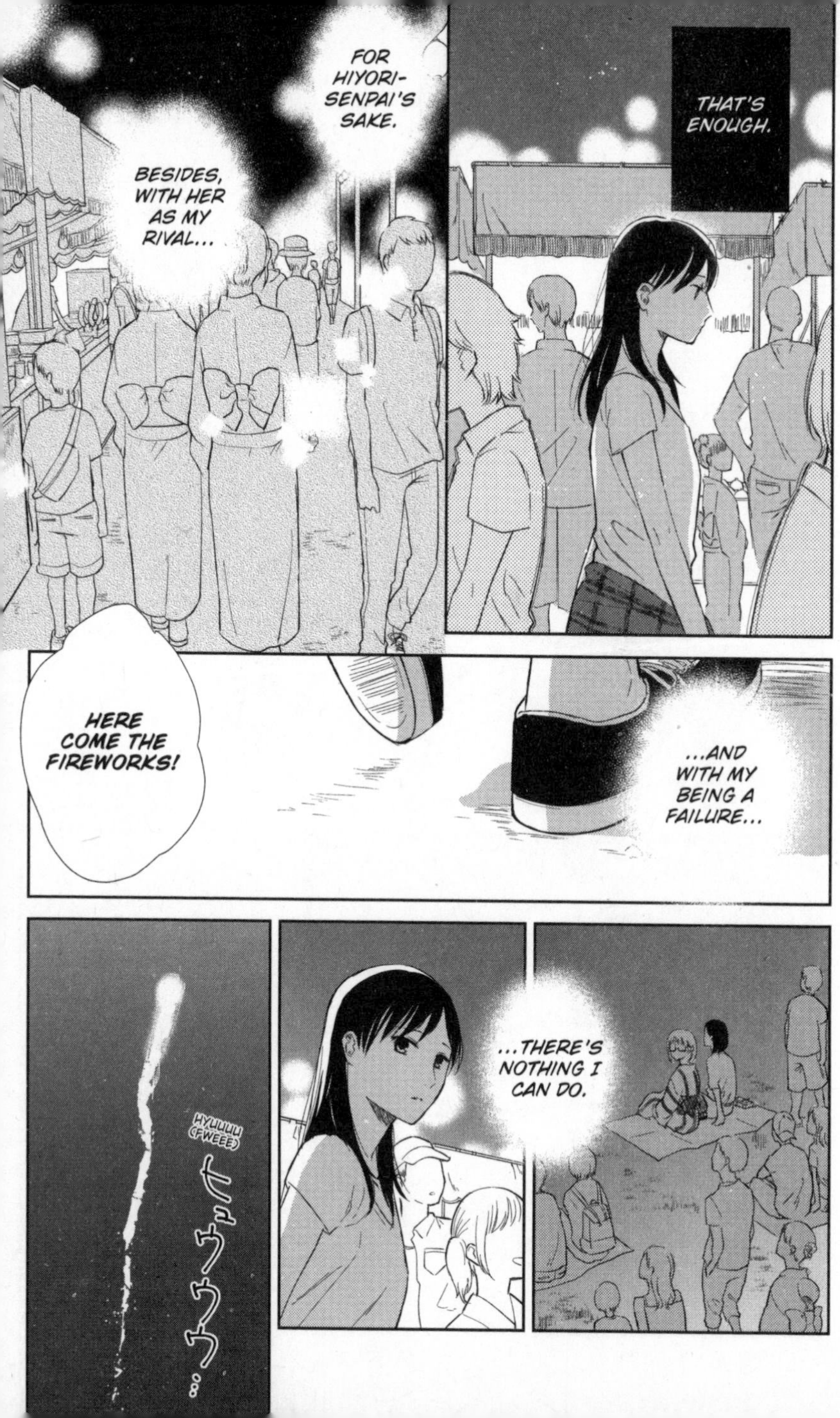
THAT'S ENOUGH.
FOR HIYORI-SENPAI'S SAKE.
BESIDES, WITH HER AS MY RIVAL...
...AND WITH MY BEING A FAILURE...
HERE COME THE FIREWORKS!
...THERE'S NOTHING I CAN DO.
ヒュウウゥ…
HYUUUU (FWEEE)

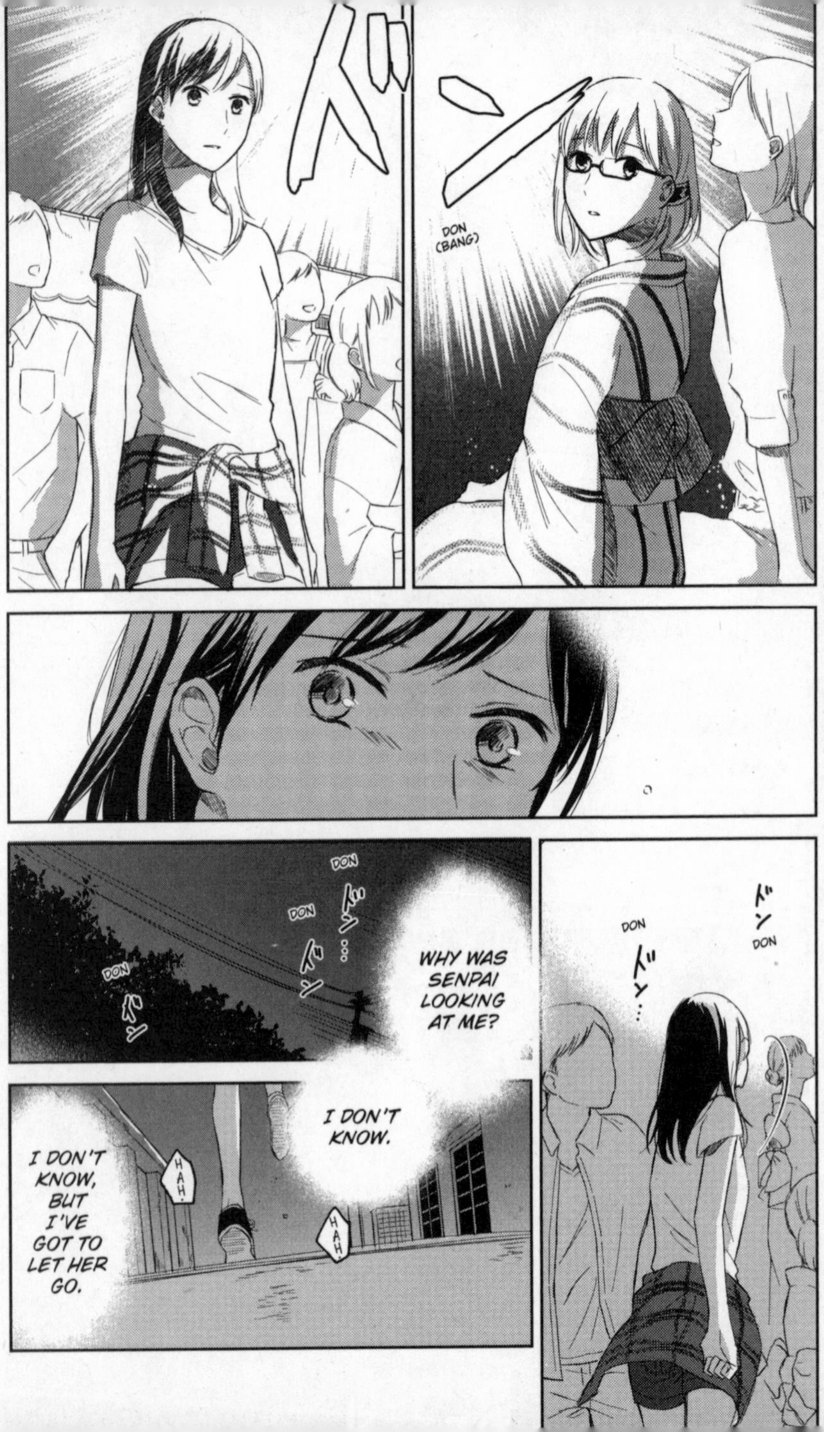
DON (BANG)
DON
DON
WHY WAS SENPAI LOOKING AT ME?
DON
DON
DON
I DON'T KNOW.
HAH.
HAH.
I DON'T KNOW, BUT I'VE GOT TO LET HER GO.

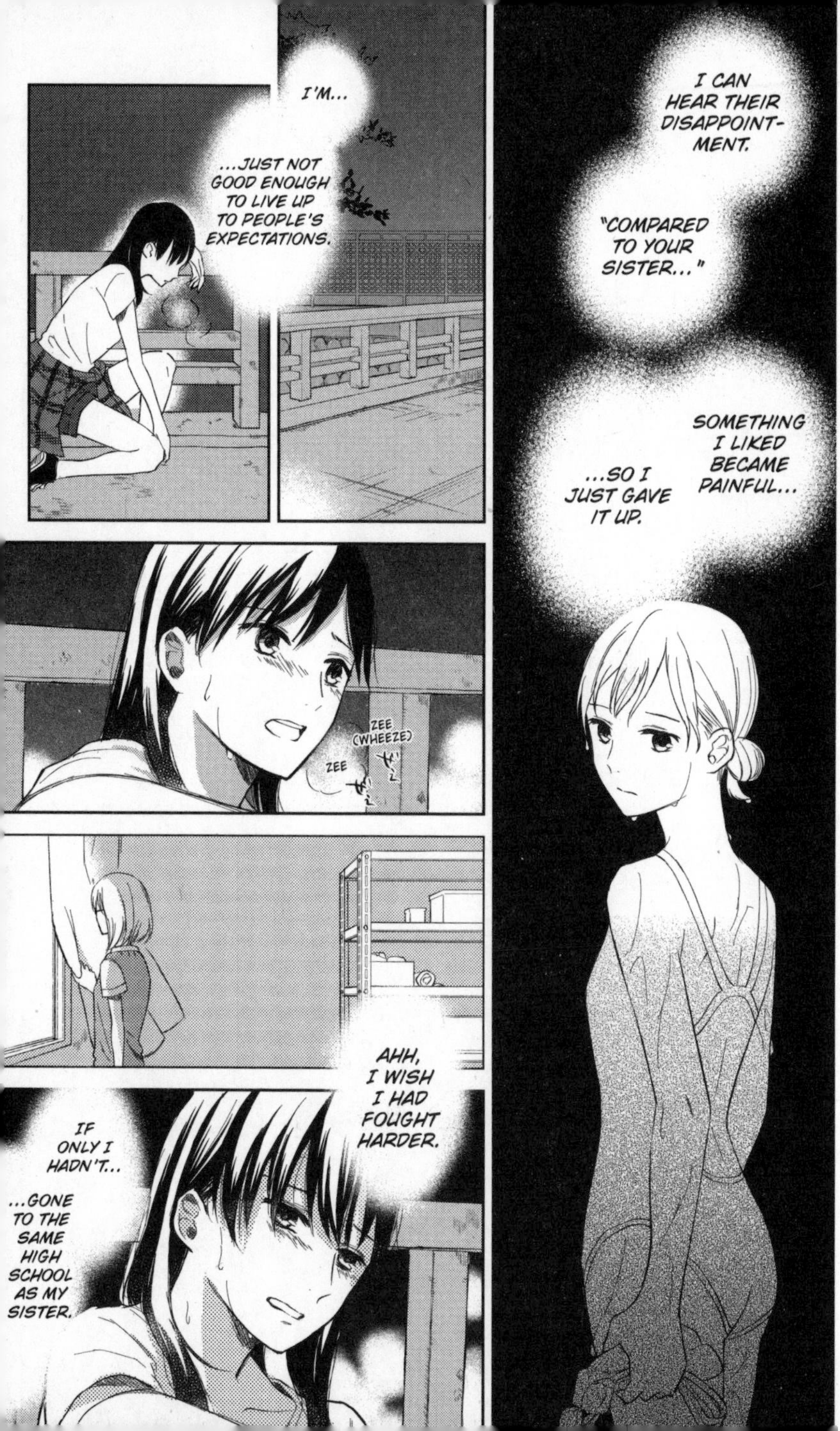
I CAN HEAR THEIR DISAPPOINT-MENT.
"COMPARED TO YOUR SISTER..."
SOMETHING I LIKED BECAME PAINFUL...
...SO I JUST GAVE IT UP.
I'M...
...JUST NOT GOOD ENOUGH TO LIVE UP TO PEOPLE'S EXPECTATIONS.
ZEE (WHEEZE)
ZEE
AHH, I WISH I HAD FOUGHT HARDER.
IF ONLY I HADN'T...
...GONE TO THE SAME HIGH SCHOOL AS MY SISTER.

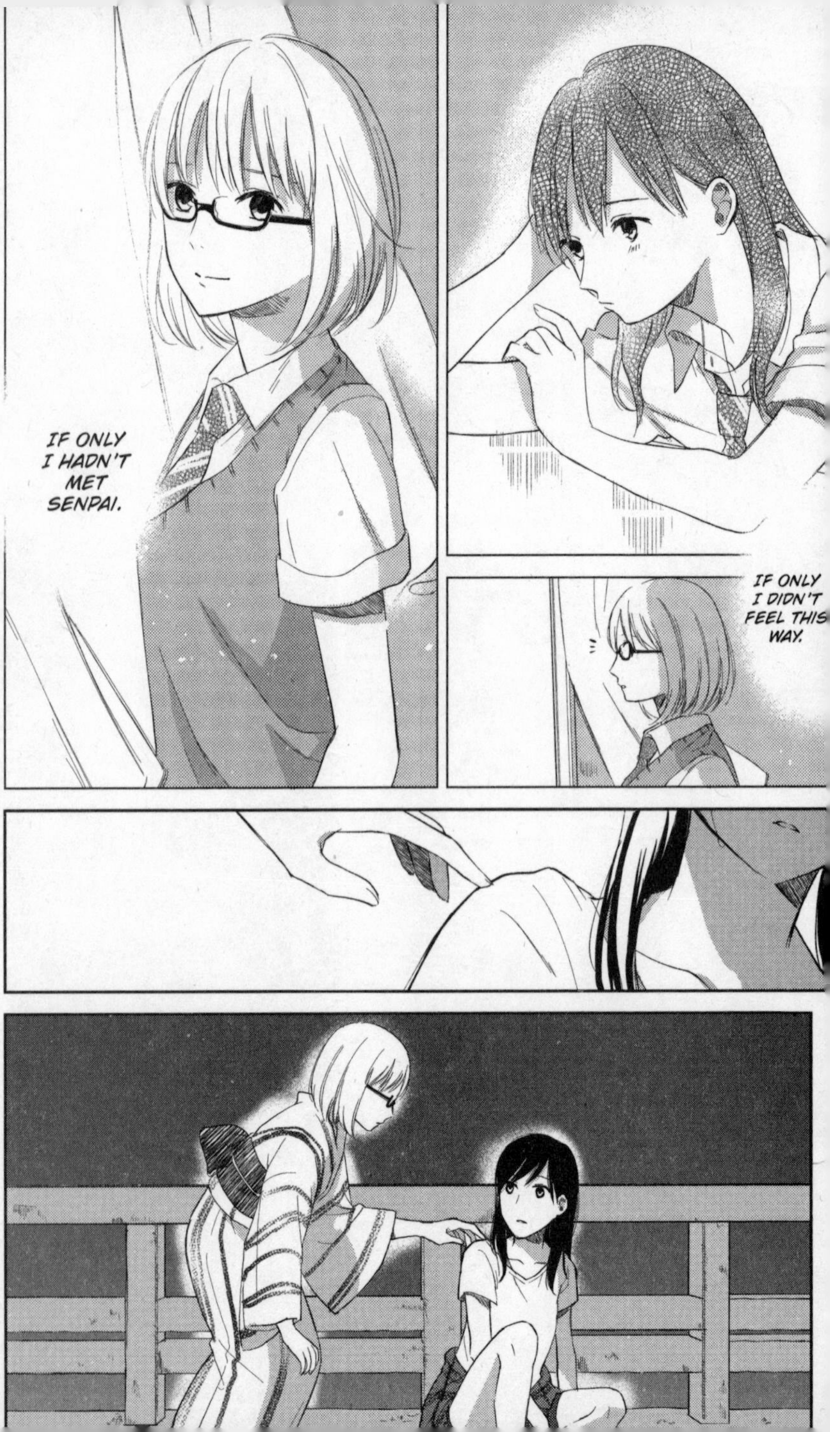
IF ONLY I HADN'T MET SENPAI.
IF ONLY I DIDN'T FEEL THIS WAY.

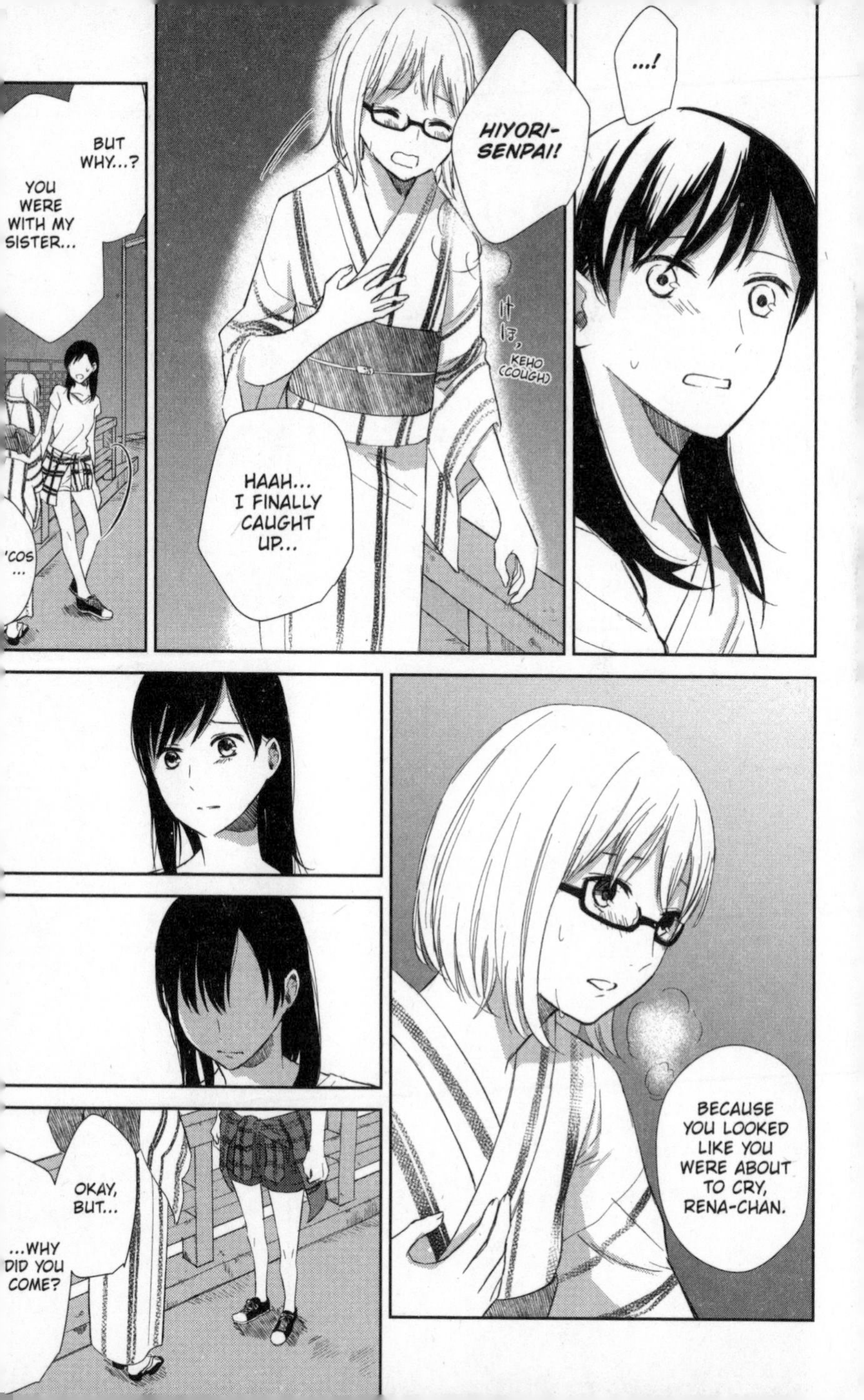
...!
HIYORI-SENPAI!
けほ,
KEHO (COUGH)
HAAH... I FINALLY CAUGHT UP...
BUT WHY...?
YOU WERE WITH MY SISTER...
'COS ...
BECAUSE YOU LOOKED LIKE YOU WERE ABOUT TO CRY, RENA-CHAN.
OKAY, BUT...
...WHY DID YOU COME?

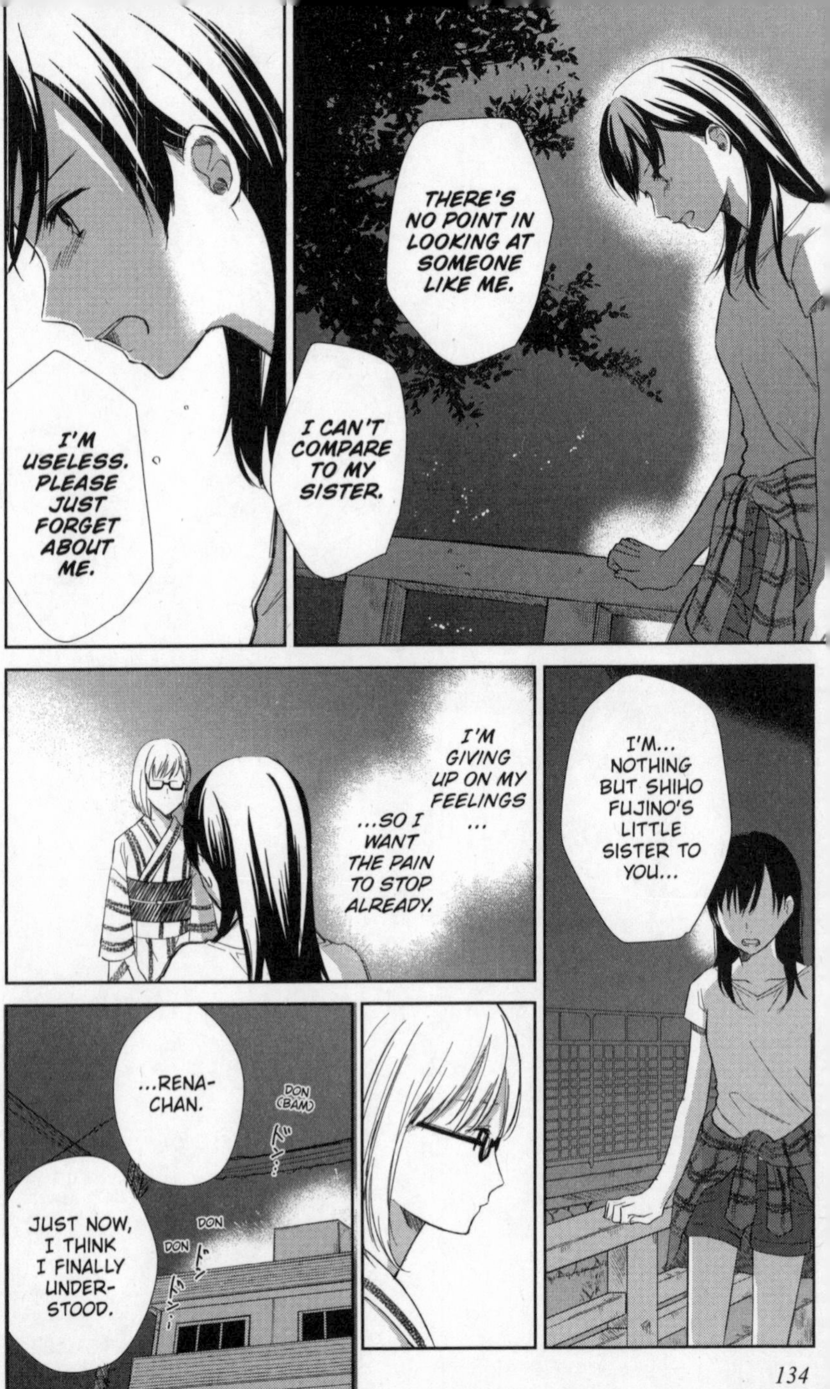
THERE'S NO POINT IN LOOKING AT SOMEONE LIKE ME.
I CAN'T COMPARE TO MY SISTER.
I'M USELESS. PLEASE JUST FORGET ABOUT ME.
I'M... NOTHING BUT SHIHO FUJINO'S LITTLE SISTER TO YOU...
I'M GIVING UP ON MY FEELINGS ...
...SO I WANT THE PAIN TO STOP ALREADY.
...RENA-CHAN.
DON (BAM)
JUST NOW, I THINK I FINALLY UNDER-STOOD.
DON
DON

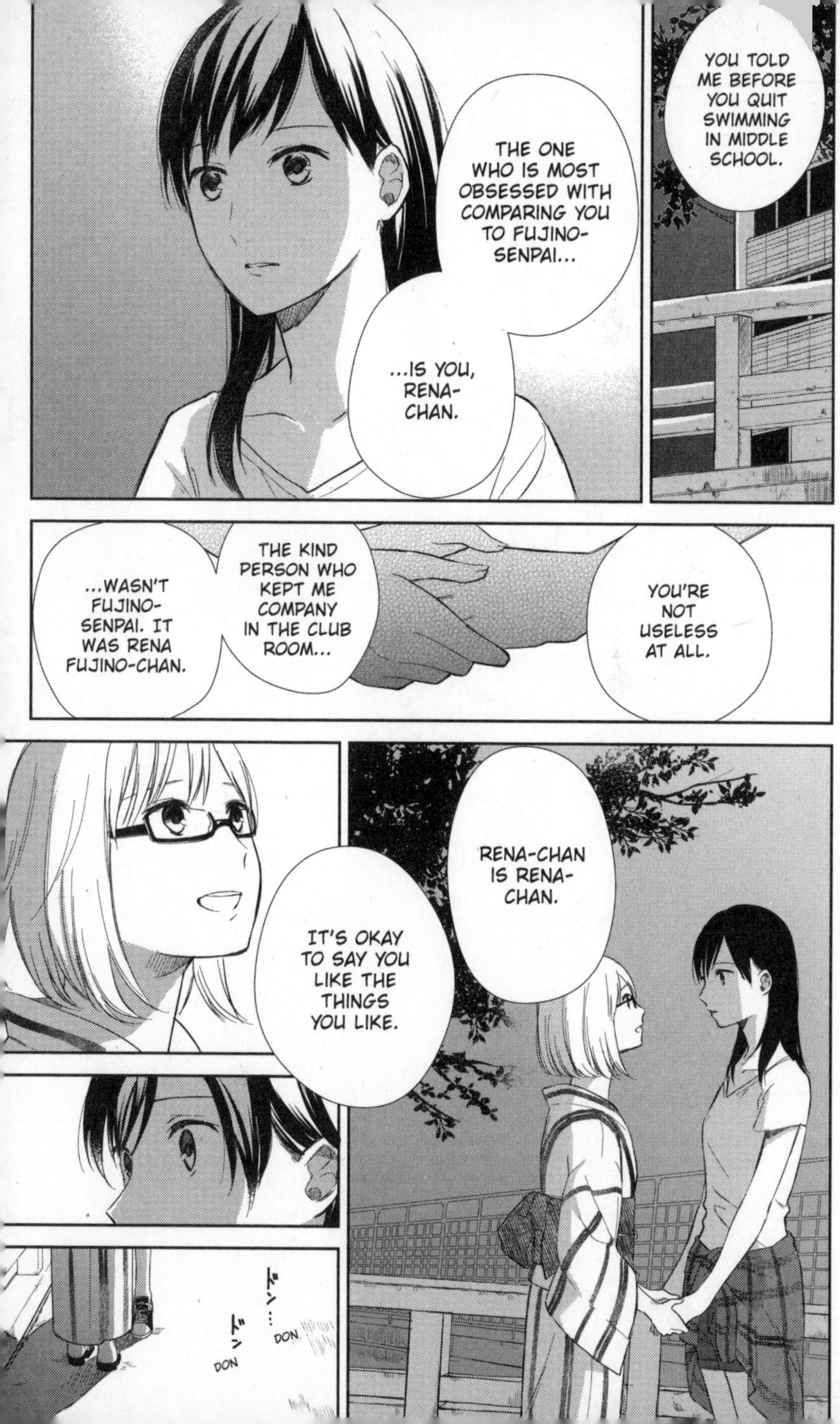
YOU TOLD ME BEFORE YOU QUIT SWIMMING IN MIDDLE SCHOOL.
THE ONE WHO IS MOST OBSESSED WITH COMPARING YOU TO FUJINO-SENPAI...
...IS YOU, RENA-CHAN.
YOU'RE NOT USELESS AT ALL.
THE KIND PERSON WHO KEPT ME COMPANY IN THE CLUB ROOM...
...WASN'T FUJINO-SENPAI. IT WAS RENA FUJINO-CHAN.
RENA-CHAN IS RENA-CHAN.
IT'S OKAY TO SAY YOU LIKE THE THINGS YOU LIKE.
ドン… DON
ドン DON

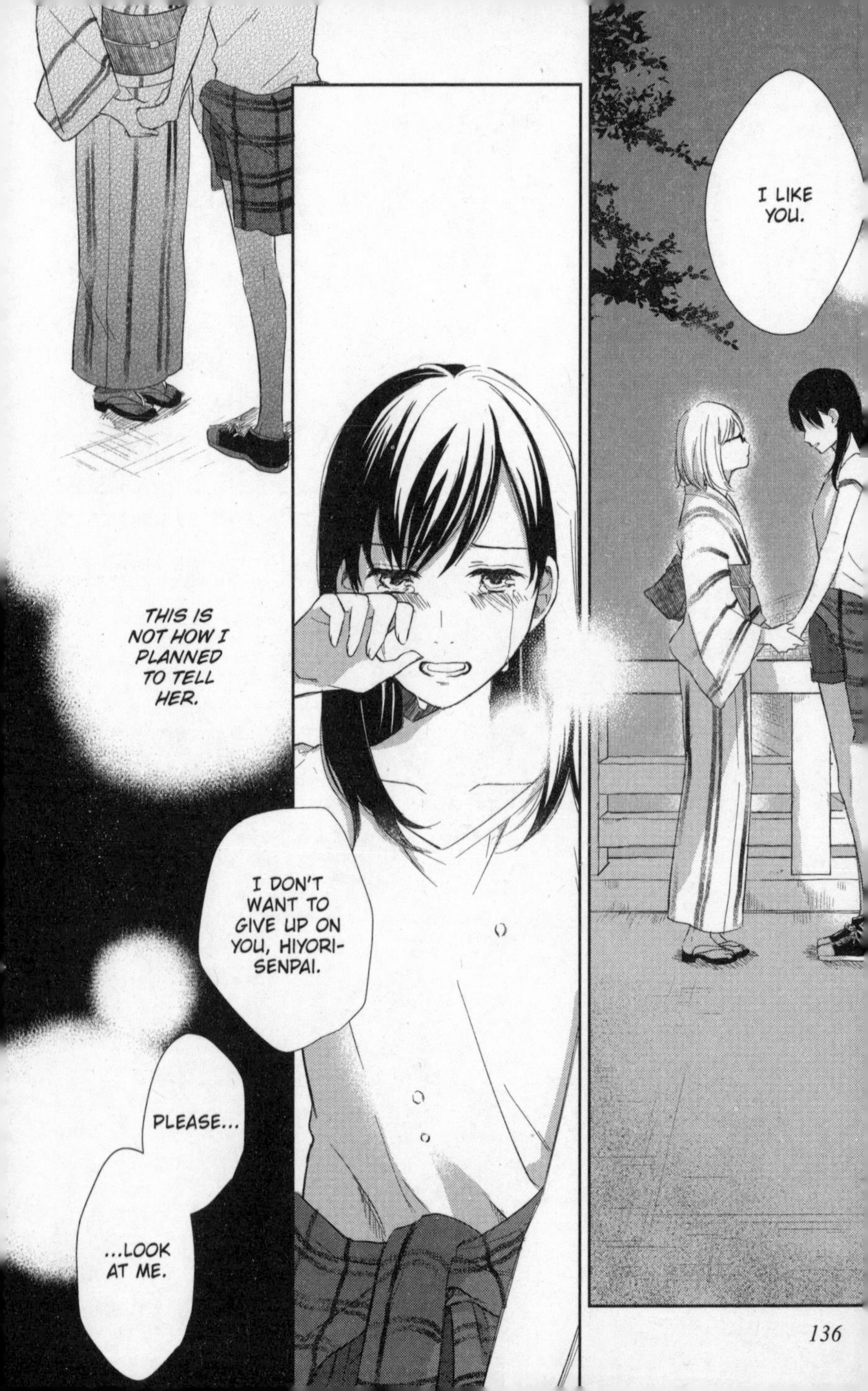
I LIKE YOU.
I DON'T WANT TO GIVE UP ON YOU, HIYORI-SENPAI.
THIS IS NOT HOW I PLANNED TO TELL HER.
PLEASE...
...LOOK AT ME.

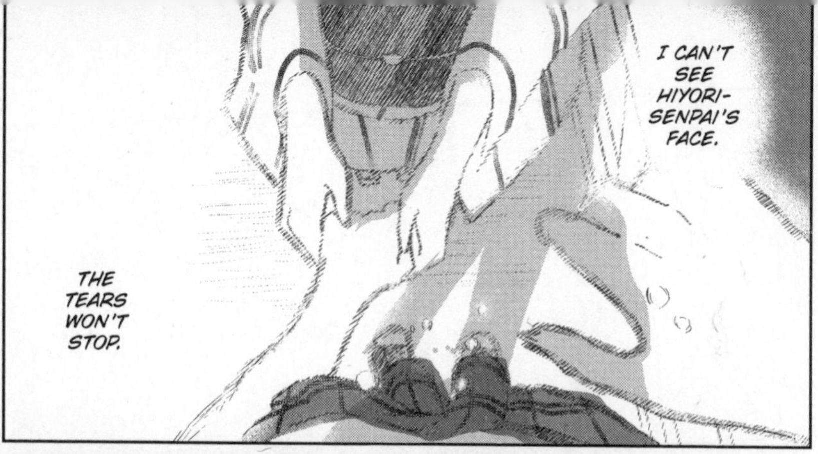
I CAN'T SEE HIYORI-SENPAI'S FACE.
THE TEARS WON'T STOP.

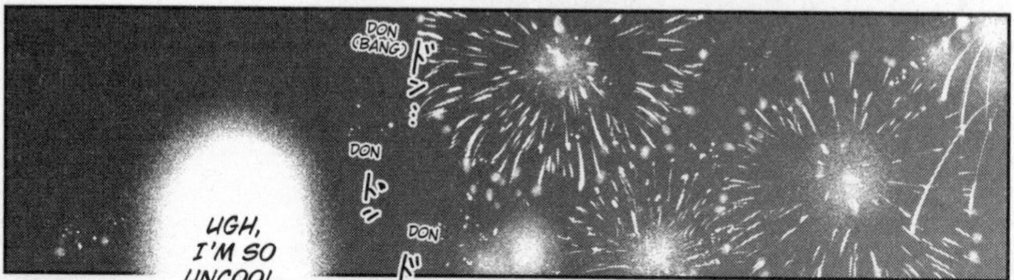
DON (BANG)
DON
DON
UGH, I'M SO UNCOOL.

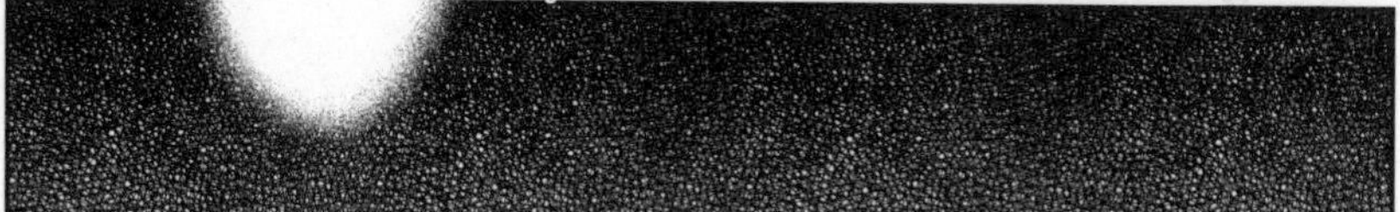

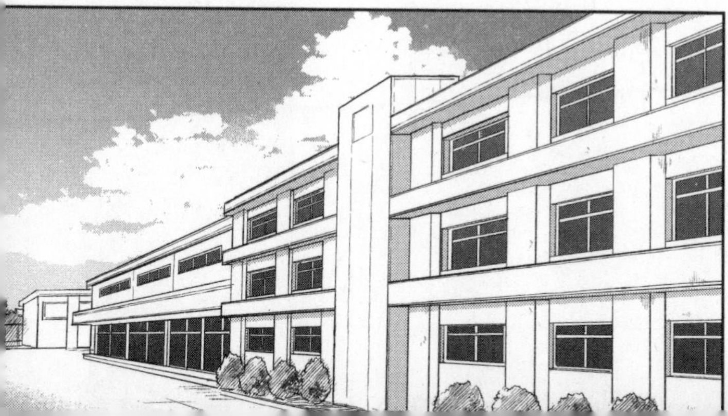

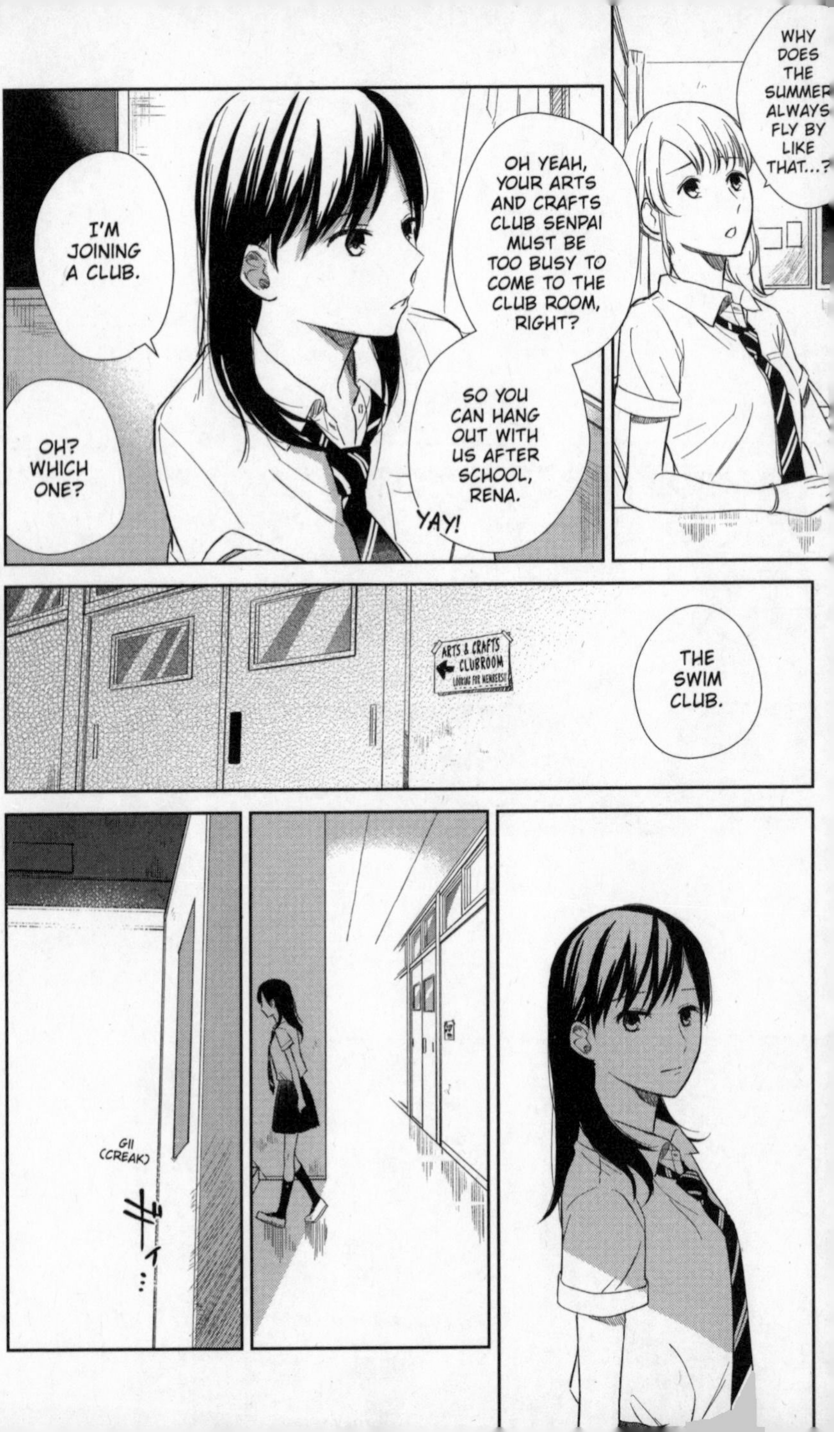
WHY DOES THE SUMMER ALWAYS FLY BY LIKE THAT...?
OH YEAH, YOUR ARTS AND CRAFTS CLUB SENPAI MUST BE TOO BUSY TO COME TO THE CLUB ROOM, RIGHT?
SO YOU CAN HANG OUT WITH US AFTER SCHOOL, RENA.
YAY!
I'M JOINING A CLUB.
OH? WHICH ONE?
THE SWIM CLUB.
ARTS & CRAFTS CLUBROOM
LOOKING FOR MEMBERS!!
GII (CREAK)
ギィ…

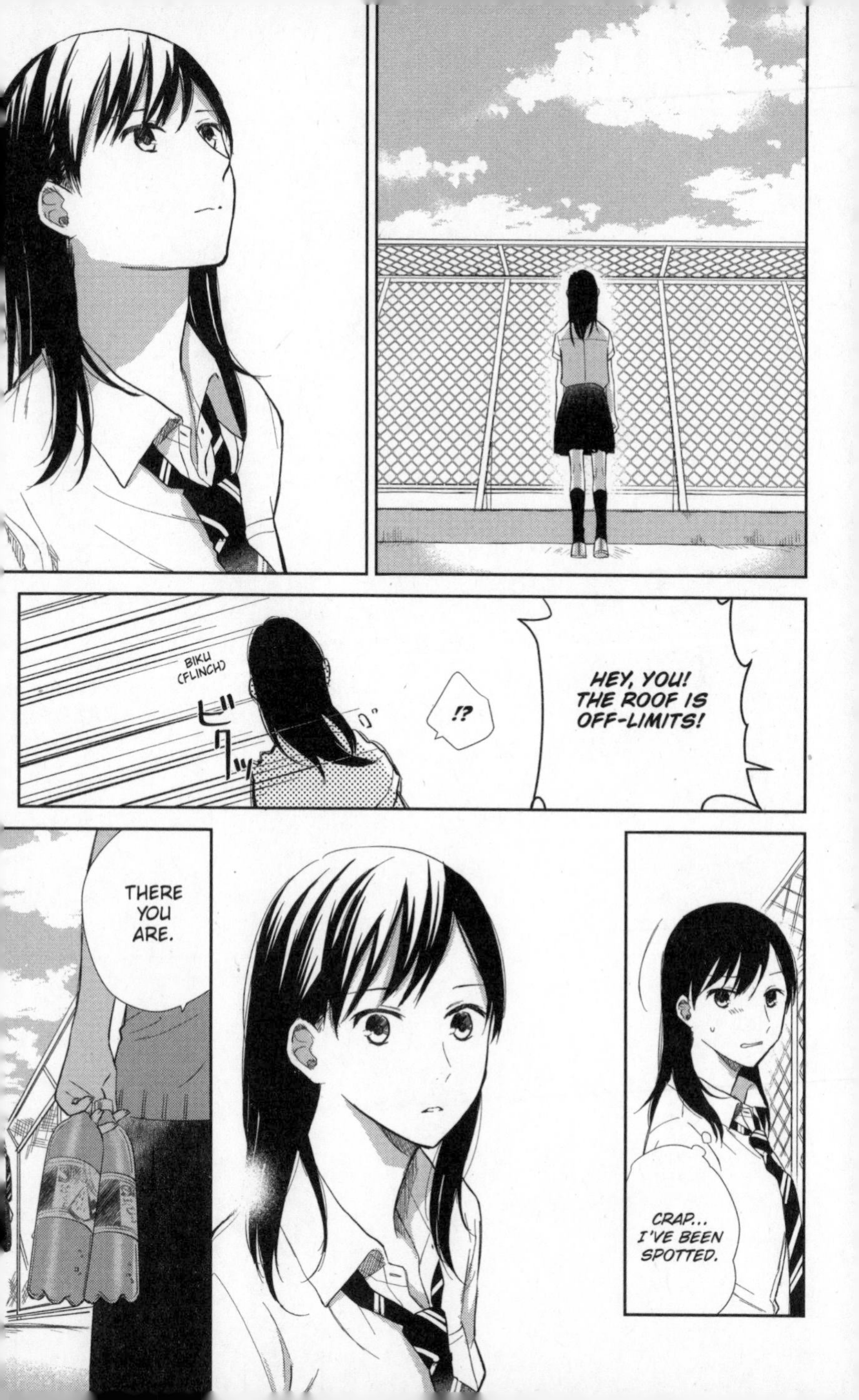
HEY, YOU! THE ROOF IS OFF-LIMITS!
!?
BIKU (FLINCH)
ビクッ
CRAP... I'VE BEEN SPOTTED.
THERE YOU ARE.

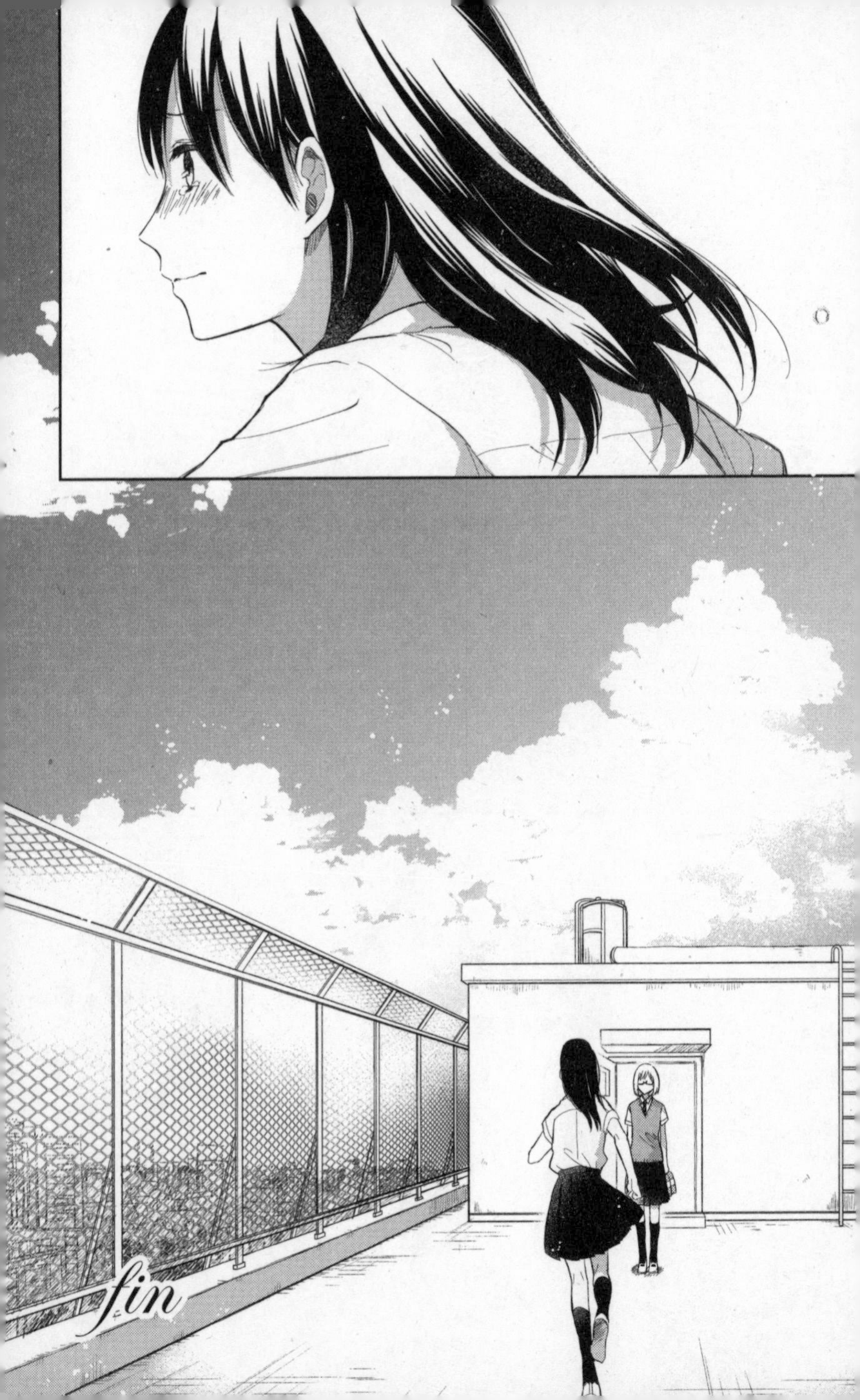
fin

éclair
blanche
A Girls' Love Anthology
That Resonates in Your Heart

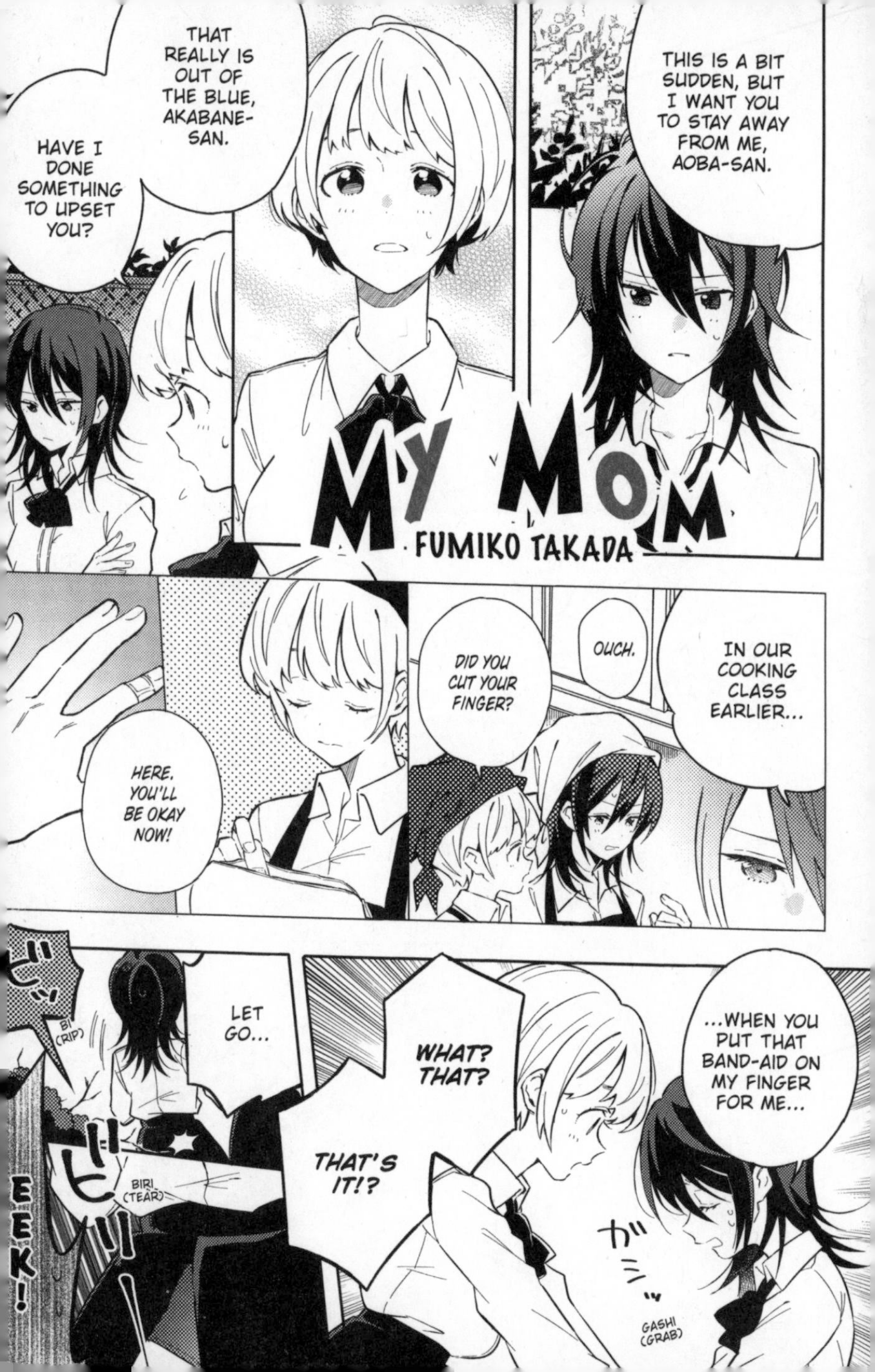
THIS IS A BIT SUDDEN, BUT I WANT YOU TO STAY AWAY FROM ME, AOBA-SAN.
THAT REALLY IS OUT OF THE BLUE, AKABANE-SAN.
HAVE I DONE SOMETHING TO UPSET YOU?
MY MOM
FUMIKO TAKADA
IN OUR COOKING CLASS EARLIER...
OUCH.
DID YOU CUT YOUR FINGER?
HERE. YOU'LL BE OKAY NOW!
...WHEN YOU PUT THAT BAND-AID ON MY FINGER FOR ME...
WHAT? THAT?
THAT'S IT!?
GASHI (GRAB)
LET GO...
BI (RIP)
BIRI (TEAR)
EEEK!

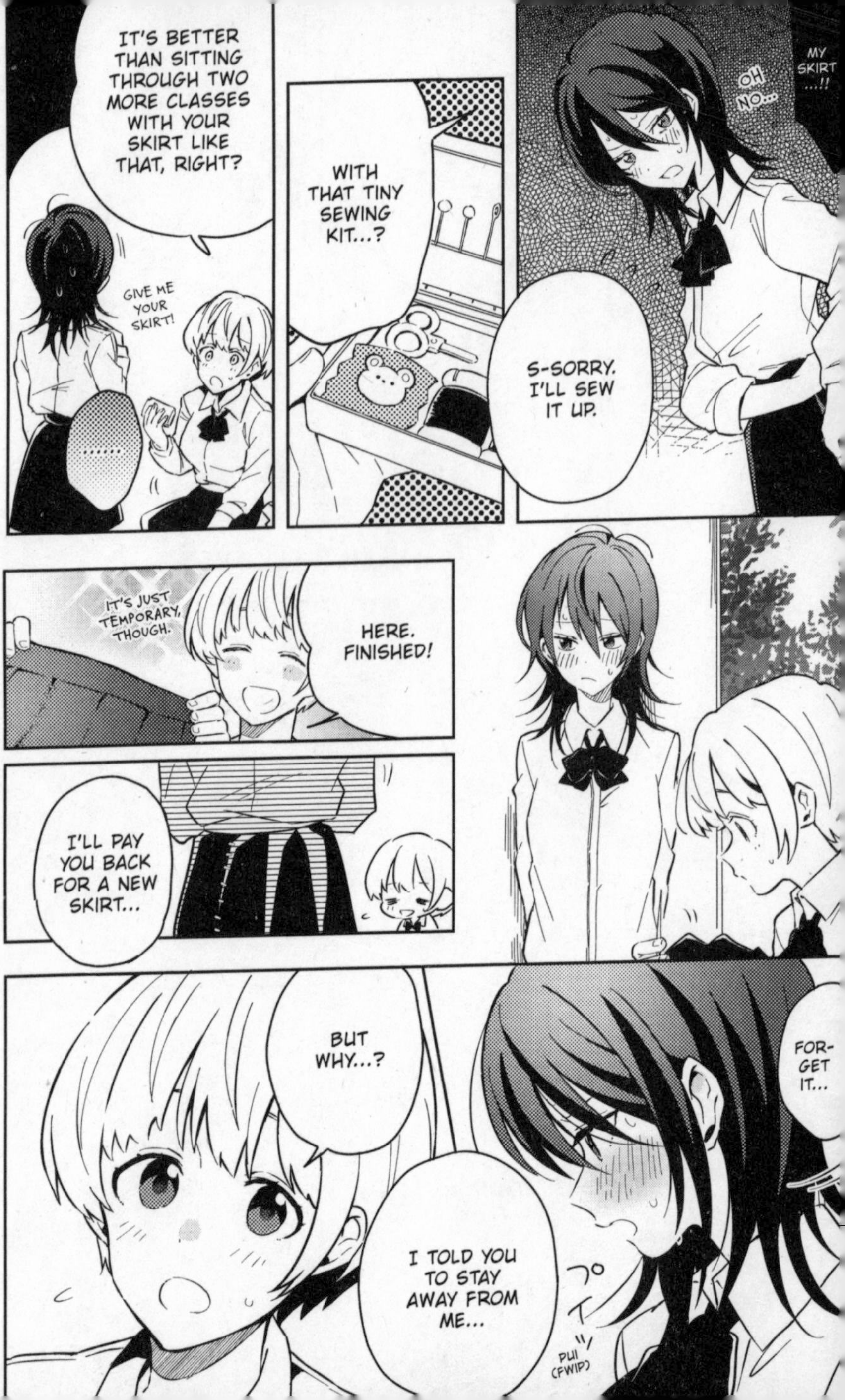
MY SKIRT ...!!
OH NO...
S-SORRY. I'LL SEW IT UP.
WITH THAT TINY SEWING KIT...?
IT'S BETTER THAN SITTING THROUGH TWO MORE CLASSES WITH YOUR SKIRT LIKE THAT, RIGHT?
GIVE ME YOUR SKIRT!
......
HERE. FINISHED!
IT'S JUST TEMPORARY, THOUGH.
I'LL PAY YOU BACK FOR A NEW SKIRT...
FOR-GET IT...
BUT WHY...?
I TOLD YOU TO STAY AWAY FROM ME...
PUI (FWIP)

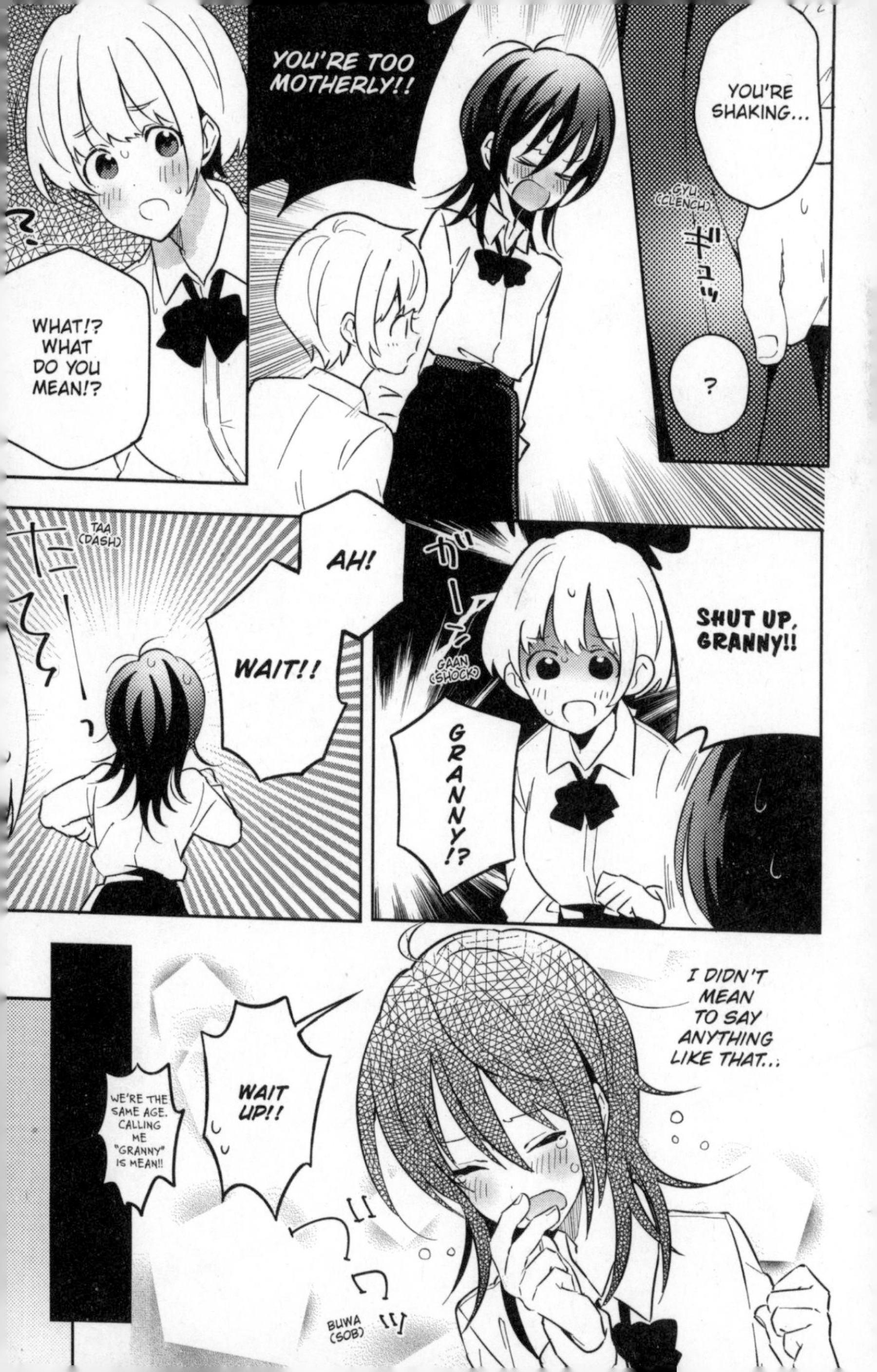
YOU'RE SHAKING...
GYU (CLENCH)
?
YOU'RE TOO MOTHERLY!!
WHAT!? WHAT DO YOU MEAN!?
SHUT UP, GRANNY!!
GAAN (SHOCK)
GRANNY!?
TAA (DASH)
AH!
WAIT!!
I DIDN'T MEAN TO SAY ANYTHING LIKE THAT...
BUWA (SOB)
WAIT UP!!
WE'RE THE SAME AGE. CALLING ME "GRANNY" IS MEAN!!

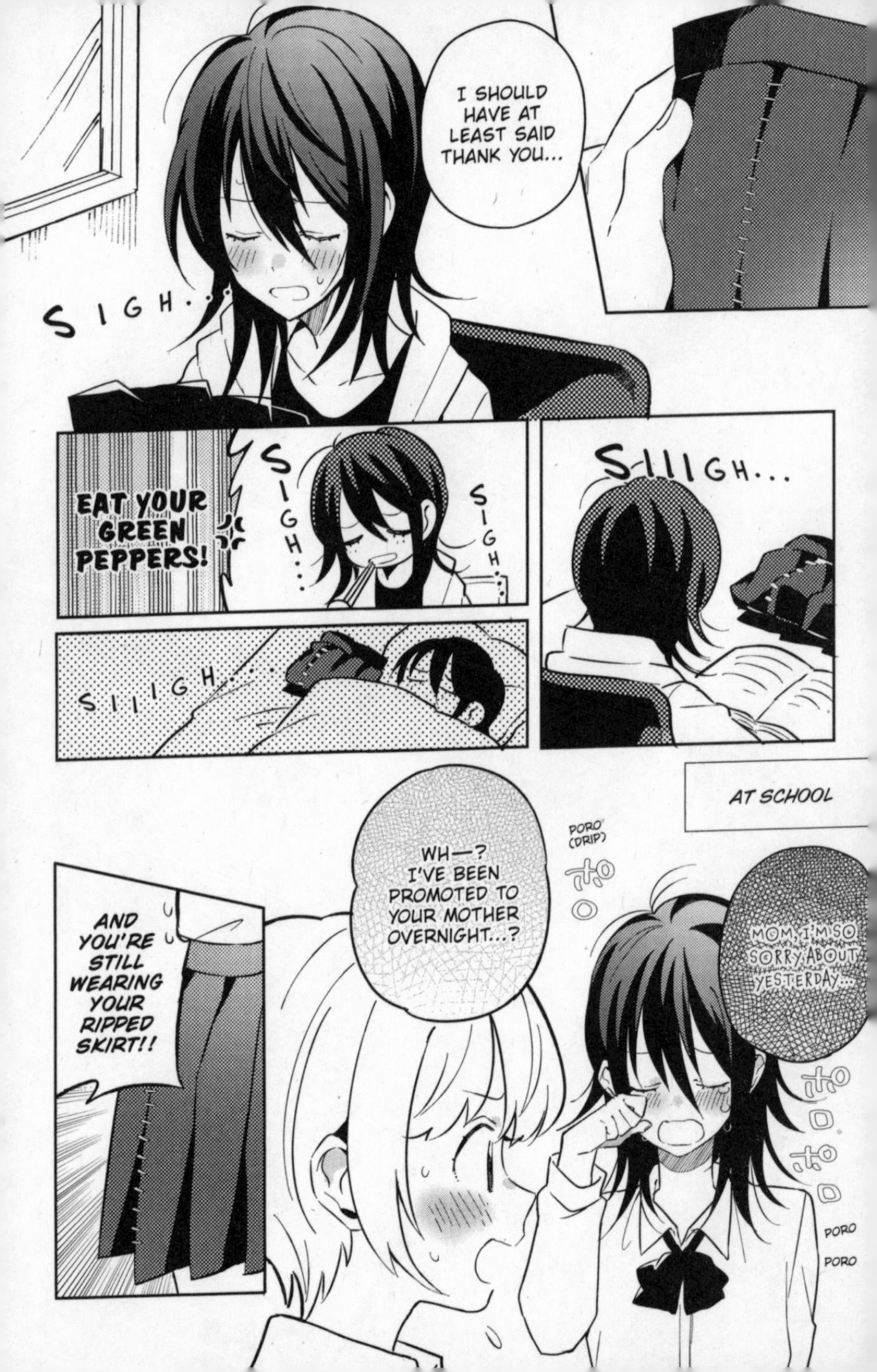
I SHOULD HAVE AT LEAST SAID THANK YOU...
SIGH...
SIIIGH...
EAT YOUR GREEN PEPPERS!
SIGH...
SIGH...
SIIIGH...
AT SCHOOL
MOM, I'M SO SORRY ABOUT YESTERDAY...
PORO (DRIP)
PORO PORO
WH—? I'VE BEEN PROMOTED TO YOUR MOTHER OVERNIGHT...?
AND YOU'RE STILL WEARING YOUR RIPPED SKIRT!!

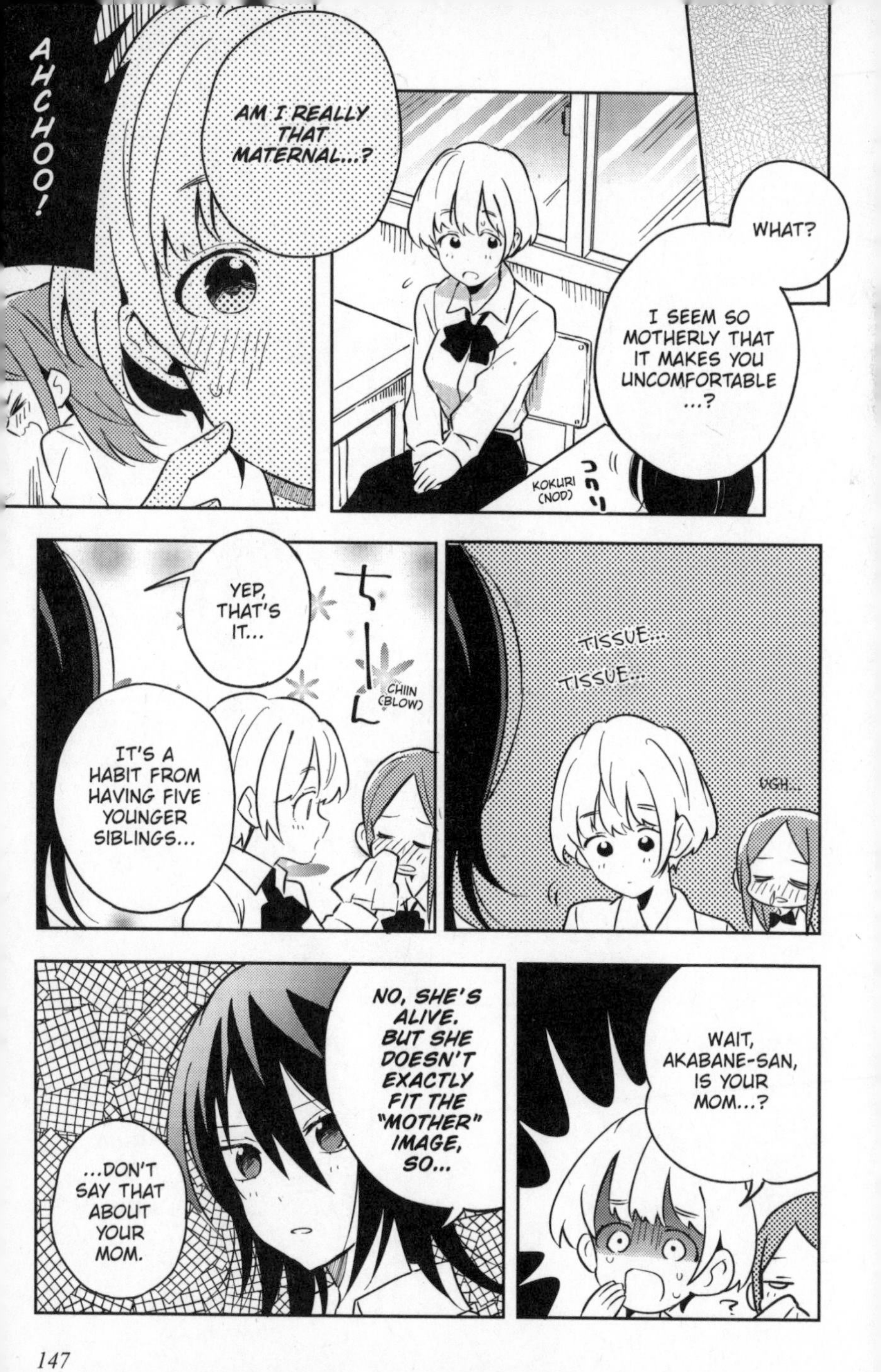
WHAT?
I SEEM SO MOTHERLY THAT IT MAKES YOU UNCOMFORTABLE ...?
KOKURI (NOD)
AM I REALLY THAT MATERNAL...?
AHCHOO!
TISSUE...
TISSUE...
UGH...
YEP, THAT'S IT...
CHIIN (BLOW)
IT'S A HABIT FROM HAVING FIVE YOUNGER SIBLINGS...
WAIT, AKABANE-SAN, IS YOUR MOM...?
NO, SHE'S ALIVE. BUT SHE DOESN'T EXACTLY FIT THE "MOTHER" IMAGE, SO...
...DON'T SAY THAT ABOUT YOUR MOM.

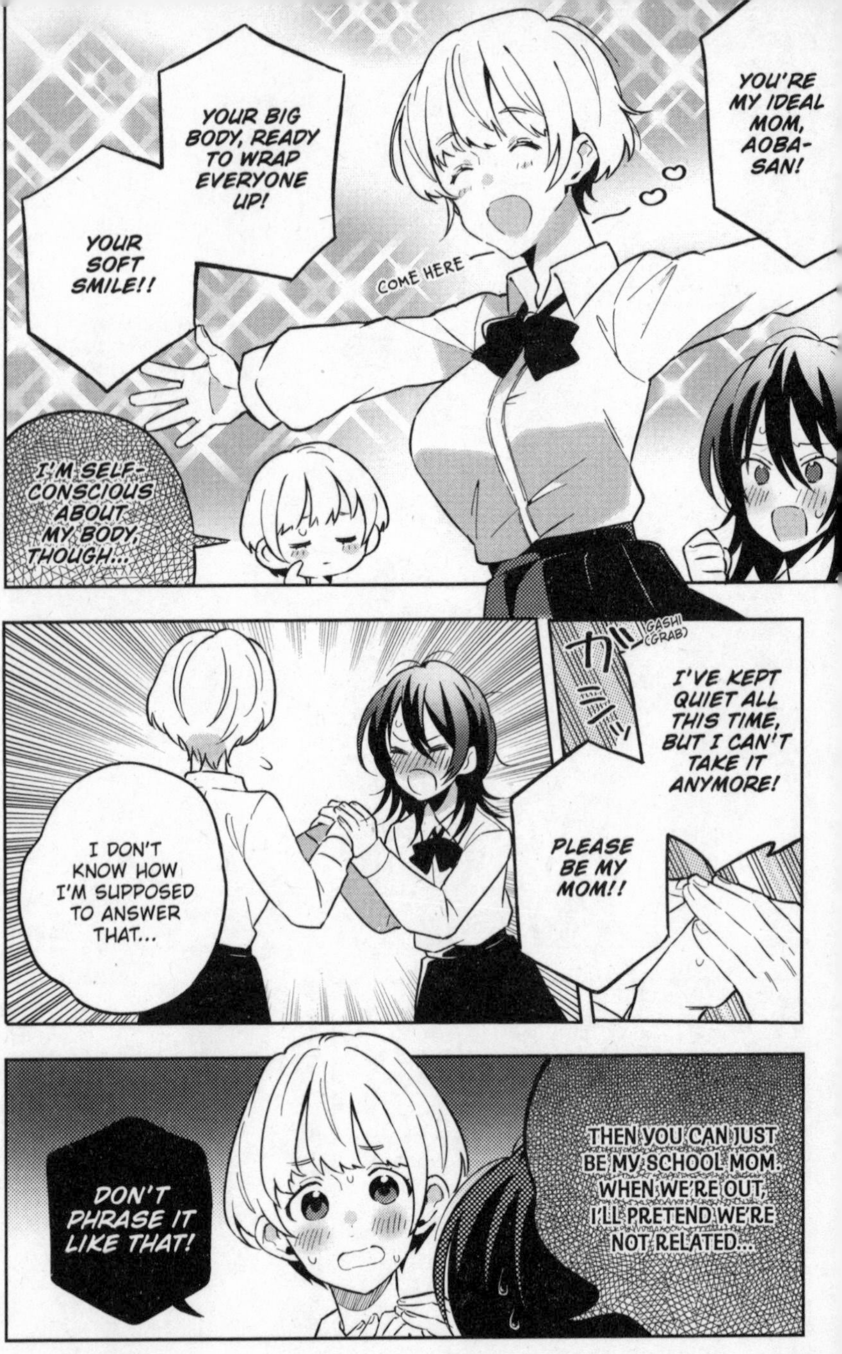
YOU'RE MY IDEAL MOM, AOBA-SAN!
COME HERE
YOUR BIG BODY, READY TO WRAP EVERYONE UP!
YOUR SOFT SMILE!!
I'M SELF-CONSCIOUS ABOUT MY BODY, THOUGH...
GASHI (GRAB)
I'VE KEPT QUIET ALL THIS TIME, BUT I CAN'T TAKE IT ANYMORE!
PLEASE BE MY MOM!!
I DON'T KNOW HOW I'M SUPPOSED TO ANSWER THAT...
THEN YOU CAN JUST BE MY SCHOOL MOM. WHEN WE'RE OUT, I'LL PRETEND WE'RE NOT RELATED...
DON'T PHRASE IT LIKE THAT!

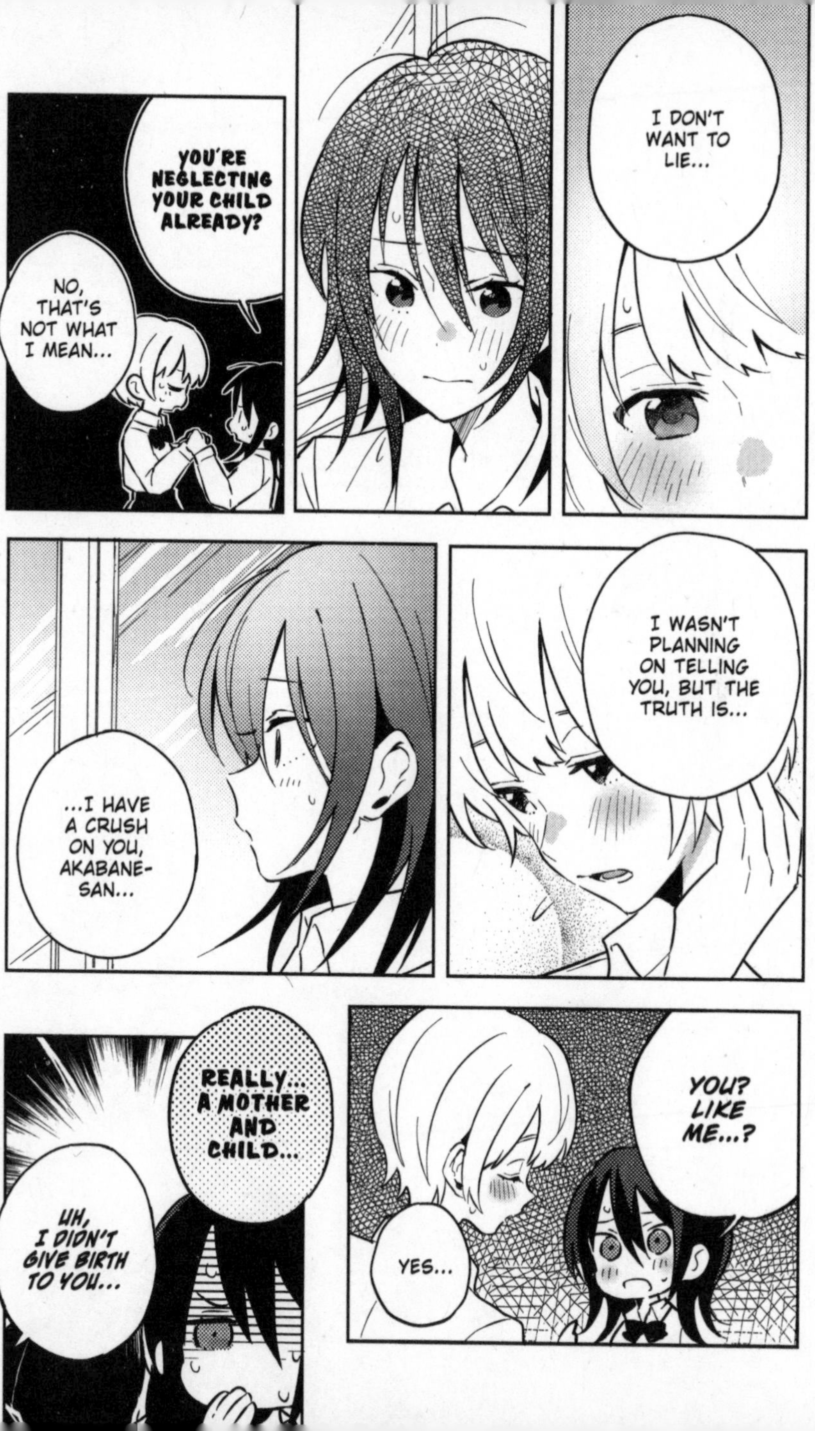
I DON'T WANT TO LIE...
YOU'RE NEGLECTING YOUR CHILD ALREADY?
NO, THAT'S NOT WHAT I MEAN...
I WASN'T PLANNING ON TELLING YOU, BUT THE TRUTH IS...
...I HAVE A CRUSH ON YOU, AKABANE-SAN...
YOU? LIKE ME...?
YES...
REALLY... A MOTHER AND CHILD...
UH, I DIDN'T GIVE BIRTH TO YOU...

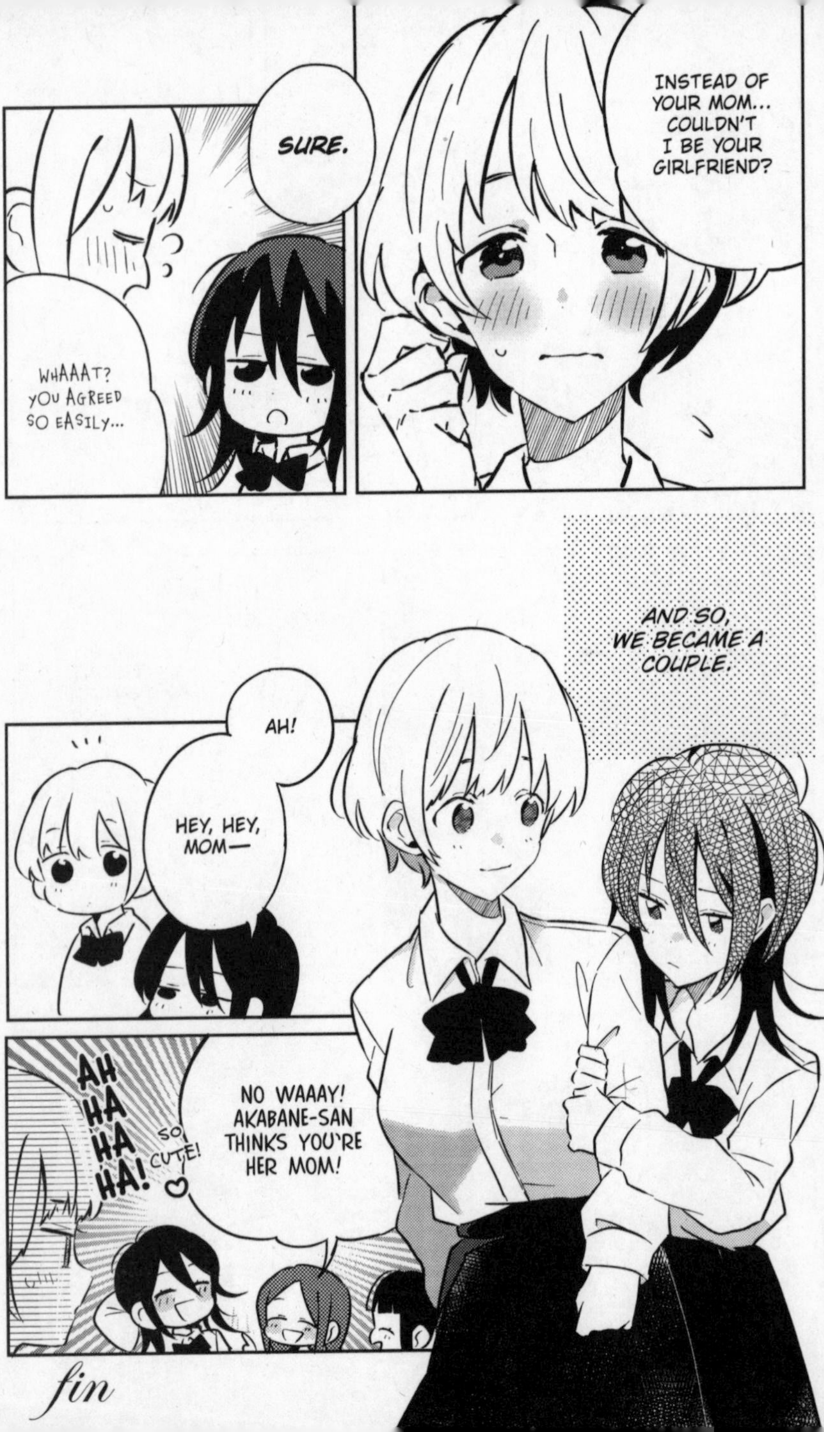
INSTEAD OF YOUR MOM... COULDN'T I BE YOUR GIRLFRIEND?
SURE.
WHAAAT? YOU AGREED SO EASILY...
AND SO, WE BECAME A COUPLE.
AH!
HEY, HEY, MOM—
NO WAAAY! AKABANE-SAN THINKS YOU'RE HER MOM!
SO CUTE!
AH HA HA HA!
fin

SHUNINTA AMANO

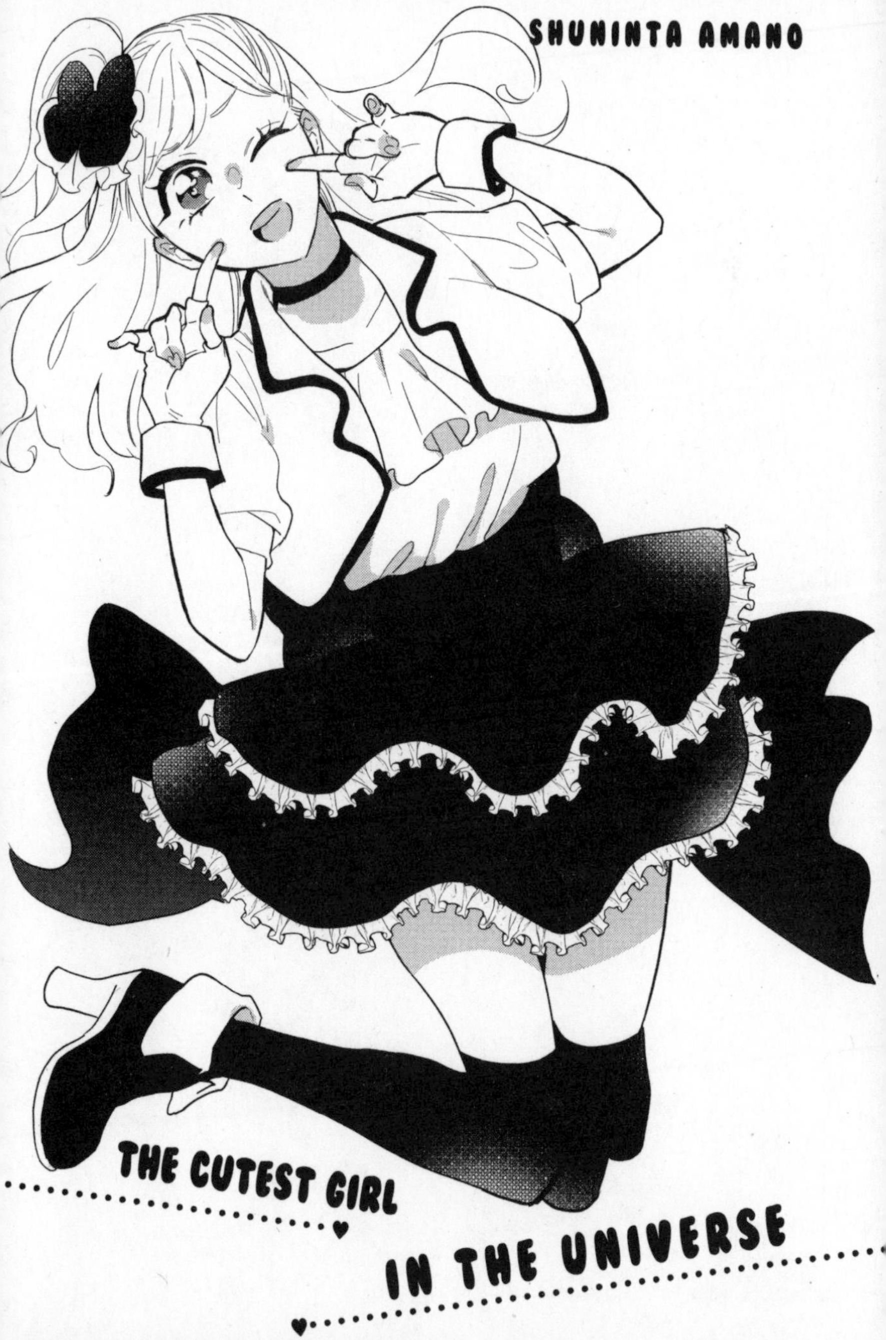

THE CUTEST GIRL IN THE UNIVERSE

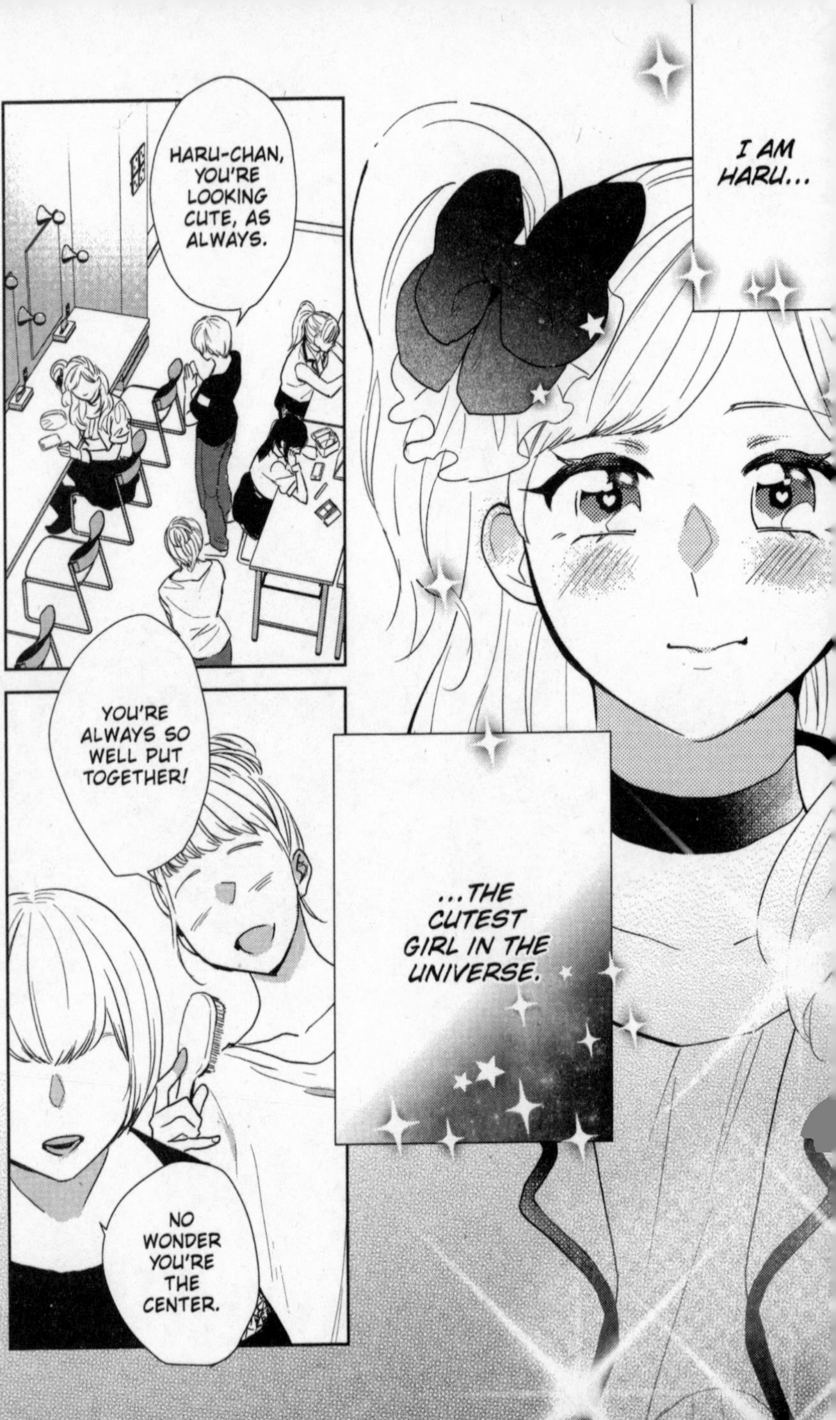
I AM HARU...
...THE CUTEST GIRL IN THE UNIVERSE.
HARU-CHAN, YOU'RE LOOKING CUTE, AS ALWAYS.
YOU'RE ALWAYS SO WELL PUT TOGETHER!
NO WONDER YOU'RE THE CENTER.

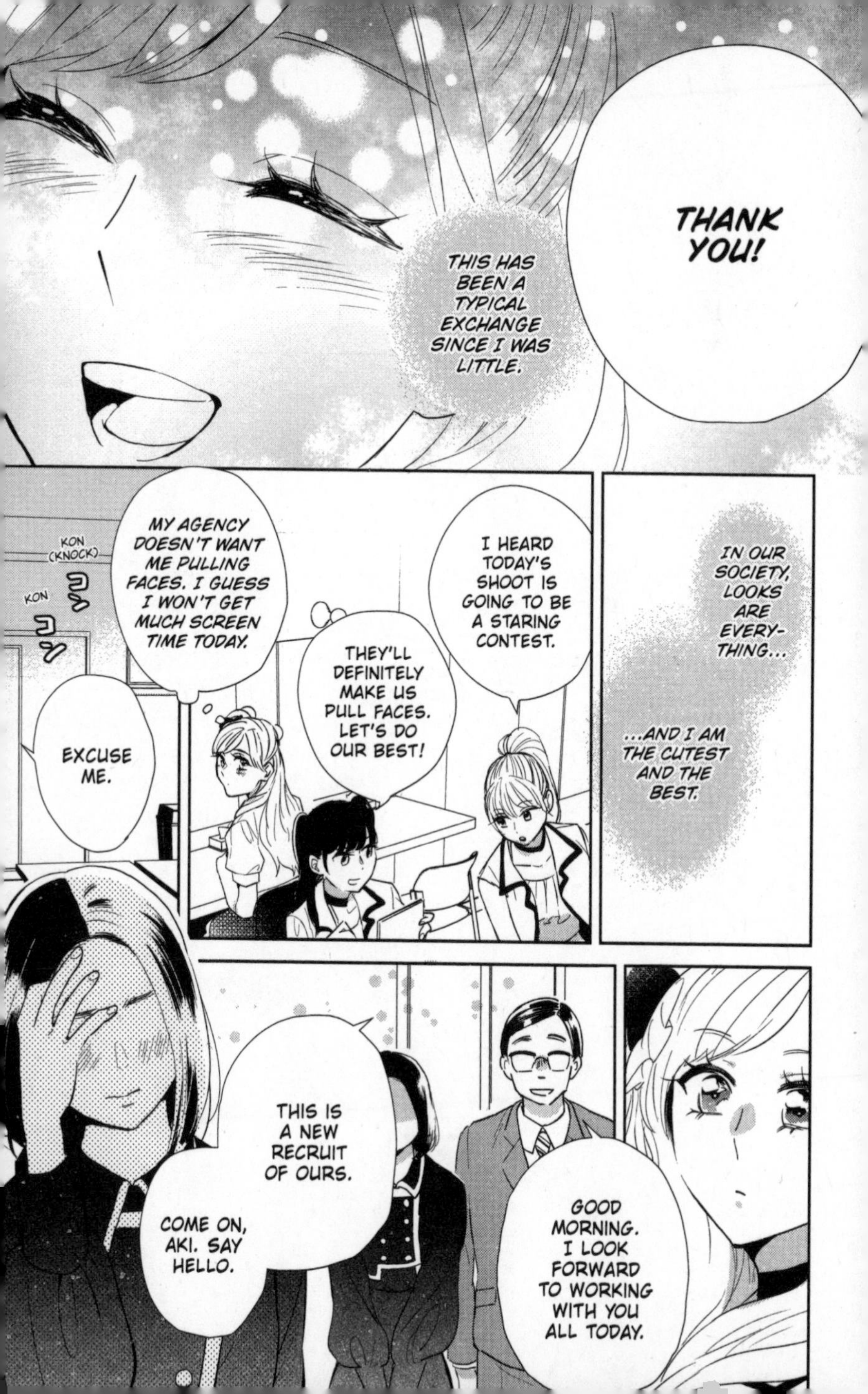
THANK YOU!
THIS HAS BEEN A TYPICAL EXCHANGE SINCE I WAS LITTLE.
IN OUR SOCIETY, LOOKS ARE EVERY-THING...
...AND I AM THE CUTEST AND THE BEST.
I HEARD TODAY'S SHOOT IS GOING TO BE A STARING CONTEST.
THEY'LL DEFINITELY MAKE US PULL FACES. LET'S DO OUR BEST!
MY AGENCY DOESN'T WANT ME PULLING FACES. I GUESS I WON'T GET MUCH SCREEN TIME TODAY.
KON (KNOCK)
KON
EXCUSE ME.
THIS IS A NEW RECRUIT OF OURS.
COME ON, AKI. SAY HELLO.
GOOD MORNING. I LOOK FORWARD TO WORKING WITH YOU ALL TODAY.

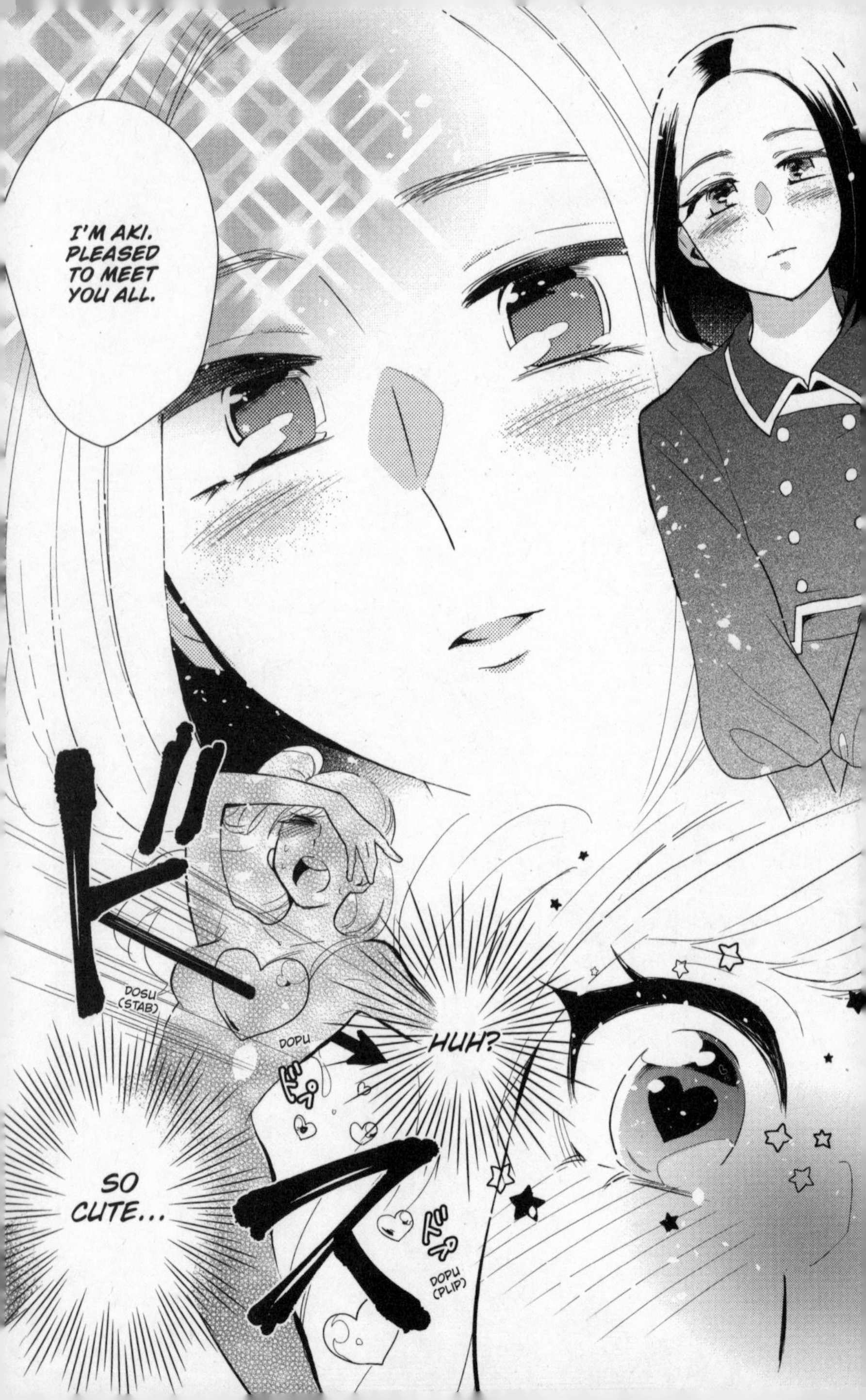
I'M AKI. PLEASED TO MEET YOU ALL.
HUH?
DOPU
DOSU (STAB)
DOPU (PLIP)
SO CUTE...

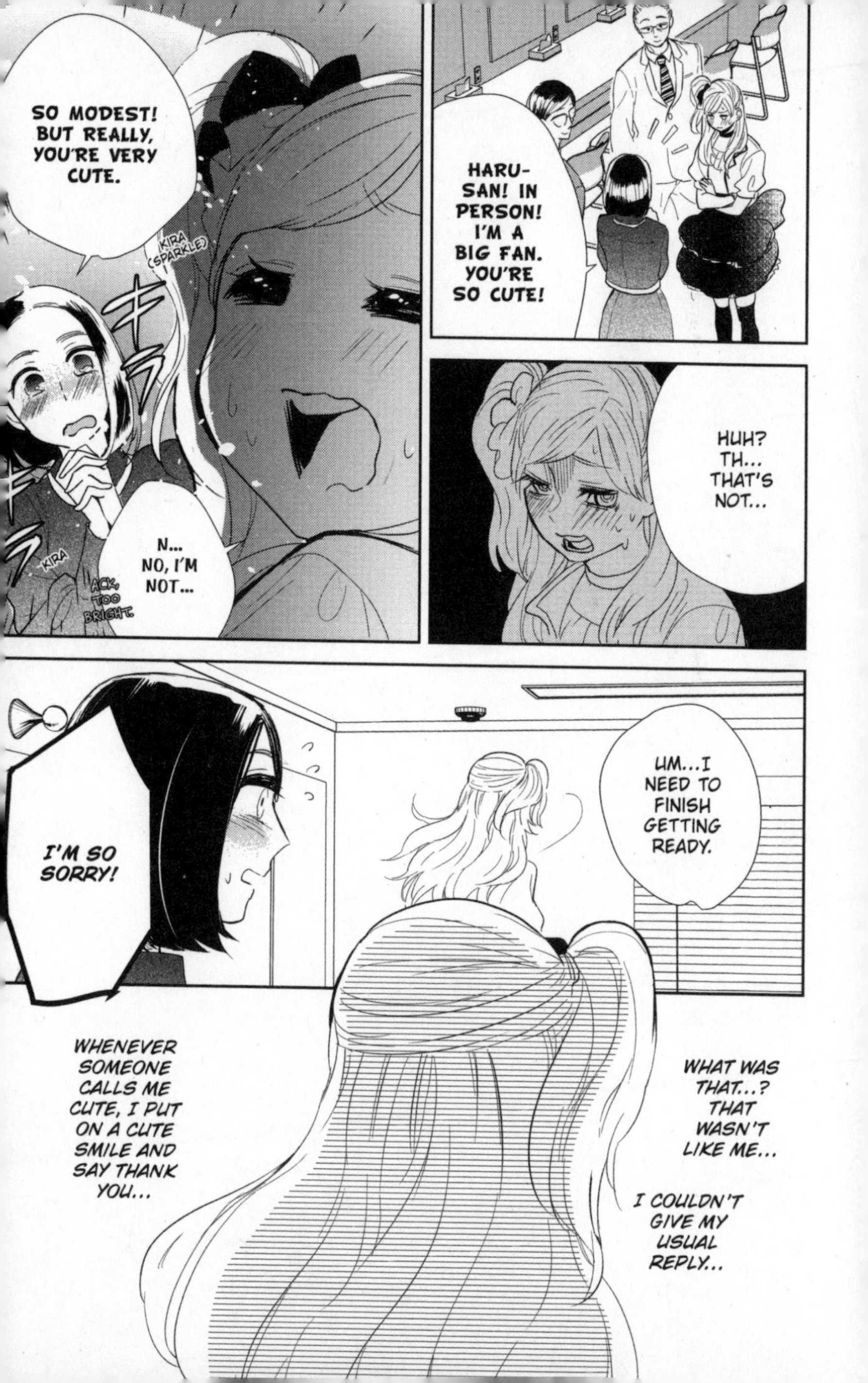
HARU-SAN! IN PERSON! I'M A BIG FAN. YOU'RE SO CUTE!
HUH? TH... THAT'S NOT...
SO MODEST! BUT REALLY, YOU'RE VERY CUTE.
KIRA (SPARKLE)
KIRA
ACK, TOO BRIGHT.
N... NO, I'M NOT...
UM...I NEED TO FINISH GETTING READY.
I'M SO SORRY!
WHENEVER SOMEONE CALLS ME CUTE, I PUT ON A CUTE SMILE AND SAY THANK YOU...
WHAT WAS THAT...? THAT WASN'T LIKE ME...
I COULDN'T GIVE MY USUAL REPLY...

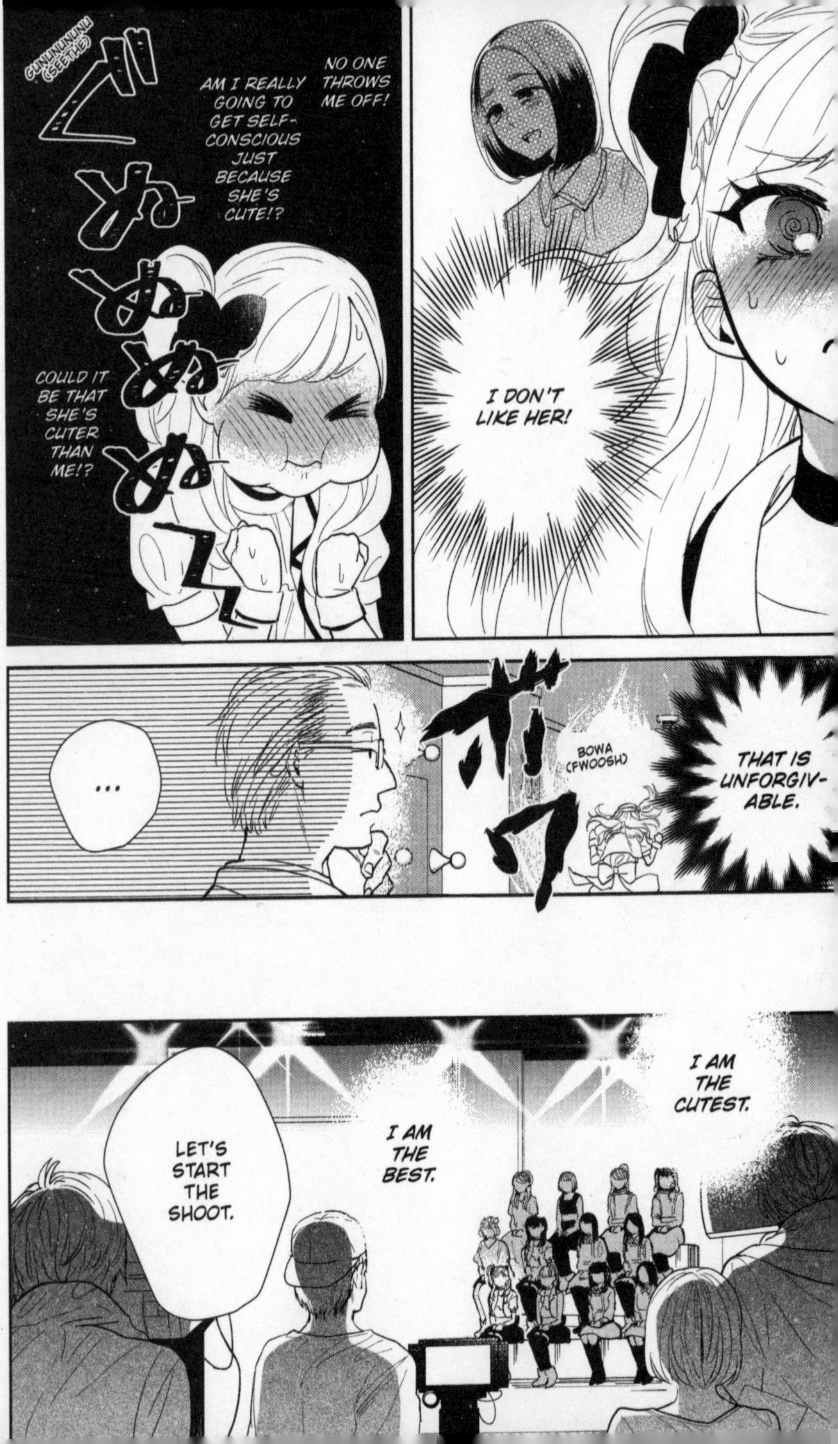
I DON'T LIKE HER!
NO ONE THROWS ME OFF!
AM I REALLY GOING TO GET SELF-CONSCIOUS JUST BECAUSE SHE'S CUTE!?
GUNUNUNUNU (SEETHE)
COULD IT BE THAT SHE'S CUTER THAN ME!?
THAT IS UNFORGIV-ABLE.
BOWA (FWOOSH)
...
I AM THE CUTEST.
I AM THE BEST.
LET'S START THE SHOOT.

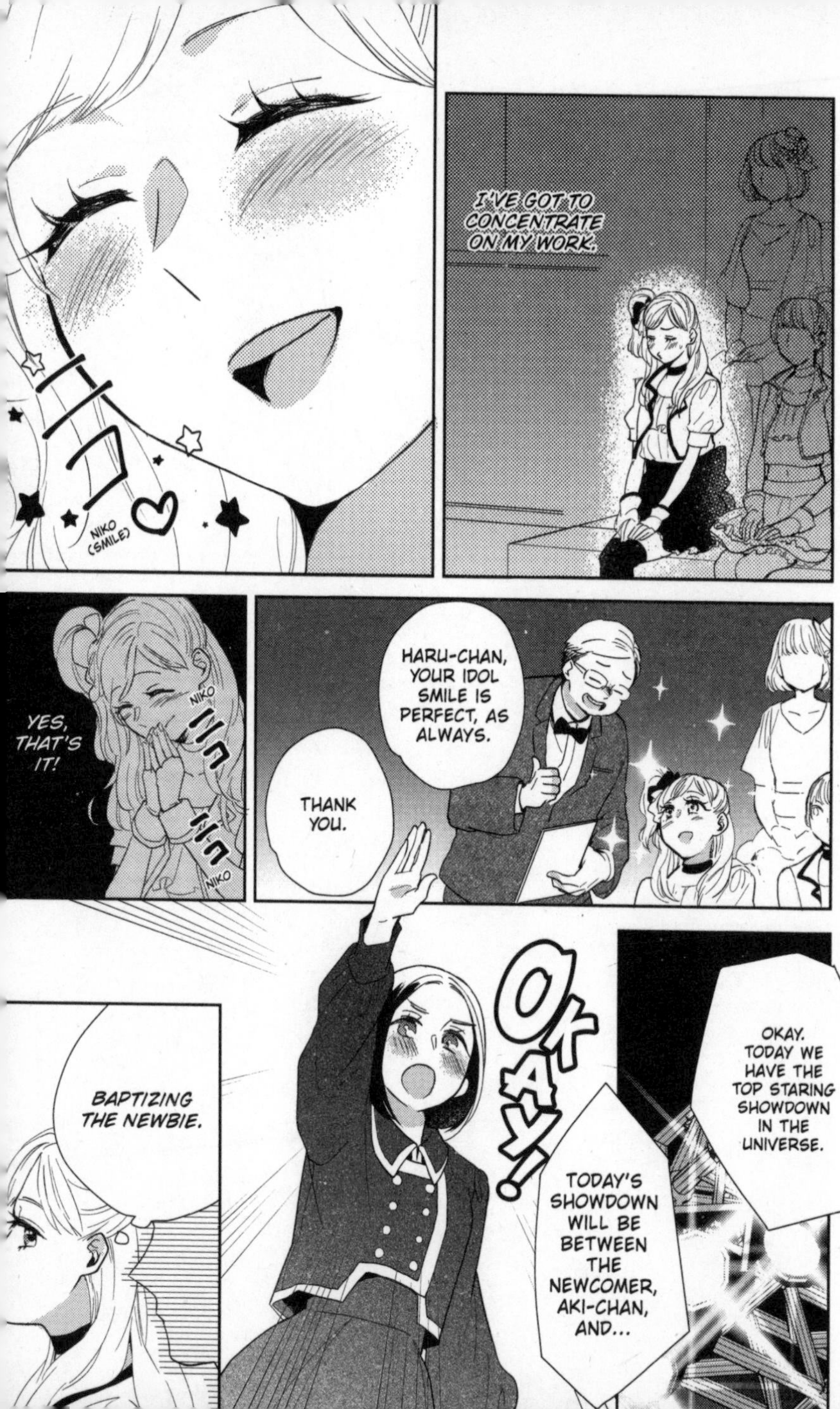
I'VE GOT TO CONCENTRATE ON MY WORK.
NIKO (SMILE)
HARU-CHAN, YOUR IDOL SMILE IS PERFECT, AS ALWAYS.
THANK YOU.
YES, THAT'S IT!
NIKO
NIKO
OKAY. TODAY WE HAVE THE TOP STARING SHOWDOWN IN THE UNIVERSE.
TODAY'S SHOWDOWN WILL BE BETWEEN THE NEWCOMER, AKI-CHAN, AND...
OKAY!
BAPTIZING THE NEWBIE.

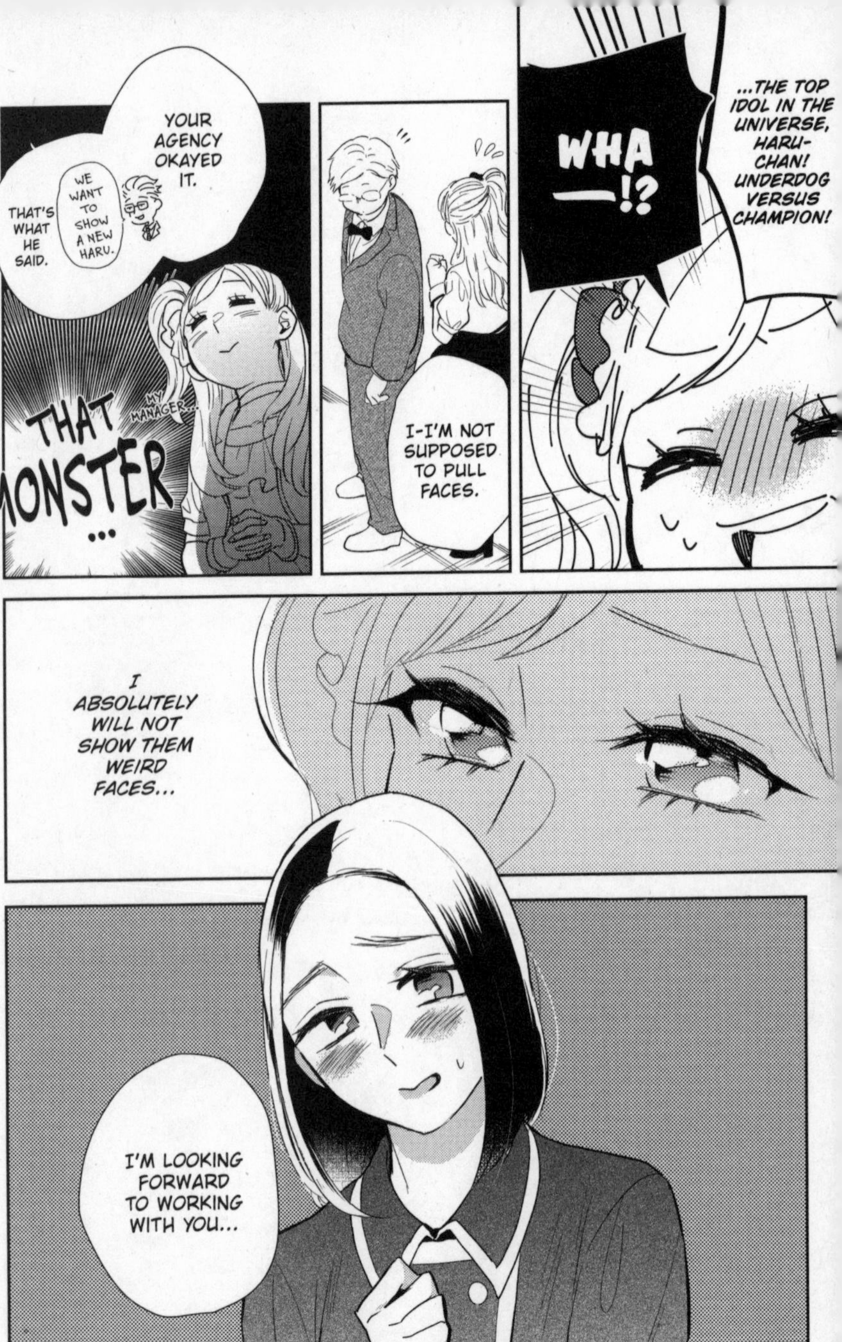
...THE TOP IDOL IN THE UNIVERSE, HARU-CHAN! UNDERDOG VERSUS CHAMPION!
WHA—!?
I-I'M NOT SUPPOSED TO PULL FACES.
YOUR AGENCY OKAYED IT.
WE WANT TO SHOW A NEW HARU.
THAT'S WHAT HE SAID.
MY MANAGER...
THAT MONSTER...
I ABSOLUTELY WILL NOT SHOW THEM WEIRD FACES...
I'M LOOKING FORWARD TO WORKING WITH YOU...

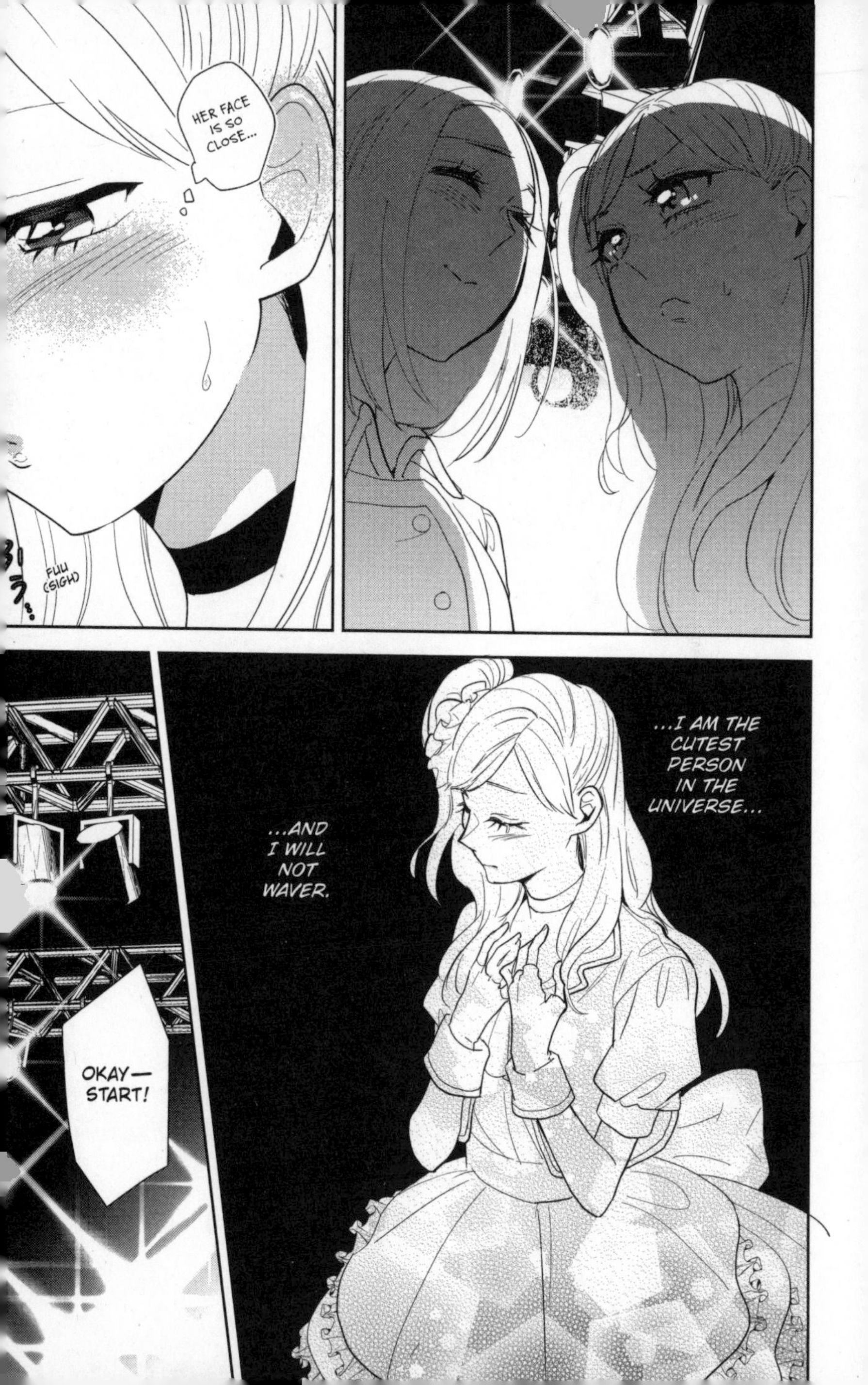
HER FACE IS SO CLOSE...
FUU (SIGH)
...I AM THE CUTEST PERSON IN THE UNIVERSE...
...AND I WILL NOT WAVER.
OKAY— START!

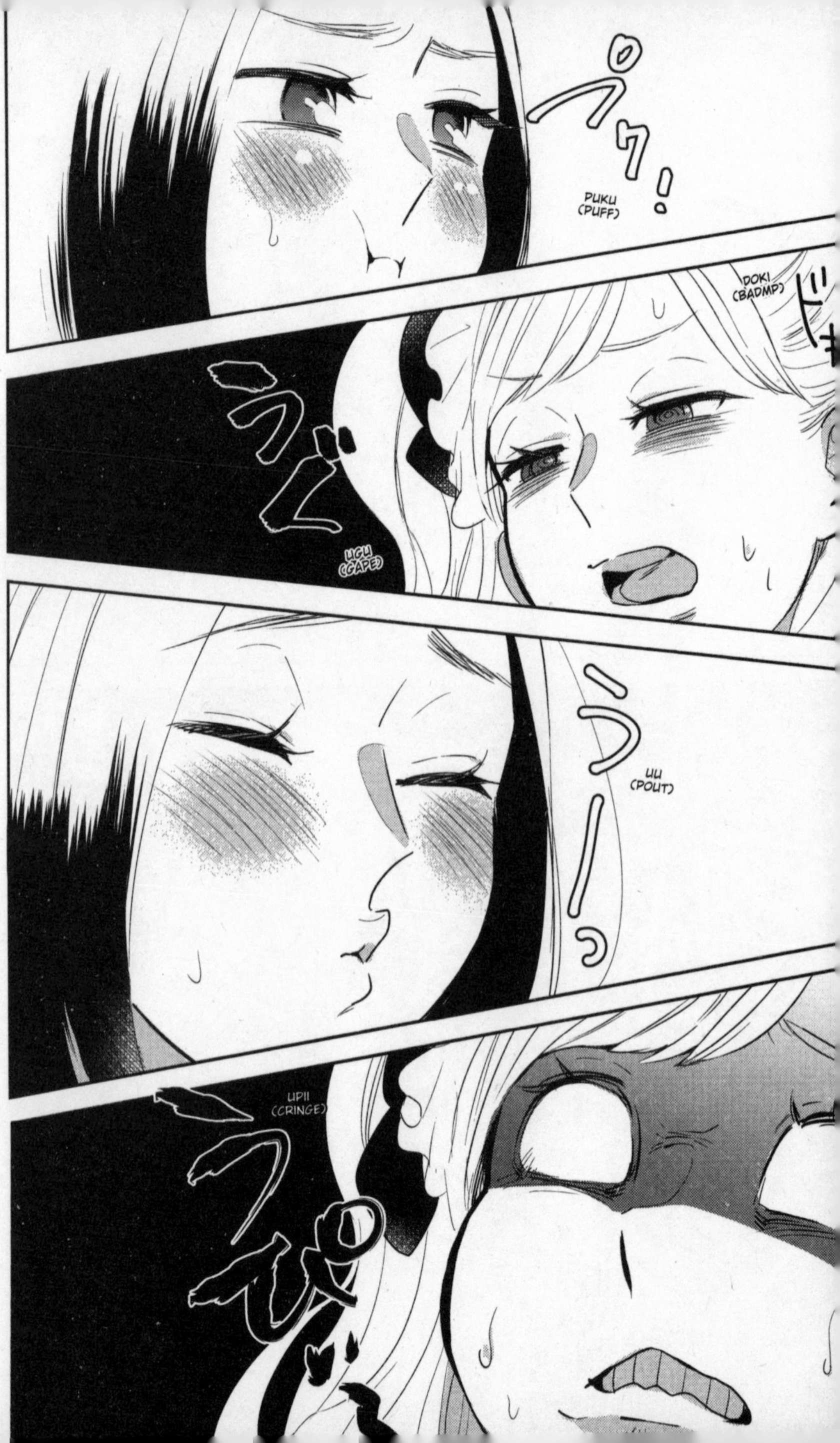
PUKU (PUFF)
DOKI (BADMP)
UGU (GAPE)
UU (POUT)
UPII (CRINGE)

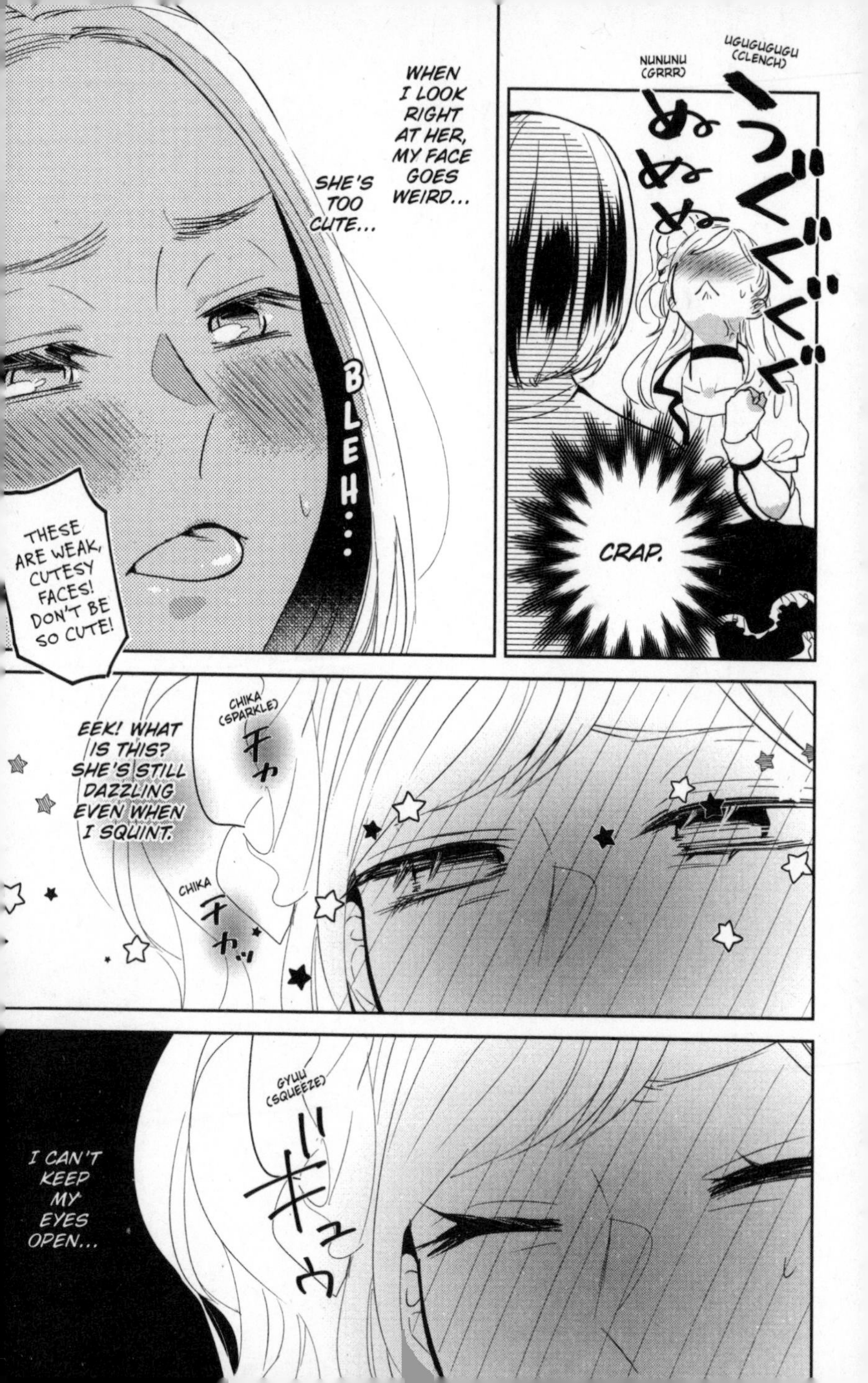
UGUGUGU (CLENCH)
NUNUNU (GRRR)
CRAP.
WHEN I LOOK RIGHT AT HER, MY FACE GOES WEIRD...
SHE'S TOO CUTE...
BLEH...
THESE ARE WEAK, CUTESY FACES! DON'T BE SO CUTE!
CHIKA (SPARKLE)
CHIKA
EEK! WHAT IS THIS? SHE'S STILL DAZZLING EVEN WHEN I SQUINT.
GYUU (SQUEEZE)
I CAN'T KEEP MY EYES OPEN...

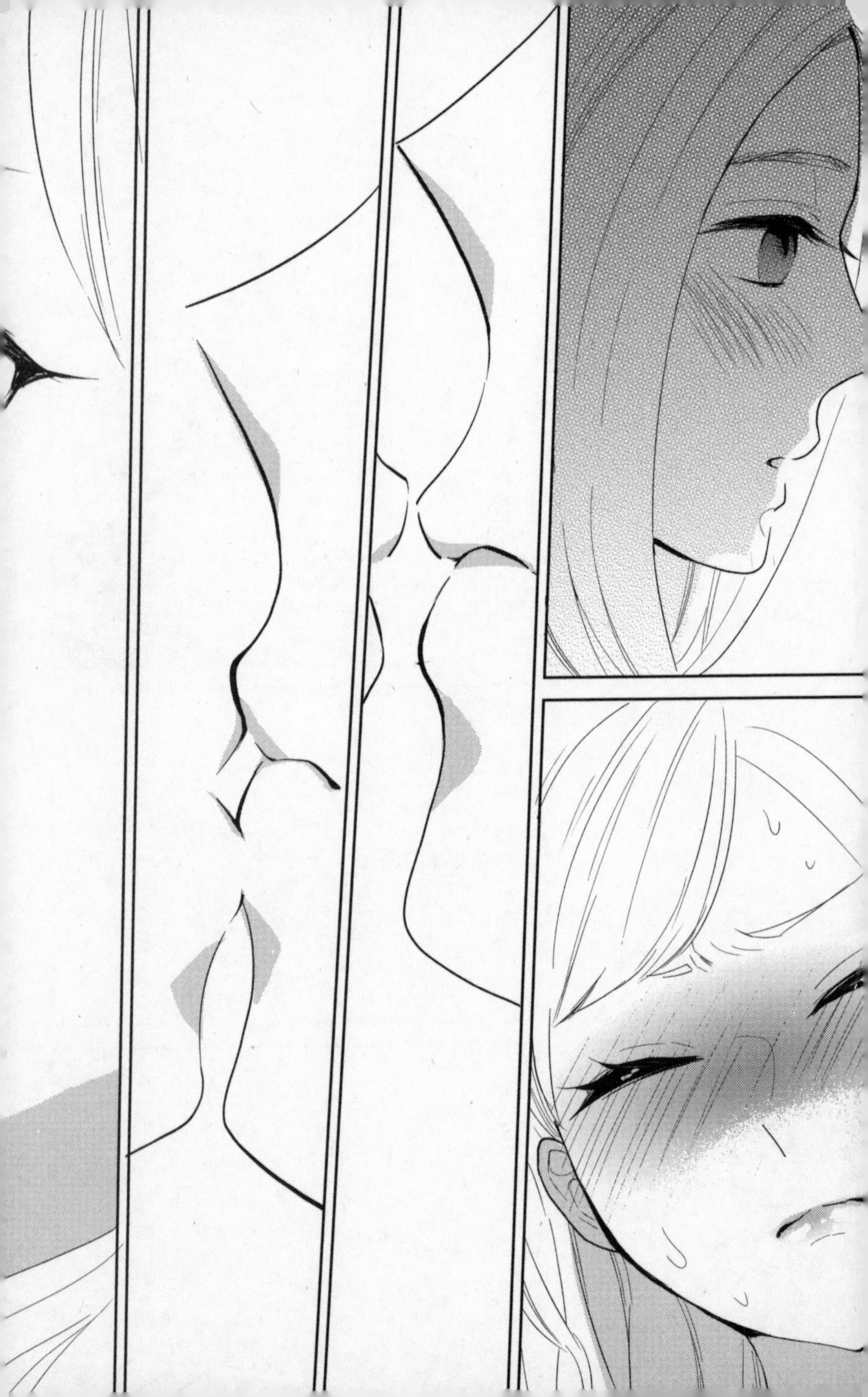

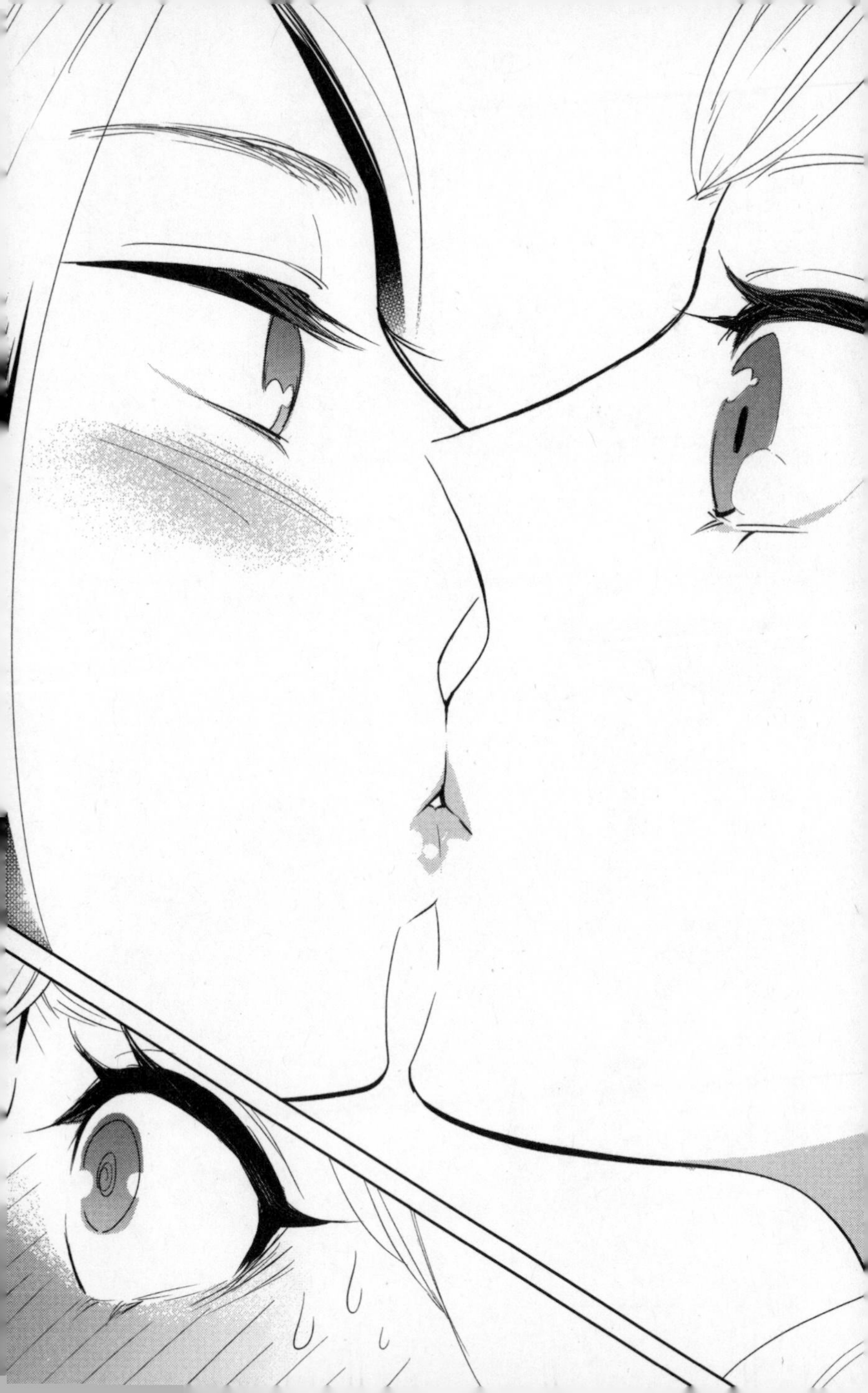

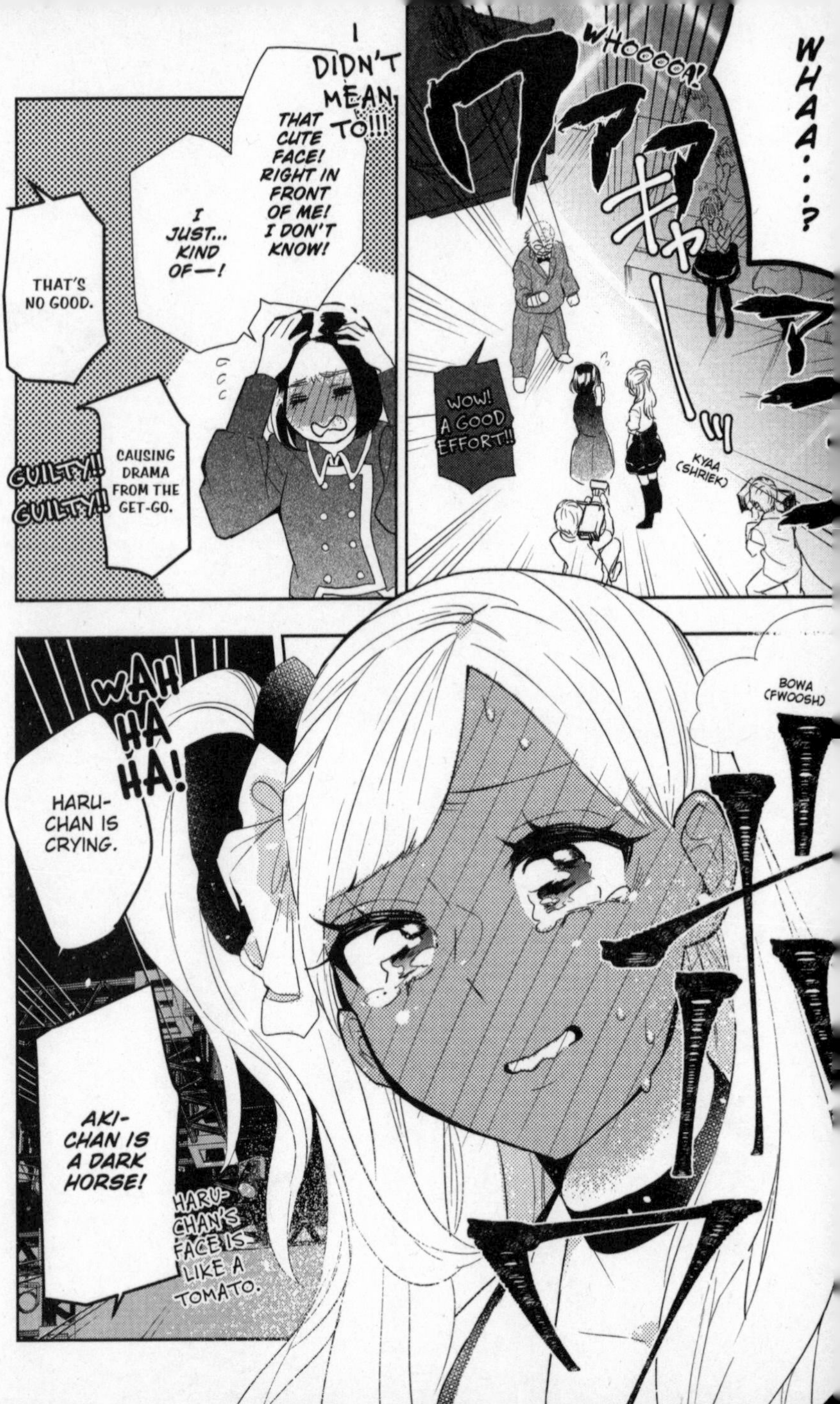
WHAA...?
WHOOOOOA!
KYAA (SHRIEK)
WOW! A GOOD EFFORT!!
I DIDN'T MEAN TO!!!
THAT CUTE FACE! RIGHT IN FRONT OF ME! I DON'T KNOW!
I JUST... KIND OF—!
THAT'S NO GOOD.
CAUSING DRAMA FROM THE GET-GO.
GUILTY!! GUILTY!!
BOWA (FWOOSH)
WAH HA HA HA!
HARU-CHAN IS CRYING.
HARU-CHAN'S FACE IS LIKE A TOMATO.
AKI-CHAN IS A DARK HORSE!

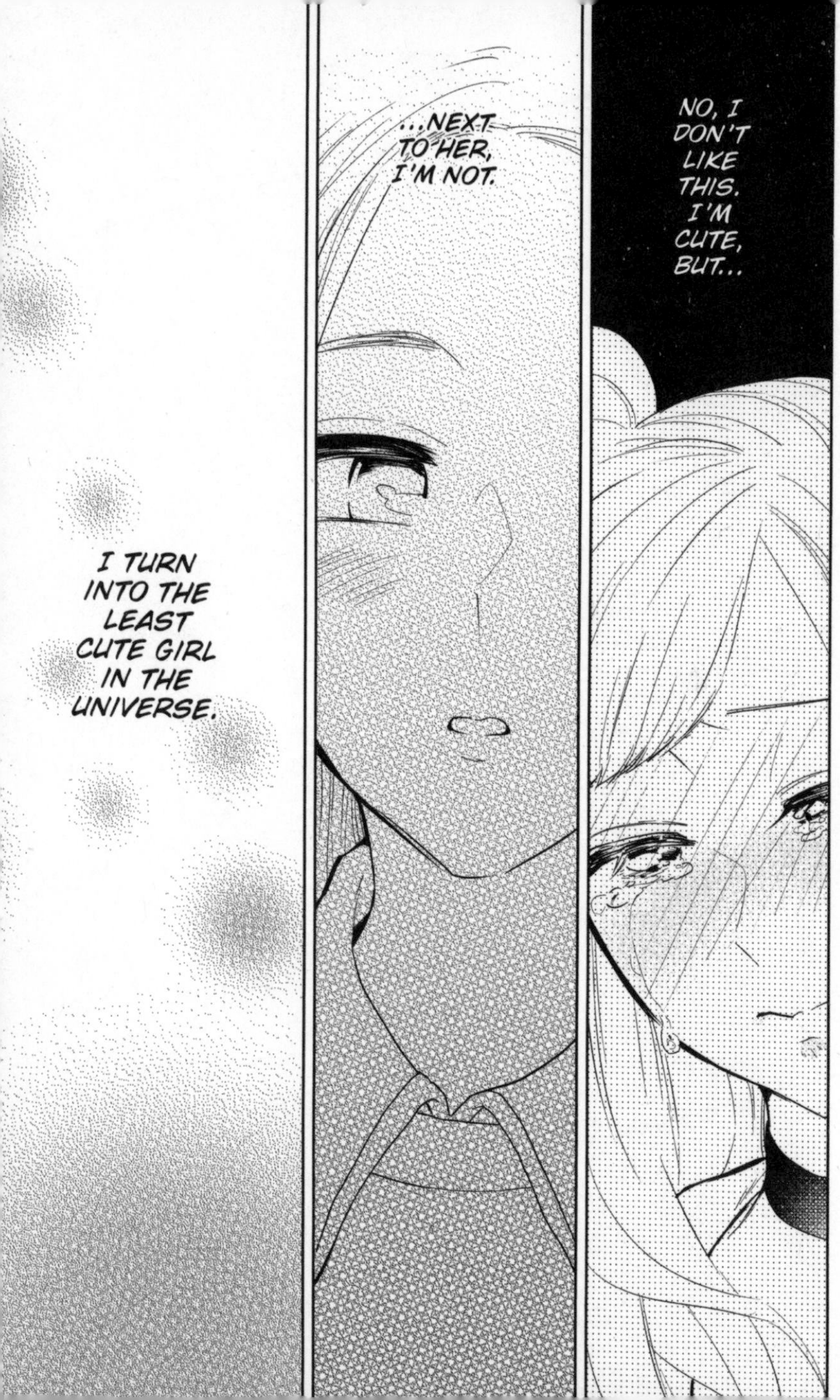
NO, I DON'T LIKE THIS. I'M CUTE, BUT...
...NEXT TO HER, I'M NOT.
I TURN INTO THE LEAST CUTE GIRL IN THE UNIVERSE.

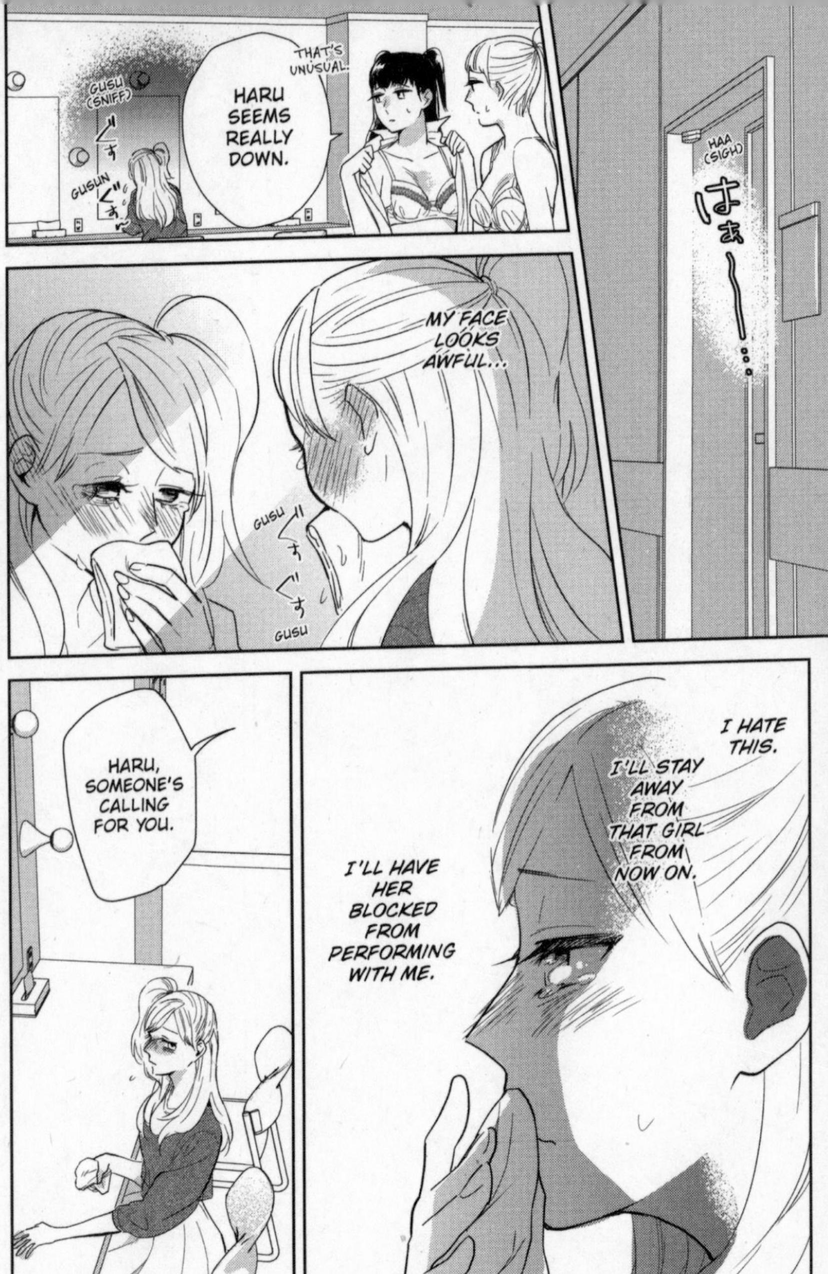
HAA (SIGH)
はぁ~...
THAT'S UNUSUAL.
HARU SEEMS REALLY DOWN.
GUSU (SNIFF)
ぐす
GUSUN
ぐすん
MY FACE LOOKS AWFUL...
GUSU
ぐす
ぐす
GUSU
I HATE THIS.
I'LL STAY AWAY FROM THAT GIRL FROM NOW ON.
I'LL HAVE HER BLOCKED FROM PERFORMING WITH ME.
HARU, SOMEONE'S CALLING FOR YOU.

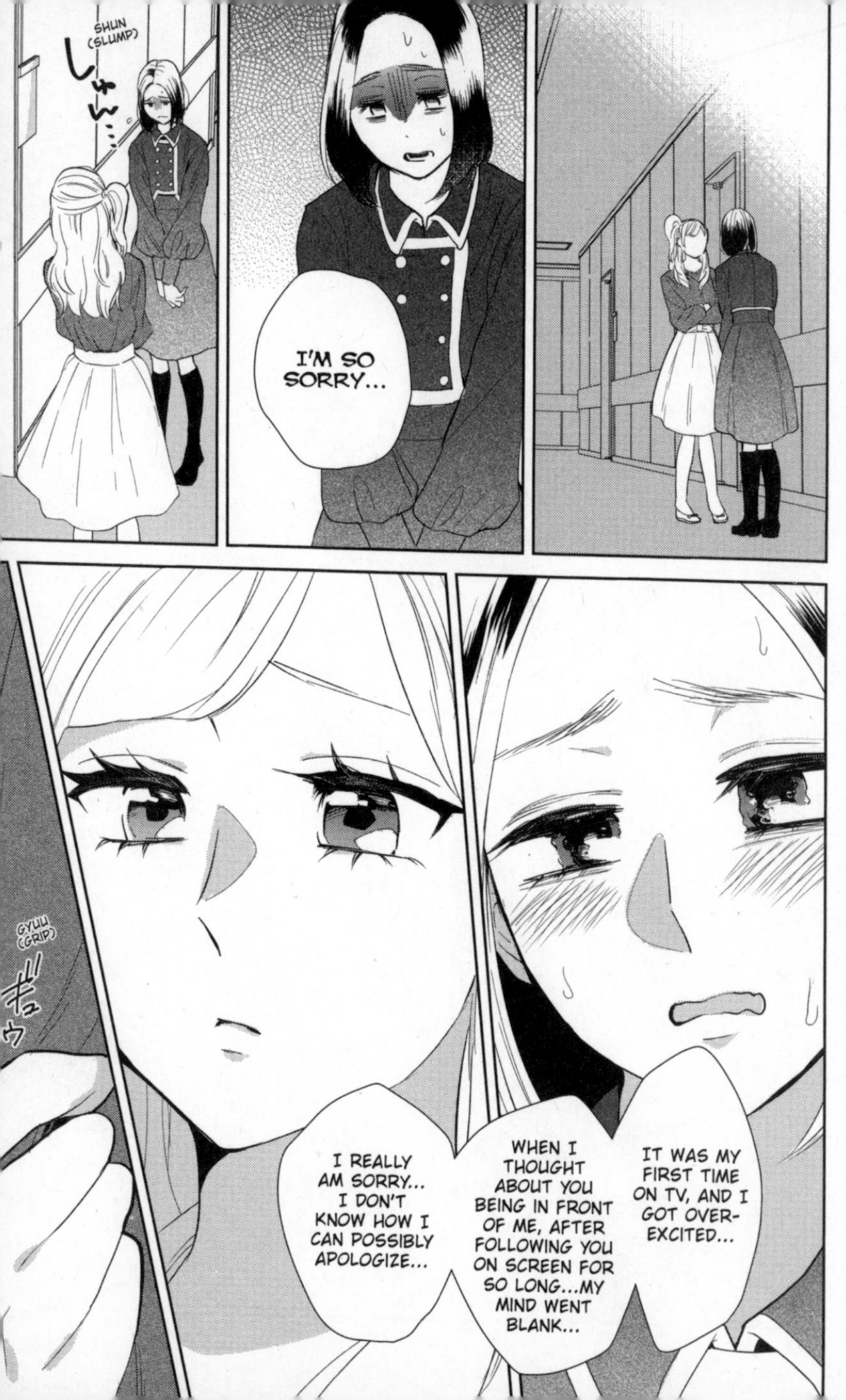
I'M SO SORRY...
SHUN (SLUMP)
しゅん…
IT WAS MY FIRST TIME ON TV, AND I GOT OVER-EXCITED...
WHEN I THOUGHT ABOUT YOU BEING IN FRONT OF ME, AFTER FOLLOWING YOU ON SCREEN FOR SO LONG...MY MIND WENT BLANK...
I REALLY AM SORRY... I DON'T KNOW HOW I CAN POSSIBLY APOLOGIZE...
GYUU (GRIP)
ギュウ

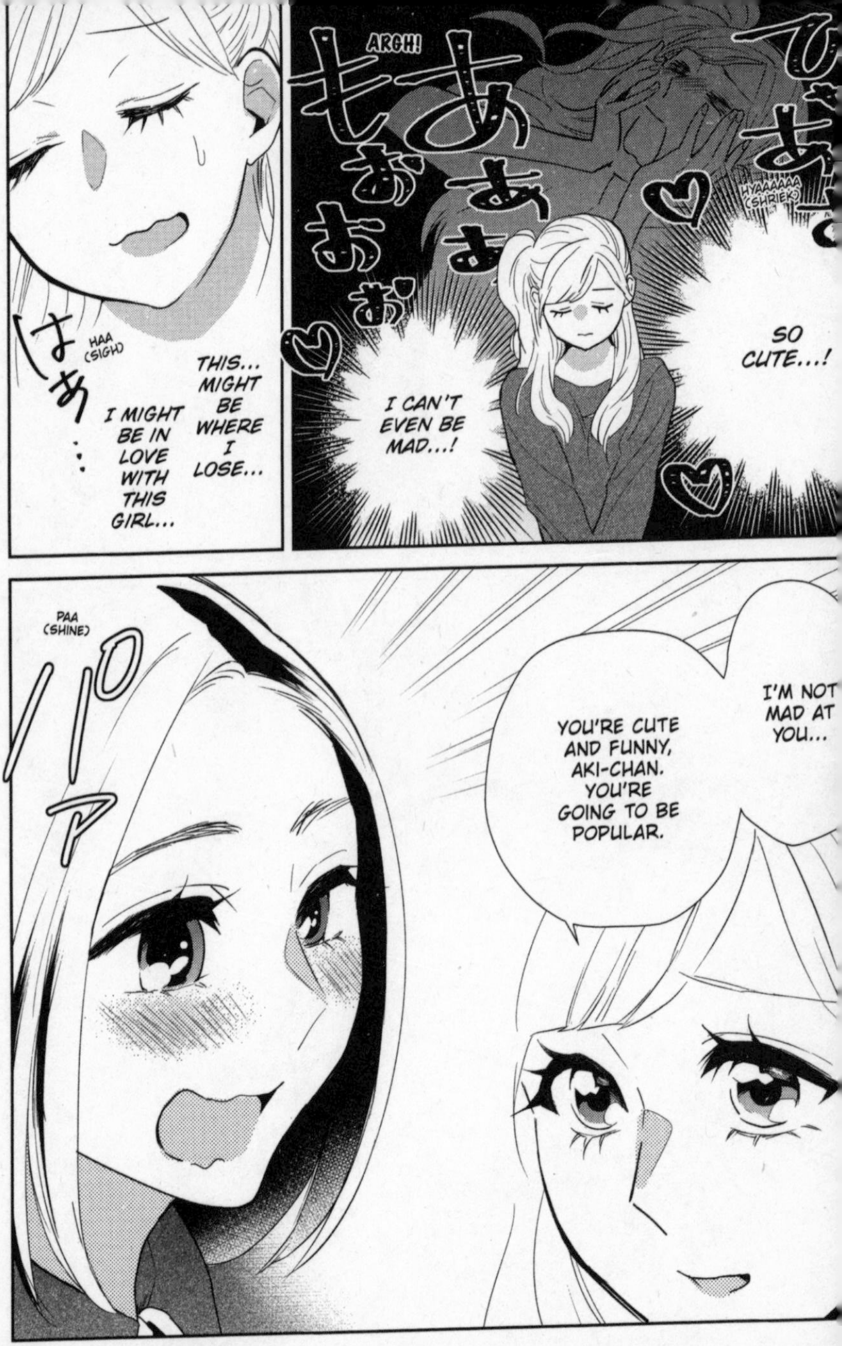
HYAAAAA (SHRIEK)
SO CUTE...!
ARGH!
I CAN'T EVEN BE MAD...!
HAA (SIGH)
THIS... MIGHT BE WHERE I LOSE...
I MIGHT BE IN LOVE WITH THIS GIRL...
I'M NOT MAD AT YOU...
YOU'RE CUTE AND FUNNY, AKI-CHAN. YOU'RE GOING TO BE POPULAR.
PAA (SHINE)

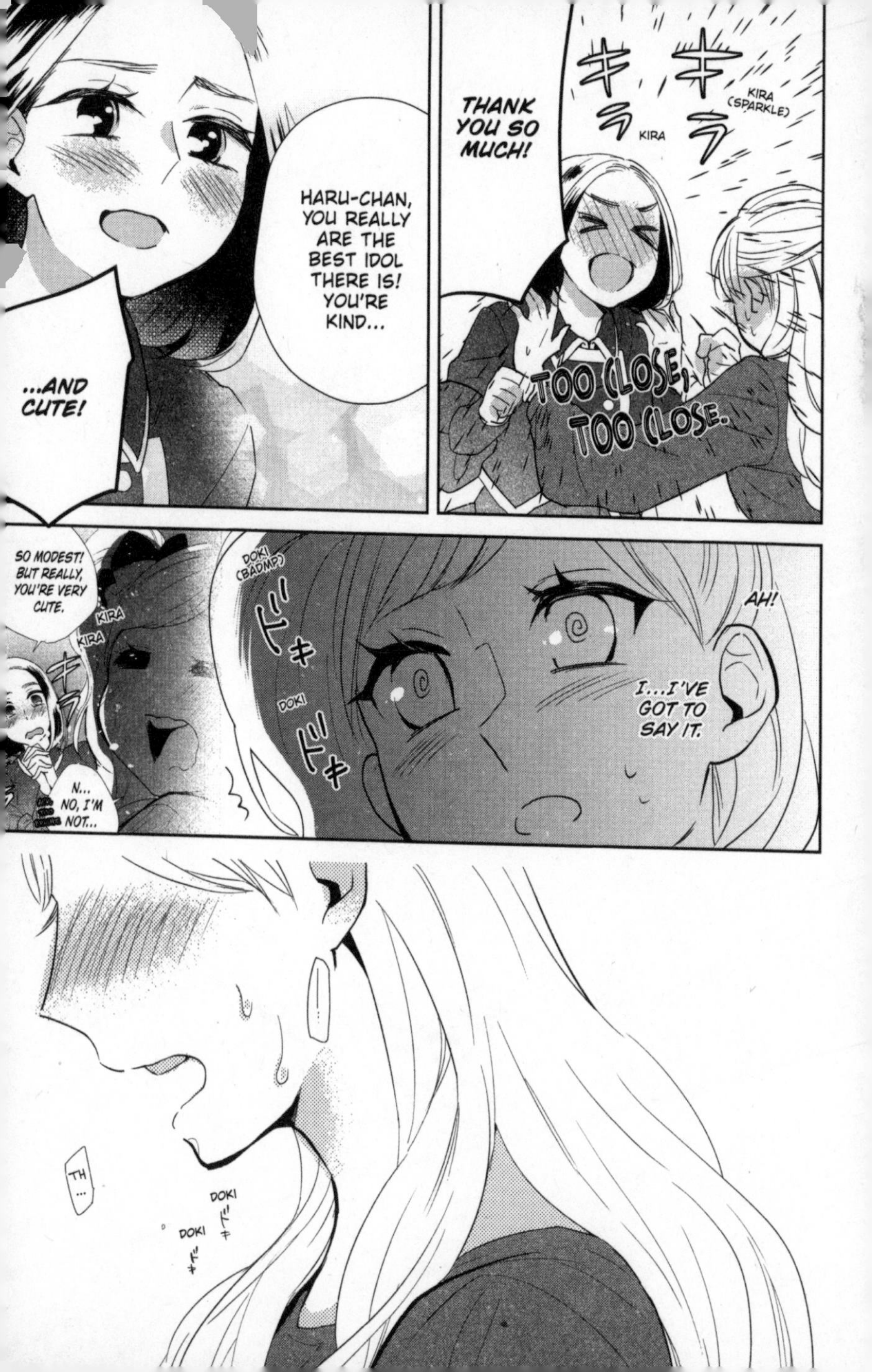
KIRA (SPARKLE)
KIRA
THANK YOU SO MUCH!
TOO CLOSE, TOO CLOSE.
HARU-CHAN, YOU REALLY ARE THE BEST IDOL THERE IS! YOU'RE KIND...
...AND CUTE!
AH!
I...I'VE GOT TO SAY IT.
DOKI (BADMP)
DOKI
SO MODEST! BUT REALLY, YOU'RE VERY CUTE.
KIRA
KIRA
N... NO, I'M NOT...
TH...
DOKI
DOKI

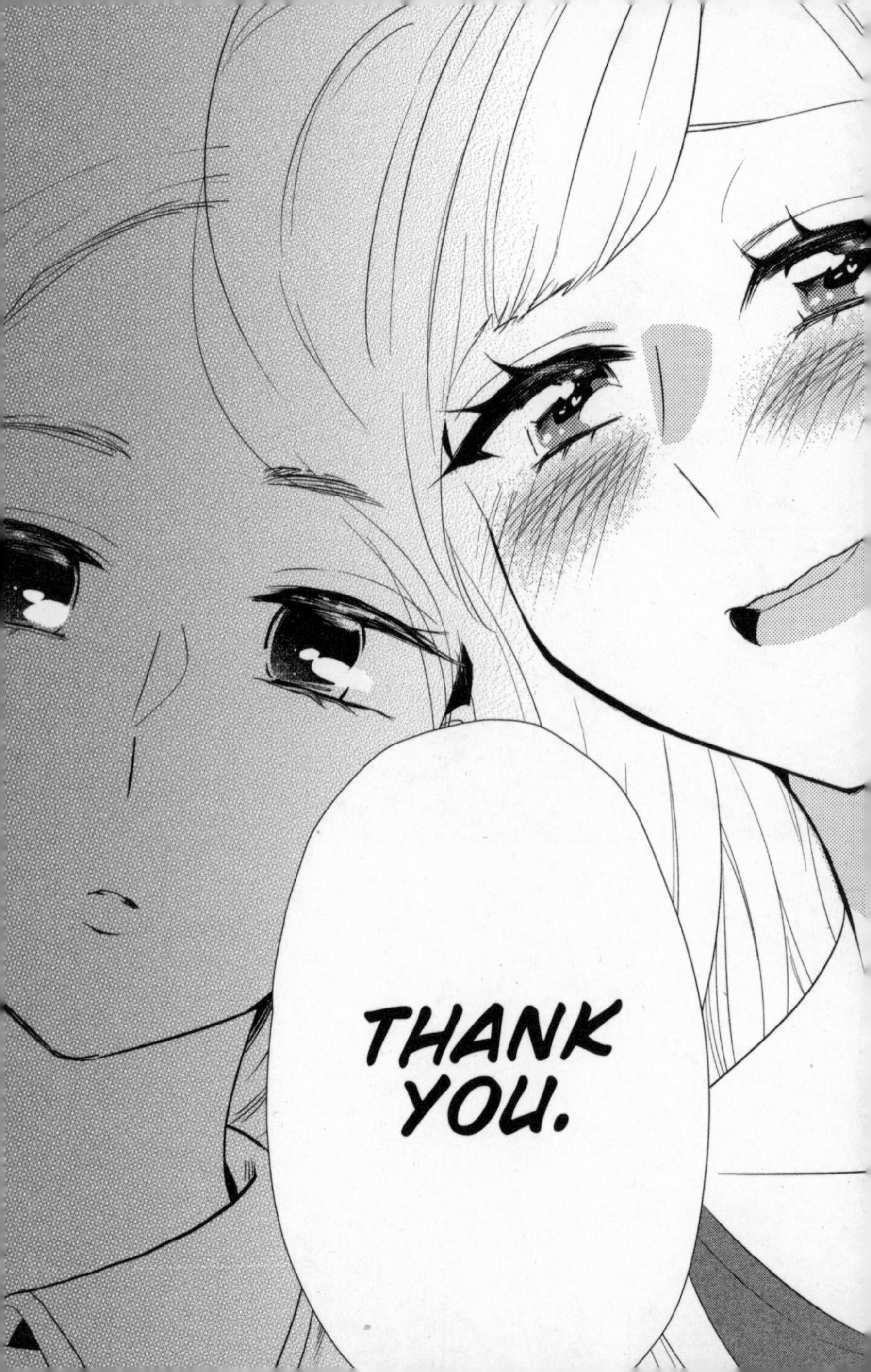
THANK YOU.

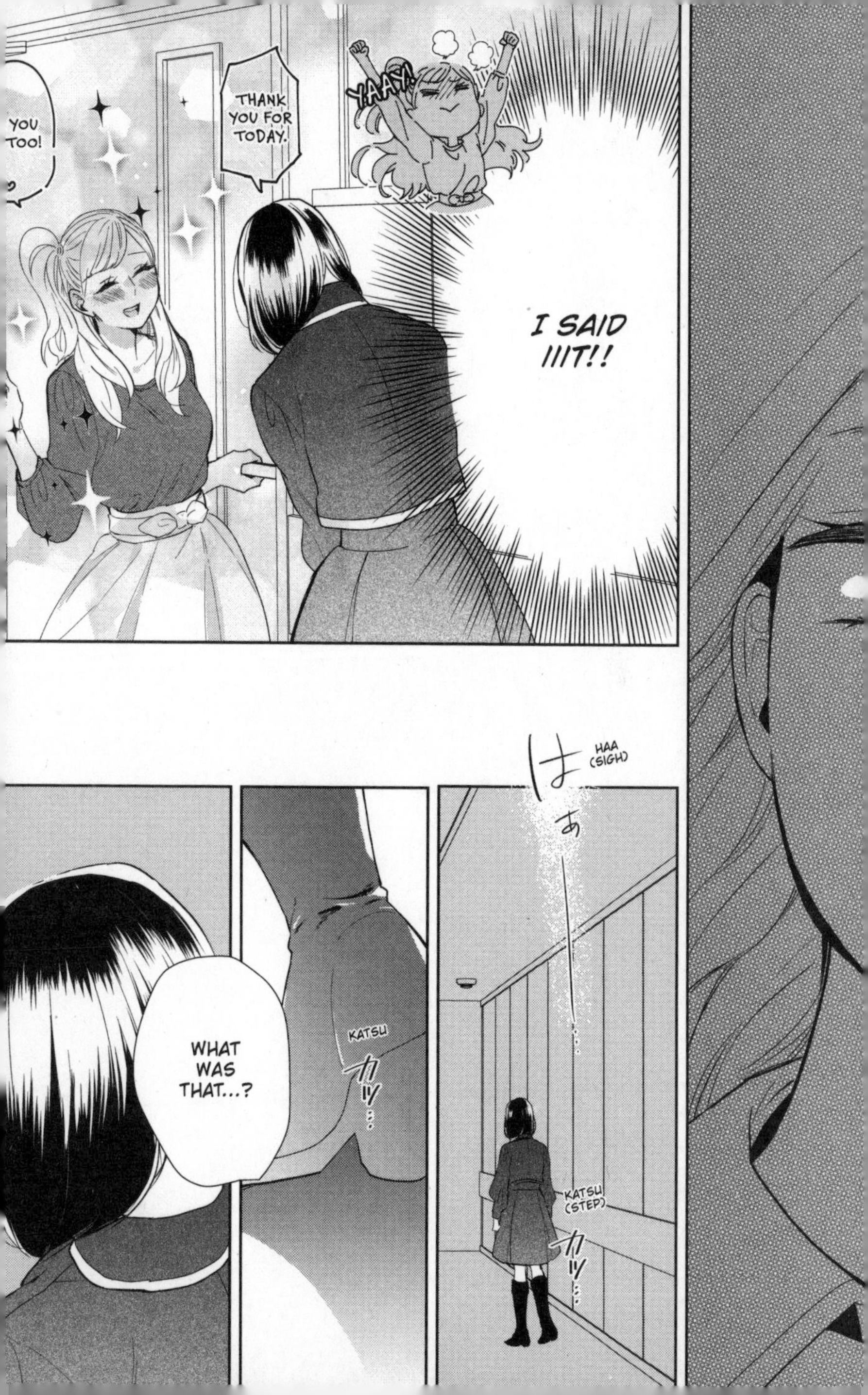
YAAAY!
THANK YOU FOR TODAY!
YOU TOO!
I SAID IIIT!!
HAA (SIGH)
はあーー…
KATSU (STEP)
カツ…
KATSU
カツ…
WHAT WAS THAT...?

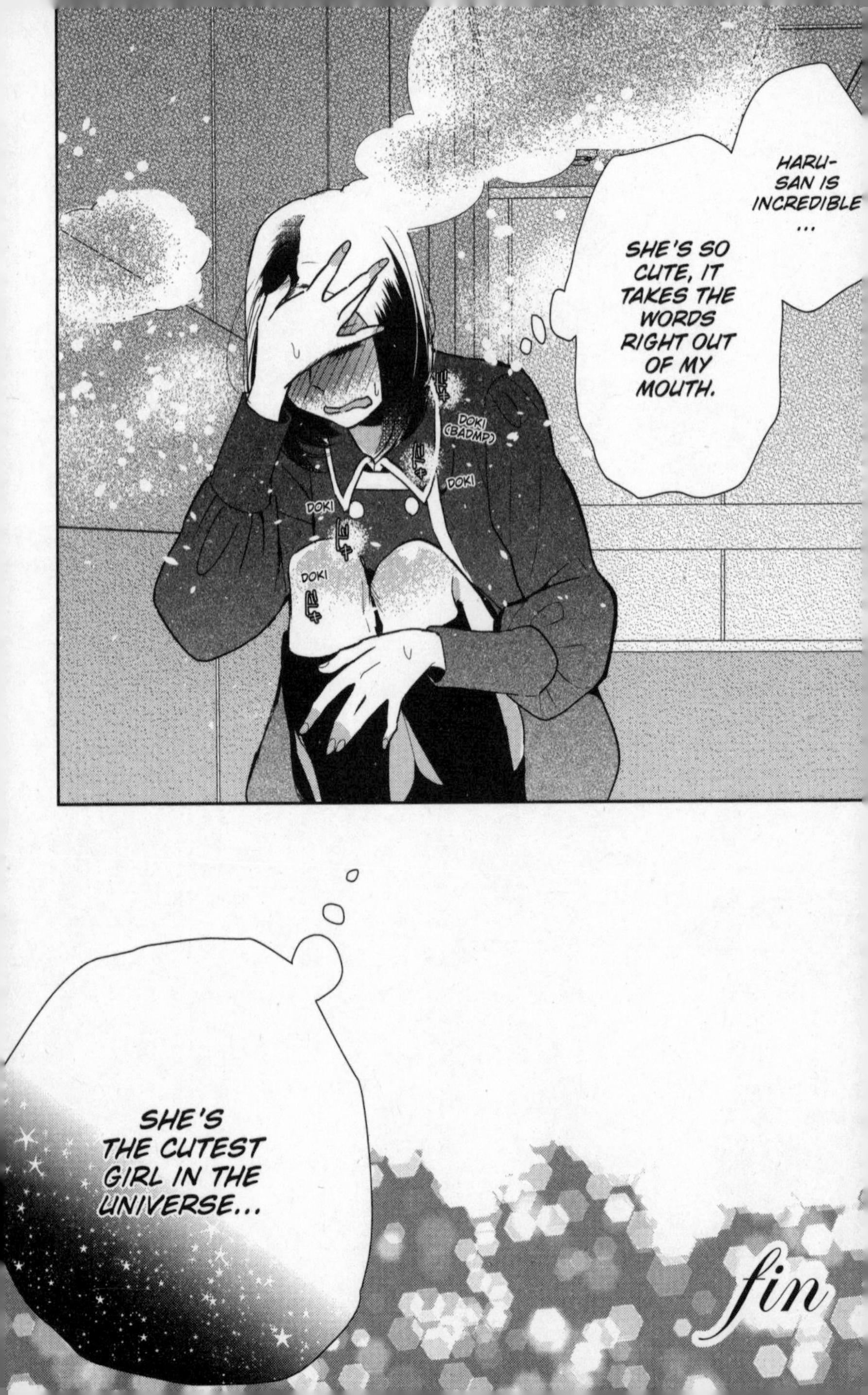
HARU-SAN IS INCREDIBLE...
SHE'S SO CUTE, IT TAKES THE WORDS RIGHT OUT OF MY MOUTH.
DOKI (BADMP)
DOKI
DOKI
DOKI
SHE'S THE CUTEST GIRL IN THE UNIVERSE...
fin

éclair
blanche

A Girls' Love Anthology
That Resonates in Your Heart

【 Graduation Piercing 】

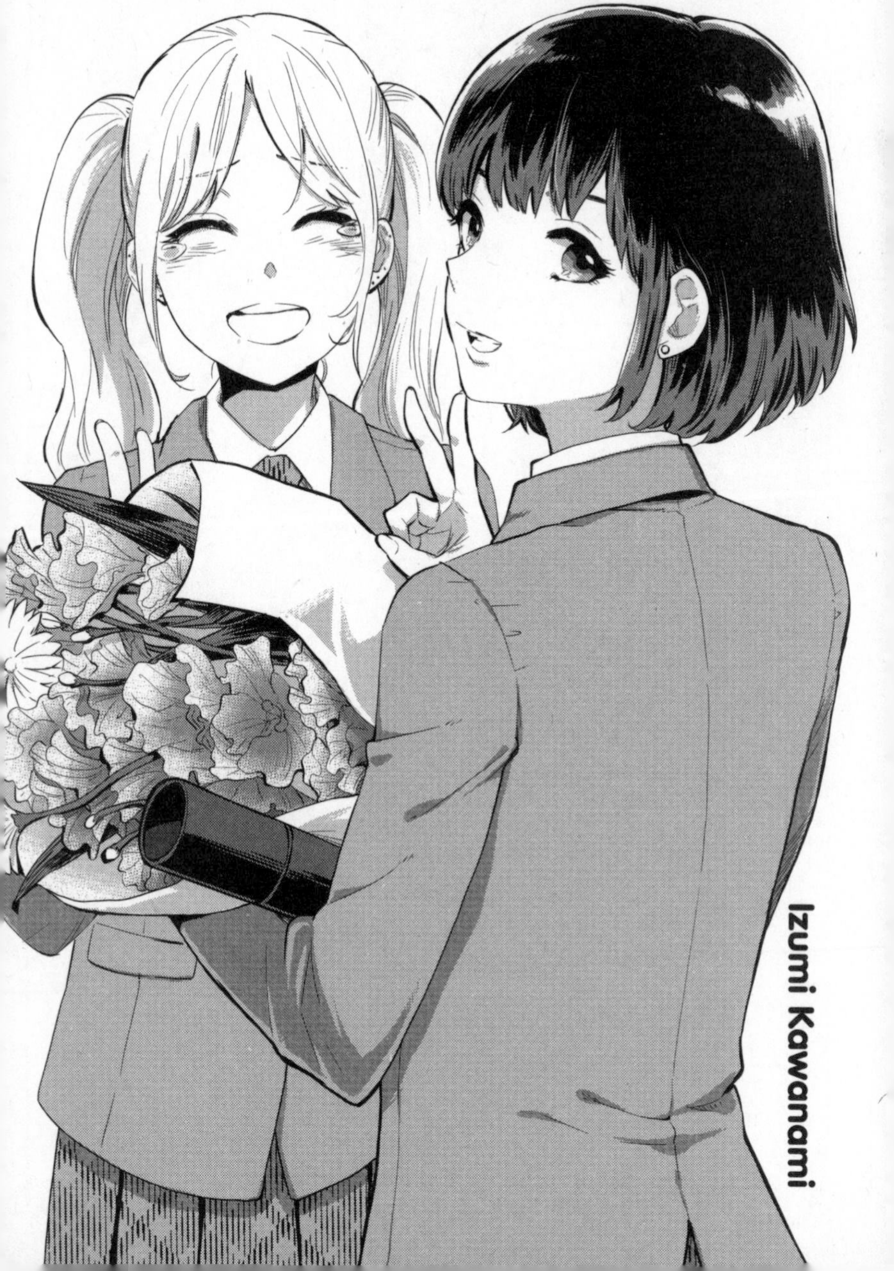
Izumi Kawanami

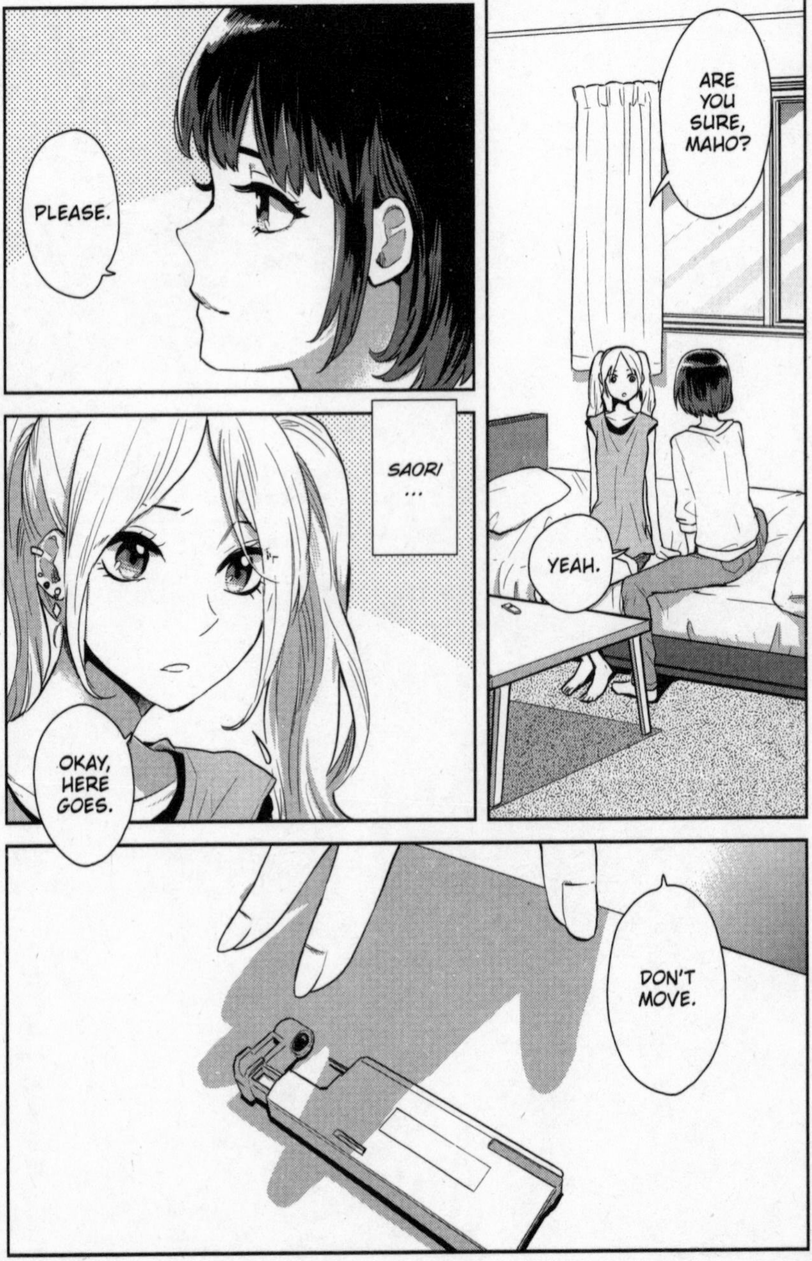

ARE YOU SURE, MAHO?
YEAH.
PLEASE.
SAORI ...
OKAY, HERE GOES.
DON'T MOVE.

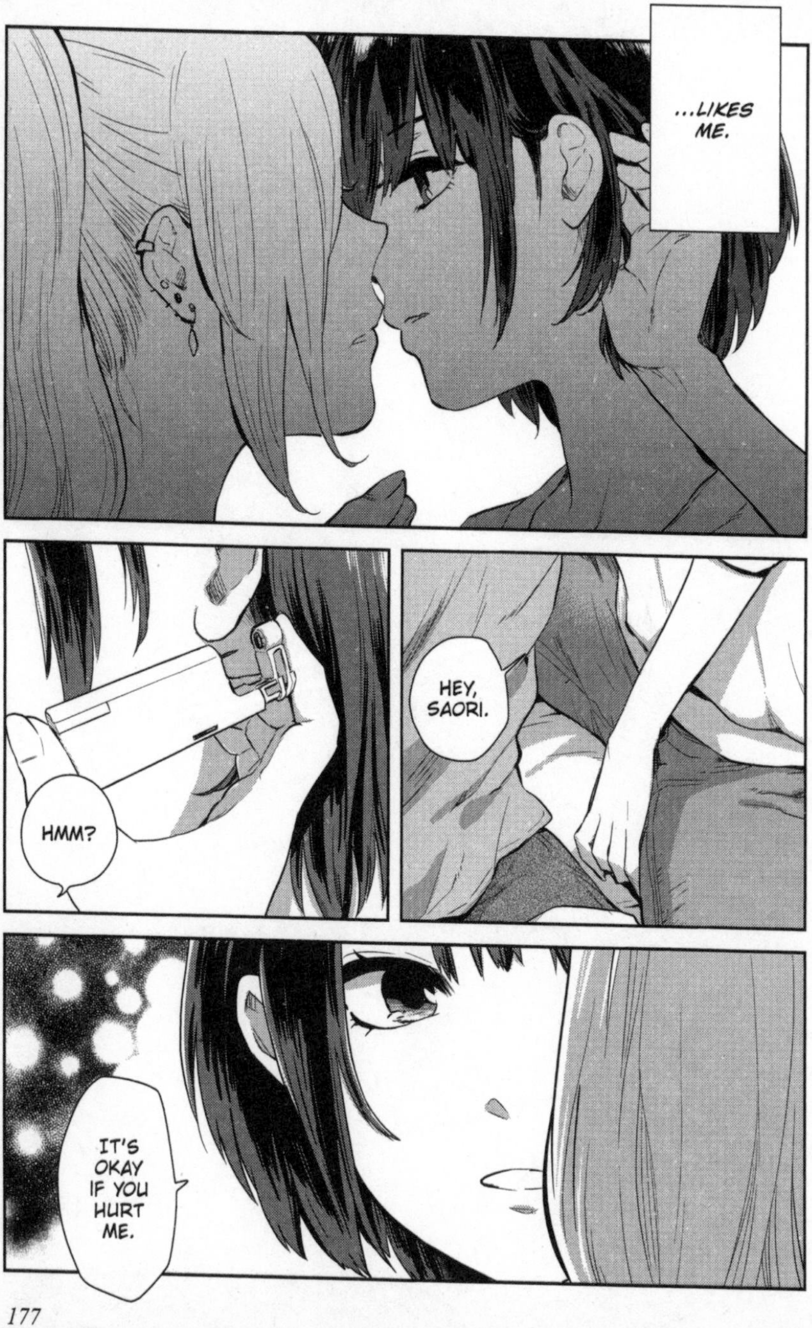
...LIKES ME.
HEY, SAORI.
HMM?
IT'S OKAY IF YOU HURT ME.

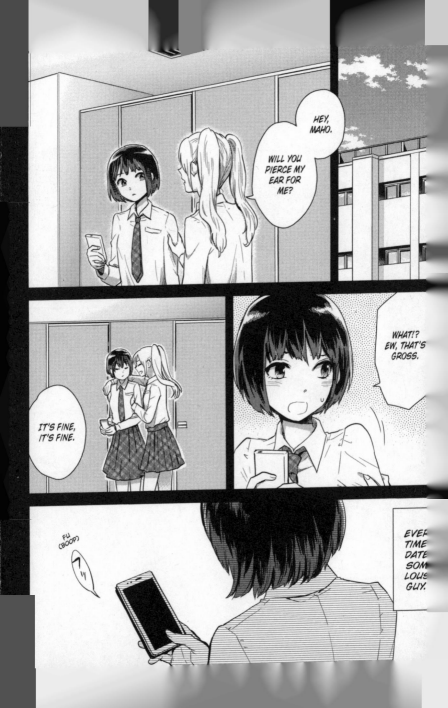

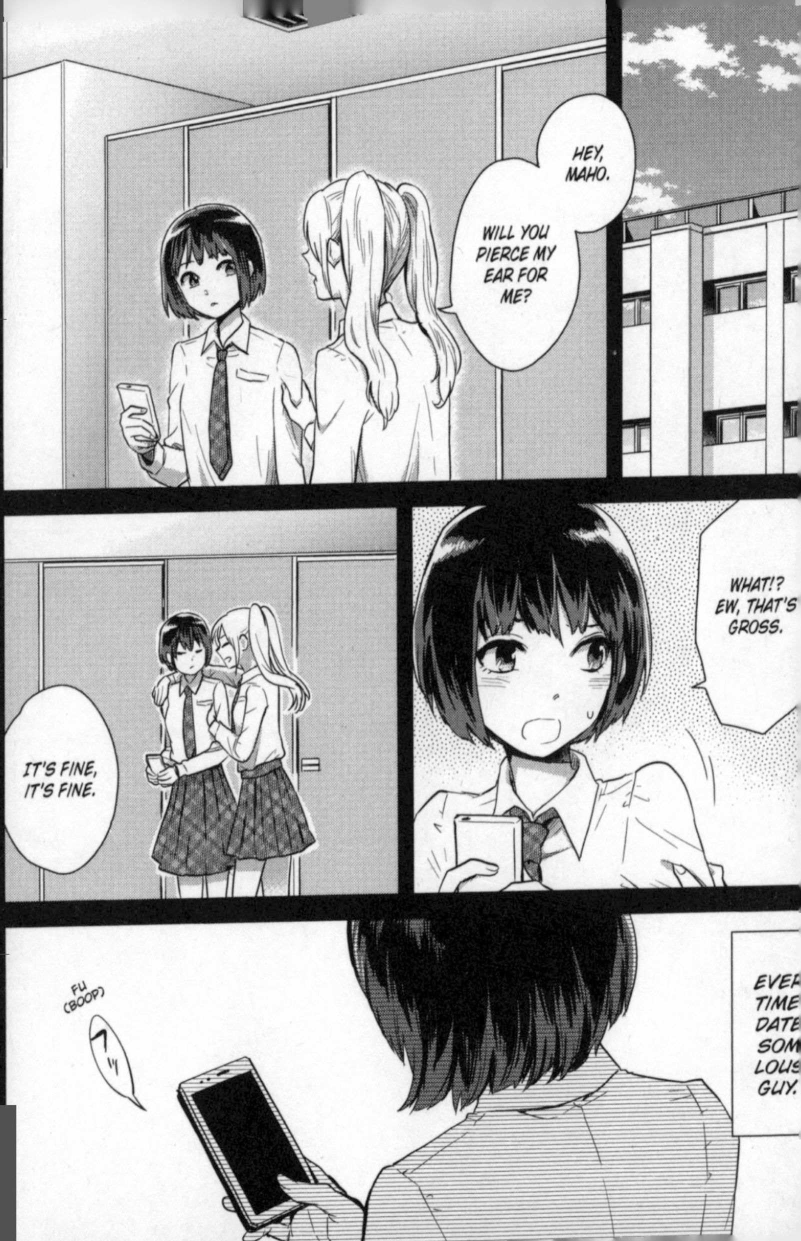
HEY, MAHO.
WILL YOU PIERCE MY EAR FOR ME?
WHAT!? EW, THAT'S GROSS.
IT'S FINE, IT'S FINE.
EVER TIME DATE SOM LOUS GUY.
FU (BOOP)
フッ

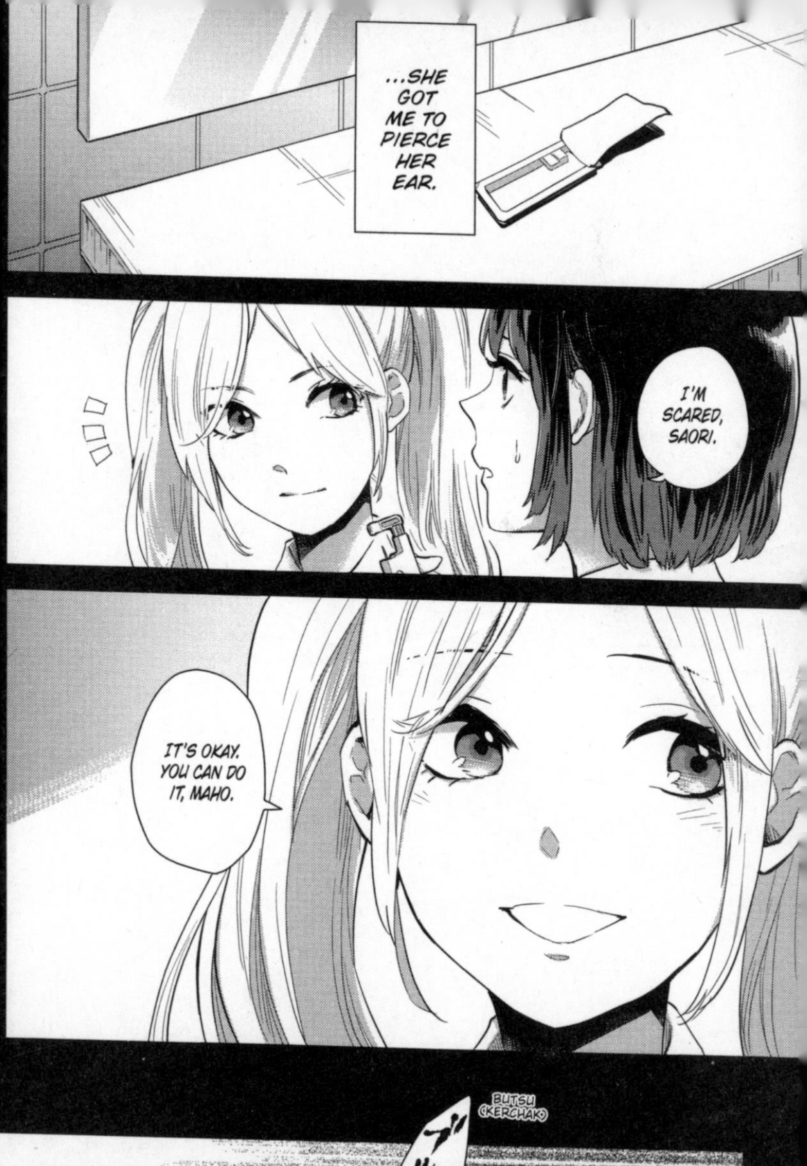
...SHE GOT ME TO PIERCE HER EAR.
I'M SCARED, SAORI.
IT'S OKAY. YOU CAN DO IT, MAHO.
BUTSU (KERCHAK)

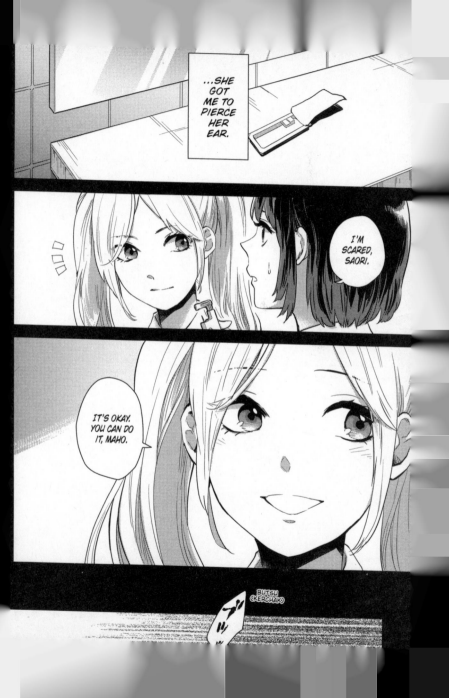

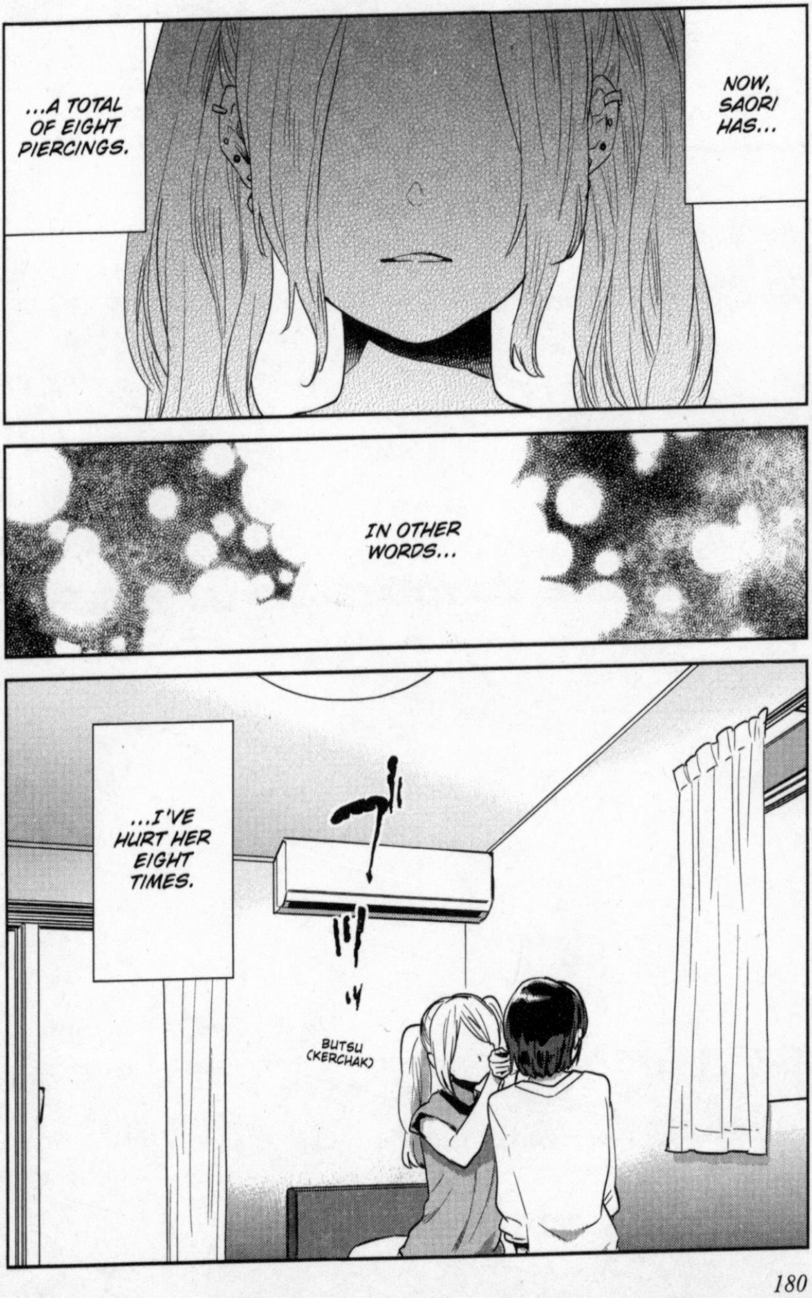
NOW, SAORI HAS...
...A TOTAL OF EIGHT PIERCINGS.
IN OTHER WORDS...
...I'VE HURT HER EIGHT TIMES.
BUTSU (KERCHAK)

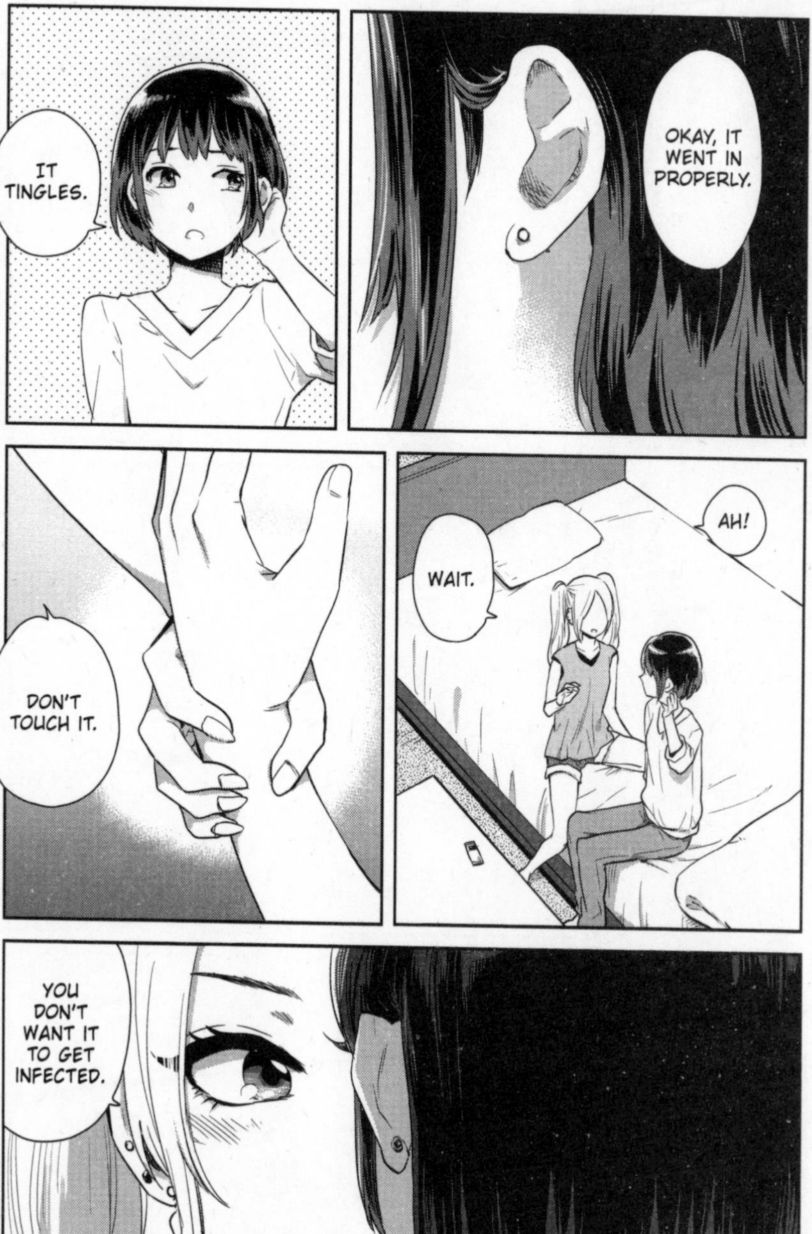
OKAY, IT WENT IN PROPERLY.
IT TINGLES.
AH!
WAIT.
DON'T TOUCH IT.
YOU DON'T WANT IT TO GET INFECTED.

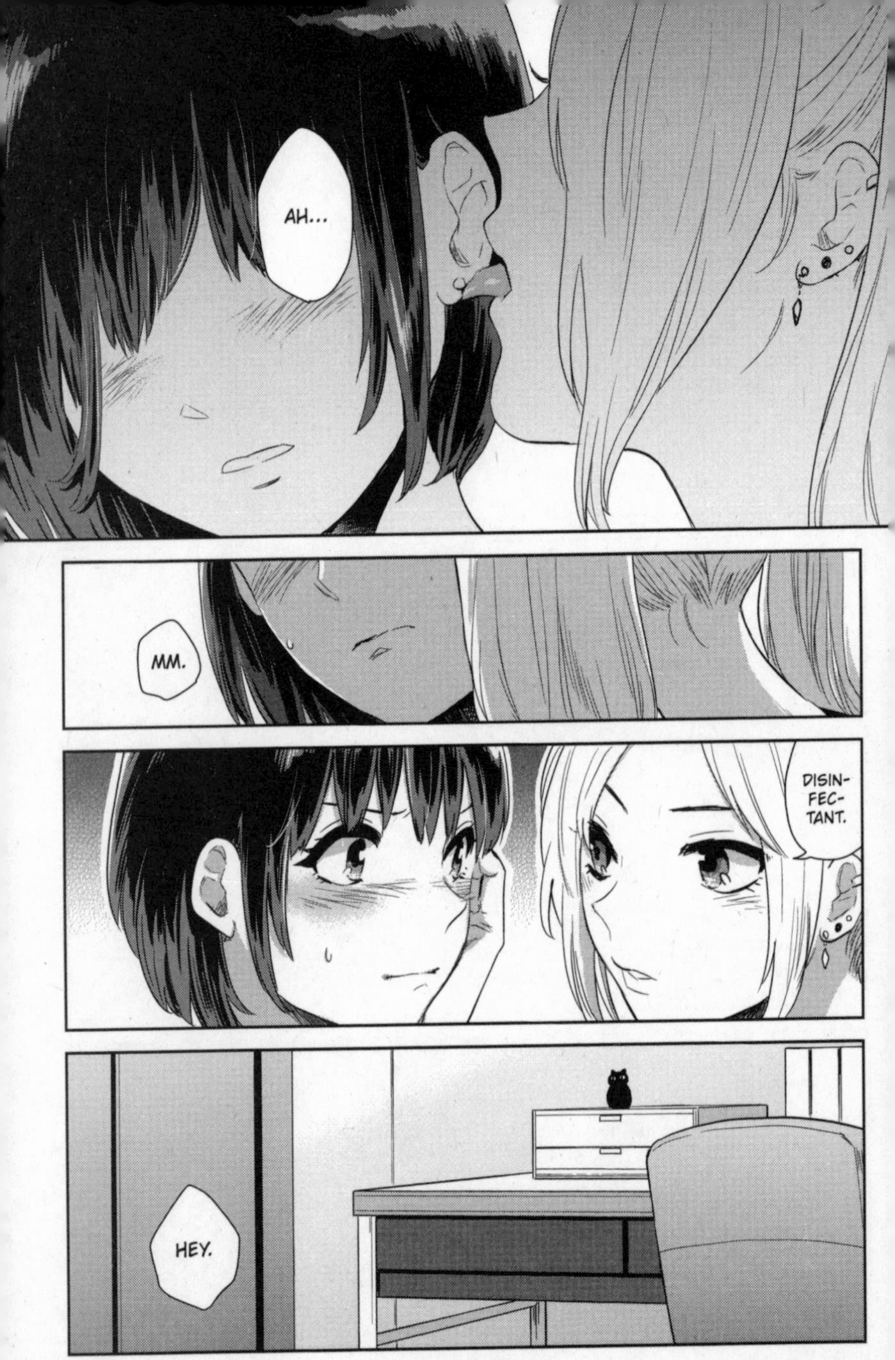
AH...
MM.
DISIN-
FEC-
TANT.
HEY.

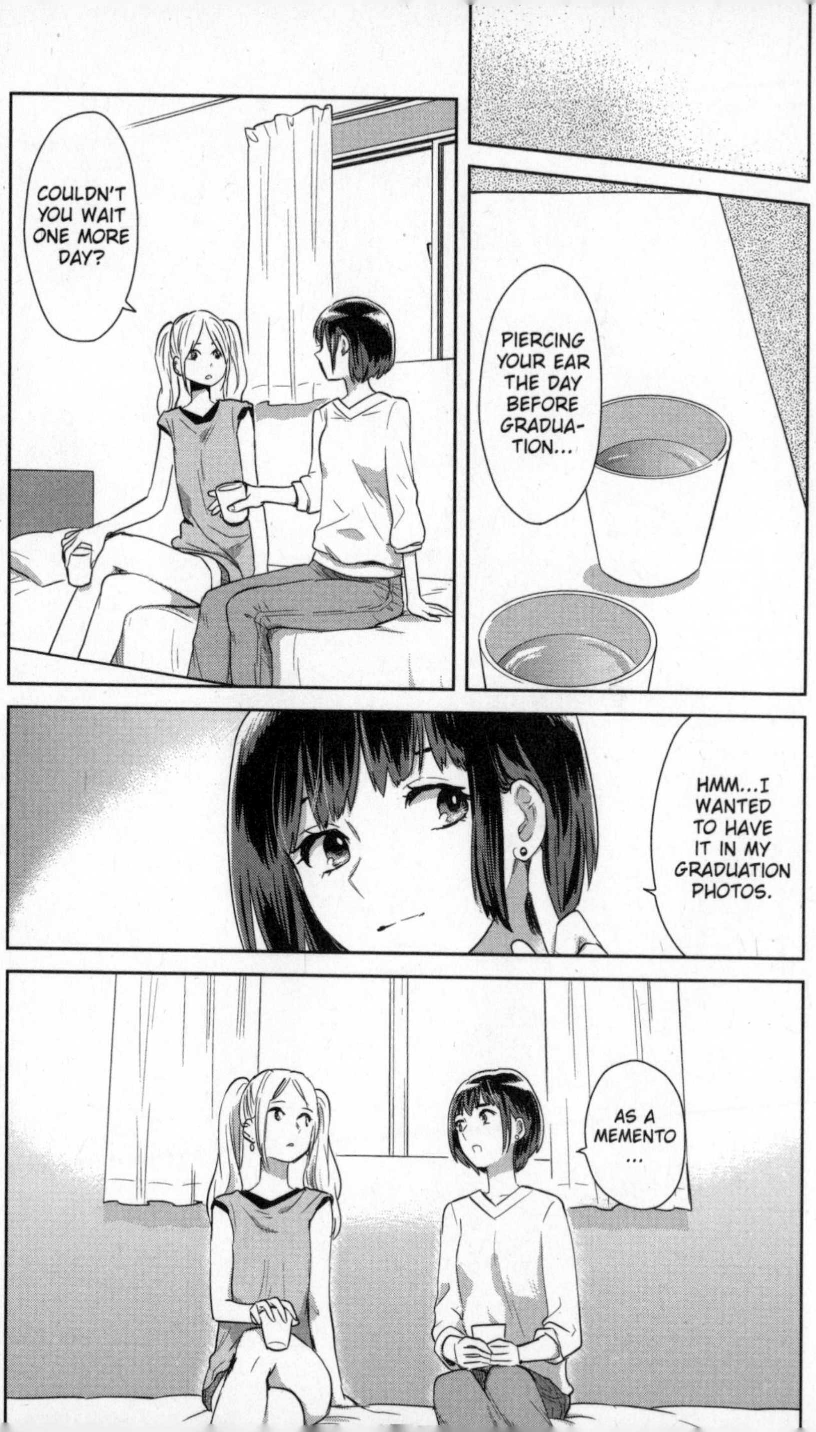
PIERCING YOUR EAR THE DAY BEFORE GRADUATION...
COULDN'T YOU WAIT ONE MORE DAY?
HMM...I WANTED TO HAVE IT IN MY GRADUATION PHOTOS.
AS A MEMENTO...

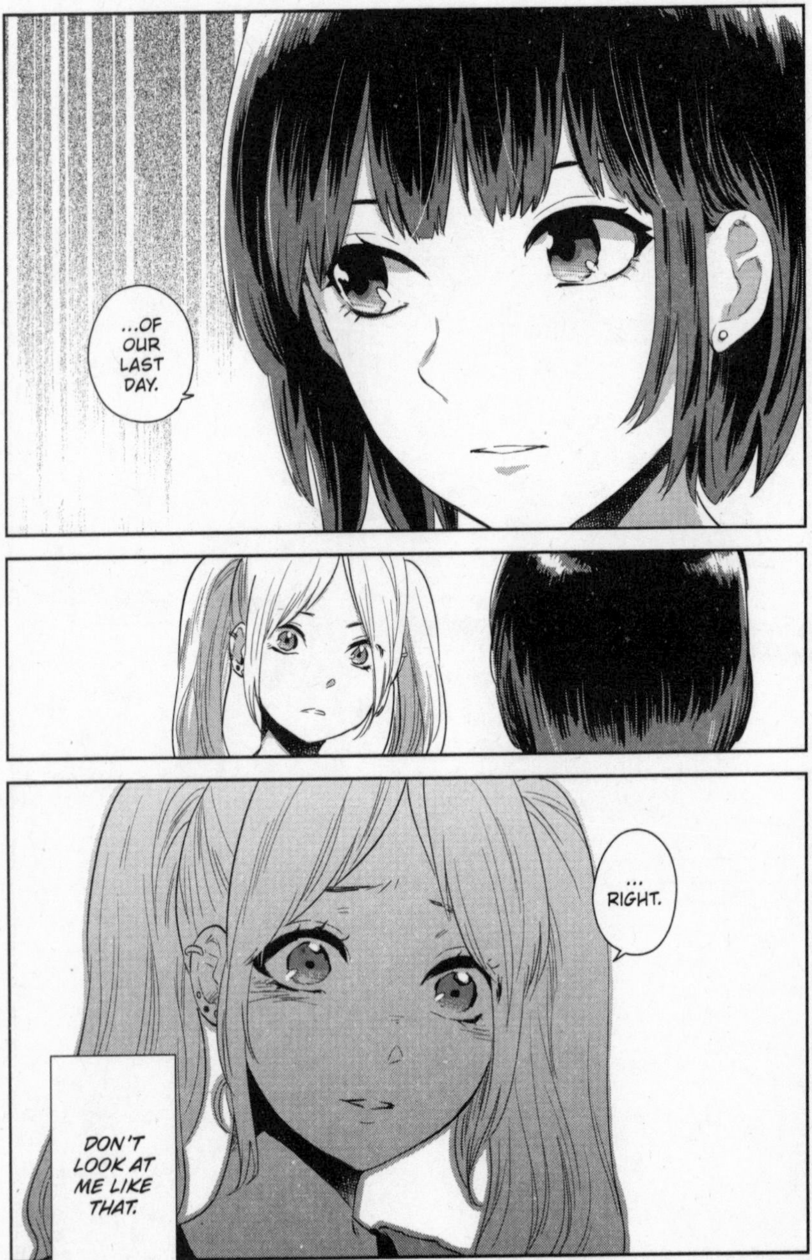
...OF OUR LAST DAY.
...RIGHT.
DON'T LOOK AT ME LIKE THAT.

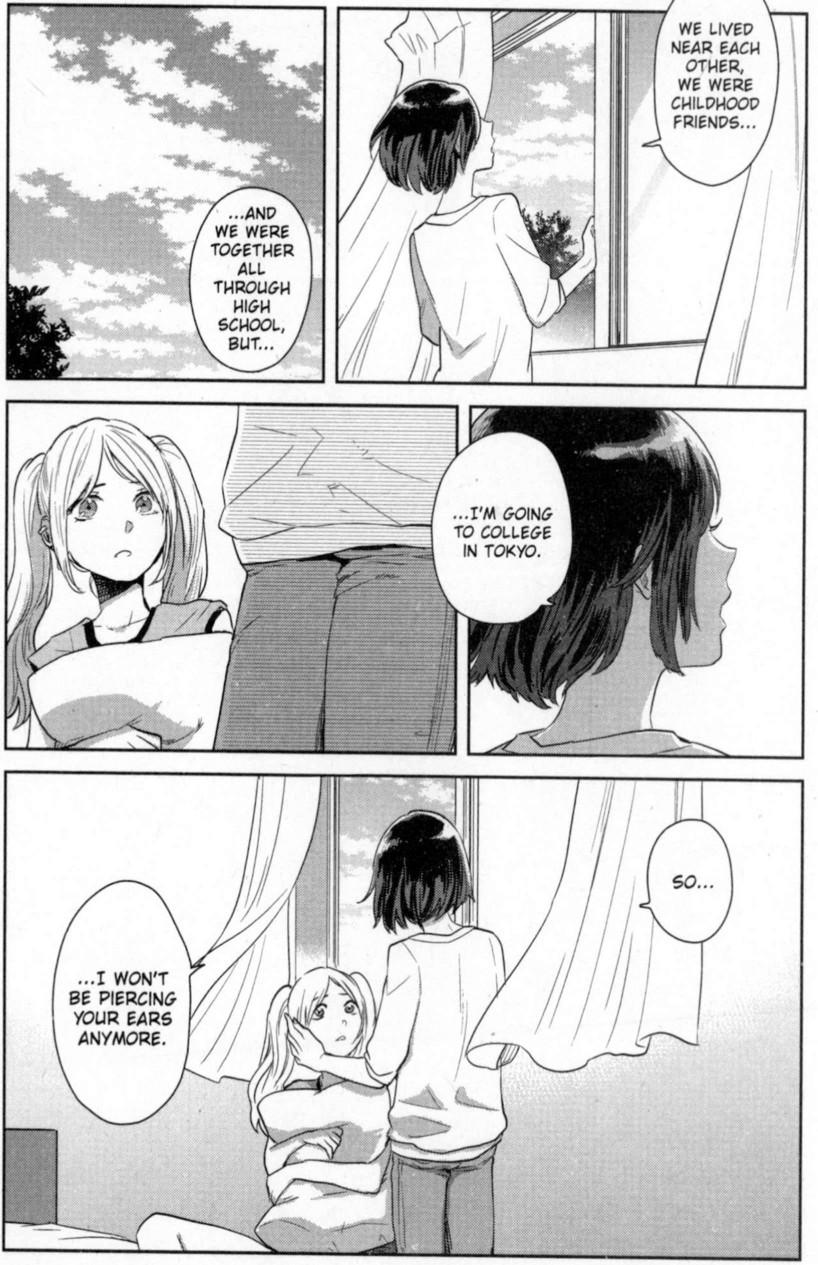
WE LIVED NEAR EACH OTHER, WE WERE CHILDHOOD FRIENDS...
...AND WE WERE TOGETHER ALL THROUGH HIGH SCHOOL, BUT...
...I'M GOING TO COLLEGE IN TOKYO.
SO...
...I WON'T BE PIERCING YOUR EARS ANYMORE.

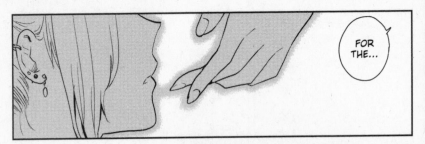

FOR THE...

...FIRST TIME...

...I FOUND SOMEONE I REALLY LIKE.

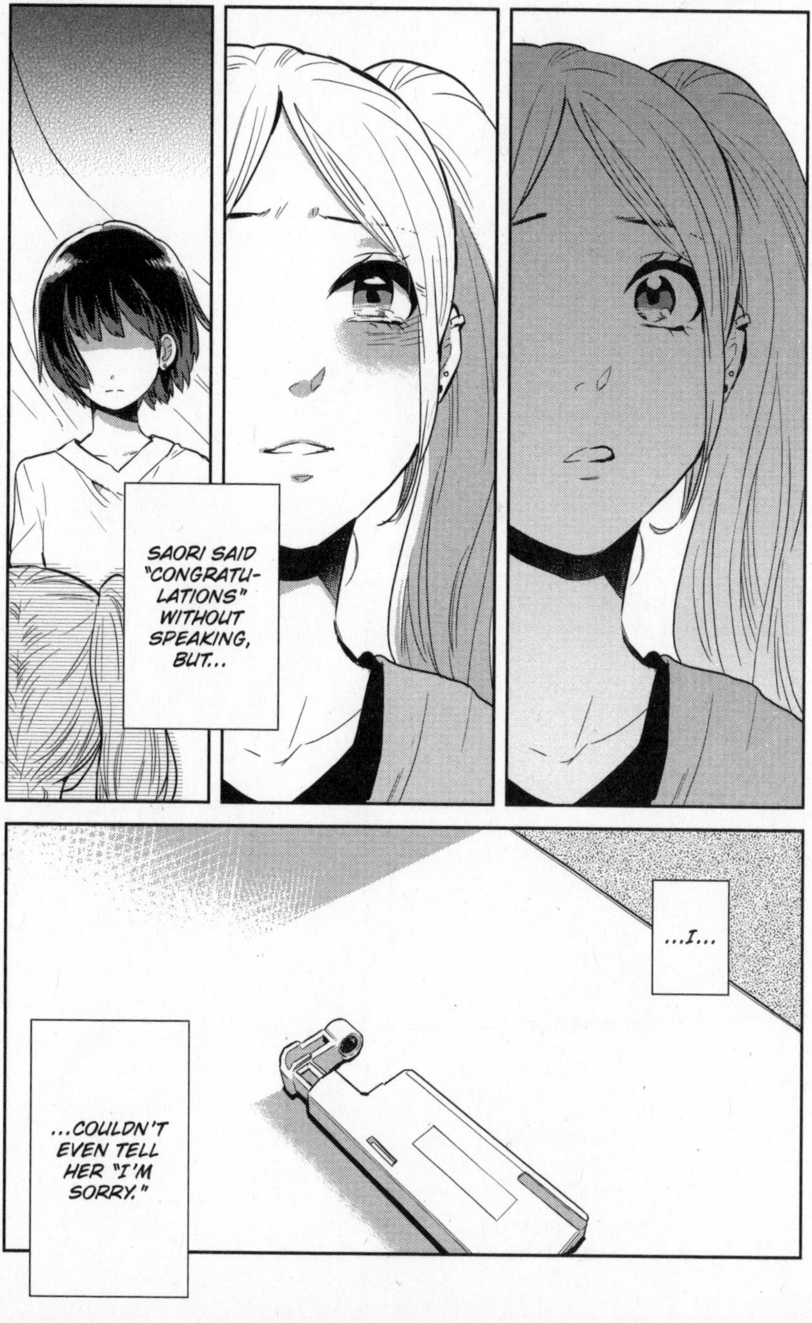
SAORI SAID "CONGRATU-LATIONS" WITHOUT SPEAKING, BUT...
...I...
...COULDN'T EVEN TELL HER "I'M SORRY."

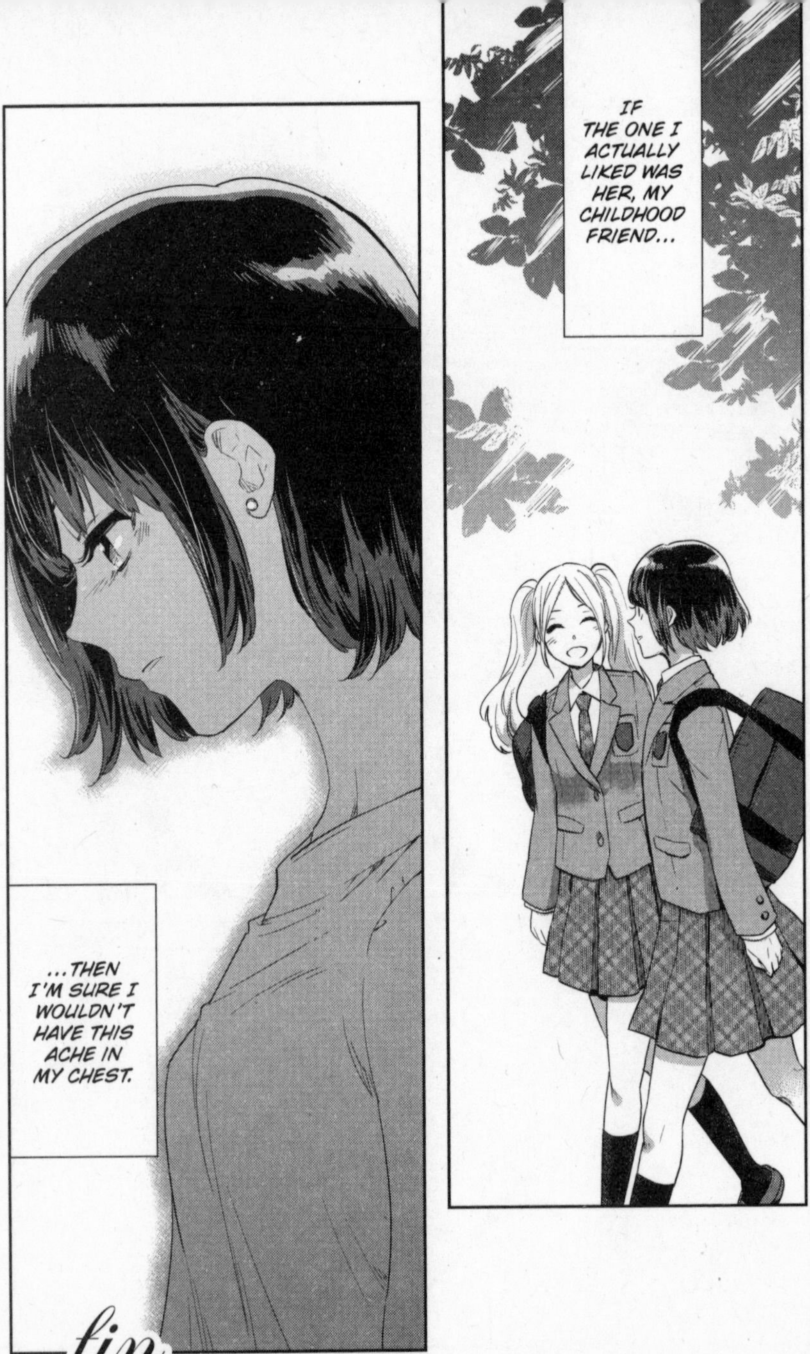
IF THE ONE I ACTUALLY LIKED WAS HER, MY CHILDHOOD FRIEND...
...THEN I'M SURE I WOULDN'T HAVE THIS ACHE IN MY CHEST.
fin

éclair
blanche

A Girls' Love Anthology
That Resonates in Your Heart

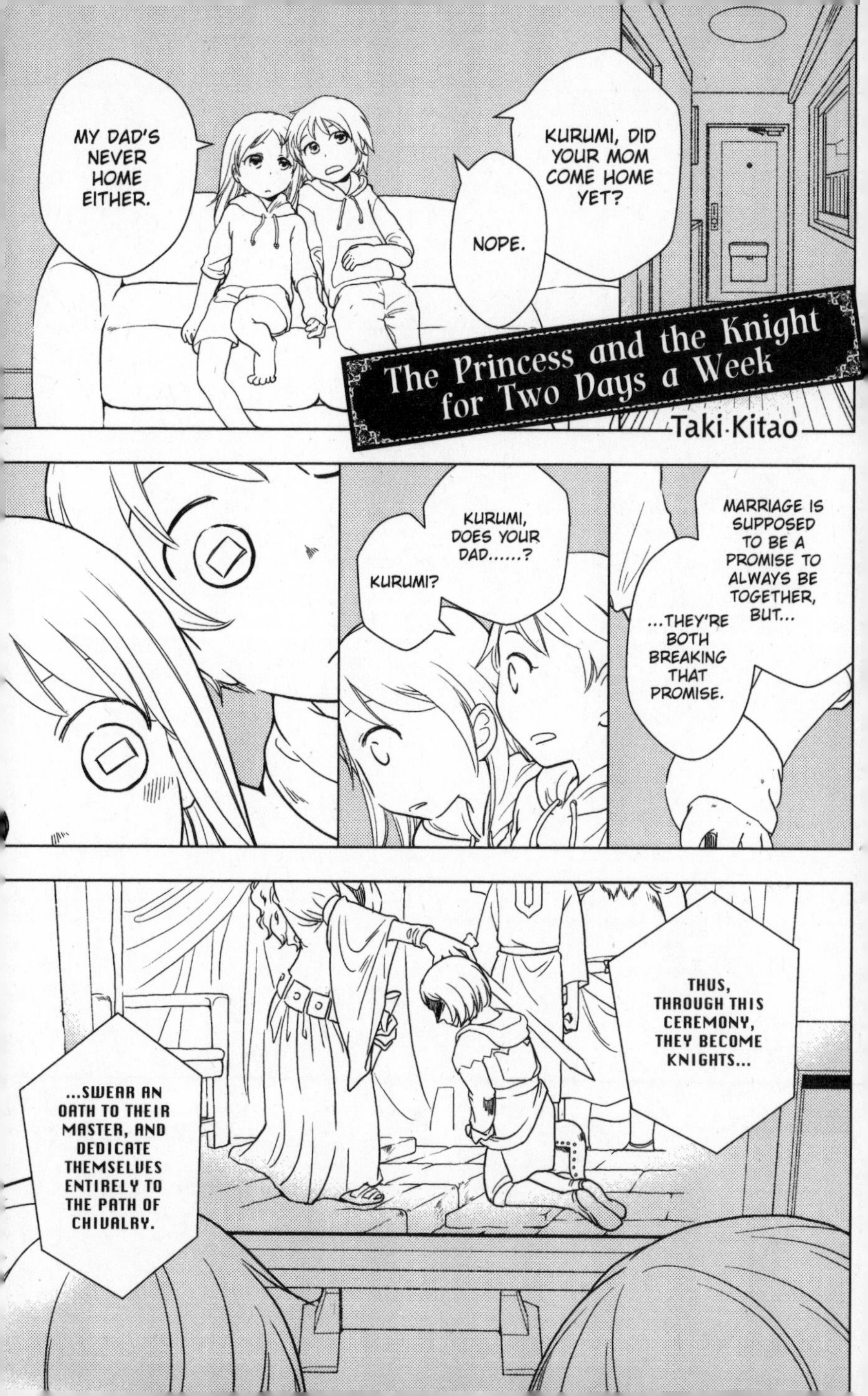
KURUMI, DID YOUR MOM COME HOME YET?
NOPE.
MY DAD'S NEVER HOME EITHER.
The Princess and the Knight for Two Days a Week
Taki Kitao
MARRIAGE IS SUPPOSED TO BE A PROMISE TO ALWAYS BE TOGETHER, BUT...
...THEY'RE BOTH BREAKING THAT PROMISE.
KURUMI, DOES YOUR DAD......?
KURUMI?
THUS, THROUGH THIS CEREMONY, THEY BECOME KNIGHTS...
...SWEAR AN OATH TO THEIR MASTER, AND DEDICATE THEMSELVES ENTIRELY TO THE PATH OF CHIVALRY.

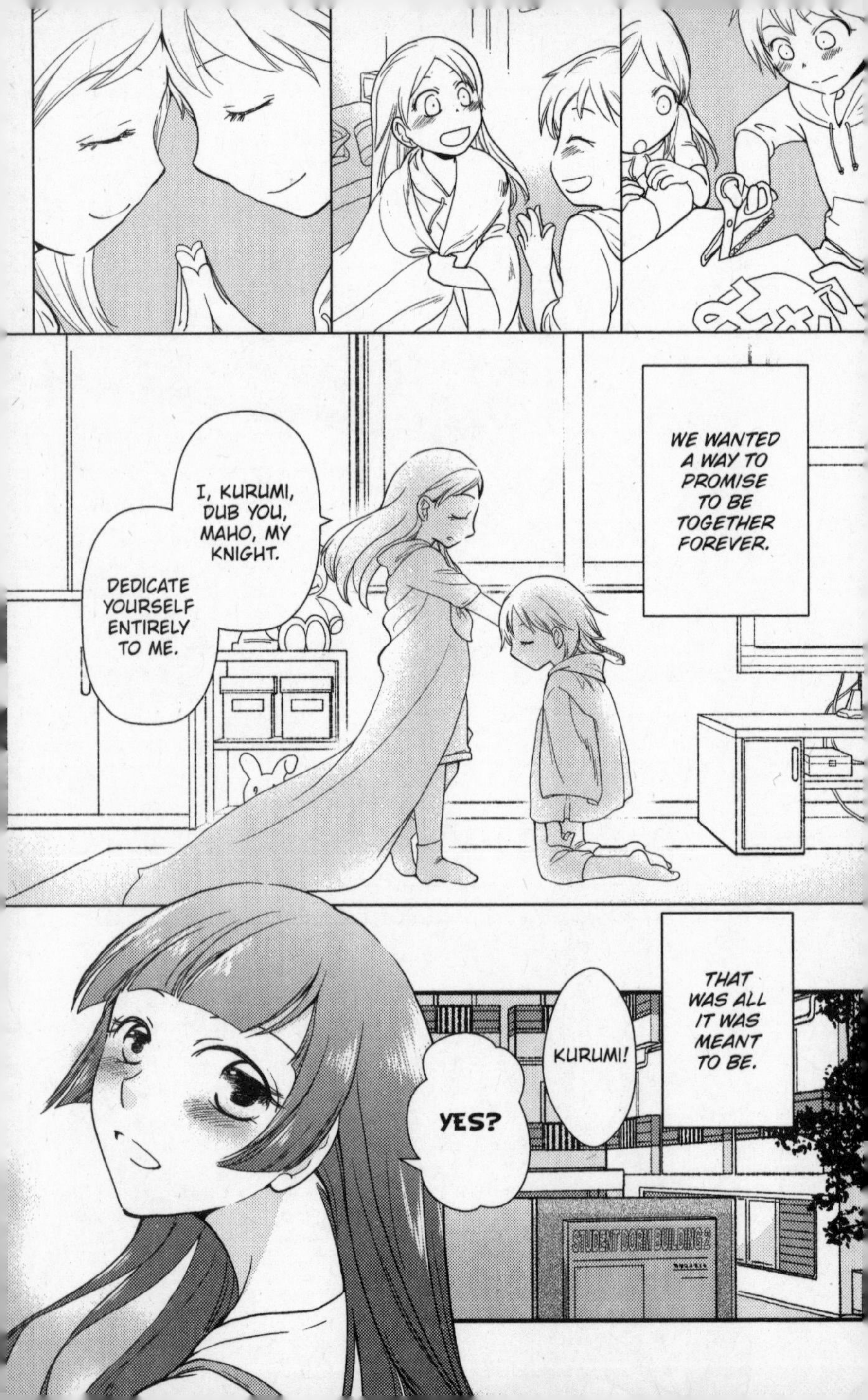
WE WANTED A WAY TO PROMISE TO BE TOGETHER FOREVER.
I, KURUMI, DUB YOU, MAHO, MY KNIGHT.
DEDICATE YOURSELF ENTIRELY TO ME.
THAT WAS ALL IT WAS MEANT TO BE.
KURUMI!
YES?
STUDENT DORM BUILDING 2

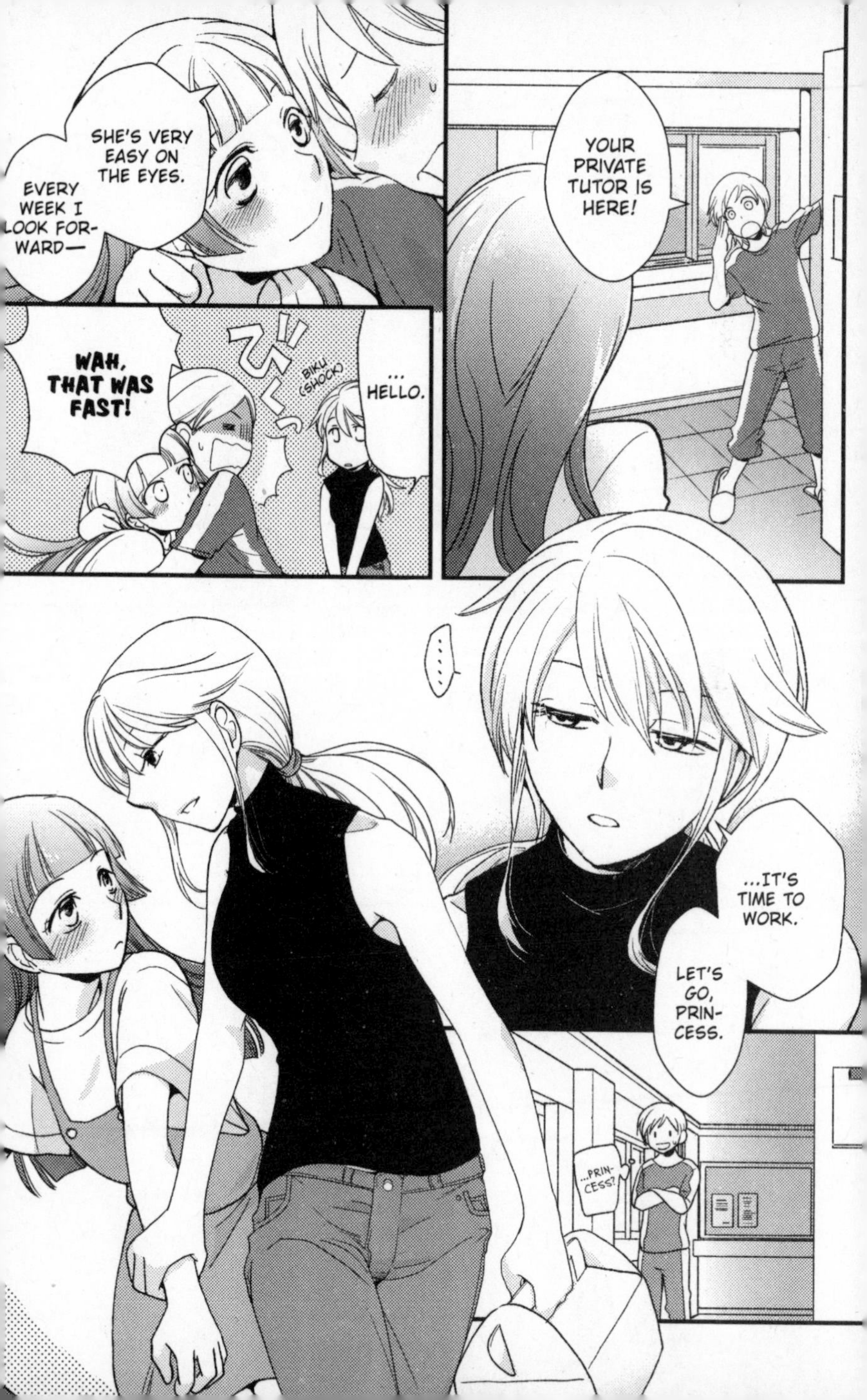
YOUR PRIVATE TUTOR IS HERE!
SHE'S VERY EASY ON THE EYES.
EVERY WEEK I LOOK FOR-WARD—
...HELLO.
BIKU (SHOCK)
WAH, THAT WAS FAST!
......
...IT'S TIME TO WORK.
LET'S GO, PRIN-CESS.
...PRIN-CESS?

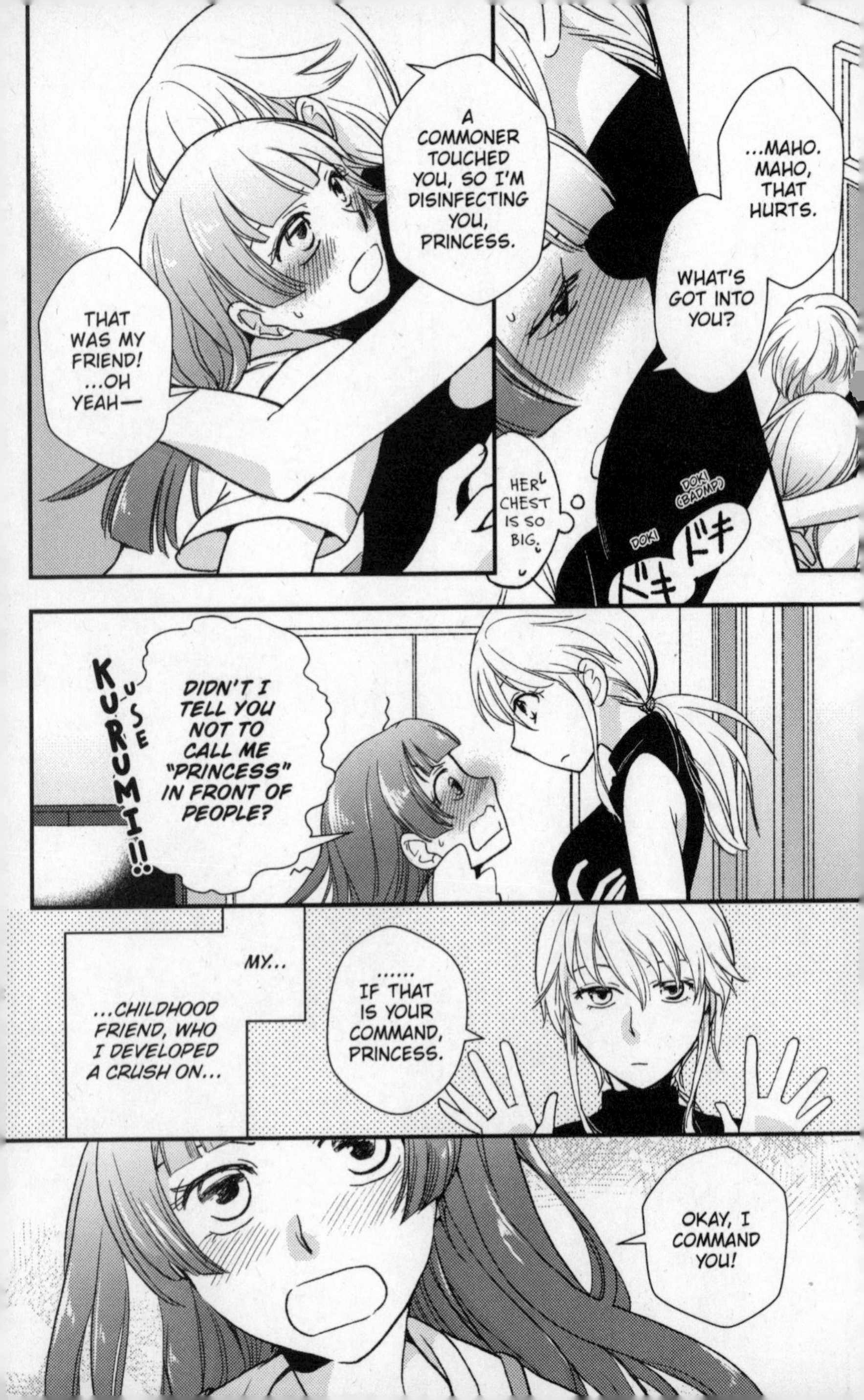
...MAHO. MAHO, THAT HURTS.
WHAT'S GOT INTO YOU?
HER CHEST IS SO BIG.
DOKI (BADMP)
DOKI
ドキ
ドキ
A COMMONER TOUCHED YOU, SO I'M DISINFECTING YOU, PRINCESS.
THAT WAS MY FRIEND! ...OH YEAH—
DIDN'T I TELL YOU NOT TO CALL ME "PRINCESS" IN FRONT OF PEOPLE?
KURUMI!!
USE
...... IF THAT IS YOUR COMMAND, PRINCESS.
MY...
...CHILDHOOD FRIEND, WHO I DEVELOPED A CRUSH ON...
OKAY, I COMMAND YOU!

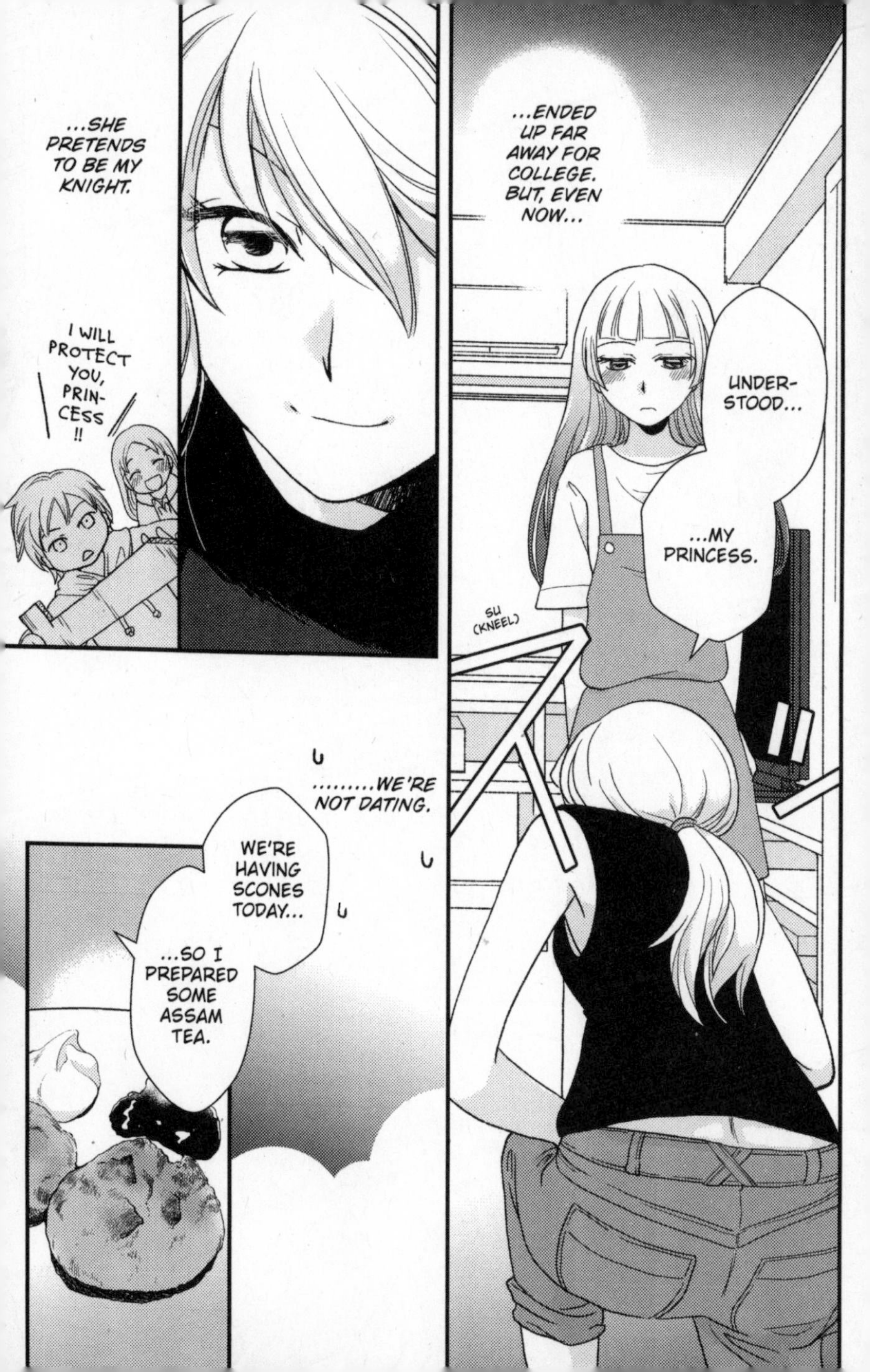
...ENDED UP FAR AWAY FOR COLLEGE. BUT, EVEN NOW...
UNDER-STOOD...
...MY PRINCESS.
SU (KNEEL)
...SHE PRETENDS TO BE MY KNIGHT.
I WILL PROTECT YOU, PRIN-CESS!!
.........WE'RE NOT DATING.
WE'RE HAVING SCONES TODAY...
...SO I PREPARED SOME ASSAM TEA.

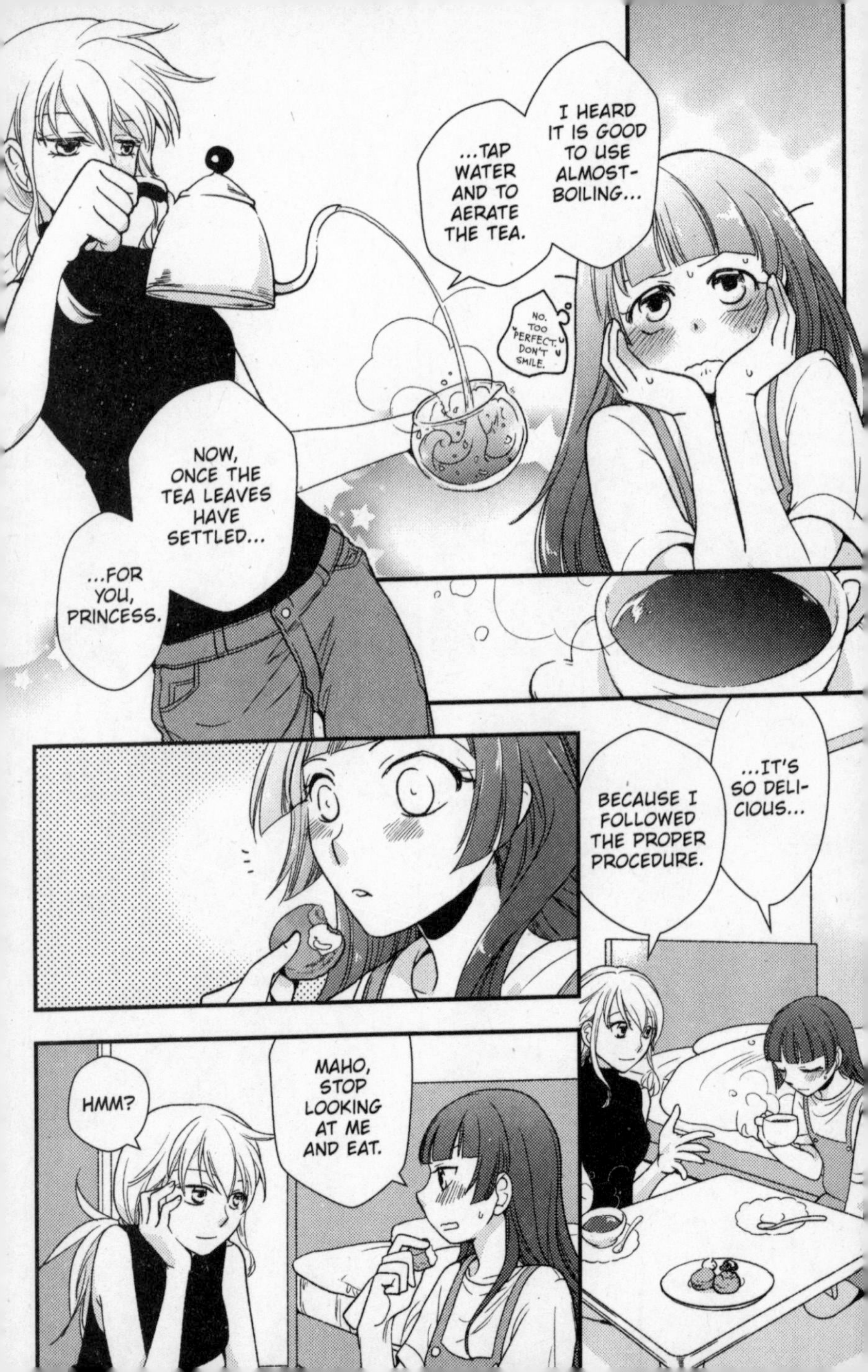
I HEARD IT IS GOOD TO USE ALMOST-BOILING...
...TAP WATER AND TO AERATE THE TEA.
NO. TOO PERFECT. DON'T SMILE.
NOW, ONCE THE TEA LEAVES HAVE SETTLED...
...FOR YOU, PRINCESS.
...IT'S SO DELI-CIOUS...
BECAUSE I FOLLOWED THE PROPER PROCEDURE.
MAHO, STOP LOOKING AT ME AND EAT.
HMM?

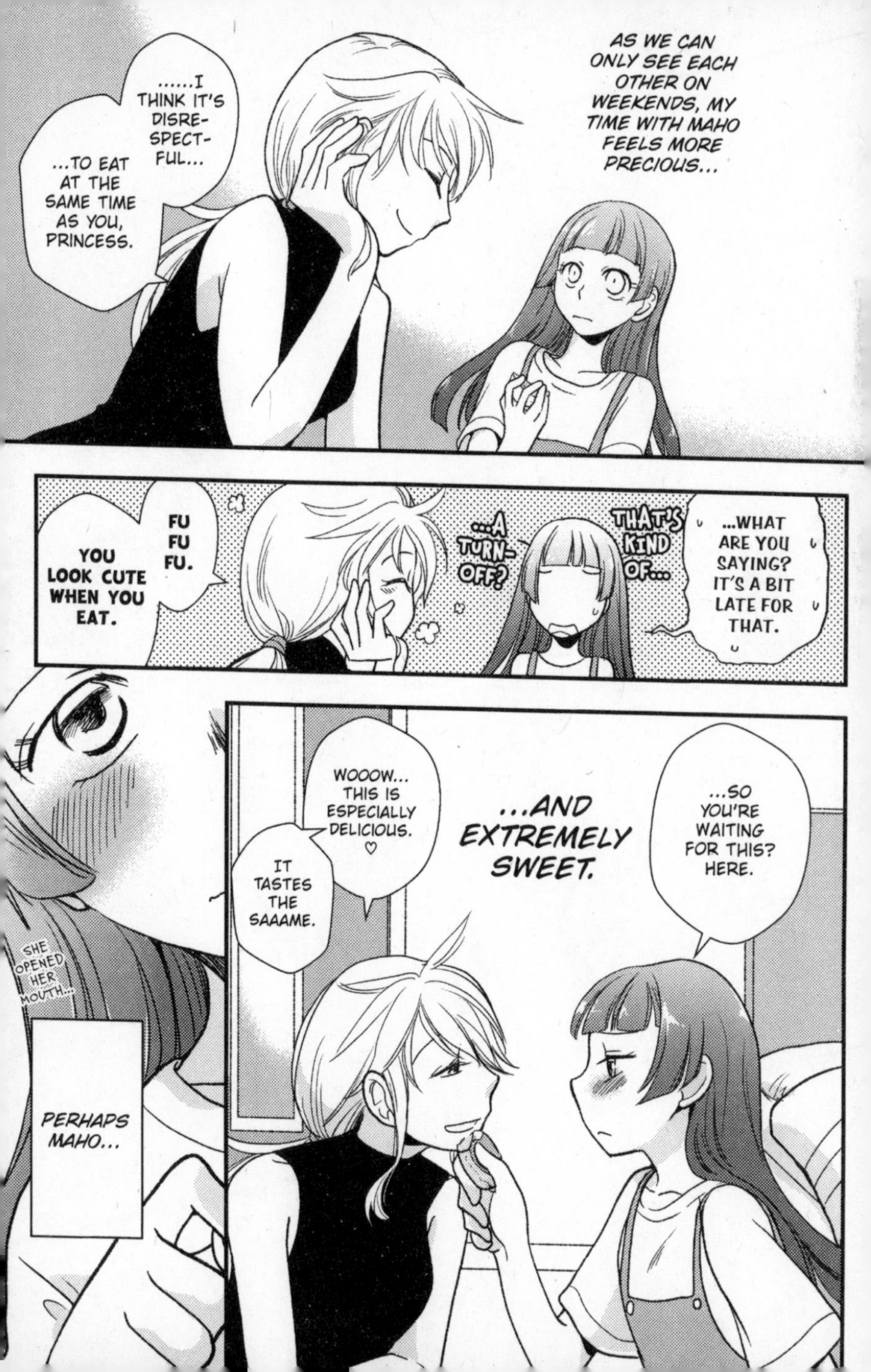
AS WE CAN ONLY SEE EACH OTHER ON WEEKENDS, MY TIME WITH MAHO FEELS MORE PRECIOUS...
......I THINK IT'S DISRE-SPECT-FUL...
...TO EAT AT THE SAME TIME AS YOU, PRINCESS.
...WHAT ARE YOU SAYING? IT'S A BIT LATE FOR THAT.
THAT'S KIND OF...
...A TURN-OFF?
FU FU FU.
YOU LOOK CUTE WHEN YOU EAT.
...SO YOU'RE WAITING FOR THIS? HERE.
...AND EXTREMELY SWEET.
WOOOW... THIS IS ESPECIALLY DELICIOUS. ♡
IT TASTES THE SAAAME.
SHE OPENED HER MOUTH...
PERHAPS MAHO...

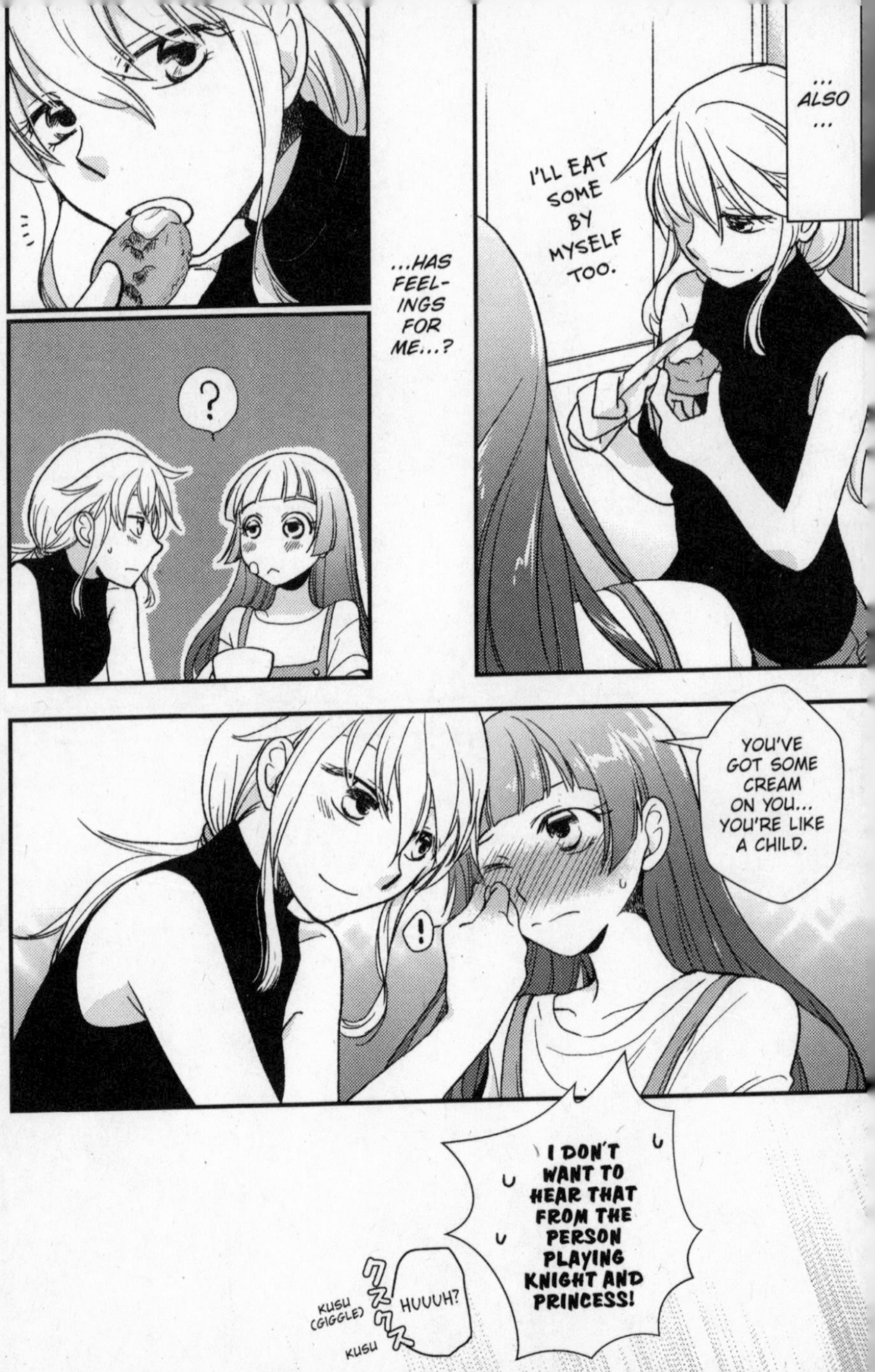

...ALSO...
I'LL EAT SOME BY MYSELF TOO.
...HAS FEEL-INGS FOR ME...?
?
!
YOU'VE GOT SOME CREAM ON YOU... YOU'RE LIKE A CHILD.
I DON'T WANT TO HEAR THAT FROM THE PERSON PLAYING KNIGHT AND PRINCESS!
HUUUH?
KUSU (GIGGLE)
KUSU

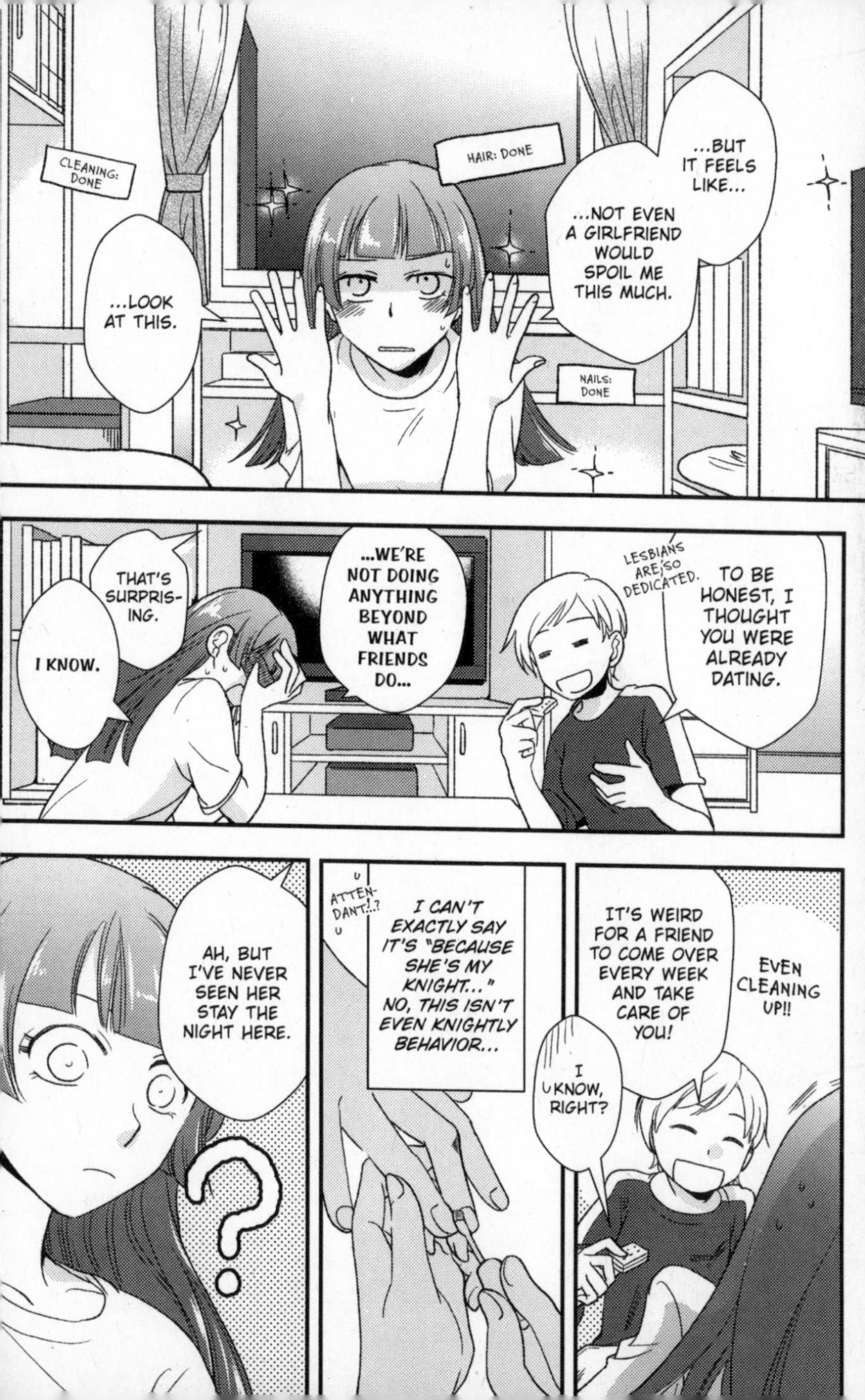
...BUT IT FEELS LIKE...
...NOT EVEN A GIRLFRIEND WOULD SPOIL ME THIS MUCH.
HAIR: DONE
CLEANING: DONE
...LOOK AT THIS.
NAILS: DONE
LESBIANS ARE SO DEDICATED.
TO BE HONEST, I THOUGHT YOU WERE ALREADY DATING.
...WE'RE NOT DOING ANYTHING BEYOND WHAT FRIENDS DO...
THAT'S SURPRIS-ING.
I KNOW.
IT'S WEIRD FOR A FRIEND TO COME OVER EVERY WEEK AND TAKE CARE OF YOU!
EVEN CLEANING UP!!
I KNOW, RIGHT?
ATTEN-DANT...?
I CAN'T EXACTLY SAY IT'S "BECAUSE SHE'S MY KNIGHT..." NO, THIS ISN'T EVEN KNIGHTLY BEHAVIOR...
AH, BUT I'VE NEVER SEEN HER STAY THE NIGHT HERE.

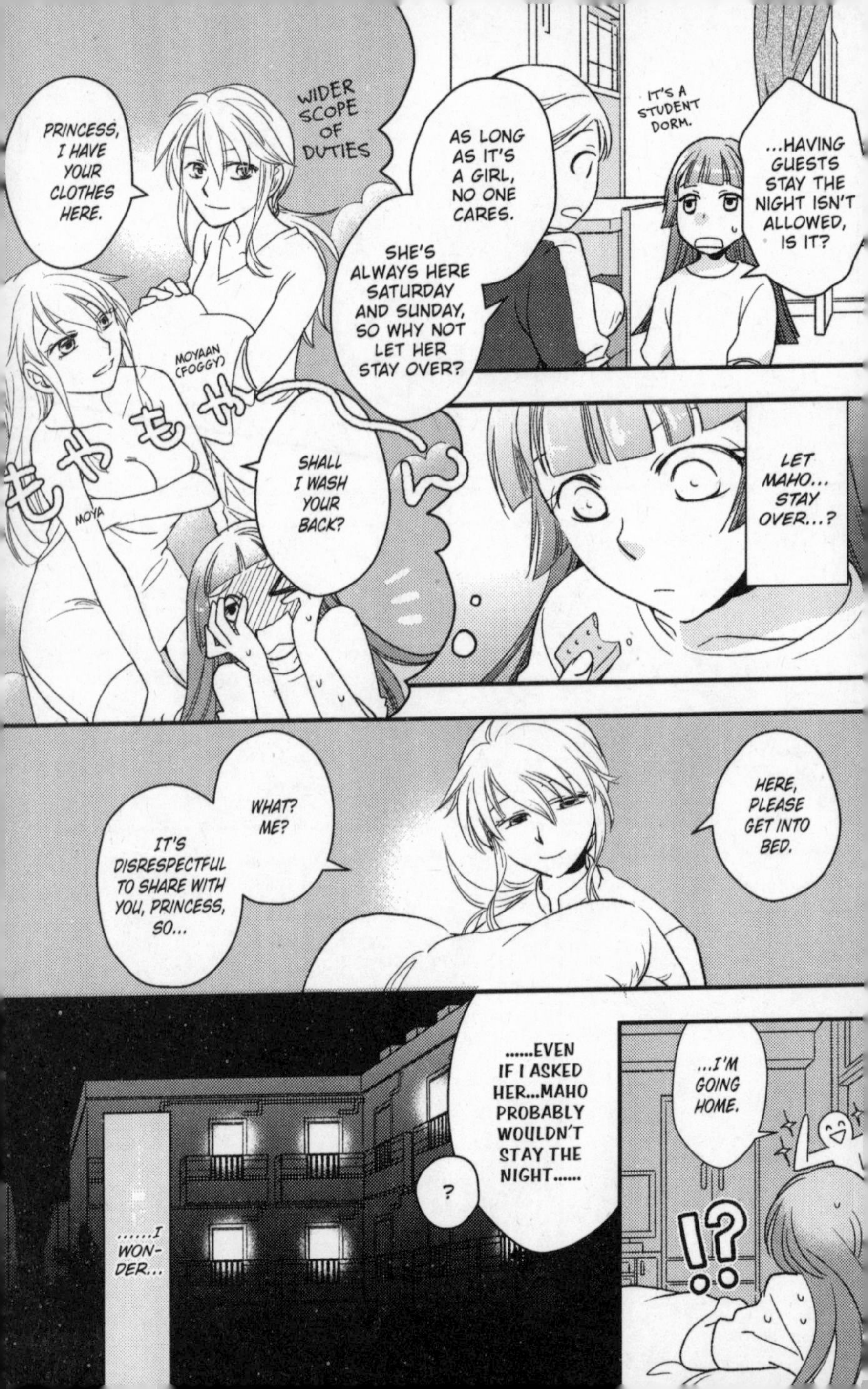
IT'S A STUDENT DORM.
...HAVING GUESTS STAY THE NIGHT ISN'T ALLOWED, IS IT?
AS LONG AS IT'S A GIRL, NO ONE CARES.
SHE'S ALWAYS HERE SATURDAY AND SUNDAY, SO WHY NOT LET HER STAY OVER?
LET MAHO... STAY OVER...?
WIDER SCOPE OF DUTIES
PRINCESS, I HAVE YOUR CLOTHES HERE.
SHALL I WASH YOUR BACK?
もやもや
MOYAAN (FOGGY)
MOYA
HERE, PLEASE GET INTO BED.
WHAT? ME?
IT'S DISRESPECTFUL TO SHARE WITH YOU, PRINCESS, SO...
...I'M GOING HOME.
!?
......EVEN IF I ASKED HER...MAHO PROBABLY WOULDN'T STAY THE NIGHT......
?
......I WONDER...

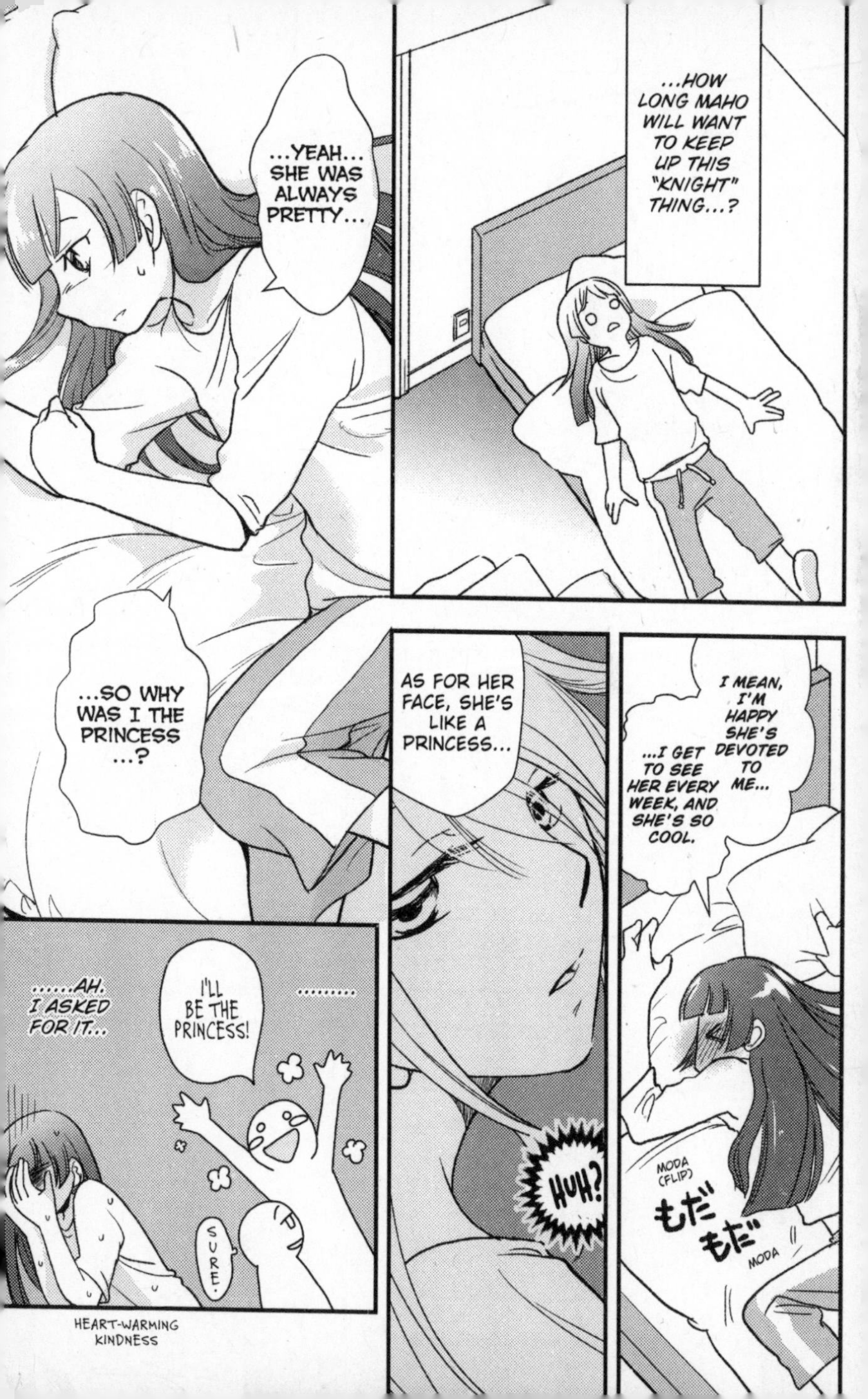
...HOW LONG MAHO WILL WANT TO KEEP UP THIS "KNIGHT" THING...?
...YEAH... SHE WAS ALWAYS PRETTY...
I MEAN, I'M HAPPY SHE'S DEVOTED TO ME...
...I GET TO SEE HER EVERY WEEK, AND SHE'S SO COOL.
MODA (FLIP)
もだもだ
MODA
AS FOR HER FACE, SHE'S LIKE A PRINCESS...
HUH?
...SO WHY WAS I THE PRINCESS ...?
....
I'LL BE THE PRINCESS!
......AH. I ASKED FOR IT...
SURE.
HEART-WARMING KINDNESS

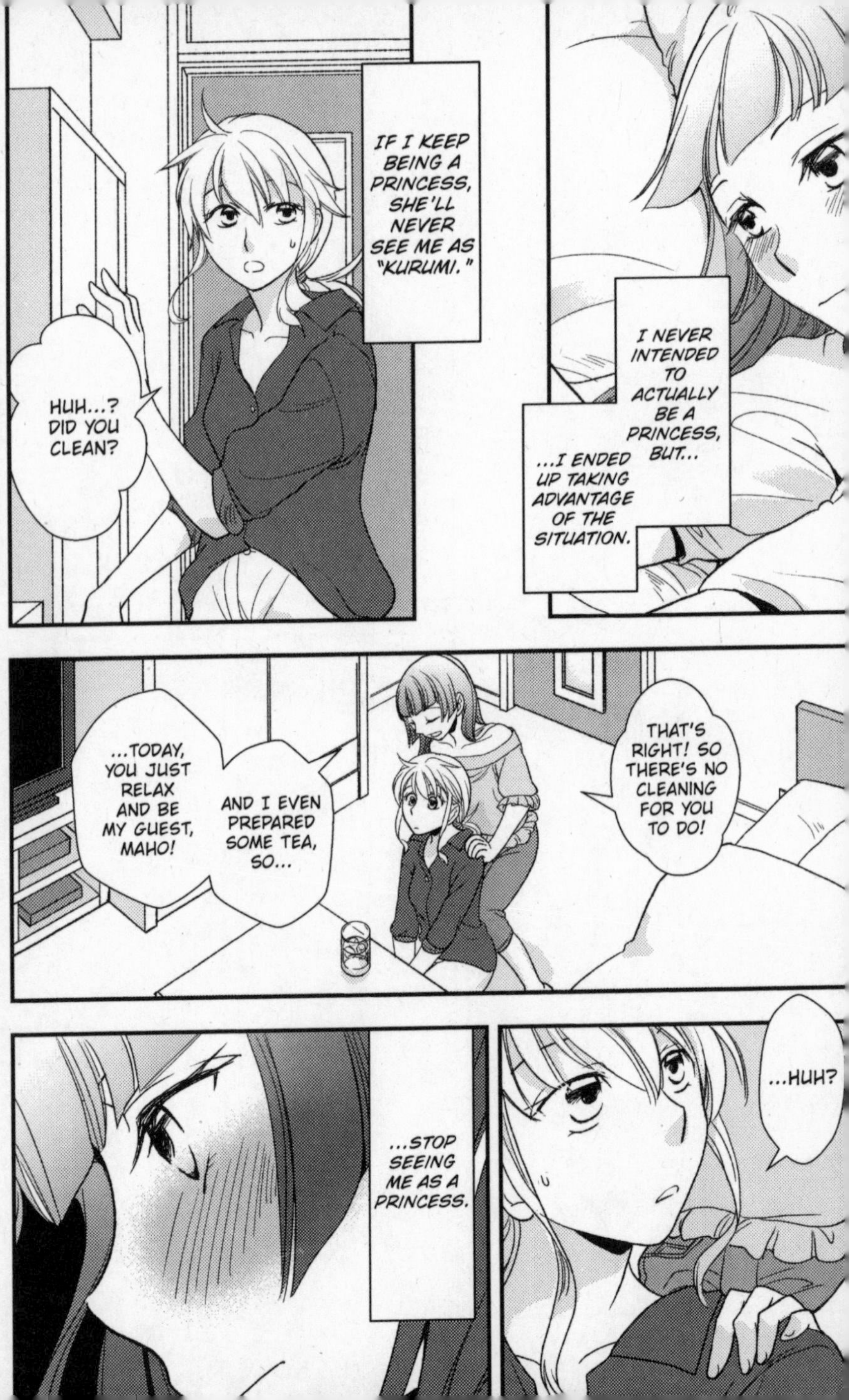
I NEVER INTENDED TO ACTUALLY BE A PRINCESS, BUT...
...I ENDED UP TAKING ADVANTAGE OF THE SITUATION.
IF I KEEP BEING A PRINCESS, SHE'LL NEVER SEE ME AS "KURUMI."
HUH...? DID YOU CLEAN?
THAT'S RIGHT! SO THERE'S NO CLEANING FOR YOU TO DO!
AND I EVEN PREPARED SOME TEA, SO...
...TODAY, YOU JUST RELAX AND BE MY GUEST, MAHO!
...HUH?
...STOP SEEING ME AS A PRINCESS.

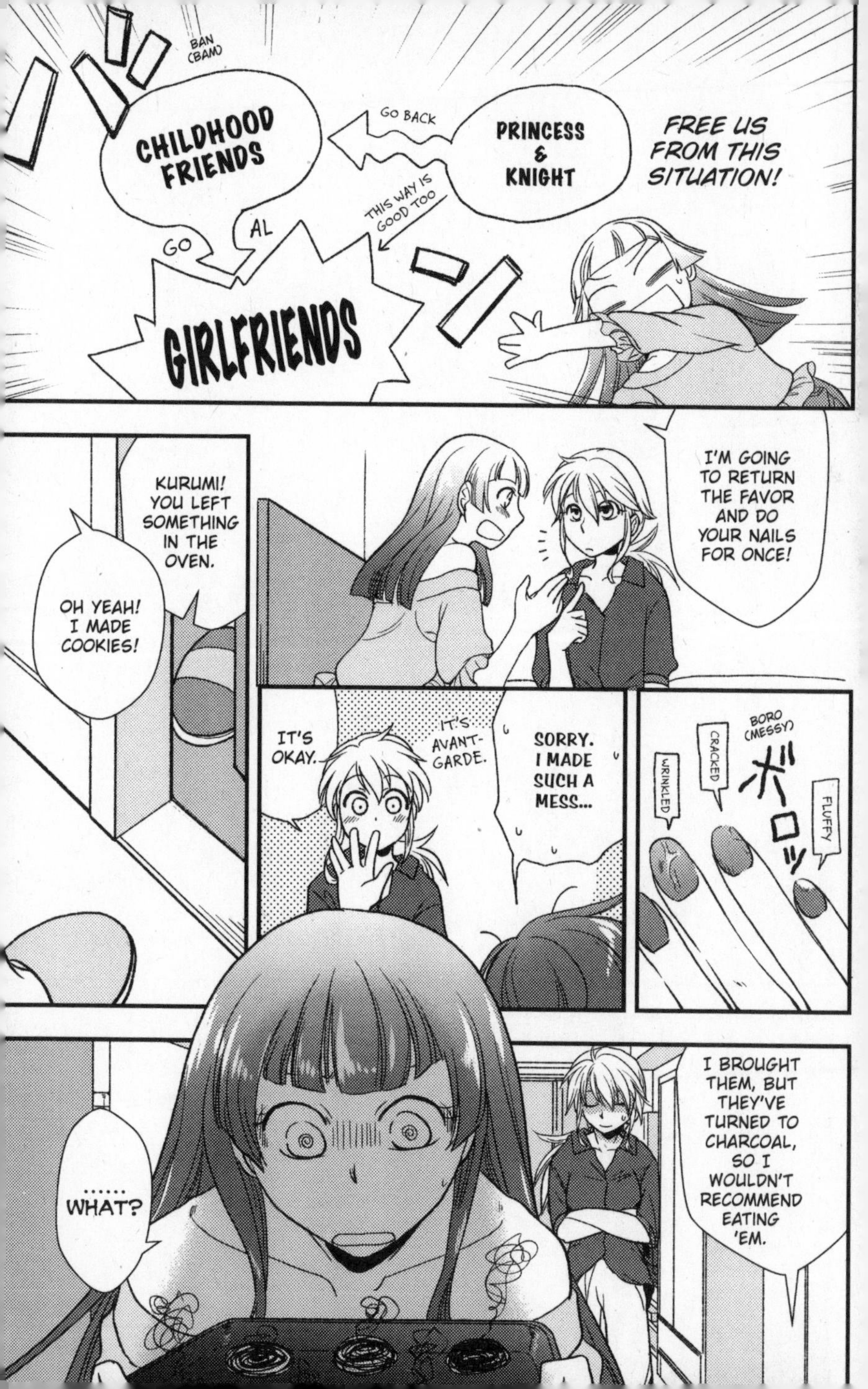
FREE US FROM THIS SITUATION!
PRINCESS & KNIGHT
GO BACK
CHILDHOOD FRIENDS
BAN (BAM)
THIS WAY IS GOOD TOO
GO
AL
GIRLFRIENDS
I'M GOING TO RETURN THE FAVOR AND DO YOUR NAILS FOR ONCE!
BORO (MESSY)
FLUFFY
CRACKED
WRINKLED
SORRY. I MADE SUCH A MESS...
IT'S AVANT-GARDE.
IT'S OKAY.
KURUMI! YOU LEFT SOMETHING IN THE OVEN.
OH YEAH! I MADE COOKIES!
I BROUGHT THEM, BUT THEY'VE TURNED TO CHARCOAL, SO I WOULDN'T RECOMMEND EATING 'EM.
...... WHAT?

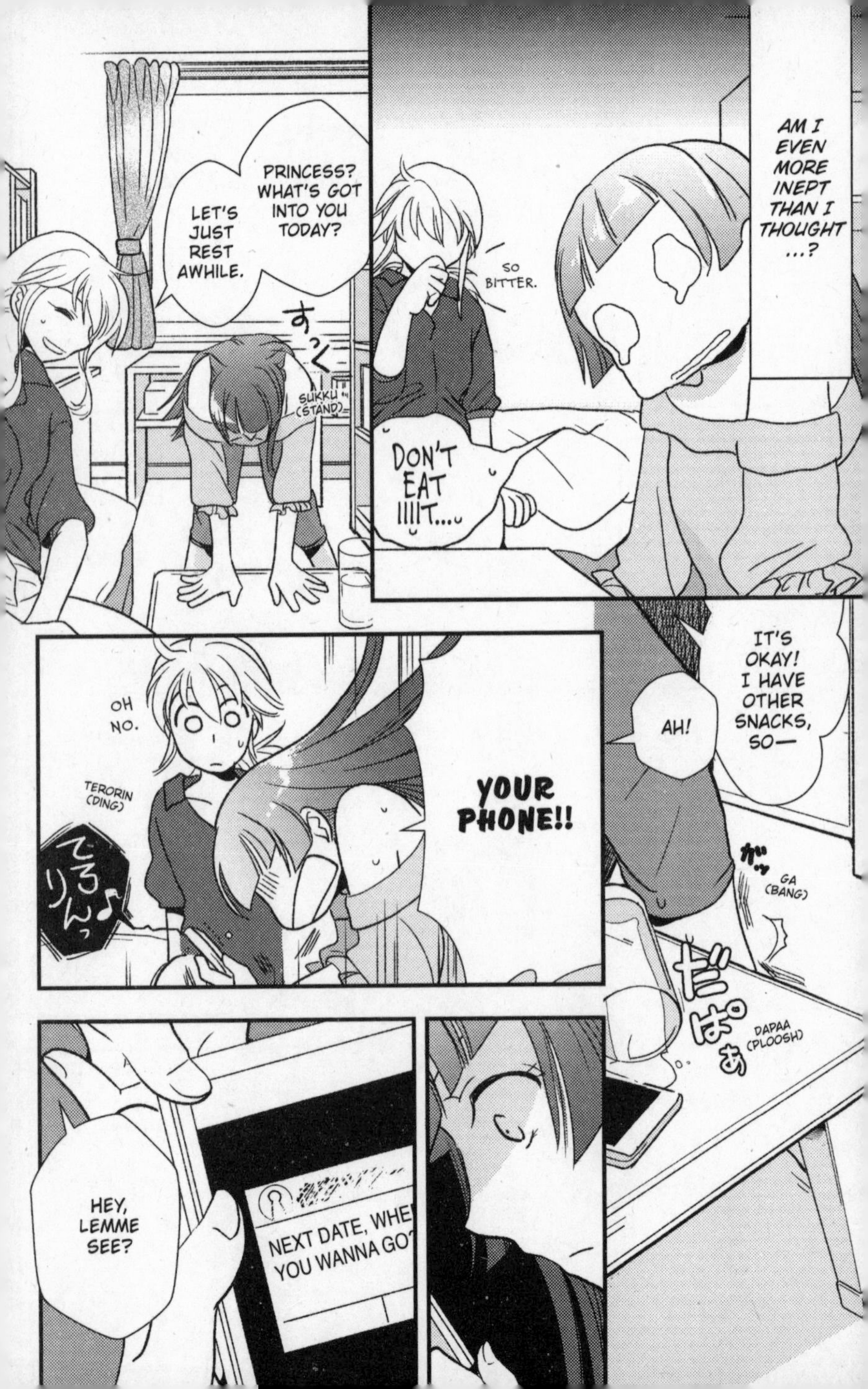
AM I EVEN MORE INEPT THAN I THOUGHT...?
SO BITTER.
DON'T EAT IIIIT....
PRINCESS? WHAT'S GOT INTO YOU TODAY?
LET'S JUST REST AWHILE.
すっく
SUKKU (STAND)
IT'S OKAY! I HAVE OTHER SNACKS, SO—
AH!
がッ
GA (BANG)
だぱぁ
DAPAA (PLOOSH)
OH NO.
YOUR PHONE!!
TERORIN (DING)
てろりんっ♪
HEY, LEMME SEE?
NEXT DATE, WHE
YOU WANNA GO

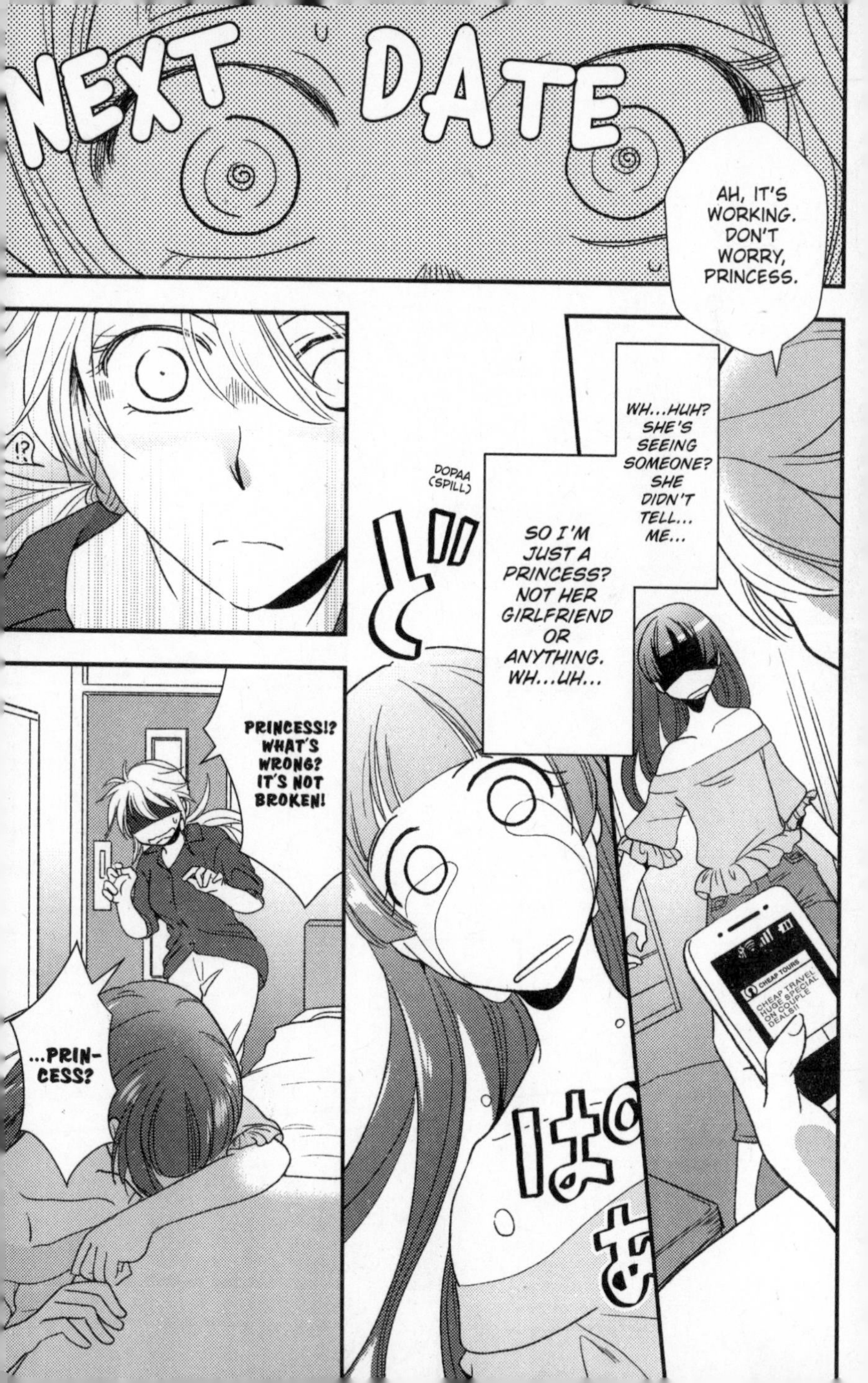
NEXT DATE
AH, IT'S WORKING. DON'T WORRY, PRINCESS.
WH...HUH? SHE'S SEEING SOMEONE? SHE DIDN'T TELL... ME...
SO I'M JUST A PRINCESS? NOT HER GIRLFRIEND OR ANYTHING. WH...UH...
DOPAA (SPILL)
CHEAP TOURS
CHEAP TRAVEL HUGE SPECIAL ON COUPLE DEALS!!
!?
PRINCESS!? WHAT'S WRONG? IT'S NOT BROKEN!
...PRIN-CESS?

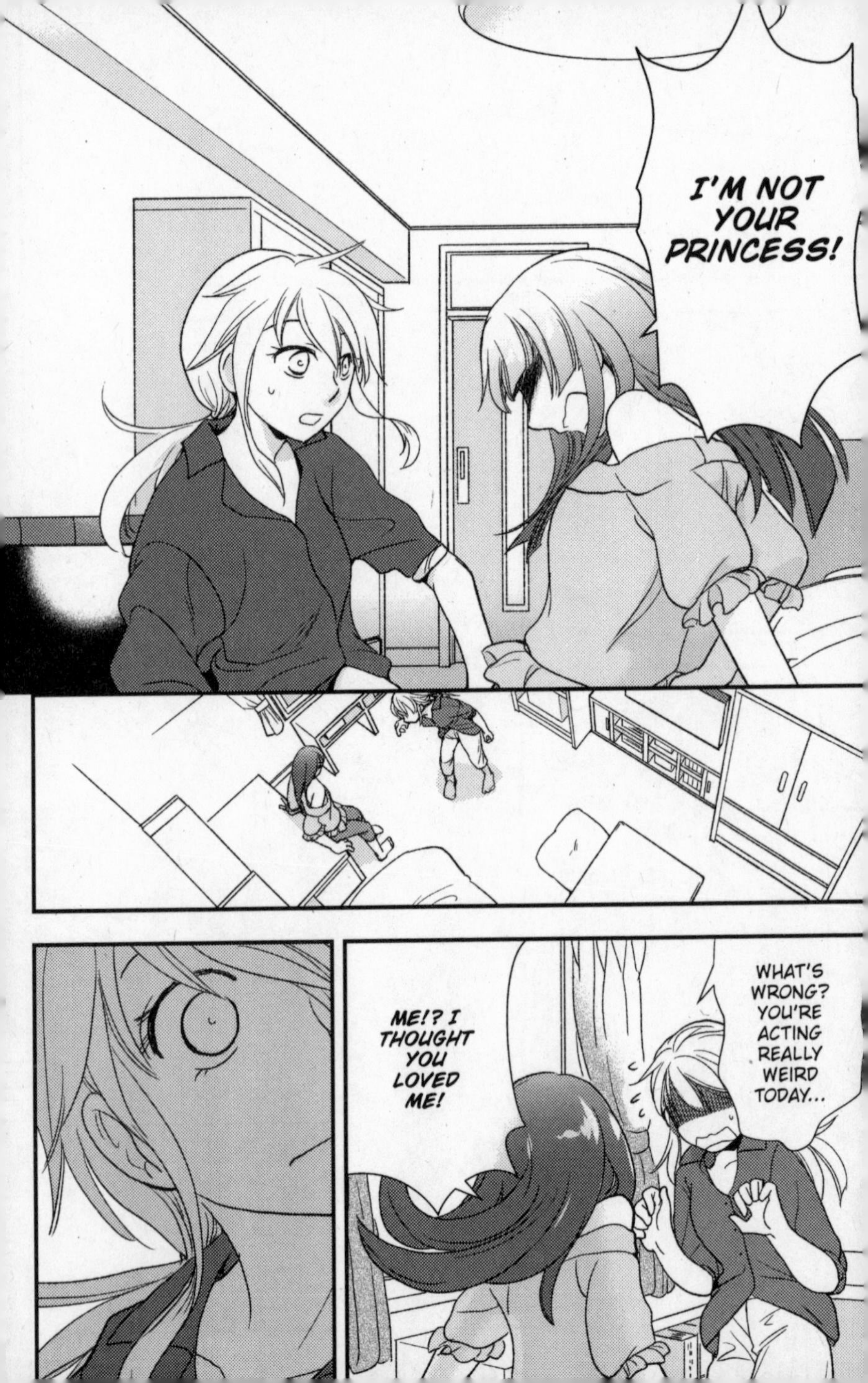
I'M NOT YOUR PRINCESS!
WHAT'S WRONG? YOU'RE ACTING REALLY WEIRD TODAY...
ME!? I THOUGHT YOU LOVED ME!

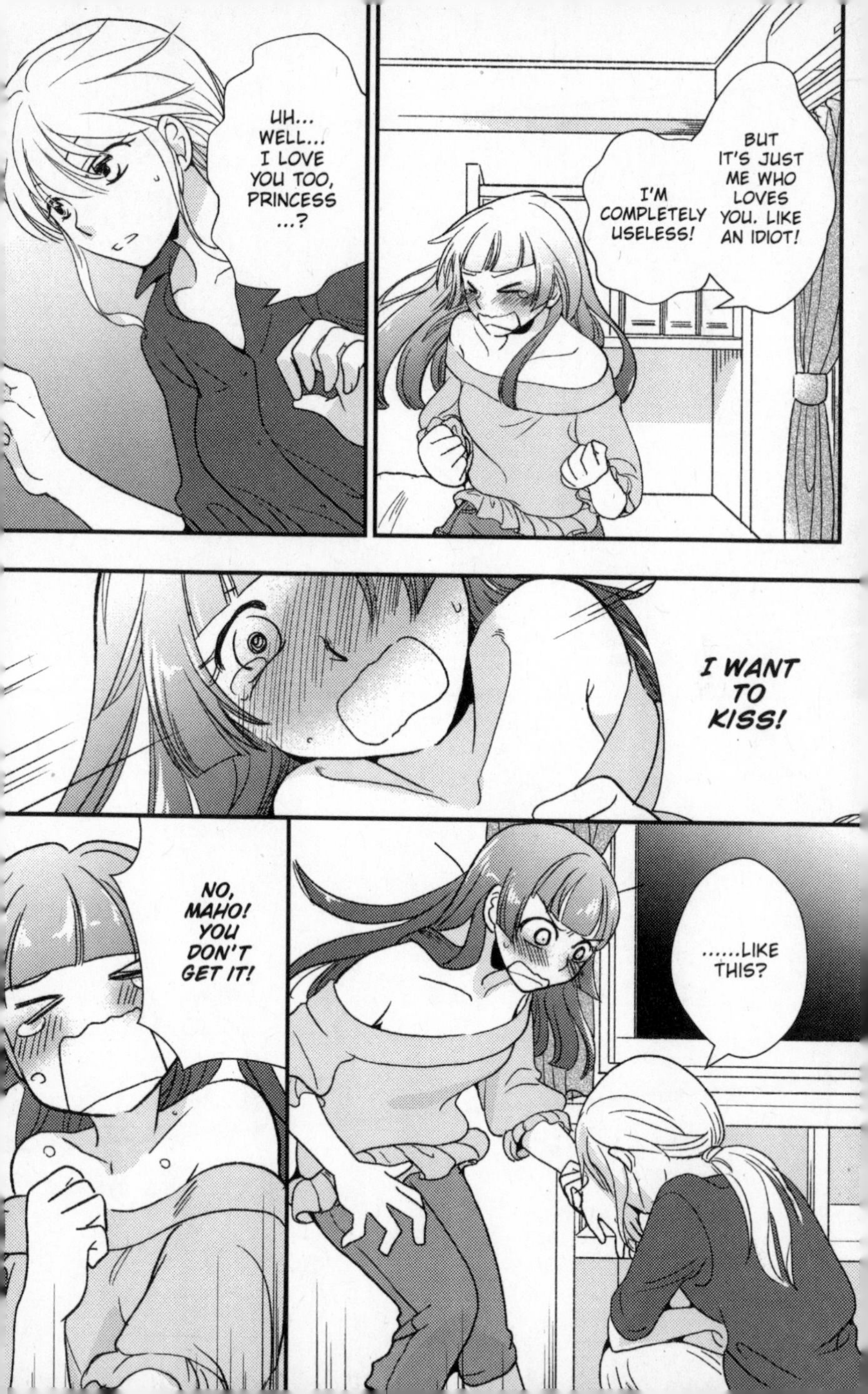
BUT IT'S JUST ME WHO LOVES YOU. LIKE AN IDIOT!
I'M COMPLETELY USELESS!
UH... WELL... I LOVE YOU TOO, PRINCESS ...?
I WANT TO KISS!
......LIKE THIS?
NO, MAHO! YOU DON'T GET IT!

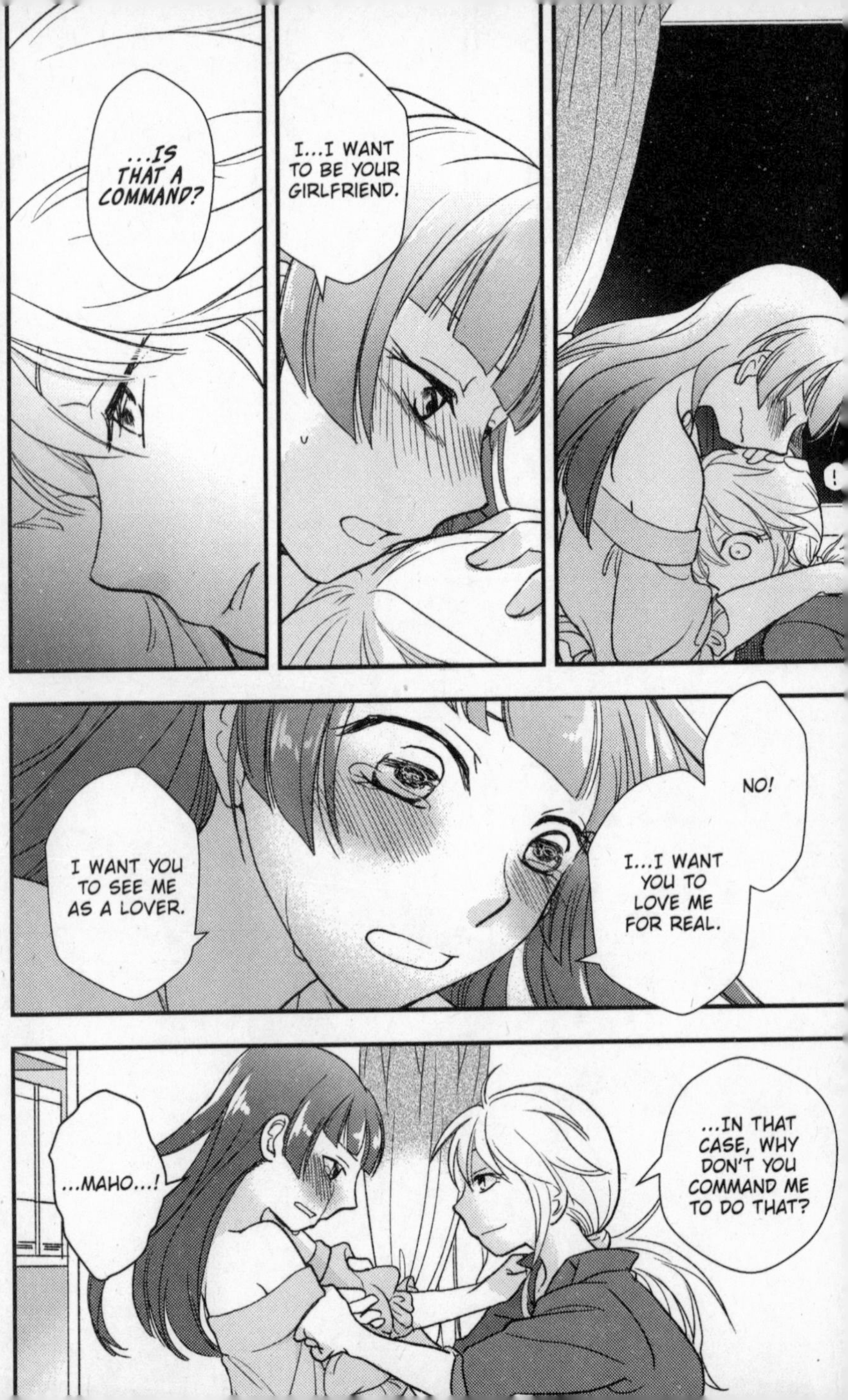
!
I...I WANT TO BE YOUR GIRLFRIEND.
...IS THAT A COMMAND?
NO!
I...I WANT YOU TO LOVE ME FOR REAL.
I WANT YOU TO SEE ME AS A LOVER.
...IN THAT CASE, WHY DON'T YOU COMMAND ME TO DO THAT?
...MAHO...!

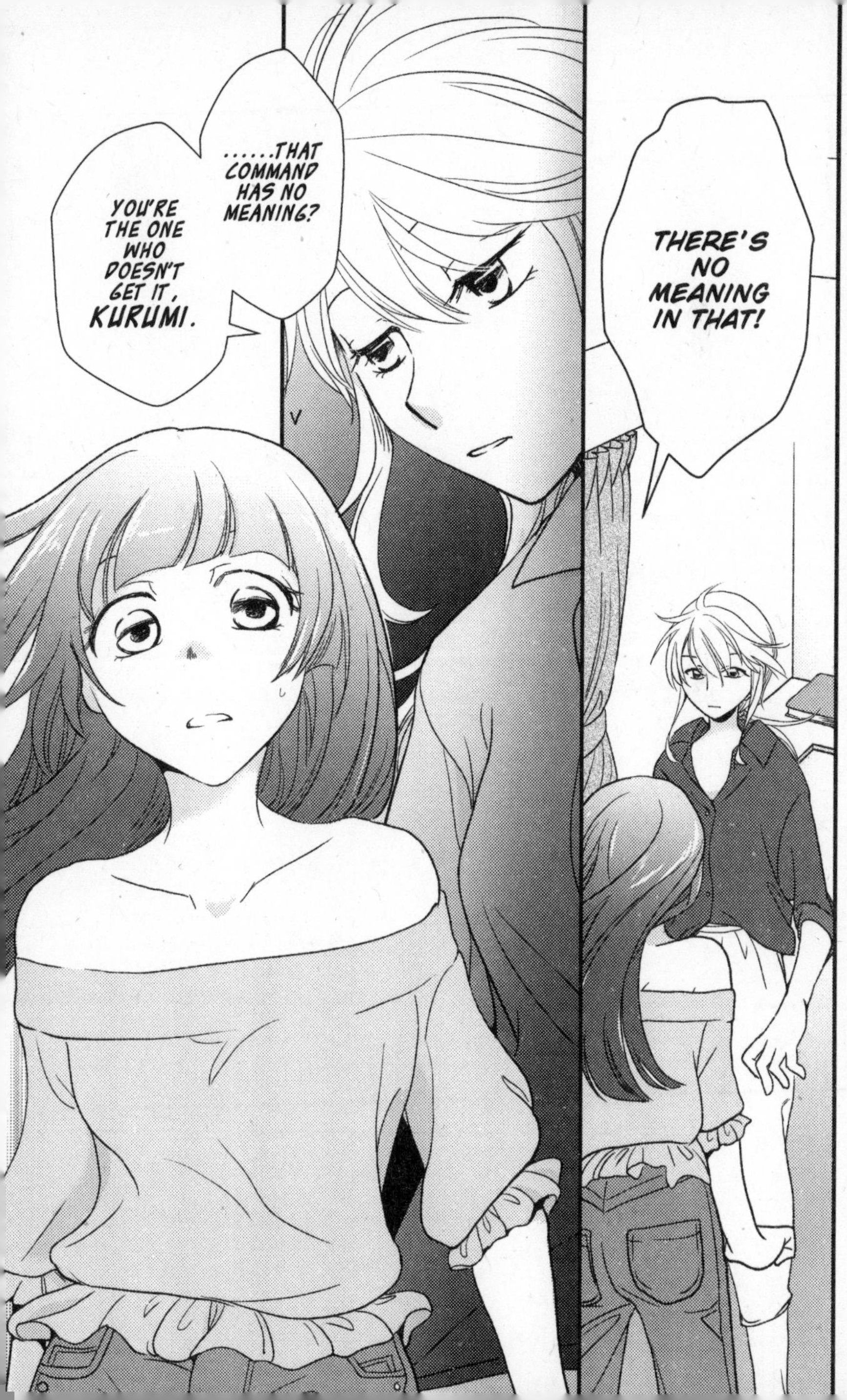
THERE'S NO MEANING IN THAT!
......THAT COMMAND HAS NO MEANING?
YOU'RE THE ONE WHO DOESN'T GET IT, KURUMI.

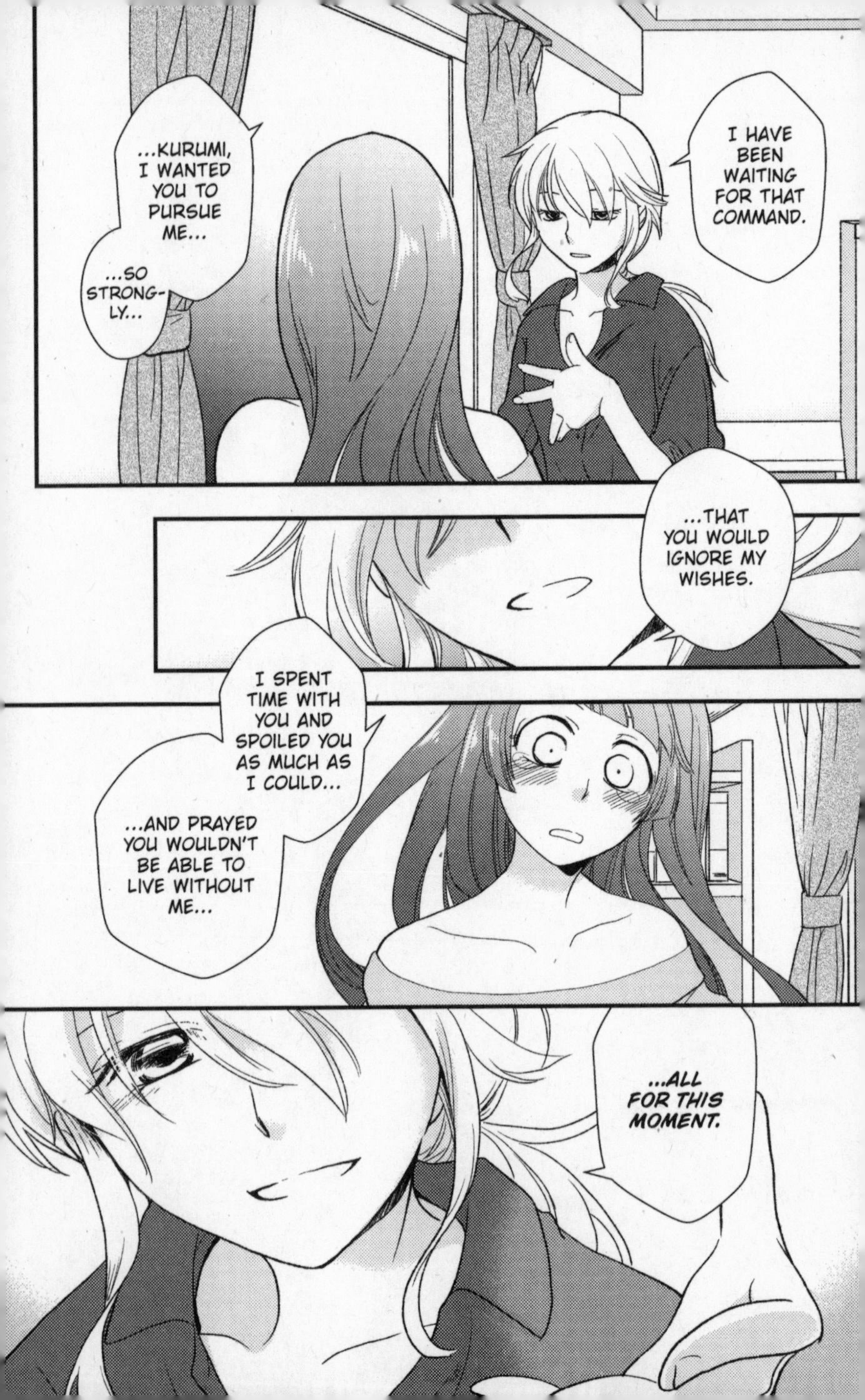
I HAVE BEEN WAITING FOR THAT COMMAND.
...KURUMI, I WANTED YOU TO PURSUE ME...
...SO STRONG-LY...
...THAT YOU WOULD IGNORE MY WISHES.
I SPENT TIME WITH YOU AND SPOILED YOU AS MUCH AS I COULD...
...AND PRAYED YOU WOULDN'T BE ABLE TO LIVE WITHOUT ME...
...ALL FOR THIS MOMENT.

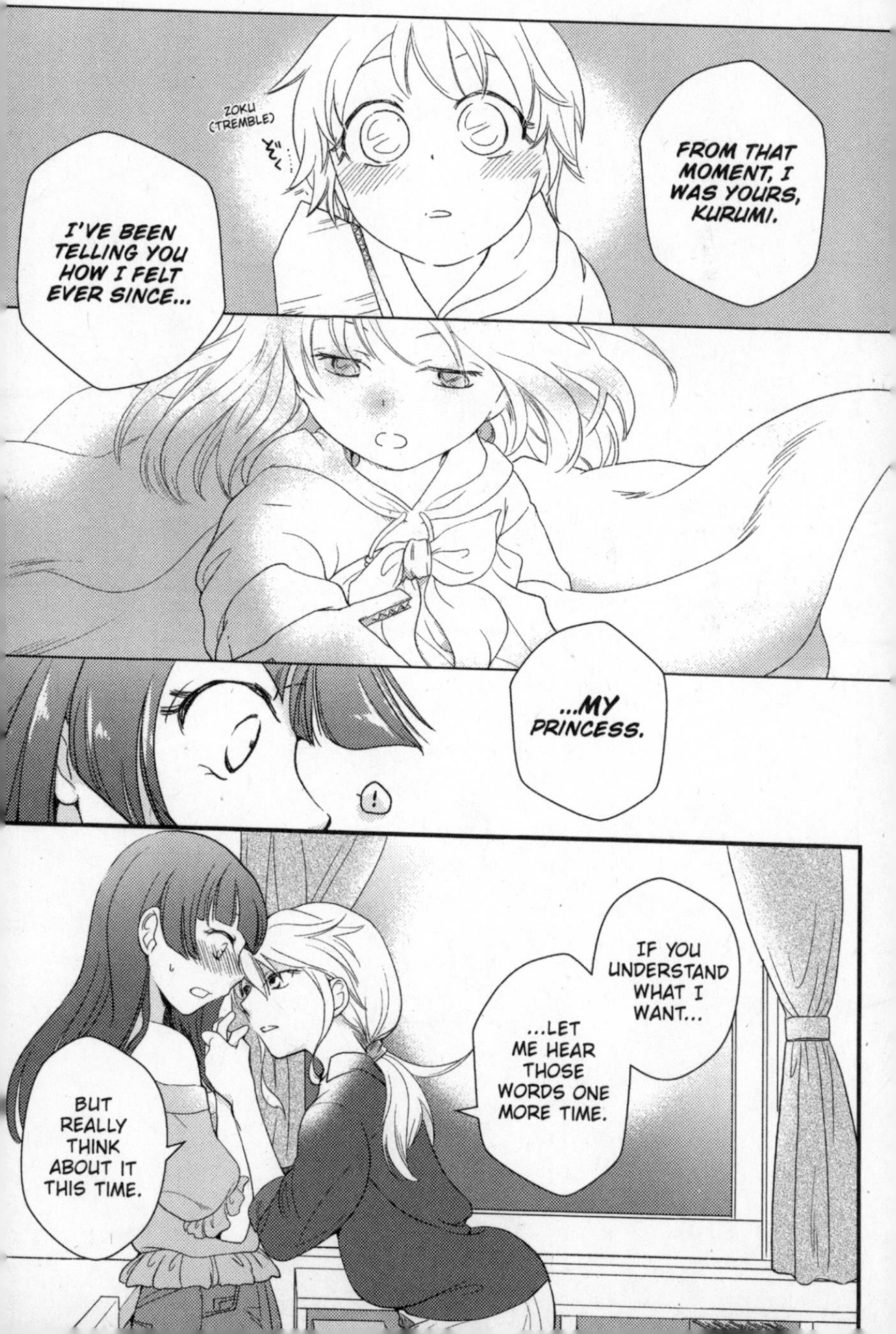
FROM THAT MOMENT, I WAS YOURS, KURUMI.
ZOKU (TREMBLE)
I'VE BEEN TELLING YOU HOW I FELT EVER SINCE...
...MY PRINCESS.
!
IF YOU UNDERSTAND WHAT I WANT...
...LET ME HEAR THOSE WORDS ONE MORE TIME.
BUT REALLY THINK ABOUT IT THIS TIME.

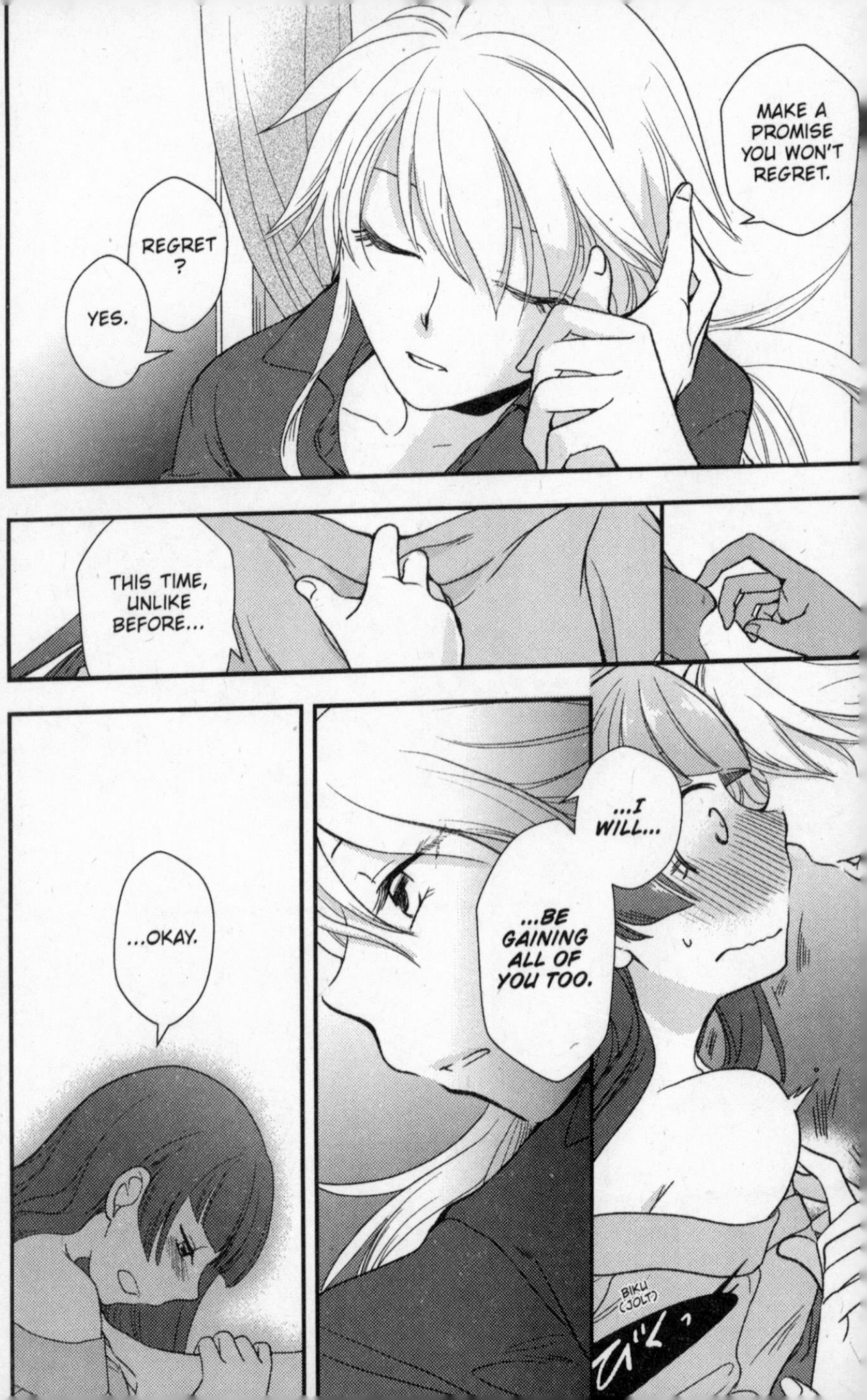
MAKE A PROMISE YOU WON'T REGRET.
REGRET?
YES.
THIS TIME, UNLIKE BEFORE...
...I WILL...
...BE GAINING ALL OF YOU TOO.
BIKU (JOLT)
...OKAY.

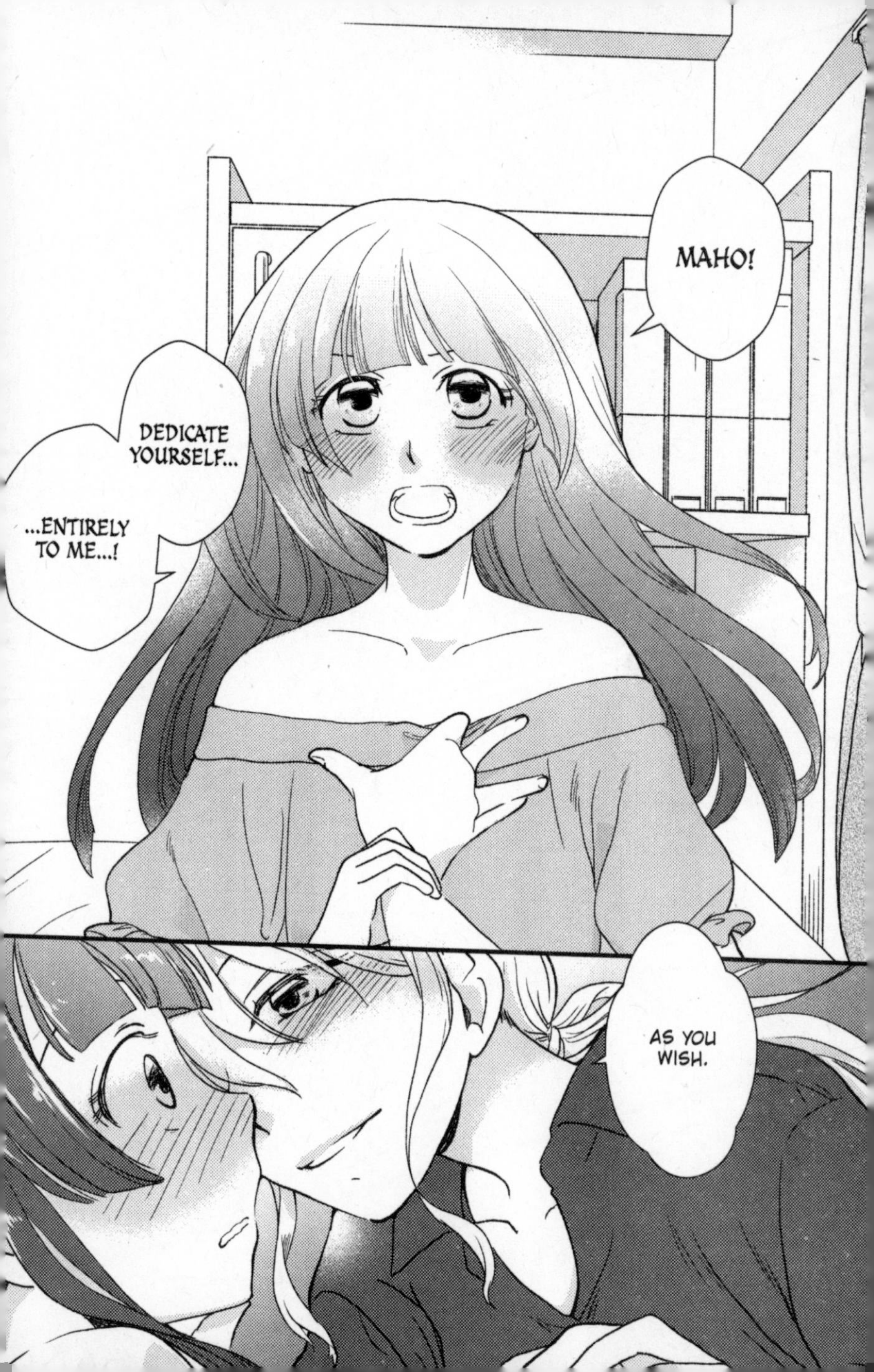
MAHO!
DEDICATE YOURSELF...
...ENTIRELY TO ME...!
AS YOU WISH.

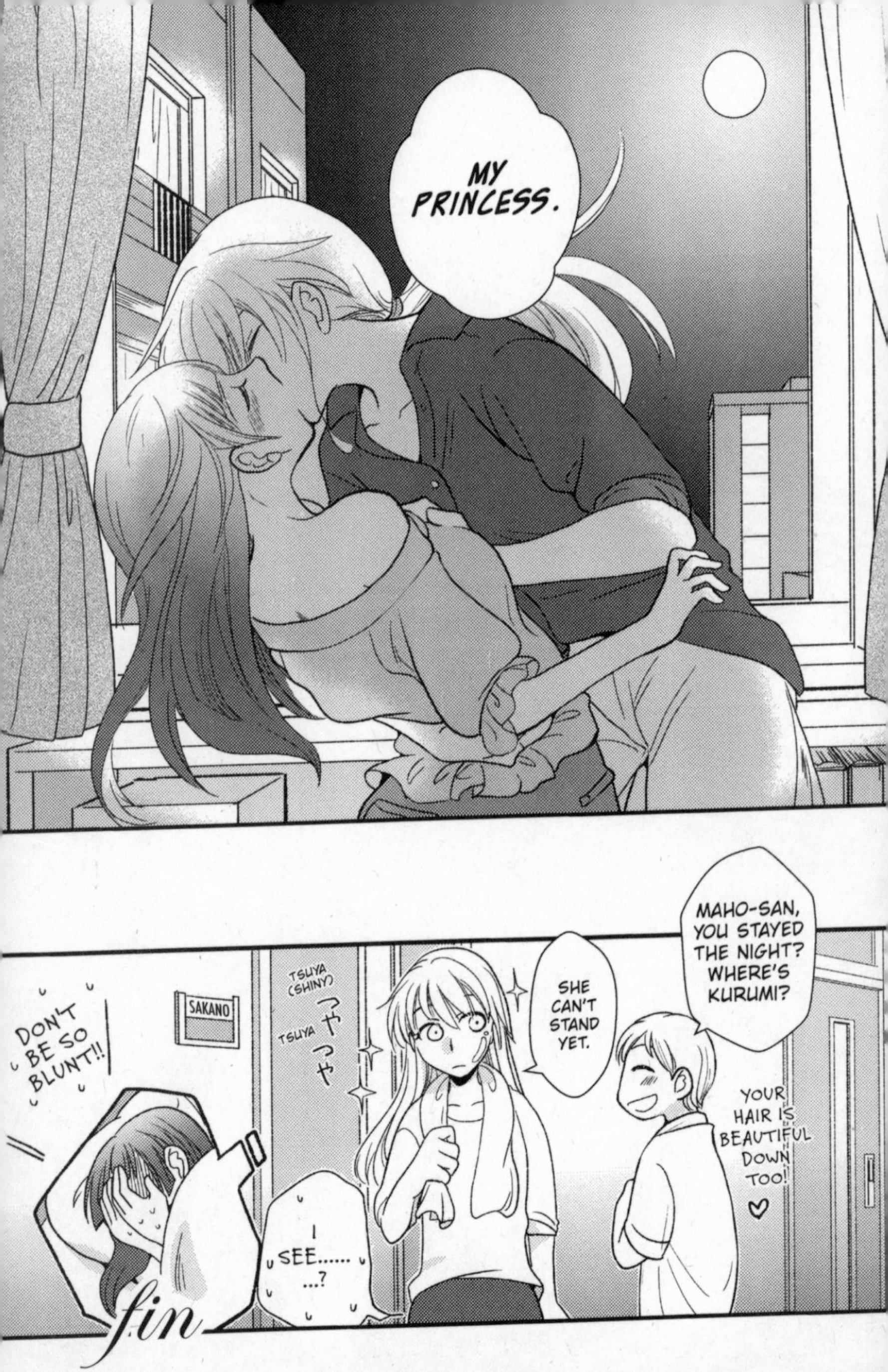
MY PRINCESS.
MAHO-SAN, YOU STAYED THE NIGHT? WHERE'S KURUMI?
YOUR HAIR IS BEAUTIFUL DOWN TOO!
SHE CAN'T STAND YET.
TSUYA (SHINY) つや
TSUYA つや
SAKANO
DON'T BE SO BLUNT!!
I SEE...... ...?
fin

éclair
blanche

A Girls' Love Anthology
That Resonates in Your Heart

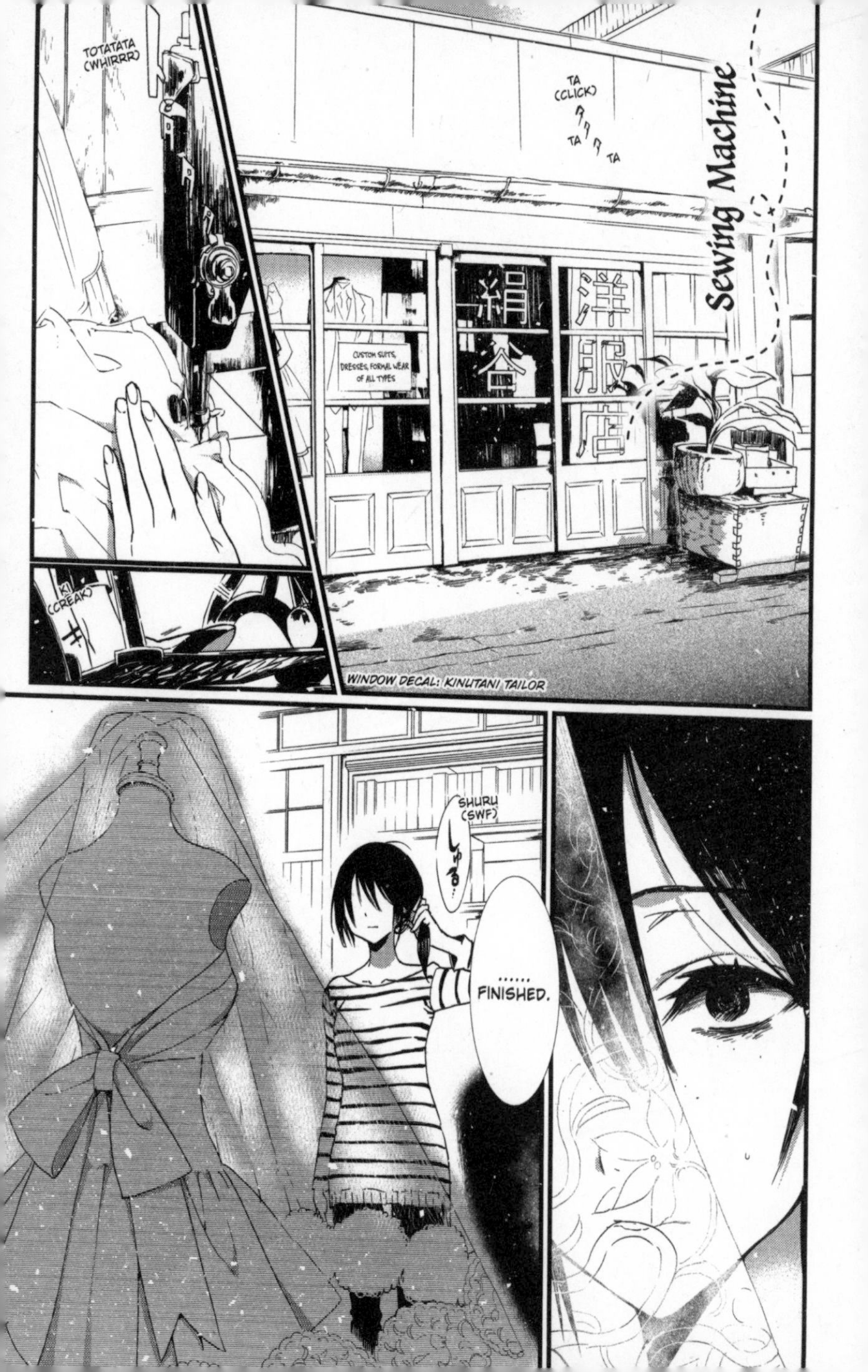
Sewing Machine
TA (CLICK)
タタタ
TA TA
絹谷洋服店
CUSTOM SUITS, DRESSES, FORMAL WEAR OF ALL TYPES
WINDOW DECAL: KINUTANI TAILOR
TOTATATA (WHIRRR)
KI (CREAK)
ギ
SHURU (SWF)
しゅる…
...... FINISHED.

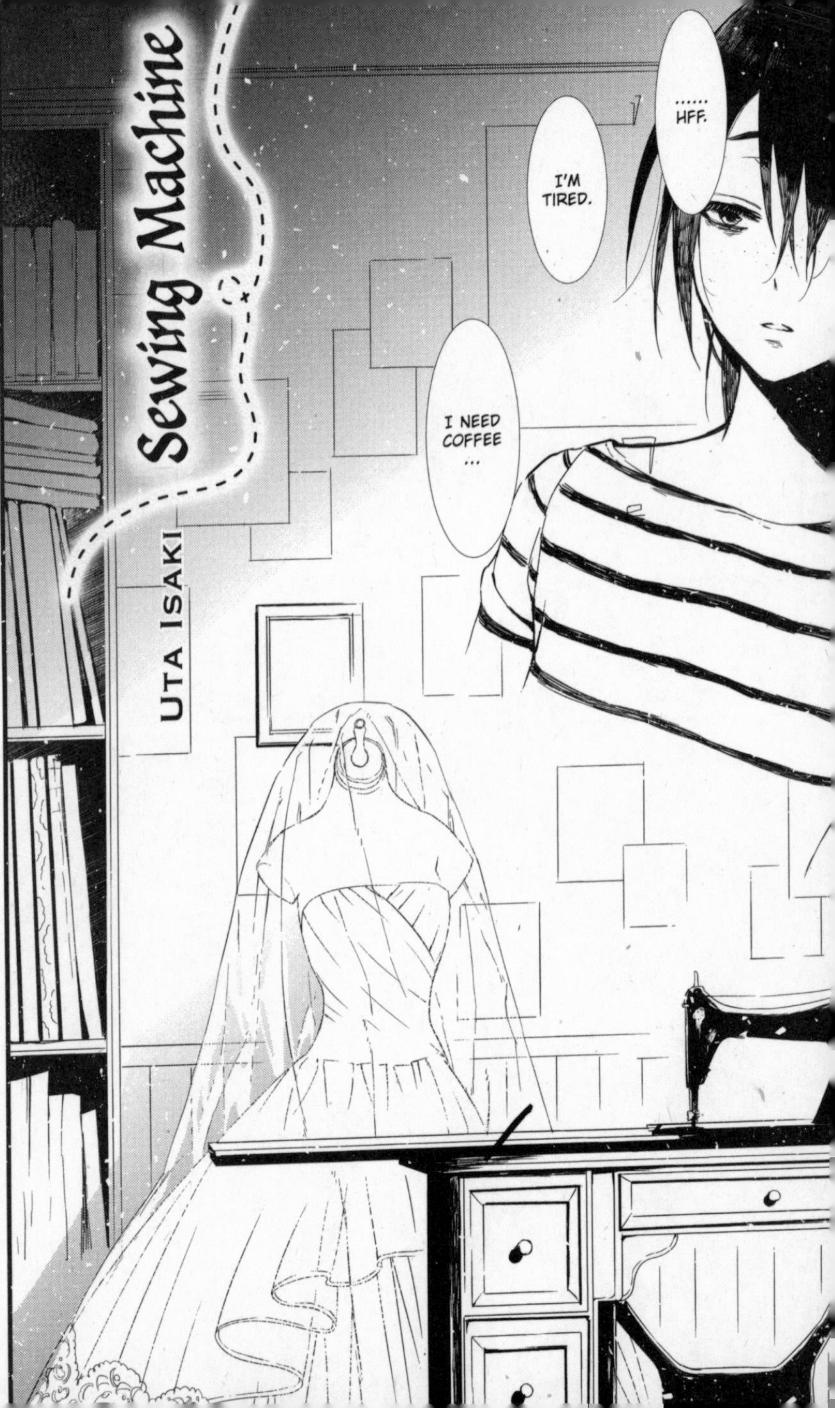
......HFF.
I'M TIRED.
I NEED COFFEE ...
Sewing Machine
UTA ISAKI

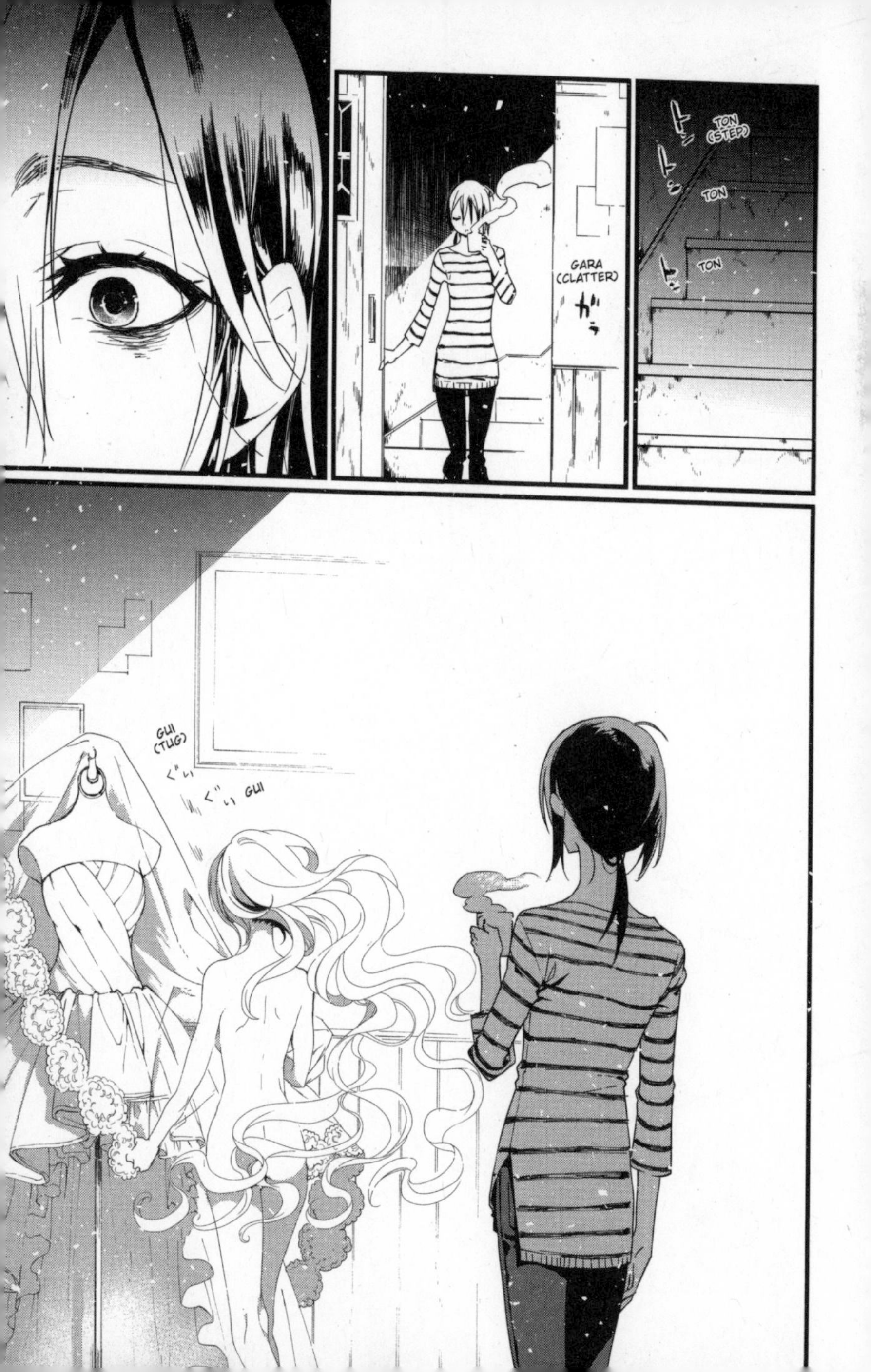
TON (STEP)
TON
TON
GARA (CLATTER)
GUI (TUG)
GUI

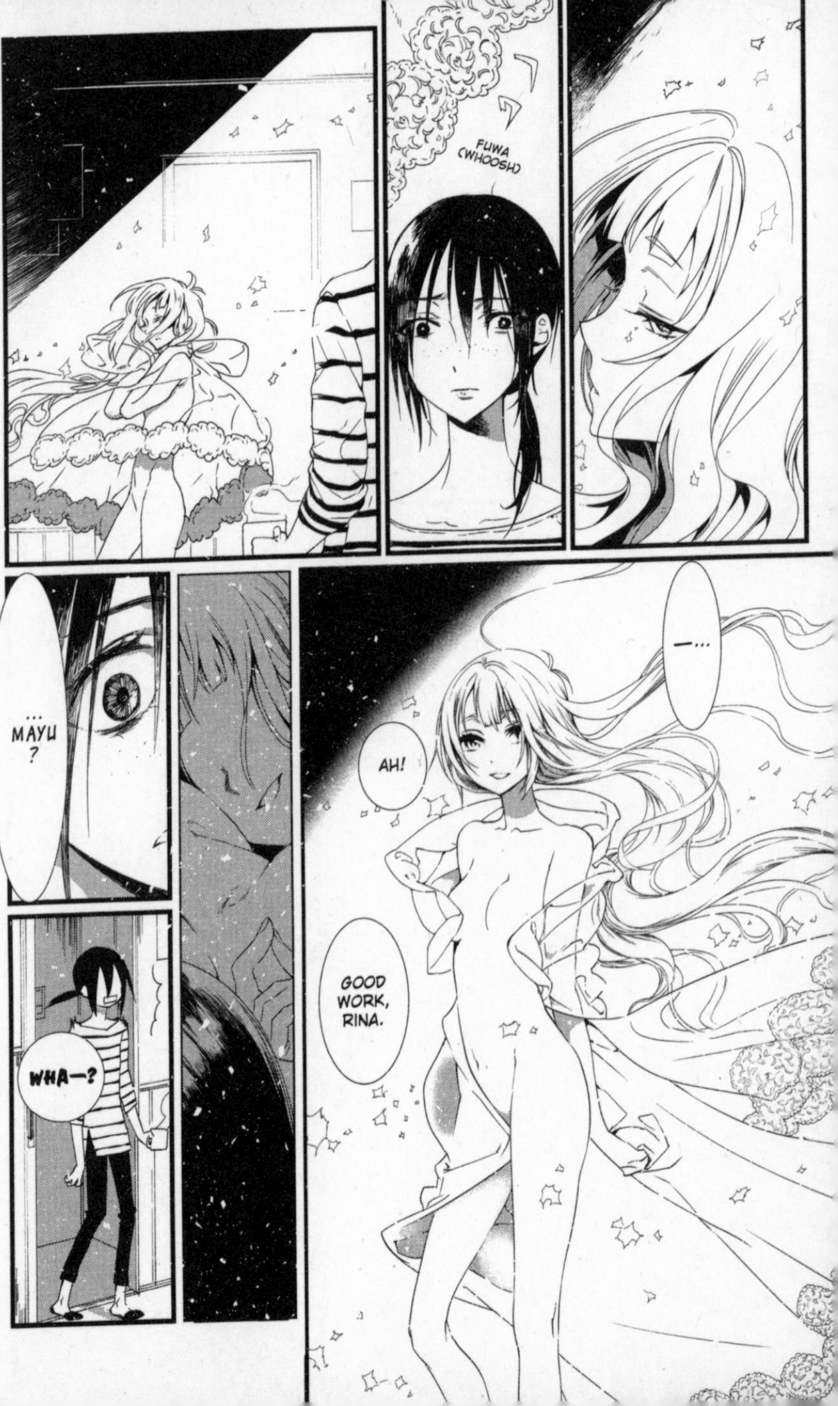
FUWA (WHOOSH)
—…
AH!
GOOD WORK, RINA.
… MAYU ?
WHA—?

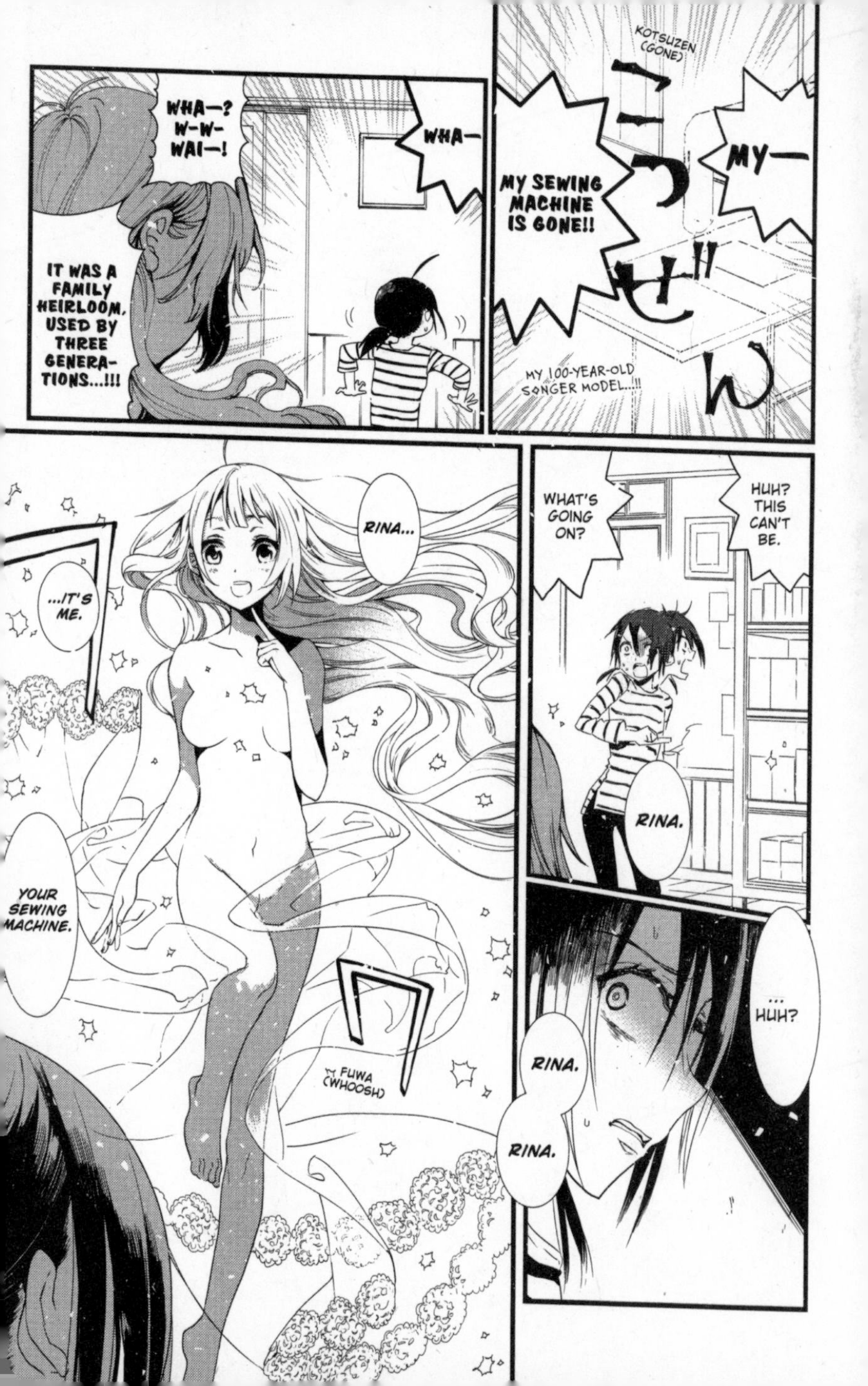

KOTSUZEN (GONE)
MY—
こーつぜん!!
MY SEWING MACHINE IS GONE!!
MY 100-YEAR-OLD SONGER MODEL...!!
WHA—
WHA—? W-W-WAI—!
IT WAS A FAMILY HEIRLOOM, USED BY THREE GENERATIONS...!!!
HUH? THIS CAN'T BE.
WHAT'S GOING ON?
RINA.
...HUH?
RINA.
RINA.
RINA...
...IT'S ME.
YOUR SEWING MACHINE.
FUWA (WHOOSH)

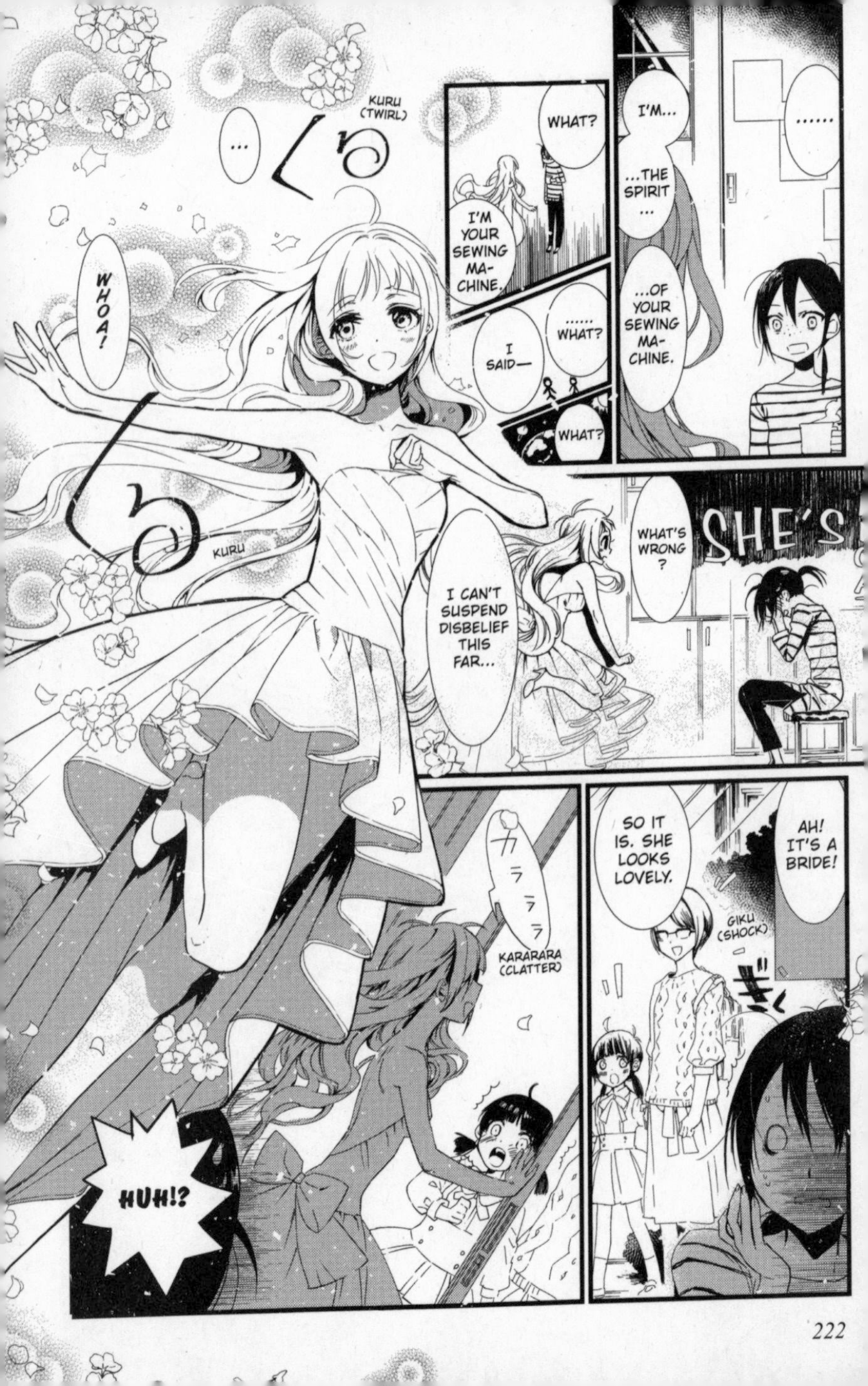

......
I'M...
...THE SPIRIT...
...OF YOUR SEWING MA-CHINE.
WHAT?
I'M YOUR SEWING MA-CHINE.
......WHAT?
I SAID—
WHAT?
KURU (TWIRL)
...
WHOA!
KURU
WHAT'S WRONG?
SHE'S
I CAN'T SUSPEND DISBELIEF THIS FAR...
AH! IT'S A BRIDE!
SO IT IS. SHE LOOKS LOVELY.
GIKU (SHOCK)
KARARARA (CLATTER)
HUH!?

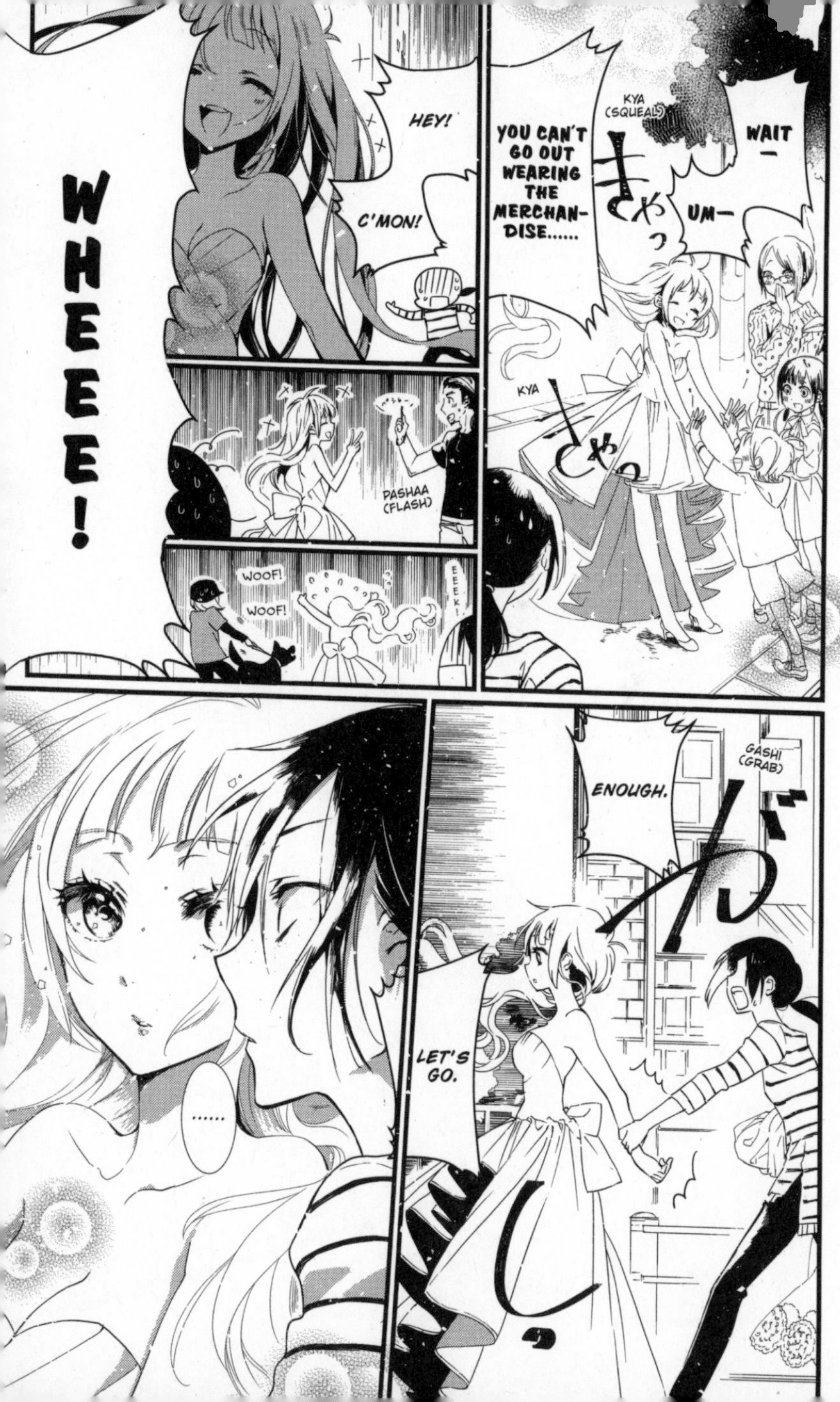
WAIT —
KYA (SQUEAL)
YOU CAN'T GO OUT WEARING THE MERCHANDISE......
UM—
KYA
HEY!
C'MON!
WHEEE!
PASHAA (FLASH)
EEEK!
WOOF!
WOOF!
GASHI (GRAB)
ENOUGH.
LET'S GO.
......

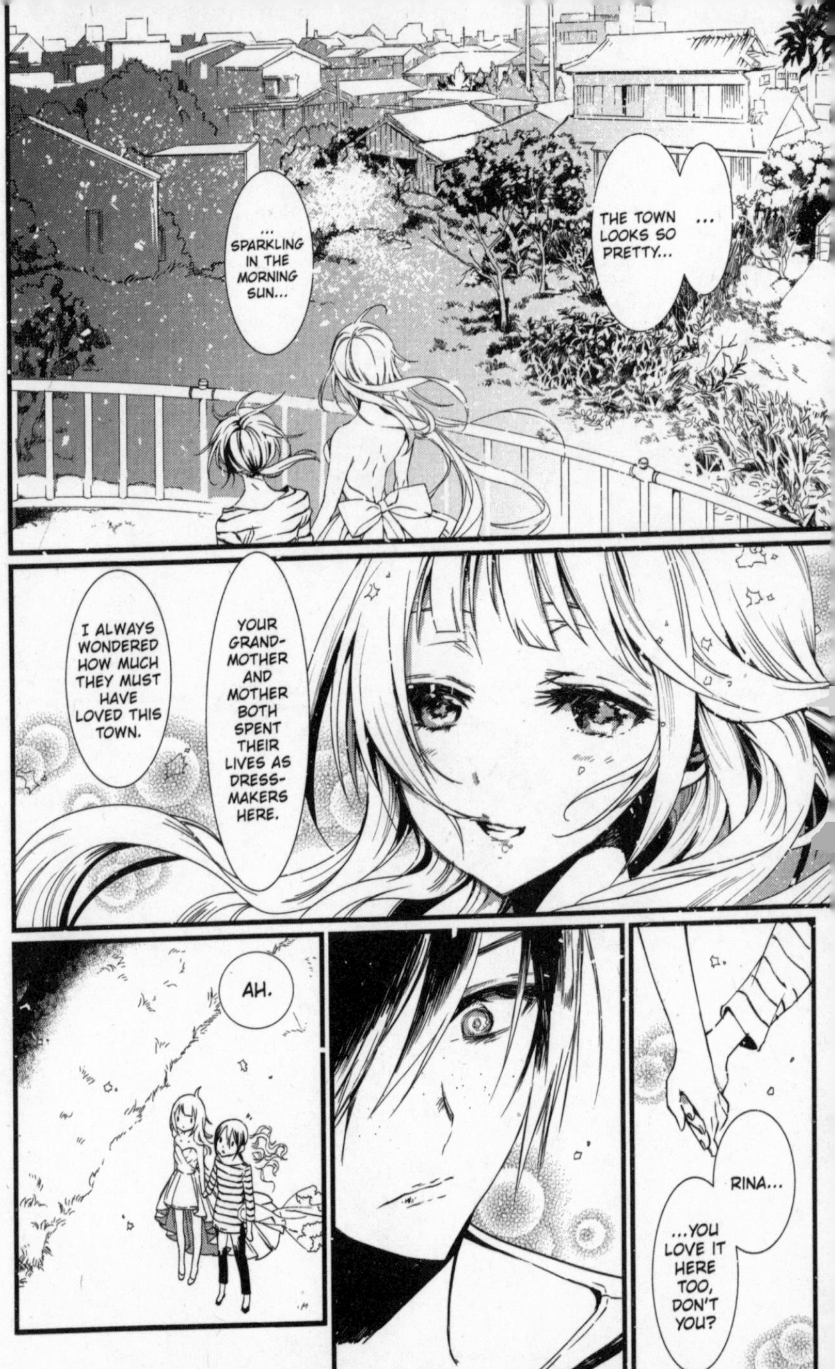
...THE TOWN LOOKS SO PRETTY...
...SPARKLING IN THE MORNING SUN...
YOUR GRAND-MOTHER AND MOTHER BOTH SPENT THEIR LIVES AS DRESS-MAKERS HERE.
I ALWAYS WONDERED HOW MUCH THEY MUST HAVE LOVED THIS TOWN.
RINA...
...YOU LOVE IT HERE TOO, DON'T YOU?
AH.

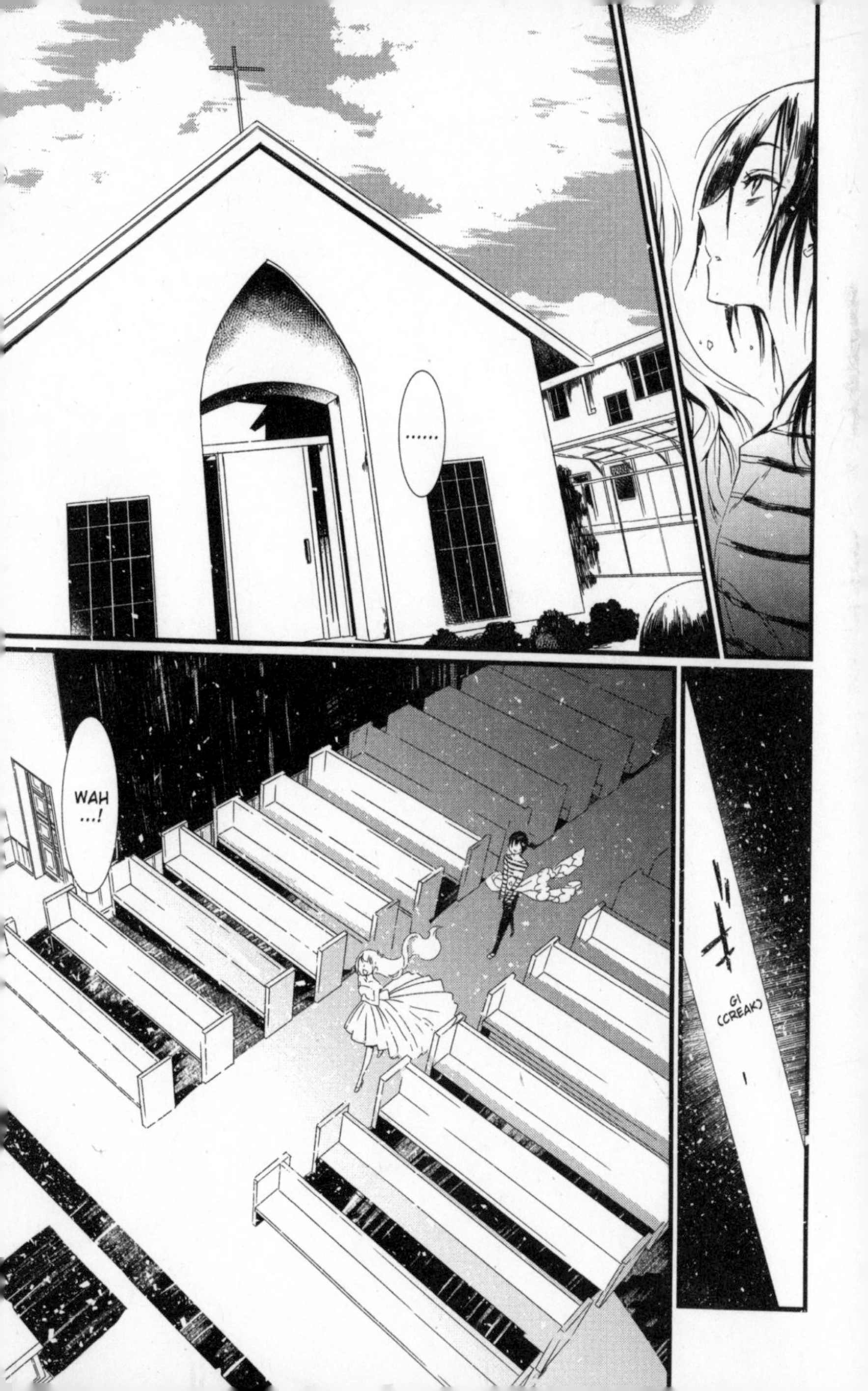
......
GI
(CREAK)
WAH ...!

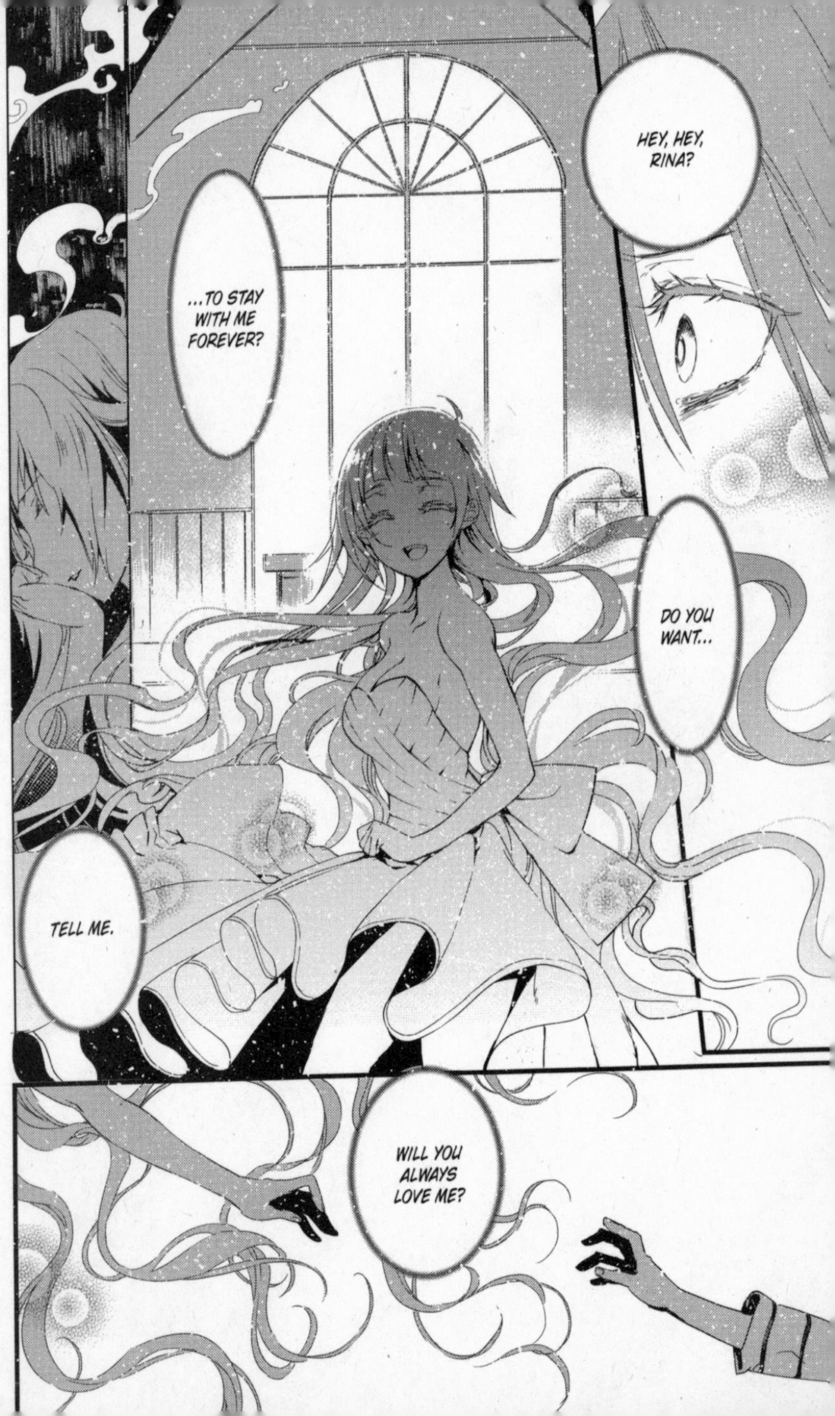
HEY, HEY, RINA?
DO YOU WANT...
...TO STAY WITH ME FOREVER?
TELL ME.
WILL YOU ALWAYS LOVE ME?

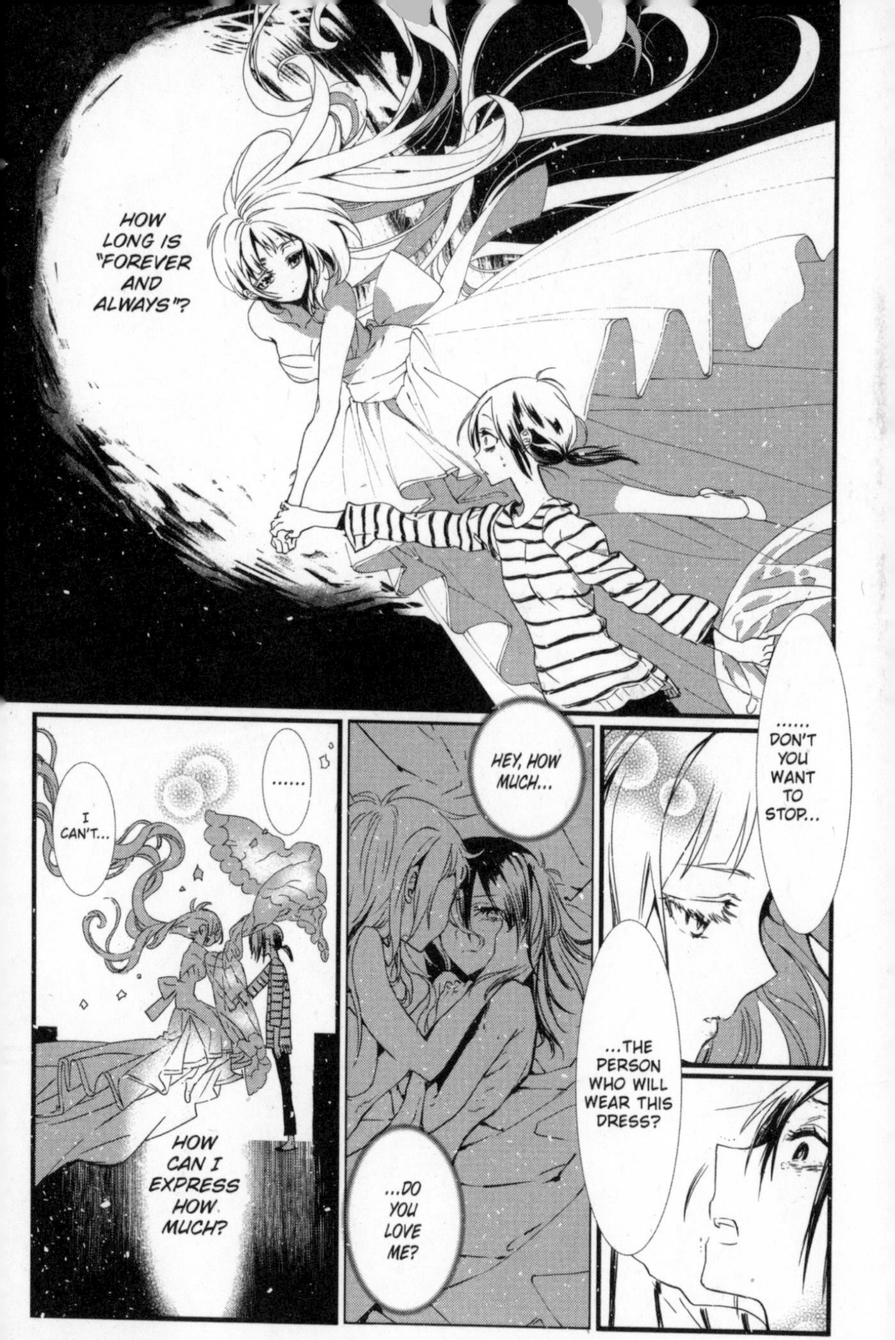
HOW LONG IS "FOREVER AND ALWAYS"?
......DON'T YOU WANT TO STOP...
...THE PERSON WHO WILL WEAR THIS DRESS?
HEY, HOW MUCH...
...DO YOU LOVE ME?
......
I CAN'T...
HOW CAN I EXPRESS HOW MUCH?

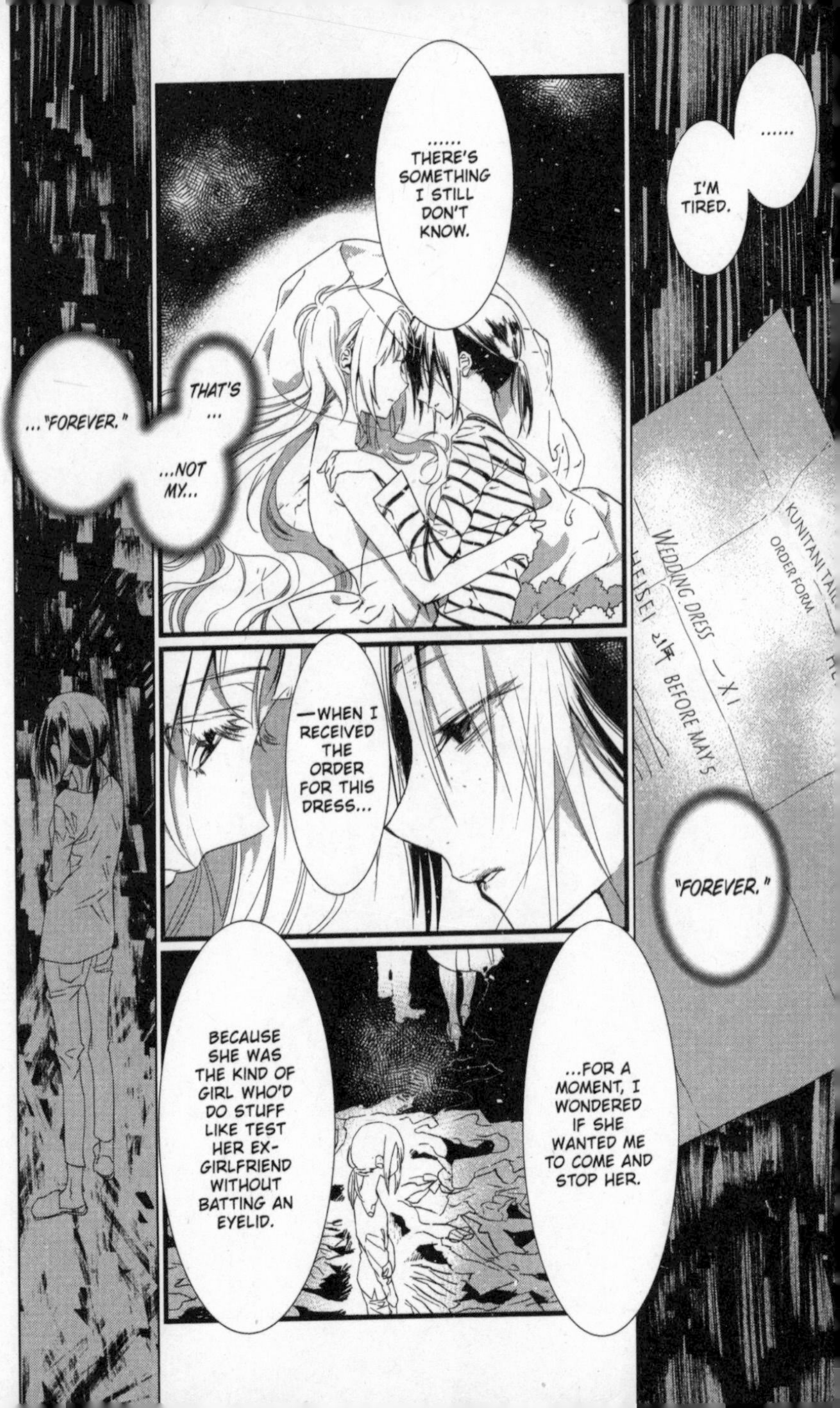
......
I'M TIRED.
ORDER FORM
WEDDING DRESS —X1
HEISEI 21年 BEFORE MAY 5
"FOREVER."
...... THERE'S SOMETHING I STILL DON'T KNOW.
—WHEN I RECEIVED THE ORDER FOR THIS DRESS...
...FOR A MOMENT, I WONDERED IF SHE WANTED ME TO COME AND STOP HER.
BECAUSE SHE WAS THE KIND OF GIRL WHO'D DO STUFF LIKE TEST HER EX-GIRLFRIEND WITHOUT BATTING AN EYELID.
THAT'S ...
...NOT MY...
..."FOREVER."

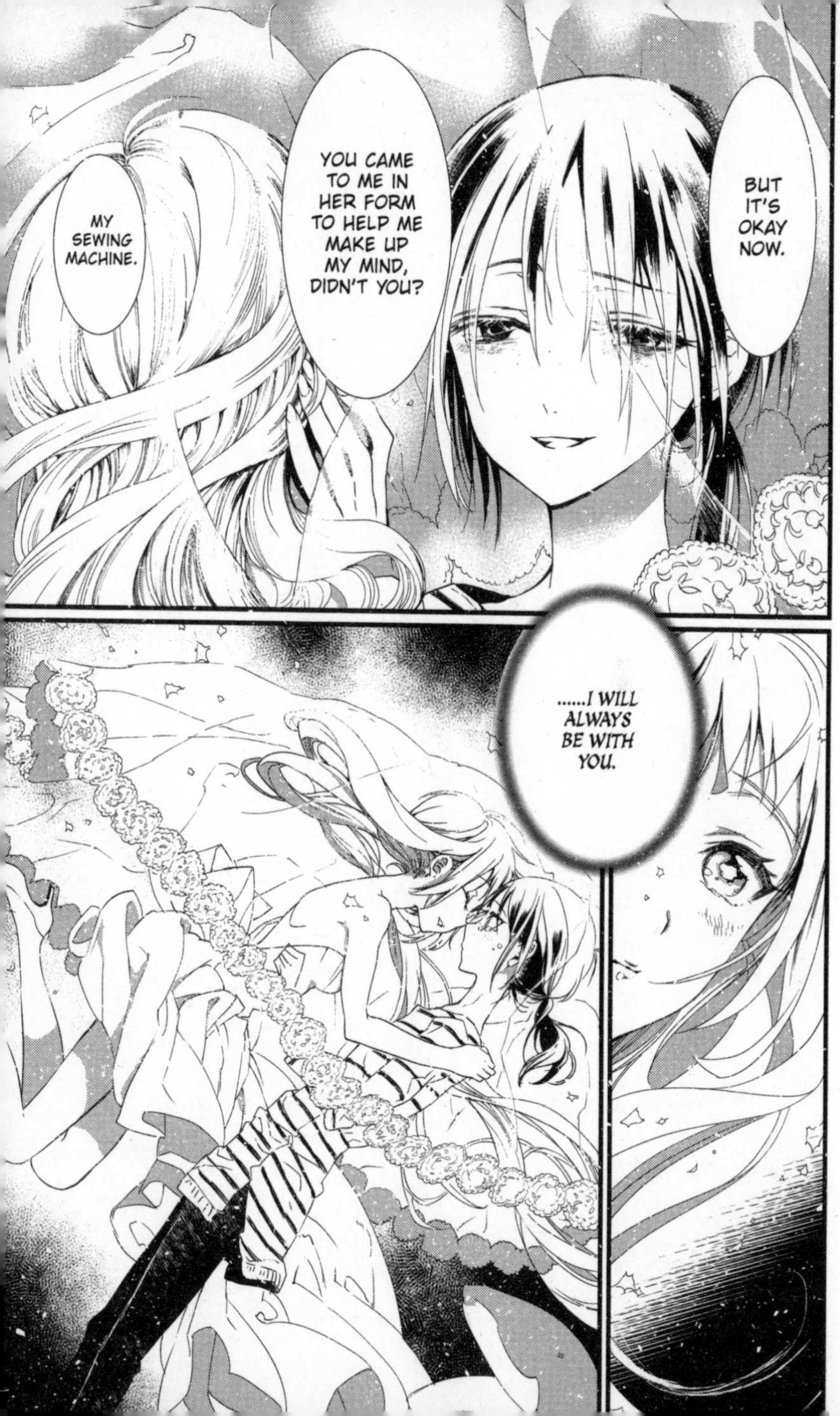
BUT IT'S OKAY NOW.
YOU CAME TO ME IN HER FORM TO HELP ME MAKE UP MY MIND, DIDN'T YOU?
MY SEWING MACHINE.
......I WILL ALWAYS BE WITH YOU.

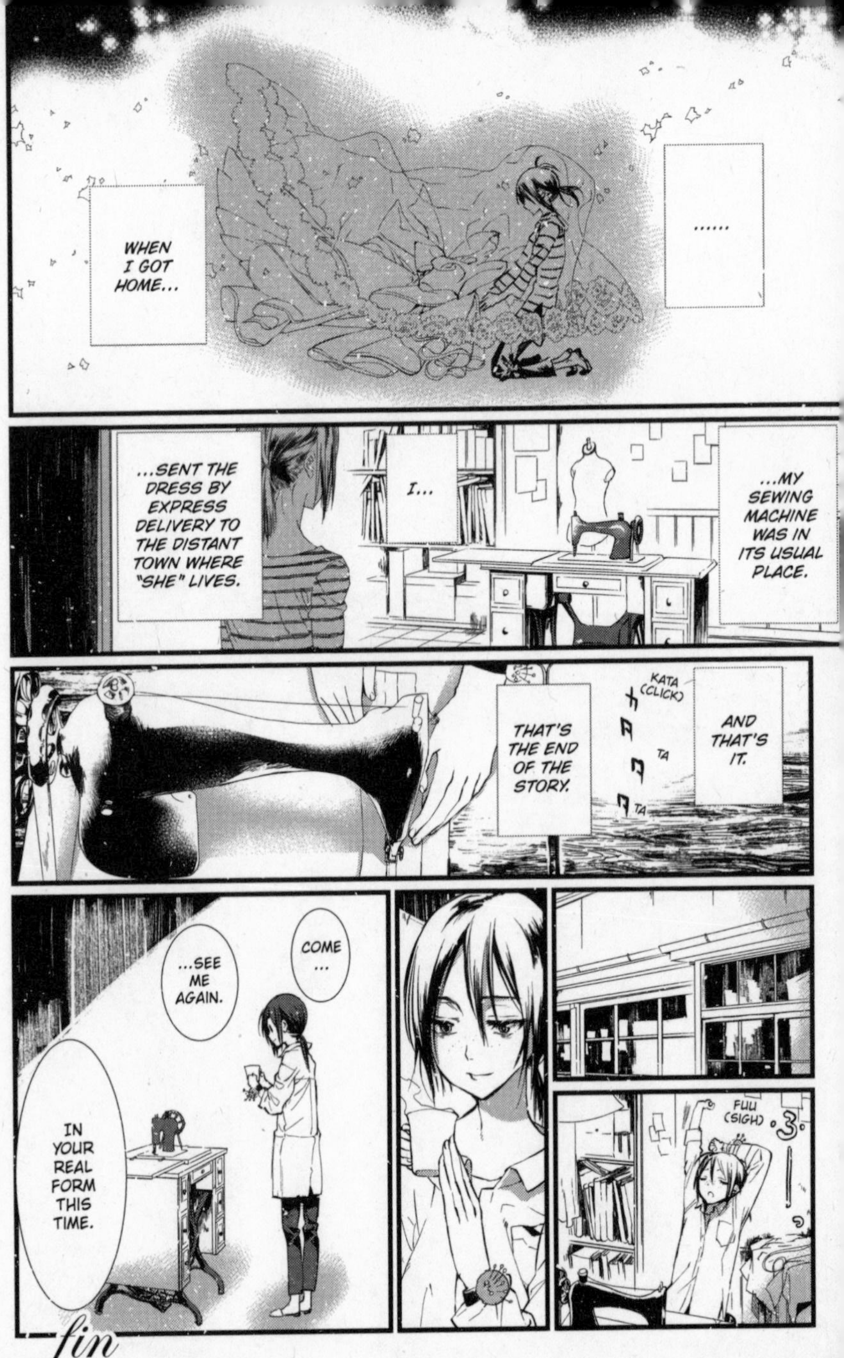
......
WHEN I GOT HOME...
...MY SEWING MACHINE WAS IN ITS USUAL PLACE.
I...
...SENT THE DRESS BY EXPRESS DELIVERY TO THE DISTANT TOWN WHERE "SHE" LIVES.
AND THAT'S IT.
KATA (CLICK)
TA
TA
THAT'S THE END OF THE STORY.
FUU (SIGH)
COME...
...SEE ME AGAIN.
IN YOUR REAL FORM THIS TIME.

fin

éclair
blanche

A Girls' Love Anthology
That Resonates in Your Heart

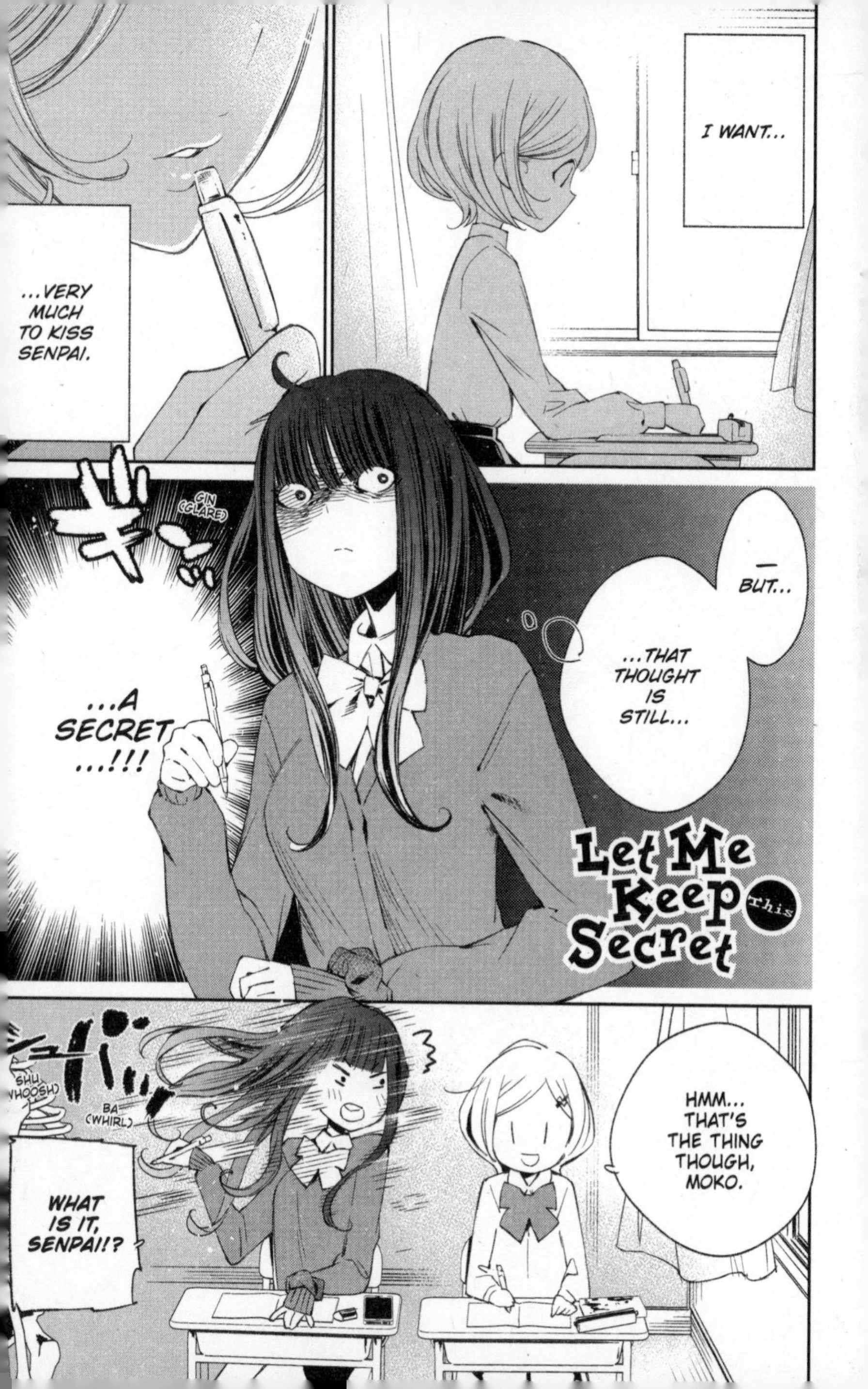
I WANT...
...VERY MUCH TO KISS SENPAI.
—BUT...
...THAT THOUGHT IS STILL...
GIN (GLARE)
...A SECRET ...!!!
Let Me Keep This Secret
HMM... THAT'S THE THING THOUGH, MOKO.
BA (WHIRL)
SHU (WHOOSH)
WHAT IS IT, SENPAI!?

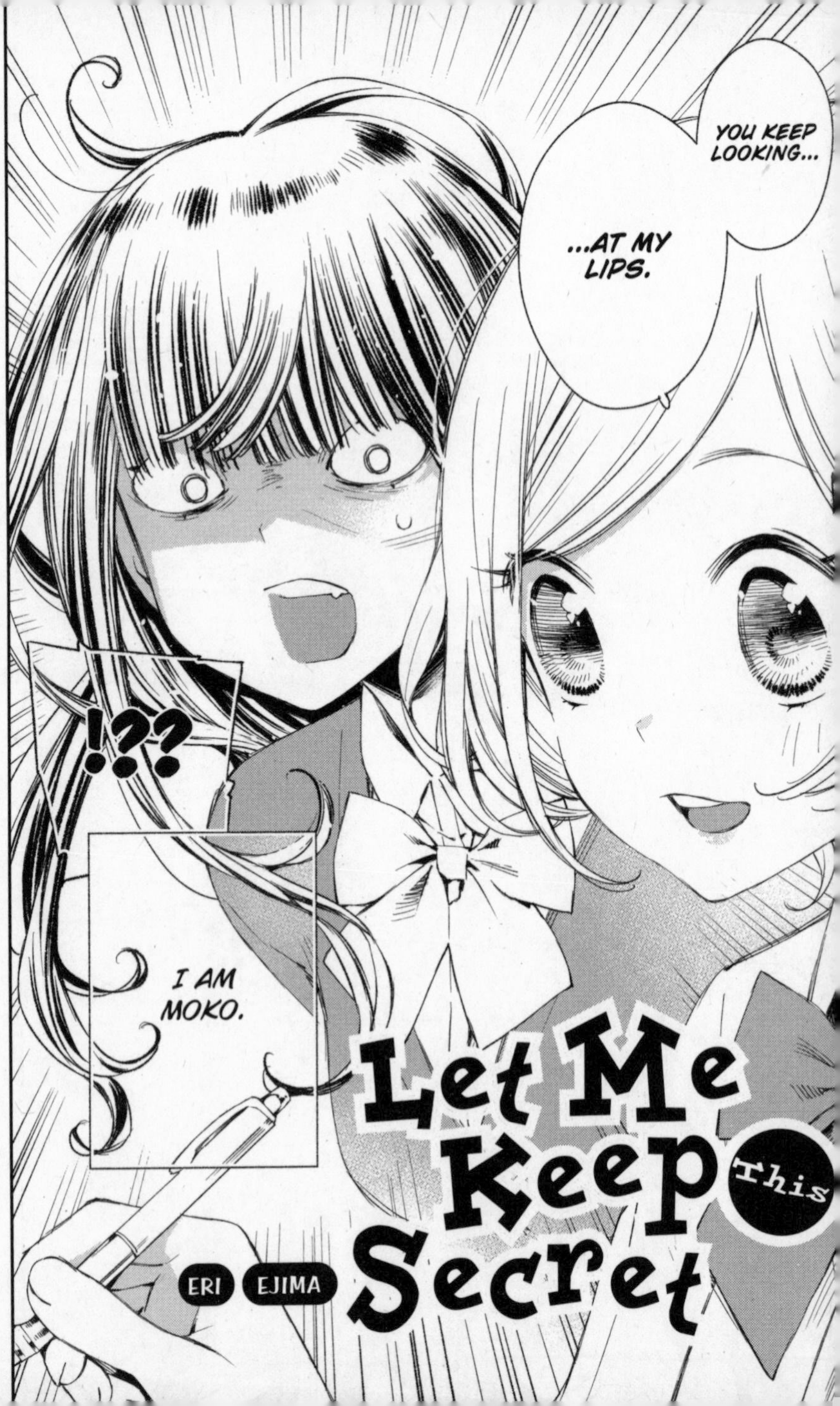
YOU KEEP LOOKING...
...AT MY LIPS.
!??
I AM MOKO.
Let Me Keep This Secret
ERI EJIMA

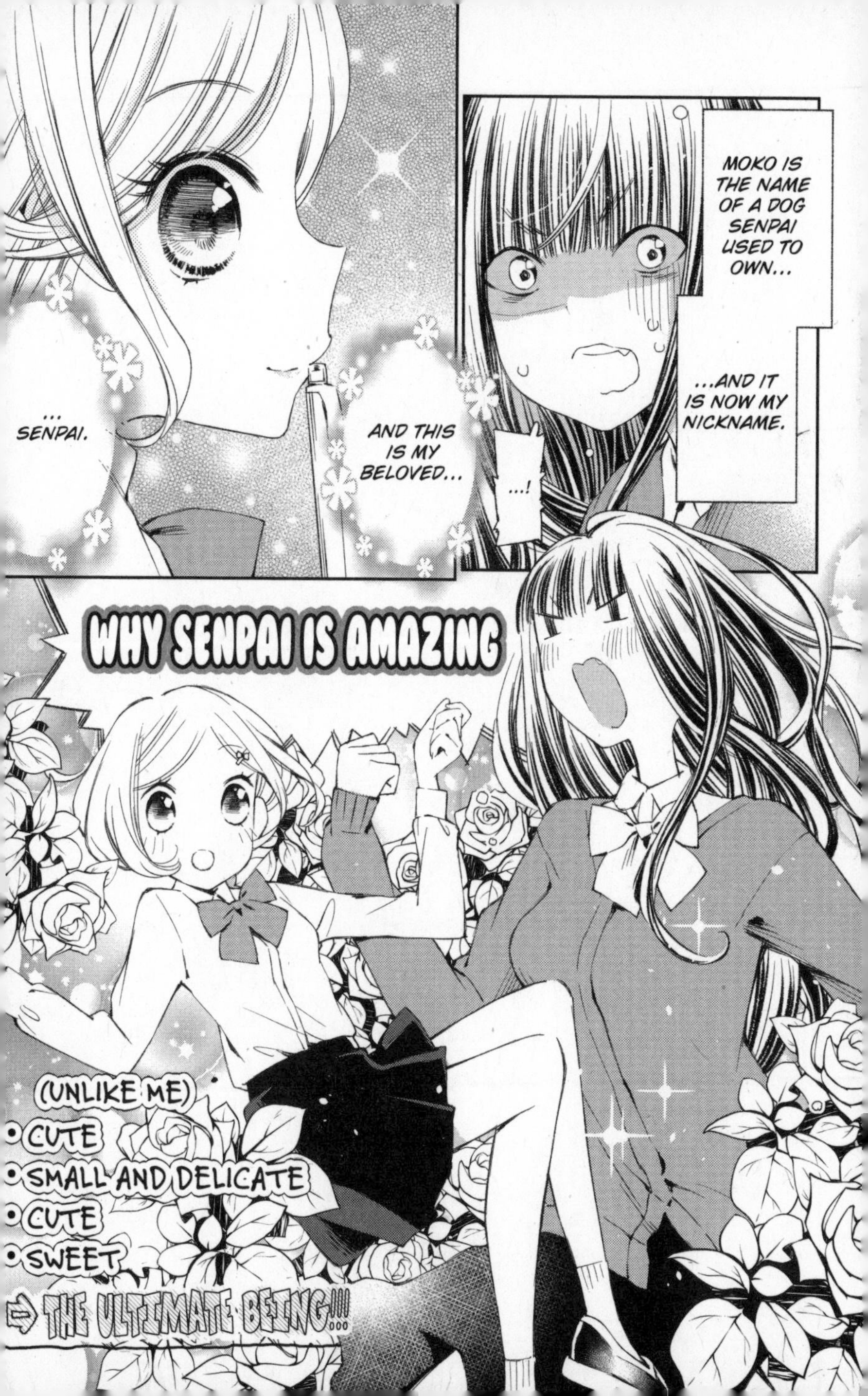
MOKO IS THE NAME OF A DOG SENPAI USED TO OWN...
...AND IT IS NOW MY NICKNAME.
...!
AND THIS IS MY BELOVED...
... SENPAI.
WHY SENPAI IS AMAZING
(UNLIKE ME)
• CUTE
• SMALL AND DELICATE
• CUTE
• SWEET
⇨ THE ULTIMATE BEING!!!

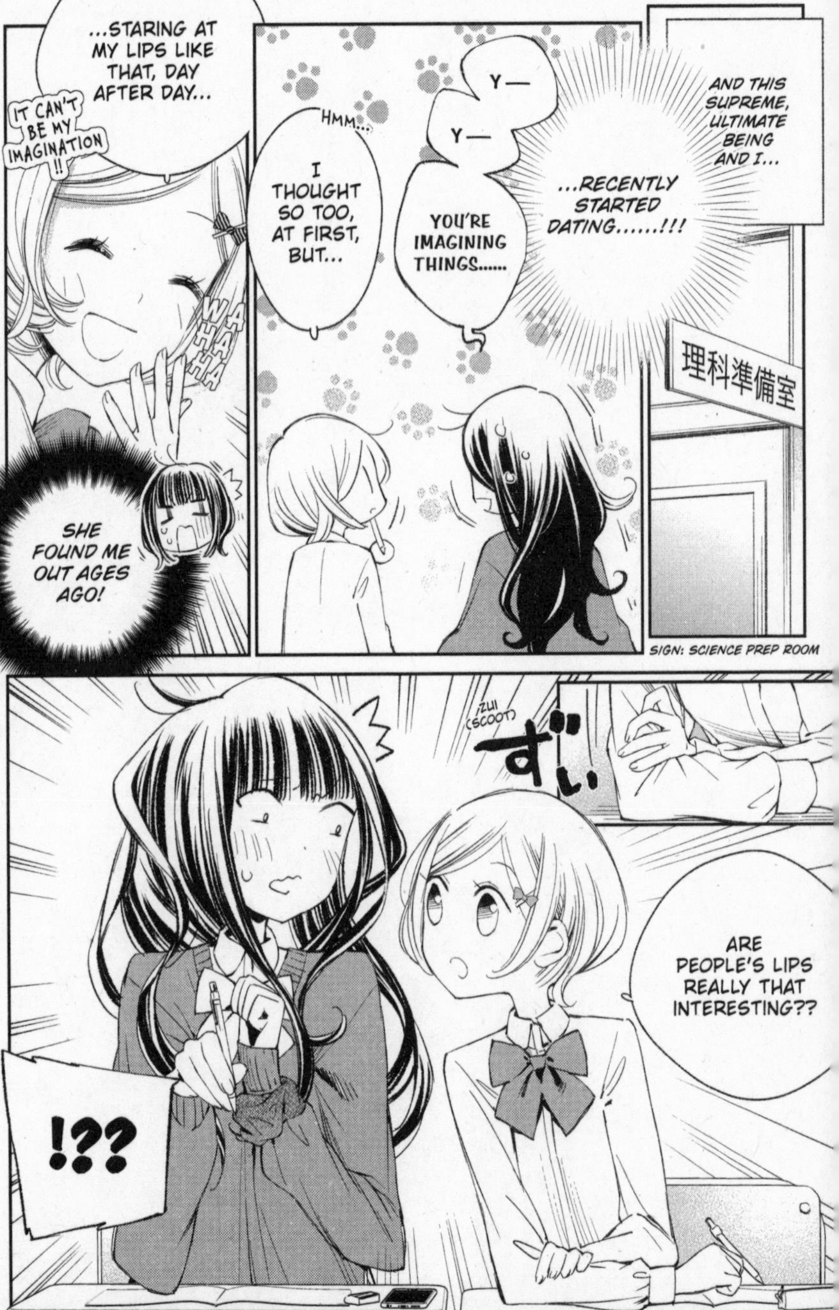
AND THIS SUPREME, ULTIMATE BEING AND I...
...RECENTLY STARTED DATING......!!!
理科準備室
SIGN: SCIENCE PREP ROOM
Y—
Y—
YOU'RE IMAGINING THINGS......
HMM...
I THOUGHT SO TOO, AT FIRST, BUT...
...STARING AT MY LIPS LIKE THAT, DAY AFTER DAY...
IT CAN'T BE MY IMAGINATION!!
WAHAHAHA
SHE FOUND ME OUT AGES AGO!
ずい
ZUI (SCOOT)
ARE PEOPLE'S LIPS REALLY THAT INTERESTING??
!??

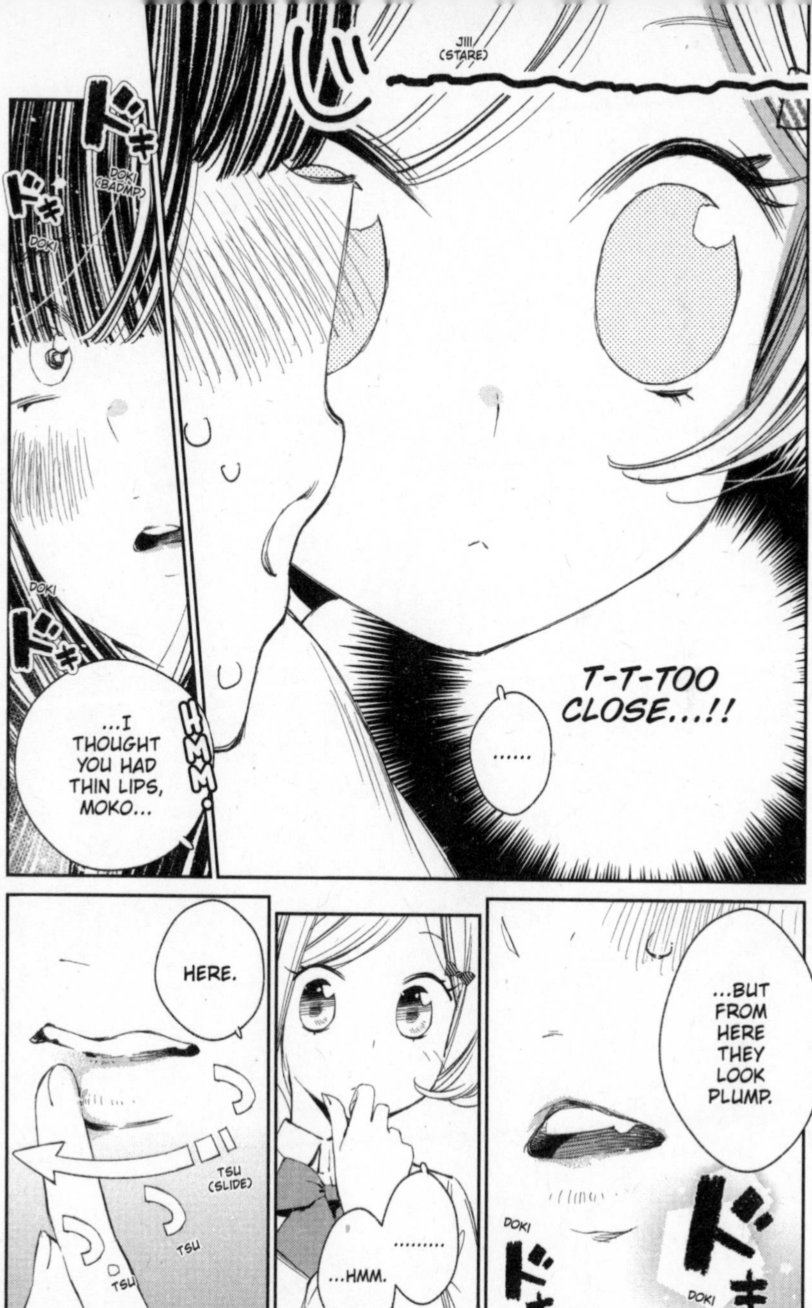
JIII (STARE)
ドキ
DOKI (BADMP)
ドキ
DOKI
T-T-TOO CLOSE...!!
......
HMMM.
DOKI
ドキ
...I THOUGHT YOU HAD THIN LIPS, MOKO...
...BUT FROM HERE THEY LOOK PLUMP.
ドキ
DOKI
DOKI
ドキ
....
...HMM.
HERE.
TSU (SLIDE)
TSU
TSU

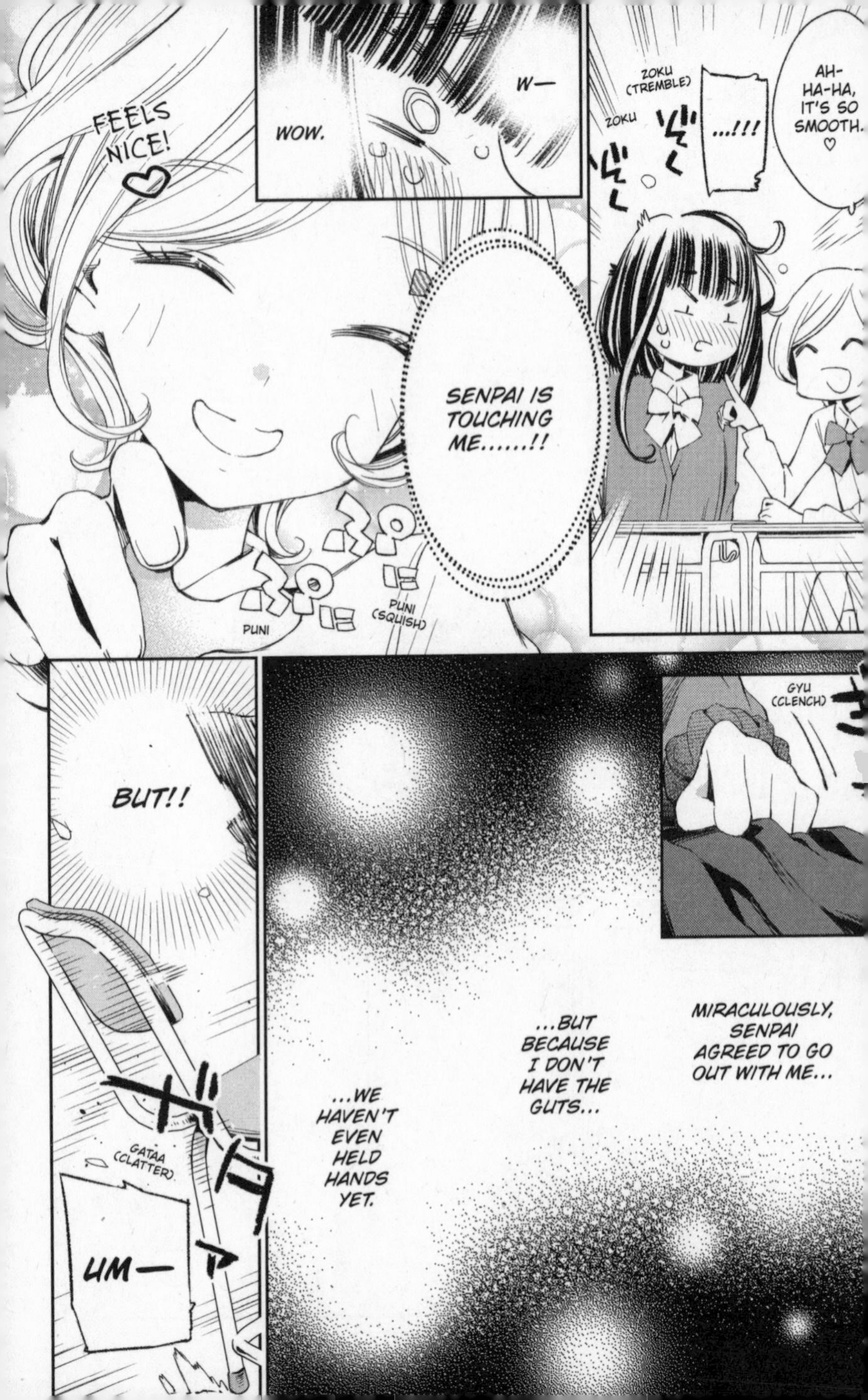
AH-HA-HA, IT'S SO SMOOTH. ♡
...!!!
ZOKU (TREMBLE)
ZOKU
W—
WOW.
FEELS NICE! ♡
SENPAI IS TOUCHING ME......!!
PUNI (SQUISH)
PUNI
GYU (CLENCH)
MIRACULOUSLY, SENPAI AGREED TO GO OUT WITH ME...
...BUT BECAUSE I DON'T HAVE THE GUTS...
...WE HAVEN'T EVEN HELD HANDS YET.
BUT!!
GATAA (CLATTER)
UM—

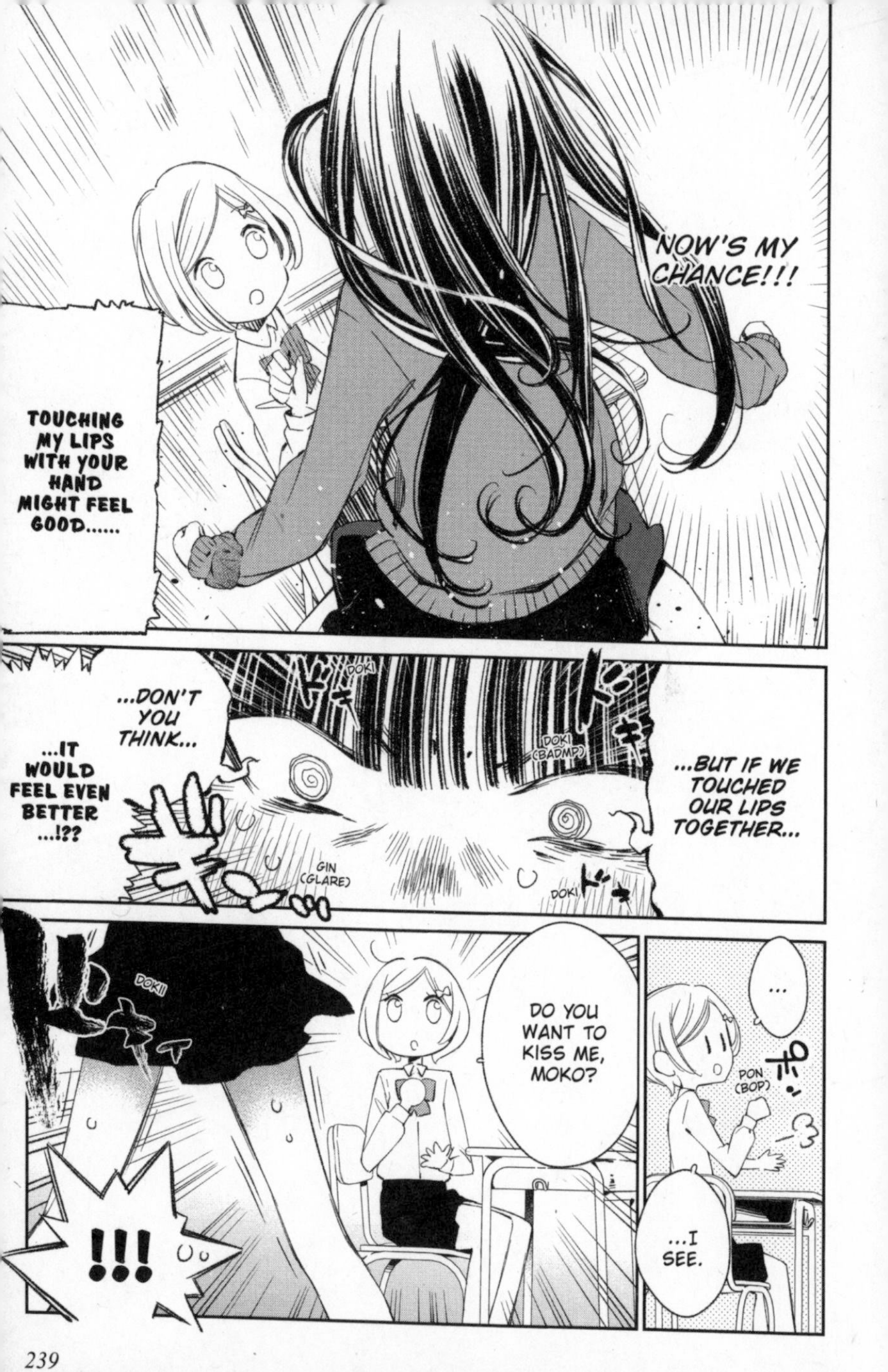

NOW'S MY CHANCE!!!
TOUCHING MY LIPS WITH YOUR HAND MIGHT FEEL GOOD......
...BUT IF WE TOUCHED OUR LIPS TOGETHER...
DOKI (BADMP)
DOKI
...DON'T YOU THINK...
...IT WOULD FEEL EVEN BETTER ...!??
GIN (GLARE)
DOKI
...
PON (BOP)
...I SEE.
DO YOU WANT TO KISS ME, MOKO?
DOKII
!!!

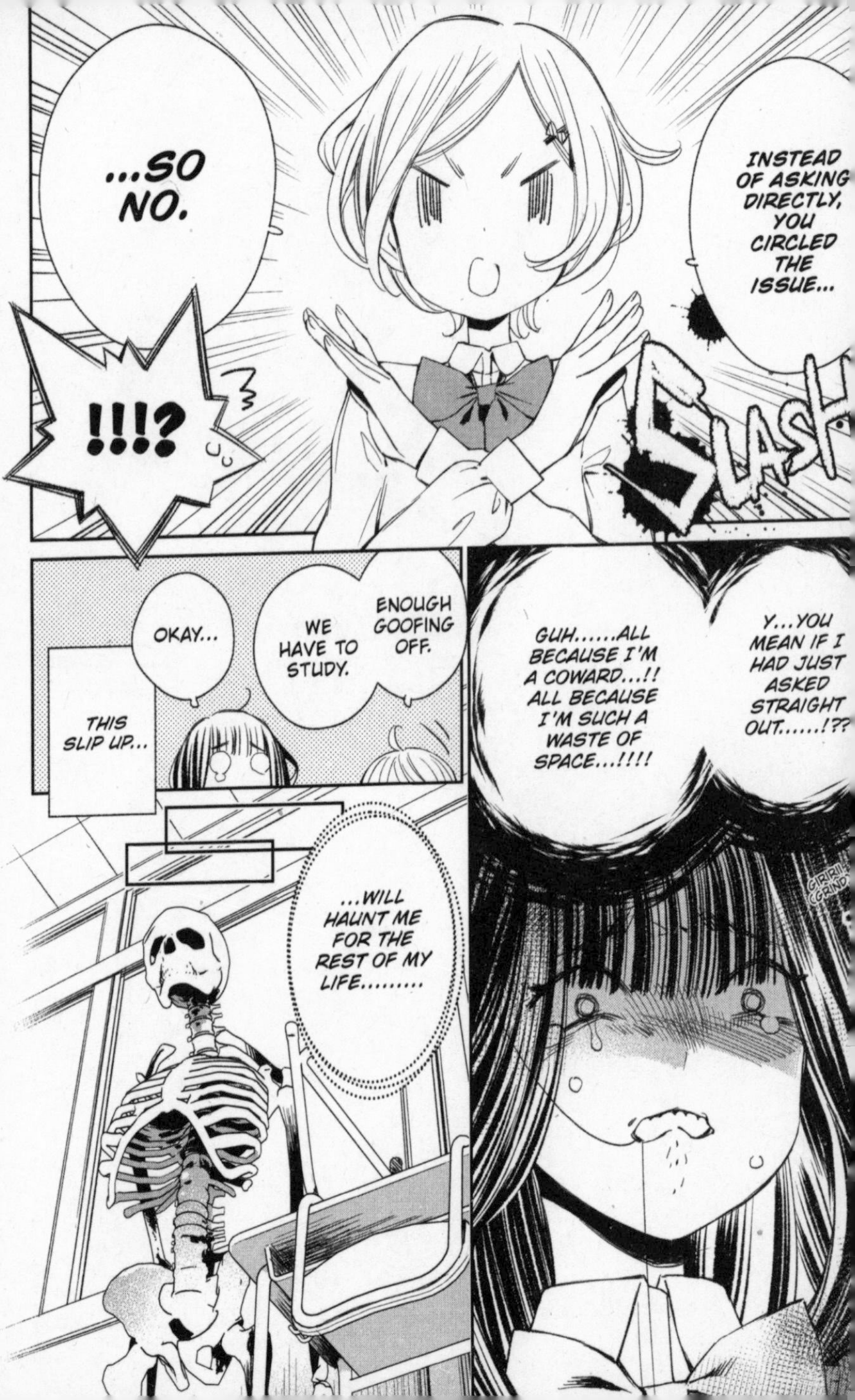
INSTEAD OF ASKING DIRECTLY, YOU CIRCLED THE ISSUE...
SLASH
...SO NO.
!!!?
Y...YOU MEAN IF I HAD JUST ASKED STRAIGHT OUT......!??
GUH......ALL BECAUSE I'M A COWARD...!! ALL BECAUSE I'M SUCH A WASTE OF SPACE...!!!!
GIRIRI (GRIND)
ENOUGH GOOFING OFF.
WE HAVE TO STUDY.
OKAY...
THIS SLIP UP...
...WILL HAUNT ME FOR THE REST OF MY LIFE.........

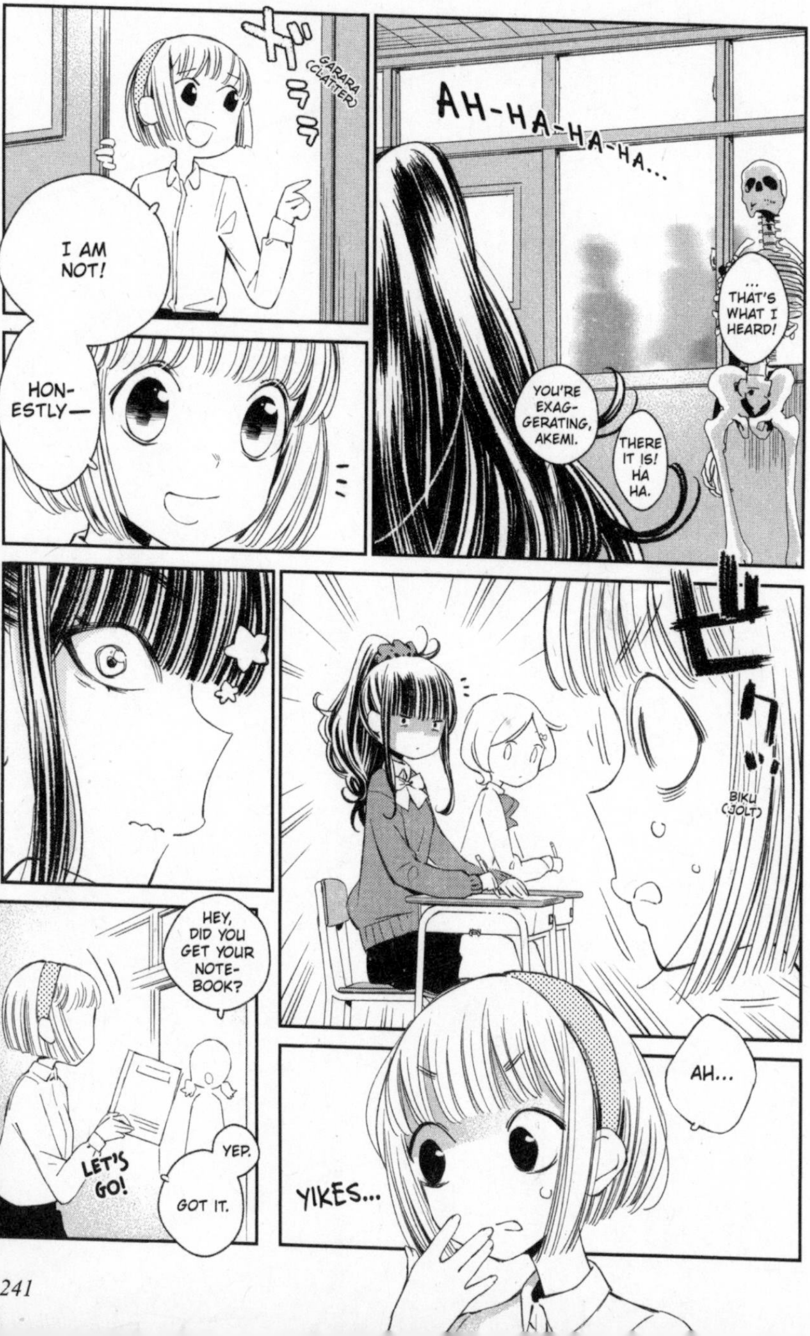
AH-HA-HA-HA...
... THAT'S WHAT I HEARD!
YOU'RE EXAG-GERATING, AKEMI.
THERE IT IS! HA HA.
GARARA (CLATTER)
I AM NOT!
HON-ESTLY—
BIKU (JOLT)
AH...
YIKES...
HEY, DID YOU GET YOUR NOTE-BOOK?
YEP.
GOT IT.
LET'S GO!

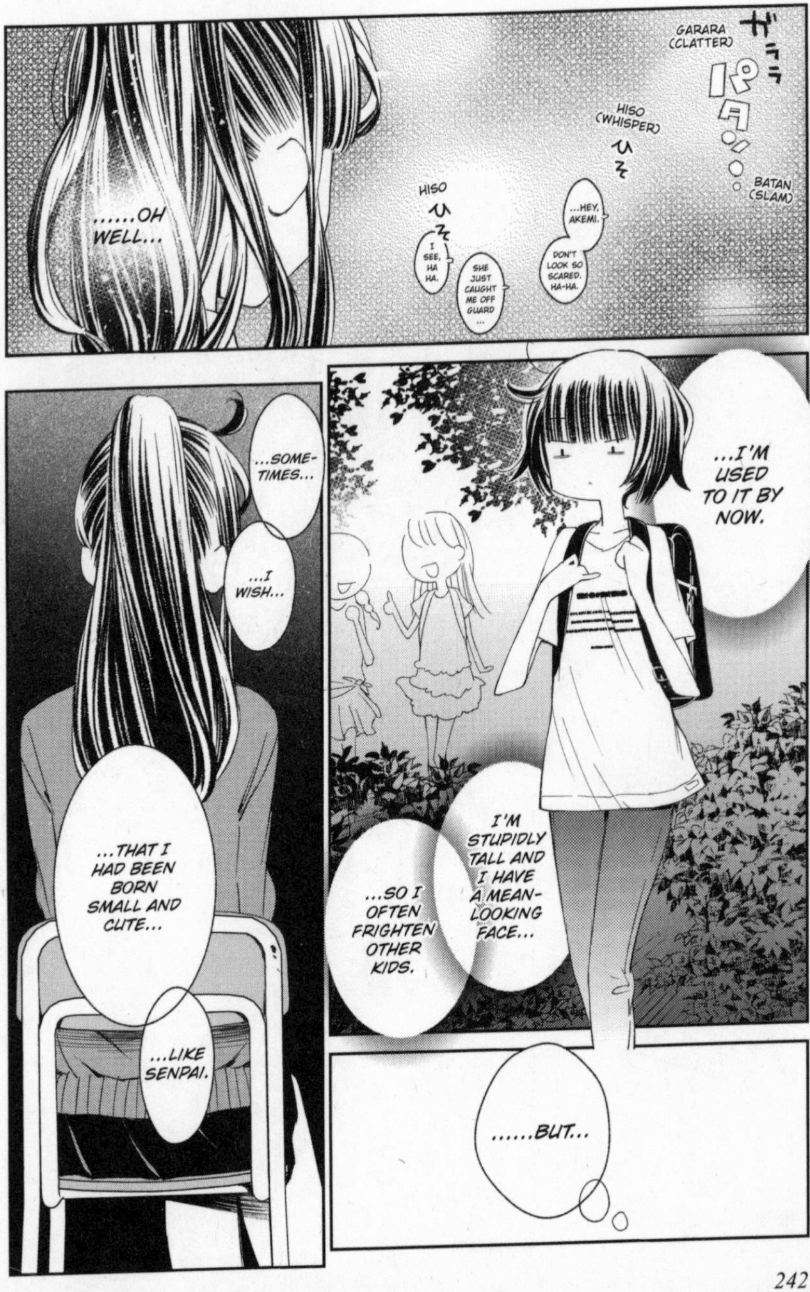
GARARA (CLATTER)
BATAN (SLAM)
HISO (WHISPER)
...HEY, AKEMI.
DON'T LOOK SO SCARED. HA-HA.
SHE JUST CAUGHT ME OFF GUARD...
HISO
I SEE, HA HA.
......OH WELL...
...I'M USED TO IT BY NOW.
I'M STUPIDLY TALL AND I HAVE A MEAN-LOOKING FACE...
...SO I OFTEN FRIGHTEN OTHER KIDS.
......BUT...
...SOME-TIMES...
...I WISH...
...THAT I HAD BEEN BORN SMALL AND CUTE...
...LIKE SENPAI.

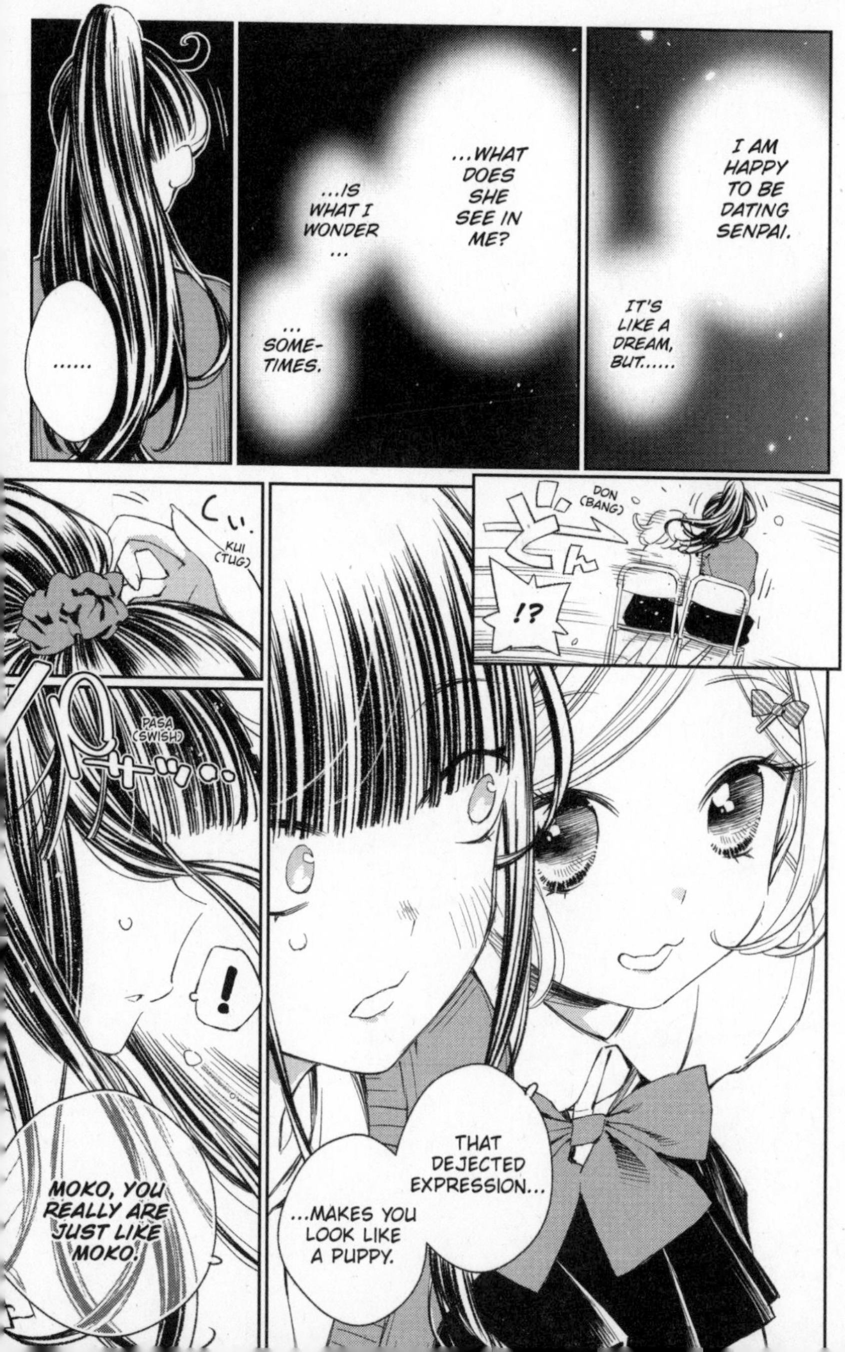
I AM HAPPY TO BE DATING SENPAI.
IT'S LIKE A DREAM, BUT......
...WHAT DOES SHE SEE IN ME?
...IS WHAT I WONDER...
...SOMETIMES.
......
DON (BANG)
!?
THAT DEJECTED EXPRESSION...
...MAKES YOU LOOK LIKE A PUPPY.
KUI (TUG)
PASA (SWISH)
!
MOKO, YOU REALLY ARE JUST LIKE MOKO.

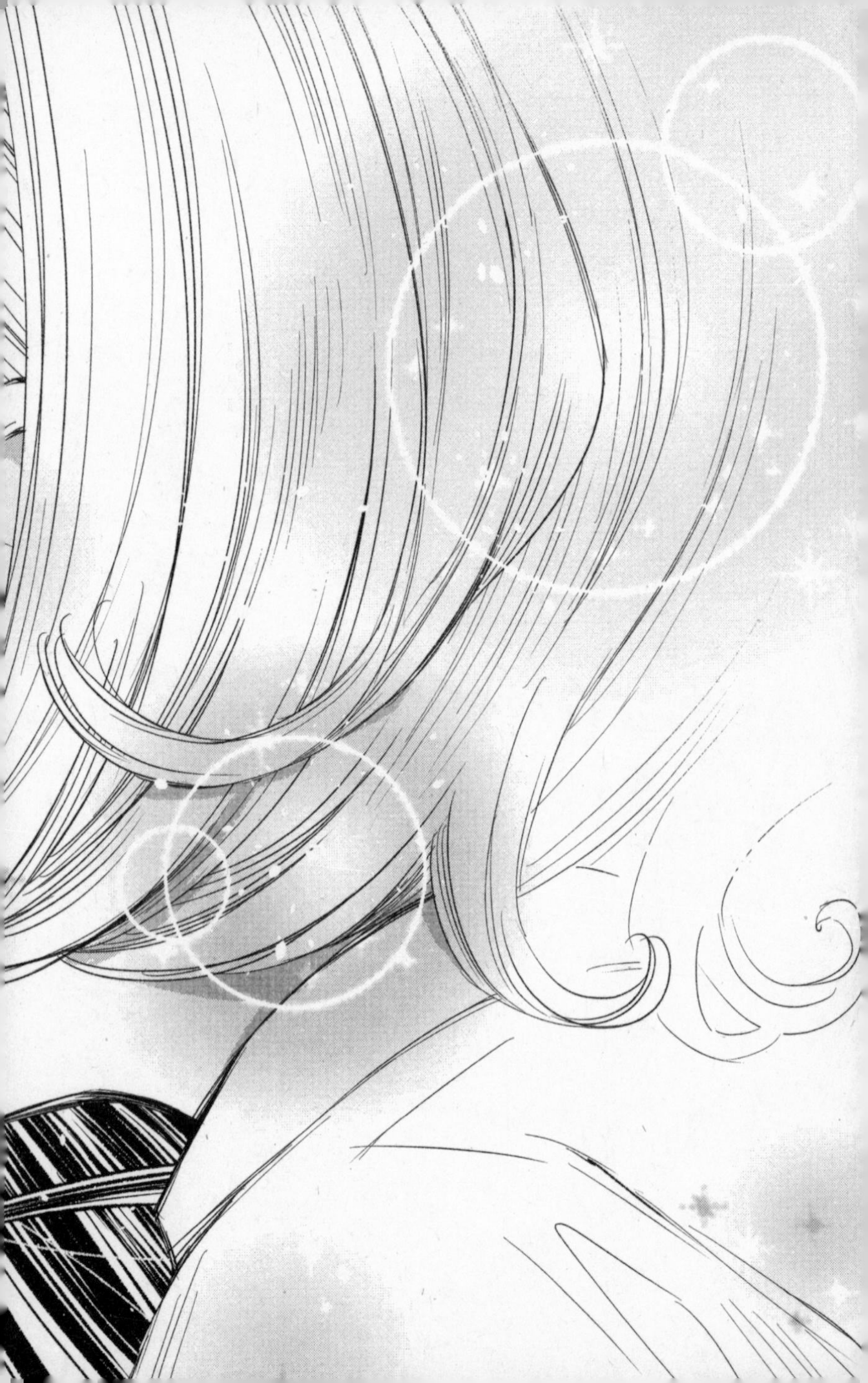

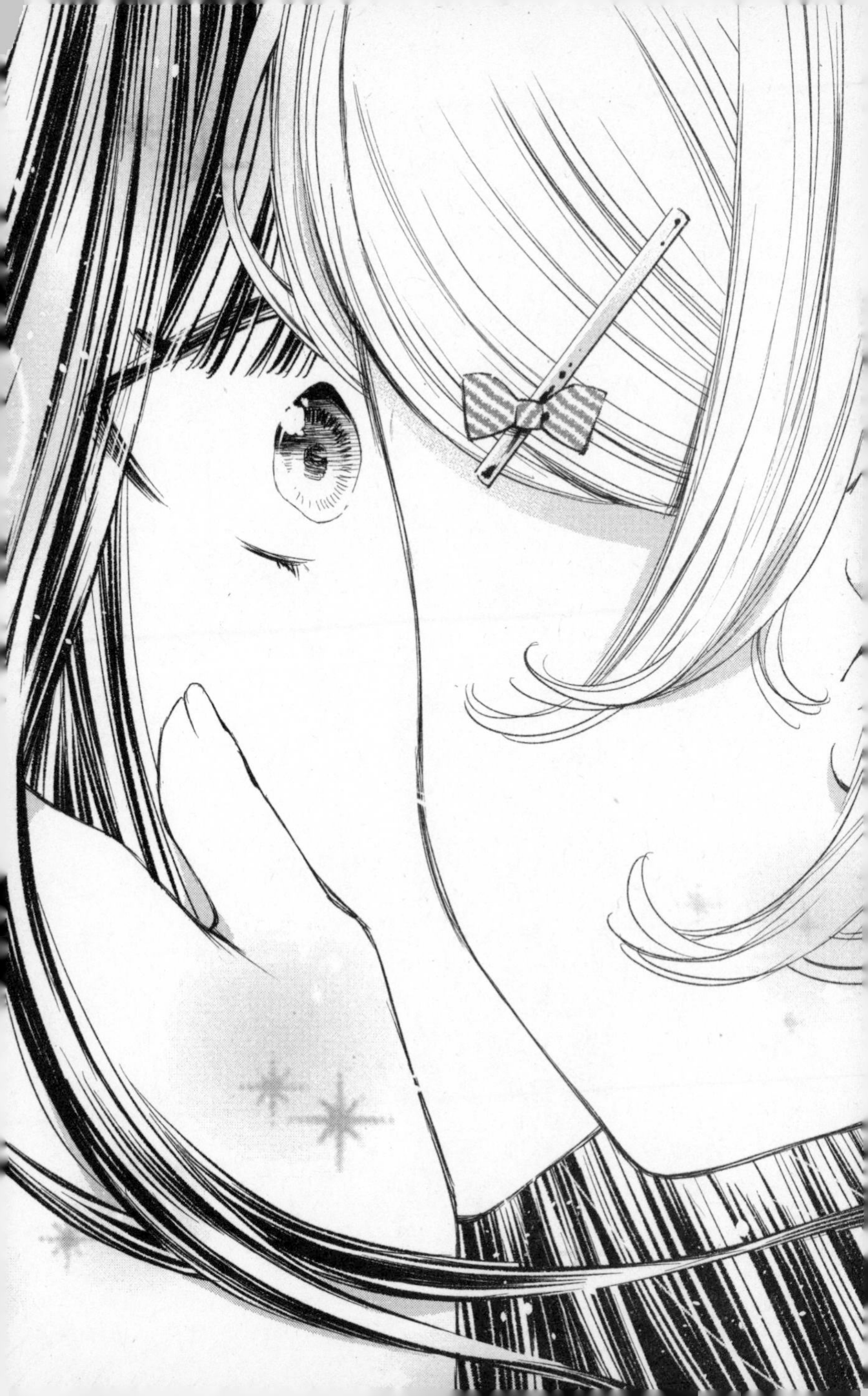

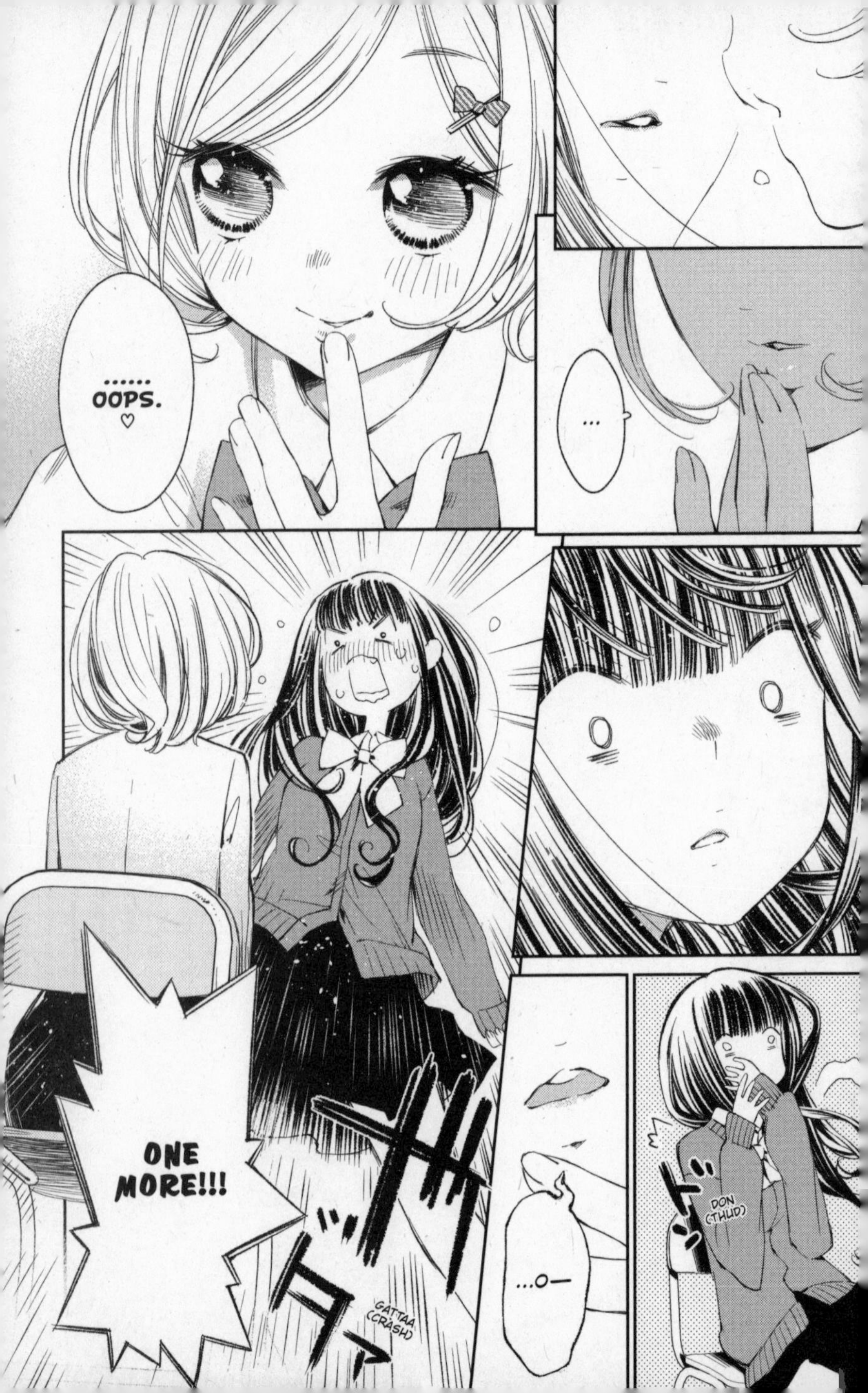
...
......OOPS. ♡
DON (THUD)
...O—
ONE MORE!!!
GATTAA (CRASH)

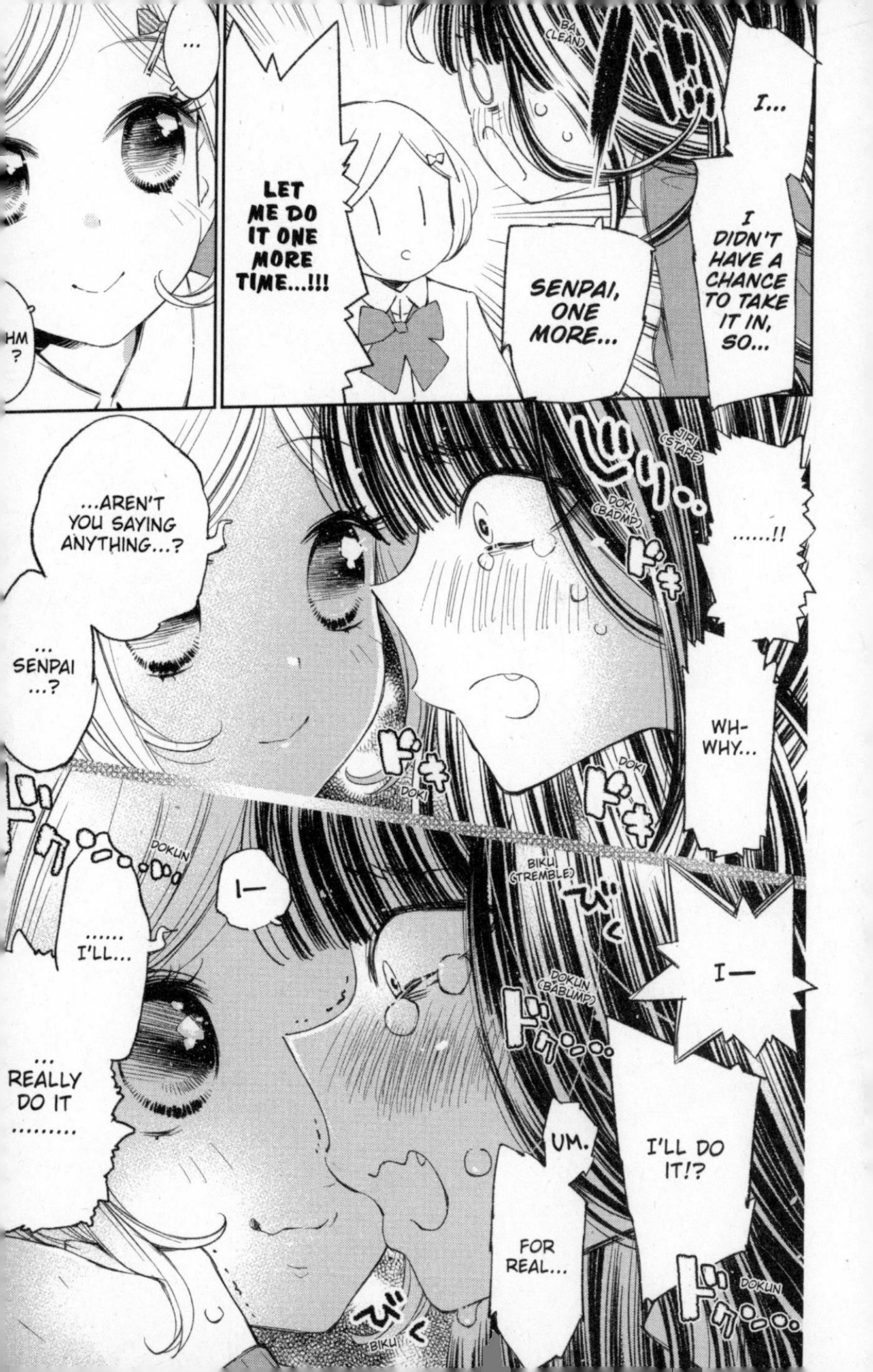

I...
I DIDN'T HAVE A CHANCE TO TAKE IT IN, SO...
BA (LEAN)
SENPAI, ONE MORE...
LET ME DO IT ONE MORE TIME...!!!
...
HM?
JIRI (STARE)
......!!
DOKI (BADMP)
WH- WHY...
DOKI
DOKI
...AREN'T YOU SAYING ANYTHING...?
... SENPAI ...?
BIKU (TREMBLE)
I—
DOKUN (BABUMP)
I'LL DO IT!?
DOKUN
UM.
FOR REAL...
BIKU
I—
DOKUN
...... I'LL...
... REALLY DO IT ....

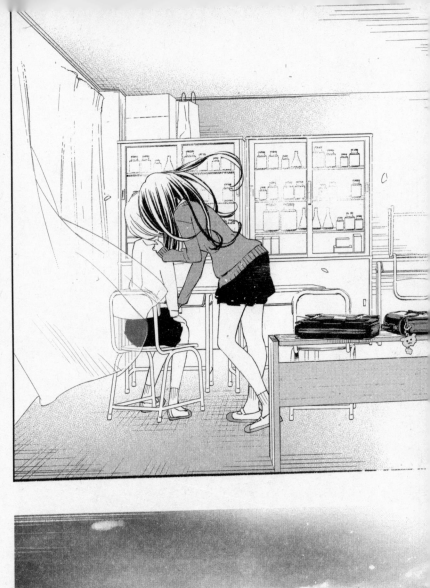

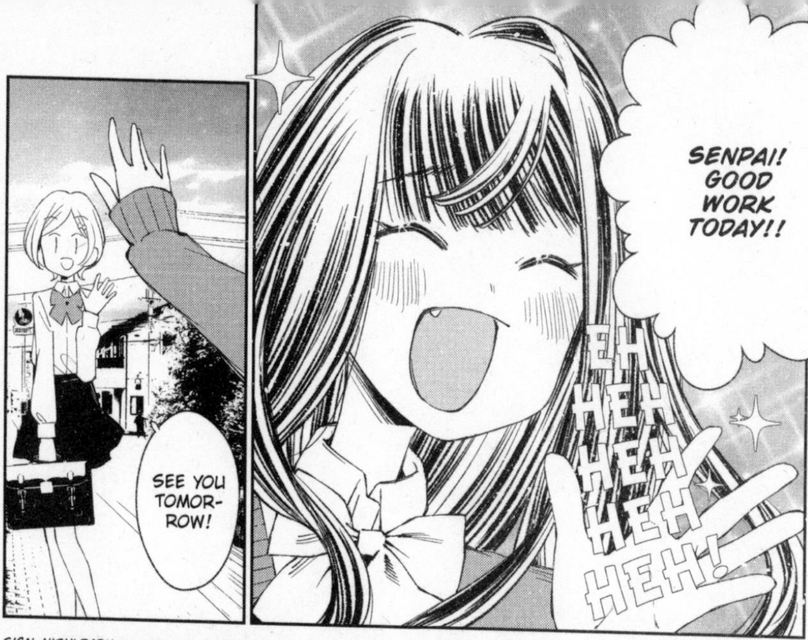
SENPAI! GOOD WORK TODAY!!
EH HEH HEH HEH HEH!
SEE YOU TOMOR-ROW!

SIGN: NISHI PARK

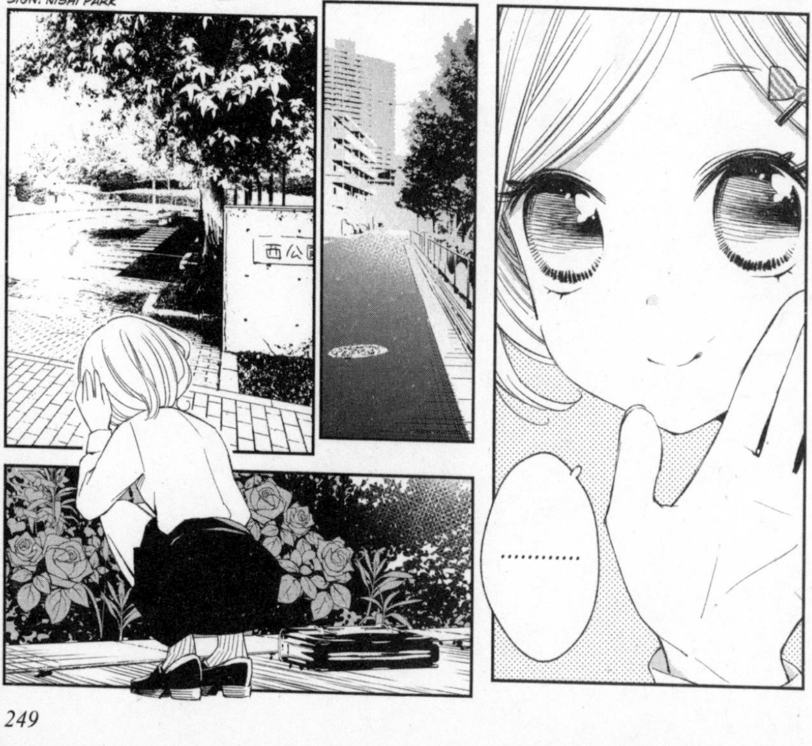
....

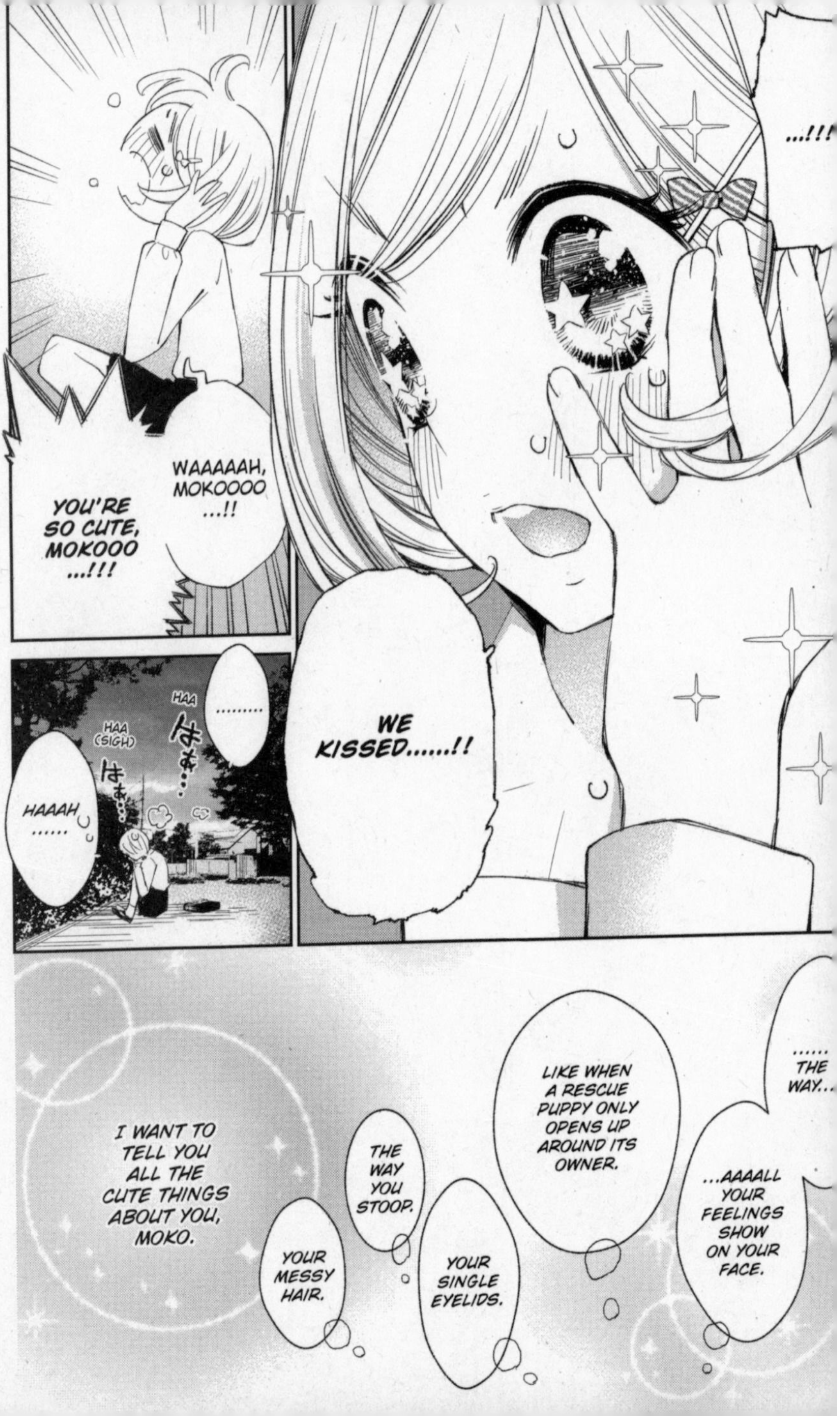
...!!!
WE KISSED......!!
WAAAAAH, MOKOOOO ...!!
YOU'RE SO CUTE, MOKOOO ...!!!
....
HAA
HAA (SIGH)
HAAAH ......
...... THE WAY...
...AAAALL YOUR FEELINGS SHOW ON YOUR FACE.
LIKE WHEN A RESCUE PUPPY ONLY OPENS UP AROUND ITS OWNER.
YOUR SINGLE EYELIDS.
THE WAY YOU STOOP.
YOUR MESSY HAIR.
I WANT TO TELL YOU ALL THE CUTE THINGS ABOUT YOU, MOKO.

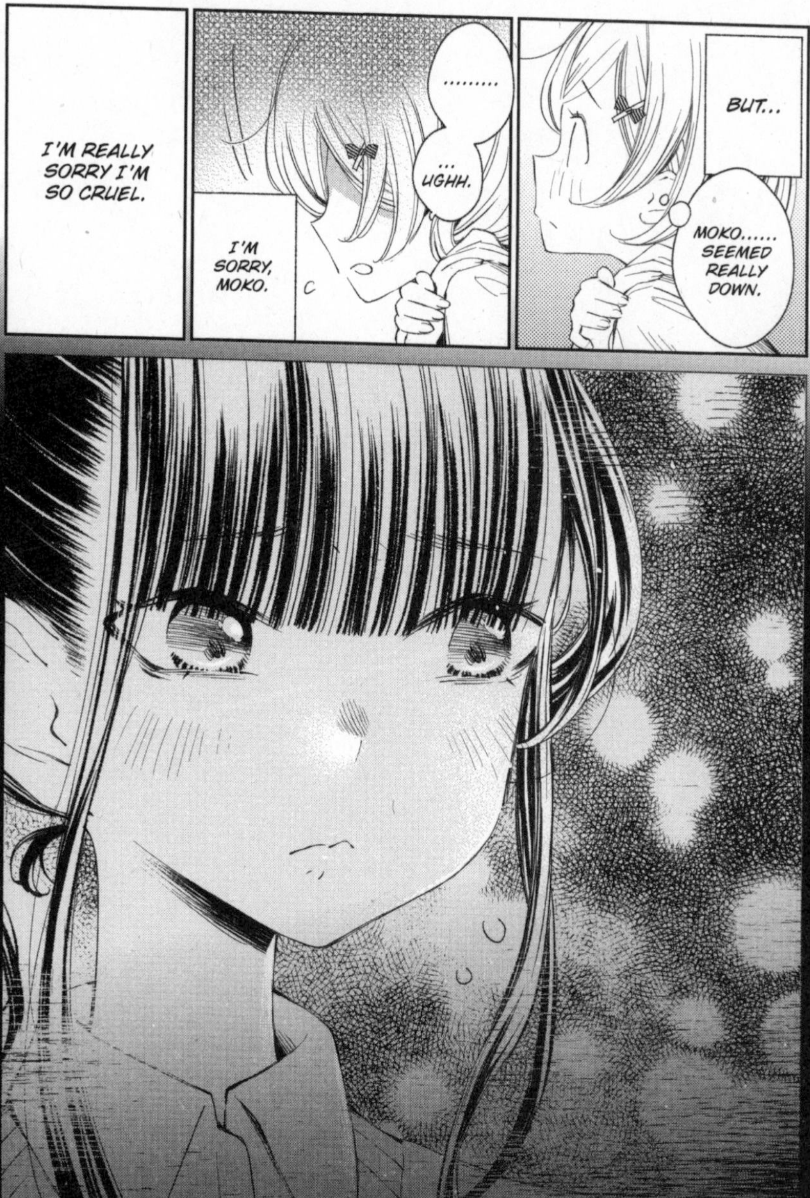
BUT...
MOKO...... SEEMED REALLY DOWN.
....
... UGHH.
I'M SORRY, MOKO.
I'M REALLY SORRY I'M SO CRUEL.

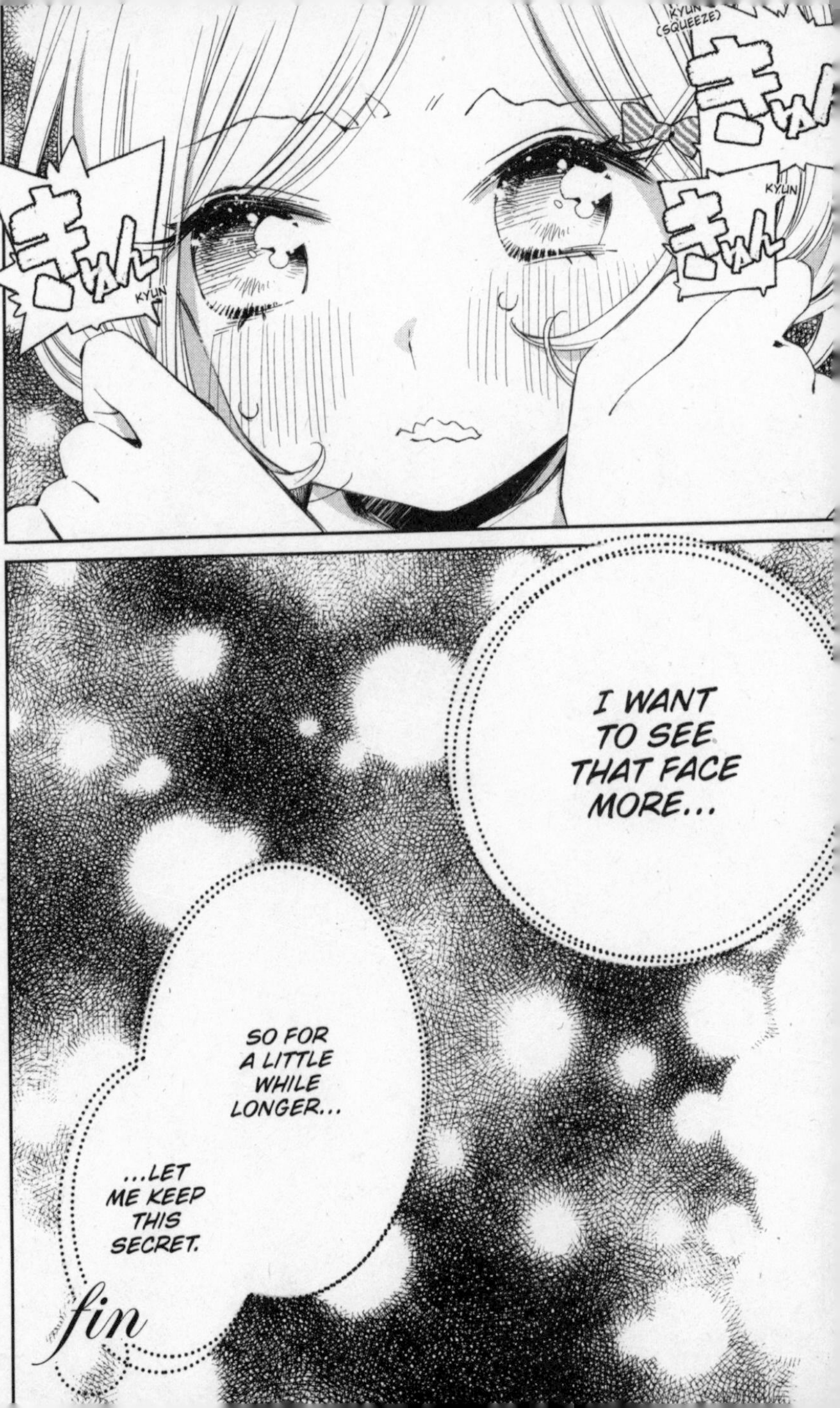
KYUN (SQUEEZE)
きゅん
KYUN
きゅん
きゅん
KYUN
I WANT TO SEE THAT FACE MORE...
SO FOR A LITTLE WHILE LONGER...
...LET ME KEEP THIS SECRET.
fin

éclair
blanche

A Girls' Love Anthology
That Resonates in Your Heart

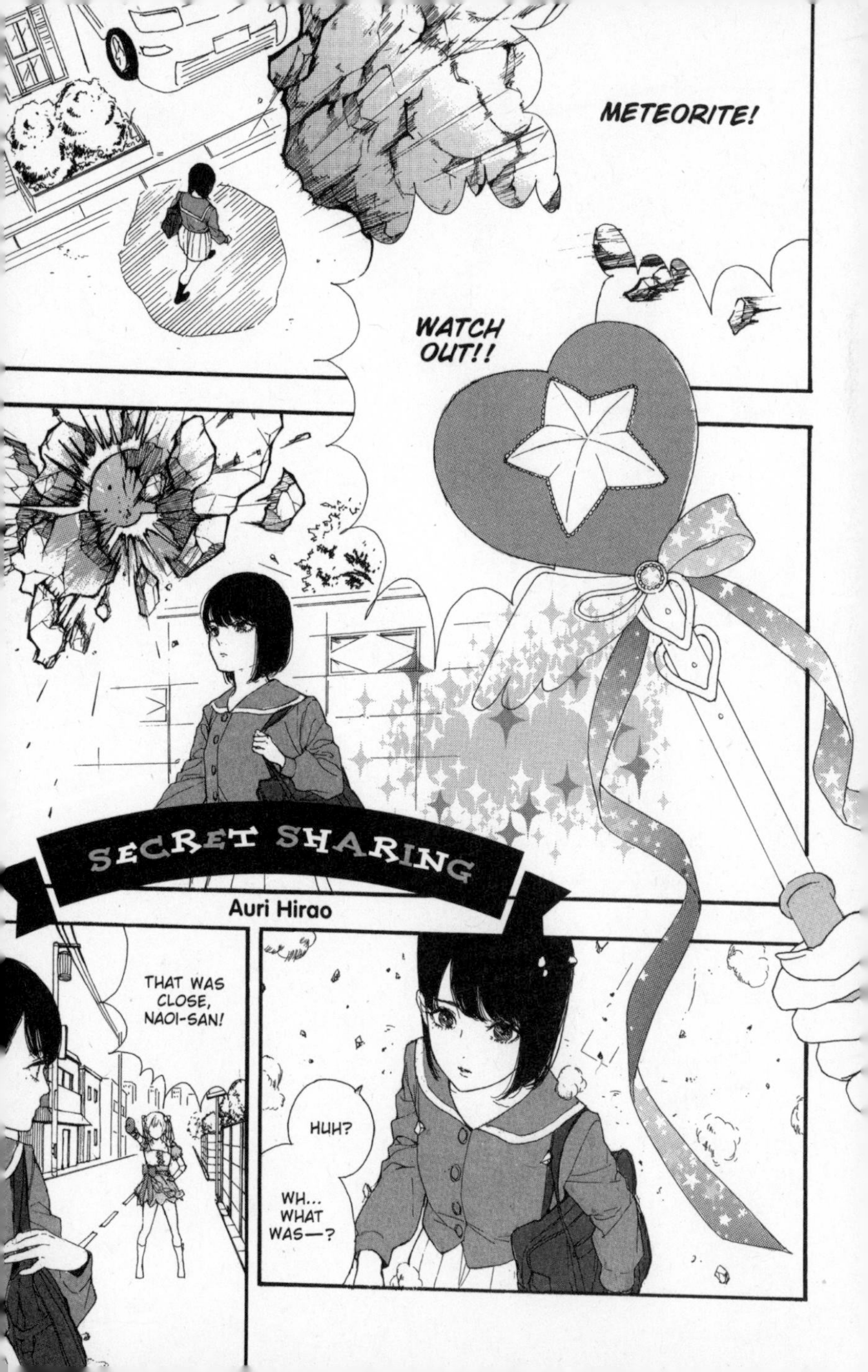
METEORITE!
WATCH OUT!!
SECRET SHARING
Auri Hirao
HUH?
WH... WHAT WAS—?
THAT WAS CLOSE, NAOI-SAN!

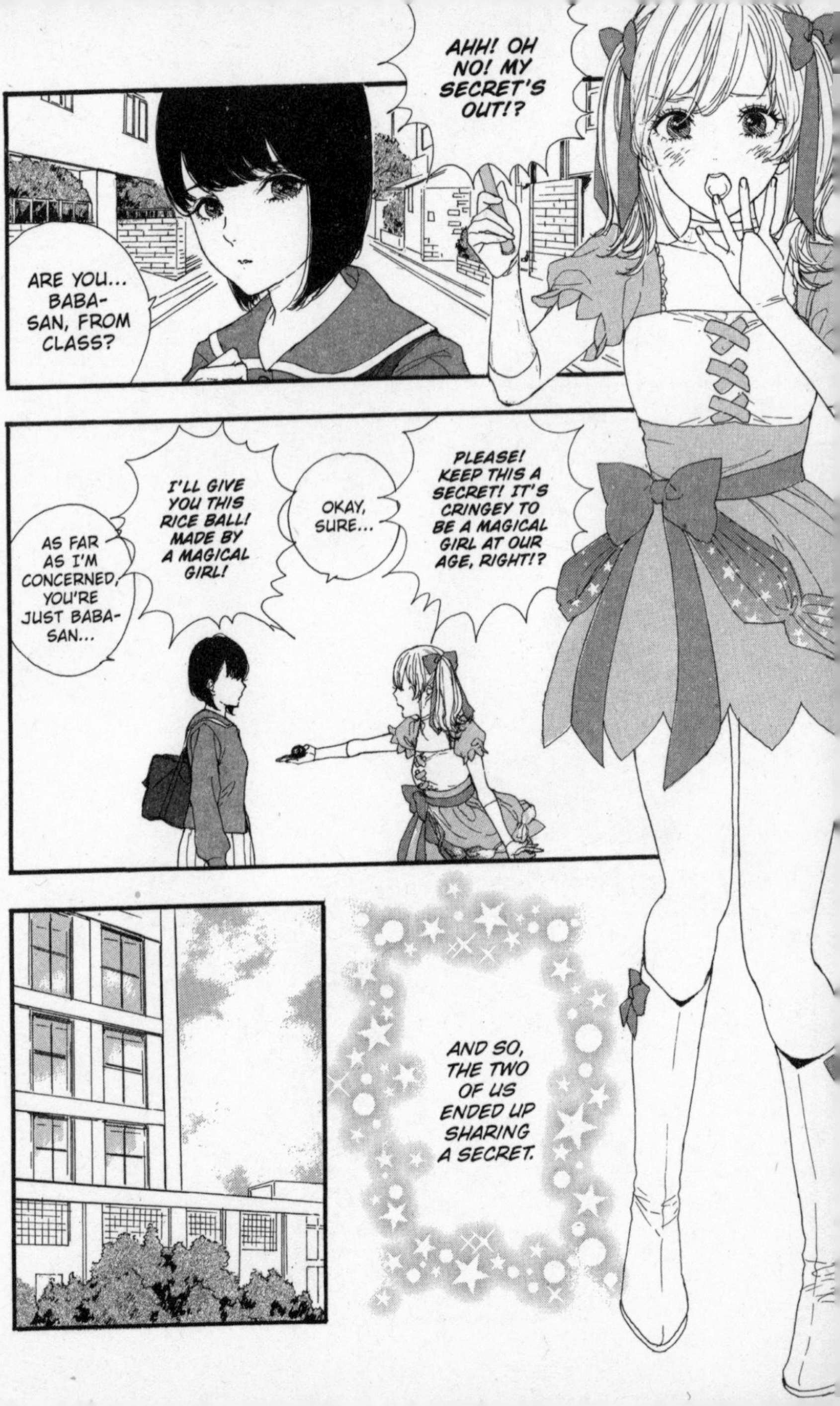
AHH! OH NO! MY SECRET'S OUT!?
ARE YOU... BABA-SAN, FROM CLASS?
PLEASE! KEEP THIS A SECRET! IT'S CRINGEY TO BE A MAGICAL GIRL AT OUR AGE, RIGHT!?
OKAY, SURE...
I'LL GIVE YOU THIS RICE BALL! MADE BY A MAGICAL GIRL!
AS FAR AS I'M CONCERNED, YOU'RE JUST BABA-SAN...
AND SO, THE TWO OF US ENDED UP SHARING A SECRET.

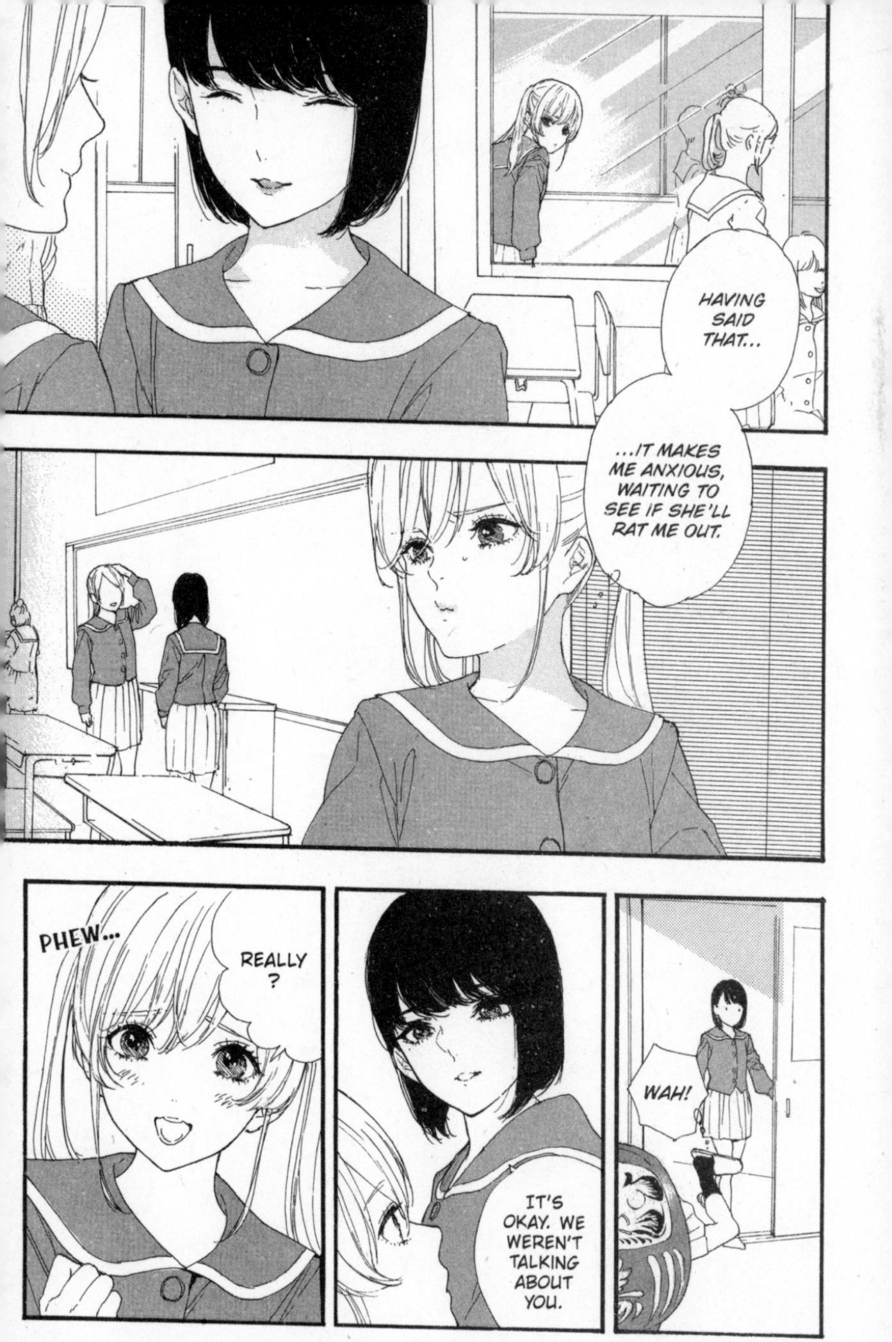
HAVING SAID THAT...
...IT MAKES ME ANXIOUS, WAITING TO SEE IF SHE'LL RAT ME OUT.
WAH!
IT'S OKAY. WE WEREN'T TALKING ABOUT YOU.
PHEW...
REALLY?

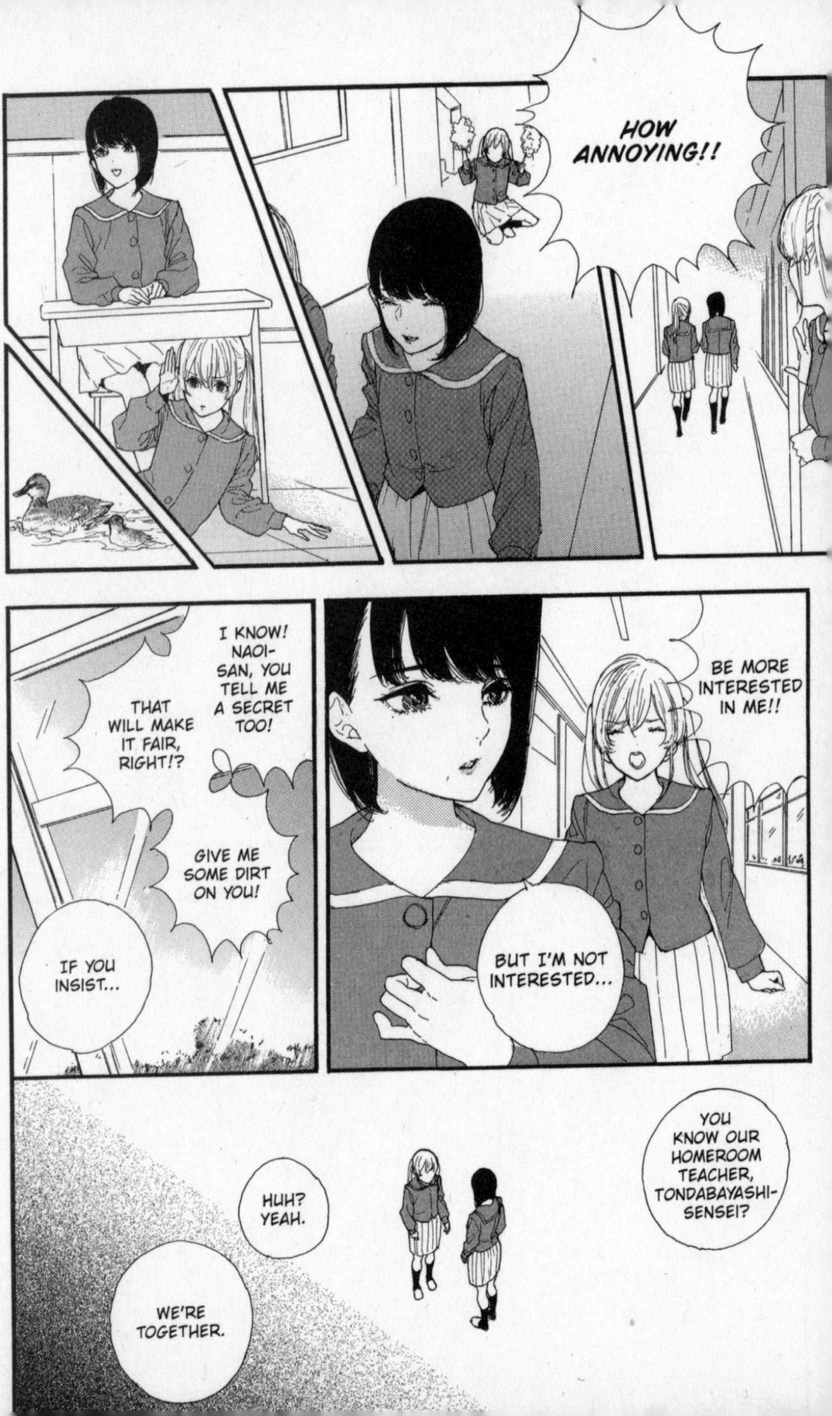
HOW ANNOYING!!
BE MORE INTERESTED IN ME!!
BUT I'M NOT INTERESTED...
I KNOW! NAOI-SAN, YOU TELL ME A SECRET TOO!
THAT WILL MAKE IT FAIR, RIGHT!?
GIVE ME SOME DIRT ON YOU!
IF YOU INSIST...
YOU KNOW OUR HOMEROOM TEACHER, TONDABAYASHI-SENSEI?
HUH? YEAH.
WE'RE TOGETHER.

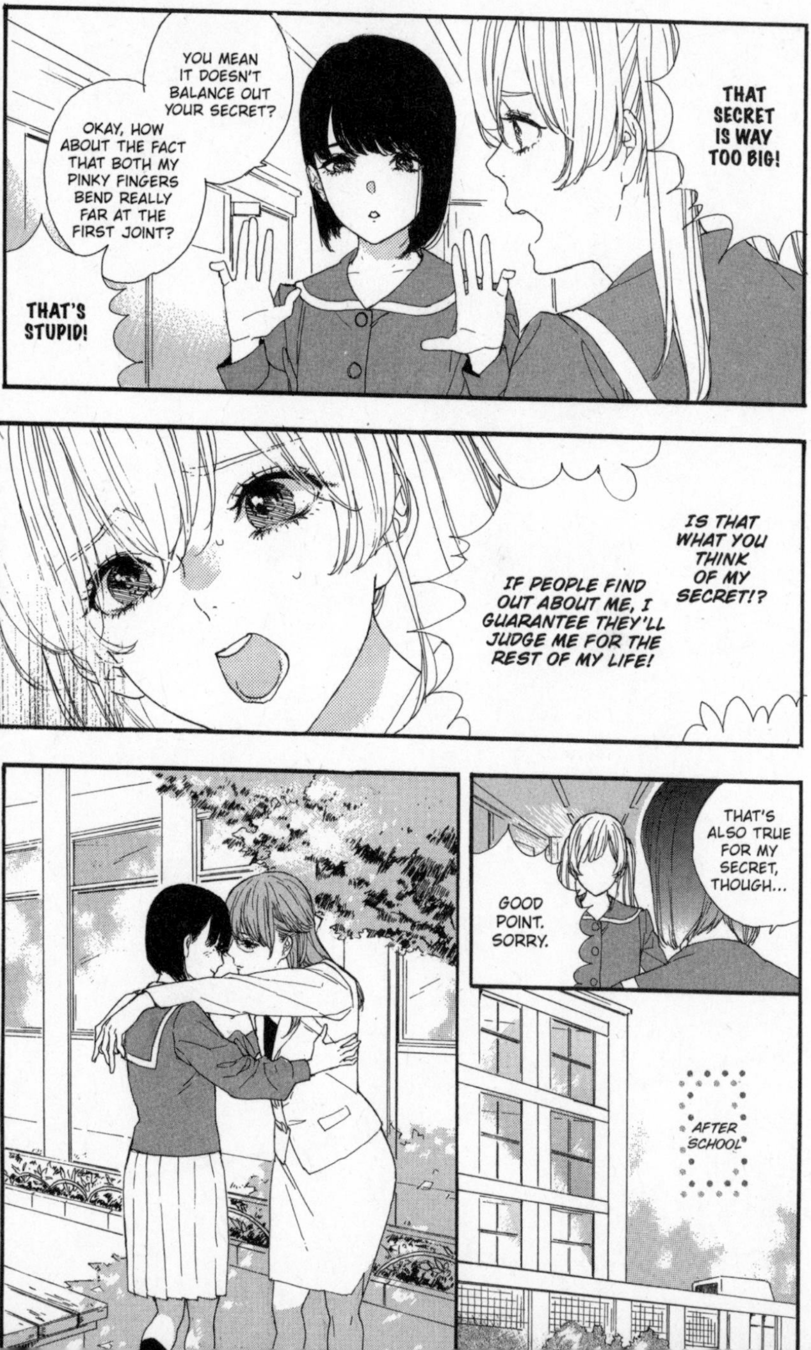
THAT SECRET IS WAY TOO BIG!
YOU MEAN IT DOESN'T BALANCE OUT YOUR SECRET?
OKAY, HOW ABOUT THE FACT THAT BOTH MY PINKY FINGERS BEND REALLY FAR AT THE FIRST JOINT?
THAT'S STUPID!
IS THAT WHAT YOU THINK OF MY SECRET!?
IF PEOPLE FIND OUT ABOUT ME, I GUARANTEE THEY'LL JUDGE ME FOR THE REST OF MY LIFE!
THAT'S ALSO TRUE FOR MY SECRET, THOUGH...
GOOD POINT. SORRY.
AFTER SCHOOL

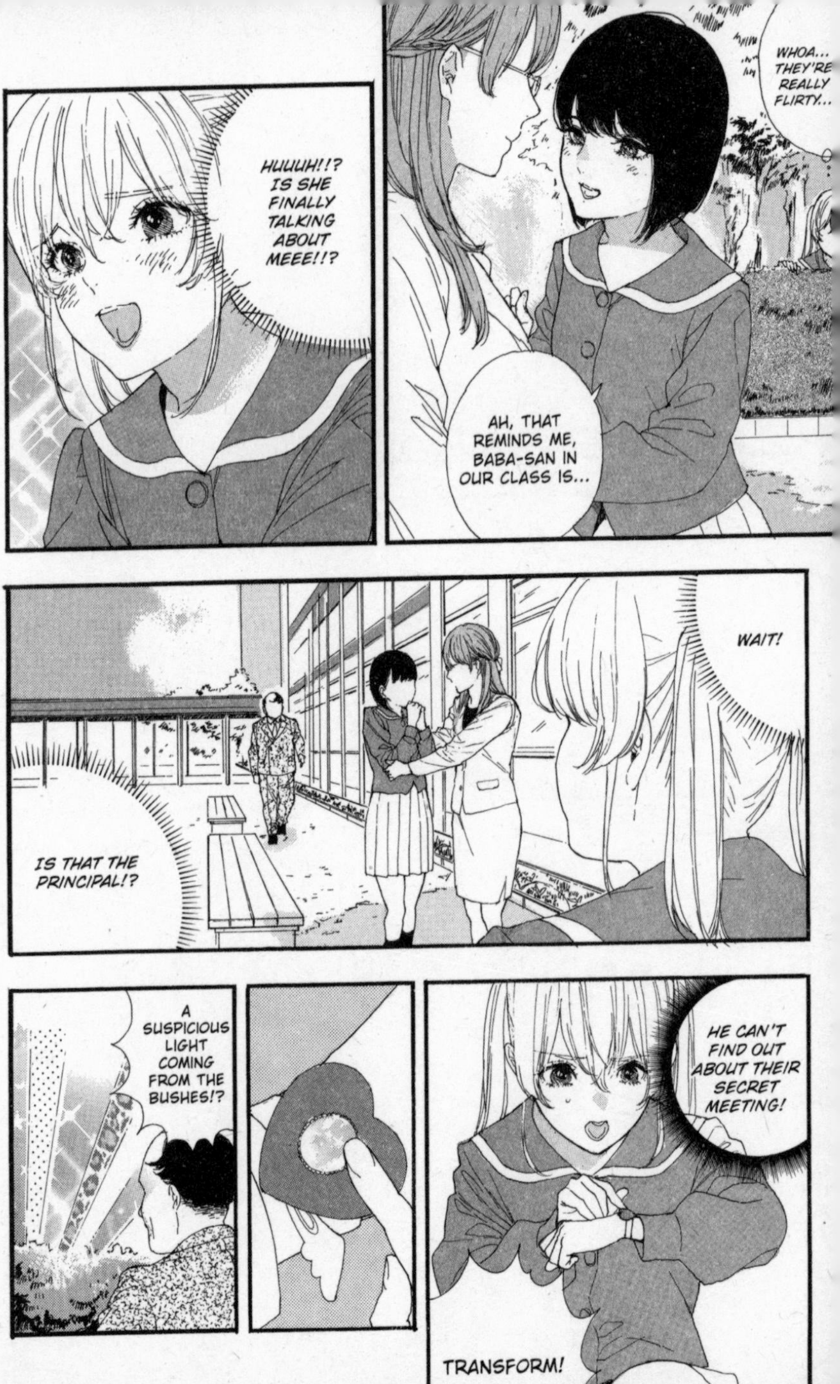
WHOA... THEY'RE REALLY FLIRTY...
AH, THAT REMINDS ME, BABA-SAN IN OUR CLASS IS...
HUUUH!!? IS SHE FINALLY TALKING ABOUT MEEE!!?
WAIT!
IS THAT THE PRINCIPAL!?
HE CAN'T FIND OUT ABOUT THEIR SECRET MEETING!
TRANSFORM!
A SUSPICIOUS LIGHT COMING FROM THE BUSHES!?

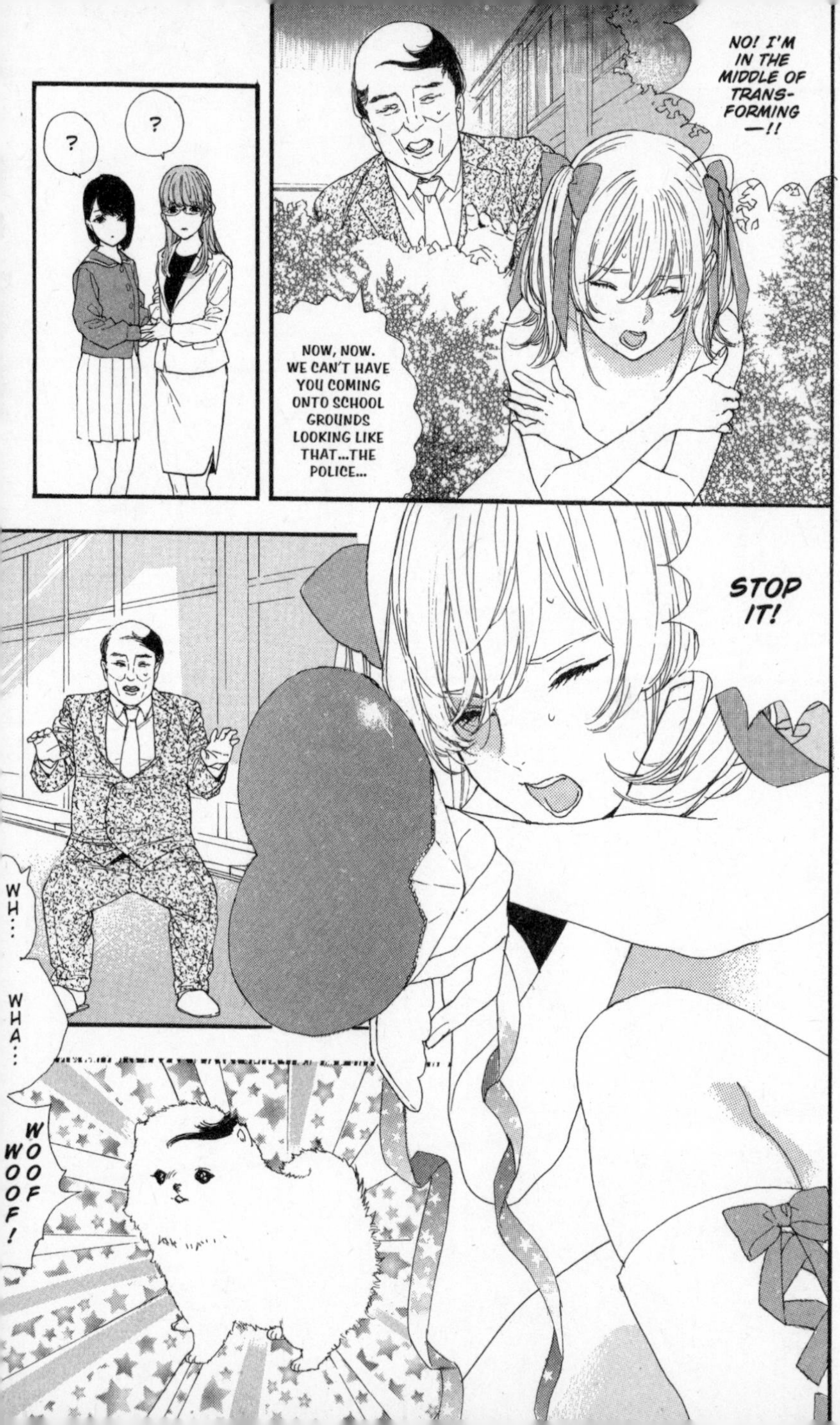
NO! I'M IN THE MIDDLE OF TRANS-FORMING—!!
NOW, NOW. WE CAN'T HAVE YOU COMING ONTO SCHOOL GROUNDS LOOKING LIKE THAT...THE POLICE...
?
?
STOP IT!
WH...
WHA...
WOOF WOOF!

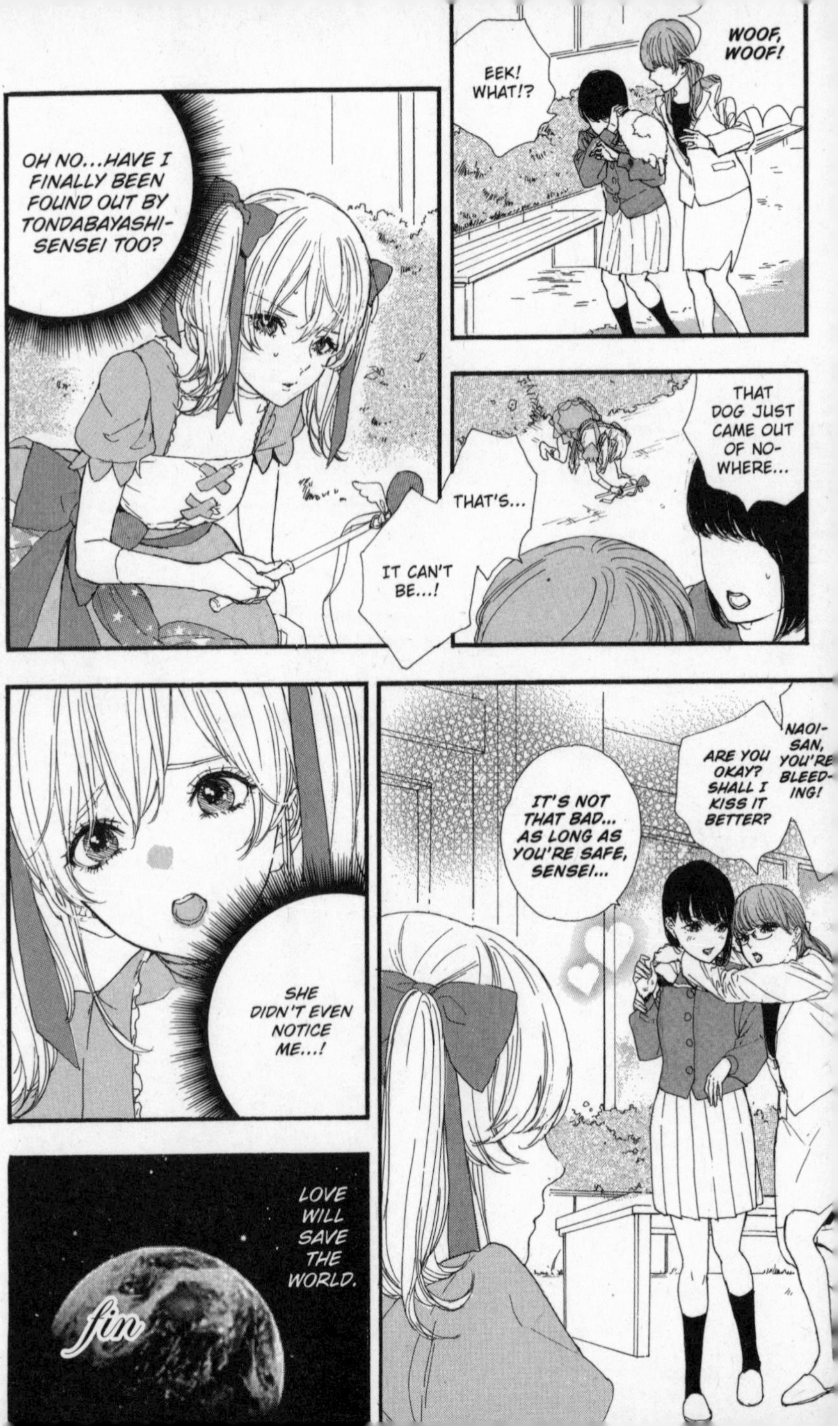
WOOF, WOOF!
EEK! WHAT!?
THAT DOG JUST CAME OUT OF NOWHERE...
THAT'S...
IT CAN'T BE...!
OH NO...HAVE I FINALLY BEEN FOUND OUT BY TONDABAYASHI-SENSEI TOO?
NAOI-SAN, YOU'RE BLEEDING!
ARE YOU OKAY? SHALL I KISS IT BETTER?
IT'S NOT THAT BAD... AS LONG AS YOU'RE SAFE, SENSEI...
SHE DIDN'T EVEN NOTICE ME...!
LOVE WILL SAVE THE WORLD.
fin

Postscript

Fly

Thank you very much for inviting me to join this wonderful project. I even got to draw the cover—I'm so happy. In illustrations, I often draw yuri with some space between the girls, but in my manga I think I managed to show what happens next with these two.

U35

Pleased to meet you. My name is U35 (Umiko). I had only ever looked at yuri works, so I am deeply grateful for this wonderful opportunity......! The time I spent drawing and fantasizing about the relationship between these two was a lot of fun.

Yutaka Hiiragi

Many years ago, I passed by a wedding hall and saw a young woman, one of the staff, sitting on a plastic chair behind the hall, blowing up a large number of balloons. The juxtaposition in that place of the joyous feeling of the hall, the fancy-colored balloons, and the girl's blank expression stuck with me. I wonder how she's doing.

Non

Thank you for inviting me back for the second installment!
The black-haired girl has a one-sided crush. Oblivious girl x girl with an unrequited crush is my favorite trope.

Musshu

Nice to meet you. I'm Musshu. Thank you very much for letting me stray into this wonderful anthology. I have started writing a manga called *Furidashi ni Ochiru!* in *Dengeki Daioh*. The story is about girls who have a close relationship. Please give it a look.

Nio Nakatani

I am not particularly a big fan of idols, but when I saw some idols live, everything except "cute" vanished from my vocabulary.

Kazuno Yuikawa

I was deeply honored to be invited back. I like troublesome girls.

Tamamushi Oku

I am extremely honored that, through *Éclair*, I was able to achieve my longtime dream of drawing something in a yuri anthology! But I got a bit too nervous and it ended up as a kind of understated piece......I'd love it if you could enjoy it with the mind-set of "It's okay, it's her first try!"

Kagekichi Tadano

Thank you for inviting me back again. I usually think about a girl and a girl, but this time I thought about a girl and a girl and a girl.

Canno	Thank you very much for inviting me to take part again. This manga is about a terrible woman and an innocent high school girl, but during storyboarding I was told "All the characters are terrible people." That wasn't my intention......I hope you enjoy it!
Kabocha	Nice to meet you. My name is Kabocha. Somehow, I managed to slip into the second book of *Éclair*. I'm grateful for that. This time the story was set in summer— apparently I like the season of summer even more than I thought. I hope you can sense the smell of a clear summer day in it.
Fumiko Takada	I didn't think I would be able to take part in this project again, so I'm very happy! I'm excited for this next volume of *Éclair* to be delivered......
Shuninta Amano	My life consists of thinking about cute girls with cute girls for every moment of every second of every minute of every hour of every day. I'm so lucky.
Izumi Kawanami	I am very happy that I was able to publish another piece in *Éclair*. I like complicated relationships between complicated girls. Please give it a look.
Taki Kitao	My favorite trope is "the handsome one usually bottoms," but my other, absolute favorite is "the servant dominating their master," so that's how this story ended up! Kurumi will probably keep being tormented by having to roleplay as a princess. I'm not saying in what way, though!
Uta Isaki	I wanted to draw a plain, skinny girl with a mean face, and this is what happened. In yuri manga, even a girl like that can be the main character, which I think is pretty open-minded. (*Éclair* is probably a special case......)
Eri Ejima	Nice to meet you! I bought a copy of the first *Éclair* as an ordinary reader and thought it would be a waste to read it all in one go, so I spread it out over a few days. It's amazing to be on the drawing side of things this time... Incidentally, I'm currently serializing *Yuzumori-san* in *Yawaraka Spirits*. It's coming out as a collected volume too, so please give it a look if you liked this one-shot. ☆
Auri Hirao	I was happy to be invited to take part again! I always get nervous and can't write anything important in the anthology comment section, so I want to be fifty centimeters taller.

Two girls, a new school, and the beginning of a beautiful friendship.

Complete series available now!

Kiss & White Lily for My Dearest Girl

In middle school, Ayaka Shiramine was the perfect student: hard-working, with excellent grades and a great personality to match. As Ayaka enters high school she expects to still be on top, but one thing she didn't account for is her new classmate, the lazy yet genuine genius Yurine Kurosawa. What's in store for Ayaka and Yurine as they go through high school...together?

Yen Press

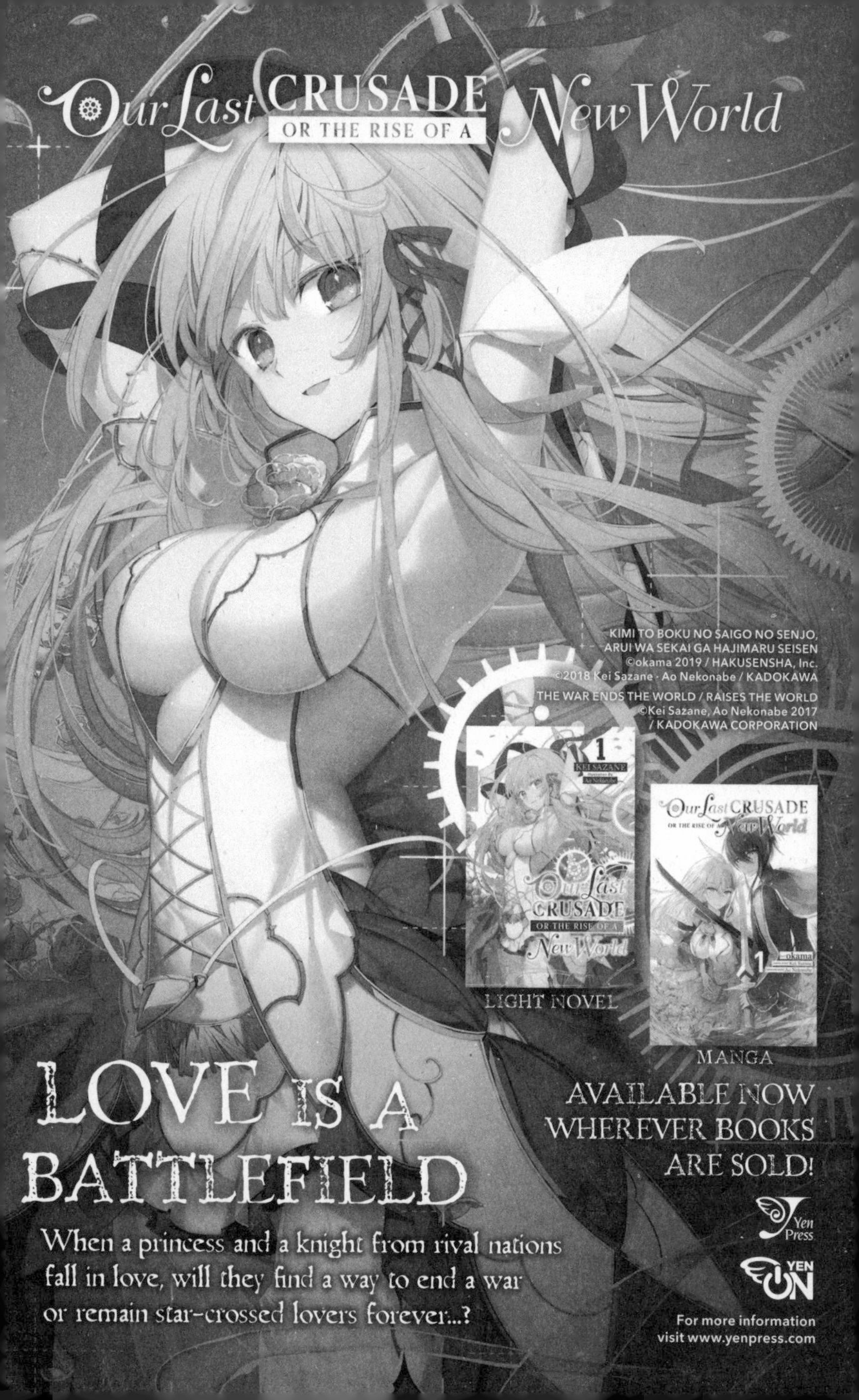
Our Last CRUSADE OR THE RISE OF A New World
KIMI TO BOKU NO SAIGO NO SENJO,
ARUI WA SEKAI GA HAJIMARU SEISEN
©okama 2019 / HAKUSENSHA, Inc.
©2018 Kei Sazane · Ao Nekonabe / KADOKAWA
THE WAR ENDS THE WORLD / RAISES THE WORLD
©Kei Sazane, Ao Nekonabe 2017
/ KADOKAWA CORPORATION
LIGHT NOVEL
MANGA
LOVE IS A BATTLEFIELD
When a princess and a knight from rival nations fall in love, will they find a way to end a war or remain star-crossed lovers forever...?
AVAILABLE NOW WHEREVER BOOKS ARE SOLD!
Yen Press
YEN ON
For more information visit www.yenpress.com

The ISOLATOR
▼ Manga

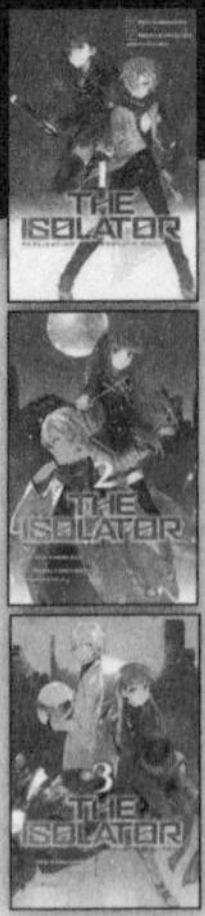
THE ISOLATOR

The ISOLATOR
▼ Light Novels

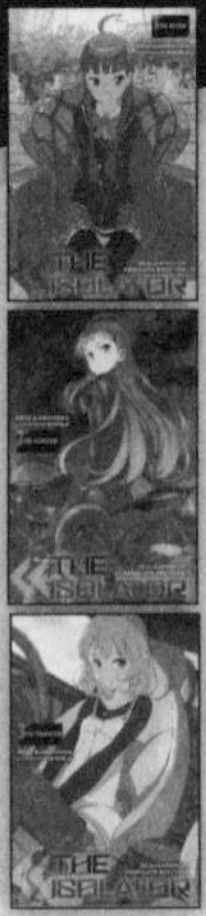
THE ISOLATOR

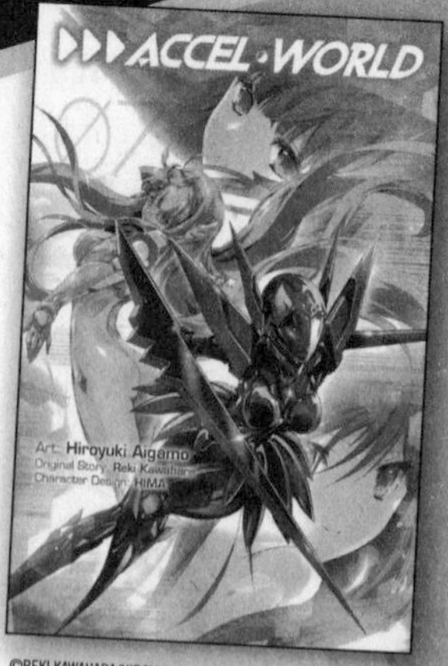
ACCEL·WORLD
Art: Hiroyuki Aigamo
Original Story: Reki Kawahara
Character Design: HIMA

▼ *ACCEL WORLD* Manga

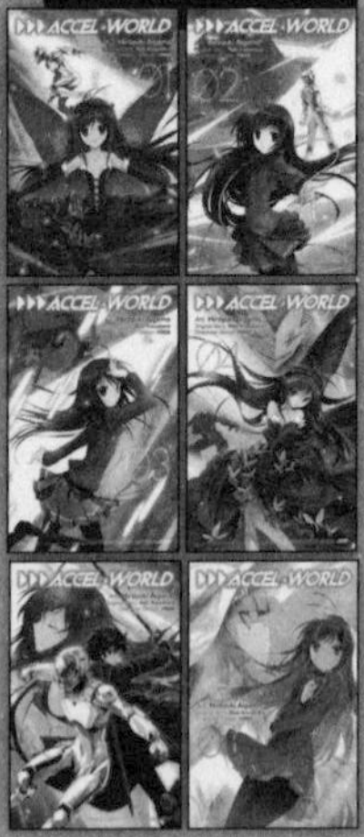
ACCEL·WORLD

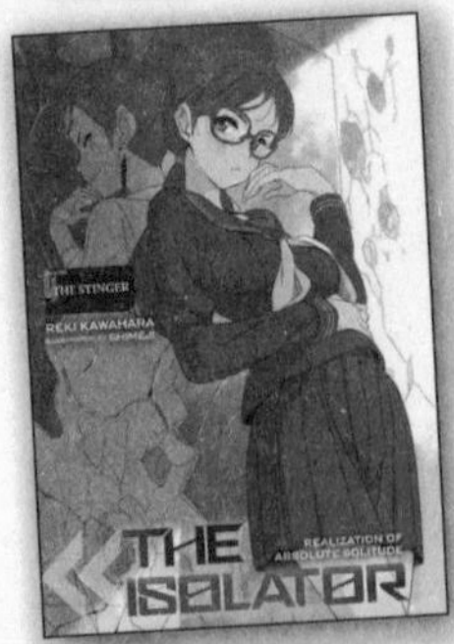
THE STINGER
REKI KAWAHARA
REALIZATION OF ABSOLUTE SOLITUDE
THE ISOLATOR

▼ *ACCEL WORLD* Light Novels

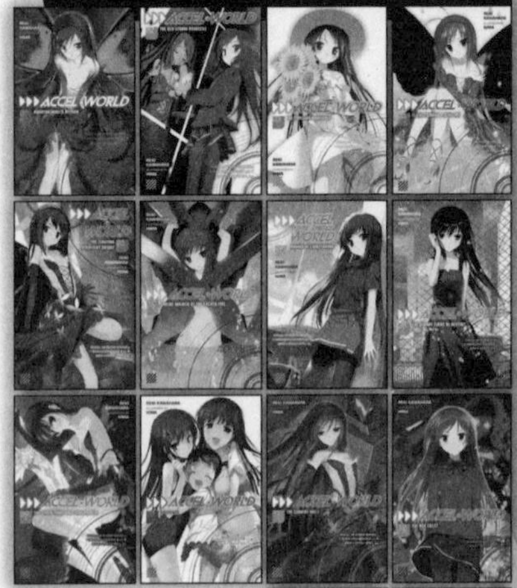
ACCEL·WORLD

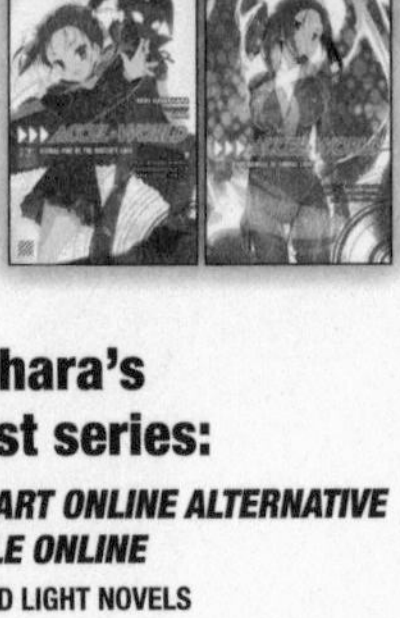
ACCEL·WORLD

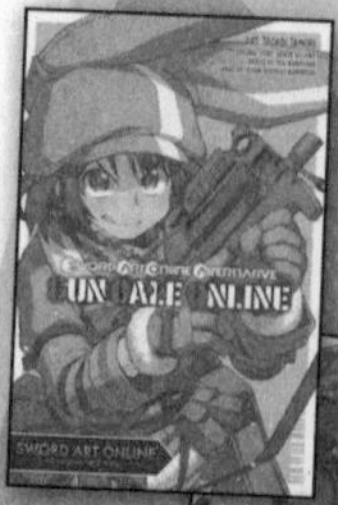
SWORD ART ONLINE ALTERNATIVE
GUN GALE ONLINE
SWORD ART ONLINE

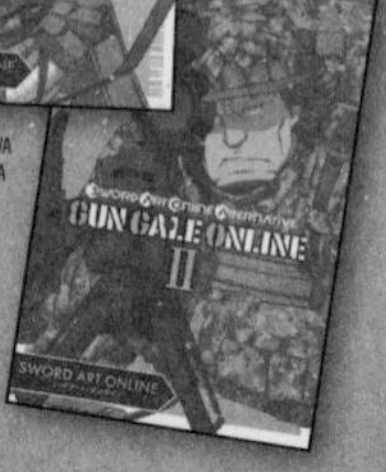
SWORD ART ONLINE ALTERNATIVE
GUN GALE ONLINE
II
SWORD ART ONLINE

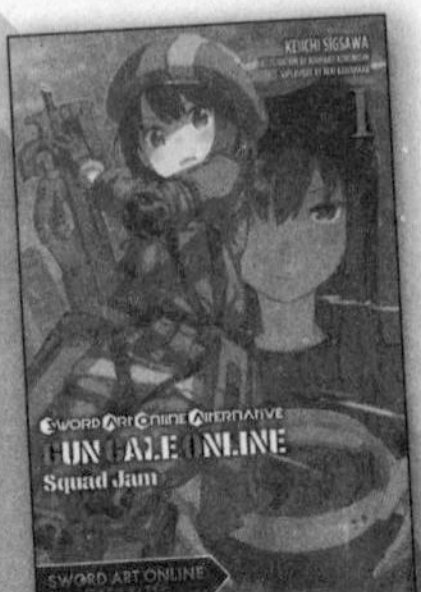
KEIICHI SIGSAWA
I
SWORD ART ONLINE ALTERNATIVE
GUN GALE ONLINE
Squad Jam
SWORD ART ONLINE

◀ **Kawahara's newest series:**

SWORD ART ONLINE ALTERNATIVE GUN GALE ONLINE

MANGA AND LIGHT NOVELS

Dive into the latest light novels from *New York Times* bestselling author REKI KAWAHARA, creator of the fan favorite *SWORD ART ONLINE* and *ACCEL WORLD* series!

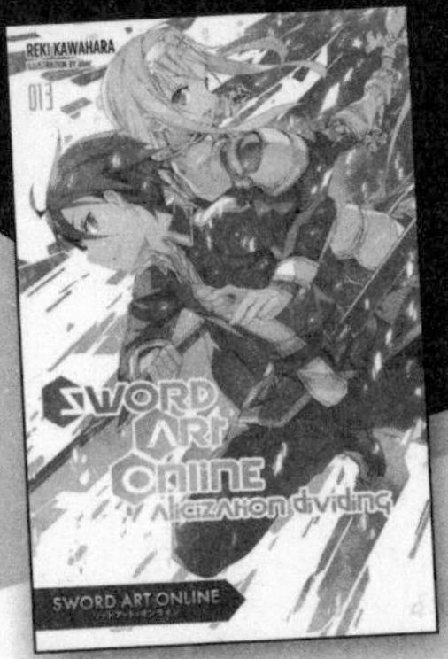

©REKI KAWAHARA ILLUSTRATION: abec

***SWORD ART ONLINE* Light Novels ▼**

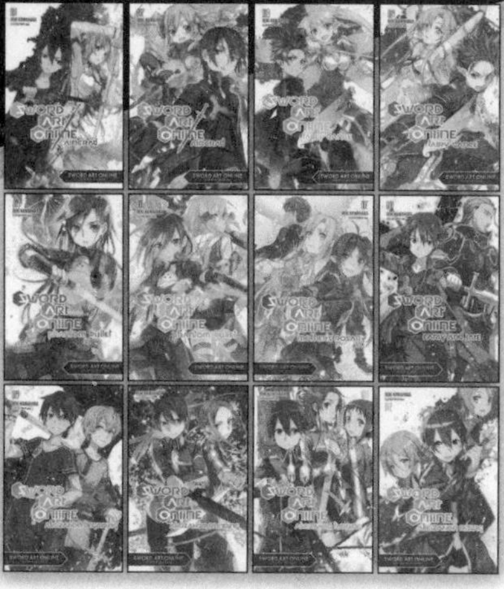

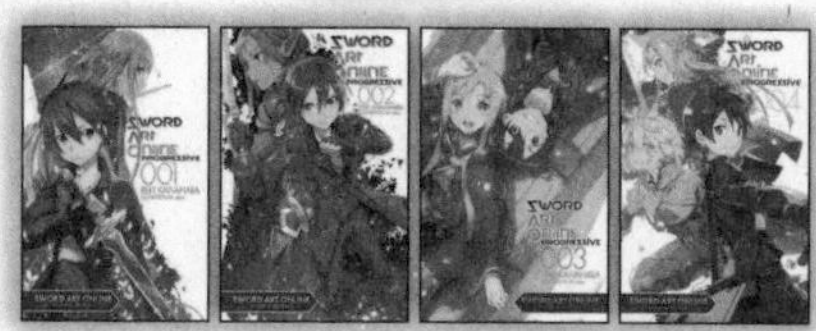

©REKI KAWAHARA ILLUSTRATION: abec

***SWORD ART ONLINE* Manga ▼**

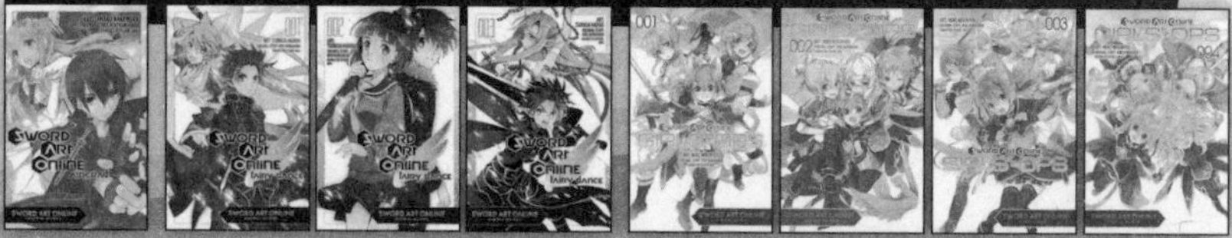

©REKI KAWAHARA/TAMAKO NAKAMURA ©REKI KAWAHARA/TSUBASA HADUKI ©REKI KAWAHARA/NEKO NEKOBYOU

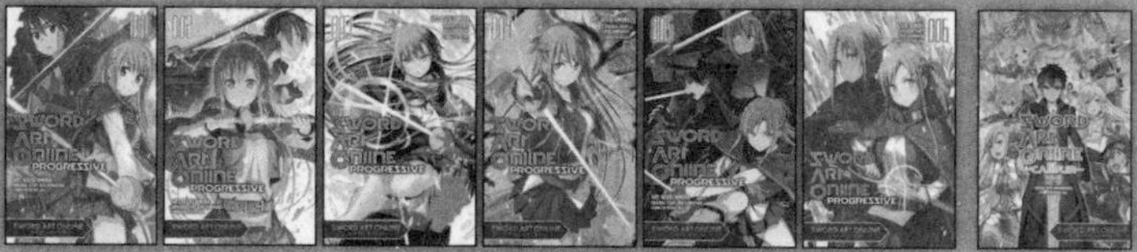

©REKI KAWAHARA/KISEKI HIMURA ©REKI KAWAHARA/CSY

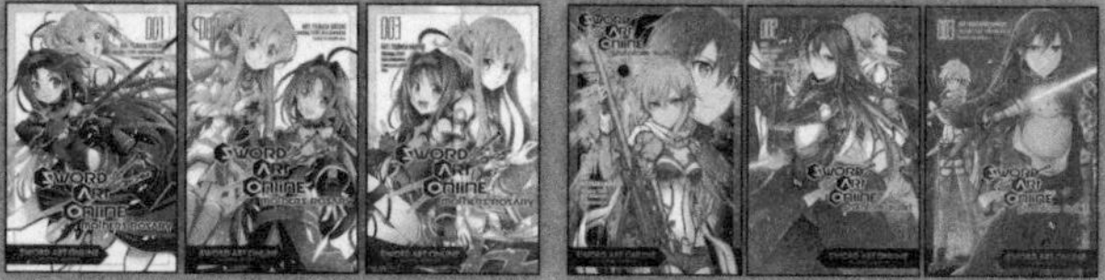

©REKI KAWAHARA/TSUBASA HADUKI ©REKI KAWAHARA/KOUTAROU YAMADA

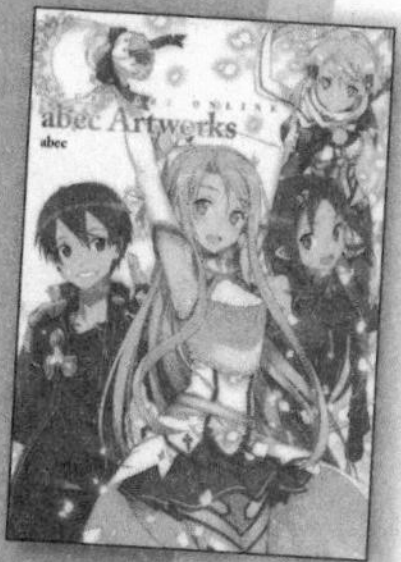

abec Artworks ▶

Featuring original, full color artwork from multiple *Sword Art Online* manga and light novels. A must for any *Sword Art Online* fan!

©abec ©REKI KAWAHARA

YEN ON Yen Press

www.YenPress.com

A fallen angel with falling grades!

Gabriel Dropout

Vol. 1–8 on sale now!

www.yenpress.com

Yen Press

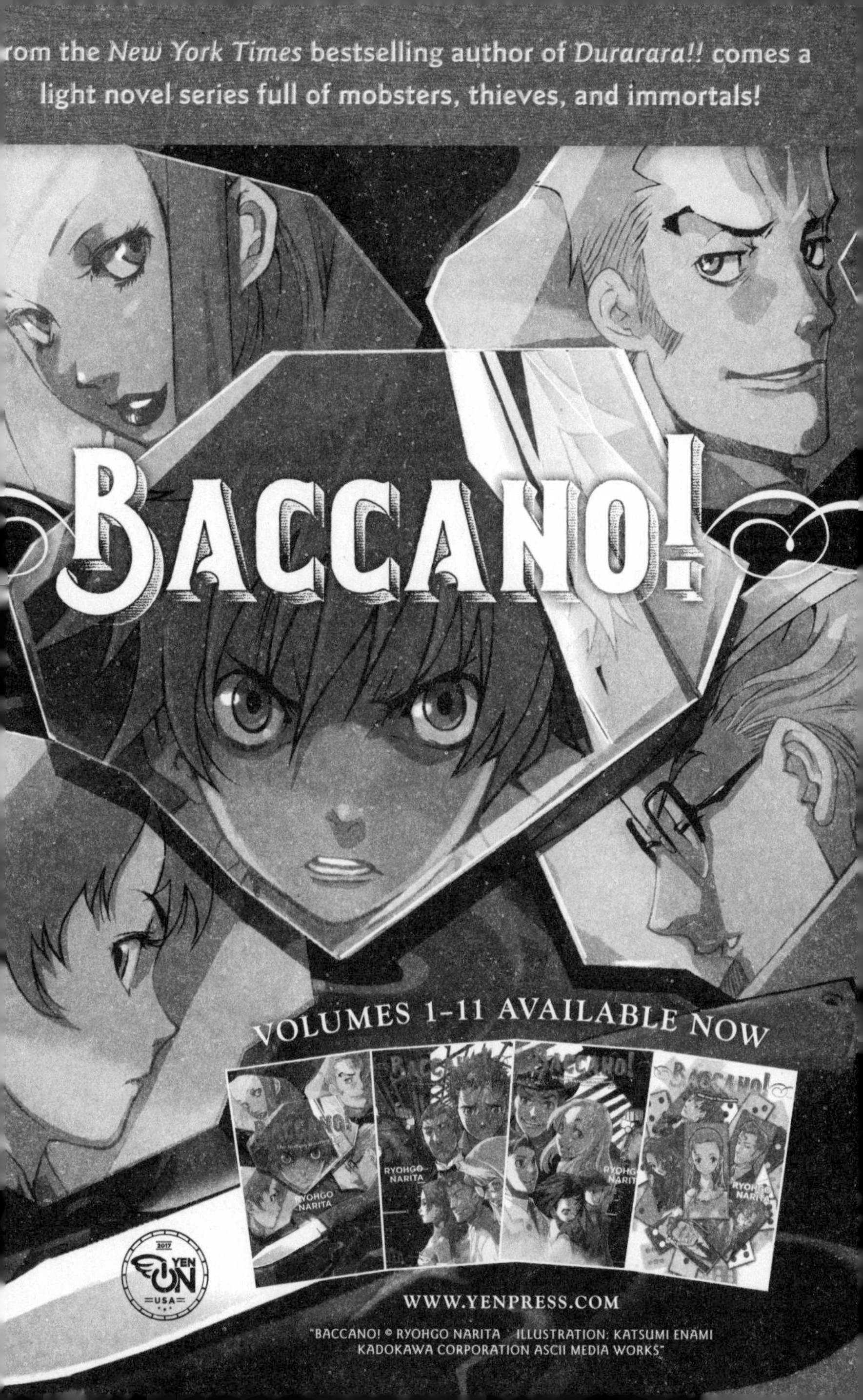
rom the *New York Times* bestselling author of *Durarara!!* comes a
light novel series full of mobsters, thieves, and immortals!
BACCANO!
VOLUMES 1-11 AVAILABLE NOW
WWW.YENPRESS.COM
"BACCANO! © RYOHGO NARITA ILLUSTRATION: KATSUMI ENAMI
KADOKAWA CORPORATION ASCII MEDIA WORKS"

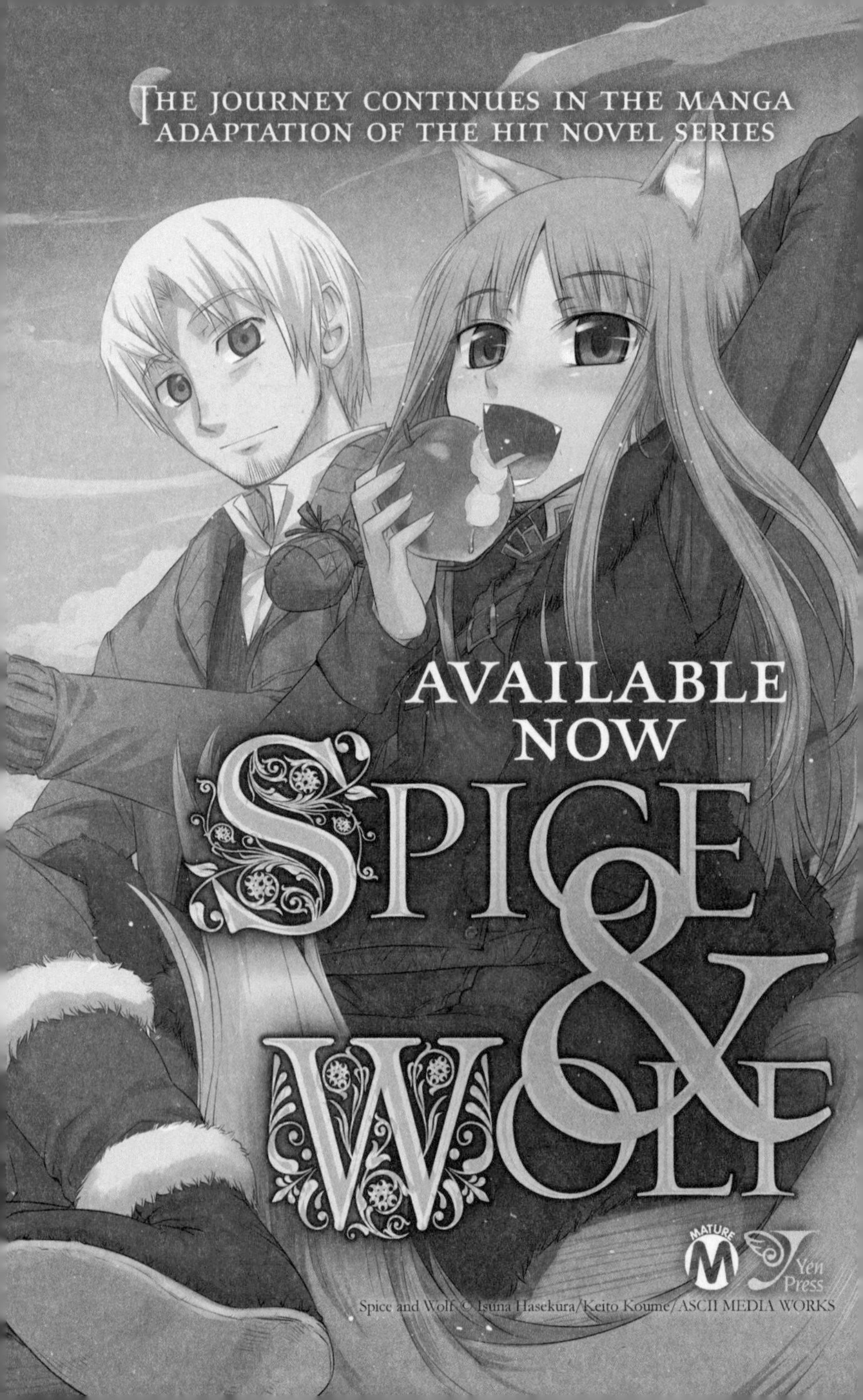
THE JOURNEY CONTINUES IN THE MANGA
ADAPTATION OF THE HIT NOVEL SERIES
AVAILABLE
NOW
SPICE & WOLF
MATURE
Yen Press
Spice and Wolf © Isuna Hasekura/Keito Koume/ASCII MEDIA WORKS

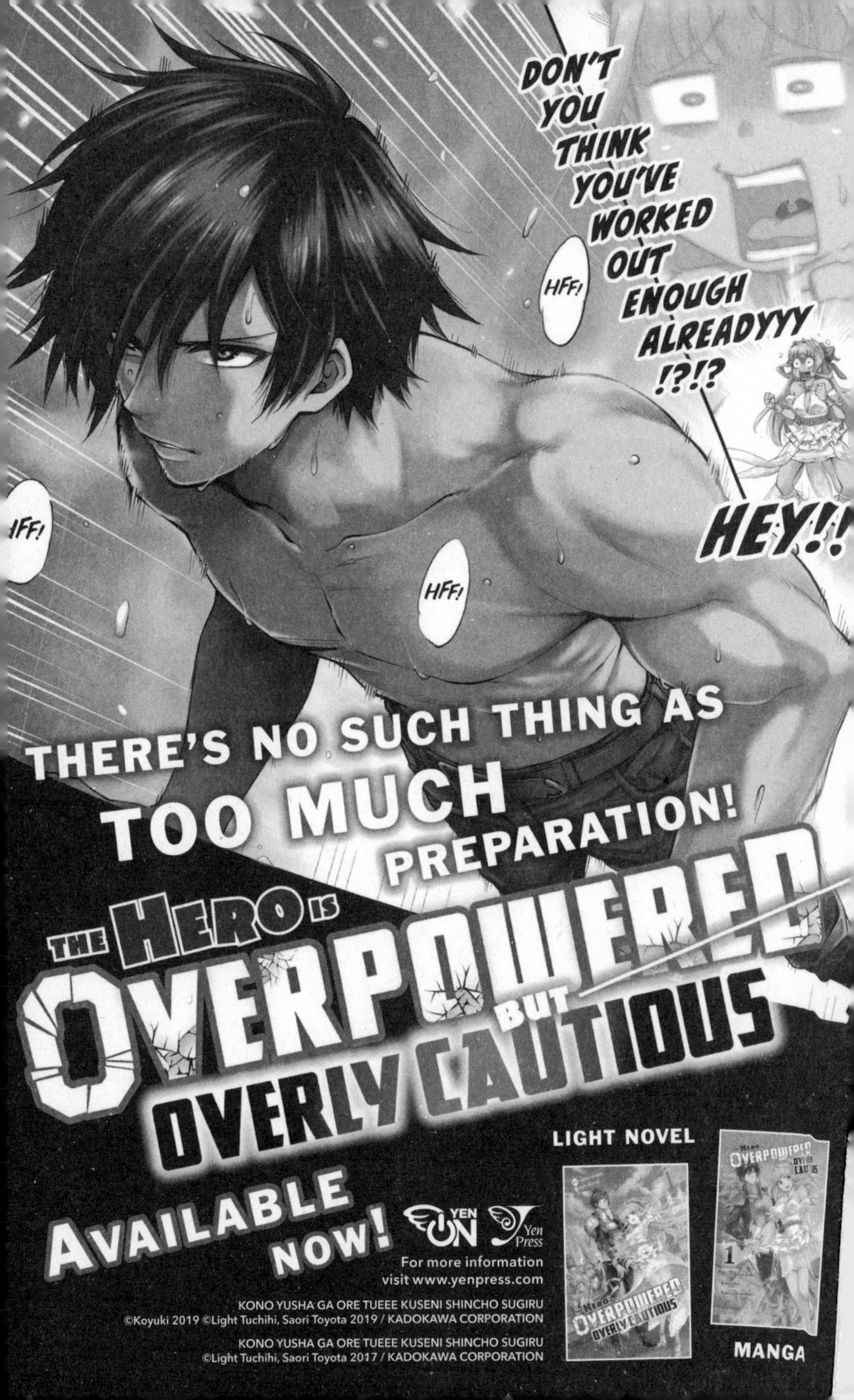
DON'T YOU THINK YOU'VE WORKED OUT ENOUGH ALREADYYY !?!?
HFF!
HEY!!
HFF!
HFF!
THERE'S NO SUCH THING AS TOO MUCH PREPARATION!
THE HERO IS OVERPOWERED BUT OVERLY CAUTIOUS
LIGHT NOVEL
AVAILABLE NOW!
YEN ON
Yen Press
For more information visit www.yenpress.com
KONO YUSHA GA ORE TUEEE KUSENI SHINCHO SUGIRU
©Koyuki 2019 ©Light Tuchihi, Saori Toyota 2019 / KADOKAWA CORPORATION
KONO YUSHA GA ORE TUEEE KUSENI SHINCHO SUGIRU
©Light Tuchihi, Saori Toyota 2017 / KADOKAWA CORPORATION
MANGA

éclair
blanche

A Girls' Love Anthology
That Resonates in Your Heart

Translation: Eleanor Summers ✦ Lettering: Alexis Eckerman

éclair blanche ANATA NI HIBIKU YURI ANTHOLOGY
©KADOKAWA CORPORATION 2017
First published in Japan in 2017 by KADOKAWA CORPORATION, Tokyo. English translation rights arranged with KADOKAWA CORPORATION, Tokyo, through Tuttle-Mori Agency, Inc.

English translation © 2020 by Yen Press, LLC

Yen Press
150 West 30th Street, 19th Floor
New York, NY 10001

Visit us at yenpress.com • facebook.com/yenpress • twitter.com/yenpress • yenpress.tumblr.com • yenpress.com/instagram

First Yen Press Edition: May 2020

Yen Press is an imprint of Yen Press, LLC.
The Yen Press name and logo are trademarks of Yen Press, LLC.

Library of Congress Control Number:
2018937031

ISBNs: 978-1-9753-5909-6 (paperback)
978-1-9753-5910-2 (ebook)

10 9 8 7 6 5 4 3 2 1

WOR

Printed in the United States of America